Comparing Theories of Child Development

THIRD EDITION

R. MURRAY THOMAS
University of California
Santa Barbara

Wadsworth Publishing Company
Belmont, California
A Division of Wadsworth, Inc.

To Shirley

Psychology Editor: Kenneth King
Editorial Assistant: Cynthia Campbell
Production Editor: Carol Dondrea, Bookman Productions
Print Buyer: Randy Hurst
Designer: Detta Penna and Hal Lockwood
Copy Editor: Betty Berenson
Illustrator: Nancy Warner and John Foster
Cover: Hal Lockwood and Wendy Goldberg, Bookman Productions
Compositor: Kachina Typesetting

This book is printed on acid-free paper that meets Environmental Protection Agency standards for recycled paper.

4 5 6 7 8 9 10—96 95 94

Library of Congress Cataloging-in-Publication Data

Thomas, R. Murray (Robert Murray), 1921–
    Comparing theories of child development / R. Murray Thomas. — 3rd ed.
       p.   cm.
    Includes bibliographical references and indexes.
    ISBN 0-534-16302-5
    1. Child psychology. 2. Child development. I. Title.
BF721.T456 1991
155.4'01—dc20   91-11267
                                                              CIP

ACKNOWLEDGMENTS

We wish to thank the following for permission to use various excerpts and illustrations.

Alston, W. P. "Comments on Kohlberg's 'From Is to Ought'" in T. Mischel, *Cognitive Development and Epistemology*. New York: Academic Press, 1971. Used by permission of Academic Press. • Ames, L. B., and Ilg, F. L. *Your Four Year Old*. © 1976 Dell Publishing Company, Inc. Reprinted by permission of the publisher. • Baldwin, A. L. *Theories of Child Development*. New York: Wiley, 1967. Used by permission of John Wiley & Sons, Inc. • Case, R. *Intellectual Development, Birth to Adulthood*. © 1985 by Academic Press. Used by permission of the publisher. • Freud, S. *An Outline of Psychoanalysis*. London: Hogarth, 1973. Used by permission of Hogarth Press Ltd. • Gesell, A., and F. L. Ilg. *Child Development: An Introduction to the Study of Human Growth*. Excerpts from Part I: "Infant and Child in the Culture of Today" copyright 1949 by Harper & Row, Publishers, Inc. Chart (list) from Part II: "The Child from Five to Ten" copyright 1946 by Arnold Gesell and Frances L. Ilg. Used by permission of HarperCollins, Publishers, Inc. and Hamish Hamilton Ltd. • Havighurst, R. J. *Developmental Tasks and Education*. Copyright © 1953 by Longman Publishing Group. Reprinted by permission of Longman Publishing Group. • Hinde, R. A. *Biological Bases of Human Social Behavior*. New York: McGraw-Hill, 1974. Used by permission of McGraw-Hill, Inc. • Ilg, F. L., L. B. Ames, and S. M. Baker. *Child Behavior*. Copyright 1981 by Frances L. Ilg, Louise Bates Ames, and Sidney M. Baker. Reprinted by permission of HarperCollins, Publishers. • Inhelder, B., and J. Piaget. *The Early Growth of Logic in the Child*. London: Routledge & Kegan Paul, 1964. Used by permission of Harper & Row, Publishers, Inc. and Routledge & Kegan Paul Ltd. • Kohlberg, L. "From Is to Ought" in T. Mischel, *Cognitive Development and Epistemology*. New York: Academic Press, 1971. Used by permission of Academic Press. • Kohlberg, L. "Moral and Religious Education in the Public Schools: A Developmental View" in T. R. Sizer, *Religion and Public Education*. Copyright © 1967 by Houghton Mifflin Company. Used by permission of Houghton Mifflin Company. • Kohlberg, L., and R. Kramer. "Continuities in Childhood and Adult Moral Development." *Human Development*, Vol. 12 (1969), pp. 93–120. Used by permission of S. Karger AG, Basel, Switzerland. • Maslow, A. H. *The Farther Reaches of Human Nature*. Copyright © 1971 by Bertha G. Maslow. An Esalen Book, used by permission of The Viking Press. • Maslow, A. H. *Toward a Psychology of Being*. © 1968 by Litton Educational Publishing, Inc. Used by permission of D. Van Nostrand Company. • Mounoud, P. "Similarities Between Developmental Sequences at Different Age Periods," in I. Levin (ed.), *Stage and Structure: Reopening the Debate*. Reprinted by permission of Ablex Publishing Corp. • Peters, R. S. "Moral Development: A Plea for Pluralism" in T. Mischel, *Cognitive Development and Epistemology*. New York: Academic Press, 1971. Used by permission of Academic Press. • Riegel, K. F. "From Traits and Equilibrium Toward Developmental Dialectics," in W. J. Arnold (ed.), *Conceptual Foundations of Psychology*. Reprinted by permission of the University of Nebraska Press. • Skinner, B. F. "Baby in a Box" in B. F. Skinner (ed.), *Cumulative Record: A Selection of Papers*, 3d ed. New York: Appleton-Century-Crofts, 1972. Used by permission of Prentice-Hall, Inc. • Skinner, B. F. *Walden Two*. New York: Macmillan, 1948. Used by permission of Macmillan Publishing Co., Inc. • Tryon, C., and J. Lilienthal. "Developmental Tasks: I. The Concept and Its Importance" in *Fostering Mental Health in Our Schools*. Copyright © 1950 by the Association for Supervision and Curriculum Development. Used by permission of the Association for Supervision and Curriculum Development. • Valsiner, Jaan. *Culture and the Development of Children's Action*. © 1987 by John Wiley & Sons, Ltd. Reprinted by permission of the publisher. • Vygotsky, L. S. *Thought and Language*. Cambridge, Mass.: Massachusetts Institute of Technology, 1962. Used by permission of MIT Press.

CONTENTS

CHAPTER ELEVEN   Vygotsky and the Soviet Tradition   319

Perspective D   *Estimating the Future of Stage Theories*   347

PART SIX   *COMPUTER ANALOGUES AND THE SELF*   365

A search for the way children gain skill in processing information and for how a child's innermost self develops

CHAPTER TWELVE   Information-Processing Theory   367

A search for the ways children's and youths' moral reasoning and moral behavior evolve

PREFACE

As suggested in the first two editions of this text, child development theorists are dissatisfied people. They are not content with existing explanations of how a child grows up, so they search for more adequate explanations. To guide their search, they set up goals at which to aim their efforts, goals that may be either stated or implied. The primary purpose of this book is to identify these goals and to describe the results achieved by more than two dozen theorists in their search. A secondary purpose is to inspect a series of issues met in the domain of child development, issues that bridge a variety of theories.

Like the earlier editions, this version of the book has the same aim in the world of theories that a three-week guided European tour has in the world of travel. I do not pretend to give a detailed, in-depth account of any one territory. Instead, I propose to: (1) suggest profitable ways to compare theories (Chapters One and Two), (2) describe key aspects of a variety of the better known theories (Chapters Three through Sixteen), and (3) analyze a series of topics related to many theories (Perspectives A through G).

Readers acquainted with the second edition of *Comparing Theories of Child Development* may be interested at the outset in learning how this new version is similar to and different from that edition. The most obvious added features are the seven perspectives, which focus on issues in the field of child development. One perspective is placed at the end of each of the last seven parts of the book—that is, Parts Two through Eight. In nearly every instance, the topic of the perspective derives from some matter that has assumed prominence in the chapters preceding it. The topics center on questions of normal development, states of consciousness, investigative methods, stage theories, types of causal factors, trends in theorizing about development, and ways of representing the essence of a theory in metaphor.

Many of the models of development that appeared in the second edition are still accorded a prominent place in this new version, but their treatment is updated. Such is the case of developmental tasks, psychoanalysis, Erikson's psychosocial theory, Piaget's model, operant behaviorism, humanistic theory, and Kohlberg's conception of moral development. Other schemes described in the former edition are offered in the present version in a much expanded form, with particular attention to newer concepts and to additional theorists who have made contributions to those schemes: commonsense attribution theory, Gesell's normative approach, Soviet theories, information processing, social learning models and contextualism (Rotter, Riegel, Valsiner), ecological theory (Bronfenbrenner), and ethology (Hinde, Eibl-Eibesfeldt). An entirely new chapter describes an integrated theory of moral development.

To make space for the added material, several features of the second edition have been dropped, including the historical treatment of Rousseauistic and Puritan theories, the research suggestions in each chapter, the annotated bibliography of additional theories, and the detailed discussion of Lewin's and Werner's work.

As noted in the first two editions, there are far more theories in the world than a single volume can accommodate. Therefore it has been necessary to select those that are most suitable. Each choice has been guided by three criteria:

1. Has the theory been popular? That is, have many people subscribed to it or at least been acquainted with it?
2. Has the theory been influential? Has it affected people's treatment of children or influenced the beliefs of other theorists?
3. Is the theory representative of a class or family of theories? Theories often fall into groups, with the members of each group being similar in certain respects and dissimilar in others. Because it is not feasible to include all variants of a particular group, I have chosen only a few theories—in some cases only one—to represent each class. In making this selection I have been influenced not only by the representativeness of a theory but also by my own tastes and interests, and thus I've included those theories that I feel are more interesting than others.

The fifteen chapters that describe individual theories are organized in seven parts. Each part reflects a key goal pursued by the theorists discussed within that part as they searched for descriptions or explanations of development more adequate than those found in existing theories. I have tried to suggest this key goal by placing at the opening of each part a phrase identifying the sort of search that links together the theorists included in that section.

When we inspect the origins of the theories discussed, we discover that they display a geographical and cultural bias. All originate in the Western world. Their roots are in Western civilization, and they have been nurtured primarily in Europe and North America. To help balance this bias, four of my former graduate students who are expert in Asian languages and cultures joined me in preparing a companion volume entitled *Oriental Theories of Human Development—Scriptural and Popular Beliefs from Hinduism, Buddhism, Confucianism, Shinto, and Islam* (New York: Peter Lang, 1988). As the term *scriptural* suggests, the book contains theories extracted from the traditional literature of five religions. Such theoretical material is supplemented by the results of interviews about human development with more than a hundred adherents of each of the religions (*popular beliefs*). The interviews were collected by the research team in India, Thailand, the Republic of China on Taiwan, the Sudan, and Japan.

Finally, a note of appreciation is due to my students and colleagues at the University of California, Santa Barbara. They have always been helpful in offering comments that have forced me to improve the clarity and accuracy of what I say and write. I am particularly indebted to Professor James Block for his intimate knowledge of trends in development theories. I wish to thank the following colleagues in other universities for reviewing this third edition of the book: Armin Arndt, Eastern Washington University; Michael Green, University of North Carolina, Charlotte; and Alastair Younger, University of Ottawa. I also wish to thank all those who read earlier versions of this book and offered valuable suggestions for improving its content: Andrew Collins, University of Minnesota; Bernard S. Gorman; Billie Housego, University of British Columbia; Jane Ledingham, University of Ottawa; James Moran, Virginia Polytechnic Institute; Ronald Mullis, North Dakota State University; Richard Newman, State University of New York at Stony Brook; Samuel Snyder, North Carolina State University at Raleigh; Judy Todd, and Eleanor Willemson, Santa Clara University.

In addition, I wish to express my appreciation for the wisdom and diligence applied to the production of this new edition by members of the Bookman Productions staff, particularly Carol Dondrea. Finally, a word of thanks is due Ken King, senior psychology editor at Wadsworth, for his strong support.

STANDARDS OF COMPARISON

Ways of analyzing likenesses and differences among theories

Since this book compares theories of child development, it is reasonable to ask at the outset, Compares theories against what standards? Or, compares them along what dimensions? The two chapters comprising Part One are designed to answer these questions.

Chapter One defines the way such terms as *facts, theory,* and *model* are used throughout the book. It also describes a variety of standards or criteria that people often use to distinguish "good theory" from "bad theory."

Chapter Two looks at theories in a different way. It reviews a range of topics or questions on which a child development theory may focus. These questions are intended as guides to identifying the contents of a theory, that is, as guides to the substantive focus of the theory.

Part One, then, suggests viewpoints from which the theories surveyed in Chapters Three through Seventeen can be analyzed at an introductory or basic level.

CHAPTER ONE

Theories, Models, Paradigms, and Such

Many people—parents, teachers, college students—often say, "I don't want a lot of theorizing. I want to know what children are really like. It's the facts of child development I'm interested in."

For such people, "theorizing" means speculating about children in the quiet of a study, producing a kind of armchair philosophy that has little or nothing to do with the way children grow up in the real world. "Facts," they feel, are practical and useful. Facts show how children really develop and why they behave as they do. For these people a book on child development theories is of no value.

The above distinction between "fact" and "theory" is not the one intended in this book. I see the relationship between the two in a different way. I consider facts or data to be either (1) discrete observations and measurements of children and their actions or (2) summaries of such observations and measurements. Here are three typical examples of discrete observations:

> A first-grade teacher poured all of the water from a bowl into a tall drinking glass, then asked six-year-old Anne if the amount of water now in the glass was the same as the amount that had been in the bowl. Anne said there was now more in the glass.

> The parents of thirteen-year-old Martin were upset because, they said, the boy acted "like a sissy." Martin did not like to play with other boys. He wore fancy rings and bracelets. His mother found him in her bedroom putting rouge on his lips and darkening his eyelids with her eye shadow. His father said, "Marty even walks like a girl."

Shortly after supper one evening, seventeen-year-old Linda received a
telephone invitation to go to a movie, but she said, "Sorry, Hank, I have
to stay in all evening to study chemistry." A few moments later she
answered another phone call with, "Okay, Larry, but only for a couple of
hours. I'll study till eight o'clock. Then we can go out for a while."

Facts or data can also be in the form of summaries of observations or
measurements: the average height of twelve-year-old girls, a list of the
reactions of five-year-olds when they first enter kindergarten, the percentage of sixteen-year-olds who have smoked marijuana.

If these are facts, then what is theory? There is no easy, definitive
answer to this question because many different meanings for theory are
found in writings on philosophy and science. For the purposes of this book,
however, I have simplified matters by adopting one definition broad
enough to encompass all the different authors that I have included. I
define theory as *an explanation of how the facts fit together*. More precisely, I
intend the process of theorizing about child development to mean the act
of proposing (1) which facts are most important for understanding children and (2) what sorts of relationships among the facts are most significant for producing this understanding. Theory is what makes sense out of
facts. Theory gives facts their meaning. Without theory, facts remain a
clutter of disorganized specks on the canvas, unconnected spots that form
no picture of how and why children grow up as they do.

Thus a book on theories of child development can serve as a practical
guide to understanding children, for it describes the underlying structure
of different beliefs about what children are like and how children should
be treated.

In this opening chapter we focus on four questions that people often
ask when they first seriously consider theories of development: (1) What
difference does it make which theory you adopt? (2) How does the term
theory relate to such terms as *model, paradigm, analogue,* and the like? (3)
What standards can be used to distinguish good theory from bad theory?
(4) Why do scholars develop different theories rather than agree on an
existing one?

THE DIFFERENCE YOUR CHOICE
OF THEORY CAN MAKE

A theory of child development can be likened to a lens through which we
view children and their growth. The theory filters out certain facts and
gives a particular pattern to those it lets in. To illustrate the way such
filtering operates, let's briefly consider how the incidents of Anne, Martin,

and Linda might be interpreted from the viewpoints of four theories presented later.

These interpretations will be much simplified since you have not yet had a chance to inspect any of the theories in detail. However, the examples still illustrate the point that the theory chosen for interpreting facts about children determines the meaning assigned to those facts. When you have read further, you will recognize the complexities the case of Anne, Martin, and Linda would involve if they were interpreted more completely.

The theorists whose lenses we will peer through are Piaget, Freud, Skinner, and certain humanistic psychologists.

A Piagetian Viewpoint

For more than fifty years a Swiss child psychologist, Jean Piaget, collected facts on how children of different ages solved reasoning problems, expressed their dreams, made moral judgments, and carried out other mental activities. He proposed that a child's modes of thought form a series of stages of intellectual growth common to all children in all cultures. We might reasonably propose then that Piagetians would interpret the cases of Anne, Martin, and Linda in terms of these stages.

For instance, we would expect an advocate of Piaget's theory to explain that Anne thought there was more water in the tall glass than in the shallow bowl because she had not yet reached the stage at which children understand conservation of volume. By "conservation" we mean that Anne does not yet recognize that the quantity of water remains the same (is "conserved") even though the height and width of the two containers differ.

When we turn to Martin's effeminate behavior, we are on less secure ground in speculating about what a Piagetian would conclude because Piaget focused little if any attention on matters of socially unconventional behavior. Piaget was more concerned with the thought processes of the typical or average child than with personal-social behavior that differed from a particular society's norms for sex-appropriate actions. However, Piaget did give a good deal of attention to children's moral judgments, to what children considered right and wrong and how they supported such decisions. Piaget identified a series of stages through which children passed in the development of moral judgment, and we might use these stages for interpreting what Martin would say in defending the rightness of his wearing lip rouge and eye shadow. In other words, by posing moral decision questions for Martin to answer, we could estimate the level of reasoning he uses to defend his actions.

When we use a Piagetian lens to view seventeen-year-old Linda's rejection of Hank in favor of Larry, we again receive little direct aid since Piaget did not theorize about sexual attraction and social interaction among adolescents. However, if we put the sexual attraction question aside and limit ourselves to the intellectual companionship aspect of Linda's choice, then we might find some aid in Piagetian theory. We could speculate that Linda may have preferred Larry because her stage of intelligence or mode of thought was more like Larry's than like Hank's. In other words, we would be estimating that youths of similar intellectual levels have a greater affinity for each other than youths of dissimilar levels.

We might also use Piagetian theory in another way to give meaning to the facts about Linda. Since Piaget identified stages of moral judgment that children pass through, we could ask Linda to explain why she thought it was right to reject Hank in favor of Larry. Then we could use her response to estimate her stage of moral judgment.

Let's turn now to a second theorist's perceptions of the same cases.

A Freudian Viewpoint

Toward the end of the nineteenth and the beginning of the twentieth centuries, Sigmund Freud devised a theory of child development based on the childhood recollections of adults that he treated for neuroses in his Vienna, Austria, psychiatric practice. Freud, like Piaget, proposed that children develop through a series of stages. However, instead of concerning himself with children's reasoning skills, Freud focused on *psychosexual* development. He identified steps in personality growth as influenced by children's ways of satisfying sexual drives from one period of childhood to another.

For example, Freud theorized that between the ages of 3 and 5, the typical child views the opposite-sex parent as a desirable love object that he or she wants to possess exclusively. In essence, the boy yearns to possess his mother and the girl her father. However, the child recognizes that she or he has been bested in this competition by the like-sexed parent. In other words, the boy's father has been the victor in the contest for the mother's sexual attention, and the girl's mother has been the victor in the competition for the father's love. To resolve this problem of yearning for the opposite-sex parent, the typical child in Freud's system seeks to acquire the characteristics of the victor. This means that the boy identifies with his father and seeks to adopt his father's traits, the traits of masculinity. In like fashion, the girl identifies with her mother and tries to behave in those feminine ways that apparently have made her mother successfully attractive. This process of identification, then, explains from a Freudian viewpoint why the typical boy develops the characteristics that his society considers masculine and the typical girl develops the characteristics considered feminine.

However, Freudians point out that sometimes the process of resolving the parental love conflict goes awry. The boy may not identify with his father's traits. Instead, he identifies with his mother's characteristics, or perhaps some other twist occurs in the normal process. Consequently the boy adopts feminine characteristics. From a Freudian perspective, we could reasonably assume that such a twist occurred in Martin's case. The boy apparently did not achieve a proper resolution of the conflict he faced in middle childhood, so that in early adolescence he is displaying sexually inappropriate behavior. To find out how this actually happened, Freudians would wish to gather information from the boy's unconscious mind— information collected by means of dream interpretation and by analyzing the free-flowing thoughts that Martin expresses while he is in a relaxed condition.

We can speculate that Freudians would see Anne's reactions also from a psychosexual viewpoint. Freudians—or at least some Freudians—would interpret Anne's reactions to the bowl and the tall glass in terms of sexual symbols. The meaning of the bowl-and-glass incident, they might say, lies in the unconscious portion of the girl's mind and relates to Anne's concerns about her own drives and the ways they are being satisfied or frustrated. In Freud's view, containers such as bowls and glasses symbolized female sex organs, whereas protruding, projectile-like objects symbolized the male. But exactly how such symbolization might fit into Anne's personality structure in the bowl-and-glass experiment would likely be unclear to psychoanalysts until they collected more information about the girl's feelings and thought processes. This information, intended to reveal the child's unconscious motives, might be gathered through the analyst's listening to Anne's comments while she played with dolls or while she recounted her fantasies.

The case of the high school girl, Linda, might be analyzed in several ways from a Freudian viewpoint. Freudians might explain Linda's behavior in terms of how the characteristics of her two suitors, Hank and Larry, compared with the characteristics of other important males in her life, particularly her father. Did Linda select Larry because he reminded her of her father and was a substitute for him in the girl's affections? Or did Linda reject Hank because he reminded her of her father and she was symbolically striking back at her father whom she resents and wishes to harm? In effect, how is Linda's reaction to the two boys related to the manner in which she has sought to resolve the desire to possess her father—a desire that ostensibly began a decade earlier at the psychosexual stage known generally as the Oedipus stage or, for girls, the Electra stage? The answer to such questions is not found in the facts of the Larry and Hank incident. Rather the answer must be sought through the collection of far more information about the nature of Linda's unconscious motives and the manner in which she has interacted with her parents over the past years.

Thus we see that the facts offered earlier about Martin, Anne, and Linda can assume quite different meanings when viewed through Freudian rather than Piagetian spectacles.

A Skinnerian Viewpoint

B. F. Skinner was an American psychologist who represents a school of thought known as *radical behaviorism.* He believed that it is more profitable to observe the factors in life that seem to influence people's behavior rather than speculate about what might be in people's minds or personalities. The basic tenets of his system are quite simple. Every time someone acts, the action is followed by a consequence. The nature of this consequence determines whether the person will act in the same way in a similar situation in the future. If the consequence is pleasant and rewarding, then the person will tend to act in the same way in the future. If the consequence is not rewarding, the person will tend to act differently. In essence, according to Skinner, the behaviors we develop as we grow up depend on the consequences that followed those behaviors in the past.

Now let us speculate about how such a theory might enable us to interpret the incidents involving Anne, Martin, and Linda. We may assume that in the past Anne has been rewarded (behaviorists would call it *reinforced* instead of *rewarded*) for concluding that when something is taller, it is larger or bigger in general. Her own experience and other people's remarks have confirmed this conclusion for her. Thus, when she sees the water reach a greater height in the glass than it did in the bowl, she draws the same conclusion that has been reinforced in the past—that there is more of the substance when it is taller. If we wish to change Anne's misconception, we need to arrange the consequences of her behavior so they no longer reinforce her unsophisticated judgment. We would arrange experiments that force her to disconfirm her conclusion about the water containers, and we would also tell her when she is right and wrong. We may even wish to furnish some external reward, such as a toy or candy, for correct conclusions and withhold such reinforcers when she makes errors in judgment. Thus, according to Skinnerian theory, we influence Anne's intellectual development by manipulating the consequences of her behavior.

When we consider Martin's behavior from a Skinnerian viewpoint, we conclude that he currently displays feminine ways because when he has done so in the past the consequences have been more satisfying or reinforcing than the consequences following masculine actions he has attempted. Not only does he currently persist in retaining past feminine acts but he can be expected to acquire even more of them in the future if the consequences of doing so are reinforced. The only way to alter his behavior pattern is to manipulate the consequences so that those following feminine acts are nonreinforcing and those following masculine acts are reinforcing or pleasurable.

In like manner we can interpret Linda's preference for Larry rather than Hank in terms of the consequences that have followed the girl's past contacts with the two boys. Apparently her relationship with Larry has been reinforced more strongly than her relationship with Hank. This greater reinforcement accounts for her preference to be with Larry.

A Humanistic Viewpoint

A humanistic psychologist's conviction about the best way to view development is quite the opposite of a behaviorist's. Rather than concentrating on children's observable actions, humanists focus on children's conceptions of themselves. The development of each child's unique *self* is a key concern, as reflected in frequent reference to the child's *identity, self-confidence, self-control, self-consciousness, self-efficacy, self-realization,* and the like. Thus the process of getting to know oneself is of central interest. Important humanistic issues are children's feelings, their loves and hates, their hopes and fears, and their expectations for the future.

As we try to interpret the descriptions of Anne, Martin, and Linda from a humanistic perspective, we find little or nothing to say about Anne and her answers during the water-in-the-glass experiment. Humanistic theory does not address issues of how children analyze physical phenomena.

In contrast, Martin's case offers ample possibilities for interpretation. Perhaps the most obvious inference to draw is that Martin's actions reveal his attempt to find his authentic identity, an attempt to actualize a unique potential that is within him and to express this potential in behavior that is self-satisfying. He obviously faces some opposition in this quest because the persona he displays fails to match the stereotype traditionally accepted as masculine in Western society. However, his chances of showing his inner nature without fear of public censure is greater today than it would have been a quarter century ago, because living as a member of the gay community has recently become far more acceptable than it was in the past. Today, Western society's legal provisions and general attitudes regarding "proper" gender behavior have grown increasingly liberal, thereby permitting both males and females to adopt ways of life that in the past were restricted to the opposite sex. Still, because of tradition, Martin can expect to continue encountering difficulties with his parents and others in his pursuit of self-actualization.

Linda's preferring Larry rather than Hank can also be explained from a humanistic point of view. She may find Larry more desirable because he enhances her own self-image. For instance, Larry may be considered a "great catch" among the high-school crowd—handsome, entertaining, wealthy, a star athlete, a student-body leader, or the like—so that Linda's sense of her own worth is fostered by Larry's attention. Being seen in public with Larry raises her social stock among her agemates. Or the way the two boys treat Linda may be the determining factor in her choice. Perhaps Larry often compliments her, so she feels attractive and capable when she is with him, while Hank makes fun of her appearance and opinions, and she finds this degrading. Or she may be influenced by how Larry's personality complements her own self-concept. For instance, if she views herself as highly capable and wanting to direct others around her, she may prefer Larry because he always does what she suggests. Or, in contrast, she may lack confidence in her own judgment, so she likes to be with Larry because he is self-assured, readily makes decisions, and adopts a protective attitude toward her. As still another possibility, Linda could be looking vaguely—perhaps unconsciously—toward marriage in the future, and she finds that Larry matches her hopes for a mate better than Hank. In summary, humanists' emphasis on the *self* and on an individual's dreams of the future offers a host of possibilities for analyzing such incidents as Linda's response to the two boys' invitations.

Before leaving our four illustrative theorists, I should state explicitly that the interpretations I have offered of the data about Anne, Martin, and Linda are not the only ones that might be drawn from the four theoretical positions. Other interpreters might find other implications in the data. Thus the conclusions I have presented are not *the* correct or definitive analyses; rather they are simply illustrations of meanings that logically could be offered from the four perspectives. Furthermore, I obviously have given only a brief glimpse of each theory, just enough to suggest how data can assume quite different meanings when different theories are used for organizing the facts. A more complete examination of each theory is found in later chapters.

THE WORD *THEORY* AND OTHER TERMS

So far in our discussion I have stayed almost exclusively with the word *theory* in referring to authors' schemes for organizing data. However, in the literature on child development a variety of terms are used, and this is a problem for newcomers to child development theory. The problem is, How do such words as *theory, model, paradigm, analogue,* and *metatheory* relate to each other? Solving the problem would be simple if all writers intended the same meaning for a given term, but such is not the case. One writer will use *theory* and *model* as synonyms; another will not. Before we move further into the analysis of theories, we need to inspect a number of these terms to see how they are used by different authors.

Of the many words we might consider, I have selected thirteen of the most common to discuss. The first six are used almost synonymously by many writers; they are *theory, model, paradigm, analogy, structure,* and *system.* The seventh is *metatheory,* a term of recent popularity that appears to have spawned a brood of related *meta* words. The last six are typically used for identifying kinds of statements made within a theory; these are *assumption, axiom, postulate, hypothesis, principle,* and *law.*

When we read about theories of child development, we must be alert to the meaning the writer explicitly or implicitly assigns to the word *theory.* For us, a theory will be any statement describing (1) which facts are most important for understanding children and (2) what sorts of relationships among facts are most significant for producing this understanding. Other writers place more restrictions on the term. For example, *theory* can be defined as a "set of statements, including (a) general laws and principles that serve as axioms, (b) other laws, or theorems, that are deducible from the axioms, and (c) definitions of concepts" (Reese & Overton, 1970, p. 117). Skinner on occasion has denied that his explanation of behavior qualifies as theory; and if a very restricted definition of the term is applied, he would appear to be correct in his denial. However, in the broad sense of the word that I have adopted in these pages, Skinner's explanation does indeed qualify as theory (Skinner, 1950).

The word *model* has become increasingly popular in recent decades as a label for theoretical proposals. However, the term has caused some confusion because one writer will use it in a broad sense while another will limit its meaning. In its broad sense, *model* can mean any tentative ideational plan of relationships among variables. At this general level, a model can be a world view (Kuhn, 1962) or a world hypothesis (Pepper, 1942) that suggests something about the basic nature of people or of reality. For example, some child development theories are founded on a machine model in contrast to others founded on a dynamic organism model. That is, one camp of theorists pictures the growing child as a machine that reacts to things done to it by the environment: The child's behavior is primarily a product of the way the environment manipulates it. The other group pictures the child as an active, seeking organism who determines his or her own behavior by internally motivated desires. In a more limited sense writers have used the word *model* to mean, for example, an exclusively mathematical or graphic representation of the way something operates (Suppes, 1969, pp. 10–17). In child development literature, therefore, we should try to decide which of these meanings the writer intends. In the following chapters I will use *model* in the same broad sense as I am using *theory*—as any scheme intended to describe relationships among variables or facts of child development.

Another common term in child development literature is *paradigm* (rhymes with either "dim" or "dime"). Some people use *paradigm* to mean only a very general model (Kuhn, 1962), an overall viewpoint or description of relationships about reality. Others use it to mean either a broad, general picture or as a more specific, more precise description of relationships among variables. In this sense, they equate *paradigm* with *model* and use the terms interchangeably. Again, it is well to determine the way an author intends the term to be used.

Theorists use the term *analogy* or *analogue* when comparing an aspect of growth to something else in order to help explain that aspect of growth. For instance, theorists may say that the mind of the growing child is like an electronic computer, consisting of a finite amount of storage space for ideas and a system for retrieving the ideas when they are needed. Or theorists may liken a highly mobile two-year-old to an inquisitive puppy that noses into everything without any notion of danger or responsibility. Analogies are thus kinds of models, in the sense of one thing representing qualities of something else. In this book, *analogy* or *analogue* will refer to a comparison between child development in a general sense and some other object or system; for example, an analogy would liken stages of growth to steps on a ladder the child ascends as the years pass.

The words *structure* and *system* are considered together for they commonly carry the same meaning. Each identifies the elements that comprise something and describes the way these elements are interrelated. Therefore a theorist's entire complex of beliefs and their interconnections can be called a system. Likewise, one segment of an overall complex of beliefs can be singled out as a separate entity with its own constituent parts and be called a system or subsystem by itself. So we can speak of Piaget's complete set of ideas about child development as his system or theoretical structure, or we can pick one segment of this complex—such as Piaget's explanation of children's play—and view it as a subsystem with its own inner workings (Hall & Lindzey, 1970, pp. 317–318).

Beginning in the 1970s, a host of new *meta* words sprang up in the human development literature: *metatheory, metamemory, metacognition, meta-analysis, metalearning, metaperception, metaprinciples,* and more. This rash of neologisms has caused some confusion since authors often fail to explain how they intend such terms. Furthermore, while there is some consistency of usage, not all authors use a given meta word with the same meaning. In contemporary human development literature *meta* is most often intended to mean "an analysis of" or "knowledge about" the subject to which the meta is prefixed. So in this sense, *metacognition* is knowledge about cognition or, in other words, "thinking about thinking." In like manner, *metamemory* is an awareness of how memory operates, and *metalearning* is the analysis of how learning occurs. Following this same pattern, *metatheory* becomes the analysis of what *theory* is about, how *theory* is developed or used. As a result, what we are doing throughout this book is *metatheory*. It is especially what I am attempting in these first two chapters.

Although most meta terms in child development literature seem to mean "knowledge about" some process, sometimes they are not intended that way. Not long ago I asked an author what he meant by *metatheory* in one of his recent articles. Did he mean "an analysis of" theory? Or, rather, was *metatheory* in this instance an overarching, umbrella theory that encompassed more specific subtheories, as some writers use the term? He said no. On this occasion he used the word to mean a precursor of "true theory," that is, a set of preliminary speculations that would not as yet qualify as tightly knit theory. So, because the meanings for meta terms have not been standardized, it is well to study a theorist's meta words with some care to estimate which meaning she or he is seeking to convey.

Next we turn to six words that refer to types of statements that may be included in a theory. They are *assumption, axiom, postulate, hypothesis, principle,* and *law.* Again, as with the words just discussed, not all writers assign identical meanings to these terms. However, we shall not take time to survey the various uses of each term. Instead we will look at the most widely accepted meaning of each.

One useful way to approach the six terms is to think of their roles within a series of four phases a theorist may go through in creating and refining a model of child development (see Table 1.1). To begin, the theorist accepts certain concepts as true without testing them. These self-evident beliefs are frequently called *assumptions, axioms,* or *postulates.* An axiom or postulate is a formal statement of the conviction on which the theorist's model will be founded. In contrast, an assumption is either informally stated by the theorist or is not stated at all. Sometimes theorists

Table 1.1 Terms and Phases in Theory Building

	Phase 1	Phase 2	Phase 3	Phase 4
	Foundation Convictions	*Model Descriptions*	*Logical Deductions*	*Conclusions*
Products of the Phase:	Axioms Postulates Assumptions	Structure System	Hypotheses	Principles Laws
The Theorist's Behavior:	Accepts certain beliefs as being self-evident.	Defines the parts of the model and their interrelations.	Suggests relationships or outcomes that reasonably might be expected if the model accurately represents the aspect of development it is supposed to describe.	Draws generalizations from evidence collected to test or estimate the accuracy of the model.

Note: Although the process of theory building can thus be described as four sequential steps or phases, in practice a theorist frequently may not move systematically through the sequence. More often than not, theorists appear to shuttle back and forth among the phases, revising here and altering there, to produce a scheme they believe provides a convincing interpretation of the facts.

are unaware that they are making certain assumptions until critics point them out.

After establishing a foundation of assumptions and postulates, the theorist erects the superstructure of the model. Typically the model, or at least certain aspects of it, is proposed in only a tentative form because the author is not sure that it represents an accurate picture of the way children develop. The author is saying, in effect, that "it seems likely that children grow up this way and for these reasons." However, she or he is not entirely sure. So to answer questions that are still puzzling about the theory's validity, the theorist composes some "if-then" statements that derive logically from the model. These yet-to-be-proven statements are usually called *hypotheses*.

One popular way to state a hypothesis is in an if-then form. For example, in Chapter Four we consider a developmental-task theory advocated by an American psychologist named Robert J. Havighurst. The theory proposes that every few years as children grow up, they meet a new set of physical-growth and social-psychological problems or *tasks* they must solve. The theory further contends that if children do not successfully solve a problem at one age level, they will have difficulty in solving tasks at higher age levels in the future. From this general proposal, we can create hypotheses to test the validity of Havighurst's notion. As one illustration, we can take the area of emotional development called "giving and receiving affection." Within this area, the preadolescent child is said to face the task of "learning to give as much love as one receives." In early adolescence, the emotional-development task the child is to accomplish is that of "accepting one's self as a worthwhile person, really worthy of love." So we now have a pair of sequential tasks in hand and are thereby able to offer the following hypothesis:

> If, by the end of late childhood, a girl has not learned to give as much love as she receives, then in early adolescence she will not accept herself as a worthwhile person, really worthy of love.

As soon as we define the key terms in this statement (such as *late childhood, as much love, early adolescence, accept herself,* and *worthwhile person*), we are ready to set up an experiment or make observations of adolescents that will test the validity of the hypothesis. In effect, we observe children to decide whether this statement—one aspect of the theory—is true in real life.

A hypothesis or tentative estimate of the real state of affairs is not always in the form of an if-then statement. It can be a simple declarative sentence that only implies the if-then condition. For example, we could rephrase our hypothesis to read:

> A girl who has not learned to give as much love as she receives by the time she reaches the end of late childhood will not accept herself as a worthwhile person, really worthy of love, during her adolescent years.

Or, as another option, the hypothesis can be phrased as a question:

> Will a girl who has not learned by the end of late childhood to give as much love as she receives be able to accept herself as a worthwhile person, really worthy of love, when she is an early adolescent?

Despite the form in which a hypothetical relationship is cast, its status in theory building is the same. It functions as a reasonable, but as yet unproven, idea whose validity needs to be examined.

When the investigators have collected enough evidence to convince themselves that a hypothesized relationship is valid, they may then draw a generalization about it that they call a "principle." Thus I am using the term *principle* to mean a generalization that is accepted as true—not because it seems self-evident but because it is supported by what the theorists believe are sound data. Or if they regard the empirical data and logic behind it as irrefutable, the theorists can accord the generalization a higher status and term it a *law* or *law of nature*.

Finally, in this discussion of terminology, I feel it is useful to make a distinction between *evidence* and *proof*. Perhaps our most basic motive for comparing theories is to discover which of them is "true" or, at least, which parts of them are "valid." We might say that we are seeking proof of the theories. In this search I find it helpful to define the terms *evidence* and *proof* in the following way:

> *Evidence* is a public thing. It consists of the arguments, the logic, the patterns of reasoning, and the facts that bear upon what it treats. This book is intended to present evidence about the theories it includes.
>
> *Proof*, in contrast, is a personal, private thing. It is a conviction that something is true.

The significance of distinguishing between these two concepts is illustrated by arguments that arise over whether a generalization should be labeled an assumption, a hypothesis, or a principle. The arguments seem to arise because the people on the two sides of the debate either (1) have different kinds of evidence at hand or (2) are convinced by different kinds or amounts of evidence. The sort of evidence one person accepts as proof of a theory may not be the same sort that another accepts. A generalization about child growth that I accept as a proven principle or law may be one that you still consider to be a hypothesis.

GOOD THEORY, BAD THEORY

Typically when we compare theories we are interested not only in learning how they are alike or different but also in judging whether one is better than another. To make this judgment, we need to decide what our standards of goodness will be. Everyone does not use the same standards for appraisal. Therefore let's review some of the more common standards people use in differentiating good theory from bad.

We will consider nine popular standards of judgment. These are not necessarily ones you *should* adopt as your own; rather they are ones you *might* adopt if they seem convincing and if they fit into your own set of values. Further, you will likely discover that they are not all of equal importance to you. You may wish to revise certain ones, eliminate others, and add a few of your own. In this way you will devise your own standards for judging child development theories.

At the beginning of this chapter the term *theory* was defined in a very broad manner. A theory, I proposed, is a description of (1) which facts are most important for understanding children and (2) what sorts of relationships among facts are most significant for producing this understanding. I noted later that some people use *theory* in a more restricted way. They usually restrict the term by adding the sort of criteria described by the nine standards that follow. For instance, some people are unwilling to call a collection of ideas a theory unless the collection is both internally consistent in structure and clearly provides for the generation of testable hypotheses. However, we will use these standards not for deciding what should be called a theory but for deciding how worthwhile or how "good" a theory is.

Standard 1: A theory is better if it accurately reflects the facts of the real world of children.

Some theorists are criticized for producing a model of development that does not accurately represent children. We will consider three reasons why a mismatch may occur between a theory and the facts of child development.

First, a theorist may draw conclusions from a study of only a few children, then improperly apply these conclusions to many children—the error of generalizing beyond the data. This criticism does not apply to the common practice of studying a representative sample of children and then extending the resulting conclusions to the larger population of children accurately reflected by the sample. Indeed, such sampling is involved in virtually all research on development. But it is an error to apply conclusions about a small group to a larger population when there is good reason to believe that the conditions of the two groups are significantly different. For instance, Arnold Gesell (Chapter Three) has been criticized for improperly generalizing conclusions from a study of children who came to his clinic at Yale University. He apparently assumed that the group of children he observed and measured were accurate representatives of nearly all other children. But there is a serious question about whether his conclusions correctly describe child growth in other cultural settings.

Likewise, in the eighteenth century, Jean Jacques Rousseau wrote at length about the nature of children, founding his beliefs on three sorts of evidence: (1) his experience as a tutor for several sons of aristocratic European families, (2) some casual observations of French peasant children, and (3) hearsay impressions of the personalities of "noble savages" in primitive cultures. Critics of Rousseau have questioned whether his descriptions of child development, based on such limited data, actually matched the experience of all the children to whom he applied his conclusions.

Second, a theory may not describe children accurately because a researcher who studies one facet of child growth may not be satisfied to limit conclusions to that facet. Instead, in an effort to discover general principles of growth that explain all sorts of behavior, the researcher applies the conclusions to explain other aspects of child growth as well. For example, he or she may measure trends in children's physical growth and then seek to apply the pattern of increases and plateaus in physical growth to other areas of development, such as social or emotional or mental development. But principles governing one aspect of development may not be the same as those governing another, so risk may be involved.

The third cause of conflict between theory and fact may arise from the researcher's faulty memory or inaccurate observation of children. Probably none of us can help being influenced by memories of our own childhood or by our casual impressions of children we have seen and talked with. Unless we are careful to use controlled observing, testing, and measuring of children, we risk allowing distorted observations from the past or from casual impressions to influence the schemes we devise for explaining development.

Standard 2: A theory is better if it is stated in a way that makes it clearly understandable to anyone who is reasonably competent ("reasonably competent" means having a suitable command of language, mathematics, and logical analysis).

More precisely, anyone with reasonable competence should be able to understand: (1) what facets or events in the real world are referred to by each part of the theory, (2) the meaning of terms used in the model, (3) the key assumptions on which the model is founded, and (4) how the explanations and predictions are logically derived from the definitions and assumptions.

This standard may appear simple and straightforward, but in practice it can be quite controversial. If we find that a theory lacks clarity, is it the theorist's fault for being obscure or confused, or is it our own fault for lacking the competence needed to understand the theorist? We usually have a higher regard for a theory whose elements we can readily comprehend.

Standard 3: A theory is better if it not only explains why past events occurred but also accurately predicts future events. Furthermore, it is better if it enables us to make accurate predictions about the specific behaviors of a particular child rather than only speculations about general growth patterns for a group of children.

People who seek to understand children are usually interested in both the past and the future. They look to the past to learn what forces in a child's life caused the child to be the way she or he is today. They look to the future to estimate what the child will probably be like in coming years.

Many theories are better suited to explaining the past than to foretelling the future. And of those that say something of the future, most are better suited to predicting general characteristics of the typical child or of children in general than they are to predicting the specific development characteristics of a particular child. However, those interested in child development—researchers, parents, teachers, physicians—more highly value a theory that produces specific predictions about a given child than one that foretells only general growth directions or yields only estimates of how the average child will turn out. It is my own belief that a social learning theorist (Chapter Nine) is better prepared to make predictions about a specific child's verbal development than are people who base their judgment solely on Havighurst's developmental-task theory (Chapter Four).

Standard 4: A theory is better if it offers practical guidance in solving daily problems of child rearing to people responsible for the welfare of children—parents, teachers, camp counselors, pediatricians, clinical psychologists, juvenile court judges, and so on.

This standard, which is a practical extension of standard 3, is considered by many to be the most important, for they are interested in theory only to the extent that it improves their own skills in understanding and treating the children they meet daily. In contrast, some theorists, and readers of theory, are not particularly concerned with translating ideas into advice on child rearing. Rather, they are searching for basic principles of human growth and behavior; the question of whether these principles will enable people to treat children with greater skill is entirely incidental.

Standard 5: A theory is better if it is internally consistent.

The essence of a theory is its structure, a description of its elements and the way they interact. Theorists choose different ways to display this framework of their beliefs. For example, although all theorists explain their models of development verbally, some supplement their verbal descriptions with mathematical symbols that permit the theory's components to be manipulated according to rules of logic. By quantifying the components, a theorist hopes to gain precision in analyzing and predicting child growth and behavior. Piaget is an example of a theorist who has sought to enhance the clarity of his verbal explanations with such symbols (Piaget, 1950).

Another way to supplement verbal description is through diagrams. For example, if a theory involves two main dimensions that interact (such as the relationship between chronological age and mental growth), then the relationship can be displayed as a simple graph, with age on one axis and mental growth on the other. More complex diagrammatic versions of theories appear in Chapters Five, Six, Twelve, and Seventeen.

Whatever the mode of presentation, however—words, mathematical symbols, or diagrams—the system, according to standard 5, should be internally consistent. A person seeking to understand the system should not have to disregard one segment of a model in order to comprehend another. The parts should all fit together logically.

Standard 6: A theory is better if it is economical in the sense that it is founded on as few unproven assumptions as possible and requires simple mechanisms to explain all the phenomena it encompasses.

This criterion is often referred to as the *law of parsimony, Occam's razor,* or *Morgan's canon,* the latter in recognition of a biologist, Lloyd Morgan, who proposed that if two explanations of a phenomenon fit the facts equally well, it is better in the long run to choose the simpler of the explanations. Note that the purpose of this standard is not to discourage theorists from formulating complex explanations of complex events—indeed, simpler explanations can prove to be inaccurate. Instead it is intended to reduce the establishment of theories with elaborate hypothesized internal mechanisms not well supported by evidence. Frequently the more complicated the theory, the more difficult it is to test, and proponents are left to support it with argument and emotion.

Standard 7: A theory is better if it is falsifiable or disconfirmable.

In scientific circles a theory is generally conceived to be an estimate of the truth rather than a definite statement of the truth. Researchers must test the validity of hypotheses derived from the theory in order to determine to what extent it does indeed explain the facts satisfactorily. Thus if a theory's hypotheses can be tested to determine whether they are true, then the reverse should also obtain—it should be possible to test that a hypothesis is false. Many scientists feel that the validity of a theory should not only be confirmable through logic and the presentation of data, it should also be falsifiable or disconfirmable.

Some theories of child development, however, do not appear to display this characteristic of falsifiability; that is, we cannot conceive of a research result that such a theory is unprepared to answer. The theory is built to explain the negative outcome of an experiment as well as the positive outcome.

I can illustrate the problem of falsifiability with the following example. Imagine that we create a theory of social development in which diet is the prime determinant of a child's social adjustment. We contend that a proper combination of B vitamins is particularly important. The proper combination produces a child who is socially constructive and amiable. The improper combination produces a child who is resentful and commits antisocial acts. Our hypothesis, in this form, becomes falsifiable when we have specified the proper and the improper B-vitamin combinations. Now we can create experiments to determine whether this aspect of the theory is valid or not. But let us add another element to our theory. We will call it the *counterpoise factor* and propose that when it is present, the B-vitamin combinations work in just the opposite way we would normally expect. By adding this factor, we have rendered our theory nonfalsifiable. If someone tries to test our theory and discovers that many children who eat the improper B-vitamin combination are socially well adjusted, we explain that in those children the counterpoise factor has been operating. Thus the theory is nonfalsifiable—it is always "correct."

Jaan Valsiner has addressed this matter of falsifiability by contending that:

> Theories are hierarchically organized systems of propositions about reality where every single proposition is related to others and follows

from some more general assumption that the theory constructor has accepted. Such systems are more likely to be adequate if they are constructed by a scientist who knows the empirical phenomenology well—in this sense many aspects of theories grow out of the author's intuitive integration of the empirical knowledge with the abstract bases of the theory. Explicit testing of the theory in the research process involves only some aspects of the theory that the constructor considers important. Depending on the theory constructor's psychological tolerance for failure, different scientists react to the disconfirmation of the selected aspects of the theory in variable ways. . . . Some may accept the disconfirmation and reject the theory. The believers in the absolute truthfulness of the data in their role as "final judges" might react in this way. Others may refuse to accept the disconfirming empirical evidence (1987, pp. 143–144).

Many researchers are uncomfortable with a theory that is nonfalsifiable, so they include standard 7 among the criteria they apply for judging the worth of theories. Among the models reviewed in this book, those of Freud and humanistic psychologists might be considered the least falsifiable.

Standard 8: A theory is better if it stimulates the creation of new research techniques and the discovery of new knowledge.

This can be called the *fertility criterion*. Some theories have been highly fertile, remarkable for the number of new vistas they have opened and the amount of research they have stimulated. As a review of child development journals will attest, a great proportion of published investigations from the 1960s through the 1980s trace their origins to Piaget's writings. Likewise, behaviorism, social learning theory, and information-processing models have been highly effective motivators of research in recent years. In contrast, the work of Havighurst and other developmental-task proponents has not generated much of a search for new knowledge.

Among researchers, this fertility factor is often regarded as the most valued function of a theory because models of development that stimulate many ideas for research will exert the greatest influence on expanding the world's store of knowledge. Such stimulation can take several forms. Perhaps the simplest form is that which leads to *direct replication studies*—empirical studies on which the original theory was based are repeated by other researchers to determine whether the same empirical outcomes and theoretical conclusions result as those reported by the original theorist. Stimulation also can lead to *hypothesis testing*, where a general principle, which is part of the theory, generates hypotheses that can be tested on actual children to determine more precisely the conditions under which the principle validly applies. A third form of stimulation is *verification studies*, where research is conducted to discover whether some theoretical proposal is borne out in real life. Verification is typically sought when a theorist's notions seem to conflict with common sense or with some other theorist's well-accepted proposal. A fourth form can be dubbed *population applicability* because the purpose of the research is to discover if an empirical finding or a theoretical conclusion based on one population of children is equally true in other populations, such as among children of different age levels, of different cultures, or of different ability levels. A fifth form is *discrepancy resolution,* referring to research designed to resolve, or at least to expose, what seem to be a theory's internal inconsistencies. A sixth form is *extended theorizing,* when a theorist's ideas stimulate another theorist to create proposals that extend beyond those of the original author, with the extended theorizing resulting in new possibilities for empirical studies.

Standard 9: A good theory is self-satisfying. It explains development in a way that we feel makes good sense.

This might be called the standard of *self-affirmation.* It is a sort of catchall that depends not only on the previous standards but also on emotional and intuitive factors that we cannot readily identify. The operation of these factors is reflected in our saying about a theory, "I just can't believe that's true" or "I can't believe that's the whole story" when we do not know exactly what it is we find dissatisfying about it. Or we may consider a theory valid because "I feel that's right" or "That rings true—it seems to be the way things are."

   Among the theories described later in this book, the one type that appears to depend most heavily on self-affirmation factors is humanistic psychology, for it is based on the theorist's belief that the individual's real world is the one she or he personally experiences. That is, the feelings and inner experiences of the child are the most important, no matter what sorts of objective factors exist in the world around the child. The development of the child's personally sensed *self* is what interests the humanistic psychologist, and this self is known only through introspection. The advocate of humanistic theory, therefore, can comfortably accept a theory because "it feels right" and "makes intuitive sense" without requiring confirmation from outside, "objective" data. On the other hand, a radical behaviorist, although she might informally say she "feels" her theory is true, does not cite this feeling as validating evidence; instead she is compelled by her theoretical position to produce observational or experimental evidence to support the theory.

   In the final analysis, of course, all theories depend on self-conviction for acceptance.

Further Standards

As noted earlier, the above nine criteria are not the only standards that can be used for judging the goodness of a theory. You may find other criteria that better suit your own tastes. Consider, for example, P. R. Thagard's (1978) three standards for appraising theories—*consilience, simplicity,* and *analogy.*

Consilience refers to how much a theory explains. One child development model is more consilient than another if it elucidates more classes of facts than the other. That is, a consilient theory not only explains the facts but "the facts it explains are taken from more than one domain" (Thagard, 1978, p. 82). Thus a theory that analyzes not only physical growth but also the development of language, social skills, and self-perceptions is more consilient than one that accounts for phenomena in only one of these domains.

Thagard's *simplicity* criterion is much like our standard 6—economy of explanation. Simplicity serves to constrain consilience, for "a *simple* consilient theory not only must explain a range of facts; it must explain those facts without making a host of assumptions with narrow application" (Thagard, 1978, p. 87). Hence, if we want our theory to meet both criteria—consilience and simplicity—we cannot properly include assumptions that apply exclusively to physical growth or ones bearing solely on language or on social skills.

Thagard's use of *analogy* as a criterion is based on his belief that comparing phenomenon X to phenomenon Z will not only serve the heuristic purpose of helping readers understand the theorist's notion of X, but it fosters the understanding of X by showing how the explanation of Z also helps explain X. Later, in Chapter Twelve, this point is made with information-processing theory, where the functioning of the human mind is likened to the operation of an electronic computer. In classical information-processing models, explaining the workings of a complex computer may also clarify how the human sensory, perceptual, and memory systems work.

If you find Thagard's proposal appealing, you may wish to add consilience and analogy to your own list of standards.

WHY DO SCHOLARS DEVELOP DIFFERENT THEORIES?

People who are new to investigating theories of development often wonder what influences theorists to propose new models. The most obvious reason is that they are not satisfied with the answers existing theories offer for the questions they believe to be important. Or they may feel that existing theories do not meet the standards they use to judge the worth of a theory. But in addition to these general reasons, we can identify several more specific ones that cause theorists to generate new perspectives on children's growth.

All theorists are affected by the field of knowledge in which they received their principal training. For example, a strong background in biological science can cause a scholar to focus more attention on children's heredity than on their environment in explaining development. In contrast, a strong foundation in sociology may influence a theorist in the opposite direction. As illustrations, the theories of Herbert Spencer and G. Stanley Hall during the late nineteenth century were affected by their study of biology, particularly by their study of Darwin's theory of evolution (Hall, 1904).

Not only do theorists' academic backgrounds influence their explanations of development, but the problems they meet in daily work also funnel their attention toward particular facts and their possible relationships. In the late nineteenth century, the puzzling cases of neurotic patients that Freud met in his psychiatric practice stimulated him to seek explanations that deviated markedly from the neurological theories popular in his day (Chapter Six). Early in this century Piaget was working in a psychological testing center in France when he became curious about the thinking processes that caused children to give certain incorrect answers to test questions. This curiosity led him to a lifelong study of the growth of children's thought patterns and to a theory that organized the facts he discovered (Chapter Ten).

The way investigators gather data also influences the conclusions they draw. Skinner distrusted the accuracy of people's reports of their own thought processes so he chose to base his conclusions on objective observations of behavior by an outsider (Chapter Eight). However, Charlotte Buhler, a humanistic psychologist, encouraged people to report their feelings, hopes, and ambitions (Chapter Thirteen). Both Piaget and Lawrence Kohlberg presented standard test questions to which children responded (Chapters Ten and Sixteen). In contrast, Freud asked adults to recount their dreams, and from their recollections he sought to reconstruct events of their childhood (Chapter Six). Thus researchers' sources of information favor their drawing certain kinds of conclusion and make it unlikely they will draw other kinds.

One of the most potent forces affecting models devised by experimental psychologists is the appearance of surprising or puzzling results in research they conduct with children. When an experiment turns out in an unexpected way, researchers are faced with the possibility that the existing theory is inaccurate and that changes are called for. This sort of influence has been particularly prominent in the work of such investigators as Albert Bandura (Chapter Nine) and Robbie Case (Perspective D, p. 000).

Finally, the personal, nonprofessional concerns of individuals also influence their proposals about development. Historical events that placed young Lev Vygotsky in the U.S.S.R. stimulated him to devise a theory of development compatible with Marxist social doctrine (Chapter Eleven). Abraham Maslow's dissatisfaction with the ways behaviorism and psychoanalysis explained his own personality and events in his daily life played a part in his creating a version of humanistic psychology (Chapter Thirteen).

In sum, a variety of factors interact to make theorists so dissatisfied with existing explanations that they formulate new models. As a result, today there are a number of major theories and a host of minimodels, and we can expect many more in the years ahead.

CONCLUSION

Chapter One is designed to accomplish four purposes:

1. Present an initial taste of several quite different theories and suggest how interpreting child behavior from each theory's point of view can result in very different conclusions.

2. Identify some general theoretical terms and the meanings that can be assigned to them.

3. Propose illustrative standards for judging the worth of a theory.

4. Note some of the factors that influence theorists to propose new schemes for interpreting child development.

The material in Chapter One should serve as a useful background for Chapter Two, which suggests a series of questions that can be asked about the contents of theories when different models of child development are being compared.

FOR FURTHER READING

The following publications are useful sources of information about theoretical terminology, criteria for judging the worth of theories, and illustrative appraisals of theories.

Baldwin, A. L. (1967) *Theories of Child Development.* New York: Wiley.

Lerner, R. M. (1986) *Concepts and Theories of Human Development.* New York: Random House.

Marx, M. H., and F. E. Goodson (eds.). (1976) *Theories in Contemporary Psychology.* New York: Macmillan.

Miller, P. H. (1983) *Theories of Developmental Psychology.* San Francisco: W. H. Freeman.

Reese, H. W., and W. F. Overton. (1970) "Models of Development and Theories of Development," in L. R. Goulet and Paul B. Baltes (eds.), *Life-Span Developmental Psychology.* New York: Academic Press, pp. 115–145.

Skinner, B. F. (1972) *Cumulative Record: A Selection of Papers.* 3d ed. New York: Appleton-Century-Crofts. (See Skinner's questioning the need for theory in the Part II selection, "Are Theories of Learning Necessary?")

Thomas, R. M. (ed.) (1988) *Oriental Theories of Human Development.* New York: Peter Lang.

CHAPTER TWO

The Contents of Child Development Theories

In comparing theories, we need to consider not only the sorts of criteria described in Chapter One but also the content characteristics. By *content* I mean both the aspects of child development on which theorists focus attention and the key philosophical and methodological convictions that undergird the model they propose.

This second chapter introduces a variety of content categories often included in theories. One aim of the chapter is to alert you to questions that child development theories frequently try to answer, so you can decide which of these questions are the most important from your viewpoint. Another aim is to illustrate the fact that not all theorists seek to answer the same questions or accord the same significance to a given question. It is important to recognize this because two theories that at first appear to be in conflict may, in fact, be merely directed at different aspects of child growth. Two ostensibly conflicting viewpoints could even, perhaps, be satisfactorily combined, as J. Dollard and N. E. Miller sought to do with behaviorist and psychoanalytic theories in their book *Personality and Psychotherapy* (1950).

In Chapter Two a number of questions that identify either the content focus of theories or their philosophical and methodological understructure are presented. The questions are organized into thirteen clusters. The names of the clusters and an overall question that encompasses the sub-questions in each are given below.

CONTENT CHARACTERISTICS

1. *Scope or range.* What age levels, aspects of development, and human cultures are the objects of the theory?

2. *Nature and nurture.* How does heredity compare with environment as a contributor to development?

3. *Direction of development.* What sorts of maturity or what future condition does the infant grow toward?

4. *Continuous versus stepwise change.* Do children grow by imperceptibly small increments or do they periodically move up from one identifiable stage to another?

5. *Original moral condition.* Is the child born moral, immoral, or amoral?

6. *Personality structure.* What are the key components of human personality, and how are these related to each other?

7. *Motivation and the learning process.* What motivates development, and by what process does a child learn?

8. *Individual differences.* How does the theory account for differences in development among children of the same chronological age?

9. *Desirable—undesirable, normal—abnormal.* How does the theory distinguish desirable from undesirable development and normal from abnormal development?

10. *Philosophical origins and assumptions.* From what philosophical viewpoint has the theory arisen, and on what assumptions is it founded?

11. *Investigative methods.* What methods has the theorist used for gathering, analyzing, and validating ideas, and how have these methods influenced the content and structure of the theory?

12. *Appeal for acceptance.* On what sort of appeal does the theorist depend for convincing people of the theory's worth?

13. *Terminology.* What special terms are used in the theory, and how do they relate to similar concepts in other theories?

Before inspecting each of these topics in some detail, we should note three characteristics of this list. First, the topics are not mutually exclusive. They overlap and crisscross. For example, when we discuss Freud's proposed structure for personality development, we necessarily consider as well his growth stages, his idea of the child's original moral condition, and his special terminology. Thus these questions are not separate entities but are simply different angles from which to view the integrated body of a theory.

Second, the list itself is not proposed as *the correct* list of topics for analyzing theories of development. It is just one possible listing, one I have found helpful for directing attention at significant aspects of theories. Other lists, different in content or organized in a different pattern, serve other people just as well.

Third, topics at the beginning of the list are more distinctly developmental than the rest. Within the broad field of psychology, practitioners are traditionally divided into several loosely defined groups: specialists in the clinical treatment of behavior disorders, specialists who compare human behavior with that of animals, specialists in research on learning, and specialists in development. This last group is the one that we are concerned with. Developmental psychologists have a dominant interest in questions about how and why people change with the passing of time or the advancement of age. In our list of thirteen topics, items 1 through 5 are most distinctly concerns of developmentalists. Items 6 through 13 are generally of equal or greater interest to practitioners in other psychological groups. Now let's turn to a more detailed explanation of the topics.

1. Scope or Range   The term *scope* is used here to identify three aspects of a theory: (a) its *age range*—the way the theory marks the beginning and end of the development period; (b) its *variety of aspects*—the number and kinds of facets stressed or included by the theory; and (c) its *cultural range*—the variety of cultures the theory proposes to describe. To discover how a particular theorist treats these matters, we can be guided by the following set of questions:

> **1.1** How are the beginning and end of the development period defined? What characteristics, such as age in years, particular changes in behavior, or changes in growth rate, define this period?

Some of the schemes discussed in later chapters are best labeled *theories of human development* since they propose structures and principles describing the entire life span, from conception to death. Others are more accurately called *theories of child development* because they focus exclusively, or primarily, on the first two decades or so of life. In this book we are concerned only with these initial two decades, regardless of whether the theory being considered extends into adulthood and old age.

Many theories use chronological age as the chief measure of child development periods, with either biological conception or birth marking the lower limit and age 18 or 21 marking the upper limit. Thus the adolescent years are typically included within the span of the term *child development,* although some writers prefer to limit the word *childhood* to the years before puberty—age 12 or 14—and *adolescence* to the years between puberty and adulthood.

Other theorists find chronological age an unsatisfactory dimension in analyzing development (Wohlwill, 1976). They use some other characteristic, such as the attainment of adult height or the emergence of specified adult behaviors, as the indicator that childhood is over. Also their boundary lines for stages of growth throughout the childhood period are set by developmental signs other than years since birth.

Some authors focus their theories on the entire range of childhood and adolescence experiences, whereas others attend to only one segment of this range.

1.2 What aspects of growth or behavior does the theory include or emphasize?

Some models concentrate on a narrow range of behavior. For example, Kohlberg (Chapter Sixteen) concerns himself solely with moral aspects, and humanistic psychologists (Chapter Thirteen) focus chiefly on the development of the self. Other theories are much broader in scope. Havighurst's scheme (Chapter Four) involves physical, emotional, moral, cognitive, and social aspects. Gesell (Chapter Three) also includes a wide range of behaviors and growth characteristics in his studies.

1.3 Does the theory propose to explain child development in all cultures or only in certain ones?

Most theorists want their model to apply to as many children as possible. In effect, they try to produce a universal theory. Their broad-ranging statements imply that they are talking about children in all places and, seemingly, in all times. Such is true of Piaget, Freud, Skinner, and many more. Other theorists state that their proposals are intended to describe development within defined cultural or geographic domains. For example, Havighurst has said that his "tasks of development" are ones faced by mid-twentieth-century American boys and girls, particularly those from the middle and upper social classes.

These three facets of a theory's scope help delineate the territory the theorist is trying to map out.

2. Nature and Nurture   Over the decades the most fundamental concern of child development theorists has been the heredity–environment issue. The terminology of the debate has varied from time to time—nature versus nurture, nativism versus cultural relativism, genetics versus social controls, maturation versus learning, innate traits versus acquired characteristics—but the basic issue has been the same: How do inborn factors compare with environmental factors in contributing to a child's development?

As demonstrated throughout most of this book, the question of what causes development is typically cast in one of these heredity–environment forms, thus implying that there are only two sources for the way a child grows up: (1) her inherited nature and (2) the way she is nurtured by parents and others. However, some theorists have proposed other possible causes as well. Before identifying these additional possibilities, we will first inspect the nature–nurture issue since it remains the central concern of most psychologists, biologists, and sociologists when they argue questions of cause. As the debate has progressed over the years, the focal question has shifted somewhat, moving first from *which one* to *how much,* and then subsequently to *in what manner* (Anastasi, 1958). We will inspect each of these in turn.

Which one? In past centuries philosophers seemed to be answering the question, Which causes developmental changes, a child's heredity *or* environment? An example from the environmentalist side of the issue is the proposal of British philosopher John Locke (1632–1704) that at birth a child's mind is a void, an unmarked page or *tabula rasa* on which the contents of the mind are sketched by the child's experiences as he grows up. At the other extreme was Rousseau (1712–1778), who considered the child's inherited "nature" to be the most influential force in determining her steps in development.

The which-one controversy can be simply illustrated as positions on either side of a fence (see Table 2.1). Traditionally the people on the heredity side have been divided into two groups: the *preformationists* and the *predeterminists.*

The distinction between preformationists and predeterminists chiefly concerns how powerful the theorist believes hereditary effects are. Preformationists believe that *all* of an individual's potentials—his or her personality, values, motives, mental abilities, and emotional makeup—exist completely formed within the infant at birth. As the child advances in age, these potentials unfold on a prearranged genetic schedule. Since all signifi-

Table 2.1   The "Which-One" Issue

| | Hereditarians | |
Environmentalists	Preformationists	Predeterminists
The child's experiences are preeminent in determining development.	Environment has no influence.	Environment has little influence.

cant elements of development are preformed, the particular environment in which the child grows up has no role in determining development. Predeterminists, however, are not so willing to dismiss the influence of a child's physical and social surroundings. They believe environment has some effect. But since they believe a child's genetic schedule is so important, they belong on the heredity side of the controversy along with the preformationists.

Actually the issue of *which one*—heredity *or* environment—determines development is rather silly since even rudimentary reasoning will show that neither factor can exert influence or even exist without the other. A child's heredity cannot display itself in a condition of nothingness, that is, in a nonenvironment. Nor can a child be spontaneously generated without ancestors, as if springing out of nowhere to be influenced by an environment. Even the most radical environmentalists and hereditarians of the past recognized the necessary existence of both factors, nature *and* nurture. So the argument actually was not *which one* but *how much*.

How much? During the nineteenth century and through the first half of the twentieth, the nature–nurture issue centered primarily on the question of how much heredity contributed to development in comparison to environment. Graphically the issue can be pictured as a line, with the heredity component above and the environment component below (see Table 2.2). A given theorist's position on the issue can be identified at some point along the line. To illustrate, we cite the famous debate that attracted the attention of American psychologists in the 1920s and 1930s concerning which factor contributed more to a child's intellectual growth, heredity or environment. By statistical methods, B. S. Burks (1928) concluded that heredity deserved 83 percent of the credit for mental ability and environment only 17. Other investigators (Leahy, 1935; Shuttleworth, 1935) also

Table 2.2   The "How-Much" Issue

	Extreme Hereditarians	Moderates	Extreme Environmentalists
Percentage of Nature's Contribution	95%	50%	5%
Percentage of Nurture's Contribution	5%	50%	95%

concluded that heredity played the major role, though the proportions they derived were somewhat different. Still other researchers, using a series of studies conducted in the midwestern United States, concluded that the opposite was true, that environment was the stronger factor in determining mental ability (Skeels, 1940; Skodak, 1939). This debate has never been settled, and the main reason may well be that the wrong question—or at least an unprofitable question—was being asked.

Investigations based on the how-much issue have led to conflicting conclusions about the same data and to interpretations of questionable usefulness. As a consequence, in recent decades there has been a strong movement among people interested in these matters to recast the key question from *how much* to *how* or *in what manner* the factors interact (Anastasi, 1958).

In what manner do nature and nurture interact? A basic tenet of this modern interactionist approach is that nature and nurture are two different dimensions, each operating 100 percent in its role. Although this approach does not really abandon concern with how much, its more important question by far is: How does the interaction of heredity and environment take place in order to produce the observed development of the child? There are a variety of answers to the question, each depending on the point of view of the particular theorist being examined. Since it is my purpose in the present chapter only to outline issues that theories treat and to pose guide questions for use in comparing theories, I will not analyze a wide array of interpretations of interaction here. Rather I will describe briefly only two views in order to illustrate the extent to which ideas about interaction can vary.

According to the first view, heredity defines the boundaries of potential development, and environment determines where, within these boundaries, a child's actual development is realized. "Heredity determines what we can do, and environment what we do do" (Montagu, 1959). Furthermore, it is assumed that the boundaries differ for different characteristics. For certain traits, such as eye color, heredity sets very narrow limits within which environmental forces—such as nutrition—can operate. For other characteristics, such as the cognitive ability to analyze complex abstract relationships, the boundaries set by heredity appear to be wide, allowing considerable room for the operation of such environmental factors as nutrition, instruction, rewards for the child who practices such analysis, and many more.

This interactionist viewpoint also assumes that the potential defined by heredity is manifested differently at different times in the child's life. For example, at puberty a genetically timed ripening occurs for the primary sex characteristics (maturing ova in girls, maturing sperm in boys, and maturing systems for delivering these cells) and such secondary sex characteristics as changes in body shape. Thus puberty produces different potentials from those available when the child was age 2 or 4 or 6.

From this interactionist perspective, the question of how much nature contributes as compared to nurture is no longer of prime interest. Instead we now seek to know (1) how wide are the boundaries set by heredity for various aspects of development—physical traits, cognitive abilities, frustration tolerance, and others; (2) what environmental forces influence the way these aspects manifest themselves in the child's structure and behavior; and (3) how this interaction of inherited potential and environmental forces operates at different stages of the child's growth period.

Some idea of how the complex interrelations of this model differ from the interrelations of the which-one and how-much approaches can be shown in the simplified diagram in Figure 2.1. Three concepts are plotted here:

1. *Genetic influence over different developmental characteristics varies from one characteristic to another.* The three characteristics shown in Figure 2.1 are height, skill at analyzing abstract relationships, and emotional control under stress. The top and bottom of each box represent, respectively, the greatest and least genetic potential that is humanly possible for that characteristic (at a certain age level). The white space in each box represents one hypothetical child's genetic potential for that characteristic.

2. *Heredity establishes boundaries of potential for each characteristic.* In Figure 2.1 the hypothetical upper limit for development—for example, the tallest that child can grow—is the upper dotted line, and the lower limit—the shortest height the child can grow to—is the lower dotted line.

3. *Environmental influences determine where within the boundaries a child's development will manifest itself.* The range within which environment can affect development is shown as the white area between the dotted lines in each characteristic. The letter *F* signifies the level of development a child will exhibit if the environmental influences are very favorable (near the upper limit). The letter *U* signifies the level of development exhibited if environmental conditions are very unfavorable (near the lower limit).

Thus in Figure 2.1 we hypothesize that there is more leeway for the influence of environmental factors in determining a child's emotional control than there is in determining either height or skill at abstract analy-

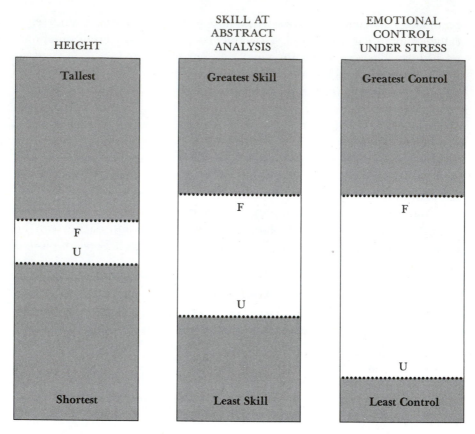

* * * * * = Hypothesized upper and lower boundaries of inherited potential
  F = Development in favorable environment
  U = Development in unfavorable environment

Figure 2.1 An Interactionist Viewpoint: In What Manner?

sis. Whether such a hypothesis is true becomes a matter of empirical investigation.

To complete this first analysis of interaction, I need to explain which environmental factors are most potent in determining how genetic potential is realized and how these forces are interrelated. I also need to describe how the interaction may vary at different stages of the child's development.

Although this first interactionist approach does not tell us, as older how-much theories did, what proportion of development is due to heredity and what proportion is due to environment, it still enables us to differentiate between "environmentalists" and "hereditarians." In terms of Figure 2.1, theorists who picture the area between the inherited-potential boundaries as narrow are hereditarians, for they believe the child's genetically designed nature does not permit much manipulation by environmental factors. Theorists who picture the boundaries as widely separated are more environmentalist, for they think environmental influences greatly affect the way development characteristics are manifested.

Let's turn now to the second way of viewing the *in-what-manner* approach to interaction. Some writers consider interaction in terms of how directly heredity influences development (Anastasi, 1958; R. M. Lerner, 1976, pp. 48–83). To illustrate, let us consider three examples of mental development that range in scale from very direct to very indirect hereditary influence.

At the very direct end of the scale is the case of a child suffering from phenylketonuria. This mental defect results from hereditary metabolic dysfunctions that are not significantly improved by changes made in the child's environment—the affected child will remain mentally defective (Anastasi, 1958, p. 198).

Heredity has a less direct influence on mental development in cases of hereditary blindness or deafness. A blind or deaf child who is raised in an environment designed for children with normal sight and hearing will typically display symptoms of retarded mental growth. Although sight and hearing cannot be restored, changes can be made in the environment to compensate for the handicap. A blind child can be given audio-recordings of books and can be taught to read by the braille method; the deaf child can be taught sign language and lip reading. These compensatory measures enable mental development to proceed far more normally.

Our third example from the very indirect end of the scale of hereditary influence concerns social stereotypes. We recognize that genetic endowment has much influence in determining a child's skin color, height, weight, facial features, acuity of senses, and so forth. People within a given culture often associate certain intellectual or personality traits with such physical characteristics. In other words, people often hold social stereotypes. If a child's facial features and her movements are usually viewed in her society as typical of sweet, clever girls, then people will often treat this child as though she were sweet and bright. Since the way people treat a child influences the way that child comes to perceive herself, we can conclude that the child's self-concept—her feeling of adequacy—is at least partially the result of social stereotypes associated with inherited physical characteristics. In effect, if the child perceives herself as clever rather than dull, she may be motivated to display higher levels of mental development than if she believed herself dull. Heredity, in this instance, has influenced mental development in a very indirect manner.

Earlier I said that although theorists who adopt one of these interactionist approaches emphasize the *in-what-manner* or *how* of the nature–nurture interaction, they have not abandoned the question of *how much*. However, they phrase the question in new ways. For instance, when Anastasi (1958, p. 206) proposed that it is best to view nature/nurture in terms of a directness/indirectness scale, she added that the more indirectly heredity influences a behavior, "the wider will be the range of variation of possible outcomes." In other words, there is not much room for environment to influence a child's characteristics that most directly depend on genetic factors. Yet environment can very much influence those characteristics that are very indirectly linked to heredity. Thus Anastasi is still posing a how-much question in terms of the amount of variability possible.

What can we say then about modern theorists' position on the heredity–environment issue? Today, most theorists consider themselves interactionists in that they think both nature and nurture are indispensable and work together to produce development. However, this does not mean that the debate has ended—theorists continue to disagree on the conditions of the nature–nurture interaction. Indeed, one of the most incendiary social controversies in American educational circles in recent years centered on the question of whether the genetic endowment of certain racial groups limits their potential mental ability compared to that of other racial groups (Hebb, 1970; Hirsch, 1970; Jensen, 1969, 1973; Layzer, 1974). Since the issues are complex and far from settled, arguments of this type can be expected to continue in the years ahead.

When we analyze theories of development, we can include such guide questions as the following:

2.1 Can the theorist be identified by such traditional labels as *preformationist, predeterminist, interactionist, hereditarian,* or *environmentalist?*

2.2 Does the theorist see some aspects of development as being more constrained by hereditary boundaries than others? For example: Are the inherited-potential boundaries narrower or the heredity connections more direct for skin color than for oral language skills (if, indeed, two such different characteristics can be adequately compared in terms of amounts)?

2.3 Does the theorist see heredity as more constraining for certain growth characteristics at different periods of childhood? For example: Are the inherited-potential boundaries for the development of reading ability different at age 6 than they are at age 12?

2.4 Does the theorist describe the process by which the interaction of nature and nurture takes place?

Earlier I noted that, in contrast to most present-day theorists, some writers have proposed further sources of influence besides heredity and environment. As examples of such proposals, there are the conceptions of a respected developmentalist, T. C. Schneirla, and two beliefs common to many of the world's major religious traditions.

Schneirla (1957) suggested that a third force affecting development is the growing organism, that is, the child itself. This influence arises from the manner in which the hereditary and environmental factors interact. For example, assume that infant A is born with a genetic structure that predisposes him to a high level of activity. As a result, he sleeps less than most babies. When he is awake he cries for his parents' attention. Although the parents seek to provide the comfort and care their son seems to require, they soon become physically tired and emotionally irritated by his irregular rest habits and demanding activity. Their irritation is reflected in the way they handle the child and in the harshness of their voices when they lose their patience. In their frustration and exhaustion, they increasingly escape by closing the door to the baby's bedroom to "let him cry it out." This treatment serves to heighten, rather than decrease, their son's activity level because the child is stimulated by his emotional distress to make even greater demands on his parents' time and patience. In effect, a cycle of interaction has been established in which the evolving characteristics of the organism—the growing child—become a significant influence—a third force—in determining the way the environment will treat him. Schneirla concluded, in essence, that "the individual seems to be interactive with itself throughout development, as the processes of each stage open the way for further stimulus-reaction relationships depending on the scope of the intrinsic and extrinsic conditions then prevalent" (1957, p. 86).

We turn now to a pair of additional influences found in concepts of development embedded in many of the world's religions. The pair are *human will* and *supernatural intervention*. In the case of will, the assumption is made that a person's life pattern is not determined entirely by genetic and environmental variables but is influenced as well by the individual's free-will choices and by how hard she tries to implement such choices. This conception of the importance of will appears in such diverse religions as Christianity, Judaism, Islam, Confucianism, Hinduism, and Shintoism, as well as in much of the commonsense or naive psychology of the general public.

The operation of *supernatural intervention* as a contributor to development is a central element in most if not all religious traditions. Adherents of such traditions believe that a person's developmental fate can be determined to a large degree by the action of destructive supernatural forces

(Satan or other evil spirits) and of constructive or salutary powers (God, Allah, Cosmic Energy, or other beneficent spirits). Sometimes the supernatural powers act on their own volition to influence people's lives. In other cases supernatural intercession is solicited by people through prayers, rituals, and offerings. This type of cause is generally given no place in such modern "scientific theories" as those described in Chapters Three through Seventeen (Thomas, 1985, p. 719). (Nevertheless, proponents of scientific theories may sometimes in their daily lives display a belief in supernatural influence. Particularly in times of danger, as during a child's illness or a threat to the family's safety, even a scientific developmentalist may appeal to a supreme power to intercede on the developmentalist's behalf.)

3. Direction of Development   The terms *growth* and *development** both imply change, and it has been one of the central concerns of theorists to identify the directions of this change.

A good example of a theory that gives central attention to directions of development is that of Heinz Werner (1961), whom we meet briefly in Perspective D in Part Five, "Estimating the Future of Stage Theories." Werner proposed that one direction of growth was from rigidity to flexibility. By this he meant that an infant displays rigid behaviors suited specifically to given situations and does not readily alter these behaviors to suit new conditions. In contrast, an adolescent's behaviors are more flexible and adapt readily to changed conditions.

Perhaps the easiest way to discover a theory's directions of development is to ask, How does the child differ from the adult? In Piaget's model, young children are very self-centered, constrained to interpret events solely from their own viewpoint. Normal adults, on the other hand, understand that different people may interpret events from rather different perspectives.

In our search for the directions described or implied in a theory, we can ask:

3.1 What aspects of behavior or growth (for example, physical growth, cognitive development, social skills) are encompassed by a particular principle or statement of direction?

3.2 What interrelationships, if any, exist between the direction of change of one aspect and that of another? For example: Does attainment of physical maturity come before the attainment of intellectual maturity? Does the differentiation of behaviors in the young child

---

**Growth* is often defined as change in size, *development* as change in the complexity and functions of the individual. However, each term may be defined as change in both size and function. It is in this second, more inclusive manner that the terms are used in this book.

proceed more rapidly than the integration of various individual actions into smoothly flowing systems of behavior?

4. Continuous versus Stepwise Change   Usually theories not only define directions of change, they tell whether this change occurs gradually in small increments or dramatically in large periodic steps (steep advances) that are followed by periods of less apparent change (plateaus). Skinner's behaviorism is an example of a theory that pictures growth as occurring in imperceptibly small increments. In contrast, other theories picture growth as shifting from one major step or stage to another. Piaget proposed steps and substeps of cognitive development. Freud identified several major psychosexual stages of growth. Havighurst proposed that children at different points in their life are confronted with particular tasks of growing up and that these tasks form a series of stages in development. In effect, the essence of many theories is found in the sorts of stages postulated and in the way the child's movement from one level to the next is viewed. The controversy about these matters among developmentalists has traditionally been known as the *continuity–discontinuity issue.*

Everyone agrees that development from one day to the next is gradual. No one claims that a twelve-year-old girl is a prepuberal child one week and a full-blown adolescent the next. In this sense growth is continuous and occurs in small increments. The real question, then, is whether, during this process, the child's structure and behavior periodically display symptoms that warrant the label of a new stage of development. Behaviorists such as Skinner answer no to this question; other theorists answer yes. Those who answer yes are then obligated to identify the traits of a stage so that, following their theories, we can recognize a new stage when we see one.

Consequently, in analyzing a theorists' position on the continuity–discontinuity issue, we first pose this question:

4.1 Does children's development proceed through a series of small, continuous increments without any dramatic changes or identifiable qualitative plateaus? Or do children develop from one recognizable stage to another?

If the answer to this first query is that children pass through stages, then we can profitably pose several more questions:

4.2 How does the theorist define *stage* or *step* or *period?*

4.3 How many stages are identified in the system, and what are the names and distinguishing characteristics of each stage?

4.4 On what aspects of life or growth do the stages focus? In other words, what dimensions of development do the stages represent? For example: Are these stages of physical growth? Of sexual development? Of socialization? Of moral judgment? Of oral language development?

4.5 Do the aspects or dimensions have the same importance at all times during childhood? For example: Are physical growth stages more prominent in the early years than they are later in childhood?

Since the matter of whether children are growing up "normally" is of interest to many people—parents, teachers, pediatricians, and children themselves—it is also useful to ask what a theory expects of developmental stages. To begin:

4.6 How are the levels or stages related to chronological age?

Of the proposals discussed in later chapters, that of Gesell's (Chapter Three) is the most specific in correlating age with growth characteristics. Gesell described in rather definite terms what the typical two-year-old is like and how his or her characteristics differ from those of the one-year-old and the three-year-old. The stages described by Piaget, Freud, and Havighurst are less closely tied to specific ages than Gesell's, and Maslow's levels of human needs (Chapter Thirteen) are even less specifically correlated with chronological age than those of Piaget and Freud.

The question of age–stage correlation is not the only one pertinent to the task of judging the normality of a child's growth. For example, a number of questions arise about the universality and invariance of stages.

4.7 Are the stages universal, that is, true for all children in all cultures? Or do children in one culture pass through different stages from those in another? Within a culture, is it possible for a child to skip what has been described as a stage, or must everyone move through the stages in a single defined sequence? If a child can skip a stage or proceed by a different path than some of his or her peers, why does this deviation occur?

Many theorists consider the stages they describe to be universal—found among all children in all cultures—and their sequence invariant. *Invariant* means that not only are the stages found in all cultures for which we have reports, but the nature of development is such that no other sequence in the pattern of growth stages is possible. Such writers as Piaget (Chapter Ten), Kohlberg (Chapter Sixteen), and Erik Erikson (Chapter Seven) have assumed invariance although this position has been questioned by some critics (Phillips & Kelly, 1975). Remember, therefore, not only to inquire about a theorist's position but also to consider whether the evidence or line of reasoning used to support that position is convincing.

Three other sets of questions can be asked about how growth rates, fixation at a stage, and regression to an earlier stage may be treated in a theory.

4.8 Does everyone go through the stages at the same pace? If not, why not?

The terms *retarded, normal, advanced,* and *gifted* have traditionally been used to describe children who are growing at particular rates compared to their age-mates, regardless of whether growth is viewed as continuous or stepwise. Question 4.8 is directed at whether a theory recognizes such phenomena and, if so, how it accounts for them.

Another question related to the rate of passing through stages is:

4.9 Can a child display typical characteristics of more than one stage at the same time? If so, why does this occur?

Some theorists (Gesell, Havighurst) make little or no mention of this possibility; others accord it considerable attention (Erikson, Piaget, Kohlberg). An example of the simultaneous presence of multiple stages is found in Piaget's subtheory about children's ideas of causality. When Piaget studied what children believe causes certain physical events in the world, he concluded that a child who accounts for cloud movements by saying elves push the clouds is operating on a lower level of thought than a child who says that air currents (rising hot air, descending cool air) move the clouds. Piaget found, however, that while a child may use fantasy beings (elves) to account for certain physical events, the same child may give naturalistic explanations (air currents) to account for others. In effect, the child is operating on two stage levels at the same time (Piaget, 1930).

4.10 Can a child's progress through the stages become arrested or fixated at a particular stage? If so, what causes the fixating? What can be done to release the fixation and stimulate progress to the next stage?

Theorists account for fixation in several ways. Gesell's system, which can be labeled a predeterminist theory, views arrested development as caused by inadequate genetic endowment. Behaviorists feel it results from inadequate stimulus from the environment. Freud's psychoanalysis views it as seated in either too much satisfaction of needs at the present stage of development or too little satisfaction.

4.11 Can a child return to an earlier stage after entering a more advanced one? If so, what causes this *regression* or *retrogression?* What can be done to help the child recover and move ahead once more?

Regression, like fixation, is of particular interest to therapists, whose task it is to assist children whose development seems to be going awry. The most popular explanation, by theorists who recognize the phenomenon of regression, is that a child slips back to an earlier stage of development when the adjustment skills developed at the present stage prove inadequate for coping with current problems. However, some theorists contend that there is no such thing as true regression. The child does not really slip back but just gives the appearance of regressing by adopting a segment of behavior from an earlier time.

Our concern with retardation, fixation, regression, and uneven development can also lead logically to another question;

4.12 If a child experiences growth problems at one stage, how may these problems influence success at subsequent levels? And how can we best deal with such problems?

For most theorists, problems that are not adequately resolved at one stage either will prevent the child from moving on to the next or will make it difficult for the child to adjust to subsequent levels. And most feel that therapy or retraining is required to correct or ameliorate the problems and thus enable the child to continue developing. However, not all theories see the issue in this same light. Theories like Gesell's, which see genetic factors as greatly restricting the range within which environmental factors can affect development, do not usually propose therapy or retraining. For instance, Gesell's model of development contains the concept of alternating "good" and "bad" years or phases of growth. This pattern of alternation is seen as a "natural" one, common to virtually all children. So problems at one level of growth are seen as instances of "going through a bad phase" that will naturally pass with time. Patience rather than therapy is needed to wait out the passing of the phase (Ilg & Ames, 1955, pp. 22–24).

In summary, twelve sets of questions have been proposed to guide our inquiry into the way a theorist handles the continuity–discontinuity issue. Although most of the questions are directed at theories that view growth as occurring in steps or stages, a number of them are also useful for understanding nonstage or continuous theories as well. For example, we can ask if a continuous growth model pictures all children as developing along the same route (4.7) and at the same pace (4.8). We can also ask if a child can become fixated (4.10) or can regress (4.11) and how growth problems can be ameliorated (4.12).

5. Original Moral Condition   An issue of greater interest in past centuries than it is today is that of the child's natural moral mode. Some theorists either state outright or imply that the child at birth, and by natural inclination, is in a particular moral condition: good (moral), bad (immoral), or neutral (amoral). The eighteenth-century writer on child development and social policy, Jean Jacques Rousseau, contended that children are innately moral. He felt that if they are to remain good, they need to be protected throughout their growing years from the corruptions of an immoral society (Rousseau, 1773). Fundamentalist Christian doctrine, in contrast, has pictured children as innately immoral, having received the sin of Adam and Eve in their psychic inheritance. Such children need a great deal of strict guidance if they are to be saved from devilish ways (*New England Primer*, 1836; Dunstan, 1961, p. 208). Freudians regard children as innately amoral—that is, without knowledge of right or wrong at birth—but with a capacity to internalize the morals of their social environment so that these values eventually become a part of their personalities, the part he labeled *superego*. Maslow, as a humanistic psychologist, viewed the child's sense of morals as being partly innate and partly learned.

Therefore, in comparing theories, we may wish to ask:

5.1 What is the original or genetically determined condition of the child: moral, immoral, or amoral? Can the newborn be some mixture of the three, depending on which aspect of development is under consideration?

6. Personality Structure   Most theories of development assume that the child has a psychological system or a sort of mental machinery, which is known by such terms as *personality, mind, cognitive structure,* or *intervening variables.* Usually this system is assumed to contain elements or functions that interact to determine the child's behavior. Part of the task of understanding development, then, consists of identifying these components and the ways they interact over the first two decades of life. Freud's system includes three key elements: the *id*, the *ego*, and the *superego*. Information-processing theorists often distinguish among such components as the *sense organs, short-term memory,* and *long-term memory.* Piaget distinguished three basic mental operations: *assimilation, accommodation,* and *equilibration.* Thus, in analyzing a theory, we may wish to ask:

6.1 What are the components of personality or of behavior?

6.2 How do the components interact and change as the child grows up?

7. Motivation and the Learning Process   In the field of psychology the topics of motivation and learning are often considered separately. However, *motivation* is typically seen as the fuel for learning, as the director of the child's attention toward what she or he will seek to learn. Therefore, since motivation can be viewed as a beginning step or condition in the learning process, I will discuss them together.

Not all theorists use the same words to identify motivating forces. However, the two most popular terms are *need* and *drive*. These terms are like two sides of a coin, two ways of looking at the same phenomenon. The word *need* implies intake, a void seeking to be filled. *Drive* implies output, pent-up energy searching for a place in which to invest or expend itself. So the need for food is the hunger drive, and the need for drink is the thirst drive. Although there is a tendency for some theorists to favor the term *need* (humanistic psychologists) and others to favor *drive* (behaviorists), in each case the intention is to identify a motivating force that energizes behavior.

In some theories little or no attention is given to describing motivating forces (Gesell in Chapter Three, Kohlberg in Chapter Sixteen). In others, motivating forces are at the center of the schemes (Freud in Chapter Six, Maslow in Chapter Thirteen).

Furthermore, some theorists conceive of a single general force that activates all behavior. In Freud's early model he called this general force *libido,* an energy arising in a component of the personality called the *id* but utilized by other components of the personality as well to fuel their functions. Freud originally pictured libidinal energy as dominantly a sexual drive. However, in his later years he altered his beliefs and suggested that development and behavior are motivated by the interaction of two contrary drives, a life-promoting force (*libido* from a source termed *eros*) that accounted for constructive events in the personality and a death-directed force (*thanatos*) that accounted for destructive ones (S. Freud, 1938, pp. 5–6).

Many theories of personality and development either explicitly or implicitly differentiate among levels of needs. For example, a commonly postulated basic need from the field of biology is that of self-preservation. But when we observe behavior, we can propose that this basic need is manifested through a variety of more specific needs, such as those for food, for oxygen, for sexual expression, and for succor (the need to be nursed, supported, and consoled) (Hall & Lindzey, 1970, pp. 174–180).

Theorists, then, differ in the number of motivating forces they identify or imply, as well as in the way they name and organize the proposed drives or needs. Therefore we may wish to include in our guide questions the following:

7.1 Does the theorist identify or imply forces that motivate behavior? If so, what are these forces and what are their characteristics?

Not all theorists who propose the existence of various drives or needs agree as to the potency of each. For instance, Freud described his general force, libidinal energy, as being preeminently sexual. An early colleague of Freud's, Alfred Adler (1870–1937), disagreed that the prepotent human drive was sexual. Although he recognized sex as a significant drive, Adler contended that the truly overriding motive in human development was a *will to power*, a striving for superiority. He wrote that "whatever premises all our philosophers and psychologists dream of—self-preservation, pleasure principle, equalization—all these are but vague representations, attempts to express the great upward drive" (Adler, 1930, p. 398).

Maslow's system (Chapter Thirteen) also recognizes differences in the potency of various motivating forces but pictures their operation in a manner different from Freud's or Adler's. Maslow suggested that a person's needs are arranged in a hierarchy, like steps on a ladder, with the lower-step needs requiring fulfillment before the upper-step needs. He relegated such survival needs as those for food, drink, and physical safety to the lower levels of the hierarchy and drives for creative expression and "self-actualization" to the upper levels.

Not only may theorists claim that some needs are more significant than others throughout life, but they may also propose that certain needs are more potent at one stage of development than at another. For instance, a need for physical protection and nurturance is often considered more important during infancy, while a need for sexual expression is considered more demanding following puberty. (See the developmental tasks of Chapter Four.)

From this discussion we can generate another set of guide questions:

7.2 If several motivating forces are identified in the theory, do all of them carry equal power and importance? If not, which are more significant and why? If they differ in potency, do their relative degrees of power change from one growth stage or one age level to another?

Most theorists agree that a child is not only motivated strongly or weakly, but is also motivated toward particular things in the environment. In other words, a motivating force not only has power but also direction. Theorists do not agree, however, about the source or cause of this direction. The question is essentially:

7.3 Which source—the child's inner needs or the environment's stimuli—is more important in determining where the child directs his or her attention?

Theorists such as Piaget and Freud credit inner needs with the greater power to direct attention, while behaviorists consider environmental stimuli to be more powerful. To a substantial degree, this difference of opinion reflects the more basic disagreement about which model each camp of theorists believes best represents human behavior. In Chapter One I noted that some theories of development are founded on the analogy of the machine, while others are based on the analogy of an organism. A machine reacts to things done to it by outside forces. It is "motivated" by environmental stimuli. An organism contains internal driving forces that seek expression in the environment; it is motivated by inner needs that direct its attention to those things in the environment that will likely fulfill the needs.

I noted earlier that motivation or stimulation is commonly considered to be a beginning step in the learning process. Exactly what steps occur after this stimulation is a matter of dispute among theorists. A behaviorist such as Skinner sketches one picture of the process, Piaget quite a different picture, and social learning proponents still another. Therefore, in analyzing theories, we can suitably ask:

7.4 In this theory, how does motivation fit into the overall picture of the learning process?

7.5 What are the necessary conditions for learning to occur? What elements or mechanisms comprise the learning process, and how do the elements interact?

8. Individual Differences   It is obvious that children of a given age level are not all alike. They differ in many ways. Theories of child development also differ in how they treat this matter of variation. Some theorists—Gesell, for example—give little recognition to the issue of differences. They talk almost exclusively about the typical child, passing over the fact that nearly all children deviate to some degree from the average. Other theories, such as behaviorism and contextualism, account more adequately for differences among individuals. Hence, to guide comparisons among theories, we can ask:

8.1 What sorts of individual differences among children are given attention in the theory?

8.2 How does the theory account for such differences? To what extent do the factors that cause differences arise from heredity or from environment, and how do the causal factors operate or develop?

9. Desirable–Undesirable, Normal–Abnormal   One of the most common practical questions asked by parents, teachers, and others who deal with children is whether a child's development is normal. Since not everyone defines the term *normal* in the same way, this question can be misleading. In one sense *normal* is used to mean "well adjusted" or "getting along very nicely." In another sense it means that the child's growth is about average for his age, or his behavior is common for his size or grade in school. We encounter problems of communication when these two meanings are mixed. For example, smoking cigarettes is very common among American youths in their upper teens and early twenties, so in this sense smoking is "normal"—that is, typical. But medical evidence suggests that smoking is not desirable, so in the sense of "getting along very nicely," smoking is not normal.

Whereas some theorists specifically differentiate between normal and abnormal growth, others only imply this distinction. They specify normal or desired goals of growth, then simply assume that deviations from the path toward the goals are undesirable.

Because matters of *normal, natural,* and *desirable* development are somewhat complex and are of considerable practical importance for child rearing, Perspective A in Part Two has been dedicated to the topic of "Distinguishing Normal from Abnormal Development."

To guide our efforts in sorting out these matters, we can ask:

9.1 Is normal or natural or desirable development defined, or at least implied? If two or more of these terms appear in the theory, are they used synonymously? If not, how are they differentiated from each other?

9.2 Is abnormal, unnatural, or undesirable development identified? If two or more of these terms appear in the theory, are they used synonymously? If not, how are they differentiated?

9.3 What causes abnormal, unnatural, or undesirable development? What, if anything, can be done to change such development into normal, natural, or desirable growth?

10. Philosophical Origins and Assumptions No theory is an entirely new creation. Each has its philosophical progenitors, and our understanding of a theory is usually enhanced by our learning something of this ancestry. Our grasp of Maslow's brand of humanistic psychology (Chapter Thirteen) is enriched by our knowing that his proposals, in part, represent his reaction against what he believed were the shortcomings of both psychoanalysis and behaviorism. We can profit from knowing that Erikson's ideas (Chapter Seven) are founded primarily on Freud's teachings but have been influenced as well by methodology and by concepts from cultural anthropology.

So we add another pair of queries to our list:

10.1 On what philosophical traditions, beliefs, and assumptions is the theory founded?

10.2 Against what beliefs is the theory reacting?

11. Investigative Methods   There is something of a chicken-and-egg relationship between a theory and its investigative methods. We never know whether (a) the theory's structure has defined the methods used for gathering data or whether (b) the data-collecting methods have dictated the structure of the theory. In any event, models of child development are heavily influenced by the investigative techniques used in producing the data they treat.

For instance, Freud's main method of collecting information was listening to neurotic adults recall incidents from their childhood and from their current dreams. Clearly the particular recollections this method evoked influenced the nature of the theory he proposed. The charge that his theory gives a gloomy, disturbed view of human development has been raised by critics who blame his choice of neurotic informants as the cause of the ostensibly pessimistic picture he paints of child growth. Likewise, his dependence on self-reports of memories and dreams as his source of data is compatible with his willingness to fashion an imaginary structure of the "mind" from which these memories and dreams are generated. In contrast, Skinner rejected introspective reports as sources of evidence and depended instead on descriptions of child behavior as recorded by an outside observer. This dedication to observable events is compatible with Skinner's unwillingness to speculate about such hypothetical elements as an unseeable "mind" or such mental components as Freud's id, ego, and superego.

Thus, in analyzing theories, we can ask:

11.1 What investigative methods are used by the theorist?

11.2 How have these methods influenced the form and content of the theory?

12. Appeal for Acceptance   Typically, theorists want others to believe their proposals. To this end they seek to present the sorts of arguments they feel will appeal to the people they want to accept their scheme. For instance, such fundamentalist Christian theorists as P. A. Captain (1984) appeal to parishioners' faith in the word of God as found in the Bible and on a set of deductions about child rearing that theologians draw from church doctrine (see Perspective D in Part Five). Classical psychoanalysts propose that, in addition to the intuitive good sense their theory makes, a person becomes convinced of its validity by going through the process of psychoanalysis. Experimental psychologists describe their experiments in detail and cast the results in statistical form, with the expectation that anyone who questions the results can carry out the same experiments and see the validity of the conclusions.

Thus different theorists use different approaches in soliciting acceptance of their schemes. Likewise, different consumers of theories consider some sorts of evidence more convincing than others. Whether you find a particular model of development more useful or valid than another depends on how well the theorist's mode of appeal matches the types of evidence you regard as most acceptable. Hence we may ask:

> **12.1** On what sorts of evidence or on what kind of appeal does the theory depend to convince people of its worth?

13. Terminology In the following chapters you will find many terms created or adopted by theorists to describe their ideas of personality structure, growth stages, and growth principles. These include *growth gradients, id, epigenetic principle, formal operations, contextualism, chaining, zone of proximal development,* and many more. Often the essence of a theorist's position is contained in the terms used. If you comprehend the terms, you understand the substance of the theorist's beliefs.

If, in our investigation of a theory, we answer the twelve clusters of questions already considered in this chapter, then we will likely have learned the meaning of most or all the key terms in the theory. But in case we have missed any, we can add two final sets of queries:

> **13.1** Does the theory have a special terminology? If so, what does each term mean?

> **13.2** Do the terms refer to concepts unique to this theory, or do they identify things for which other theorists have used different words?

CONCLUSION

In Chapter Two, a series of questions has been proposed that can be asked about the contents and philosophical underpinnings of theories we wish to analyze and compare. This list does not include all the questions that could be asked; it contains ones I feel are of general interest. You may wish to add others that focus on matters of particular importance to you.

In the following chapters separate theories are described. In organizing each chapter I have sought, as far as space permits, to answer the questions posed in Chapter Two. However, none of the chapters is designed as a sequential list of answers to these questions, with topic 1 presented first and topic 13 last. Such a catalogue pattern would make the chapters read too much like catechisms. Therefore each chapter is presented in a form intended to give the essence of the theorist's approach in a logical and interesting fashion. In the process, as many of Chapter Two questions are answered as is feasible. Some chapters do not treat certain questions because the theorist or theorists did not ask such questions. In other instances a topic plays such a small part in a particular theory that it was not worth discussing in this introductory level volume.

Now, with the perspectives of Chapters One and Two in mind, we move to the theories themselves.

FOR FURTHER READING

You may wish to find additional topics and questions to supplement the list given in this chapter. If so, your most convenient source may be child development textbooks. Chapter titles and topic headings in such books often imply questions the authors believe are important for theorists to answer. Thus an inspection of titles and headings can suggest additional guide questions. Furthermore, under such headings you often find concise answers to the questions as seen from various theorists' points of view.

To aid you in this search, the following list of representative sources is suggested:

Bee, H. L. (1989) *The Developing Child*. New York: Harper & Row.

Belsky, J., R. M. Lerner, and G. B. Spanier. (1984) *The Child in the Family*. Reading, MA: Addison-Wesley.

Branthwaite, A., and D. Rogers (eds.). (1985) *Children Growing Up*. Philadelphia: Open University Press.

Broughton, J. M. (ed.). (1987) *Critical Theories of Psychological Development*. New York: Plenum.

Cole, M., and S. R. Cole. (1989) *The Development of Children*. New York: W. H. Freeman.

Damon, W. (1983) *Social and Personality Development: Infancy through Adolescence*. New York: Norton.

Fisher, K. W., and A. Lazerson. (1984) *Human Development: From Conception through Adolescence*. New York: W. H. Freeman.

Hetherington, E. M., and R. D. Parke (eds.). (1988) *Contemporary Readings in Child Psychology*. New York: McGraw-Hill.

Jahoda, G., and I. M. Lewis (eds.). (1988) *Acquiring Culture: Cross Cultural Studies in Child Development*. London: Croom Helm.

Mussen, P. H., J. J. Conger, and J. Kagan. (1984) *Child Development and Personality*. New York: Harper & Row.

PART TWO

FOUNDATIONS FOR CREATING THEORIES

A search for how to describe development and for how people draw commonsense interpretations

Two foundation blocks on which formally constructed theories of development are erected are (1) descriptions of how children change with the passing years and (2) commonsense interpretations people draw from observing children's growth and behavior.

Gesell's and Havighurst's Descriptive Schemes

Consider, first, the matter of descriptions. People's attempts to understand their world begin with observations of how things appear. Only after they can describe appearances do people begin speculating about how one thing relates to another and what causes things to change. Thus descriptions of appearances serve as a foundation for theorizing about relationships and processes. This order of events — description precedes theorizing — is true in both everyday living and scientific investigation. And such is the case with theories of child development, which are founded on descriptions of children's physical characteristics and their behavior at different age levels.

Prior to the late nineteenth century, the observations on which almost everyone based beliefs about child development were rather casual. Even such influential writers as the French social philosopher Jean Jacques Rousseau (1712–1778) and the German founder of the kindergarten movement, F. W. A. Froebel (1782–1852), were unsystematic in compiling their perceptions of child characteristics. Then, by the late eighteenth century, initial efforts were directed by several European scholars at applying methods of natural science in collecting and manipulating observations of human growth. Dietrich Tiedemann (1748–1803) is credited with producing the first psychological diary of the growth of a young child. Another German, Friedrich August Carus (1770–1808), attempted to develop a general science of life span psychological development. A Belgian astronomer and statistician, Lambert Adolphe Quételet (1796–1874), proposed sophisticated methods for analyzing multiple influences on human development. And the English author of *On the Origin of Species*, Charles Darwin (1809–1882), in 1877 published a diary of child growth entitled *Biographical Sketch of an Infant*, a work now considered one of the best early efforts at careful observation of human development.

Subsequently, in the United States in 1891, G. Stanley Hall published "The Contents of Children's Minds on Entering School," thereby launching a tradition that dominated child development investigation in the United States during the first half of the twentieth century. This is the tradition of measuring and observing groups of children and then summarizing the results in the form of averages for different age levels. Studies of this type have focused on a wide array of children's characteristics, ranging from measurements of height and weight, through the testing of mental and physical skills, to observations of social relations, sleep habits, and outbursts of anger. The number of such published studies from around the world runs into many thousands. They have been called *normative, descriptive* investigations because they describe the normal, in the sense of average, status of children on specified characteristics at different age levels. The summarized results of these studies typically are labeled *descriptive norms* or *age norms*.

The theorist who best exemplifies the normative-descriptive school of child development is Arnold Gesell, a physician and child psychologist who in the early 1900s studied under Hall at Clark University before setting up a clinic at Yale University to conduct descriptive research on children. Gesell's apparent intention was to chart with as great care and thoroughness as possible children's characteristics at each age level in a great many facets of their lives. A brief review of Gesell's work is given in Chapter Three.

A second approach to describing milestones on the road to maturity is illustrated in Chapter Four. The approach, known as *developmental-task theory*, grew in the 1930s and 1940s in the United States within the progressive education movement that dominated the educational thought of that era. Like Gesell, leaders of the developmental-task approach tried to identify the typical steps in development at different age periods in many aspects of growth—physical, intellectual, social, and emotional. But, unlike Gesell, developmental-task adherents did not systematically measure, test, and observe children who were chosen as typical representatives. Rather they based their growth stages on data drawn from a great variety of sources: empirical studies like those from Gesell's clinic, anthropological and sociological investigations, observations by teachers of children in school, commonsense ideas about child raising, and others. Furthermore, whereas Gesell was most interested in describing what children are like at different age levels, the developmental-task theorists were more interested in speculating about what children are trying to accomplish during each successive age period. The term *developmental task* was created to reflect the theorists' conviction that growth should be viewed as the child's seeking to achieve new goals or perform new tasks at each new stage of development.

In sum, Gesell endeavored to describe what children are like. And advocates of the developmental-task approach not only wished to describe what children are like at each phase of growth, they also sought to infer from these descriptions the sorts of goals they felt children were pursuing or the needs they were seeking to fulfill by their behavior.

The tradition of normative-descriptive studies in which Gesell played such an important role continues to be very active today. Likewise, although the peak of developmental-task theorizing was reached in the early 1950s, the movement still continues to exert a significant influence on curriculum development in schools and on child development textbooks.

Heider's Analysis of Commonsense Theory

A second foundation of formally constructed theories is the set of estimates that nearly all people adopt in order to explain why children grow up as they do. This collection of ideas that most people hold about how children develop is usually called *commonsense* or *naive psychology*. Fritz Heider (1896–1988), an American psychologist, proposed that this collection is not simply a scattering of beliefs but rather is founded on an intuitive theoretical framework that can be analyzed and described. Principal elements of this framework, as depicted by Heider, form the commonsense model of development presented in Chapter Five.

Since the term *common sense* has different meanings for different people, it is important at the outset to clarify our definition of it.

In ancient Greece, Aristotle proposed that there were five external senses—sight, hearing, taste, smell, and touch—plus a common sense, located in the heart, which served as the coordinating center for the other five. Remnants of this belief are still found in our language in such statements as, "She learned it by heart." Later philosophers relocated the common sense in the brain. However, in Chapter Five, the term *common sense* is not used with this meaning.

For many people, common sense refers to convictions held by a person because the truth of such beliefs is self-evident. If we need no special training or special instruments to arrive at a conclusion about something we see or hear or smell, then we usually say our conclusion is "just common sense." We believe that anyone in his "right mind" would come to the same conclusion. In Chapter Five, this sort of common sense—self-evident conclusions—is part of what I intend.

For the other part of my meaning, common sense is equated with the term *popular opinion*. To some people common sense means an idea that everybody, or nearly everybody, subscribes to, whether it is obvious or not. In our culture, for example, the fact that the earth is a sphere is common sense today, though that "fact" is not obvious to the eye. Nor was that "fact" common sense at the time of Columbus.

Thus in Chapter Five the phrase "a commonsense view of child development" identifies those beliefs shared by a large proportion of society—with many of the beliefs being self-evident conclusions.

Although at first this definition of commonsense theory may appear uncomplicated, we will see, when we analyze specific convictions, that people do not all agree on what they believe about children's growth and development. Differences of opinion are especially apparent in large, complex modern societies in which scholars have both the time and desire to speculate and conduct research about the nature of humanity. These thinkers come up with ideas that sometimes conflict with the common sense of the populace. But as the novel ideas are communicated, many people become convinced of their validity and join this new school of thought. Such splintering of common sense into different camps can be expected to occur more frequently in societies that are blessed, or burdened, not only with the leisure time for speculation but also with highly penetrating mass communication devices—television, radio, newspapers, magazines, and books. Smaller, more isolated, and cohesive societies subscribe to a more commonly accepted set of convictions about children than do larger, more disparate ones. Therefore, as we consider one version of commonsense theory, there may be a problem of consensus.

Furthermore, the common sense outlined in Chapter Five applies chiefly to societies that have evolved from European roots. How closely this version represents common sense in traditional African, Asian, Native American, and Pacific Island cultures is only partially known (Thomas, 1988).

Another aspect of naive psychology that deserves attention was described by an American developmental psychologist, A. L. Baldwin (1967, p. 38):

> It is important to realize . . . that naive psychology is not a stated theory but a body of beliefs about human behavior. Only the systematic description of naive psychology gives it the look of a theory.

Thus we are interested not just in the commonsense beliefs themselves but in the systematic way they are analyzed. However, we may ask whether such everyday beliefs about children deserve a chapter in a book on formal theories. Aren't naive assumptions too ordinary to warrant serious discussion? There are at least three reasons why they are not and why they do indeed deserve attention.

First, commonsense psychology is the sort that all of us use, either entirely or to a great degree, in dealing with children during the routine of daily living. A study of the structure and content of naive notions of development should help us analyze the strengths and weaknesses of such notions. As a result, we may be able to alter at least some of the least defensible aspects of our commonsense opinions and perhaps substitute more valid ones.

Second, the analysis of common sense can help us understand the nature of more formal theories of development because those theories often include many commonsense assumptions. After we observe the way psychologists such as Heider analyze naive beliefs, we will be better prepared to recognize the naive-psychology aspects of other theories we study.

Third, formal theories, in a sense, are often the reactions of theorists against naive-psychology notions that they believe are in error. Thus, when we recognize the commonsense ideas theorists are reacting against, we are better equipped to understand the formal theories. In effect, naive psychology serves as one of the foundations on which formal theories are constructed.

V. L. Lee (1988, pp. 17–18, 25) has characterized this relationship between common sense (ordinary knowledge) and formal theorizing (scientific knowledge) in the following manner:

> Scientific knowledge is extraordinary knowledge. It is knowledge of phenomena beyond ordinary observation. Probing beyond ordinary observation is part of what we ask and expect of a science. . . . We should expect inquiry to start in what is known and deliberately to surpass it. We want an academic psychology that can provide extraordinary knowledge and that can link its extraordinary knowledge step-by-step to the foundation given in ordinary psychology. . . . Ordinary psychology is constitutive of our experience of conduct and it is not easily set aside.

For these reasons, then, a chapter on commonsense psychology is of value in a modern-day book on theories of development.

First Key Issue: Normal, Natural, Desirable Development

The final segment of each of the following parts of this book is dedicated to a discussion of one key issue, called a "Perspective," in the realm of child development. The issue chosen for Part Two concerns the normality or desirability of development. I selected such a topic because so many of the people responsible for the care of the young want to know how to decide if the development of a child or an adolescent is *normal* or *natural* or *proper* or *desirable*. Should such words be used as synonyms, or is it better to distinguish among them? And if they should be differentiated, how is this best accomplished? More specifically, what popular options are available for defining these terms, and what are the advantages and disadvantages of each option?

Why this issue fits properly into Part Two should become apparent after you have read Chapters Three, Four, and Five.

CHAPTER THREE

Gesell's Descriptive Growth Gradients

The chief goal of some investigators has been to chart the steps or stages through which children advance as the years pass. The question guiding these efforts has been: What are children's characteristics at different age levels in physical, mental, social, emotional, and other facets of growth? Influential representatives of this tradition have been Arnold Gesell and his colleagues, who worked first at the Yale University School of Medicine and later at the Gesell Institute of Child Development in New Haven, Connecticut. Their findings have been reported in a series of books extending from 1912 into the 1990s.

Gesell was born in 1880 in Wisconsin, where he was educated and eventually took a college degree in teaching before earning a Ph.D. in psychology at Clark University in Massachusetts in 1906. In 1911 Gesell was appointed to the Yale faculty as an assistant professor of education. At the same time he established the Clinic of Child Development, which he directed during the next thirty-seven years. While at Yale he earned a doctorate in medicine (1915), and his clinic was attached to the school of medicine. After Gesell's retirement, several of his co-workers set up a private institution near Yale in New Haven, naming it the Gesell Institute of Child Development. Gesell served as a consultant to the clinic from 1950 through 1958. He died in 1961, but the work of his clinic has continued since that time.

Over the decades, Gesell and his colleagues pursued the task of describing the observable changes in child growth and behavior from birth into adolescence. Although their principal concern was with development after birth, the group also conducted studies on prenatal growth stages.

This chapter reviews the following theoretical themes that dominated Gesell's work: (1) aspects of development on which the research focused, (2) the primacy of genetic determinants, (3) cycles of behavior, and (4) the manner of accounting for individual differences. The chapter then continues with (5) practical applications of growth gradient studies, (6) an assessment of the Gesell group's work, and (7) a postscript concerning lessons to learn about the nature and use of normative-descriptive data.

ASPECTS OF DEVELOPMENT

The research portion of Gesell's work has consisted mainly of studying "fifty or more" children, each brought to the clinic to be examined yearly from infancy through age 10. "Most of these children were of high-average or superior intelligence, and came from [New England] homes of good or high socioeconomic status. . . . A special group of fourteen children, who attended an excellent private school in a small Connecticut town, were examined at semiannual intervals from ages six through nine" (Gesell et al., 1977, p. xiv). In books published by the Gesell group, there is occasional mention of other children seen in the institute's clinic and in schools, but no data are furnished about the numbers of children, their age levels, or their cultural backgrounds.

To carry out their investigations, Gesell and his staff created an array of tests, measuring procedures, and techniques of observation that would enable them to describe children's status in a wide range of growth areas. The research team gathered information about children in the clinic and also interviewed parents to learn about the children's behavior at home. These data enabled the group to describe *maturity traits* and developmental steps, called *growth gradients,* for the typical child in ten major areas, with each area defined by the subcategories shown in parentheses in the following list (Gesell et al., 1977, p. 58):

1. *Motor characteristics* (bodily activity, eyes and hands)
2. *Personal hygiene* (eating, sleeping, elimination, bath, dressing, health, somatic complaints, tensional outlets)
3. *Emotional expression* (affective attitudes, assertion, anger, crying, and related behavior)
4. *Fears and dreams*
5. *Self and sex*
6. *Interpersonal relations* (mother-child, father-child, child-child, siblings, family, grandparents, groupings in play, manners)

7. *Play and pastimes* (general interests, reading, music, radio, television, movies)

8. *School life* (adjustment to school, classroom demeanor, reading, writing, arithmetic)

9. *Ethical sense* (blaming and alibiing; response to direction, punishment, and praise; responsiveness to reason; sense of good and bad, truth and property)

10. *Philosophic outlook* (time, space, language and thought, death, deity)

An inspection of this list shows that Gesell adopted a multifaceted view of children rather than concentrating on one or two aspects of growth. And the fact that the topics cover growth areas that are of daily concern to parents and teachers helps account for the popularity of his books. When a mother worried about whether a particular kind of behavior was typical or "normal" for her child, she could turn to one of Gesell's volumes for an answer. The writing style of the most widely read books was adjusted to the reading tastes of parents. The volumes were not composed of statistical tables, showing the frequency of certain behaviors or of the number of children above and below the average at a given level. Instead, Gesell and his staff digested the statistics and turned them into specific statements of what a child was like at a given age. For example, here are typical descriptions of an aspect of behavior—children's fears—for ages 5 and 6 from a volume by two of Gesell's closest co-workers, Frances L. Ilg and Louise B. Ames.

> *5-year-olds:* Not a fearful age. More visual fears than others. Less fear of animals, bad people, bogeymen. Concrete, down-to-earth fears: bodily harm, falling, dogs. The dark. That mother will not return.
>
> *6-year-olds:* Very fearful. Especially auditory fears: doorbell, telephone, static, ugly voice tones, flushing of toilet, insect and bird noises. Fear of supernatural: ghosts, witches. Fear that someone is hiding under the bed. Fear of the elements: fire, water, thunder, lightning. Fear of sleeping alone in a room or of being only one on a floor of a house (1955, pp. 172–173).

Thus the main body of books issued from the Gesell clinic was composed of such "typical traits and growth trends of each age . . . summarized in a 'Behavior Profile' " (Gesell & Ilg, 1949, p. 2). In addition, Gesell and his co-workers expressed three important convictions that warrant our attention: (1) that development is primarily a product of genetic factors,

(2) that better and worse years alternate systematically in child growth, and (3) that there is a clear correlation between a child's body type and personality. These are the matters to which we now turn.

THE PRIMACY OF GENETIC DETERMINANTS

In the heredity–environment controversy, Gesell and his co-workers belong in the predeterminist camp. Over the decades, they have firmly maintained the conviction that the dominant causal factors in child growth and behavior are the biological structure of the child and the genetic time clock that establishes when particular physical and mental characteristics will ripen. In the 1980s, consistent with the position espoused by Gesell in the 1930s and 1940s, the directors of the Gesell Institute explained that:

> At the time we first wrote this book [1955], many psychologists were still blaming parents for any and all kinds of aberrant or even mildly undesirable behavior. . . . [But now] most child specialists and most behavior clinics have stopped blaming "emotional factors in the home" and general parental ineptitude for the majority of child behavior problems. Child specialists are becoming increasingly biologic in their interpretations of behavior. It is our belief that as knowledge about the human body and its functioning increases, and as emphasis shifts from blaming parents and other aspects of the environment to an understanding of biological function, much of the troublesome behavior that has bothered parents in the past can not only be understood and dealt with effectively but may actually be prevented in the first place (Ilg, Ames, & Baker, 1981, pp. vii–viii).

In light of this belief in the primacy of genetic determination, it is hardly surprising that Gesell and his staff saw their most important mission to be that of compiling descriptions of physical and mental characteristics at each age level. The resulting catalog of average, normal characteristics could inform parents, teachers, and pediatricians of the traits they might expect to see unfold with each year of growth.

CYCLES OF BEHAVIOR

Gesell's group also labeled each year of development as either better or worse. They proposed that the better and worse phases appear in recurring cycles and are essentially the same for all children—or for nearly all. The term *better stage* has been applied to any year in which the child appears to be in good adjustment or in good balance, both within herself and with the people in her world. The term *worse stage* has been given to years during which the child is unhappy and confused within himself and at odds with his social and physical environments. For example: "We have defined the major cycles of growth that take place from two to five, from five to ten, and ten to sixteen, and in each we see the same sequencing of alternating stages of equilibrium and disequilibrium, inwardizing and out-wardizing of behavior" (Gesell et al., 1977, p. xi).

As Table 3.1 shows, the first cycle of alternating better and worse ages begins at age 2 and ends at age 5. The next cycle starts at age 5 and lasts until age 10. The third cycle begins at age 10 and continues through age 16.

Since the Gesell group envisioned the characteristics of the better and worse years to be determined by internal maturational factors, their advice to parents and teachers concerning what to do about the worse years was basically to be patient and wait until the inevitable bad times passed. Therapy, which Freudians might suggest, or retraining, which behaviorists would recommend, was not proposed. "We can try to smooth over the child's 'worse' stages. . . . But if we can accept . . . these extremes . . . as necessary parts of growth, and not blame them on somebody (teacher, other parent, neighbor, child himself), we will be looking at things realisti-cally" (Ilg & Ames, 1955, p. 17).

Table 3.1   Alternation of Stages of Equilibrium and Disequilibrium in Child Behavior

Stages of Child Behavior				
First Cycle	*Second Cycle*	*Third Cycle*		
Age	*Age*	*Age*	*General Personality Trends*	*Quality of the Age*
2	5	10	Smooth, consolidated	Better
2½	5½–6	11	Breaking up	Worse
3	6½	12	Rounded, balanced	Better
3½	7	13	Inwardized	Worse
4	8	14	Vigorous, expansive	Better
4½	9	15	Inwardized-outwardized, troubled, "neurotic"	Worse
5	10	16	Smooth, consolidated	Better

Table adapted from Ilg and Ames, 1955, p. 22.

INDIVIDUAL DIFFERENCES

When a system like Gesell's is described, with children at each age level depicted as so much alike in so many ways, the question of individual differences among age peers comes up. In acknowledging the existence of exceptions to their descriptions of typical characteristics, Gesell and his colleagues inserted in their writings such comments as: "The prevalence of significant variations [is] recognized at every turn" (Gesell & Ilg, 1949, pp. 1–2). And: "When we describe characteristic behavior for any given age, we do not mean that all children of that age will behave in just that way all of the time. In fact, some of them rarely behave that way" (Ilg, Ames, & Baker, 1981, p. 15).

The manner in which the Gesell Institute staff has rationalized children's individual differences within this system of alternating better and worse years is illustrated in a passage about four-year-olds. As Table 3.1 illustrates, age 4 (like ages 8 and 14) is viewed as a "better" year during which the child is vigorous and expansive. These two traits result in a tendency for the child to go "out of bounds" (a tendency that parents and teachers might consider strange evidence for a *better* year). Then the authors account for any four-year-old behavior that deviates from this normative description by proposing that a given child: "may quite normally reach this 4-year-old out-of-bounds stage a little ahead of time or a little behind time or may be of such a gentle nature that even at his worst he does not go far out of bounds. Or he may be of such a vigorous nature that at *every* age he is more or less out of bounds" (Ilg, Ames, & Baker, 1981, p. 15).

Other than the foregoing occasional comments, seldom is more specific mention made in these writings of deviations from the typical traits, particularly in books written before 1950. In later volumes (Ilg & Ames, 1955; Ilg, Ames, & Baker, 1981; Ames & Haber, 1990), the authors have given somewhat more recognition to individual differences by first describing typical traits and then identifying two or three types of children that represent deviations from or variations of these traits. In addition, the writers have offered suggestions about what might be done to help the deviant make a better adjustment. As an example, the following is part of Ilg and Ames's discussion of eating behavior:

> Some children live to eat. They are the round, often plump children. They are rarely feeding problems. But there are others who rarely think of eating. They are the small, petite, or even scrawny children. Hunger may come often to them but it is usually sharp and shortlived. These children do better on small, frequent meals, even five or six a day. . . . They gain weight very slowly but are active and healthy, more healthy, often, than the larger robust children (Ilg & Ames, 1955, p. 91).

This passage illustrates three characteristics frequently found in publications emanating from the Gesell Institute. First, any differences among children at a given age are described in terms of two or three types of children, in this case the plump and the petite or scrawny, with the implication that all children fit into either the basic category for their age or into one of the deviant groups. Second, little or no attempt is made to suggest any environmental factors that might have contributed to a child's becoming one of these types, the implication being that children are naturally that way because of their genetic structure. Third, when advice is offered about what can be done for children whose type deviates from the average, the advice does not derive from principles inherent in Gesell's theory. Rather the advice either qualifies as common sense or derives more logically from studies or theories of other workers in the field of child behavior.

In view of the dominant role the Gesell Institute members have assigned to heredity in all aspects of development, it is easy to understand why they turned to William Sheldon's theory of *somatotypes* to account for personality differences among children. (Sheldon's proposal attracted a modicum of attention in the 1940s, but it has never been viewed by most psychologists as an adequate way to describe or explain development.) In Sheldon's opinion, there are three basic body types among people, or at least three tendencies. He labeled these the *endomorph,* the *mesomorph,* and the *ectomorph* (Sheldon, 1940, 1942).

The person who is predominantly *endomorphic* tends to be fat, soft, and round. Sheldon proposed that this body build is accompanied by a personality type that displays a love of comfort and relaxation, of food, of the company of other people, and of affection.

The *mesomorph* has big bones and heavy muscles. This type loves vigorous muscular activity and is assertive, wishing to dominate others in social situations.

The *ectomorph* is thin, fragile, poorly muscled. This personality is restrained, inhibited, oversensitive, seeks concealment, and avoids social contact.

Although Sheldon agreed that few people are entirely one of these body types, he claimed that everyone tends toward one or the other. The Gesell group, subscribing to the Sheldon position, has stated that:

> Whether we approach an understanding of individuality through measuring the way that the body is built or through an observation of the way that the individual behaves, we come to the conclusion that individuality is largely inborn. . . . Accept the fact that no matter how "well adjusted" he is, your thin, wiry ectomorph will probably be at heart a shy, quiet individual who prefers to remain relatively inconspicuous. That your well-built, heavily muscled mesomorph will be active, competitive,

noisy, relatively insensitive. That your plump, pear-shaped endomorph will be jolly, friendly, sociable, easygoing, but will have little desire to compete and dominate (Ilg, Ames, & Baker, 1981, p. 68).

The Gesell staff has allowed some room for the influence of the environment by adding: "All of this does not mean that human behavior is *entirely* determined by hereditary factors. What it does mean is that the body structure provides the raw material out of which personality is formed" (Ilg & Ames, 1955, p. 55). Nevertheless, despite this passing recognition of environmental influences, the dominant theme throughout all of the Gesell Institute's work is that the prime factor in shaping development, both for the average child and for types deviating from the average, is the child's genetically set maturation schedule.

PRACTICAL APPLICATIONS

Among the practical contributions of the Gesell Institute have been the staff's methods of assessing the growth levels of babies submitted for adoption and of children applying for entrance to kindergartens.

But perhaps of greater note is the fact that Gesell's work, and that of similar investigators, has furnished standards in many aspects of development against which children may be compared to indicate how "normally" they are growing. The widespread attraction of books offering descriptive norms demonstrates that such studies as Gesell's have been enthusiastically welcomed by parents and teachers who seek to understand child development. As an example of the popularity of the books, the 1976 edition of *Your Four Year Old* had been reprinted seventeen times by the late 1980s (Ames & Ilg, 1976).

However, critics have charged that the naive, imprecise, and unscientific way in which the Gesell group has presented their normative material can seriously warp parents', teachers', and pediatricians' interpretations of child development. The nature of such criticism is explained in the following appraisal of the Gesell group's work.

GESELL'S CONTRIBUTIONS: AN ASSESSMENT

Among professionals who study child development, the height of interest in Gesell and his normative-descriptive studies extended from the 1920s into the 1940s. Since that time, the activities of the Gesell Institute have been of little or no interest to most serious workers in the field, even though books written by the institute staff continue to be widely read by parents and, in some cases, by early childhood teachers. The reasons why

this work drifted into disfavor among serious theorists, empirical researchers, and clinicians can be explained in terms of the nine appraisal standards
suggested in Chapter One.

My ratings of Gesell's work may appear to form a strange pattern since
I have given his approach high marks on five of the nine criteria, yet have
judged his theory overall as not very satisfying. To explain these conclusions, let's consider first the higher ratings.

With few exceptions, the Gesell group's beliefs are described quite
clearly (item 2). But important among the exceptions is the confusing use
of the word *normal*. For each year of childhood and early adolescence, the
authors describe typical characteristics of children. Readers are told that
these characteristics form *age norms,* meaning what usually can be expected
of children at that time of life. For example:

> Child behavior, for all reasonably normal children, does develop in a
> highly patterned way. . . . [But] Age norms (our story of what behavior is
> like at the different ages) are only *averages*. So, if we say that a certain
> behavior is characteristic of four years of age, and your four-year-old has
> not reached this stage yet, you should not feel that you have cause to
> worry. Your child may be, and quite normally so, a little slower than the
> average in his development (though the quality of his behavior might be
> quite superior, indicating that a fine potential will express itself in time).
> . . . "Now I know he's normal" is what many parents say when they read
> our often seemingly somewhat lurid descriptions of what behavior can
> be like at different ages. This is why we write for you, hopefully to
> prepare you for, and to make you feel comfortable with, the many
> sometimes rather remarkable ways in which even completely normal
> children behave as they grow older (Ames & Ilg, 1976, pp. 12–13).

Thus children who fit the *maturity traits* that form the age norms are, by
definition, "normal." But children who deviate from these age norms are
also "normal." So questions arise: Are there no criteria for distinguishing
normal from abnormal? Under what conditions should adults view a child's
growth and behavior as warranting special intervention rather than only a
laissez-faire attitude—letting nature take its course? When is action, not
just patience or complacency, called for? Because of the contradictory way
the Gesell group has continued to apply the concept of normal development, I have rated the theory less than perfect in its clarity. (See Perspective A following Chapter Five, where we tackle the task of differentiating
among concepts of *normal, natural,* and *desirable* development.)

Generally, I find Gesell's work internally consistent (item 5). However,
I have rated the theory slightly below "very well" because of the muddled
use of *normal* and because his approach is so weak in accounting for
individual differences among children of the same age. Among the Gesell

Institute's detailed descriptions of what all children of a given age are expected to be like, I find it curious to meet such occasional incongruous statements as "The schools' present greatest need . . . is to treat each child as a human being and not as a subject who must be made to fit into preconceived patterns which are all too often not relevant to the individual" (Gesell et al., 1977, p. x).

Gesell's work is readily falsifiable (item 7). His growth gradients and descriptions of behavior by age levels are the result of empirical findings, so their accuracy can be checked empirically. Furthermore, the validity of the proposal that "*Better* or *worse* behavior tends to alternate with the ages in a fairly lawful sequence of unfolding" (Ilg, Ames, & Baker, 1981, p. 7) can be determined by a researcher who prepares careful definitions of *better* and *worse* and then observes behavior of children of different age

Gesell's Theory

How well do I think the theory meets the standards?

The Standards	*Very Well*	*Moderately Well*	*Very Poorly*
1. Reflects the real world of children		X	
2. Is clearly understandable	X		
3. Explains the past and predicts the future	Specifically X	Accurately X	
4. Guides child rearing	Specifically X	Accurately X	
5. Is internally consistent	X		
6. Is economical		Simplistic X	
7. Is falsifiable	X		
8. Stimulates new discoveries		X	
9. Is self-satisfying			X

levels to see how closely such behavior matches the definitions. In a similar manner, the proposed correlation between body build and personality characteristics is amenable to empirical testing.

Item 8 gets a rather high rating in recognition of the influence Gesell's work has exerted on other researchers in the field of development. During the years of his greatest productivity, he devised a variety of testing and observation procedures, particularly for use with very young children, which have been admired for their precision and ingenuity. His procedures have become part of commonly used scales for judging development over the first year or so of life. Not only are his research methods still used in normative studies, but much of what he learned about the early years of growth continues to be respected. Burton L. White, a Harvard University authority on infancy, wrote in 1971, "In this country, the most widely utilized source of information on the behavior of the human infant is probably the work of Arnold Gesell" (White, 1971, p. 7).

The rating on item 6 for the degree of economy Gesell's system displays represents a compromise between (1) his extremely simple, and in that sense economical, explanation of the causes of development and (2) the oversimplicity of the explanation. Although Gesell did not devise an unduly elaborate array of untested assumptions on which to erect his explanations, he did ignore a mass of research evidence that suggested environmental influences were far more important than his system recognized. As E. Zigler has commented:

> It is difficult to refer to [Gesell's scheme] as a theory. It appears rather to be a grand view having but a single construct, maturation. . . . Within such a framework, no other choice exists than to make the norms discovered through empirical investigations into explanatory devices . . . [so that] explanation is thus reduced to a labeling process. . . . The vacuousness and conceptual inadequacy of such a procedure has frequently been noted (1963, pp. 359–360).

In effect, the system is not overly complex, so it appears economical. In reality, however, it is unconvincingly simplistic. So I have rated it rather low on item 6.

On item 1, concerning how well a theory reflects the real world of children, Gesell deserves credit as an empiricist for founding his beliefs on observations of actual children, not imagined ones. He did not speculate about what children might be like or should be like. However, his penchant for reducing his observations to convenient averages or statements concerning typical characteristics at each age level distorts the picture of the real world of children. At any age level, and on any dimension of development, there are marked variations among children. Reporting of only averages, or at best merely noting subtypes of children who deviate from the average, gives an unrealistic picture of the growth status of many children at every age level.

Besides the problems of Gesell's reporting only typical characteristics of children, there is also a question of how accurately his developmental norms represent children in general. The question concerns both the number and the cultural background of the children on whom he based the norms. The exact number of boys and girls seen in the clinic is not specified in Gesell's major publications, but the total at each age level in the longitudinal studies apparently was no more than a few dozen. Furthermore, the children were from New England families interested enough in Gesell's research to bring their children to the clinic periodically for testing and observation. This method of sampling might well bias the results since there might be systematic differences between these families and those that did not participate in the clinic's studies. Indeed, Gesell pointed out that the preschool children in his group were above average in intelligence. Thus there is reason to doubt that the typical behaviors recorded for this sample give a realistic picture of children from other geographic and cultural settings.

Of course, this question about the representativeness of the sample is really not a serious issue when viewed from Gesell's predeterminist perspective. Since he believed that development depends heavily on heredity rather than environment, he could reason that it is unnecessary to choose children from different cultural environments—environment has little influence. It is necessary only to observe enough children to convince yourself that you have included the few major genetic types that make up the population. Thus Gesell was willing to generalize his observations to all children. But because I agree with those researchers who state that environment does exert an important influence on development, I have concluded that Gesell's sampling procedures were inadequate.

By balancing Gesell's admirable care in studying real children against his practice of describing only typical behaviors of a sample of New England children, I decided to rate his scheme only moderately realistic (item 1).

Both item 3 (explains past, predicts future) and item 4 (guides child rearing) are given two marks. The first mark in each case is for the degree of specificity of Gesell's system. In his system a child's past development is explained as the result of the natural unfolding of the preset genetic pattern. A child's future growth is described in terms of the typical characteristics of the age in which we are interested. Gesell's guides to child-rearing practices are equally definite. Basically we should let nature take its course. If the child's current development seems unsatisfactory, it is because the child is in one of the worse years, and patience on the part of adults is required until the stage passes. For such specificity Gesell's system rates high marks.

However, in terms of the accuracy of his explanations of the past, predictions for the future, and child-raising recommendations, he is rated further down the scales. I disagree with his practice of limiting his attention to "average" or "typical" behavior for an age group. Probably no child is average or typical in every way. Each child has a pattern of characteristics that makes up his individuality. Group averages are of limited use in explaining a child's past, predicting his future status, and suggesting what should be done to guide his development. The faith that researchers during the first half of the twentieth century placed in the value of normative group studies that yielded average scores (called *nomothetic* studies) has decreased in recent decades. More attention has been given recently to devising methods of investigating the growth of the individual child (called *idiographic* studies), particularly for purposes of prediction and child-rearing guidance.

Not only do I question Gesell's heavy dependence on typical behaviors, but I also question his crediting the environment with such a meager role in shaping development. In later chapters we will inspect the work of theorists who marshal evidence and a line of reasoning that suggest that environmental factors are extremely important in fashioning child growth, and much of this evidence I find convincing. Gesell's neglect of children's physical and social surroundings reduces the accuracy of his explanations of the child's past, predictions of her future, and recommendations for guiding her upbringing. For these reasons I have marked items 3 and 4 in the low to moderate range for accuracy.

Finally, I judge Gesell's system overall to be in the low to moderate range in terms of being self-satisfying (item 9). I respect his practice of making careful firsthand investigations of children and his devising techniques for carrying out such studies. However, these contributions do not sufficiently compensate for his overdependence on maturation and his overconcentration on "typical" behavior to warrant a higher rating.

POSTSCRIPT: NORMATIVE-DESCRIPTIVE LESSONS

The foregoing review of work emanating from the Gesell Institute can suggest lessons to learn about the nature of normative-descriptive information and about the use of such information in rearing children. The following overview is organized around a series of key concepts relating to normative statements.

Normative-Descriptive Statements Defined

Normative statements are descriptions of the extent to which people who fall within a given classification possess a particular characteristic. Example 1: The average height of five-year-old American boys is 42.9 inches. Example 2: During the 1980s, adolescent girls accounted for nearly half of all out-of-wedlock births in the United States (Romig & Thompson, 1988, p. 134).

Class Types   The most common category or classification for reporting normative data is chronological age. However, age itself is not a *cause* of developmental change but simply a surrogate for a cause, that is, a correlate of some cause that is less convenient to observe or chart. The "actual" or "true" cause may be a genetically timed change in the child's bodily structure or hormone production. Or it may be a particular experience that children commonly have around a given age level, such as the experience of being taught to read in the early years of schooling. Age, in effect, is accepted as a handy though imprecise indicator of these more-difficult-to-observe variables.

Complex Classes   A classification can be defined by one characteristic, such as age or sex, or by a combination of two or more characteristics. Examples of complex classes are ones combining:

Age, sex, and ethnic status. For example: sixteen-year-old Filipino males or eight-year-old second-generation Italian girls.

Grade level, socioeconomic status, and geographic location. For example: fourth-grade pupils in a lower-socioeconomic-class school in the Harlem district of New York City.

Gender, a developmental characteristic, a time period, and nationality. For example: among American girls during the 1970s, the first nonpathologic menstruation (the menarche) occurred between ages 9 and 16 (Bullough, 1981).

Knowing the classification on which normative information has been founded is important for determining whether that information can properly be applied to an individual child or a group of children we have in mind. This is the issue of *suitable sampling*. The question is: To what extent is the child to whom we wish to apply the normative data similar to the sample of children on whom the data were originally founded? The word *similar* in this case means "comparable in ways that significantly influence the data."

To illustrate this point, consider the matter of children's language development. Assume that we have obtained normative descriptions of children's vocabularies and sentence structures at different age levels. If we believe that children's vocabulary and syntax are significantly influenced by the language spoken in their homes, by their social-class subculture, and by their general intelligence, then it would be useful to have information about how these variables were distributed among the children on whom the age norms were founded. In other words, we would profit from having complex-class data (age, home language, social-class status, intelligence scores). Such information helps us know how well the characteristics of our particular child match such significant variables in the normative group.

The Gesell studies mentioned in this chapter suffer from the authors' failure (1) to stress sufficiently the significant variables displayed by the sample children on whom their data were based and (2) to caution readers that the conclusions derived from their studies should be used for comparison purposes only with other children who are similar on those variables. In other words, the Gesell group appears to imply that their conclusions can properly be applied to all children in all places and at all times.

Norms as Averages or Percentages

Normative-descriptive information is most commonly reported as either (1) the average amount of a characteristic manifested by a class of children or as (2) the proportion of children within the classification who display the characteristic. The most common statistic for reporting the average or *central tendency* of a group is either the *arithmetic mean* or the *median.*

Examples of Averages   In the early 1930s, the average age at which infants in California could first walk alone was 11.7 months (Malina & Roche, 1983). At age 6, the mean height of six-year-old American boys whose parents averaged 5.8 feet tall was 3.9 feet, while the mean height of six-year-old American boys whose parents averaged 5.3 feet tall was 3.6 feet (Lowrey, 1978).

Examples of Percentages   Studies in the mid-1980s of drug use by U.S. high school seniors showed that 61 percent had tried an illicit drug and 40 percent had tried some drug other than—or usually in addition to—marijuana (Johnston, O'Malley, & Bachman, 1986, p. 17). A study of urban American teenagers showed that over the decade 1965–1975, the rates of premarital intercourse increased by 50 percent for white males and 300 percent for white females. By age 16, one-quarter of white males and females had engaged in intercourse, as had 90 percent of black males and nearly 50 percent of black females (Chilman, 1983, p. 79).

Data on Variability

Knowledge of the amount of variability within a group is usually as important as knowledge about the group average. Variability is typically reported in terms of how much members of the group deviate from the average. The most common statistic for this purpose is the *standard deviation.* However, the *distance between two percentiles* (such as between percentile 10 and percentile 90) can also tell whether the group is spread out or bunched together. The usefulness of variability information can be illustrated if we wish to know how a five-year-old girl, whose height is 3.68 feet, compares in height to her age mates. A normative study of five-year-old girls tells us that the median (the child at the half-way point in the group) height is 3.57 feet, that the 75th percentile is 3.62 feet, and the 90th percentile is 3.75 feet (Hamill, 1977). Thus our girl is about halfway between the 75th and 90th percentiles, so she is taller than perhaps 80 or 85 percent of five-year-old girls.

Predicting from Normative Data

Normative information is commonly used for predicting how likely a newly met member of a class (perhaps a newly met two-year-old Hopi girl) will possess a given characteristic. The following three rather obvious generalizations can help guide such predictions.

1. The Proportion of a Characteristic within a Class   The greater the percentage of children in a class who possess a given characteristic, the more confidently we can predict that a newly observed member of the class will also possess that characteristic.

For example, studies have shown that 90 percent of U.S. girls whose first pregnancy has come in their early teens continue to live with a parent or close relative (Furstenburg, 1981). This datum enables us to predict with a great deal of assurance that the next young teenage mother we encounter will be living with a close relative. In contrast, we would be less confident in predicting the likely cause of mental deficiency in a newly met child if we learn that a biological cause can be identified in only around 25 percent of children diagnosed as mentally retarded, while the causes for the remaining 75 percent are attributed to unknown or environmental factors (Bricker, 1986, p. 148).

To summarize, the closer a percentage approaches 50 percent, the less confidence we can place in a prediction that a newly met child will display the characteristic in question. In contrast, the closer the percentage approaches 100 percent, the greater our assurance that the child will possess the characteristic.

2. Effect of Variability of Prediction The greater the overlap of a characteristic from classification A to classification B, the less confidence we have in predicting that someone in class A will display the characteristic while someone in class B will not.

Consider, for example, the matter of children's reading ability, which is often described in terms of grade levels. A student who reads as well as the average eighth-grader is said to be reading at the eighth-grade level. A question now can be asked about how much overlap exists between the students in one grade and those in another grade in reading skill. In other words, if we learn that a boy reads at the eighth-grade level, how confidently can we assume that he actually is in the eighth grade? Or, to put it another way, what proportion of eighth-graders read at that level rather than at the seventh- or ninth-grade level? A study of 975 eighth-graders in two junior high schools of a small western U.S. city revealed that only 9 percent of those students read at the eighth-grade level on a nationally standardized reading test (Thomas & Thomas, 1965, p. 307). Of the 975, slightly more than 11 percent read as well as the average seventh-grader, and 10 percent read at the grade-six level. Smaller numbers read at grade levels five, four, and three. Then, above grade eight, 10 percent read at grade level nine, 13 percent at ten, 13 percent at eleven, and 20 percent at the twelfth-grade level or higher. In effect, the reading ability of the 975 eighth-graders extended over a range of more than ten grades. Such variability in reading skill within the classification *eighth-graders* warns us that we risk making a serious error if (1) we assume that a newly met eighth-grade girl will necessarily read at the eighth-grade level and if (2) we then assign her to read a textbook written for the average eighth-grader. The great overlap among grades also suggests that many sixth-, seventh-, ninth-, and tenth-graders will read at the eighth-grade level.

The books issued by the Gesell Institute have consistently committed the error of proposing that certain developmental attributes are unique characteristics of specific age or grade levels—and are absent or very rare at other ages or grade levels. For instance, in describing children's emotional expression at sequential ages, the Gesell group has stated that seven-year-olds have "little sense of humor," eight-year-olds "have a high humorous sense," nine-year-olds enjoy humor, and the humor of ten-year-olds is "usually not funny from an adult point of view" (Gesell et al., 1977, pp. 284–285). Even casual observations of children at different age levels reveal the absurdity of such sweeping generalizations. If we wish to produce accurate normative descriptions of children's sense of humor at sequential stages, then our research will require: (1) precise definitions, with illustrative examples, of types of humor; (2) a description of the environmental settings under which each type is displayed in children's lives; and (3) the percentage of each type observed within a defined sample of children at each age level. In contrast to the Gesell conclusions, other researchers' studies of humor and of play do not yield the kinds of simplistic statements about each age level that typify the Gesell growth gradients (Chapman & Foot, 1976; Pepler & Rubin, 1982; Vawkey & Pellegrini, 1984). Instead, such investigations show considerable overlap of humor types from one age level to another, along with some general trends from early to late childhood and into adolescence. In other words, accurate normative descriptions will reflect the sorts of individual differences among children that have been given no more than lip service in the Gesell Institute publications.

3. The Precision of Normative Statements   All normative statements offer quantitative information about an aspect of life, but the statements vary greatly in their level of precision. The least precise are ones in which the quantity is expressed as a nonnumerical adjective *(many, a few, most, several, some)*, as an adverb *(occasionally, significantly, unduly, typically, barely, slightly, often)*, or as a noun (a *majority*, a *number*). There are several reasons for such imprecision. Perhaps the most common is that the person offering the statement has constructed the normative description from unsystematic observations collected in daily life. For example, an experienced teacher may conclude that "Most six-year-olds can't sit still for very long" or "Lots of high school girls hate swimming class because they don't want to get their hair wet."

Imprecise statements can also result from a textbook writer inspecting a variety of research studies, then trying to summarize the gist of the studies in an easy-to-remember form. For instance, one published study may report that 20 percent of children treated in clinics for minor phobias completely recovered as the result of accustoming the child to the object of the phobia. Another study may report a 36 percent recovery rate, a third a 23 percent rate, and a fourth a 61 percent rate. From these figures, an easy-to-recall verbal summary might be drawn: "In most cases a strong minority profit from such treatment." Slightly more precision can be lent to the statement if it is rephrased as: "The rate of recovery from the disorder ranged from nearly one-quarter to slightly over one-half of the clients" (Thomas, 1990, p. 41).

Another reason that quantities are so often expressed in nonnumerical terms is that the people who issue the statements are unsure about how faithfully the data collected on the normative sample will apply to other children of the same age, gender, or ethnic background. Thus the use of terms such as *frequently* or *occasionally* may simply be an expression of caution.

However, in general, normative descriptions cast in precise numerical form are more helpful than vague quantitative statements. The absence of numerical information in the Gesell Institute publications seriously diminishes the worth of the group's research results.

The Lessons Summarized

Normative-descriptive information provides a significant portion of the building materials from which theories of child development are constructed. (Other building materials are the assumptions about *ontology* [the nature of existence] and *epistemology* [the nature and methods of human knowledge] on which a theory is based.) In effect, the quality of a theory depends to a considerable extent on the accuracy and clarity of its foundational normative information. As proposed in the foregoing paragraphs, such accuracy and clarity are more likely to result if the published normative descriptions:

1. Identify significant characteristics of the sample of children on whom the norms were based. Such information helps us estimate how appropriate the norms—and any theory founded on the norms—will likely be for explaining the development of particular children we have in mind.

2. Provide information about both the average status of members of the group and the degree to which the members spread out from the average. In other words, we can profit from learning: (a) the extent of individual differences within the normative group and (b) the amount of overlap between one class of children (such as one age level) and another.

3. Are in numerical form rather than cast only as imprecise verbal quantities.

FOR FURTHER READING

Ames, L. B., and C. C. Haber. (1990) *Your Eight Year Old.* New York: Dell. This book exemplifies the publications that members of the Gesell Institute have written for each age level to answer parents' child-rearing queries.

Gesell, A., F. L. Ilg, L. B. Ames, and G. E. Bullis. (1977) *The Child from Five to Ten.* New York: Harper & Row. This volume presents the Gesell Institute interpretation of child development. It includes detailed descriptions of maturity traits and growth gradients.

CHAPTER FOUR

Havighurst's Developmental Tasks

According to the developmental-task theory, the process of living, from birth to death, consists of an individual's working her way from one stage of development to the next by solving problems that are met at each stage. These problems, common to virtually everyone in a particular culture, are life's *developmental tasks*. If a person is successful in achieving each task, she is happy and receives the approval of her society. This success builds a good foundation for accomplishing later tasks. If the individual fails with a task, she feels unhappy, society does not approve, and she faces difficulty with later tasks (Havighurst, 1953, p. 2).

Examples of developmental tasks at the first stage of life, infancy, are learning to walk and learning to talk. Examples from middle childhood are learning the physical skills necessary for ordinary games and developing the fundamental skills of reading, writing, and calculating. Examples from later adolescence are achieving emotional independence from parents and preparing for an occupation.

Developmental-task theory is not the product of a single theorist. The basic idea underlying the scheme and the identification of important tasks began in the 1930s and evolved during the 1940s among groups of child psychologists and educators who played leading roles in the Progressive Education Association in the United States.* The theory was subsequently cast in its most systematic and extensive form by Robert J. Havighurst in his 1953 volume entitled *Human Development and Education* and by Carolyn

---

*Havighurst (1953, pp. 328–333) credits the following people with contributions to the developmental-task concept: Frankwood Williams, Lawrence K. Frank, Carolyn Zachry, Erik Erikson, Fritz Redl, Caroline Tryon, Jesse Lilienthal, Stephen M. Corey, Peter Blos, Daniel Prescott, Evelyn Duvall, and Reuben Hill.

Tryon and Jesse Lilienthal in two chapters of their 1950 work *Fostering Mental Health in Our Schools*. The picture of the theory sketched in the following pages is based mainly on these two sources.

Although the developmental-task model found its greatest popularity in the 1940s and 1950s in the field of education, it has continued to influence child psychologists and educators and has periodically stimulated the publication of new books in Europe and America founded on the concept.

The following brief overview of the theory treats five topics: (1) characteristics of tasks, (2) timing of tasks, (3) evidence to support the theory, (4) practical applications, and (5) research challenges.

CHARACTERISTICS OF TASKS

The term *developmental task* was apparently coined in the 1930s by people prominent in the Progressive Education Association. It was adopted and popularized by Havighurst in the 1940s and 1950s because, in discussions of adolescent development, he said he had "seen so much misunderstanding result from the use of the equivocal term 'needs' as a central concept" (1953, p. 330). He felt that the new term *developmental tasks* better described what young people were attempting to do as they grew up. According to Havighurst, the developmental tasks of life are pursuits that:

> constitute a healthy and satisfactory growth in our society. They are those things a person must learn if he is to be judged and to judge himself to be a reasonably happy and successful person. A developmental task is a task which arises at or about a certain period in the life of the individual, successful achievement of which leads to his happiness and to success with later tasks, while failure leads to unhappiness in the individual, disapproval by society, and difficulty with later tasks (1953, p. 2).

What are the tasks at different age levels? How many are there? Havighurst said that the number is somewhat arbitrary. It depends both on the way a person chooses to specify them and also on the particular society the person is talking about. For instance, the task of learning independent locomotion can be seen either as a single complex task composed of sub-activities (creeping, walking, trotting, running, hopping, jumping) or as six different small tasks.

Some tasks arise mainly from the biological nature of humans and thus will be found in all human societies. Their form is essentially the same in all cultures. Other tasks derive their characteristics from the unique cultural patterns of a given society; these either exist in different forms in different societies or else are found in some cultures but not in others. A task like learning to walk, which depends primarily on genetically determined growth factors, is essentially the same in all societies and arises at about the same time in a child's life. However, the task of selecting and preparing for an occupation is a complex one in highly industrialized societies that are characterized by much specialization and division of labor, while in nonindustrialized societies in which nearly everyone is a farmer or hunter or fisher, the task of choosing a vocation is perhaps simpler and is achieved at a younger age than in the industrialized society. Furthermore, the tasks of learning to read and write, which are so important in highly literate cultures, do not even exist in preliterate ones.

Consequently, lists of developmental tasks will not be the same for all cultures, and the items in the lists identifying a culture's tasks will be determined to some degree by the personal value systems of the people who prepare them. Havighurst admitted that the description of tasks he produced was "based on American democratic values seen from a middle-class point of view, with some attempt at pointing out the variations for lower-class and upper-class Americans" (1953, p. 26).

Havighurst felt that, in applying the developmental-task approach to children's education, it is most useful to define six to ten tasks at each stage of development. One such application is shown in Table 4.1, which is adapted from a table by Tryon and Lilienthal. The chart contains ten general categories or types of tasks. These categories are listed in the far-left column. To find the specific tasks in each category at each age level, look to the right of the category name.

For example, consider the first category, that of the child's achieving an appropriate dependence–independence pattern in growth. In the second column from the left, we find two specific tasks the infant faces in this category: (1) establishing one's self as a very dependent being and (2) beginning the establishment of self-awareness. For children at the stage of early adolescence (fifth column), we find one task described in this category, that of establishing one's independence from adults in all areas of behavior. In a similar manner we can find the specific tasks for each growth stage in any of the ten task categories.

Just as the number of tasks is somewhat arbitrary, so also are the stages through which an individual's development is traced. Tryon and Lilienthal identified five stages from birth to around age 20. Havighurst, however, divided the entire life span into six stages: (1) infancy and early childhood (birth through age 5), (2) middle childhood (ages 6 through 12), (3) adolescense (ages 13 through 17), (4) early adulthood (ages 18 through 30), (5) middle age (ages 31 through 54), and (6) later maturity (ages 55 and beyond).

No matter how the stages are defined in terms of age levels, tasks at each stage arise from three sources: (1) the biological structure and function of the individual, (2) the particular society or culture in which the individual lives, and (3) the personal values and aspirations of the individual. Havighurst called these the biological, the cultural, and the psychological bases of development. Three examples of biologically based tasks are: (1) learning to control the elimination of one's bodily wastes, (2) learning to accept one's physical sex changes in adolescence, and (3) learning to behave appropriately toward the opposite sex. Three tasks originating mainly from the pressures of society are: (1) learning to read and write, (2) learning to respect other people's property, and (3) accepting the responsibility to do one's share of the work in group projects. Two tasks arising in later adolescence chiefly from the personal values and motives of the individual are: (1) selecting an occupation and (2) establishing one's philosophical or religious convictions.

To guide people who wish to analyze the anatomy of each task for themselves, Havighurst recommended a series of questions that fall under five categories: task definition, biological basis, psychological basis, cultural basis, and educational implications. Specifically, he recommended that we try to answer these queries about a given task.

Nature of the task: How is it defined?

Biological basis: What can the biological sciences tell us about this task? How is a person's physical maturation related to achieving it? How do individual biological differences influence achievement of the task?

Psychological basis: What can psychology tell us about the task? How is the person's mental development related to it? How do the values and aspirations of the individual influence her or his achievement of the task? How is the task related to individual mental and personality differences? How can success or failure in accomplishing the task influence personality?

Cultural basis: What can sociology and social anthropology tell us about the task? How does the task vary from one culture to another? How is the task defined in the upper, middle, and lower social classes?

Educational implications: What are the responsibilities of general education for helping children and youth accomplish this task? How well are these responsibilities now being met? How might the educational system do a better job of helping young people achieve the task? (Havighurst, 1953, p. 17.)

To learn how Havighurst himself used these questions as guidelines for the complex job of delineating tasks, see his *Human Development and Education* in which he offers detailed analyses of the key tasks he identified for six periods of the life span.

THE TIMING OF TASKS

For any theory involving stages of development, an important question to ask is, How crucial is it that a child pass through a stage at the time designated as normal or usual? In other words, are there critical stages? In his theory, Havighurst differentiated between two general categories of tasks: ones that arise only at a particular time and must be completed at the time and ones that are continuing tasks whose fulfillment the individual works on for many years. In the first category are such tasks as learning to walk and talk, learning how to eliminate bodily wastes in an acceptable manner, and selecting a vocation. In the second category are such long-term, recurrent tasks as learning to participate as a responsible citizen and learning a feminine or masculine role. These recurrent tasks, however, have substages that are to be completed at given times in the child's and adolescent's development.

According to Havighurst, it is critical that the child pursue and succeed with most, if not all, tasks at the time designated for them. To support this opinion, he cited studies of children "who were denied human companionship during their first few years of life and therefore did not learn to talk" (1953, p. 3). He suggested that such cases furnish at least some evidence that if the task of learning to talk is not accomplished during the second year of life, it may never be accomplished successfully. Hence the second year of life is seen as the critical period for achieving initial speaking skill. Furthermore, failure with a task during its critical period causes difficulties in performing later tasks related to the one that was failed. Failure in learning to talk, for example, will prevent the child from learning to read and write and from understanding many concepts normal to children at later stages of growth.

The model for this concept of timing tasks was drawn by Havighurst from evidence about the biological development of humans, particularly development in the prenatal, embryonic stage. In the embryo, the organ that does not arise at its proper time not only damages its own chance of developing but "endangers the whole hierarchy of organs" (1953, p. 3). Havighurst then extended this generalization to all of the bio-socio-psychological tasks treated in his scheme. "If the task is not achieved at the proper time it will not be achieved well, and failure in this task will cause partial or complete failure in the achievement of other tasks yet to come" (Havighurst, 1953, p. 3).

EVIDENCE TO SUPPORT THE TASK THEORY

Adherents of the developmental-task concept of child growth base most of their theorizing on normative studies and on their own casual observations of children and adolescents. Also, Havighurst acknowledged that the psychoanalytic ideas of Erik Erikson influenced the sorts of tasks he defined regarding the development of a self-concept in the early years of growth. And, as noted, Havighurst found it convenient to derive growth principles from biological studies and then to extend these principles to encompass social and psychological development as well. However, he regarded this extension more as a plausible hypothesis than a description of absolute truth.

In an effort to test the hypothesis that biological growth principles could be extended to other areas, he and his colleagues conducted a study of fifteen boys and fifteen girls in a small American town over a period of six years. The children were age 10 when the study began and age 16 when it was completed. To make the study broad in scope, the researchers used a variety of assessment techniques, including interviews with pupils and their parents, sociometric tests, projective tests (the Rorschach, Thematic-Apperception, and sentence-completion tests), observational reports by teachers and other adults, essays and checklists from the pupils, tests of aptitude and intelligence, ratings of personality, and measurements of physical growth.

The five developmental tasks on which the study focused were: (1) learning an appropriate sex role, (2) achieving emotional independence from parents and other adults, (3) developing a conscience and a set of values, (4) getting along with age-mates, and (5) developing intellectual skills.

At the end of the study, the researchers concluded that, in general, success with one task was correlated with success in others, although the amount of relationship varied with the types of tasks. For example, there was a high relationship between getting along with age-mates and developing a scale of values. However, the relationships were only moderately high for other tasks, such as learning an appropriate sex role (which correlated only $r = .61$ between ages 10 and 13). In most cases success with a task at one age would be followed by good performance on the task at later ages although the relationships were not so strict as to "rule out any possibility of improvement on the part of a poor performer as he grows older" (Havighurst, 1953, pp. 290, 325–326).

The research team also found some evidence to support the concept of compensation. A child might make up for poor performance on one task by good performance on another. However, such children seemed to be exceptions to the general rule, so that "the number of people who are using

Table 4.1 The Tasks of Five Stages of Development in Ten Categories of Behavior

	Infancy (Birth to 1 or 2)	Early Childhood (2–3 to 5–6–7)	Late Childhood (5–6–7 to Pubescence)	Early Adolescence (Pubescence to Puberty)	Late Adolescence (Puberty to Early Maturity)
I Achieving appropriate dependence–independence pattern	1. Establishing oneself as very dependent being 2. Beginning to establish self-awareness	1. Adjusting to less attention; becoming independent physically (while remaining dependent emotionally)	1. Freeing oneself from primary identification with adults	1. Beginning to establish independence from adults in all behavior areas	1. Establishing oneself as independent individual in an adult manner
II Achieving appropriate giving–receiving pattern of affection	1. Developing a feeling for affection	1. Developing ability to give affection 2. Learning to share affection	1. Learning to give as much love as one receives; forming friendships with peers	1. Accepting oneself as worthwhile person, worthy of love	1. Building strong mutual affectional bond with possible marriage partner
III Relating to changing social groups*	1. Becoming aware of the alive vs. the inanimate, the familiar vs. the unfamiliar 2. Developing rudimentary social interaction	1. Beginning to develop ability to interact with age-mates 2. Adjusting to family expectations for child as member of the social unit	1. Clarifying adult world vs. child's world 2. Establishing peer grouping and learning to belong	1. Behaving according to shifting peer code	1. Adopting adult-patterned social values by learning new peer code

IV Developing a conscience	1. Beginning to adjust to expectations of others	1. Developing ability to take directions, to be obedient in presence of authority 2. Developing ability to be obedient in absence of authority (conscience substitutes for)	1. Learning more rules; developing true morality		1. Learning to verbalize contradictions in moral codes, discrepancies between principle and practice; resolving these problems responsibly
V Learning one's psycho-socio-biological sex role		1. Learning to identify with adult male and female roles	1. Beginning to identify with same-sex social contemporaries	1. Strong identification with one's own sex 2. Learning one's role in heterosexual relationships	1. Exploring possibilities for future mate; acquiring "desirability" 2. Choosing an occupation 3. Preparing for future role as responsible citizen

*Tryon and Lilienthal, 1950, pp. 77–89. I have not dealt with the developmental tasks of relating to "secondary" social groups. As the child grows and develops, he or she must relate to groups other than the family and peers—to school, community, nation, world. There are not yet sufficient data to enable us to delineate the specific developmental tasks in this area.

Table 4.1   The Tasks of Five Stages of Development in Ten Categories of Behavior (continued)

	Infancy (Birth to 1 or 2)	Early Childhood (2–3 to 5–6–7)	Late Childhood (5–6–7 to Pubescence)	Early Adolescence (Pubescence to Puberty)	Late Adolescence (Puberty to Early Maturity)
VI Accepting and adjusting to a changing body	1. Adjusting to adult feeding demands 2. Adjusting to adult cleanliness demands 3. Adjusting to adult attitudes toward genital manipulation	1. Adjusting to expectations based on improving muscular abilities 2. Developing sex modesty		1. Reorganizing self concept in the face of significant bodily changes 2. Accepting one's appearance	1. Learning appropriate outlets for sexual drives
VII Managing a changing body and learning new motor patterns	1. Developing physiological equilibrium 2. Developing eye-hand coordination 3. Establishing satisfactory rest–activity rhythm	1. Developing large muscle control 2. Learning to coordinate large and small muscles	1. Improving skill in use of small muscles	1. Controlling and using "new" body	
VIII Learning to understand and control the physical world	1. Exploring the physical world	1. Meeting adult restrictions on exploration and manipulation of expanding environment	1. Learning more realistic ways of studying and controlling physical world		

IX. Developing an appropriate symbol system and conceptual abilities	1. Developing pre-verbal communication 2. Developing verbal communication 3. Rudimentary concept formation	1. Improving one's use of the symbol system 2. Great elaboration of concept pattern	1. Learning to use language to exchange ideas or to influence 2. Beginning to understand casual relationships 3. Making finer conceptual distinctions; thinking reflectively	1. Using language to express and clarify more complex concepts 2. Moving from the concrete to the abstract; applying general principles to the particular	1. Reaching one's potential level of reasoning
X. Relating oneself to the cosmos		1. Developing a rudimentary notion of one's place in the cosmos	1. Developing a scientific approach		1. Formulating a workable belief and value system

good achievement in one task to compensate for poor achievement in another must be quite small" (Havighurst, 1953, p. 322).

This investigation of the developmental-task theory, conducted with a very small sample of children, is apparently the most intensive and best controlled study designed to test the theory. Thus belief in the theory remains grounded mainly in normative studies—what the average child is like at different age levels—and in the logic or reasonableness of the scheme.

PRACTICAL APPLICATIONS

Applications of developmental-task theory have been of several kinds. One has been in the form of efforts to improve school curricula and out-of-school programs for children. As curriculum planners have sought to suit schoolwork to pupils' needs, they have assessed how well the subject matter and activities of the current curriculum match the developmental tasks identified for children at different age levels. In this way improvements have been made in parts of the course of study that apparently had not previously contributed toward the achievement of important tasks (Tryon & Lilienthal, 1950). Leaders in charge of extracurricular and out-of school programs for young people have also used task analysis in selecting activities to be included in their programs.

As a further type of application, authors of child development textbooks in both America and Europe have described childhood from a developmental-task perspective (see, for example, Bernard, 1970; Hurlock, 1968; Muller, 1969; Travers, 1977). Their assumption has been that an understanding of tasks children are attempting to accomplish will help parents and teachers to be more patient with such attempts and to provide activities that help the young succeed in their endeavors.

In addition, researchers working in particular fields have adopted the notion of developmental tasks as a productive way to approach their specialized realms of interest. An example is A. Godin's (1971) proposed sequence of five developmental tasks in Christian education. The first task consists of the child's discovering Jesus at the center of God's plan in history, an accomplishment that becomes possible only when the child's *historical consciousness* is awakened around age 12 or 13. Second is the task of comprehending that Jesus was not simply a historical figure but is a continuing symbol of God's present-day actions. In Godin's opinion, this comprehension first becomes possible around age 13. Godin's third task is that of the child's gradually abandoning a magical view of religion in middle adolescence and replacing it with true faith in God's plan. Fourth is the task of progressively leaving behind the notion that moral behavior earns favors from God. This notion is replaced by the adolescent's growing desire to do good works because they are an expression of humanism, without expecting God to provide gifts in proportion to the works performed. The fifth task, to be met in later adolescence and early adulthood, is that of freeing one's Christian beliefs from the parental images of mother and father.

A second example of applying the developmental-task concept outside the realm of Havighurst's model appears in E. M. Duvall's book *Family Development* (1971) in which she organizes her presentation around developmental tasks of the family. Duvall's model is founded on the premise that families grow through predictable stages that can be analyzed in terms of the development of both the individual family members and the family as a unit.

In summary, some applications of the developmental-task approach have involved using the original sets of tasks from Havighurst and his colleagues as the bases for educational and child-rearing practices. Other applications, such as Godin's and Duvall's, have consisted of creating entirely different tasks and then basing analyses and educational practices on this new set.

DEVELOPMENTAL-TASK THEORY: AN ASSESSMENT

In keeping with the mode of assessment used in the previous chapter, I will use the nine assessment standards described in Chapter One to appraise developmental-task theory.

I have rated developmental-task theory high on item 1 because Havighurst offers a realistic picture of the cultural group to which he restricted his particular list of tasks. That is, his list is intended to represent the developmental tasks of mid-twentieth-century, middle-class, American children and youths. My observations of such children suggest that Havighurst's claim that these young people are seeking to accomplish his list of tasks is reasonable.

I have also rated the developmental-task system high for its clarity of explanation (item 2) and its internal consistency (item 5). Likewise, the theory appears to fulfill the criterion of economy (item 6), for it does not require a large number of untested assumptions as its foundation when a smaller number would suffice. While it is not unduly complex, neither is it overly simplified, as I feel Gesell's system is. Havighurst has gone to considerable length to analyze for each task the biological, social, and personal-psychological roots from which he proposes the tasks have grown.

On items 3 (explains past, predicts future) and 4 (guides child rearing) I have rated the theory in the moderately well range. It does, in a general way, predict the future for a child by describing tasks that seem common to all children in a given culture. Thus it suggests on what areas of life children at different stages will be focusing attention. Likewise, if a child seems maladjusted at a particular stage, developmental-task theory suggests what tasks were possibly not achieved adequately in the past and are thus causing difficulties with present tasks. However, the theory is more a way of describing behavior, of telling what children are like in their interests and concerns at different age periods, than a way of explaining why a child is behaving in a particular manner at the present time. In short, the theory is more descriptive than explanatory, as is Gesell's system. If you ask how biological factors interact with environmental factors to yield a particular behavior, developmental-task theory does not provide a clear answer.

Developmental-Task Theory

How well do I think the theory meets the standards?

The Standards	Very Well	Moderately Well	Very Poorly
1. Reflects the real world of children	X		
2. Is clearly understandable	X		
3. Explains the past and predicts the future		X	
4. Guides child rearing		X	
5. Is internally consistent	X		
6. Is economical	X		
7. Is falsifiable		X	
8. Stimulates new discoveries		X	
9. Is self-satisfying		X	

In terms of child rearing, the theory tells what sorts of problems children may be expected to face while growing up, but it does not offer much useful advice to parents and teachers about how to promote successful achievement of the tasks. The most useful implications for child rearing to be drawn from developmental-task theory seem to be that (1) we should recognize the nature of children's tasks at each age period and provide opportunities for them to practice solutions of the tasks, (2) we should be patient with children's attempts to solve the problems inherent in the tasks, and (3) we should furnish them information and training in skills that can promote accomplishment of the tasks.

As for item 7, the theory appears to be only moderately falsifiable. Some of its key hypotheses are testable, as was demonstrated in Havighurst's study of how satisfactory accomplishment of earlier tasks seems to influence the achievement of later ones. However, other aspects of the theory are not falsifiable. For example, how can we determine what the proper number of tasks and grouping of tasks should be for a given culture? Or, how do we identify with confidence which task or combination of tasks is being pursued in a specified segment of behavior, such as in a girl's agreeing to stay home and wash clothes for her mother rather than going to a movie with her friends? Identifying the tasks that are ostensibly motivating a particular series of actions or developmental changes involves a large measure of personal opinion. Testing the validity of personal interpretations made in matching tasks with behaviors would seem to be, in many cases at least, impossible. In this sense, then, developmental-task theory does not appear to be falsifiable, and the theory is rated moderately low on this scale.

The developmental-task approach has been fertile (item 8) in the sense of providing a useful scheme for revising school curricula and for offering parents and teachers another way of looking at children's developmental needs. And even though the developmental-task model has not been a particularly fruitful source of empirical studies over the decades, it still continues to serve as a conceptual framework for a limited number of researchers. For example, A. Palmonari, M. L. Pombeni, and E. Kirchler (1990) have studied the influence of peer groups on adolescents' attempts to cope with developmental tasks. D. A. Dangelo (1989) inspected the way changing times have affected the roles assigned to adolescent females in literature that concerns adolescents. M. Ittyjerah and A. Samarapungavan (1989) studied the performance of congenitally blind children in cognitive developmental tasks. And R. Fuchs (1988) investigated the culminating effects of success and failure in learning activities that involve developmental tasks. However, when compared to Freud's psychoanalysis or Piaget's cognitive theory, the developmental-task approach ranks very poorly on research fertility, so I have rated it low for that reason.

Finally, how self-satisfying is the theory (item 9)? It is limited in terms of its capability to explain rather than just describe behavior. And it is not precise in identifying tasks and matching them to segments of behavior. Furthermore, it has not opened new vistas for investigation; or at least few researchers have seen it as a fertile source of new discoveries. Despite these limitations, though, the developmental-task perspective is useful for interpreting children's behavior. The idea that children are struggling to achieve the goals implied in the tasks makes sense to me. Balancing these shortcomings of the theory against its usefulness as a way of viewing children, I have rated it as moderately self-satisfying.

FOR FURTHER READING

Havighurst, R. J. (1953) *Human Development and Education.* New York: Longmans, Green. The most complete analysis of the developmental-task approach available.

CHAPTER FIVE

Commonsense Attribution Theory

As explained in the introduction to Part Two, a "commonsense" view of child development identifies those beliefs shared by a large proportion of society, with many of the beliefs being self-evident conclusions. Of course, members of the general public have not assembled their collection of convictions into an organized theory. However, psychologists have managed to infer from people's behavior the major dimensions of this assortment of convictions and have described how the dimensions appear to interact. A version of this inferred belief system is what I am referring to as *commonsense attribution theory*. It "deals with the rules the average individual uses in attempting to infer the causes of observed behavior" (Jones et al., 1971, p. x).

We could adopt any of several ways to construct a commonsense theory of development. We might conduct a poll, asking a sample of people to answer questions about children. We might collect folklore, proverbs, and traditional sorts of advice about child raising, and then search for the pattern of concepts that underlies them. We could observe adults as they interact with children or as they talk about children and then estimate what theory of child nature is implied in such action and talk. We might analyze a society's laws relating to children, on the assumption that laws reflect a common set of beliefs for that society. Or we could use all of these approaches. However, due to space limitations, in this chapter we will use only two: an analysis of typical daily talk and an inspection of a few key laws that relate to children.

For the analysis of talk, our basic guide will be the work of Fritz Heider (1896–1988), as later enhanced by the theorists who followed his lead.

Heider was born in Vienna, was raised in Graz (Austria), and after completing doctoral studies in 1920 went to Berlin where he came into direct contact with such Gestalt psychologists as Kurt Lewin (1890–1947). In 1931 Heider accepted an appointment to work with another German Gestaltist,* Kurt Koffka (1886–1941), at Smith College in the United States. After nearly two decades at Smith, Heider moved to the University of Kansas to continue his mission of discovering the underlying framework of the naive psychology that seems to guide the way most of us account for human behavior (Weiner, 1980, p. xv). The principles he derived are described in *The Psychology of Interpersonal Relations* (Heider, 1958). However, because his description focuses primarily on adults and not on children, it is necessary in this chapter to extend his treatment to show how commonsense psychology views a child's developmental changes from one age level to the next. In making this extension, I have depended not only on people's everyday language but also on civil and criminal laws commonly found in modern American communities.

It is important to realize that there is no single version of commonsense theory and that this chapter is designed only to suggest some of the main lines of naive theory and to illustrate the way Heider and his followers have identified such lines. The material included here falls far short of reflecting the complexities of various forms of such theory.

The present-day derivative of Heider's naive psychology is called *attribution theory,* meaning a scheme that attempts to explain how and why people attribute human behavior to particular causes. Using the term *attribution* to distinguish this model from others may seem a bit odd since essentially all theories of human development or personality attribute human thought and action to those factors the theorists regard as the most potent causes. For example, Freudians attribute much of development to the ways the child's inner drives interact with such agents of the environment as parents. Behaviorists attribute development to the way the consequences of a child's present actions will influence the way the child acts in the future. However, even though all theorists "attribute," it is the particular line of theorizing set off by Heider that is typically referred to as attribution theory, so I am using the term *commonsense attribution theory* to

---

*In the German language, the term *Gestalt* means *configuration.* The term is used in reference to any organized group of items whose patterning gives the group a significance or meaning that is more than simply the sum of the individual items. In the realm of child development, Gestalt theorists adopt a *holistic* or *field* view. They consider the child to be a unified, integrated organism. To the Gestalt theorist, a new stimulus or experience does not merely add a new element to the child's store of actions or knowledge, leaving the previous elements undisturbed; rather, each new experience alters the relationship of many or all the existing elements that have made up the personality to this point, so the patterning of the whole personality is influenced.

identify one model of development built on Heider's work. In preparing the version offered in the following pages, I have combined Heider's proposals with contributions from E. E. Jones and K. E. Davis (1965), H. H. Kelley (1967, 1971, 1972, 1973), and K. G. Shaver (1975). I have also included elements derived from my own observations of the way people talk about children and adolescents.

THE CAUSES OF HUMAN ACTION

The central question that commonsense psychology seeks to answer is: Why do people act as they do? When this question is translated into child development terms it becomes: How and why does the pattern of children's behavior change as they grow up?

Shaver (1975, p. 29) has suggested that the motive behind all human effort to estimate causes arises from the need to simplify the "perceptual world by *explaining* the present and past behavior of others and by *predicting* with some degree of accuracy what those people are likely to do in the future." As children grow up, the frequency with which they themselves make causal attributions increases as their attribution scheme (their commonsense theory) becomes more complex and increasingly similar to the basic principles embraced by most adults in their society.

According to Heider and his followers, the way people simplify the problem of explaining their perceptual world is by reducing to a small number the causal factors they believe are part of the individual person and the environment. The behavior of children and adults is then interpreted in terms of how these factors interact. In the version of attribution theory reviewed here, the significant properties of the person are: ability, intention, motivation, conscience, emotional dispositions, and an aptitude for empathy (the skill of experiencing life from the viewpoint of other people). The significant properties of the environment are: opportunity, task difficulty, environmental coercion, and situation and role prescription. The theory also makes room for the operation of such indeterminate influences as luck and supernatural intervention.

To suggest the flavor of the raw materials from which such a theory is constructed, I have prefaced the analysis of these factors with a fictitious conversation, a typical chat about children that might be overheard in many U.S. neighborhoods. Phrases from this conversation will be used later to illustrate, from the viewpoint of commonsense attribution theory, the convictions about child behavior that underlie people's daily interactions. Examples will also be drawn from phrases often heard in other everyday conversations.

TALK ABOUT CHILDREN—GRIST FOR COMMONSENSE PSYCHOLOGY'S MILL

Mrs. Campbell and Mr. Young meet in a supermarket.

Mr. Young: What do you think of the kids' third-grade teacher? I think she's expecting too much of them. My son Freddie says hardly anyone in the class can do the math. Have you seen the problems she gives?

Mrs. Campbell: Yes, Doris brings work home every day. But luckily she seems to get it done all right without my help.

Mr. Young: She must be pretty smart.

Mrs. Campbell: It's not just that. She works hard at it, too. I guess having to compete with her twelve-year-old brother has caused her to try hard. He's good at physical activities but kind of average in school work, so she seems to want to show that she's good with her brain. She tries to get attention that way.

Mr. Young: Oh, yes, your son. I saw in the paper that he's on the football team.

Mrs. Campbell: Well, he's crazy about sports. But getting on the team isn't much of a distinction. Nearly every boy who showed up was put in uniform.

Mr. Young: But isn't he some kind of a star?

Mrs. Campbell: Well, for the first couple of weeks he was the starting quarterback. He's growing up fast—tall and strong for his age, and he throws the ball well. But then he had a streak of bad luck. He sprained his ankle, and that put him out for over a week. Since then the coach hasn't given him a fair chance to show what he can do. The poor kid's spending every game on the bench.

Mr. Young: That's too bad. But I'm surprised he sticks with it when he isn't allowed to show his stuff.

Mrs. Campbell: Well, he did talk about quitting. He's really trained hard for this team, so sitting on the bench seems such a waste of energy and talent. But when he mentioned quitting to the other kids, they called him chicken, so he decided to stick it out. But he really hates it.

Mr. Young: What a shame. Isn't there something you could do?

Mrs. Campbell: Oh, I can't bring myself to say anything. It's the coach's job to decide who plays and who sits.

Mr. Young: By the way, I see you didn't bring your baby with you.

Mrs. Campbell: No, I left him at home with Doris.

Mr. Young: Really? Aren't you afraid to leave a nine-year-old in charge of such a small baby?

Mrs. Campbell: Oh, no. Doris is very good at it, and she likes it. And she likes the compliments she gets for doing a good job.

Mr. Young: Well, that's brave. I don't think I'd let our daughter Charlene try that, even at fourteen. It's not that Charlene can't do it. It's just that she's always thinking of something else—mostly boys and loud music. Well, I'd better get going. I left Charlene out in the car. She's fiddling with all the gadgets, pretending she's driving. She just can't wait till she's 16 to get a driver's license. God willing, she'll be less flighty by then so I won't have to be criticizing her all the time about the way she drives. But I guess that goes with being a parent of a teenager.

Mrs. Campbell: I'm through shopping. I'll walk out with you. (*They push their shopping carts out the door and into the parking lot.*)

Mr. Young: Is that your dog in the car?

Mrs. Campbell: Yes, that's Mollie. Watch. She'll sit up and wave her paw when she sees me. She'll want a treat. She knows I always get dog biscuits at the market. Say, isn't one of those paper sacks in your cart getting wet?

Mr. Young: Oh—oh, the milk carton must be leaking. And the sack's coming apart. I'll have to go back and get a plastic bag.

APPLYING AN ATTRIBUTION THEORY

The components of our version of causal-attribution theory are displayed in Figure 5.1. With the conversation between Mrs. Campbell and Mr. Young in mind, we'll inspect each of the components in turn.

The *self,* represented in Figure 5.1 by the box at the left, is the subconscious conception of personality held by a perceiver who seeks to explain the causes of events observed in the environment. In the present case, there are two perceivers, Mrs. Campbell and Mr. Young. We are assuming that they both believe that the listed *dispositional properties* are the personality traits that chiefly determine how children and adults act under various environmental conditions. In the box at the right, I have distinguished three types of environments: those composed of humans, of higher animal species (such as dolphins, cats, dogs), and of inanimate objects (such as houses, cars, shopping bags). I have identified four characteristics of such environments that people, in their commonsense psychology, often conceive to be causes of events. The box at the bottom is assigned two sorts of forces—luck and supernatural interventions—that people may include in their causal attributions. The elements comprising each of these three sources of cause are defined below.

The Self—The Perceiver's Dispositions

A central concept in Heider's system of analysis is the "can do" or personal power aspect of personality. In Heider's analysis of people's conversations,

The Self—The Perceiver's Dispositional Properties	The Environment

1. Mental ability, comprised of
  1.1 Intelligence
  1.2 Maturation rate
  1.3 Experience that produces knowledge of:
    1.3.1 the effects of various actions and
    1.3.2 the presumed desirability of such effects
2. Physical ability, comprised of
  2.1 Body build
  2.2 Maturation rate
  2.3 Exercise and nutrition
3. Intention
4. Motivation
5. Conscience—ought forces
6. Emotional dispositions
7. Empathic attitude
	A Types of Environments
	  A.1 Humans
	  Same dispositional properties as those of the perceiver
	  A.2 Higher animal species
	  Modifications of dispositional properties of humans
	  A.3 Inanimate objects
	  Devoid of human dispositional properties
	
	B Characteristics of Environments
	  B.1 Opportunities and restrictions
	  B.2 Task difficulty
	  B.3 Environmental coercion
	  B.4 Situation and role prescriptions

Indeterminate and Supernatural Influences

1. Luck, chance
2. Supernatural forces—God, Satan, astrological conditions, etc.

FIGURE 5.1   Framework of a Commonsense Attribution Theory

beliefs about personal power are reflected in the terms *can* and *cannot* ("Hardly anyone in the class can do the math." "It's not that Charlene can't do it.") Personal power has several components. The most important is *ability,* represented as items 1 and 2 in the self portion of Figure 5.1. Other components that exert a minor influence are *attitudes* (represented in Figure 5.1 as *emotional dispositions*), *social status,* and such *temporary personal conditions* as fatigue.

We begin our analysis with ability. During an average day, a typical teenager uses many specific skills or abilities in performing tasks. However, in commonsense psychology, these abilities are not all discrete and unconnected. Instead, they seem to fall into two categories, mental and physical. It is not uncommon for people to believe that a youth can have one level of ability in the mental realm and another in the physical. For example, it seems reasonable that a twelve-year-old boy might be a fine football player but not much of a scholar and that his nine-year-old sister might be the opposite. But it seems less common for people to see that within either category a youth's subabilities may vary. In short, people seem to think that mental ability is all-encompassing, a unitary skill or aptitude that covers all intellectual task performance. So Mr. Young, on hearing of Doris's skill in mathematics, concludes that Doris must be smart in general. Mrs. Campbell, too, reflects this idea of an all-encompassing mental ability by saying that Doris is "good with her brain." The belief that abilities are divided into physical and mental realms that are each unitary rather than composed of rather discrete subskills is widely accepted, even though the belief is somewhat at odds with present-day theory and empirical evidence (Gardner, 1983; Kail & Pellegrino, 1985; Pellegrino & Varnhagen, 1985).

Consider, next, people's ideas about three factors that contribute to mental ability—intelligence, maturation rate, and experience. The term *intelligence* is typically used to identify a child's inherited potential for being "smart" or "bright." This potential is recognized as maturing over time, with some children's maturation rates being faster than others'. As intellectual potential advances, experience with the world is necessary to equip the child with a storehouse of knowledge, particularly about the effects that different actions will produce and about the presumed desirability of those effects (Shaver, 1975, pp. 45–46).

The factors that make up physical ability parallel the components of mental ability—body build, maturation rate, and the experiential factors of exercise and nutrition. A person's basic body build, in the sense of neuromuscular potential, is usually assumed to be inherited. This potential evolves over time, with the maturation rate for some children differing from that of others ("He's growing up fast—tall and strong for his age.") Experience, in the form of exercise and nutrition, also contributes to physical ability ("He's really trained hard for this team.")

As people try to understand and predict their own and others' behavior, they are interested in knowing whether a person's ability is high, medium, or low. It is therefore useful for us to examine three kinds of information on which this judgment is based. This analysis involves presumed relationships between personal power and the environmental factor of *task difficulty*.

The first clue to ability level is the proportion of other people who can perform the task or tasks we have in mind. Specifically, if only a few people can perform the task, then any individual who does so is credited with having high ability. The main cause of success is thought to reside in the individual's personal power, and consequently that individual is accorded respect. But if nearly everyone can perform the task, then we conclude that it was easy, and those people who perform it successfully are not credited with much ability. In fact, the cause of success is not attributed to the person at all but to the environment. We believe the individual succeeded because environmental factors were in his or her favor.

A second important factor in judging ability is a knowledge of the people who have already performed the task. This matter is far more significant for assessing ability in childhood and adolescence than in the adult years because children's physical and mental skills increase noticeably with age, while adult skills are thought to be stable until the declining years. So in naive psychology we seek to learn the ages of the people with whom a given child is being compared. It is considered fairest to compare the child with age peers—often age-mates of the same sex. However, it is frequently useful to compare the child with older or younger children as well. A young child who performs as well as an average child several years older is credited with high ability and is labeled gifted, bright, or even genius. An older child who performs no better than an average child several years younger is said to be retarded, deficient, or handicapped.

A third sort of information that tells us about ability level is the amount of effort exerted to perform a task, in other words, a child's strength of motivation. The child who succeeds with ease is credited with greater ability than the one who has to struggle and strain to accomplish the same job.

Temporary conditions, such as fatigue and illness, influence how a person performs on a given occasion, but these conditions do not decrease the true ability attributed to that individual.

To close this brief look at commonsense notions of personal power, note three of the most significant assumptions underlying naive psychology's view of child development:

1. Abilities are considered rather permanent attributes of an individual. They do not change over the short term.

2. Abilities increase, sometimes regularly and sometimes in spurts, over the period of childhood and adolescence. To a great extent, the study of child development is the study of the manner in which abilities increase. A child described as a "problem learner" in school is usually one whose abilities are not increasing at the rate considered desirable.

3. Abilities are determined by both heredity (for example: "His good memory is from his mother's side of the family") and environment ("It was easy for her to learn to read with all those books in her

house"). However, the proportion that each of these two sources contributes to various abilities and the manner in which the two interact are not clear.

Consider, now, the next two dispositional properties of the self— *intention* and *motivation*. Not only must children have the personal power to perform, they must also *want* to do it. So "can" and "try" are both necessary for action.

Intention refers to whether or not a child has purposely chosen to act in a given way. Intention is a crucial factor in commonsense psychology since estimates of whether or not children "meant to do it" determine the esteem or blame they incur. Children whose behavior is interpreted as reflecting good intentions are credited with "good character," while those who seem directed by bad intentions get a reputation for "bad character." Although the notion of intention underlies a great quantity of people's judgments of children, usually the term *intention* is not used outright but, instead, is simply implied: "She seems to want to show that she's good with her brain." "He's crazy about sports." "He did talk about quitting." "It's not that Charlene can't do it. It's just that she's always thinking of something else." Children who do something wrong are less likely to be censured if it seems they "didn't mean it." Likewise, when something that children have done turns out well, they receive little or no credit if it appears that it was not on purpose but "just happened" or "he did it accidentally." Because the assignment of credit and blame depends so heavily on apparent intentions, the way people attribute intention to children has a critical influence on child rearing, schooling, law enforcement, counseling, peer relations, and the like. Shaver (1975, pp. 28–29) has observed that:

> from the psychologist's point of view, to be attributionally valuable, an action must be judged to have originated from an intention. . . . Ultimately, the careful perceiver will rely on his assessment of the circumstances surrounding the action, on his other knowledge of the actor, and on his own past experience as an actor in similar situations to arrive at a choice of an intention behind the action.

The fourth property of self, *motivation*, is used here to mean the amount of effort invested toward carrying out an act. This amount is typically considered to be under the child's intentional control, as reflected in such remarks as "He just doesn't try hard enough" or "When she puts her mind to it, she plugs right along till it's done." Sometimes, however, the fact that children do not accomplish some act is attributed not to their lack of trying, but rather to their limited reservoir of energy: "She was too worn out to finish." Children are credited with having "good character" if they have impressed others with the amount of effort they seem to apply to tasks they face. For instance, the pupil who is thought to have limited ability will often be awarded higher marks in school tasks if he appears to have tried hard. And parents who wish to impress others with their children's good character often insert motivation ascriptions into conversations: "She works hard at it, too" and "He's really trained hard for this team."

The next two properties of self, *conscience* and *emotional dispositions,* influence the intent and motivation that comprise the "try-to" aspect of personality.

Conscience is an internalized set of social rules or standards, of do's and don'ts that Heider has called *ought forces* (1958, pp. 218–243). When children violate the rules, they "feel bad." When they abide by the rules, they "feel good" or "feel proud" or "have a clear conscience." Most people believe the contents of conscience are not innate but, instead, are gradually acquired from the environment—from adults, from peers, and from mass communication media over the period of childhood and adolescence ("At his age, he still doesn't know any better" or "She's just now learning to be responsible"). Conscience functions as both a stimulator of action ("If she hadn't helped her injured friend, she would have felt terrible") and an inhibitor ("Oh, I can't bring myself to say anything—it's the coach's job to decide who plays and who sits").

The sixth postulated property, *emotional dispositions,* is a catch-all collection of feelings that influence both the direction of people's intentions and the effort they put into the tasks they attempt. Such dispositions include desires and fears, interests and prejudices, likes and dislikes: "He's crazy about sports." "Doris is very good at it, and she likes it." Shaver (1975, p. 29) has contended that, for purposes of explaining and predicting someone's behavior, identifying a *dispositional attribution* is superior to identifying an intention because "it provides an answer to the question 'Why?' that is a more fully satisfactory explanation, and at the same time is a better estimate of future action."

Finally, the term *empathic attitude* refers to people's ability to see and feel things from the perspective of someone else—what George Mead (1934) referred to as "taking the role of the other." Shaver (1975, p. 23) suggests that "Individual differences in perceivers' ability to make interpersonal judgments accurately are probably related to differences in experience, intelligence, and empathic ability."

With the components of the self now described, we next consider the roles of environments in attribution theory.

Environments—Types and Characteristics

The three types of environments listed in Figure 5.1 are identified by the kinds of elements that comprise them: humans, higher animal species, and inanimate objects. My reason for distinguishing between the first and third of these should be obvious. The humans who inhabit the social world all possess the traits that comprise the self, whereas the objects that make up the physical world have none of those traits. This difference is clearly of great import when people attribute cause. For example, when Mr. Young's grocery sack began to split, he accounted for the cause by speculating that a carton of milk was leaking, but he did not attribute ability, intention, motivation, or emotional dispositions to either the carton or the sack. If we pressed him to explain the cause, he probably would have cited factors in the inanimate world—the effect of moisture on paper as compared to plastic, the damage incurred in the manufacture or transport of milk cartons, and the like. On the other hand, he attributed self properties to his daughter Charlene when he explained why she fiddled with the gadgets in the car.

The second type of environment proposed in Figure 5.1, *higher animal species,* has been included to illustrate the fact that people often ascribe many, if not all, human dispositional properties to higher animal species whose characteristics appear to approximate properties of the human self. Mrs. Campbell was indulging in such anthropomorphic reasoning when she implied that her dog Mollie exhibited intelligence, intention, and emotional dispositions: "She'll want a treat. She knows I always get dog biscuits at the market." We might then propose the following commonsense attribution principle: The farther down that a species is located in the phyla of the animal kingdom, (1) the less likely people will attribute human properties to a member of that species and (2) the more likely characteristics of inanimate objects will be ascribed to that creature. Hence, it is improbable that Mrs. Campbell would speak of garden slugs or paramecia with the same empathic spirit she displayed when talking about Mollie.

Next, let's consider the four environmental characteristics or functions included in Figure 5.1. First, social and physical environments can either open opportunities (at age sixteen Charlene can get a driver's license) or restrict opportunities ("Since then the coach hasn't given him a fair chance to show what he can do").

Some tasks are more difficult to accomplish than others. Hence, if a child cannot perform a task, or can do so only with great effort, the task can be blamed for being too difficult and the child will be held faultless. As already noted, people's judgments of the "objective" difficulty level of tasks are typically based on what proportion of children of the same age, size, and sex can succeed with the task. If many can accomplish it, and particularly if they do so with little effort, then the task is considered to be easy; a child succeeding with that task will receive little or no credit for intelligence, physical ability, or for trying hard ("Getting on the team isn't much of a distinction. Nearly every boy who showed up was put in uniform"). On the other hand, a child who fails at tasks that most age-mates accomplish is blamed for low ability, for lack of intent, or for insufficient effort.

The third hypothesized function is *environmental coercion,* meaning pressures (ought forces) exerted by children's social and physical surroundings that impel them to act in approved ways or else prevent them from acting in unacceptable ways ("When he mentioned quitting to the other kids, they called him chicken, so he decided to stick it out"). Environmental coercion has an intimate link to conscience since most people believe that children gradually learn the rules of their society and incorporate these rules into their own personalities as habits and as the contents of conscience. This is the *socialization* process. Parents, teachers, pastors, the police, and others seek to effect such socialization (1) by offering direct instruction and models of behavior and (2) by imposing consequences (rewards and punishments) that will motivate children to acquire values deemed desirable and to eschew those deemed improper. As examples of consequences, Mrs. Campbell observed that Doris "likes the compliments she gets for doing a good job" and Mr. Young hoped "I won't have to be criticizing Charlene all the time about the way she drives." Ultimately, a youth is considered to be appropriately socialized—socially mature—when society's do's and don'ts have assumed the form of an internalized moral gyroscope in that individual's personality.

The final pair of environmental characteristics are *situation* and *role prescriptions.* The theory proposes that people often base their estimates of cause on their notion of how situations and social roles affect children's behavior. Situational attributions are reflected in such remarks as "He was very subdued because he was in church" or "She was able to muster unusual strength to carry her friend to safety." People's regard for role prescriptions are reflected in such comments as "It's the coach's job to decide who plays and who sits" and "I guess that goes with being a parent of a teenager" or "Don't expect too much of him since he's still a small child."

Indeterminate and Supernatural Influences

In addition to seeing causes in the self and in the social and physical environment, many people include two further sets of factors in their causal ascriptions. The first is an amorphous category that represents the attributer's puzzlement about what factors are actually responsible for an event. The words *luck, chance,* and *fate* signify a speaker's admission that the cause of an event is inexplicable. Mrs. Campbell was avoiding any self or environmental reasons for her son's injury when she proposed that "a streak of bad luck" had produced his sprained ankle and his subsequent confinement to the bench. As for Doris's math assignments, "luckily she seems to get it done all right without my help."

Sometimes an apparent lack of convincing causes in self-properties or in the environment prompts people to locate causes in supernatural forces—God, the devil, evil spirits, astrological configurations, and the like ("God willing, she'll be less flighty by then"). Ascribing cause to such influences has important implications for the ways people will attempt to influence children's development. If they believe a self-characteristic (lack of intention, insufficient motivation) caused a child to fail at a task, they will often directly enjoin the child to pay attention and exert more effort. Or if they believe the environment has failed to furnish suitable opportunities, they may seek to rearrange the environment so opportunities become available. But if they think God is in control of the child's performance, they probably will pray for help rather than work directly with the child or the environment.

Summary

Thus a *commonsense attribution theory* is a proposal about the likely structure of reasoning that, at a subconscious level, determines how most people in a society account for why things happen as they do. Key components of this postulated structure, as inferred from the way people talk about affairs of the day, are displayed in Figure 5.1 and defined briefly above. However, an essential element of the theory is missing—a description of the actual way people assign causes on a particular occasion. That is, what is needed is an explanation of which components are involved in a given decision about cause, including an interpretation of the weightings or degree of force that various components in the interaction contribute to the decision. (The only segment above that directed any attention to interactions was the description of how people judge ability as it relates to task difficulty.) However, engaging in a detailed analysis of such interactions requires far more space than this chapter allows. Hence this issue of interactions is noted but not pursued. (You may wish to try your hand at performing such analysis by listening to a conversation in which the participants offer estimates of the cause of some child or adolescent behavior and then speculating about which components of Figure 5.1 are likely involved in the causal attributions the participants offer and which components likely exerted the greatest influence on their decisions.)

THE DEVELOPMENT OF PEOPLE'S COMMONSENSE THEORY

We may well ask how the members of a society adopt such a mode of ascribing cause. In response, I would suggest that the contents of commonsense theory are not innate but, instead, are acquired gradually as the infant progresses through childhood and adolescence. The lessons children learn over the years result from their being directly instructed by adults and peers, from their overhearing adults and peers talk about other people's behavior, and from their reading books and watching television. The content of such lessons is then corroborated, and perhaps revised, by the child's direct observations of people in action. In short, an individual's subconscious theory evolves in keeping with the rate of the child's neural maturation and the range of the child's experiences with the social and physical world.

Commonsense attributions can vary from one society to another, according to prevailing notions of cause embedded in the society's philosophical foundations. For instance, the naive theory acquired by a typical child in a society with a strong Confucian (China, Korea) or Shinto (Japan) foundation will more often credit a person's motivation as the cause for success or failure than would be the case in North America and Western Europe, where environmental factors are frequently considered more significant (Munro, 1977; Stevenson, Azuma, & Hakuta, 1986; Thomas, 1988).

IMPLICATIONS OF THE THEORY FOR THE TREATMENT OF CHILDREN

From naive psychology's factors that account for action, we can draw several implications about child rearing to guide adults' treatment of children. For instance, if we want to help a child complete a task at which she is currently failing, we first need to estimate which of three factors—ability, task difficulty, or effort—is causing the failure. Then we can try to remedy the faulty condition of the identified factor.

If we think the child is striving as well as she is able and that her ability cannot be improved very readily, then we logically should attempt to reduce the difficulty of the task so she can succeed. To reduce the task's difficulty level, we can either do part of the task ourselves or break it down into smaller steps she can manage. However, in many cases we either cannot or do not wish to simplify the task. Then we may concentrate on improving the child's ability through training. In other cases we may conclude that the child's abilities are sufficient, that she either has not focused on the task (direction of motivation) or has not tried hard enough.

So we try to convince the child that the task is something she really wants to do. We might try logic, cajoling, promises of rewards, or threats of punishment to motivate her to action (Heider, 1958, p. 123).

If this line of reasoning appears too obvious to be worth analyzing, it is not surprising. It's all common sense.

CHILDREN'S INTERPRETATIONS OF THEIR OWN BEHAVIOR

So far we have looked only at ways adults use commonsense psychology in explaining children's behavior. But equally important, or perhaps even more important, is children's use of commonsense psychology as a foundation for their own attitudes and behavior. One child may consistently avoid engaging in new experiences because he has a very low regard for his ability or personal power in relation to virtually all unfamiliar tasks. People perceive him as being "painfully shy" because of his "negative self-concept," his "low level of self-esteem and self-efficacy," or his "general feelings of inferiority." Another child may be willing to try some tasks but unwilling to try others. She may account for this difference by contending that some of the tasks are easy but others are too hard, or else she may attribute the difference to the factor of motivation: "I like to do these things, but those others don't interest me." Still a third child appears to have unflagging confidence in his personal power so that he eagerly takes on any new task and then attributes any failures to not having tried hard enough the first time (Weiner, 1974).

The importance of understanding a child's system of attributions lies in the observation that people do not behave on the basis of reality but rather act on the basis of their perceptions of reality. That is, they act on their attributions. Thus what stimulates a child to try a task is not the *objective fact* that she can succeed; instead it is her *belief* that she can do it. Hence, from this view of human development, an important measure of a child's or youth's personal maturity is how closely his or her pattern of attributions fits conditions of the real world. This measure is reflected in the question, How accurately can an individual predict the outcome of a task performance when he or she really tries (exerts strong effort) to accomplish the task? The child who predicts more accurately—that is, who correctly estimates the relation of personal power to the difficulty level of tasks—is regarded as the more mature.

PRIVILEGE AND RESPONSIBILITY

Like other theories of development, commonsense theory depicts child growth in terms of stages. The three most general stages are *infancy, childhood,* and *adolescence.* The borders between them are distinguished by relatively sudden physiological and psychological changes. An infant or baby crosses the border into childhood when he becomes "more of a real person" through learning to walk and talk around age 1½ or 2. The child crosses the border into adolescence or teenage status when sexual functions mature and such secondary sex characteristics as voice change, a spurt in height, body hair, and changes in skin texture show up around the ages of 12 to 15.

Paralleling these marks of physical maturation are a series of changes in privilege and responsibility that society regards as suitable for the growing child. Consequently one way to analyze directions or stages of development from a commonsense perspective is to do so in terms of the sorts of privileges and responsibilities that are added at different age levels.

The phrase *growth in privileges* here means increased opportunities to engage in a wider variety of activities, particularly activities the child considers desirable. In other words, she can do more things that she would like to do. *Growth in responsibility* means that the child incurs the obligation to carry out, under her own initiative or supervision, additional tasks that society considers proper, constructive, and desirable. In naive psychology, responsibility is composed of what Heider has called *ought forces* (1958, pp. 218–243). These are attitudes regarding the duties people fulfill that are shared widely by a community. Such duties are necessary for providing individuals with a stable, predictable social environment in which to live, in the same way that "man can operate in the physical environment only when physical laws hold" (Heider, 1958, p. 229).

As suggested by the folk saying, "With each privilege you incur a responsibility," common sense conceives privilege and responsibility to be the opposite ends of a balance scale. Throughout children's development, their increasing abilities enable them to do more things for themselves, so they gradually are permitted by their society to carry out a greater variety of actions and make more decisions on their own. But as children gain privileges, society—primarily in the form of parents and teachers—adds oughts or duties. Much of the conflict between children and adults during the first two decades of life comes from (1) children wanting more privileges at an early age and (2) adults seeking to postpone the privileges or to impose responsibilities before children want them.

Since the most commonly agreed upon gauge of developmental level is chronological age, society uses age for defining when children's abilities (and sense of responsibility) are sufficient to permit them to try certain tasks or make certain decisions. Some of these age expectations are in the form of custom, such as the custom in certain Christian churches of having children gain church membership at around age 12. Other expectations are formalized as laws and regulations. By inspecting these laws, we can see what the common sense of the day considers to be proper steps or stages of development. For example, the stage of early childhood is typically distinguished from later childhood by school entrance laws. In the United States children are both permitted and obligated to attend school around age 5 or 6. Such formal laws reflect commonsense perceptions of steps in development. Less formal regulations, such as the school's curriculum guidelines, delineate substages within the major steps. For instance, it is common in American schools to focus kindergarten activities on broadening the children's experience with their physical and social world and less on formally teaching them reading, writing, or arithmetic. But when children enter first grade at age 6 or so, they are expected to begin reading, writing, and formally analyzing quantitative concepts.

Criminal law reflects the commonsense belief that children before puberty are not yet reasonable or responsible beings, and even after puberty they are not considered to be entirely reasonable. The California penal code states that children under age 14 are not capable of committing actual crimes unless there is "clear proof that at the time of committing the act charged against them, they knew its wrongfulness." So the excuse that "she didn't know what she was doing" is sufficient for not prosecuting a child as a "reasonable" adult would be prosecuted. Between ages 14 and 17, youths are still considered only partially responsible beings, so that when they commit unlawful acts they are labeled delinquents rather than criminals and are processed through special juvenile courts. Furthermore, many states prohibit the public press from publishing the names of youths under age 18 who are involved in crimes, in the belief that prior to 18 an adolescent is still not fully responsible and does not deserve public blame and shame.

The number of laws, both civil and criminal, that use age 18 as the cutting point for various privileges and responsibilities suggests that common sense today defines the period of childhood and adolescence as extending from birth through age 17, even though in American society many youths are still not economically independent of their parents by age 18. There is a general expectation, or hope, that all youths will graduate from high school, and this usually occurs around age 18. In recent years the legal voting age was lowered from 21 to 18. One result of this was to make the voting age more closely coincide with the age at which boys acquire the privilege or obligation to fight and die for their country (age 17—voluntary enlistment; age 18—registering for conscription).

In effect, laws and customs reflect common notions of steps in development, with each step representing a point at which abilities and children's acceptance of ought forces are sufficient for them to be accorded new privileges and responsibilities. However, reaching the designated age for taking a step is not a guarantee that a privilege or responsibility will actually be provided. Other measures of development are also used. Before a child is considered ready for first grade, for example, he is tested or observed to determine whether he has the abilities needed to succeed at typical first-grade tasks. And Mr. Young's daughter, Charlene, is not guaranteed a driver's license at age 16. The girl's driving skill and knowledge of traffic laws will also be tested, and she will be denied a license until she has proven her skill. On the other hand, privileges are sometimes given before the minimum age level is reached. An adolescent who is slightly underage but who can prove her driving skill and a compelling need to drive (such as to provide the family income) may be given a driver's license before age 16. In sum, age is the main criterion of developmental sufficiency in commonsense psychology, but other criteria are also used to accommodate individual differences in children's ability.

Thus commonsense psychology proposes (1) generalizations that describe the average child and (2) minor amendments that describe children who deviate from the average. These conclusions that form a society's naive view of development are found in the customs, regulations, and laws that apply to life in the home, in the school, and in the wider community.

PRACTICAL APPLICATIONS

When the word *practical* is defined as "something firmly tied to the realities of daily living," then commonsense attribution theory by its very nature is indeed practical since it represents the framework of assumptions that underlie the way people in everyday life account for how and why children develop as they do. Furthermore, when *practical* is defined as "something useful in the solution of daily problems," commonsense theory again qualifies as practical for it explains the system of reasoning people employ as they interpret children's behavior. For example, if we know from commonsense theory about the interaction that most people assume exists among ability, task difficulty, and trying hard, we are better prepared to understand the structure of parents' reasoning as we hear them explain why their child is or is not developing satisfactorily.

Another practical function of commonsense theory is its potential usefulness in revealing to us the structure of our own unstated assumptions about children's growth. As a consequence of such self-revelation, we may newly recognize that certain of our underlying beliefs, when carefully analyzed, prove to be contradictory or perhaps inconsistent with research evidence. Armed with this increased awareness, we may be able to devise a more logical version of attribution theory, a version that properly fits with our personal system of values and the available facts about children's growth.

NAIVE PSYCHOLOGY: AN ASSESSMENT

This appraisal of commonsense theory is based on the nine evaluation standards used previously. My estimates of how well naive theory meets the standards are given as marks on the nine scales; then my explanations for the ratings are given. Again, because your value system or your weighing of the evidence may differ from mine, you may well arrive at a different pattern of ratings and may wish to prepare your own rating sheet.

The logic behind my ratings may be easier to follow if we begin with item 5, the degree of internal consistency in the theory. There is necessarily

Naive Theory

How well do I think the theory meets the standards?

The Standards	Very Well	Moderately Well	Very Poorly
1. Reflects the real world of children	X		
2. Is clearly understandable		X	
3. Explains the past and predicts the future		X	
4. Guides child rearing	X		
5. Is internally consistent	X		
6. Is economical		X	
7. Is falsifiable		X	
8. Stimulates new discoveries	X		
9. Is self-satisfying		X	

considerable consistency among the assumptions on which people conduct their everyday treatment of children. Otherwise child rearing would be far more chaotic than it is. However, as Heider has pointed out, one can also criticize naive theory and its sources of data for "the many contradictions that are to be found in this body of material, such as antithetical proverbs or contradictions in a person's interpretation of even simple events" (1958, p. 5). Which is the proper guide to child raising: "A little love and kindness goes a long way" or "Spare the rod and spoil the child"? How does a teacher reconcile the contradictions in his observation that "she really doesn't have the ability to do it, but she tries so hard that she is able to overachieve"? In judging item 5, then, the substantial consistencies in naive theory are balanced against what seem to be a substantial number of contradictions, and the theory is rated in the upper portion of the moderately well segment.

There are at least two ways of looking at item 2, regarding the clarity of naive theory. First, naive psychology is not some scientist's creation. It is the set of assumptions upon which people base their treatment of children. So a first way of viewing the issue of clarity in item 2 is reflected in the question, Are the assumptions about children that comprise common sense clearly understood and agreed upon within a given society? I believe the answer to this is that the contents of commonsense psychology are only moderately clear. People in a society have different assumptions about what makes sense in terms of child development. Even within a given person's set of assumptions there are contradictions, as illustrated above. However, there is considerable clarity about many aspects of naive psychology. If there were not, we would have far more conflict in our society than we do.

A second way to look at the clarity issue is illustrated by the question, Have psychologists who analyze naive theory clearly described all of its characteristics? Heider made a good start toward clarifying the structure of commonsense views, writers such as A. L. Baldwin (1967) extended Heider's general system to focus it more distinctly on childhood, and a large body of literature has grown up over the past few decades to expand attribution theory still further (Worchel & Cooper, 1979). However, much of the contemporary literature focuses on adults rather than on children so that many aspects of children's use of naive psychology remain to be investigated.

Therefore from both points of view—from people's understanding and agreeing upon the nature of commonsense beliefs and from psychologists' descriptions of the underlying structure—I have estimated that naive theory is only moderately clear.

Now to item 1: Does naive theory accurately describe the real world of childhood and adolescence? I believe that to a great extent it does. As Heider has observed, "The ordinary person has a great and profound understanding of himself and of other people which, though unformulated or only vaguely conceived, enables him to interact with others in more or less adaptive ways. . . . Intuitive knowledge may be remarkably penetrating and can go a long way toward the understanding of human behavior" (1958, p. 2). However, there are, at the same time, some notably unrealistic aspects to commonsense views. One of the most obvious is the tendency for people to attribute happenings in a child's development or behavior to a single cause. A careful analysis of events illustrates that any event results from multiple causes, with some causes exerting more influence than others. Past arguments about whether nature or nurture caused a particular development exemplify this commonsense tendency to attribute a happening to a single cause. Baldwin has written that "in many ways this feature of naive theory is its most insidious error and creeps most easily into attempts to develop a better, more scientific theory of human behavior" (1967, p. 75).

There are numerous other aspects of naive theory that bring into question its accuracy in describing children. For example, studies in recent decades of intellectual abilities have furnished a mass of evidence that contradicts the commonsense notion that the level of ability in one subarea of mental life will be the same in all other subareas. As a consequence, psychologists have moved increasingly away from a single general intelligence test that yields one overall intelligence quotient and have moved instead toward the use of multiple-factor tests that yield separate scores for each of several types of mental skills (Gardner, 1983; Harris & Harris, 1971). Likewise, studies of children's reading readiness contradict the belief that the time when all children are ready to begin reading is when they enter first grade (Durkin, 1976).

Thus, balancing the strengths of naive theory against its weaknesses in terms of describing children realistically, I rated the theory in the upper portion of the moderately well segment.

Related to a realistic view of children are item 3 (explaining the past, predicting the future) and item 4 (guides child-rearing practices). Since naive theory is better prepared to explain past events than to predict future ones, it cannot achieve a top rating for its ability to guide child rearing. As Baldwin has pointed out, the theory's weakness in predicting the future behavior of children rests to a great extent on two of its prominent characteristics. First, it does not specify all of the conditions or causes that interact to bring about an event or an aspect of development. For this reason, if the cause it does identify is not the most powerful of those actually operating, then the prediction will be in error.

Second, naive theory assumes that the child has a *free will*. The issue of free will is an old one in philosophy, one that has never been resolved satisfactorily. The concept of free will is usually discussed in connection with the contrasting or contrary concept of *determinism,* which has long been a basic tenet of the physical sciences or what is known as the *scientific method.* Determinism is a belief that everything that happens has been absolutely set or established by preceding conditions and could not have turned out any other way. In effect, if you know all the causal factors, you can make an exact, error-free prediction of what will happen. In contrast, the concept of free will holds that determinism may be true for strictly physical phenomena, such as thunderstorms and the growth of violets, but events that involve human decisions are influenced as well by the individual's freedom to make a choice. In effect, in human events a knowledge of preceding conditions or causal factors enables us to estimate likely outcomes, but we still must consider the individual's free will. The issue of determinism versus free will is a complex one. Here I simply point out that the idea of free will poses problems for naive theory when the theory is used as the basis for predicting future child behavior. No matter how much is known about causal conditions in a child's life, if the child has freedom of choice, errorless predictions of future development or behavior are not possible. This fact limits the value of naive theory for child-rearing purposes. When we treat a child a given way, we never know for sure how the child will interpret our actions and choose to respond.

Therefore, even though naive theory contains a lot of folk truths that, over the generations, have enabled people to guide children's development with some measure of success, it also has shortcomings that limit the accuracy of its predictions and child-guidance suggestions. Hence I rate naive theory in the moderate range for items 3 and 4.

Item 6 was difficult to mark because in some ways naive theory is too economical. That is, it makes what appear to be simplistic assumptions about aspects of development that seem to require more complex explanations. You may recall from Chapter One that Morgan's canon states: A theory is better if it is economical in the sense that it is founded on as few unproven assumptions as possible and requires rather simple mechanisms to explain all the phenomena encompassed by the theory. Naive theory violates this standard by failing in some ways to provide the simple mechanisms and in other ways to explain all the phenomena. In failing to fulfill the attribute of simplicity, naive theory may be too complex—for example, it still accepts certain assumptions about the divisions of the mind held over from faculty psychology. In failing to fulfill the attribute of explaining all the phenomena, naive theory may be too simple or simplistic.

Let us consider this charge of oversimplification in more detail. Baldwin (1967, pp. 64–70) has illustrated this problem with examples focusing on matters of perception and intentional action. He points out that the assumption is made in naive psychology that everyone perceives things in the same way. In other words, the child's perceptual equipment is like a television camera, recording sight and sound the way "they really are." And everyone's camera records events in the same way. (This assumption underlies the practice in courts of having witnesses describe what they perceived so the judge and jury can determine what "really" happened.) But today a growing body of research suggests that perception is far more complex than naive theory would suppose. In effect, naive theory neglects the complexities of the phenomenon and proposes an overly simple picture of what apparently occurs.

Baldwin charges that, in like manner, common sense fails to explain adequately the relationship between a person's intention and his actions. This objection leads us to the traditional philosophical issue of *teleology*. In a teleological explanation, the main cause of an event is found in the future rather than in the past or present. Instead of specifying the past and present conditions that have caused a young child to speak a few words, the teleological approach identifies some future purpose or outcome that has "caused" the speech behavior. For example, a child learns to speak because she now will be able to communicate her wants more adequately. Or, adolescents seek sexual mates out of a need to reproduce and thus preserve the human species for the future. Although this line of logic may at first appear reasonable, it is not in keeping with basic rules traditionally followed in the natural sciences. In the natural sciences, a cause does not appear in the future, that is, a cause does not appear before its effect. Thus, for people who want child development theory to adhere to the tenets of biological and physical sciences, the teleological aspects of naive theory are an embarrassment, just as are the beliefs in free will and single causal factors.

There are, of course, theorists who say that human behavior follows different laws (at least to some degree) from those governing nonhuman events. For these theorists, including the humanistic psychologists (Chapter Thirteen), teleological causation and free will are not objectionable features of commonsense psychology.

In terms of its economy of explanation, then, naive theory oversimplifies certain aspects of development, thus violating part of item 6, and I have rated it only moderately well.

As for item 7, falsifiability, parts of the theory are testable or disconfirmable, and other parts are not. Although many research studies conducted over the past century on child development represent successful efforts to test the validity of commonsense views, some important aspects of the theory have not as yet appeared testable or falsifiable. These aspects have depended for their confirmation on personal opinion or faith. Two examples of such aspects are the concepts of free will and teleological causation. Balancing these positive and negative factors against each other, I rated item 7 in the moderately well range of the scale.

The highest rating has been given to item 8 in recognition of the great fertility of commonsense beliefs for stimulating new discoveries. As mentioned earlier, in the last analysis, all new theories and new research have resulted from people's dissatisfaction with commonsense answers or from people's attempts to defend naive theory in the face of attacks on it. Furthermore, the sort of analysis of commonsense theory carried out by Heider and his disciples has itself led to the growing body of research called *attribution theory*.

Finally, naive theory is, overall, moderately self-satisfying (item 9). Although much of my own treatment of children is based on commonsense notions, in many ways this common sense fails to answer my child development questions adequately and I am left discontented with naive theory. This discontent serves as a sufficient stimulus for learning what more formal theories, such as the ones in the following chapters, offer.

FOR FURTHER READING

Heider, F. (1958) *The Psychology of Interpersonal Relations.* New York: Wiley. Heider describes what he conceives to be the theoretical framework on which people's commonsense psychology is founded.

Heider, F. (1983) *The Life of a Psychologist: An Autobiography.* Lawrence, Kans.: University of Kansas Press. The author describes the geographical and intellectual routes he traveled to arrive at attribution theory.

Shaver, K. G. (1975) *An Introduction to Attribution Processes.* Cambridge, Mass.: Winthrop.

DISTINGUISHING NORMAL FROM ABNORMAL DEVELOPMENT

How can decisions be made about whether development is normal, natural, proper, or desirable?

The question of what kinds of growth and behavior are normal at each stage of childhood and adolescence is obviously of great concern to people who daily engage in the care and guidance of the young. Not only is the question of great interest, but it is also one of considerable confusion, partly because such words as *normal* and *natural*—and their opposites, *abnormal* and *unnatural*—are not assigned the same meanings by everyone. Even greater confusion results when people who use the terms have not decided for themselves precisely what they intend. Consequently, students of child development can profit from both (1) recognizing the varied meanings that such words can carry and (2) deciding precisely what criteria they themselves wish to apply in clarifying their use of the terms. These two matters are the focus of this perspective.

DIVERSE MEANINGS OF *NORMAL, NATURAL,* AND *DESIRABLE*

In the realm of child development, there are two common uses of *normal:* (1) statistical similarity or frequency and (2) desirability or acceptability. The first refers to how much a child's condition is like the condition of others of the same category. Typical categories are ones defined by such characteristics as age, sex, grade in school, ethnic background, birth order, socioeconomic status, and the like. The second use of *normal*—that of desirability or acceptability—refers to how closely a child's condition matches the value system of the person making the judgment about normality. In this second sense, *normal* means *approved, admirable, satis-*

117

factory, proper, acceptable, and the like. It is possible for a child to be normal in the first sense and abnormal in the second, or vice versa. An eight-year-old with an intelligence quotient of 150 could be judged statistically abnormal but normal (or supranormal) in terms of desirability. A sixteen-year-old could be judged statistically normal in the use of marijuana (in a community in which 70 percent of the age group has used the drug) but abnormal in the sense of desirable behavior.

There are also alternative uses of *natural.* One is the degree of statistical similarity to others of the same category. The other is the likelihood that development will progress satisfactorily without special intervention. Consider, first, the statistical usage. If some characteristic of a child is found very frequently in the group of which the child is a member (age group, ethnic group, intelligence-level category, or some other), then the child's development is judged to be statistically natural, meaning "what is most likely to be expected." This meaning is implied in such remarks as: "She's growing up quite naturally" or "It's just natural to pass through a phase like that." Gesell's growth gradients and Havighurst's developmental tasks would qualify as indicators of such natural development. Whatever is common at an age level is *natural.*

Consider, now, the second use of natural, which is the course of development that can be expected if the influences on the child's life continue in the usual pattern. In other words, if no special intervention or treatment is instituted to alter the child's life, such-and-such outcomes will probably result. For example, if the teenager's wisdom teeth are not extracted now, the other teeth will naturally become jammed together, causing both an improper bite and an unpleasant appearance. If the seven-year-old's parents continue to praise her for the friendly way she greets visitors, she will naturally develop a pleasing social manner.

However, child-rearing difficulties can occur if people fail to distinguish between the foregoing two meanings of *natural.* Problems arise whenever people interpret "statistically natural" as always implying "the way things *should* be." This is the error of confusing "is" with "ought," an error illustrated in the tendency of Gesell and his colleagues to interpret normative descriptions at different age levels as *natural,* thus requiring no special intervention to alter the course of development. The remedy for such an error lies in recognizing that statistically common or natural events need to be inspected carefully in order to determine how desirable they are in relation to the values held by the person making the judgment. In some instances, development should not be allowed to continue in its present or *natural* course. Instead, steps should be taken to intervene. However, in other instances, even though the present growth characteristic is not the most desirable, experience demonstrates that no special intervention at this time would likely correct the condition, so it is best to "let nature take its course."

The two most common situations in which nonintervention with unsatisfactory development is warranted are those in which (1) particular internal maturation changes are necessary before the desired development can occur and (2) changes in the environment that will remedy the present unsatisfactory condition are bound to appear without special intervention. Consider, for example, the vestiges of "baby talk" or indistinct enunciation that often remain in the speech of four- or five-year-olds. Studies of children's speech patterns at successive age levels have shown that articulation deviations from "standard" speech usually disappear during the early years of elementary school without specific remedial measures. As H. Winitz (1969, p. 60) has noted, the great majority of children naturally arrive at producing nearly all sounds correctly by 8 years of age. This *natural correction* apparently results from a combination of factors, including: the advancing internal maturation of the child's auditory-perception mechanism, which equips the child to detect differences between his or her enunciation and that of other people, and the increasingly mature speech of the child's age-mates, which serves as a model the child chooses to emulate, particularly if age-mates and school personnel voice their disapproval of "baby talk." From such observations as this, we can derive a rule of thumb for deciding when to let nature take its course:

> (1) If the genetically timed internal maturation of the child's nervous system and musculature (necessary for a desired type of behavior) has not yet occurred, then it is appropriate to await such maturation rather than to adopt special efforts to produce the behavior ahead of its maturational schedule. Pressuring children to perform at levels beyond their present maturational capacity may not only be futile, but it may damage children's sense of worth and self-confidence. (2) If changes that typically can be expected to occur in a child's environment are ones that will probably correct an existing undesired characteristic, then it is unnecessary at the present time to adopt remedial measures to alter that characteristic.

The reciprocal of this prescript can then serve as a guide to when intervention is advisable for changing the "natural" course of events:

> Even though a particular characteristic of a child's present development is *natural* (in the sense of frequent or common among other children at this stage of life), special efforts to alter that characteristic are warranted if (1) the characteristic is judged to be unsatisfactory, (2) the child's

maturational capacity is sufficient to achieve the desired improvement, and (3) it is unlikely that factors in the child's environment will "naturally" change in ways that will remedy the objectionable characteristic.

DECISIONS ABOUT *NORMAL* OR *NATURAL* AS *SIMILAR* OR *FREQUENT*

A question that now can now be asked is what kinds of evidence a person needs for deciding if a child's development is *normal* or *natural* in the statistical sense of *similar* or *frequent*. I would propose three kinds.

The first is a description of where children are spread along a particular dimension (such as weight by age, smoking habits by gender and age, child abuse by gender, or English-language fluency by ethnic designation). The description is most helpful when it is in the form of a distribution showing the percentage of children at different points along the dimension. The distribution can be equally helpful if it is summarized in the form of the group's average (mean or median) and extent of variability (standard deviation or distance between percentiles 20 and 80). Or, when information is offered in dichotomous or trichotomous form (yes–no or often–sometimes–never), the results are typically in the form of percentages of people in each subcategory.

The second kind of evidence needed is a description of where our particular child or adolescent stands in relation to the group, such as how the child's height, weight, or score on an oral English-language test compares to the group's status or *norms*. These first two types of evidence are objective, in the sense that anybody making the decision would arrive at the same conclusion.

The third type consists of the line of reasoning that establishes the cutting point on the distribution that distinguishes normal from abnormal (or natural from unnatural) or that stipulates degrees of normality (*very normal, somewhat normal, slightly abnormal, very abnormal*). This is not an objective judgment. Instead, it is a decision reflecting the values held by the person making the appraisal. Hence it calls for support in the form of a rationale explaining the values on which the decision is founded. A convincing rationale is what I find missing in the writings of such people as Gesell and his colleagues who work in a normative-descriptive mode.

DECISIONS ABOUT *NORMAL* AS *DESIRABLE* OR *ACCEPTABLE*

Establishing criteria that define *normal* (or *natural*) as *desirable*—or at least as *acceptable*—is a subjective act that can differ greatly from one person to another. The source of the criteria is the set of values held by the definer and, as such, the criteria require clarification (1) of the elements that go into the definition and (2) of the proper sources of evidence for making a decision about the normality of a given child's growth. Apparently many people seat their judgments of such normality on vague, intuitive impressions instead of specific, rational standards (when *rational* means *under conscious cognitive control*). I believe it is important for teachers, parents, counselors, and pediatricians not to be satisfied with amorphous, subconscious conceptions of such normality but to clearly identify what they believe constitutes desirable or acceptable development.

One way to begin explicating the components of such a conception is to offer a general definition of *normal,* then to explain the line of logic supporting the components. The following general definition illustrates this process:

> Children are developing normally (properly, desirably, satisfactorily) when: (1) they feel that they are fulfilling their own needs at least moderately well, (2) their behavior does not unduly encroach on other people's rights and opportunities, (3) they fulfill those responsibilities typically held as reasonable for people of their ability (physical and mental) within their particular social environment, and (4) their personal characteristics do not cause other people to treat them in ways which harm them physically, psychologically, or socially or which deny them opportunities [equal to the opportunities enjoyed by their peers] to pursue their ambitions (Thomas, 1990, p. 50).

This definition is the one to which I subscribe. I thus become obligated to explain the values on which I base the four components. My rationale, then, is as follows.

1. Fulfilling One's Own Needs

This first criterion derives from two convictions: (1) that each child has physical and psychological needs that, when satisfied, bring feelings of joy and contentment and that, when frustrated, bring feelings of misery and distress and (2) that the child deserves to have these needs met as promptly and as thoroughly as conditions permit. The term *conditions,* in this case, refers to the way children's needs and abilities interact with environmental factors. It is clear that infants, with their very limited abilities, must depend almost entirely on other people to satisfy needs. But as time passes, and children's internal maturation combines with experience to foster rapid growth in abilities, they depend less and less on the services of others for need satisfaction.

It is apparent that the goal of prompt need fulfillment can never be perfectly achieved because two or more competing needs can arise simultaneously or, as is so often the case, the environment does not permit immediate satisfaction. In early childhood, mother may be doing the laundry at the moment the toddler seeks solace. In later childhood, the girl scout may be far from a doctor when she suffers a sprained ankle during a hike in the mountains. In adolescence, the teenage girl and boy may find their sexual urges rising as they sit next to each other in the school library. Thus the goal of immediate need satisfaction can, at best, only be approximated, but I still hold it as an ideal to pursue. I believe that children who unduly suffer unmet needs are not developing properly.

2–3. Respecting Others' Rights and Bearing One's Own Responsibilities

In contrast to the introspective nature of the first criterion, the second and third standards represent perceptions from society's viewpoint. The rationale supporting these two standards holds that no one, except the rare hermit, lives alone. Instead, people live in interdependent groups, sharing common territories and dividing up the tasks of daily living, cooperating, and competing. Under these conditions, if the greatest good is to result for the greatest number, individuals cannot be concerned exclusively with indulging their own desires without regard for others. It thus becomes a matter of enlightened self-interest for people to recognize that, in the long run, their own needs will be best satisfied if they permit others to exercise the same rights that they themselves enjoy. Furthermore, their own needs will be best met if they, and all other members of the society, bear a fair share of the responsibility to perform the tasks that make the society operate efficiently. Criteria 2 and 3, in effect, represent the social aspect of satisfactory development. From the viewpoint of the group, individuals who fail to abide by society's customs are not developing properly.

4. The Importance of Societal Attitudes and Socioeconomic Opportunities

Frequently children's failure to achieve optimal development is caused by their being treated in prejudicial ways by others. Restrictions are placed on their opportunities to reach their desired potential. The fault, in many instances, lies in other people's basing their judgments of a child or youth on normative impressions or stereotypes. This can occur when a general conclusion about an easily identified group—Catholics, Jews, Blacks, Irish, Latin-Americans, adolescents, overweight children, the homeless—is applied to every member of the group in equal measure. In other words, individuals who bear the group label are not judged on their own characteristics but are branded with a generalization about "those kinds of people." As a result, opportunities for individuals can be restricted. Parents can determine their children's playmates and can influence which boys their adolescent daughter dates. Teachers and club leaders can decide which children will work together and how privileges, praise, and blame are meted out. Employers establish who gets a job and who is assigned to which tasks. Finally, children and teenagers themselves play a highly significant role in deciding which groups their age peers will be allowed to join. In short, failure of a child to develop in the most desirable way can be due to prejudicial attitudes of people in the environment who control opportunities for growth, self-expression, and need fulfillment.

SOURCES OF INFORMATION ABOUT DESIRABLE DEVELOPMENT

My purpose in proposing the foregoing criteria has not been to suggest that my definition is *the* right one. A review of theories in this book will reveal other definitions reflecting somewhat different values. My intention, then, is to illustrate the process of stating a definition and defending it with a line of reasoning.

A definition at such a level of specificity can also serve as a guide to the types of information a person will need for answering such questions as: Is this child developing properly? Am I expecting too much of that teenager? Do I really have anything to worry about? Should I be trying some special intervention or should I just let nature take its course?

Some of the needed information may be in the form of summary statements about groups—information about children and youths at different age levels as provided by researchers working in the normative-descriptive modes of Gesell and Havighurst. For example, in applying the four standards suggested above, it can be helpful to have normative information about (1) needs and developmental tasks that are especially prominent at different age levels (first criterion), (2) the typical abilities of children at successive ages and the accompanying rights and responsibilities that society holds for those age stages (second and third criteria), and (3) stereotypical attitudes held within the society about ethnic, religious, gender, and age groups (the fourth criterion). Such normative information provides a useful starting point—a set of probabilities—which then need to be verified and refined by information about the particular child whose development we are seeking to evaluate. In other words, normative data provide a rough guess about what factors may influence the development of a child during a given age period. What is next required is precise information about this specific child. Such information can be gathered through observing and interviewing the child, questioning people who know the child, and administering tests that can reveal something of the child's physical skills, cognitive abilities, views of social relationships, emotional responses, and perceptions of self.

In summary, then, I have suggested that normative-descriptive studies of children at different age levels are useful for showing where a given child or adolescent stands in relation to age-mates. However, knowing that a child is close to the group average or is distant from the average does not tell if that child's development is *proper* or *satisfactory* or even *acceptable*. Judgments about the desirability of a given child's growth depend on the particular values that underlie the judge's standards of appropriate development.

PART THREE

THE PSYCHOANALYTIC
TRADITION

A search for developmental causes
and cures of neuroses

From the viewpoint of the general public, the most unsettling theory of child development proposed during the past century has been Sigmund Freud's psychoanalysis. In the late 1800s and throughout the 1900s many people were shocked by Freud's contention that sexual motives—with sex interpreted in a broad sense—underlie much if not all human behavior. More shocking still is the notion of infantile sexuality. To the lay public and medical profession of the late 1800s and early 1900s, the idea that little children have sensuous thoughts that are important determinants of their personal and social adjustment is clearly a distortion of the truth at the hands of a dirty-minded neurotic (S. Freud, 1917, pp. 323–325, 1938, p. 9; Hartmann, 1959, p. 11).

Not as morally shocking but no less disturbing personally was Freud's suggestion that much of the time we do not consciously know why we act the way we do. Instead of behaving as rational beings, we are driven and manipulated by primitive urges and by traumas from our past that reside in what Freud called our *unconscious mind*. In the sixteenth century, Copernicus had already insulted humanity by suggesting that the earth is not the center of the universe. Darwin had carried the insult further by proposing that humans are descendents of lower forms of life and therefore not the divine, unique beings that they had led themselves to believe. Now Freud pushed insult another step by contending that a person's conscious mind was neither master of his fate nor captain of his soul; instead, each person was a victim of unconscious drives.

However, over the years since Freud first put forth his theory, he has gained a substantial following of believers. His work, and the revisions of it by later generations, now represents a major branch of psychology. Indeed,

125

many of his key ideas have nearly achieved the status of common sense. For these reasons, the psychoanalytic tradition deserves a prominent place in a survey of theories of child development.

Chapter Six presents central concepts of the theory as Freud himself devised them. The chapter ends with a brief description of contributions subsequently made by Freud's third daughter, Anna, specifically concerning the childhood portion of the overall theory.

Chapter Seven illustrates a major extension of psychoanalysis by a disciple of Freud, Erik Erikson. Of the various revised versions of psychoanalysis fashioned during the twentieth century, Erikson's has been the most significant for the field of child development, particularly for the years of adolescence.

CHAPTER SIX

Sigmund Freud's Psychoanalysis

Often we will best understand how a theorist arrived at a model of development if we recognize the sequence of experiences that were instrumental in guiding the direction of his theorizing. Since this seems particularly true in the case of psychoanalysis, let's begin the account of Freud's model by looking briefly at the medical puzzles that stimulated him to speculate about the nature of children and the forces that determine their development.

Sigmund Freud (1856–1939) was an Austrian neurologist who, early in his career of private medical practice in Vienna, encountered some very perplexing cases. Patients came to him with a variety of ailments, such as paralysis of the hand or aches or blurred vision, which could not be explained by traditional physiological knowledge. Although the patients' symptoms suggested that nerve tissue had been damaged, examination showed the nervous system to be intact.

How could people suffer such ailments without any organic impairment of the nervous system? While Freud was pondering this problem, he learned about the work that Jean Charcot was conducting on hypnotism in Paris. Charcot had shown that under a hypnotic spell people could be told that they would have one or another bodily symptom after they awakened from the hypnotic state, but would not remember the cause of this symptom. They would not recall that they had received a suggestion under hypnosis. And, indeed, after coming out of hypnosis, they did exhibit the suggested symptoms, such as paralysis of a leg, numbness of the skin, or deafness. Charcot, in addition, was able to use hypnosis to relieve people of certain symptoms. Under hypnosis, patients were told that they no longer suffered the ailment that had brought them to the clinic. Upon awakening, at least some of these patients had lost the symptom of which they had complained (S. Freud, 1910, p. 21).

Freud's interest in Charcot's experiments was so great that he spent the year 1885–1886 in Paris studying the methods and effects of hypnosis. At the same time, he asked questions that might explain these curious phenomena: What relation might there be between the strange cases Freud faced in his medical practice and the cases Charcot exhibited in his clinic? How must human personality be structured and how must mind be related to body in order to cause such things to occur (S. Freud, 1910, pp. 16–22)?

To answer these queries, Freud, over the next several decades, developed his psychoanalytic theory of personality. Included in the theory is a conception of child development that has exerted significant influence over a number of areas of child psychology today—child psychiatry, counseling children and adolescents, nursery school teaching methods, and research in child development. Certain concepts from Freudian theory have now been generally accepted by psychologists, educators, and social workers, and even by those who reject most of psychoanalytic theory. In effect, Freud's views have had a decided influence on people concerned with raising children.

Psychoanalytic theory in its entirety is quite complex. Not only does it have many ramifications but adherents of psychoanalysis often disagree with each other on important issues. Freud himself altered the theory in major ways on several occasions. For these reasons, the following discussion presents only a simplified sketch of the theory's main elements.

The early part of the chapter is divided into descriptions of (1) levels of consciousness, (2) the apparatus of mental life, (3) psychosexual stages of child development, and (4) the development of consciousness and ego strength. After these, there are (5) a brief review of some contributions to psychoanalytic theory and practice by Anna Freud, (6) practical applications, and (7) an assessment of the theory.

LEVELS OF CONSCIOUSNESS

Early in the process of formulating his theory, Freud proposed that each person has an *unconscious* aspect of mind in addition to the conscious aspect of which the individual is aware. By *unconscious* Freud meant a sort of mental receptacle for ideas, a receptacle from which the individual cannot recall ideas at will. These ideas, of which we are unaware, influence our actions just as much as if they were conscious. In effect, much of what we do arises from unconscious motivation (S. Freud, 1923, p. 4).

The concept of an unconscious state of mind was not entirely new in the field of philosophy. An occasional theorist over the centuries had postulated such an aspect. However, it was Freud who elaborated the concept and assigned it a central role in behavior.

By proposing the unconscious, Freud was able to account for other-wise unexplainable disorders suffered by his patients. He hypothesized that a person who faces a distressing, unsolved problem in daily life will find the problem psychologically painful. So the individual's personality, to escape this pain of unresolved conflicts, automatically resolves the problem by pushing the distressing thoughts out of consciousness. The patient actively "forgets" the matter. But Freud believed that such forgotten material does not leave the mind. Instead, it is only relegated to an unconscious condition—in other words, it is "repressed"—to keep the sufferer una-ware of its existence and, consequently, enable the person to feel more at peace. But the problem, now unconscious, continues to agitate, and it expresses itself in devious ways. One mode of expression can be a bodily ailment, such as a headache or paralysis of some part of the body. So it was that Freud concluded that the strange symptoms displayed by his patients were caused by unresolved mental conflicts that seethed insistently in their unconscious minds. Not only were these bodily disorders, which he called *conversion hysteria symptoms,* the consequence of repressed mental conflicts but so, Freud believed, was the entire array of neurotic symptoms, an array including phobias, obsessions, compulsions, and anxieties.

To alleviate such symptoms—in effect, to cure the neuroses—Freud proposed that the repressed conflict, which had originated in a problem of development earlier in the patient's life, had to be brought into conscious-ness. The patient had to recognize the origin of the difficulties and verbal-ly relive the original conflict situation, but this time work out the conflict in a constructive, emotionally satisfying manner and thus be cured of the neuroses.

In order to make his therapeutic scheme work, Freud had to devise a process for uncovering the unconscious conflicts and presenting them so that patients would accept the conflicts as true and deserving of serious attention. Early in his career Freud tried different means for uncovering unconscious conflicts. He began with hypnosis but, as he later reported, "I soon came to dislike hypnosis, for it was a temperamental and . . . mystical ally" (Freud, 1910, p. 22). Hence he gave it up in favor of free association and dream interpretation.

The process of *free association* consists of encouraging the patient to relax, usually on a couch, and to describe free-flowing thoughts without editing them. The analyst listens to hours of such narration in order to locate underlying themes of conflict that are hints or symbols of hidden problems. By using the process of relaxed, free association, the therapist is assuming that "the repressed wishful impulse . . . is on the look-out for an opportunity of being activated, and when that happens it succeeds in sending into consciousness a disguised and unrecognizable substitute for what had been repressed" (Freud, 1910, p. 27). It is the analyst's task to unmask the significant elements of the patient's narration and reveal them for what they really are in the individual's past development.

In a like manner, Freud used *dream interpretation* as a window, albeit murky and distorted, for viewing the contents of the unconscious. He believed that during sleep, a censor force, which seeks to prevent unconscious conflicts from entering consciousness, is not as alert as during waking life. So dreams, in Freud's scheme, are products of the person's trying to satisfy wishes and solve problems during sleep. The dream serves as an audiovisual symbol of unconscious urges pressing for expression into consciousness. The analyst is skilled in interpreting dreams in a way that reveals the nature and source of the patient's unconscious conflicts (Freud, 1900).

The significance of Freud's reliance on free association and dream interpretation is twofold. First, both techniques were tools crucial to the conduct of his system of therapy. Second, and more important for our present purposes, they served almost exclusively as the sources of data about childhood on which he erected his model of development. Rather than spending his time directly observing children in the process of their development, Freud spent endless hours listening to adult neurotics produce memories of childhood. On these memories, extracted from free associations and dreams, he built his picture of sexual growth.

In addition to introducing a view of the mind as consisting of both conscious and unconscious aspects, Freud also distinguished two levels of unconsciousness. One level, he said, contains those ideas that are not in consciousness at the moment, that are latent. We can recall them, "bring them to mind," if we choose, even though it may take a bit of effort. This first level Freud labeled the *preconscious*. The second level contains the truly repressed ideas, those held down purposely by the personality's resistance forces because allowing them to enter consciousness would be too painful for the conscious personality to face. This second level, deeper and less accessible than the preconscious, is the *true* or prototype unconscious in the Freudian scheme. In a sense, then, the preconscious is a shadow zone between the open, bright conscious and the closed, dark unconscious (Freud, 1923, pp. 4–5). A person has thoughts or ideas at each of these levels.

THE PSYCHIC APPARATUS

The levels of consciousness serve as a sort of three-tiered arena in which a person's psychic life takes place. Within the psychical arena, the three main functionaries that compete and cooperate to produce this performance were conceived by Freud to be the *id,* the *ego,* and the *superego.* In the course of a child's development, these three do not appear simultaneously. The id comes first—it is already present at birth. The ego develops out of the growing infant's efforts to satisfy needs through transactions with the environment. Some years later the superego develops as an internal representative of the rules and values of the environment.

The way the development of the id, ego, and superego becomes intertwined with stages of the child's psychosexual growth is rather complex. In order to make this development easier to grasp, I will divide the explanation into two parts. The first, which comprises this section on the psychic apparatus, treats the nature and functions of the id, ego, and superego. The second, in the next section, describes their relation to the psychosexual growth stages that Freud proposed.

As a preface to these matters, we need to recognize that all behavior, physical and psychological, needs energy to activate it. In psychoanalytic theory the sources of all energy are the instincts, with *instinct* defined as an inborn factor that gives force and direction to psychological activities. For at least three decades Freud experimented with various conceptions of instincts. Then in 1920 he settled on a basic pair of motivating forces—the *life* and *death* instincts—which he thought vied for expression and supremacy in directing psychic behavior throughout a person's life span. The influence of the life instinct is reflected in constructive acts, in acts of love and altruism. The influence of the death instinct is displayed in destructive acts, in hate and in aggression. Freud applied the word *libido* to the psychic energy deriving from the life instinct, but he coined no parallel term for the energy emitting from the death instinct (Freud, 1920).

From the viewpoint of the instincts, the process of living consists of a continual competition between the opposing life and death forces—love against hate, life preservation against self-destruction. Often a mode of behaving represents a fusion of the two, as when aggression against a threatening enemy (motivated by the death instinct) preserves one's life and promotes one's welfare (which is the objective of the life instinct). Although throughout childhood and well into adult life the evidences of the life instinct appear to be the more prominent, the ultimate victory obviously goes to the opposing force, when, at life's close, the organism loses all animation and returns to the passive inorganic state that is the ultimate aim of the death instinct.

Now that we have the pair of basic instinctual energy sources in mind, we turn to the psychic apparatus through which the forces are invested or expended. In psychoanalytic theory, the personality of the newborn consists of a single operating component called the *id*. It is at the unconscious level and "contains everything that is inherited, that is present at birth, that is laid down in the constitution—above all, therefore, the instincts" (Freud, 1938, p. 2). It is within this id that libido builds up as a sort of pressure, searching for expression. Seen another way, libidinal energy arising from the id assumes the form of *needs* that demand fulfillment. The expenditure or release of libido is experienced by the infant as pleasure. The blocking of libidinal release is experienced as pain. So the id operates on the *pleasure principle,* which says: "Get as much pleasure as possible as soon as possible without regard for anyone else or anything else in the world." In its converse form the principle becomes: Avoid as much pain as possible.

Hence psychoanalysis pictures the newborn baby as all id, seeking only to satisfy its needs for food, for drink, for warmth, for elimination of body wastes, for freedom from skin irritants, and for affection, affection in the sense of being cuddled by its mother or mother substitute. The newborn's awareness of its condition and of the world is ostensibly very fuzzy. Freudians suppose that a baby does not distinguish among objects in its environment, nor does it recognize a difference between itself and other people or things. The newborn is aware only of discomfort or pain, which signals unfulfilled needs that require attention. The only observable methods the infant has for reacting to these pain or tension signals are crying, mouthing, and randomly moving its arms and legs.

But as time passes and the infant's experience with the world increases, more precise awareness of the environment begins to develop. The earliest level of awareness results in the *primary process,* which is the baby's act of creating in its memory an image of an object that will fulfill a need. For example, when the newborn feels hunger pangs, he automatically cries until someone feeds him. The food reduces the tension of hunger, and the baby experiences pleasure. As days pass, this cycle of hunger, feeding, and tension reduction is played over and over, so that gradually the taste, smell, feel, and sight of the food and of the feeder (usually the mother) are stored as images in the baby's memory. As a result, the infant, by means of the primary process, can now imagine those things that will bring a particular variety of satisfaction or a particular mode of expending libidinal energy.

It is important to recognize that the primary process is a rather chaotic, irrational mode of thought that does not distinguish between reasonable and unreasonable need-fulfilling images. The concern of the id and its primary process thinking is to gain satisfaction, regardless of whether or not the method of satisfaction is practical or will be tolerated by the environment. What the personality next requires, then, is a component that recognizes the nature of the environment, as well as the demands of the id, and can, therefore, provide realistic methods of investing energy. This second component of the psychic apparatus is called the *ego*. Freud postulated that the ego arises from, or separates out of, the id and is fueled by libidinal energy from the id. In effect, the id's primary process develops images of things that fulfill needs, but the image is only an initial, incomplete step toward satisfaction. Another agent, the ego, is required to bring the dream into reality. Freud explained that "the ego is that part of the id which has been modified by the direct influence of the external world through the medium" of conscious perception (Freud, 1923, p. 15). Furthermore, he proposed:

> It is to this ego that consciousness is attached; the ego controls the . . . discharge of excitations into the external world; it is the mental agency which supervises all its own constituent processes, and which goes to sleep at night, though even then it exercises the censorship on dreams (1923, p. 7).

Hence the ego serves as a decision maker that tries to negotiate a satisfactory solution to the conflicting demands that come on the one side from the id (which says "I want") and on the other side from the environment or "real world" (which says "You'll get it with a minimum of cost or pain only under these conditions"). Whereas the id works on the pleasure principle, the ego operates on the *reality principle,* which can be stated as: Recognize the conditions and demands of the real world and then seek methods of fulfilling the id's needs that are acceptable in such a world.

To play its role of negotiator, the ego is constantly assessing the kinds and strengths of needs arising from the id and at the same time assessing the conditions of the environment. From this assessment, the ego attempts to devise behaviors that represent the best compromise between the id and the outside world. Or, as is sometimes the case, the ego must negotiate a compromise among several demands coming simultaneously from the id, such as the demands of hunger and fatigue arising at the same moment.

We noted that the id, by means of the primary process, associates certain objects with need fulfillment. These associations are stored as memory images. It is now up to the ego to turn the images into reality. This problem-solving act is called the *secondary process.* The individual's skills of perceiving, remembering, analyzing, and taking action develop from this constant interaction among (1) the id's needs, (2) the maturing bodily organs, such as eyes and ears, and (3) the ego's increasing awareness of the complexities of the world.

The Superego's Role

Our next concern is with the third component of the psychic apparatus, the *superego*. Early in a child's life the rules of the world—the rules of *do* and *don't*—are enforced by the environment. The infant, in Freud's system, has no inborn inner voice telling her what is right and what is wrong. In effect, the child is born neither moral nor immoral, but *amoral*. She has no knowledge of good or bad. Her morality is simply that of getting pleasure (as demanded by the id) in a manner that will avoid punishment or pain (a manner arranged by the ego). The very young child, therefore, does not automatically feel bad or guilty or ashamed when she transgresses one of society's expectations. She feels bad only when the consequences of her behavior are either the withholding of rewards or the application of punishment. It is usually the child's parents who produce her good and bad feelings by manipulating the system of rewards and punishments she will experience.

Although children are not born with knowledge of what is good and what is evil, they are born with a capacity for two things: (1) to develop internal values and (2) to feel good (pleased and proud) when they abide by these values and to feel bad (sad, ashamed, and guilty) when transgressing them. Over the years of childhood and adolescence this capacity acquires contents in the form of moral values the child adopts from the environment. It is this third component of the growing personality that Freud labeled *superego*. How and why the superego appears and grows are matters intimately involved in the psychosexual stages of development and will be discussed in connection with them. For the present we will restrict our attention to the role the superego plays in the mental life of the older child and adolescent.

Just as Freud pictured the ego as developing out of the id, so he saw the superego arising from the ego (Freud, 1923, pp. 18–29). He explained:

> This new psychical agency continues to carry on the functions which have hitherto been performed by the people in the external world: It observes the ego, gives it orders, judges it and threatens it with punishments, exactly like the parents whose place it has taken (1938, p. 62).

Freud conceived of the superego as having two aspects, the *conscience* and the *ego ideal*. The conscience represents the "should-nots" of the child's world, the things for which he has been punished. The ego ideal represents the "shoulds," the positive moral values the child has been taught. Whereas the very young child must be punished for transgressions and rewarded for good behavior by his parents, the maturing child gradually does not need outside sanctions. His superego plays the punishing and rewarding roles for him. For disobeying the values he has now accepted as his own, the child's conscience punishes him with guilt, shame, and fear. For abiding by his moral values, his ego ideal rewards him with feelings of self-righteousness, self-praise, and pride.

With the addition of the superego to the id and ego, the apparatus of the mind is complete. The behavior of older children and adolescents is thus a result of the way the ego has negotiated a settlement among three conflicting sources of demands: (1) the id, which insists on immediate fulfillment of wishes, (2) the environment, which sets conditions under which wishes can be satisfied without punishment, and (3) the superego, which presses the youth to live up to a set of moral values he has incorporated from his parents and from other significant people in his world.

Mechanisms of Defense

As the ego develops over the years, it evolves techniques or habits for accommodating the conflicting demands made on it. A strong, mature ego uses direct means to accomplish this. It frankly admits the nature of instinctual demands, environmental forces, and the superego's commands. Then it proposes forthright, reasoned ways to effect a solution that satisfies each source of demand to an acceptable degree. But an ego that is weak, still childish and immature, slips into using more devious techniques of adjustment, techniques that Freud called *defense mechanisms*. The ego, in effect, seeks to fool itself and others concerning the state of affairs it faces, for it feels inadequate to solve the conflict among the demands that confront it.

The most significant defense technique, *repression*, has already been described. It is the automatic, nonconscious process of pushing distressing matters out of consciousness and into the unconscious. Although repression clears the conscious mind of worries, the repressed material continues to foment distress in the unconscious and produce the sorts of neurotic symptoms that Freud met in his medical practice.

A second mechanism is *sublimation*, the substitution of a culturally higher, socially more acceptable mode of expressing sexual or aggressive energy. Such altruistic acts as caring for children or aiding the sick, or such artistic endeavors as writing poetry or performing a ballet, are viewed by Freudians as substitutes for direct sexual behavior.

A third defense technique is *regression*, which consists of returning to an earlier, more primitive mode of adjusting to problems. A person may turn to this device when facing a new or distressing situation. As a simple example, a twelve-year-old girl feels frustrated when her mother criticizes her in public, so the girl begins sucking her thumb or the corner of her handkerchief as she did when she sought solace as an infant.

A mechanism that has been readily adopted into commonsense understanding is that of *projection*. When a child senses within his own personality a motive of which he is ashamed or which he fears, he may not admit its existence consciously to himself, but instead he may constantly see this motive in other people. He attributes to others those unacceptable acts and feelings that his own id urges him to express. Thus the child who harbors hate in his own unconscious will accuse others of hating him, claiming at the same time that he himself bears no malice. Likewise, a person who is repressing strong sexual desires of which he is ashamed will assume that others are trying to seduce or assault him sexually.

The device called *reaction formation* has been particularly useful to psychoanalysts, for it enables them to explain behavior that would otherwise appear to refute typical predictions that derive from the theory. Reaction formation consists of a child's adopting behavior that is just the opposite of an instinctual urge. For instance, a child may act compulsively clean, avoiding dirt and frequently washing her hands and changing her clothes. The direct interpretation of such behavior is that the child desires to be clean—cleanliness is her basic need. But Freudians would suspect something different. Since in their theory the basic drives involve such sensuous pleasure as sexual stimulation and bowel and urinary functions, they would propose that the child is not motivated by a basic cleanliness need. Instead, she really wants to become soiled, to mess around in dirt and feces, but she has been punished by her parents for expressing such desires so now she feels her basic urges are wicked. To control them, she represses the original desires and in her conscious life adopts the opposite sort of behavior as a desperate means of mastering the urges of which she is ashamed. In short, her behavior represents a reaction against her instinctual drives.

Three more defense mechanisms can be briefly described. *Compensation* is a device by which the child seeks to overcome a personal or environmental barrier by substituting success in some other realm of life than the one in which he suffers the weakness. *Rationalization* consists of giving a socially acceptable reason for a behavior that actually was motivated by a less honorable reason. *Escape* is leaving the scene of a distressing experience. The escape can be either physical, such as a girl's running away from home, or psychological, such as a youth's retreating into daydreams in school when the lesson is confusing.

These defense mechanisms, which are only some of those identified by Freud and his followers, illustrate the kinds of strategies the ego employs to satisfy, as well as possible, the conflicting demands made on it.

Now that we have identified the main components of the psyche and their functions, we can look at the psychosexual growth stages involved in the development of these components.

THE PSYCHOSEXUAL STAGES OF DEVELOPMENT

To account for the sorts of dreams and memories of childhood that his patients described, Freud produced a model of child development that featured a series of growth stages. The current neuroses of his patients, he thought, were the result of inadequate solutions to the problems the individual had faced as a child at one or more of these stages. He labeled these growth steps *psychosexual phases* because he believed the development of the personality—the *psyche*—was crucially influenced by the manner in which the child learned to expend sex energy (libido) from one period of life to the next. In other words, Freud proposed that the most significant emotional experiences during childhood and adolescence are those associated with expending libido in relation to a series of particularly sensitive zones of the body on which children's attention focuses at different points of development. These *erogenous zones,* in chronological sequence, are the mouth, the anus, and the genital organs. At the time a particular zone is the chief focus for the release of libido, the child not only derives sensuous (sexual, in a broad meaning of the term) pleasure from use of the zone, but her relationships with other people are heavily influenced by the way they respond to her attention to the zone. In essence, Freud proposed that the personal-social relationships the child develops—her feelings about herself and others, and her ways of treating herself and others—are founded in the experiences the child has at each psychosexual stage. Personality problems that arise as the child seeks to work her way through a stage may go unresolved, be repressed by the frantic ego, and continue to agitate within the unconscious and cause neuroses for years afterwards.

Although the number of developmental periods identified between birth and adulthood may vary slightly from one psychoanalytic theorist to another, all of them cite at least five major stages: oral (ages 0–1), anal (ages 2–3), infantile-genital (ages 3–4 or so), latency (ages 4 or 5 to puberty), mature-genital (from midteens to adulthood). We will examine these stages and the substages involved in several of them.

Birth: The Traumatic Beginning

Birth is not a stage of growth, but it is a highly significant event in psychoanalytic theory because it is regarded as the first great shock of the child's life. In the Freudian view, the newborn is overwhelmed with stimulation from the environment into which he or she emerges from the womb. The reaction is intense fear, for the undeveloped ego has no means to cope adequately with such a flood of stimuli. The birth trauma, then, is the prototype of all subsequent fear-producing situations the child will meet as he grows to old age. When later in life he is confronted by extreme stimuli, either extreme instinctual demands or extreme pressures from the environment, and his existing ego techniques are ineffective for mastering the stimuli, the original fear occasioned by the birth trauma will be reactivated, and he will revert to infantile behavior. Consequently, according to Freudian theory, an easier birth, involving less shock upon entering the world, can be expected to build less fear into the unconscious of the growing child, and he may be able to face frustrating experiences later in life with greater emotional control.

Stage 1: The Oral Period (Ages 0–1)

The psychoanalytic model of the child pictures the newborn not as a passive slab of damp clay on which environmental experiences will engrave a personality structure but as a dynamic energy system pressing to expend its energy. Or more precisely, the id of the neonate is seeking to invest libidinal energy in images of objects that will satisfy the instinctual needs and bring the pleasure of release. This act of investment (the primary process of the id) is called *cathexis*. When the id channels energy into an image of an object, it is said to be *cathecting* that object.

Following birth, the natural initial object for cathexis is the mother's breast or a suitable substitute because it is through the mouth that the newborn must now obtain life-sustaining nourishment. She must also use her mouth and nose for breathing. The nerve endings in the lips and mouth are particularly sensitive and offer the infant special pleasure. Freud wrote:

> The baby's obstinate persistence in sucking gives evidence at an early stage of a need for satisfaction which, though it originates from and is instigated by the taking of nourishment, nevertheless strives to obtain pleasure independently of nourishment and for that reason may and should be termed *sexual* (1938, p. 11).

The adequacy with which the child satisfies the need for food, drink, and breath gives him his first impressions of the world and of his relation to it. Not only is his personality influenced by how soon and how completely the pent-up libidinal energy is released, but the atmosphere associated with how these needs for release are either met or neglected affects him also. If his mother holds him affectionately and soothingly during the feeding process, the child will pass through the oral period in a happier, more confident state than if he is never cuddled and if there are distressing sounds and sights bombarding him while feeding.

In addition to taking the food and drink, the oral zone is used by the infant to investigate the parts of the world she can reach. She examines most objects by putting them to her lips or into her mouth. Freud suggested that the basic reason the child mouths objects is that she wishes to *incorporate* them and thus to control and master them.

The infant's personality, being mostly pleasure-seeking id, begins to distinguish *me* from *not-me* (evidence of a growing ego) by regarding pleasure-giving objects as *self* and non-pleasure-giving objects as *non-self*.

Some psychoanalysts divide the oral period into two substages, the early or *receptive stage* and the late or *biting stage*.

The receptive stage covers the first few months of life when erotic pleasure is derived from sucking, swallowing, and mouthing. At this time the infant is rather passive and plays an extremely dependent role. If his feeding and other dependency needs are not adequately met or if great conflict is associated with them, a residue of unfulfillment and conflict is repressed into the unconscious to reveal itself in subsequent years, often as neurotic overdependency or a compulsive habit of trying to "take in" other people and objects. In essence, Freudian theory sees the experience the child has with satisfying instinctual drives at a particular psychosexual stage as forming a model for attitudes or relationships that may be carried over to later life.

The biting stage occurs during the latter portion of infancy when teeth are erupting and gums are harder. The dominant zone of gratification is still the mouth, but at this point the act of touching things with the lips or of swallowing is not as satisfying as biting or chewing. As the infant's perceptual skills mature, she begins to recognize the features of outside objects more clearly. She now recognizes that one object, such as mother, can have both pleasure-giving and pain-giving functions. Mother gratifies hunger when the baby cries. But mother also has to carry out other activities in her life, so she cannot satisfy the baby's demands immediately all the time, and the baby finds this postponement painful.

As a result, the infant develops his first *ambivalent* feelings. He both loves and hates the same object. Freudian theory proposes that the child's early ambivalent feelings and sadistic tendencies are expressed in biting — biting his mother's breast, people's fingers, toys, and the like. If progress through this stage is incomplete, so that the infant experiences insufficient satisfaction of biting needs and has inadequate opportunities to express ambivalence without unduly painful repercussions, then a residue of conflict remains in the unconscious to disturb the individual in later life. If the child's progress through the latter oral stage is arrested—that is, if he becomes *fixated* at this point in psychosexual growth—then he may evidence such fixation as an adult through a pattern of "biting" criticism of others or by frequently "chewing out" people around him.

This phenomenon of fixation can occur at any of the psychosexual stages. Freudians hold that fixation—carrying into later life those modes of libidinal gratification suited to an earlier stage—can be the result of either too little or too much satisfaction at the stage in question. If the child's attempts at libidinal investment in an erogenous zone are frustrated, so there remains pent-up energy and inadequate satisfaction, then fixation may occur in the form of a constant seeking to gain the satisfaction in symbolic ways in subsequent years. In contrast, if so much satisfaction with a given erogenous zone is experienced so that the child does not wish to abandon this pleasure by moving ahead to mature forms of libidinal expression, then fixation may again be the result. At each psychosexual stage, the child progresses most satisfactorily if she gains enough pleasure to move ahead without dragging along a residue of unfulfilled needs, yet does not gain so much satisfaction that she is unwilling to advance.

Stage 2: The Anal Period (Ages 2–3)

During the second and third years of life, much of the attention of child and parents typically focuses on establishing proper control of the bowels. This time of life is usually called the anal period because the prime concern is with expelling and retaining feces. However, it is sometimes referred to as the *anal-urethral period* because control of urinary functions is also involved. Thus the dominant zones of gratification or libido investment become the anal cavity, the sphincter muscles of the lower bowel, and the muscles of the urinary system.

The shift of the child's attention to the anal area does not mean that the expression of instinctual energy via the oral zone has stopped. It means, rather, that anal activities usually become of major concern for both child and parent. In response to questions about the sequence of the oral, anal, and genital stages, Freud wrote:

> It would be a mistake to suppose that these three phases succeed one another in a clear-cut fashion. One may appear in addition to another; they may overlap one another, may be present along side of one another (1938, p. 12).

In the anal period, much of the child's important contact with adults and much of the emotion adults express toward him are related to toilet training. Like the oral stage, the anal period can be divided into two subperiods, the first concerned with pleasure in expelling feces and urine and the second with retaining these materials.

During the *expulsion stage* the child meets her first serious experience with an external barrier (parents' coercion to have the child control the bowels) to an instinctual cathexis (wishing to defecate). If the child is to accomplish bowel and bladder control, the ego must apply resistance to the child's urge to eliminate at the moment she feels the need. Thus the ego must borrow libido from the id to energize the resistance. Such a use of libidinal force by the ego—or at a later stage, by the superego—is called *countercathexis* or *anticathexis*. In short, the cathexis or energy investment of the id in the pleasurable release of defecation must be countered by an opposing cathexis of the ego if the child is to meet the parents' demands for cleanliness and thus retain their love.

This is a crucial time for the child to learn to earn love, praise, and approval. If the period is not handled properly by parents—if they harshly impose cleanliness standards before the child is physiologically prepared to control the bowels and bladder, for example—then the child's personality will retain vestiges of fear, guilt, and defiance. The repressed conflict may produce an adult who is compulsively regular and clean or, in contrast, one who is bitter and, in a symbolic sense, voids and urinates on others in his social interaction. The frequent use of the words *crap, shit,* and *bullshit* among adults is said to reflect a measure of fixation at the anal stage.

In the second half of the anal period, the child has learned to *retain* feces and urine at will. She now gains sensuous satisfaction by holding in, that is, by keeping the product she values. Freudians suggest that the child's idea of things having value comes from this period, and inadequate passage through the stage may show up later in life in acts of hoarding and collecting things.

Stage 3: The Infantile-Genital Period (Ages 3–4 or so)

The boy's penis and the girl's clitoris and vulva become the key objects of erotic pleasure during the third major psychosexual period. It, too, can be divided into two phases.

During the first phase, called the *phallic stage,* the child discovers that fondling the genitals, titillation, and masturbation (but without orgasm) give erotic pleasure. The child next associates fondling the genitals with a love object with whom he or she wishes to have some sort of sexual relations. For the boy, Freud says:

> The object that has been found turns out to be almost identical with the first object of the oral pleasure-instinct, which was reached by attach-

ment (to the nutritional instinct). Though it is not actually the mother's breast, at least it is the mother. We call the mother the first *love*-object (1917, p. 329).

While the boy is viewing his mother as the desired object, he is at the same time recognizing that he cannot have her all to himself, for his father is the successful competitor for her affections. The resulting psychological conflict—wanting to possess mother but prevented from doing so by the powerful father—has been labeled the *Oedipus complex* or *Oedipus conflict.* The girl is in the opposite situation, wanting her father as her love partner but being defeated in this contest by her mother. The resulting conflict for the girl has been called the *Electra complex,* but both the boy's and girl's problems are usually subsumed under the Oedipus label.

During this period the child experiences strong ambivalent feelings, seeking the parent of the opposite sex as a lover, but at the same time both fearing and loving the parent of the same sex. An adequate resolution of the Oedipus situation occurs when the child rejects the sexual feelings toward the taboo object, the opposite-sex parent, and, at the same time, identifies with the parent of the same sex. By identifying with the same-sex parent, the child both assuages feelings of fear of reprisal and incorporates the traits of the same-sex parent, the traits that made that parent win the love of the other. In effect, the boy identifies with his father and seeks to adopt his father's characteristics. The girl does the same with her mother. This is the way Freudian theory accounts for the development of masculine and feminine characteristics that fit the mode of the society into which the child is raised.

It is during this process of solving the Oedipus conflict by repressing sexual desires and adopting parental characteristics that the superego evolves. To control what he now considers his dangerous sexual urges, the child incorporates parental values into his personality. These values, in the form of a superego that separates out of the ego, enable the child to reward and punish himself and thus control his own behavior in the absence of outside authority figures.

If the Oedipus conflict is not adequately resolved through repression of sexual impulses and identification with the like-sex parent, remnants of the conflict remain in the unconscious to distort the personality of the adolescent and adult. For instance, homosexuality sometimes has been explained as the child's identifying with the other-sex parent and thus modeling his or her subsequent living habits and sexual tastes after the opposite-sex parent rather than the same-sex one.

The resolution of the Oedipus complex leads into the second portion of the infantile-genital stage, called the *latency period.* Since this time of latent eroticism is so different in its manifestations from the early infantile-genital stage, I treat it as a major period by itself.

Stage 4: The Latency Period
(from Ages 4 or 5 to Puberty at Ages 11–13)

During this period, the dominant zone of gratification is still the genital area, but this is usually not displayed in the child's behavior, for both the boy and girl are repressing expressions of sex in order to solve the Oedipus conflict. The child has cathected or adopted both the gratifying and punishing parts of the parents and thus considers talk and displays of sex to be "nasty." The boy stops masturbating because he is afraid of being punished by having his penis cut off, and the girl stops because she is afraid of losing parental love. According to Freud (1938, p. 10), the child falls "victim to *infantile amnesia*" and "forgets" (by use of repression) the sex urges and activities of the first five years of life.

Throughout the years of latency the child's interests in working and playing primarily with children of his or her own sex is a manifestation of efforts to control sexual thoughts. This period has sometimes been called the *gang age* because children seldom voluntarily form groups that include the opposite sex. Because of this same-sex tendency in social relationships, the period is also referred to as the *homosexual phase*, although the homosexual relationships often do not involve any overt sexual acts. Indeed, the rejection of "sex" which the child so strongly evidences at this time in order to control Oedipal tendencies can preclude even thinking about physical displays that might be construed as sexual, whether the object of these displays is a same-sex or opposite-sex peer. In effect, the superego serves as a strong, moralistic internal representative of parental, and thus societal, rules. Playing by the rules both in games and in other daily activities becomes a matter of great importance to children in this phase of growth.

Solving the Oedipus conflict and working through the latency phase successfully is a difficult, stressful task, and often children fail to complete it successfully. Some become fixated at this stage, so that in adult life they never feel comfortable around the opposite sex, and they may avoid sexual relations with the opposite sex or else perform sexual activities in an emotionally detached or aggressive manner.

Stage 5: The Mature-Genital Period
(from Ages 14–16 to 18 or 21)

The maturing of sexual functions at puberty and beyond is signaled in girls by menstruation and such secondary bodily changes as the rounding of the

breasts and the growth of underarm and pubic hair. The parallel maturation in boys is shown by growth of the genital organs, the appearance of
sperm cells, nocturnal emissions of semen (often accompanied by erotic
dreams), lowering of the voice pitch, and the growth of underarm, facial,
and pubic hair.

The primary zone of erotic pleasure or libidinal cathexis is still the
penis in the boy and the clitoral area in the girl, but now the gratification
involves sexual orgasm. Whereas during the latent period the child was
interested primarily in peers of the same sex, now the attention turns to the
opposite sex. In mature sexuality the dominant erotic activity becomes
copulation with a partner of the opposite sex. To make the transition from
the rejection of sex at the latency phase to the wholehearted pursuit of
heterosexual activity is typically a psychologically demanding challenge,
particularly in societies that have erected moral barriers against intercourse
between unmarried people, especially between adolescents. And such was
the case in the late nineteenth-century Viennese society from which Freud
drew so many of his patients on whose psychoanalytic histories he erected
his theory.

The process of working through the problems of this transition successfully not only enables the youth to gratify sexual instincts in a mature
fashion but also gives her or him a less egocentric, more objective perspective of the world in general. The superego has been well formed, with its
appropriate conscience and ego ideal. The ego operates on the reality
principle, having developed direct modes of solving life's problems and not
depending unduly on defense mechanisms.

However, it is during this final stage of psychosexual development that
society's rules about the conditions under which sexual intercourse is permissible often press youths to adopt sublimation as a defense mechanism.
That is, the adolescent abstains from copulation and substitutes instead
artistic or philanthropic activities to express sexual drives indirectly. The
substitute may be writing poetry, reading literature, singing or playing a
musical instrument, caring for children, aiding the handicapped, engaging
in sports, or the like. (The question of whether such sublimation actually
does satisfy sexual urges is an unsettled issue, still debated among psychoanalysts and among psychiatrists of other persuasions.)

The Stages and Therapy

Freud's concept of stages is the key to the practice of psychoanalysis as a
method of aiding both children and adults who suffer neuroses, with
neuroses meaning psychic disorders that are distressing but do not cause the
person to view the world in a seriously distorted way, as is the case in

psychoses. The task of the therapist is to use free association and dream interpretation to search back through the patient's psychosexual history to locate the stage at which unresolved conflicts were repressed. Through analysis the therapist hopes to reveal to the patient the original causes of the repressed problem and, by consciously reviewing the original conflicts, to help the patient recognize them for what they are and to integrate this new understanding into the personality. In short, the conflict is dug up and relived both intellectually and emotionally. When this process is complete, the neurotic symptoms that brought the patient to the psychoanalyst are expected to disappear. Thus psychoanalysts do not attempt to change neurotic symptoms directly, which they believe is folly but, rather, to find the repressed conflict that is causing the symptom. They believe that when the conflict is resolved and psychologically integrated, the symptoms will evaporate. Treating a symptom directly, they say, does not solve the problem but at best only causes the patient to substitute a different symptom for the one that has been treated. The underlying cause, they insist, must be found and relived realistically. (As we will see in Part Four, behaviorists believe quite the opposite.)

TWO FACETS OF DEVELOPMENT

Now that the main features of Freud's model have been described, we will consider two aspects of it in more detail. The discussion will illustrate something of the complexity of Freud's speculation about development and also show how these aspects—the development of consciousness and of ego strength—fit into the overall framework.

The Development of Consciousness

In Freud's system, the conscious aspect of mental life does not burst forth in its mature, ultimate state at the time of birth or during infancy. Instead, both consciousness and the preconscious develop over the years as the personality is influenced by increasing internal maturation and by ever-widening experiences with the world. This development is perhaps best explained in terms of the relationship that evolves among the levels of awareness (conscious, preconscious, unconscious) and the apparatus of mental life (id, ego, superego).

One of the major challenges Freud faced over the last two or three decades of his life was that of describing clearly the way levels of consciousness interacted with the id, ego, and superego as the child grew up. As he admitted, his attempts at solving this riddle met with only partial success because of the difficulty of penetrating such tangled and clouded territories as the preconscious and unconscious. "And the profound obscurity of the background of our ignorance is scarcely illuminated by a few glimmers of insight" (Freud, 1938, p. 20). Nevertheless, he did depict something of what he saw with the aid of such glimmers, and Figure 6.1 attempts to diagram this. (For Freud's sketches of the adult mind, see 1923, p. 14; 1933, p. 111.)

The diagrams, based on Freud's opinions about the course of personality development in the Western industrialized society he knew best, sketch the anatomy of the mind at three age levels—one month, three years, and twelve years.

Shortly after birth the mind of the newborn in Freud's system is nearly all unconscious, with the unconscious dominated by the instinctual urges arising from the core of the id. Indeed, throughout life the commanding functionary in the unconscious is the id, operating on the pleasure principle without regard for the rules of the outside world. At this beginning stage of life the ego, as arbitrator between instinctual demands and the realities of the outside world, is as yet very small and weak. Only a tiny part of the ego can properly be called conscious, for the young infant has but an embryonic, vague awareness of its existence.

When we identify the ego as the operative of the personality that takes action in the real world to expend instinctual energy from the id, then it is reasonable to assume that the predominant portion of the ego shortly after birth must be preconscious and/or unconscious. This assumption is based on the observation that most—or perhaps all—behavior of the newborn is performed without conscious intent. The neonate does not have to decide

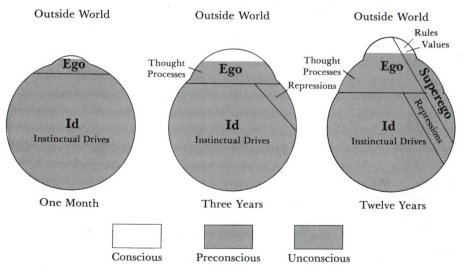

Figure 6.1 Developmental Trends in the Structure of the Mind

to make the heart beat, the lungs breathe, the lips suck, the eyelids close under strong light, or the arms and legs wiggle. These are all done automatically. But as time passes, the internal maturation of the neural system and sensations from the outside world press the infant to become increasingly aware of what possible actions may fulfill needs arising from the unconscious sources. The child also becomes more skilled in choosing from among these possibilities those acts that are likely to bring the greatest satisfaction at the least expense in terms of pain. In short, the reality principle on which the ego operates begins to guide more of the infant's behavior.

By age 3 the child's transactions with the world have improved the clarity of consciousness and greatly expanded the area of the preconscious. At this point we can identify more precisely the characteristics of the conscious and the preconscious and describe their interactions.

The conscious—sometimes called the *system perceptual conscious*—is what the individual is attending to at the moment. It is what we are presently aware of seeing, hearing, feeling, or thinking about. The conscious is the outermost surface of the mental apparatus, the part in immediate contact with the outside world. The conscious is the nucleus of the ego (Freud, 1923, pp. 9, 18).

The images or ideas on which our attention is focused at the moment are limited in number and scope. We cannot keep many things in consciousness at one time. Rather, the images are like a sequence of individual pictures; each appears momentarily, then shifts in form or passes by to make way for the next. This notion of the kaleidoscopic nature of the conscious is reflected in the phrase *stream of consciousness*. However, once the images pass, they are not gone forever. Either we can purposely bring them to mind again by recalling them to the stage of consciousness, or else they may intrude from without (as sense impressions on the eyes and ears from sources in the environment) or extrude from within (as thoughts and feelings that rise into our awareness from we know not where). However, whether from an outside or an inside source, these things that catch our attention must have one characteristic: They must be *perceptible*. They must assume a recognizable form as an image or a verbal symbol or word construction. In other words, amorphous, raw sensations from one's unconscious cannot be perceived until they are cast either as *mental images* (pictorial or auditory forms as in dreams) or as *verbal symbols* or *word presentations* (words, phrases, and sentences that have been attached to sensations recorded from the outside world).

Functions of the Preconscious   With this logic in mind, let us consider the reasons why Freud postulated the existence of a *preconscious* as an intermediary between the conscious and the unconscious. Freud envisioned the unconscious (chiefly the domain of the id) as the receptacle for instinctual energy, for ill-defined needs and urges. But he also needed a receptacle for material that was not in the mind at the moment but that could be recalled at will. So, as the storage area for memory traces of conscious perceptions from the past, for material not at the moment "conscious" but yet available to be retrieved if desired, he created the preconscious. Whereas the unconscious was pictured mainly as the operating arena for the id, the preconscious was described as basically under control of the ego.

In addition to being the storage area for retrievable memory traces, the preconscious was pictured as the processing chamber in which the ego receives amorphous urges from the id and recasts them into the image or verbal form required for their perception by the conscious ego. Recall that before the conscious ego can find ways to satisfy inner needs through trafficking in the real world, the needs must be put into perceptible shape. Freud proposed that this act of translating was performed by preconscious molding procedures that "we may—roughly and inexactly—sum up under the name of thought-processes" (Freud, 1923, pp. 9–10). It seems likely that what he meant by *thought-processes* are those mental acts known as analyzing, synthesizing, denoting, identifying, evaluating, and such.

In speaking of things arising from the unconscious and seeking expression, Freud distinguished between the route taken by ideas and the route taken by feelings. While ideas need to be processed by the preconscious, clothed by it in the recognizable raiment of familiar images or word presentations before they can appear in consciousness, feelings do not. Rather, they are emitted directly into consciousness from the unconscious (Freud, 1923, pp. 12–13).

Having identified the conscious and preconscious roles performed by the ego, we can now understand more clearly the differences between the mental maps for the one-month-old and three-year-old in Figure 6.1. The neonate's preconscious barely, if at all, exists, and the conscious is very limited in scope and clarity. But by age 3 the conscious is more extensive and acute, and the preconscious is far larger, in the sense of containing rapidly increasing numbers of memory traces drawn from experiences in the world. Furthermore, the preconscious has acquired certain of its contents—particularly its thought processes—from the unconscious. As the hypothetical twelve-year-old mind also illustrates, this trend of the preconscious becoming more complex over the years continues throughout the period of child and adolescent development. Greater internal maturation of the neural system interacts with more and more experiences in the outside world to produce more memory traces and more sophisticated thought processes.

The Dynamics of Repression   A comparison of the diagrams of the one-month-old and three-year-old minds also shows that the ego has now added something of its own to the unconscious. This something consists of psychologically painful thoughts that have been repressed into an unconscious condition by the ego because it found them too unbearable to maintain in consciousness or preconsciousness but did not know how to eliminate or solve them in a satisfactory conscious manner. We assume that these repressed materials at age 3 are seated in anxieties that arose during the oral and anal stages (from birth through about ages 2–3) from conflicts with the parents. For example, in Freud's view parents' unreasonable and often harsh demands for bowel and bladder control when the child is not yet ready for such control can cause the child to feel inadequate and to fear the loss of parental love. Since the child's weak ego cannot solve the conflict on the conscious level, the ego frantically relegates the painful events to the unconscious. And, as the diagram of the twelve-year-old mind suggests, we can assume that the amount of repressed material will increase by that age due to the psychic conflicts experienced during the Oedipal period around ages 3 to 5 and thereafter.

In summary, then, throughout the early years of life, the child's conscious grows in clarity, and the ego builds up a supply center of recallable memories from past perceptions, memories deposited in an expanding preconscious. At the same time, particularly painful problems that the immature ego is ill prepared to master are pushed out of consciousness to be actively held in the unconscious by means of energy borrowed from the id. The supply of psychic energy available for conducting conscious and preconscious affairs is thus depleted by this diverting of energy for purposes of repression. Furthermore, as noted earlier, such repressed problems are really postponed rather than solved, for they continue to seethe and to express themselves out of the unconscious in deviant ways, such as neuroses.

The third diagram, the hypothetical twelve-year-old mind, also shows the new functionary, the superego, which has grown out of the ego during the Oedipal period of middle childhood. Freud proposed that the superego starts developing around age 3, or perhaps slightly earlier, in which case a sliver of its influence could have been included in the diagram of the three-year-old mind. The superego at the conscious and preconscious levels appears as the set of conscious values or rules of living that guide the older child's behavior even when parents, teachers, and police are not present. But the existence in the adolescent's psyche of free-floating anxiety and of vague feelings of guilt and shame that are not attached to any particular event suggests that the superego has an unconscious aspect as well. In effect, the older child or adolescent can "feel bad" without knowing why. This means, in Freud's scheme, that the youth has incorporated into her personality certain parental expectations that she does not consciously recognize. Apparently these expectations or standards are ones associated with traumatic early experiences that have since been repressed.

Thus, as the child grows up, the relationships among levels of consciousness and the psychic operatives (id, ego, and superego) shift so that the child gains increasing control over his fate. At the same time, he is victimized by repressions that sap his psychic energy, divert his attention from reasonable conscious action, and cause distressing, illogical thoughts and behavior.

Developing Ego Strength

Closely tied to the processes I have just described is the matter of developing a strong ego. Although Freud did not describe ego strength in exactly the terms used here, it seems reasonable to assume, from all he wrote about the ego, that the following definition faithfully reflects his opinion: A strong ego is one that has at its command sufficient adjustment techniques to: (1) fulfill the id's instinctual needs without neglecting or unduly postponing any need and, at the same time, (2) satisfy the expectations imposed on the individual by both (a) the physical and social environments and (b) the individual's superego.

A weak ego, in contrast, is one that lacks sufficient conscious methods of expending instinctual energy that are acceptable to the environment and superego. A weak ego, faced by conflicting demands that it cannot consciously satisfy, reverts to its emergency technique of repression. Consequently, the weaker a person's ego, the more repressions we can expect to accumulate in the unconscious to plague him—unless, of course, some outside agent, such as a parent or other caretaker, intervenes to reduce the number of demands pressed upon the ego from the environment. It is in this matter of intervention that Freud's concept of ego strength bears important implications for child-raising practices.

The newborn's ego is very weak. It has only a few, simplistic methods for arbitrating the conflict between id demands and environmental requirements. The child will require far greater neural maturation and experience with the world to develop the broad array of sophisticated adjustment methods that mark the strong ego. If the neonate is to survive and is to avoid storing up a dangerous cargo of repressions to bear through life, she requires a lot of outside help from parents and others. Although there is nothing these outside agents can do to control the instinctual drives arising from the id, they can do something about the environment. Their aid in reducing the weak ego's burden of decisions can take two general forms. First, parents can provide the infant with certain things that she cannot obtain by herself, such as food and warmth. They can also furnish, in gradual steps, opportunities for the child to exercise her body and her perceptual system so that she learns to comprehend and act on her world in increasingly effective ways. Second, parents can protect the infant from intense stimuli that could overwhelm her perceptual capacities, stimuli that frighten her because she cannot understand or control them. Examples of such stimuli are loud noises, flashes of light, loss of support so the child suddenly drops, angry arguments and fights, and the like. But perhaps even more important is the parental role of protecting the young child from societal expectations that are beyond the child's capacity to fulfill. It was in relation to this role that Freud particularly criticized European child-rearing practices of his day. He felt that since nothing could be done to lessen the instinctual-drive demands on the weak ego, it was necessary for society to permit these drives freer direct expression in the early years of life instead of strictly censoring such expression.

> From a biological standpoint the ego comes to grief over the task of mastering the excitations of the early sexual period, at a time when its immaturity makes it incompetent to do so. It is in this lagging of ego development behind libidinal development that we see the essential precondition of neurosis; and we cannot escape the conclusion that neuroses could be avoided if the childish ego were spared this task—if, that is to say, the child's sexual life were allowed free play, as happens among many primitive peoples (Freud, 1938, p. 57).

While Freud proposed that fewer repressions and subsequent neuroses would develop if sexual urges (including sucking and biting in the oral stage and bowel and urinary activities in the anal stage) were allowed "free play," he proposed as well that civilization as we know it would not have developed under such free-expression conditions. He believed that the early "damming up" of the sexual instinct forced the growing child and subsequently the adult to redirect at least a portion of this energy into other channels through the adjustment technique of sublimation. This redirecting or sublimating process, he felt, caused many of the developments of our culture, since diverted libido was put to the task of fueling inventions, art works, literary creations, social service, and the like (Freud, 1938, p. 58). So in this sense, the variegated culture that we enjoy has been paid for, at least partially, by repressions by a weak ego early in life.

What, then, does all this mean for parents and other caretakers who wish to guide child growth in ways that promote the development of a strong ego and keep at a minimum repressions that will cause distressing neurotic symptoms? The answer, from a psychoanalytic viewpoint, consists of five principles. Both actual parents and surrogate parents should:

1. Recognize the nature of instinctual urges and accept the desirability of permitting expression of the urges.

2. Recognize the normal psychosexual stages of development and the sorts of conflicts the child faces at each stage.

3. Provide at each developmental stage enough opportunities for the child to satisfy instinctual drives within an atmosphere of understanding, but not furnish so much satisfaction that the child becomes fixated at that point and is unwilling to move ahead to the next stage.

4. Furnish plenty of nurture and protection to the infant in the early years so that the child's weak ego is not overwhelmed by the physical environment and societal standards.

5. As time passes, provide increasing amounts of guidance (teaching) in problem solving so that the ego develops an ever-expanding repertoire of conscious adjustment techniques to fill all kinds of instinctual demands under all sorts of environmental conditions.

In summary, the theory Freud devised to explain the origins of adult neuroses yielded, as a by-product, a number of general principles for guiding the normal personality development of children at all stages of the growth process, including the development of a strong ego.

Now that we have considered key elements of Freud's model of child development, we will look briefly at the sorts of contributions his daughter Anna made to his work.

ANNA FREUD'S PSYCHOANALYSIS OF CHILDREN

Sigmund Freud's model of child development was not constructed from direct observations of children. It was fashioned from the free associations and dreams of the neurotic adults he treated. However, Freud's daughter Anna (1895–1982) spent a major part of her adult life as a psychoanalyst working directly with children. She was a rather strict adherent of her father's theory, but she found it desirable to clarify and embellish certain aspects of it on the basis of her experience treating childhood neuroses. Her additions to Freudian theory were not published as a single, comprehensive treatise, but appeared instead as occasional articles and speeches over a period of forty years, from the 1920s to the mid-1960s. These scattered works have since been brought together in five volumes as *The Writings of Anna Freud* (1974).

The kinds of contributions she made can be illustrated with three examples; these concern: (1) the psychoanalytic treatment of a child while his or her superego is still being formed, (2) the value of direct observations of children, and (3) implications of psychoanalysis for raising the normal child.

Status of the Superego

Like her father, Anna Freud explained that many adult neuroses result from an overly punitive superego. It is the task of the psychoanalyst to help the patient reorganize the contents of the superego so they fit reality more adequately and do not pose unreasonable standards to which the individual is forced to aspire. In the adult neurotic, this rebuilding task is long and painful, for the superego has, since the time of early adolescence, become a powerful component of the personality, highly resistant to alterations. But in the older child or early adolescent, the superego is yet in the process of formation. The child is still in a state of transition between (1) receiving orders or values from her or his parents or parent figures and (2) receiving orders from the evolving superego, which has not yet separated from either the ego or its external sources (parents, peers, teachers).

Adult psychoanalysis need involve only the patient and the analyst. However, in Anna Freud's opinion, childhood neuroses are best treated by the analyst working both with the child and with such important agents of his environment as parents and teachers. By changing parents' expectations for, and treatment of, the child, the analyst hopes to influence the contents of the as-yet-dependent superego and cure the neurosis with greator speed than would be possible in an adult, whose overly demanding superego has already solidified. Thus the analyst who works with children manipulates the environment in addition to re-forming the relationships within the child's personality among the id, ego, and superego (A. Freud, 1974, vol. I, pp. 57–58).

Direct Observations of Children

In adult psychoanalysis, the source of the therapist's information is almost exclusively the patient's talk about herself. However, children are not as adept at explaining, upon command, their past history, worries, and fantasies. Thus Anna Freud recommended that in child analysis dream interpretation should be supplemented with information provided by the child's family and by the therapist's observations of the child's actions. By noting patterns of feeding, sleep, illness, play, and the like, the analyst can select aspects of behavior that, according to psychoanalytic theory, grew out of the earlier oral, anal, and infantile-genital periods. Therefore in child analysis certain types of observations can serve as substitutes for the free-association data on which the analysis of adults' psychological problems is usually founded (A. Freud, 1974, vol. V, pp. 95–101).

Psychoanalysis and Child-Rearing Practices

In 1956 Anna Freud stated, "While we are unable to alter the innate givens of a human being, we may be in the position to relieve some of the external pressures which interact with them" (1974, vol. V, pp. 265–266). She believed that psychoanalytic theory could make a major contribution toward the relief of such external pressures by helping parents gain "insight into the potential harm done to young children during the critical years of their development by the manner in which their needs, drives, wishes, and emotional dependencies are met" (1974, vol. V, p. 266). She then explained that the types of help psychoanalysis had already provided included: (1) the sexual enlightenment of children, (2) recognition of the role of conflict, conscience, and anxiety in the development of the child—a recognition that resulted in parents' limiting their authority over the child, (3) freedom for the child to express aggression, (4) recognition of the importance of the mother-infant relationship, and (5) an understanding of the mother's role as an auxiliary ego for the growing child.

In summary, Anna Freud extended psychoanalytic theory by adding to it a variety of conclusions she extracted from her direct observations of, and therapy sessions with, children at several stages of their development.

PRACTICAL APPLICATIONS

Freudian theory has been applied to the treatment of children in at least three major ways—in general child-rearing practices, in schooling at the early childhood level, and in modes of therapy.

Over the past few decades, psychoanalytic suggestions have exerted substantial influence on the child-rearing views of "concerned and well-read" adults, especially in Europe and America. These suggestions have focused on children's emotional needs, particularly in the areas of sex and aggression, and on such concepts as unconscious motivation. For instance, from the Freudian proposals about the oral stage comes the recommendation that infants be given plenty of opportunities to be cuddled and to satisfy their sucking needs, especially at feeding times. From beliefs about the anal phase comes the recommendation that toilet training should not be attempted too early, nor should it be enforced in a punitive fashion. Furthermore, toilet training should not be accompanied by distressing emotional outbursts from parents or even by half-disguised expressions of disgust, which the child interprets as threats of the withdrawal of parents' love if the child does not perform how, when, and where the parents desire. There are also suggestions about how adults can best react to children's sexual curiosity during the years of childhood and adolescence. And from Freud's proposals about unconscious motivation, parents have increasingly come to expect that a child may not be aware of the true reasons he acts as he does because the stimuli for the acts may be repressed intentions. Thus, when the child is asked to explain why he has acted in a given manner, the reasons he offers may simply be rationalizations, that is, socially acceptable explanations for behavior that actually derives from ignoble motives.

In the realm of formal education, nursery school and kindergarten practice in particular has been influenced by Freudian beliefs about sexual curiosity, nontraumatic toilet training, the symbolic meaning of children's play with water and such messy substances as mud and finger paints, children's needs for such physical contact as hugging and stroking, their inquisitiveness about the usually hidden body parts of the opposite sex, and the importance of teachers as role models with whom the child may identify.

Techniques of psychotherapy for disturbed children have also been strongly affected by psychoanalytic theory. In order to understand the dynamics of interaction among members of the child's family, therapists provide dolls that can represent family members and then interpret in psychoanalytic terms the child's dramatic play with the dolls. In other cases the child is asked to draw a picture of her family and to talk about the relationships among the members and how she feels about them. Furthermore, children's use of such play materials as punching bags and wet clay has been interpreted as revealing the sources of a disturbed child's shame, hate, distrust, or fear. Use of such materials has also been judged of cathartic value, relieving in socially acceptable ways the child's pent-up distress.

FREUDIAN THEORY: AN ASSESSMENT

My assessment of psychoanalytic theory in terms of the nine appraisal standards is given on the accompanying rating scale. My explanation for these ratings begins with the item I rated the highest and then moves to those I rated lower.

There can be little doubt that Freudian theory deserves high marks for its success in stimulating new discoveries (item 8). It has been the basis for hundreds of articles reporting clinical studies of children's development.

usually in the form of analyses of deviant types of development. It has also motivated investigators to launch new journals dedicated entirely to psychoanalytic topics and to write scores of books that offer extensions, embellishments, or revisions of the theory. Especially during the decades of its greatest popularity (the 1940s into the early 1960s), the Freudian model furnished numerous ideas for investigations by experimental psychologists, including such prominent behaviorists as J. Dollard and N. E. Miller (1950) and R. Sears, L. Rau, and R. Alpert (1965).* Even though the enthusiasm for psychoanalytic theory among psychologists has dampened since the scheme's heyday, there still continues to be lively interest in the theory, an interest that has stimulated a regular output of clinical and experimental investigations, new interpretations, and debate. For the seven-year period between early 1983 into 1990, *Psychological Abstracts* cites 4,567 journal articles on psychoanalysis, with 45 of them on child psychoanalysis and 18 more on child development issues.

The second highest rating, on item 4, is my estimate of the substantial influence psychoanalytic suggestions have exerted on the child-rearing views as summarized above under practical applications. Frequently, specific beliefs about child raising derived from Freudian theory appear as topics in both professional and popular publications and in the mass media.

However, although psychoanalytic theory offers guidance for handling children's emotional growth, it offers little or no help for directing children's academic (cognitive) development or physical growth, except in cases of physical ailments suspected of having a psychological origin. The rating on item 4, therefore, is a balance between Freudian suggestions about emotional development and a lack of suggestions about cognitive and physical growth.

As for the theory's clarity (item 2), I estimate that it deserves a mark slightly above the middle of the scale. Freudians explain the system's main components rather clearly, I feel, at least in general. And Freud's practice of illustrating these components with examples from cases of people undergoing psychoanalysis helps communicate what he intends. But when we move beyond the basic outline of the theory's structure, many puzzles appear, calling for greater clarification. As one illustration of confusion, E. Nagel has complained that the Freudian:

> Sometimes describes the main theoretical components of the mental apparatus as "units of functions," and suggests that unconscious drives are like dispositions. But he also declares that these components possess

---

*For summaries of experimental studies, see Frenkel-Brunswik (1954), Hilgard (1952), Holt (1989), and Kris (1947).

Freudian Theory

How well do I think the theory meets the standards?

The Standards	Very Well	Moderately Well	Very Poorly
1. Reflects the real world of children		X	
2. Is clearly understandable		X	
3. Explains the past and predicts the future	Specificity X		Accuracy ?
4. Guides child rearing		X	
5. Is internally consistent		X	
6. Is economical		X	
7. Is falsifiable			X
8. Stimulates new discoveries	X		
9. Is self-satisfying		X	

> energies and conflict with one another—though without explaining in what sense functions can be charged with energies or dispositions can be engaged in conflicts (1959, p. 46).

In short, when we inspect the psychoanalytic model of child development in detail, we find it can profit from a good deal of additional clarification.

The issue of clarity is also related to item 1 (reflects real world of children), which I have rated slightly below the center. I believe that in Freud's favor are his (1) bringing to public view the importance and commonality of sexual interests in childhood and adolescence, (2) identifying defense mechanisms children develop, (3) describing children's ambivalent feelings—hate combined with love—toward parents and others close to them, and similar proposals. Observations of children's behavior would appear to substantiate these findings as phenomena in real children's lives (Hilgard, 1952).

But balanced against such items, which are confirmable by direct observation or assessment, is a large portion of Freudian theory that has not been substantiated in such an open or public manner. Some critics have been particularly blunt in their charges that psychoanalysts have failed to conduct the investigations that will convincingly test the theory's proposals. M. Scriven has written that:

> As a set of hypotheses it was a great achievement 50 years ago; as no more than a set of hypotheses it is a great disgrace today. . . . It is in fact the most sophisticated form of metaphysics ever to enjoy support as a scientific theory (1959, pp. 226–227).

Part of the difficulty with Freud's model as an accurate reflector of real children's development lies in the source of data on which he founded his theory. He did not directly observe, test, or measure children during their years of growth, as did many other theorists. Actually, there were at least four somewhat "slippery" steps between his data and the growing child. That is, his process of collecting data during therapy sessions with neurotic adults involved: (step 1) the analyst's *interpreting* from his viewpoint or through his "lens" (step 2) ostensibly *symbolic* material derived from (step 3) reported *dreams* and *memories* of neurotics about (step 4) *ostensible experiences* from their childhood one or more decades earlier. In view of this mode of gathering information, the theory's data base might be a distortion of typical children's actions, thoughts, and emotions during each phase of growing up. I am skeptical about how well it represents real children's development, and I share the opinion of those critics who ask that the Freudian model be supported more adequately with publicly verifiable evidence.

Probably the main reason psychoanalytic theory has been difficult either to verify or to refute is not that its adherents are stubbornly defensive or are inept researchers (though in some instances this may be the case), but that many of its key elements, including the unconscious, repression, reaction formation, and symbolism, seem to render it nonfalsifiable. These elements have caused critics to harbor "the suspicion that Freudian theory can always be so manipulated that it escapes refutation no matter what the well-established facts may be" (Nagel, 1959, p. 44). Since I share this suspicion, I have rated psychoanalysis at the bottom on item 7 (falsifiability).

Imagine that we wish to check the validity of the concept of the Oedipus conflict, and will do so by interviewing adolescents about the sexual ideas they had during their earlier childhood years. If the adolescents' answers corroborate the notion that the father–daughter, mother–son "family romance" is widely spread, we might consider these answers as evidence supporting the Oedipus-complex concept. But let us say that we get just the opposite results from our interviews. The adolescents, seeking to be as truthful as possible, rarely have any memories of Oedipal strivings. Can we then interpret this as evidence against the notion of a universal Oedipus conflict? Freudians would say no. They would contend, instead, that the negative responses show that the earlier sexual urges have been repressed into the unconscious, so the adolescents' denial of such thoughts is proof of both the Oedipus complex and of the defense mechanism of repression. Under these conditions, there is no way to test the validity of the Oedipus concept through the retrospective interview that Freudians use as the source of evidence about how children develop.

The concept of reaction formation poses the same problem for assessing the theory. Reaction formation is the defense mechanism that occurs when a person is driven by an urge or wish (id) that conflicts with her moral values (superego), and to solve the conflict she (ego) represses the urge and behaves as if her motives were just the opposite. A child's overt sex play is seen as direct evidence of the proposed libidinal energy. But the opposite behavior—puritanical avoidance of sex—is interpreted as an expression of exactly the same libidinal or sexual energy but expressed through the mechanism of *reaction formation*. Likewise, both the child who habitually fights (displaying direct aggression) and the one who is the habitual pacifist (showing reaction formation) are seen as driven by the same aggressive urge (death instinct). Once more, an appraiser of the theory is at a loss in deciding how to handle a model that derives identical conclusions from diametrically opposed data.

The role of symbols in Freud's scheme presents other puzzles. Freud proposed that a person's ego, in cooperation with the superego, censors repressed material that seeks to arise from the unconscious into consciousness. But he also said that repressed wishes can sneak past the censor in disguise, that is, in symbolic form. For instance, I noted in Chapter One that Freud considered any elongated, projectile-shaped object that appeared in a dream to be a symbol of the male penis. An open, containerlike object symbolized the female vagina (Freud, 1900). In a similar fashion, Freud interpreted many other images from dreams as symbols, rather than as direct descriptions, of events in people's daily lives. So Freudians, with this notion of symbolism in their analytic armory, can interpret all sorts of thoughts that people express as support for their theory.

So, Freud's model of child development and personality structure may be correct, but the game of verification is unmanageable if it must be played with the elastic ground rules permitted by the inclusion of such concepts as the above. The fairly low mark given for item 5 (internal consistency) is also primarily a result of these considerations.

On item 6, whether the theory is economical, I have marked Freud's theory near the middle. While some aspects of his model appear to be direct, economical ways to explain the phenomena on which he focuses, others appear to me unduly complex. There should be simpler ways to account for the phenomena in question. For instance, there should be less confusing and simpler ways to account for fixations than to claim that they are caused by both over- and undersatisfaction of needs at a given psychosexual stage. Furthermore, there should be simpler ways to account for the prepuberal child's personal-social behavior than the Oedipus complex that Freud proposed. This is not to say Freud is wrong, but the same phenomena can be attributed to simpler sets of factors.

The difficulty experienced in giving a reasonable rating on item 3 (explains the past and predicts the future) is reflected by the two marks on the line. The mark for specificity is at the high end of the scale, principally because Freudian explanations of what psychosexual events occurred earlier in an individual's life, and why they occurred, are quite specific. Psychoanalysis emphasizes the past history of development as uncovered through free association and dream interpretation. But psychoanalytic predictions of the future are usually sketched in a more general way, often in terms of possible deviant development that might occur if the child's needs during upcoming psychosexual stages are not dealt with wisely by the adults who most affect the child's life. In consideration of the theory's very specific explanations of the past and more general predictions of the future, I have marked it relatively high for *specificity*.

However, *accuracy* of explanation and prediction is quite a different matter. For the sorts of reasons given in the discussion of falsifiability I am skeptical about the validity of explanations founded on the theory. On the basis of this skepticism, I have used a question mark as a rating in the lower range of item 3. The theory needs better validation.

Finally we come to the self-satisfying quality of Freud's model (item 9). In the case of psychoanalytic theory, this ninth standard is of particular importance because Freud's proposals have depended so heavily on personal affirmation for their acceptance. By *personal affirmation* I mean the "feeling" that psychoanalytic theory does indeed describe the way one's personality evolves and functions. Or as S. Hook has noted (1959, p. 213), some Freudians' response to criticism has been that "psychoanalysis may be unscientific, but it is true." And to some degree I must admit to sharing such a feeling. Despite the shortcomings of Freudian theory when judged against common scientific criteria like the foregoing standards, much of the theory makes a kind of existential sense to me. I believe in the unconscious, in repression, in our use of defense mechanisms, and in many other concepts the theory includes. But I remain skeptical about still other aspects of the model. For these reasons, I have rated it in the middle of the scale for item 9.

FOR FURTHER READING

The first two books are paperbacks offering concise, simplified, and accurate accounts of psychoanalytic theory.

Hall, C. S. (1954) *A Primer of Freudian Psychology.* New York: World. This is a systematic description of psychoanalysis as a theory of personality development. Hall has based his account on material drawn from a variety of Freud's writings.

Stafford-Clark, D. (1967) *What Freud Really Said.* London: Penguin. A description of the evolution of Freud's ideas, including summaries of several of his most significant publications.

The next two items are translations of Freud's own writings. The first of these is a seventy-five-page summary of psychoanalytic theory written near the close of his career. The second is a thirty-volume edition of his complete works, useful for its detail and for the picture it offers of Freud's revisions over a period of nearly five decades.

Freud, S. (1938) *An Outline of Psychoanalysis.* London: Hogarth, 1973.

Freud, S. (1964) *The Standard Edition of the Complete Psychological Works of Sigmund Freud.* James Strachey, translator and editor. London: Hogarth. In thirty volumes.

The most complete source of Anna Freud's works is the following collection:

Freud, A. (1974) *The Writings of Anna Freud.* New York: International Universities Press. In five volumes.

Recent assessments of Freudian tradition are found in:

Anthony, E. J. (1986) "The Contributions of Child Psychoanalysis to Psychoanalysis." *Psychoanalytic Study of the Child,* Vol. 41, pp. 61–87. A summary of Anna and Sigmund Freud's views about such contributions.

Holt, R. F. (1989) *Freud Reappraised: A Fresh Look at Psychoanalytic Theory.* New York: Guilford.

CHAPTER SEVEN

Erikson's Variation on Freud's Theme

Erik Homburger Erikson (born 1902) is a German-born psychoanalyst whose self-imposed mission has been to extend and refine Freud's notions of personality development, with particular attention to child development.

Three of the most significant features of Erikson's refinement have been his proposals regarding:

1. The development of the *healthy personality,* in contrast to Freud's emphasis on the growth and cure of neurotic behavior.

2. The process of socializing the child into a particular culture by passage through a series of innately determined *psychosocial stages* that parallel Freud's psychosexual stages.

3. The individual's task of achieving *ego identity* by means of solving specified identity crises at each psychosocial stage of growth.

Erikson's professional career began in Vienna, where he graduated from the Vienna Psychoanalytic Institute before coming to the United States in 1933. He entered clinical practice in the United States, became a citizen in 1939, and over a period of four decades made significant contributions to the literature on psychoanalysis, personality theory, educational practice, and social anthropology.

Much of Freud's theory—the existence and nature of the unconscious, the tripartite composition of the mind (id, ego, superego), psychosexual stages, and more—was accepted by Erikson as valid. Since he accepted these concepts, Erikson wrote relatively little about them. Instead, he centered his work on those facets of psychoanalytic theory he believed required extension and, to some degree, revision. In discussing Erikson's contributions, I concentrate on the key additions he proposed, not on his entire system of beliefs. These additions are: (1) the nature of a healthy personality and of ego identity, (2) the epigenetic principle, and (3) stages of psychosocial growth and the identity crises. Finally, there is an assessment of Erikson's ideas from the viewpoint of someone who works with children and is interested in theory construction.

EGO IDENTITY AND
THE HEALTHY PERSONALITY

Erikson agreed with those critics of Freud who claimed that Freud had focused only on neurotic personalities and, in consequence, had neglected to define the nature of healthy personalities or to trace their pattern of development. Erikson sought to right this imbalance, and he began by identifying the characteristics of the healthy personality. These characteristics would be the goals and signs of desirable human development.

One statement of such characteristics that Erikson found suitable was that of Marie Jahoda, an American psychologist who believed that a healthy personality *actively masters* the environment, shows a certain *unity of personality,* and is able to *perceive* the world and self *correctly* (Erikson, 1968, p. 92). The newborn child displays none of these characteristics. The healthiest adult personality displays them all. Thus, in Erikson's view, "childhood is defined by [the characteristics'] initial absence and by their gradual development in complex steps of increasing differentiation" (1968, p. 92).

Phrased in a different way, "growing up" is a process of achieving *ego identity.* In Erikson's system, ego identity has two aspects. The first or inner-focused aspect is the person's recognition of his own unified "selfsameness and continuity in time" (Erikson, 1959, p. 23). It is knowing and accepting oneself. The second or outer-focused aspect is the individual's recognition of and identification with the ideals and essential pattern of his culture; it includes sharing "some kind of essential character with others" (Erikson, 1968, p. 104). The person who has attained ego identity has a clear picture and an acceptance of both his inner essence and the group culture in which he lives.

Since, in Erikson's view, human development consists of moving from nonego identity to ego identity, his picture of the developmental process features a description of "conflicts, inner and outer, which the vital personality weathers, re-emerging from each crisis with an increased sense of inner unity, with an increase of good judgment, and an increase in the capacity 'to do well' according to his own standards and to the standards of those who are significant to him" (Erikson, 1968, p. 92).

THE EPIGENETIC PRINCIPLE

Studies of the development of the human organism while it is still in the mother's womb have suggested that it develops from a single fertilized cell and follows the same general stages as all human organisms, until, after about nine months, a highly complex, multicellular baby with many differentiated but coordinated parts is born. The entire pattern of development, it is believed, is governed by a genetic structure common to all humans. In other words, the genes establish a construction plan and timetable for the development of each part.

Studies of physical development after birth suggest that the genetic plan does not stop with birth. Rather, the sequence of development of such skills as crawling and walking and such characteristics as adolescent breast growth in girls and facial hair in boys has been established by the genetic plan. These characteristics arise at a particular time in life according to a preestablished time schedule that is little affected by environmental influences.

The term *epigenetic principle* has been given to this belief that everything that grows is governed by a preset construction plan: "Out of this ground plan the parts arise, each part having its time of special ascendency, until all parts have arisen to form a functioning whole" (Erikson, 1968, p. 92).

Many people have accepted the principle as a guide to understanding physical growth. But Erikson extended the principle to social and psychological growth as well, proposing that personality appears to develop also according to steps "predetermined in the human organism's readiness to be driven toward, to be aware of, and to interact with a widening radius of significant individuals and institutions" (1968, p. 93). He recognized that this interaction would be somewhat different from one culture to another since the different cultures in which children grow up can vary in many significant ways. However, he held that personality growth follows a sequence of "inner laws" that set the potentialities for the kinds of significant interactions the child will achieve with the people and institutions she does meet in her particular culture.

In short, Erikson proposed that it is the nature of the human species to pass through an identifiable series of psychosocial stages as the individual grows up, stages determined genetically, regardless of the culture in which the growth occurs. The social environment, however, does have a significant effect on the nature of the crises arising at each stage and on the success with which the child and adolescent will master the stage.

THE GRID OF PSYCHOSOCIAL STAGES

Erikson accepted Freud's set of psychosexual stages as a basically valid description of the key concerns of personality development from infancy to adulthood. However, Erikson felt that the Freudian formulation was incomplete in at least four respects.

First, he thought Freud gave too little recognition to the socialization of the child, particularly to the various patterns of behavior that different cultures consider desirable—patterns the child needs to adopt or adapt if he is to be given the approval of the group within which he grows up.

Second, Erikson believed there are stages of development after adolescence that Freud failed to recognize. Thus Erikson defined more clearly four additional levels from puberty and beyond.

Third, Erikson believed the interaction of the individual with her social environment produces a series of eight major *psychosocial crises* the individual must work through in order to achieve eventual ego identity and psychological health. Since Freud had not defined crises in a clear fashion, Erikson did so.*

Finally, Erikson believed that the concepts of development could be better understood if they were cast in the form of a grid or matrix; such a grid had not been employed by Freud. Erikson produced a number of such grids to clarify the interaction and correlation among various aspects of development. One of these "worksheets," as he called them, is produced in an adapted form as Table 7.1

Among Erikson's most significant additions to child development theory is his proposal that an individual undergoes eight psychosocial crises during development. These are listed in column A of Table 7.1. Each crisis or stage is phrased as a struggle between two opposite or conflicting personality characteristics. The trait of *trust* vies for dominance over *mistrust* in the infant's personality. At the next stage, the trait of *autonomy* struggles for ascendancy over *shame* and *doubt*. Six subsequent crises mark the next six stages of psychosocial growth to full ego identity or psychological maturity in the adult.

Although these conflicting traits or tendencies are cast in the form of absolutes, such as "absolute trust" versus "absolute mistrust," in reality they form graduated scales in the personality. Complete trust appears at one end of the scale line and complete mistrust at the other. Between these extremes are gradations that the individual may attain. In reality, no one reaches either extreme. Each personality represents some mixture of self-trust and mistrust, as well as some combination of trusting and mistrusting

*Note that Erikson's version of Freudian stages in Table 7.1 and Table 7.2 adds one stage to those described in Chapter Six. That is, Erikson inserted *puberty and adolescence* between Freud's *latency* and *mature genitality* stages, and he moved *mature genitality* from the later teen years into the twenties.

Table 7.1 A Psychosocial Development "Worksheet"

Stage Number	Column A Psychosocial Crisis	Column B Radius of Significant Relations	Column C Psychosocial Modalities	Column D Freud's Psychosexual Stages	Column E Approximate Ages in Years
I	Trust versus mistrust	Maternal person	To get To give in return	Oral-Respiratory, Sensory-Kinesthetic (Incorporative Modes)	0–1
II	Autonomy versus shame, doubt	Parental persons	To hold on To let go	Anal-Urethral, Muscular (Retentive-Eliminative)	2–3
III	Initiative versus guilt	Basic family	To make (going after) To "make like" (playing)	Infantile-Genital, Locomotor (Intrusive, Inclusive)	3–6
IV	Industry versus inferiority	"Neighborhood" and school	To make things (completing) To make things together	Latency	7–12 or so

Stage Number	Column A Psychosocial Crisis	Column B Radius of Significant Relations	Column C Psychosocial Modalities	Column D Freud's Psycho-sexual Stages	Column E Approximate Ages in Years
V	Identity and repudiation versus identity diffusion	Peer groups and outgroups; models of leadership	To be oneself (or not to be) To share being oneself	Puberty and Adolescence	12–18 or so
VI	Intimacy and solidarity versus isolation	Partners in friendship, sex, competition, cooperation	To lose and find oneself in another	Mature Genitality	The 20s
VII	Generativity versus self-absorption	Divided labor and shared household	To make be To take care of		Late 20s to 50s
VIII	Integrity versus despair	"Humankind" "My kind"	To be, through having been To face not being		50s and beyond

Adapted from Erikson, 1959, p. 166.

other people and the world in general. Consequently one way of describing the configuration of a given child's or adolescent's personality within Erikson's system would be to identify where, along each of these scale lines, the individual stands at any particular time.

Before we consider each of the stages in more detail, let's examine the other columns in Table 7.1 so the relationship between this material and the psychosocial crises is clear.

Column B of Table 7.1 lists the expanding circle of significant people with whom the growing child interacts. The particular crisis the child or adolescent faces at a given stage is worked out through interaction with the people or the social setting identified in column B as appropriate to the crisis.

Column C suggests those acts on which the growing child's attention concentrates at each crisis stage, and column D indicates which psychosexual step correlates with each act. Thus, during Freud's oral stage of earliest infancy, the baby concentrates on the acts (psychosocial modalities) of getting and giving in return. At the psychosexual stage of puberty, stage V, the young person concentrates on the acts of being oneself and sharing being oneself.

Keeping this worksheet in mind, we will consider in more detail the nature of Erikson's eight successive psychosocial crises or phases (Erikson, 1959, pp. 65–98).

Basic Trust versus Basic Mistrust

Erikson proposed that a sense of *trust*—being able to predict and depend upon one's own behavior and the behavior of others—is derived primarily from the experiences of the first year of life. In other words, a child's fundamental attitude about the dependability of the world is built chiefly on the relationship established as an infant during the oral or incorporative stage when feeding and mouthing objects is of prime importance. The most important person in the infant's life at this juncture is the mother or mother substitute. The particular point on the trust–mistrust scale that the child ultimately reaches will depend to a great extent on the quality of his relationship to the maternal figure during this first year out of the womb. If the infant's need for food, for exercising the lips and gums and the sucking mechanism, is frequently frustrated, the infant will begin life more toward the mistrust end of the scale. If the quality of affectional relationships at this time is poor, with the mother emotionally rejecting the baby while tending to its physical needs, the sense of trust will be damaged. This sets a poor foundation for the trust–mistrust ratio on which the child is to build the rest of his or her life.

As to how permanent the damage done at this early stage will be, Erikson said that the manner in which this first crisis, like the succeeding ones, is settled at the crisis period is not necessarily unalterable for the rest of the person's life. Damage to the sense of trust that occurs by an unsatisfactory infant-mother relationship during the first year of life can be repaired somewhat in later years by the child's enjoying a particularly trustworthy social environment. However, the damage will not be completely undone by later positive experiences. In like manner, an infant who establishes a secure attitude of trust during the first year may have this attitude shaken in later years by experience with undependable people who are significant to him. But he will still retain a measure of self-trust and feel a trust of others founded on his success in passing through the trust–mistrust crisis of infancy. This principle of the permanence of influences during a crisis period is valid as well for the other crises faced at subsequent stages of growth.

Autonomy versus Shame and Doubt

In parallel with Freud's psychosexual anal stage during the second year of life, Erikson proposed a second psychosocial crisis. This second stage is influenced by the child's maturing muscle system, with an increased ability to expel or retain things, particularly bodily wastes. Evacuating the bowels and bladder not only causes the child to feel good but gives her a growing sense of power through control over the evacuation system.

In Erikson's opinion, the child's new sense of power is the basis for his developing a sense of autonomy, of being able to do things for himself. At the same time he runs the risk of trying too much too soon and thereby attracting the censure of those around him. Thus during this period the child requires a delicate balance between (1) parental firmness that lets the child know he has a trustworthy world that will prevent him from overstepping the bounds and (2) parental flexibility and patience that allows him gradually to gain bowel and bladder control at a pace commensurate with his understanding and the conscious control of his sphincter muscles. If outer control is too rigid or too early, demanding he control bowel and bladder before he is able, the child will be faced with "a double rebellion and a double defeat" (Erikson, 1959, p. 68). He is powerless to manage his bowels and powerless to control his parents' actions. So he either seeks satisfaction by regressing to oral activities—sucking his thumb, whining, and demanding attention—or he fakes progression by becoming hostile and willful. He may pretend that he has achieved control by rejecting others' aid, even though he really lacks the ability to be so independent.

Erikson proposed that parents who impose strict bowel training on the two-year-old may influence the child to become an overcompulsive adult who is stingy and meticulous with love, energy, time, and money. This overcompulsive behavior is accompanied by a lasting sense of doubt and shame. In contrast, firm but gradual and kindly bowel training can aid the child in developing a sense of *self-control without loss of self-esteem* and produce an adult with a strong but socially acceptable sense of autonomy (Erikson, 1959, p. 68).

Initiative versus Guilt

During the fourth and fifth years of life, the child gains more skill in using language, in moving about, and in handling things. As a result, his imagination expands to encompass "so many things that he cannot avoid frightening himself with what he has dreamed and thought up. Nevertheless, out of all this he must emerge with a sense of *unbroken initiative* as a basis for a high and yet realistic sense of ambition and independence" (Erikson, 1959, p. 75).

This is the time of the Oedipus conflict, when the conscience develops and serves as a control on initiative. Fear of sexual impulses toward the opposite-sex parent causes feelings of guilt. In order to navigate through this period successfully, the child needs the guidance of parents and teachers who understand the trials the child is facing. Through such understanding, the important adults in the child's life can alleviate the hatred and guilt the child may feel. This permits the "peaceful cultivation of initiative, a truly free sense of enterprise" (Erikson, 1959, p. 82). The child's mental and physical skills, unfettered by overbearing guilt, permit her to go after life in a self-confident way.

Industry versus Inferiority

Throughout the Freudian latency period, in the years before puberty, the child wants to get busy with activities worth his attention and to pursue these activities with his peers. In Erikson's opinion, children during the elementary school years need and enjoy hours of make-believe games and play, but they become dissatisfied with too much of this and want to do something worthwhile. They want to earn recognition by producing something, to gain the satisfaction of completing work by perseverance.

If adults pose tasks for children that they can accomplish and that they recognize as interesting and worthy, and if the adults furnish the guidance needed for completing the tasks, then the children have a better chance to come through the latency period with a sound sense of industry. However, if the child has not solved the Oedipal conflict or if family life has not prepared him or her well for school life, the period can produce just the opposite—a sense of inadequacy and inferiority. Feelings of inferiority may also occur if the things the child has already learned to do well are considered insignificant by the teacher and classmates. Furthermore, in Erikson's opinion, the child may have potential abilities that, if not evoked and nurtured during latency, may "develop late or never" (1959, p. 87).

Identity versus Identity Diffusion

Of all the growth stages, the one on which Erikson focused the greatest attention in his writing is the period of adolescence, particularly the onset of adolescence. During the early teens, with the arrival of puberty, the body grows rapidly and changes in curious ways. These changes are disturbing to both girls and boys. Their social roles take on new form, and the views they held of themselves in childhood no longer fit their new appearance and their new feelings for the opposite sex. In addition, adults and peers adopt new expectations for them as they move from childhood into youth. The confusion this creates for the incipient adolescent has been labeled the *identity crisis* by Erikson.

During this period the results of earlier years' experiences should lead to a successful integration of the individual's basic drives with her or his physical and intellectual endowment and opportunities in life. In effect, the child's development over the first dozen or so years should now synthesize to give a sense of *ego identity* or self-definition.

> The sense of ego identity, then, is the accrued confidence that one's ability to maintain inner sameness and continuity is matched by the sameness and continuity of one's meaning for others. Thus, self-esteem . . . grows to be a conviction that one is learning effective steps toward a tangible future, that one is developing a defined personality within a social reality which one understands (Erikson, 1959, p. 89).

Furthermore, the young adolescent should gain an increasing strength of purpose and understanding of reality as she recognizes that her own way of dealing with life—her way of mastering reality—is a proper variant of the ways in which other people successfully deal with their lives.

The great danger of this period has been termed either *role confusion* or *identity diffusion* by Erikson (1963, p. 261; 1959, p. 92). The youth does not know who he is to himself or to others. As a defense against a sense of identity diffusion, adolescents may overidentify with heroes or cliques and with crowds and causes; they can temporarily lose their own individuality. They help one another during these years of confusion and of unclear

occupational direction by clustering together, by stereotyping themselves
in their clothes and speech, in their ideals, and in their idols and enemies.
They are frequently intolerant of others outside their clique. In search of
self, they often come into conflict with parents, siblings, and others close to
them while refighting "many of the battles of earlier years, even though to
do so they must artificially appoint perfectly well-meaning people to play
the roles of adversaries" (Erikson, 1963, p. 261).

Youths who solve the problems of the adolescent years come through
with a strong sense of their own individuality and a recognition that they
are acceptable to their society. Those who fail to work their way through
the identity crisis continue to display in later life such marks of immaturity
as intolerance, clannishness, cruel treatment of people who are "different,"
blind identification or loyalty to heroes and idols, and the like.

Three Adult Stages

With his description of the adolescent identity crisis, Erikson carried the
narrative of psychosocial development through the second decade of life.
However, unlike Freud, he did not stop at this point in describing personality growth. Rather, he added three more stages, depicting key conflicts
faced by adults in their early, middle, and later years. Since our chief
concern in this book is with growth through the teenage years, I will not
dwell on the three adult stages but will simply mention the nature of the
crises faced at those levels.

The transition from adolescence to adulthood is accompanied by the
crisis of *intimacy and distantiation versus self-absorption.* Or, phrased another
way, it is a crisis of intimacy and solidarity versus isolation. In Erikson's
view, the youth who emerges from adolescence with a reasonable sense of
her own identity is then prepared to establish a nonexploitative intimacy,
sexually and intellectually, with a companion of the opposite sex. The
youth whose identity is secure is also prepared to defend his or her rights
and individuality against attackers. This ability to defend oneself is termed
distantiation by Erikson. In his words, distantiation is the readiness to
"repudiate, to isolate, and if necessary to destroy those forces and people
whose essence seems dangerous to one's own" (1959, p. 95). Youths who
fail at this stage are unable to establish intimate relations with a companion,
so they retreat into self-absorption.

During the second adult stage, the psychosocial conflict involves
generativity versus stagnation (or generativity versus self-absorption). Sexual
partners who find true genitality (capacity for orgasmic potency with a love
partner of the opposite sex) wish to combine their personalities in producing and caring for offspring, a condition that Erikson labeled *generativity.*
Such partners are not simply absorbed in their own welfare.

In later years of adulthood the crisis involves *integrity versus despair and disgust*. The older person who achieves integrity is one who accepts his own life cycle and "is ready to defend the dignity of his own life style against all physical and economic threats" (Erikson, 1959, p. 98).

These, then, are the eight stages of development as conceived by Erikson in his theory of psychosocial periods. Since he introduced this scheme in 1959, he has periodically embellished it with additional propositions. For instance, in *Insight and Responsibility* (Erikson, 1964) he expanded his picture of positive ego development by describing a series of human *virtues,* which he identified as "qualities of strength."

> I . . . speak of Hope, Will, Purpose, and Competence as the rudiments of virtue developed in childhood; of Fidelity as the adolescent virtue; and of Love, Care, and Wisdom as the central virtues of adulthood (Erikson, 1964, pp. 113, 115).

These virtues, he said, are an expression of the integration of the psychosexual and psychosocial growth schedules. Each virtue has its particular time of arousal and emphasis in the hierarchy of epigenetic growth stages. For example, Erikson has postulated that the virtue of *hope* arises during early infancy, that of *will* around ages 2 and 3, and that of *purpose* in the preschool years of age 3 to 6. Furthermore, each virtue builds upon those that have developed before it. "Will cannot be trained until hope is secure, nor can love become reciprocal until fidelity has proven reliable" (Erikson, 1964, p. 115). The meanings assigned to these virtues by Erikson and their relationship to the psychosexual and psychosocial stages are displayed in Table 7.2.

Roles of Heredity and Environment   When a theorist suggests that such traits as hope, fidelity, and wisdom trace their essential development to specified age periods that are universal for all children, two questions arise about the theorist's beliefs concerning the roles of heredity and environment. First, does the theorist mean that all children inherit a time-schedule mechanism that preordains the sequence in which character traits evolve and the time when each trait becomes of primary developmental import? Second, does he mean that the actual form each trait assumes is inherited, and that, consequently, the child's social environment has little or no effect on the nature of the hope, fidelity, and wisdom that the child will display in her personality?

In response to these queries, Erikson would say yes to the first and no to the second. Yes, he does mean that the epigenetic principle establishes the sequence and the general time when particular psychosexual and

Table 7.2 Stages in the Development of Virtues

Stage Number	Column A *Freud's Psychosexual Stages*	Column B *Erikson's Psychosocial Crises*	Column C *Erikson's Virtues or Qualities of Strength*	Column D *Approximate Ages in Years*
I	Oral-respiratory	Trust versus mistrust	*Hope:* The enduring belief that fervent wishes can be fulfilled despite "the dark urges and rages which mark the beginning of existence"	0–1
II	Anal-urethral	Autonomy versus shame, doubt	*Will:* The constant determination to exercise both free choice and self-restraint, despite the shame and doubt experienced during infancy	2–3
III	Infantile-genital	Initiative versus guilt	*Purpose:* The "courage to envisage and pursue valued goals uninhibited by the defeat of infantile fantasies, by guilt and by the foiling fear of punishment"	3–6
IV	Latency	Industry versus inferiority	*Competence:* The free use of skill and intelligence in completing tasks, "unimpaired by infantile inferiority"	7–12 or so

Stage Number	Column A Freud's Psychosexual Stages	Column B Erikson's Psychosocial Crises	Column C Erikson's Virtues or Qualities of Strength	Column D Approximate Ages in Years
V	Puberty and adolescence	Identity and repudiation versus identity diffusion	*Fidelity*: Sustaining freely pledged loyalties despite contradictions in value systems	12–18 or so
VI	Mature genitality	Intimacy and solidarity versus isolation	*Love*: "Mutuality of devotion forever subduing the antagonisms inherent in divided function"	The 20s
VII		Generativity versus self-absorption	*Care*: Concern for obligations "generated by love, necessity, or accident"	Late 20s to 50s
VIII		Integrity versus despair	*Wisdom*: "Detached concern with life itself, in the face of death itself"	50s and beyond

Adapted from Erikson, 1964, pp. 115–134.

psychosocial concerns appear in center stage, demanding primary attention. But no, the form that a given trait assumes is not determined by the child's genetic nature. Instead, the way a psychosocial concern is resolved and the way the personality characteristics that the child or youth comes to display are formed depend on the way she or he interacts with the social institutions of the particular culture. So while Erikson postulates that the crucial time for the development of hope arises during infancy for all people, he says that the degree of hope or optimism the individual child achieves is determined by the way that child is treated during the first year of life. And such treatment varies greatly from one society to another and from one family to another. In effect, Erikson accords a very prominent role to the culture as an influence on the form that psychosocial traits assume as children grow up.

Toys and Reasons   The importance of social institutions in the sculpturing of the child's personality has also been emphasized in another, more recent extension of Erikson's theory described in *Toys and Reasons* (Erikson, 1977). The general subject of Erikson's attention in this book is human play, with the term *play* used in a very broad sense. According to Erikson children are engaging in their play when they use imagination to devise mental models of their place in their expanding world. These models are visions designed by children to make sense out of their feelings and skills in relation to the array of puzzling stimuli that impinge on them from without. At each stage of development such play or the creation of such visions functions as a tool to help the individual solve the psychosocial conflict on which she or he is focusing at that stage.

Three aspects of Erikson's conception of play are of particular note. First, play in this sense is not an activity limited to the period of childhood, but rather is pursued throughout the entire life span. Nor are these imaginative, playful acts simply pastimes—something nonserious to do when we are not engaged in the work of life. Instead, such acts, during either working time or leisure time, are marks of the lifelong "human propensity to create model situations in which aspects of the past are re-lived, the present represented and renewed, and the future anticipated" (Erikson, 1977, p. 44). Therefore the child is playing when he builds a structure of blocks or dramatizes with dolls an encounter in the life of a family, but the physicist is also playing when she fashions a model of the universe, and the army general is playing when devising a battle strategy and conducting war according to the "rules of the game."

Second, although the psychological purpose of play is to enable the individual to organize and master her own existence, play cannot fulfill this purpose if conducted only in a solitary setting. There is an essential social quality to much if not all play. In Erikson's view, the individual's imaginative models or mental pictures of herself in her world need to be shared with and affirmed by others. The growing child does not achieve identity or self-concept in isolation but through the interplay of her imaginative creations with those of significant people in her environment. For the preschooler, this interplay can be the child's producing a visual construction with toys and blocks in the presence of an understanding observer. In spontaneous dramatic play with peers, the child has her model situation affirmed and clarified by other children participating in the drama in a way that makes sense to them all—they have produced a shared vision of their world. The games of school-age children are also microcosms—miniature, imagined worlds with defined roles, goals, boundaries of time and space, and rules that define the right way to do things. So also are the games of adults, whether in the form of sporting events and parlor pastimes or in the form of maneuvers in national politics and war (Erikson, 1977, pp. 53–64).

Third, within any society, as time passes, the dominant shared visions or world views assume rather permanent form. Each individual or each generation does not create entirely new ones. The dominant models become traditional and ritualized, and people who share these ways of viewing themselves within their world become convinced that theirs are the right ways or best ways. To perpetuate such models, the institutions of the society—the family, church, school, social club, mass communication media, judiciary, business organizations, and government—teach the viewpoints and rituals to the young. In this way one group of people perpetuates a culture or pattern of rituals and world views that differs from the patterns perpetuated by other groups.

Whereas the biologically inherited genes differentiate the human species from such other species as chimpanzees and hummingbirds, it is the set of socializing institutions within a given culture that causes differences between the people in that society and the people in another society. These resulting groups of people, each marked by the attitudinal and ritual signs of its own culture, are what Erikson has called *pseudo-species:*

> By pseudo-speciation, then, we mean a sense of irreversible difference between one's own and other "kinds," which can attach itself to evolved major differences among human populations or, indeed, to smaller and smaller differences which have come to loom large. In the form of man's "in"-group loyalties, such a specific sense of being elect—as a tribe or nation, creed, class, or ideology—can contribute to the highest achievements in citizenship, courage, and workmanship and can, in fact, weld together in new loyalties (*civis Romanus,* Christian love) previously inimical entities. In the form of new "out"-group enmities, on the other hand, it can express itself most variably—in mortal hatred as well as in phobic avoidance, or in sheer clannishness (Erikson, 1977, pp. 76–77).

Of the various aspects of play, as Erikson has used the term, the one facet on which he centers particular attention in *Toys and Reasons* is that of *ritualization*. He has fitted various forms of ritualization into his stages of the life cycle, tracing each form from its beginnings in childhood and adolescence to its form in the adult world. Erikson's chart of the ontogeny of ritualization is shown in Figure 7.1. As the chart suggests, the evolution of ritualization according to the epigenetic schedule proceeds as follows.

The earliest beginning of ritual in infancy has been labeled *mutuality of recognition* by Erikson, for the first social interaction in the infant's life involves the infant's needs being cared for by parents, particularly by the mother. By means of the child-care ritual—the mother's touch, her smile, the name she gives the child—a mutual mode of recognizing each other and of affirming their identities and relationship develops. This initial ritual serves as the foundation for subsequent rituals of mutual recognition and bonding that will mark later stages of life: the relationship between teacher and pupil, club or gang leader and group member, chieftain and warrior, political figure and citizen, God and believer. Erikson proposes that people are born with the need for such "regular and mutual affirmation and certification" and that its absence can radically harm an infant (Erikson, 1977, p. 88). He has called this aspect of ritualization the *numinous,* for it represents reassurance for the individual through familiarity and mutuality in relation to an object or personage of devotion. Among the institutions of adult society, that of organized religion most obviously represents the numinous:

> The believer, by appropriate gestures, confesses his dependence and his childlike faith and seeks, by appropriate offerings, to secure the privilege of being lifted up to the very bosom of the divine which, indeed, may be seen to graciously respond, with the faint smile of an inclined face (Erikson, 1977, pp. 89–90).

This first aspect of ritualization, the numinous, develops throughout life and combines with subsequently developed rituals to form the complex that makes up the cultural patterns the child's personality acquires.

The second aspect, arising at age 2 or 3 in relation to the toilet-training stage, is that of discriminating good from bad. From these early years the rituals involved with making judgments develop until they reach their most formal version in the procedures of judicial courts. Hence Erikson has applied the word *judicious* to this second sequence of imaginative models of a culture.

The third sort of ritualization is seated in the dramatic play of the preschool years, ages 3 through 6, when the child's new sense of guilt at the

Infancy Age 0-1	Early Childhood Age 2-3	Play Age Age 3-6	School Age Age 6-12	Adolescence Age 12-18	Elements in Adult Rituals	Principal Societal Institutions in Adult Life*
Mutuality of recognition					Numinous	Church, family
	Discrimination of good and bad				Judicious	Court of law
		Dramatic elaboration			Dramatic	Stage, movies, television, literature
			Rules of performance		Formal	School, craft training agency, licensing agency for vocations
				Solidarity of conviction	Ideological	Political group, church, military
					Generational sanction	Marriage, guardianship, professional training and licensing agencies (for teachers, physicians, clergy, etc.)

*The institutions in adult life are partly quoted directly from Erikson and partly the present author's extrapolations from the general tenor of Erikson's analyses.

Figure 7.1 Stages in the Development of Ritualization (Adapted from Erikson, 1977, pp. 85–114) time of the Oedipus conflict motivates the child to seek a resolution of the conflict through imagined dramas. For example, in his clinical experience with children, Erikson has observed them use toys as elements in creating a narrative with a plot that includes conflicts that are finally resolved. These are the elements—plot, conflict, resolution—that make up the sophisticated adult versions of ritualization performed on the stage, in motion pictures, and on radio and television. Effective drama is a vision of reality condensed in space and time and experienced by the audience as "unbearably personal and yet miraculously shared" (Erikson, 1977, p. 102).

A fourth element of ritualization, emphasized during the elementary school years (ages 6–12), is that of *methodological performance*. During this stage the child is assigned a series of tasks that prepare him to master the skills and work habits that will enable him to participate in the economic and technological life of the society, be it agricultural, industrial, commercial, or literary. This stage is the beginning of the child's learning to gain satisfaction through competently performing the formal tasks of the society. This "work role which we begin to envisage for ourselves at the end of childhood is, under favorable conditions, the most reassuring role of all, just because it confirms us in skills and permits us to recognize ourselves in visible works" (Erikson, 1977, p. 106).

A fifth element that enters at the time of adolescence is the adoption by the growing youth of a set of convictions that tie together in a coherent manner (1) the psychosocial identity she has achieved up to this point and (2) the structure and expectations of the adult culture. Erikson has identified two varieties of ritual prominent during these years. First are the *spontaneous "rites"* by which adolescents ritualize relations with their peers and mark their subculture as distinct from childhood and adulthood. Second are the *formal rites,* such as school graduation and joining the church, which represent the passage into, and adoption of, adult status and values. The solidifying of convictions during adolescence leads to the development of the mature ideologies of adult life.

The final stage in the evolution of ritualization is *generational sanction* because as the youth achieves adult status he is officially authorized through such rituals as marriage and guardianship to take on the teaching, productive, and curative roles for a new generation of children. Whereas the child and adolescent are the objects of rituals supervised by adults, the new adult now becomes the ritualizer for the young. The evolution of ritualization for the growing years is now complete.

Erikson's unflagging desire to enrich the psychoanalytic model prompted him at the end of the eighth decade of his own life to publish yet another view of growth, this time a retrospective account from the vantage point of old age, an unraveling of the stages of development from the final phase of life back to birth (Erikson, 1982). In this work he reiterates his confidence in psychoanalytic inquiry as the most profitable method for depicting how human personality develops.

PRACTICAL APPLICATIONS

In the main, the applications described in Chapter Six for Freudian theory are the same as those for Erikson's extension of psychoanalysis. Like Freud's model, Erikson's variation has guided general child rearing, influenced early childhood education, and generated techniques of therapy for disturbed children. In particular, Erikson's description of an adolescent identity crisis has influenced parents' treatment of adolescents and has encouraged school personnel to help students master the crisis by means of life-adjustment courses and study units on self-understanding in social studies and literature classes (Tyler, 1986). A *Psychosocial Stage Inventory* founded on Erikson's model has been used in research on the adjustment of children and youths in various societies (Gray, Ispa, & Thornbury, 1986; Rosenthal, Moore, & Taylor, 1983; Sandor & Rosenthal, 1986). Techniques of therapy for disturbed and learning-disabled adolescents have also been affected by Erikson's attention to youths' struggle for identity (Pickar & Turi, 1986; M. Rose, 1986).

ERIKSON'S VERSION OF PSYCHOANALYSIS: AN ASSESSMENT

Since Erikson's theory is an extension of the psychoanalytic model and is in essential agreement with it, the evaluation of Freudian theory at the end of Chapter Six is also applicable to Erikson's theory in most respects. Therefore, rather than repeat the assessment from Chapter Six, I will confine my appraisal in the following paragraphs to ways in which Erikson's views and contributions differ from Freud's. But before identifying differences, I should note that the work of both men has continued to occupy a very prominent place in the teaching of psychology in recent years. An inspection of fourteen popular child development textbooks showed that the authors most frequently mentioned were Piaget, Skinner, and Erikson (Hogan & Vahey, 1984). A survey of the author indexes in twenty-four introductory psychology texts found that the five names cited most often, in descending order, were Freud, Piaget, Skinner, Bandura, and Erikson (Knapp, 1985).

As for Erikson's particular contributions, he has been acclaimed for his detailed definitions of psychosocial stages and the proposed identity crisis of adolescence, and has been credited as well with significant contributions to psychoanalytic research methodology. Among the complaints critics have launched against Freud is the charge that he was anthropologically naive. By this they mean that he based his theory on a very narrow range of personalities, assuming that the themes of neurotic behavior and thought he found in his patients were an accurate reflection of the modes found in the rest of humanity. In effect, critics have questioned how accurately the patients met in a late-nineteenth-century Viennese psychiatric practice, who were mainly women of upper-middle-class Jewish society, represent people in general. Erikson, in contrast, drew the cases on which he based his speculations from a far wider geographical sampling than Freud. Erikson was a psychoanalyst in Europe, but he also participated in intensive studies of cases at the Harvard Psychological Clinic, of infants suffering neuroses at the Yale University Department of Psychiatry, of normal adolescents in northern California, of Sioux and Yurok Indians, and of numerous other Americans. Furthermore, he focused more attention on normal development than did Freud, particularly the normal development of the healthy self or ego in personal and social relations.

Erikson also furthered the development of *psychohistory,* which is the analysis of the psychological development of individuals by the use of what they have written and said and by reports of their actions. Perhaps the most notable of his analyses of world figures have been those of Martin Luther (1958) and Gandhi (1969). His purpose in these endeavors was to identify significant relationships between the life histories of great leaders and "the historical moment of their emergence" (Erikson, 1975, p. 10). In particular, he concentrated on "the powers of recovery inherent in the young ego" (Erikson, 1958, p. 8).

This same concern for the influence of the broad social setting on personality development caused Erikson to seek ways for elucidating and verifying impressions derived from the psychoanalytic interview. He saw sociological and anthropological research techniques as serving to help clinicians recognize the importance of the social environment in which their data are obtained.

> Clinical evidence, finally, will be decisively clarified, but not changed in nature, by a sharpened awareness (such as now emanates from sociological studies) of the psychotherapist's as well as the patient's position in society and history (Erikson, 1964, p. 80).

As for its stimulation value, Erikson's model continues to attract the interest of empirical investigators and theorists alike. The sorts of studies that his work has inspired others to pursue in recent times include: comparative concepts of the *self* (Tuttman, 1988), conceiving of the *self* in terms of successive ego growth rings related to Eriksonian development stages (Hamachek, 1985), the social adjustment of Australian adolescents from varied ethnic backgrounds (Rosenthal, Moore, & Taylor, 1983), a validation of Erikson's model among South African blacks and whites (Ochse & Plug, 1986), late-adolescent identity as related to self-esteem (Dusek, Carter, & Levy, 1986), identity and intimacy crises (Sandor & Rosenthal, 1986), an expanded formulation of Erikson's view of ego formation (Cole & Levine, 1987), a reconceptualization of Erikson's development cycles (Logan, 1986), and an extended account of intimacy in Erikson's theory (Franz & White, 1985).

All of the foregoing points I would put on the credit side of the assessment ledger. On the debit side I find the same basic problems of scientific validation described in the assessment of Freud's theory. For example, not everyone has found the evidence cited in support of Erikson's proposed psychosocial crises to be convincing. Some of the difficulties with the evidence are reflected in the following questions: Isn't the major evidence in favor of Erikson's scheme mainly in the form of his interpretation of selected, illustrative clinical cases—cases of individuals in therapy, of such figures as Luther and Hitler, and of such groups as Sioux Indians? And couldn't another theorist find as convincing a variety of illustrations as these to suggest that psychosocial crises come in quite a different order than that suggested by Erikson? For example, why is the crisis of autonomy versus shame necessarily set in the second year of life? Couldn't we easily find behaviors at other ages that could reasonably be interpreted as symptoms of an autonomy crisis, behavior such as the striving for independence that appears to mark the years of adolescence?

In conclusion, Erikson's writings about development have generated much discussion in psychological circles and have attracted the admiration of many readers who have found his insights true in their own experience. But many of his proposals, like Freud's, must be accepted on faith, faith in the theorist's interpretive skills and in his authority rather than on experimental and observational evidence that would more clearly compel readers to arrive at the same conclusions. Of course, this charge can be made against many other theories of development as well.

FOR FURTHER READING

The two books by Erikson that most directly describe his overall theory of development are:

(1963) *Childhood and Society,* 2d ed. New York: Norton.
(1968) *Identity: Youth and Crisis.* New York: Norton.

Volumes illustrating the manner in which Erikson embellishes his basic theory with further proposals are:

(1977) *Toys and Reasons*. New York: Norton.

(1982) *The Life Cycle Completed*. New York: Norton.

For a biographical study of the theorist, see:

Coles, R. (1970) *Erik H. Erikson: The Growth of His Work*. New York: Little, Brown.

IDENTIFYING STATES OF CONSCIOUSNESS

Of what significance for human behavior are states of consciousness, how can one state be distinguished from another, and how do nonconscious mental functions develop during the first two decades of life?

Over the past century the topic "states of consciousness" or "levels of consciousness" has intermittently been in favor and out of favor with theorists. When in favor, the matter has inspired assorted proposals about the nature and development of consciousness states. To illustrate how such an issue has been addressed in various theories, the following perspective (1) reviews diverse conceptions of conscious and nonconscious mental operations, (2) considers problems of identifying nonconscious states, and (3) suggests how nonconscious aspects of mind may develop throughout childhood and adolescence.

VARIED CONCEPTIONS OF CONSCIOUSNESS STATES

One convenient way to describe beliefs about consciousness is by differentiating among three categories of theories: (1) ones that deny the existence of *nonconscious* or *unconscious* psychological processes, (2) ones that do not address the consciousness issue but, nevertheless, permit inferences about the possible existence of multiple states, and (3) ones that directly propose a system of states or levels and identify their characteristics.

The Absence of Nonconscious Mental Activity

An initial problem in this debate is how best to define the term *conscious*. Among popular choices are:

Dictionary definitions, such as (a) *awareness*—which means recognizing one's own existence, sensations, feelings, thoughts, and surroundings or (b) having one's mental processes fully active" (Flexner & Hauck, 1987, p. 432).

Philosophers' and psychologists' proposals, such as (a) *attention* is the "criterion of consciousness" so that consciousness and attention become nearly synonymous (Boring, 1963, p. 231), or (b) the term *conscious* refers to people's conceptual thought—and because concepts assume the form of words, *conscious mental activity* is that variety of thought that people can express in words (Dreikurs, 1950, p. 50).

An advantage of the dictionary definitions and the one offered by Boring is that, while their looseness may beg for greater precision, they still convey a sense of truth that people can verify in daily experience—equating *conscious* with the act of "paying attention" seems to make intuitive sense. An advantage of Dreikurs' proposal (*conscious = concepts = words*) is that his definition provides a neatly measurable distinction between conscious and nonconscious cognition—any psychological event that can be expressed in words is conscious, and any that cannot be put in words is unconscious. But critics could charge that this meaning is too narrow since it excludes cognitions or intuitions that people "are aware of" but cannot readily explain.

My aim in mentioning alternative notions of *conscious* is not to catalog all intended meanings nor to judge one as better than another for all purposes. Rather my intent is only to point out that people who speak of *conscious* or *consciousness* do not all agree on what these terms mean, so it is useful to discover what a given theorist presumes when talking about such matters.

Consider, now, theorists who have contended that mental life is entirely conscious so there can be no such thing as unconscious mental operations. Psychology had taken the form of philosophical speculation until, in the latter 1800s, it assumed the character of an empirical science in the laboratories of Wilhelm Wundt (1832–1920) in Germany in 1879 and of E. B. Titchener (1867–1927) in America in 1895. In the opinion of these pioneers, the human mind is able to observe all of its own inner workings. Hence the approach to understanding mental functions should consist of a type of introspection by which trained observers attempt to analyze their own percepts, memories, and thoughts and to describe these phenomena in terms of elementary sensations, images, and feelings. This version of psychological science became known as *structuralism* since the investigators' purpose was to identify the structures of the mind. Structuralism provided no place for nonconscious psychic activities.

The denial of nonconscious mental events was carried even further when John B. Watson's (1878–1959) revolutionary article "Psychology as a Behaviorist Views It" (1913) launched the behaviorism movement that would dominate much of psychological activity over the next half century, particularly in America. Watson rejected any such concepts as *mind* and *thought*. Psychology, he said, was strictly the science of observable behavior, so there could be no *intellect* or *mentality*. People's supposed *mental activity* was no more than silent speech, as evidenced by barely perceptible movements of the speech organs when people were ostensibly "thinking." Thus Watson's extreme behaviorism not only eliminated the possibility of unconscious mental events but of conscious ones as well. R. S. Woodworth, president of the American Psychological Association in 1914, is credited with observing that psychology had "lost its soul" when structuralist theorists divorced psychology from religious philosophy; now, thanks to Watson, psychology had "lost its mind" (Roback, 1964).

Inferred States of Consciousness

Information-processing theory illustrates a model of development that typically does not allude to matters of consciousness but, nevertheless, permits speculation about states of consciousness implied by the theory's structure. As we will see in Chapter Twelve, information-processing models portray mental activity as a procedure that involves (1) receiving stimuli from the environment, (2) transmitting and storing coded messages in the neural system, and ultimately (3) activating muscles to produce observed behavior. Each of these phases can be analyzed into constituent substages, some of them conscious, but others unconscious in that they operate without the individual's intent or awareness. For example, in such a stimulus receptor as the eye or ear, a crude filtering action takes place that identifies certain gross characteristics of a stimulus. The person experiencing the stimulus does not intend to perform such filtering nor is even aware that it is occurring. The performance is automatic, and in that sense is unconscious. In like manner, a variety of other functions of the information-processing system are equally unintentional, automatic, and unrecognized. As J. F. Kihlstrom has explained:

> Certainly a good deal of mental activity is unconscious in the strict sense of being inaccessible to phenomenal awareness under any circumstances. In conversational speech, for example, the listener is aware of the meanings of the words uttered by the speaker but not of the phonological and linguistic principles by which the meaning of the speaker's utterance is decoded. Although we have conscious access to the products of these mental processes—in that we are aware of the meaning of the utterance

... and can communicate this knowledge to others—we have no conscious access to their operations. . . . One thing is now clear: consciousness is not to be identified with any particular perceptual-cognitive functions such as discriminative response to stimulation, perception, memory, or the higher mental processes involved in judgment or problem-solving. All of these functions can take place outside of phenomenal awareness (1987, pp. 1447, 1450).

Just as information-processing theory can thus be analyzed to reveal its implied levels of consciousness, so also can other models of development that do not directly describe consciousness states. Such is true of Piaget's scheme, Soviet theories, humanistic proposals, and more.

Outright Claims for States or Levels of Consciousness

Although Freud can be credited with popularizing "the unconscious," it is clear that he neither invented nor first discovered the notion of unconscious mental actions. For centuries philosophers had speculated about such matters. And at the time Freud's career began, an active dialogue about the unconscious was already being conducted among scholars in both Europe and America, as suggested by L. L. Whyte's (1960) list of more than forty authors who preceded Freud in writing about the unconscious mind.

Over the years the most common way of categorizing states of consciousness has been to divide mental events into two types, *conscious* and *unconscious*. Earlier I pointed out the lack of agreement about the meaning of *conscious*. But that lack is far exceeded by differences of opinion regarding the term *unconscious*. Furthermore, some authors, not content with the bipartite conscious/unconscious division, have embellished their theories with additional components. Freud imposed a *preconscious* between the conscious and unconscious, and Carl Jung postulated a *racial unconscious* undergirding each individual's personal unconscious (Jung, 1963).

It is apparent that such differences of opinion are nothing new. H. Ellenberger notes in his *The Discovery of the Unconscious* (1970) that European thinkers by 1900 had already ascribed four separate functions to the unconscious mind. And R. C. Fuller (1986) lists these as:

(1) The conservative function of recording memories and registering perceptions which often escape conscious attention; (2) the dissolutive function, as evidenced by hypnotic behaviors and the multiple or split personalities of schizophrenic patients; (3) the creative function of innovative or inspirational thinking; and (4) the mythopoetic function of fabricating inner romances, fantasies, or dreams which give psychic life a kind of autonomous reality apart from events that transpire in the physical universe (p. 4).

Psychologist D. B. Klein (1977, pp. 171–178) has sought to dispel some of the confusion about nonconscious processes by describing additional ways authors have used the term *unconscious*. The last pair of the following six ways are associated with Jung and Freud, the two theorists best known for making unconscious processes an intimate part of their models of development.

1. *Ignorance.* When we are aware of our desires (such as wanting to sleep or wanting something sweet to eat) but fail to recognize the precise metabolic conditions that stimulate these desires, we are said to be "unconscious of" or "ignorant of" the physiological causes of our desires.

2. *Inattention.* Perceptual distraction may cause people to be "unconscious of" what is going on around them. For example, a mother shouts to her ten-year-old son as he plays tag with friends, but the boy fails to answer because he is concentrating so intently on the game that he remains oblivious of his mother's call. Or, during a class discussion, a high school teacher asks for a girl's opinion, but the girl is unable to respond because she was distracted by her own thoughts when the teacher posed his question.

3. *Subliminal stimulation.* The obverse of inattention is people's unconscious reception of stimuli of which they are unaware. Even though they are not aware of attending to a stimulus, such as a word flashed for an instant on a television screen, they are nevertheless affected by it. This notion of subliminal influences requires the assumption that there is a threshold or borderline—called the *limen*—between conscious and unconscious levels of stimulus perception. According to Klein: "In the area of sales promotion these modes of stimulation have been regarded as 'hidden persuaders.' Whether they ought to be classified as subconscious rather than unconscious influences is a moot point. As subthreshold modes of stimulation they may be classified as subconscious, but as influences eluding awareness they might be classified as being unconscious" (1977, p. 172).

4. *Conditioning.* A phenomenon related to subliminal stimulation is classical conditioning. For instance, a two-year-old girl has burst into tears when, on each of three occasions, she has been knocked to the ground by a neighbor's barking dog. A week later, as her parents watch an evening television drama, the child begins to cry as she hears a dog bark on the TV program. As interpreted from the viewpoint of conditioning, the child's being knocked to the

ground (unconditioned stimulus) produced her original fright and weeping (unconditioned response). And because barking accompanied each attack, any barking she now hears (conditioned stimulus) is sufficient to set off the weeping (conditioned response). Since the child did not consciously intend to associate barking with weeping, the automatic establishment of such an association qualifies as an unconscious mental event.

5. *Jung's collective unconscious.* Carl Jung (1875–1961), a compatriot of Freud until they parted company in 1912, proposed that all humans inherit residual psychic impressions that derive from

> the experiences of remote ancestors in coping with recurrent situations of crucial biological significance. These would be experiences directly related to survival in the history of the human race and thus have to do with themes of universal appeal. The resulting racial memory or collective unconscious is presumed to render mankind sensitive to thoughts of spirits, gods, storms, motherhood, birth, mother earth, monsters, sunshine, and whatever else may have impressed preliterate man as a force for good or evil (Klein, 1977, p. 175).

According to Jung, this phylogenetic unconscious provides a foundation of inclinations—referred to as *archetypes*—for how to think and act, with the inclinations then fashioned into behavior by the individual's own direct experiences with the world.

6. *Freud's states or levels of consciousness.* Throughout this perspective I have referred to *states* and *levels*. I have done so because these words—following Freud's lead—are convenient categories for directing our discussion and not because everyone who has written about such matters has pictured consciousness in terms of states or levels.

Freud's voluminous written works spanned more than sixty years (from age 21 to age 82), so it is hardly surprising that he occasionally changed his opinion about such an elusive topic as the unconscious. In delineating the architecture of the mind, he spoke sometimes of levels, with the preconscious deeper than the conscious, and the unconscious deeper yet. At other times he spoke of states: "We must be prepared . . . to assume the existence in us not only of a second consciousness, but of a third, fourth, perhaps of an unlimited number of states of consciousness, all unknown to us and to one another" (1915b, p. 170). Periodically he used a spatial analogy, comparing the unconscious to a "large anteroom, in which the various mental excitations are crowding upon one another," then picturing consciousness as a smaller reception room adjacent to the anteroom (Klein, 1977, p. 177). On still other occasions Freud avoided speaking of levels, states, or places and referred instead to mental "systems" and to "psychical acts which lack consciousness" (Freud, 1915b, p. 170).

But more important than his metaphors and labels are the characteristics Freud assigned to various states of consciousness. I believe that identifying such characteristics is best performed in terms of the most prominent version of his model of the mind—the tripartite structure of conscious, preconscious, and unconscious described in Chapter Six. The attributes of mind are displayed in Table B.1.

Thus the past century has witnessed a considerable ebb and flow in the debate over types and levels of consciousness. That debate not only continues today but is bound to endure into the future. These issues will likely never be settled because of the difficulties encountered in trying to pin down such evasive entities as *preconscious* and *unconscious* in order to comprehend them. This problem of how to identify *nonconscious* events is our next concern.

IDENTIFYING AND COMPREHENDING NONCONSCIOUS STATES

Because alleged nonconscious functions are, by definition, beyond the realm of direct inspection, the task of judging the validity of different theorists' views of the preconscious, subconscious, or unconscious becomes most elusive. Since such functions cannot be witnessed immediately, their existence must be inferred. This leads to the question: From what kinds of evidence do theorists draw their inferences about the nature of nonconscious mental events?

An examination of our earlier list of nonconscious functions suggests that theorists may base their inferences on three sources of evidence: (1) people acting without conscious intent and then being unable to identify the source of their actions, (2) the failure of people to respond to stimuli, and (3) presumed symbolic behavior. The first two may be employed by proponents of nearly any variety of theory, except for extreme behaviorism. The third is particularly associated with such theories as Jung's and Freud's.

1. A lack of conscious intent may be revealed when people are asked "Why did you do that?" and they answer "I guess I did it without thinking" or "I didn't even realize I did it" or "I suppose it's kind of automatic." This sort of evidence is used to support inferences

Table B.1   Attributes of Freudian States of Consciousness

Conscious	*Preconscious*	*Unconscious*
Type of psychic function Secondary process—the reality principle Complex, rational thought that recognizes demands of surrounding environment	Pleasure principle translated into reality principle Complex, rational thought that recognizes demands of surrounding environment	Primary process—the pleasure principle Complex thought unchecked by logical contradiction, causal association, or knowledge of outside world
Use of Psychic Energy Expends energy	Expends energy	Generates and expends energy
Types of Psychic Contents Acknowledged sensations, perceptions, and decisions; emotions and feelings A portion of the superego	Adjustment mechanisms, recallable memories, all readily available items of information at individual's disposal Censor guarding the gate between the unconscious and conscious A portion of the superego	Instinctual drives, wish impulses, repressed sexual memories, other repressed memories, and items still unidentified; no emotions
Storage Capacity for Psychic Contents Very small	Moderately large	Very large, perhaps infinite
Sense of Time Sense of past, present, future	Sense of past, present future	No sense of time
Values Positive and negative attitudes, doubts, personal convictions	Attitudes, doubts, personal convictions	No negative attitudes, no doubts, no personal convictions

Abstracted from Archard (1984, p. 25), Freud (1915b), and Klein (1977, pp. 186–189).

about unconscious mental functions underlying conditioned responses, certain creative endeavors, subliminal stimulation, hypnotic behavior and multiple personalities, and acts practiced to a level of automaticity, as observed in a skilled typist, pianist, chauffeur, or athlete.

2. Failure to respond to stimuli, in the sense of inattentiveness, can be interpreted as evidence of a hypothetical, unconscious mental filtering system that blocks all stimuli from consciousness except for the single stimulus on which the individual is concentrating at the moment. Some authors have proposed that a malfunction of such a filtering mechanism accounts for some children having difficulty attending to academic tasks in school because they are so easily distracted by irrelevant sights and sounds around them. In other words, a faulty filter allows too many stimuli to invade consciousness, thereby destroying the child's concentration on an assigned task (Thomas, 1989c, p. 188).

3. The phrase "presumed symbolic behavior" refers to the proposal that contents of the unconscious cannot reveal themselves to the conscious mind in their original form but, instead, must disguise their true nature. In other words, thoughts that arise in consciousness may not be what their appearance suggests but, rather, can be symbols of something different. In Jung's analytic theory, the items in consciousness can be representatives or embodiments of vague predispositions (related to pain, birth, death, sun, darkness, power, women, men, sex, magic, and the like) inherited from ancient ancestors and now residing deep in a racial unconscious. In Freud's psychoanalytic theory, items in consciousness can symbolize distressing, and now repressed, memories of sexual events from the past that are too threatening to the individual's conscious sense of well-being to be admitted into consciousness in their true form. The only opportunity for the psychic energy of such repressed material to expend itself occurs when the unacceptable memories mask their actual identity in symbolic garb, thereby rendering themselves acceptable to consciousness. Evidence that items in consciousness are actually camouflaged material from the unconscious has been sought in a host of phenomena—dreams, slips of the tongue, perceptual mistakes, bodily ailments, posture and movements, responses to projective devices (ink-blot tests, word-association tests, unfinished sentences), artistic productions, and the like.

Perhaps the greatest danger in using presumed symbolic behavior as a window to the unconscious lies in the fact that the interpreter of symbols is "only human" and not an objective, omniscient evaluator. Might not the Jungian analyst or Freudian psychoanalyst be projecting his or her own unconscious contents onto the client's behavior when interpreting that behavior as symbolic?

In summary, then, theorists' conceptions of the nature of nonconscious mental activities represent inferences that do not yield readily to empirical verification. This difficulty has caused Fuller (1986, p. 5) to contend that "Inasmuch as 'facts' about the unconscious cannot be ascertained empirically, theories which purport to explain men's and women's depths have almost entirely been shaped by philosophical and cultural factors." To illustrate this point, he cites the cool reception psychoanalytic theory received in America during the early decades of the twentieth century, and he proposes that "the ideological incompatibility between Freud's tragic view of life and the optimistic bent of the American mind was sufficient to account for the reluctance of academic psychologists to give psychoanalysis a more serious reading. . . . American psychology is the creation of a cultural tradition which esteems vigor and flexibility; it consequently resists trammeling the self with a complex inner structure" (pp. 124–125).

Even among the Americans who did embrace psychoanalysis, there was a tendency to revise those aspects of Freud's theory that appeared to deny the mind's positive, progressive, and creative powers. Such revisionism caused Freud to observe that the popular view of psychoanalysis in America "is no evidence of a friendly attitude toward the subject or a particularly broad dissemination of, or profound understanding of its teachings" (Oberndorf in Fuller, 1986, p. 120).

In discussing other theories, Fuller cites additional support for his proposition that the philosophical preferences of a society affect the image of the unconscious espoused by theorists in that society. For instance, he observes that in the rise of humanistic psychology during the 1960s (Chapter Thirteen) the movement's American trendsetters envisioned an unconscious core of personality whose power "gives the individual an innate potential for self-enhancement (i.e., successful adaptation to the physical and social environments) and self-transcendence (i.e., adaptation to some supranatural environment)." This notion that the "unconscious is the aesthetic medium through which the individual can align himself with an immanent life force" is a conviction Fuller traces back to the writings of the colonial theologian Jonathan Edwards (1703–1758), the philosopher-poet

Ralph Waldo Emerson (1803–1882), and the psychologist-philosopher William James (1842–1910) (Fuller, 1986, p. 155).

If Fuller's proposal is correct, then we can expect new theories of the future to reflect their authors' cultural settings in their inferences about unconscious mental activities.

HOW NONCONSCIOUS FUNCTIONS DEVELOP

My final task here is to speculate about how, from the viewpoint of different theories, nonconscious mental operations emerge during the first two decades of life. I have chosen information processing and psychoanalysis as the two theories to use for briefly illustrating a way of estimating which of a theory's unconscious contents and functions are innate and which are acquired. *Innate characteristics* are considered to be of two types: (1) those that are fully operative at birth and (2) those that arise at some point during childhood according to a genetic time schedule *(internal maturation)*. *Acquired characteristics* are the unconscious aspects of personality derived from the child's transactions with the environment.

An Information-Processing Example

In the simplified version of information-processing theory depicted in Figure B.1, cognitive functions assume the following pattern: (a) goals rise in long-term memory, (b) sensory receptors (mainly eyes and ears) search the environment for stimuli pertinent to the goals, (c) as the stimuli impinge on the receptors, gross features of the stimuli are identified (feature detection and pattern recognition) and sent as coded messages to (d) short-term working memory, where the configuration of the stimuli is compared to analogous coded images stored in long-term memory, so that an interpretation can be constructed regarding what the received stimuli mean. The product of this interpretation can then (e) be stored in long-term memory and/or (f) lead to immediate overt action in the environment. The contents of long-term memory fall into two categories: *declarative knowledge* and *procedural knowledge*. Memories in the form of declarative knowledge are of two sorts. First is *episodic knowledge,* meaning knowledge of specific objects (people, places) and events (a birthday party, graduation from elementary school) that the child experienced in the past. Second is *semantic knowledge,* comprised of abstract conceptions not limited to any particular time or place (judging distances, recalling names, catching a ball, estimating people's moods). In contrast to declarative knowledge, procedural knowledge consists of that "repertoire of skills, rules, and strategies

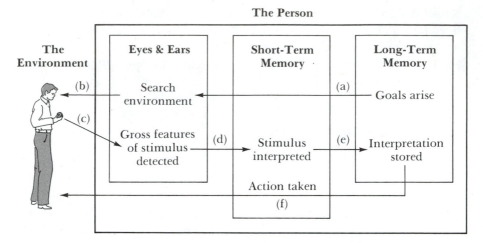

Figure B.1   A Simplified Version of Information Processing

that operate on declarative knowledge in the course of perception, memory, thought, and action" (Kihlstrom, 1987, p. 1446).

With this model of the mind before us, we are prepared to speculate about the sources of its unconscious aspects during childhood and adolescence. For the purpose of this exercise, *conscious* will be defined as "any knowledge we can bring into awareness and, preferably, describe in some manner." *Unconscious,* as the obverse, refers to any knowledge or function that we cannot bring to awareness. Thus all declarative knowledge has the potential for being conscious, in that the individual can become aware of it under the right circumstances (goals from long-term memory link with stimuli from the environment to energize declarative contents into consciousness). However, "procedural knowledge is not available to introspection under any circumstances. Thus, procedural knowledge appears to be unconscious in the strict sense of the term. We are aware of the goals and conditions of procedures, and the products of their execution, but not of the operations themselves" (Kihlstrom, 1987, p. 1446).

Now to the question of how and when, during the first two decades of life, unconscious knowledge develops. To begin, theorist J. A. Fodor (1983) has suggested that the mind contains an array of innate modules governing basic domains of mental functions, such as language, visual perception, and muscular coordination. These modules are genetically "hardwired" into the nervous system and do their work outside of conscious awareness and voluntary control. However, the modules are not entirely operational at birth. Instead, they gradually realize their potential as the child's neural system matures and the child engages in an expanding variety of encounters with the environment. For example, the evolution of language usage in childhood has been traced across cultures, revealing similar stages of language acquisition among all children, regardless of the particular vernacular used in their environment—Chinese, English, Spanish, Malay, Urdu, or some other (Drum, 1990). This evidence is cited to support the notion that inherited propensities that underlie such mental procedures are universal (characteristic of the entire human species), unconscious, and evolve by gradual stages. Furthermore, the pace at which one type of innate function matures can differ from the pace of another, so that a trait such as depth perception will be achieved sooner than will the use of complex language structures.

Distinctive from innate mental functions are those cognitive procedures acquired through experience. For instance, in the case of learning a skill, such as tying a shoelace, the activity is initially conscious as the child intently concentrates on each step of the process. But the act eventually becomes automatic, rendered unconscious by virtue of practice. The number of such skills increases at an accelerating rate as children grow older and their internal neural maturation combines with experience to extend the child's ability to manage more and more aspects of the environment. We might then offer this proposition: The point in a child's development that a particular cognitive function will be acquired and transposed into the form of an unconscious habit is governed by (1) the present maturational level of the neural system, (2) the state of that part of the child's experiential history necessary for learning the skill, (3) an opportunity for encountering the skill, (4) the child's level of motivation for gaining the skill, and (5) sufficient practice to make the skill automatic. The first two events provide the *essential readiness* for acquiring the skill. Not until they are in place can the remaining three steps occur, which may be immediately after readiness is sufficient, or it can be years later or perhaps never.

Such a line of reasoning as the above illustrates how, from the perspective of one version of information processing, inferences can be drawn about the way unconscious mental contents are acquired during childhood.

A Psychoanalytic Example

Consider the attributes listed under the Freudian unconscious in Table B.1. From among them, I would estimate that three are fully operative at birth—the energy-generating function (instinctual drives), the wish impulses, and the primary process (pleasure principle)—because all three are necessary for launching and sustaining development. Other than these, the rest of the personality attributes in Table B.1 are no more than potentials at the time of birth. Freud maintained that the original state of the personality is entirely unconscious and that the preconscious and conscious levels will gradually arise out of this primary state as a result of the maturing of the nervous system and the child's interactions with the world.

As the months and years advance, the child's progressive neural maturation combines with environmental experiences to determine when a variety of the acquired aspects of personality appear. For example, although Freud rarely spoke directly about intelligence, he did state that a sufficient (though unspecified) level of intellectual development is necessary before defense mechanisms can be acquired. He wrote that repression, as an ego-defense function of the preconscious, is not "present from the very beginning, and it cannot occur until a sharp distinction has been established between what is conscious and what is unconscious: the essence of repression lies simply in turning something away, and keeping it at a distance, from the conscious" (1915a, p. 147). He believed that other adjustment mechanisms, such as denial and reaction formation, did not require the same level of cognitive complexity as repression and thus could be learned at a somewhat younger (though unspecified) age (Klein, 1977, p. 148).

As soon as repression is operative, memories of unacceptable desires and behavior (chiefly of a sexual nature) accumulate in the unconscious. The quantity of repressions and their potency depends chiefly on the wisdom of those in charge of raising the child. According to psychoanalytic theory, the more demanding and punitive child-rearing practices are, the greater the number and the potency of repressions. Which events will be repressed is determined by the ego operating at the preconscious level. And this decision is governed to a great extent by the composition of that specific child's superego, which imposes standards of right and wrong that are not innate but are acquired, particularly at the time of the Oedipus conflict, around ages 3 to 5.

CONCLUSION

During much of the twentieth century, formal concern with nonconscious mental processes was found almost exclusively in psychoanalysis and in its onetime bedfellows, the theories of Jung and Alfred Adler. However, as the cognitive psychology movement has gained ascendence over behaviorism, psychoanalysis, and humanistic psychology during the final quarter of the century, there appears to be a growing interest in identifying and understanding varied states of consciousness within the proliferating cognitive psychology paradigms. As developmental theorists move into the twenty-first century, this interest seems bound to grow.

BEHAVIORISM AND SOCIAL LEARNING PERSPECTIVES

A search for the way principles of learning explain development

Some psychologists have felt very uneasy about theories that propose *mental elements,* such as soul, ego, or conscious. They are also uneasy about hypothetical *mental functions*—repression, epigenesis, needs, dispositions, and the like. The trouble, they say, is that they are not convinced that these supposed elements and functions really exist, or at least not in the form that various speculators have proposed. It is clear that no one has ever seen or directly measured such things as mind or the unconscious. Another problem is that one theorist who writes about mentality or personality often posits very different elements and functions than do other theorists. And if mind is unavailable for inspection, how do we know which theorist is right?

It was this sort of doubting that motivated John B. Watson (1878–1959) to publish his article "Psychology as a Behaviorist Views It" (1913) and thereby launch the *behaviorism* movement in psychology. Watson and his followers felt that it is both misleading and unprofitable to study some cogitator's fantasies about what the structure of a person's mind or unconscious might be like. They proposed, instead, that it is much more objective and scientific to observe the way people act under different environmental conditions. The observations can then be organized, analyzed, and stated as principles that are intended to explain the behavior. In short, proponents of this point of view claim that the proper business of psychology is to identify the observable conditions that influence the behavior of humans and nonhuman organisms.

Since the time of Watson's early advocacy of behaviorism, the movement has attracted many followers and has spawned numerous subgroups. Behaviorism dominated experimental psychology, particularly in the United States, from the 1920s until well into the 1960s. And while far less popular today, the movement still continues to be an influential force. In Part Four we consider several varieties of behaviorism as they apply to child development. Chapter Eight focuses primarily on B. F. Skinner's operant conditioning and on Sidney Bijou and Donald Baer's application of this approach to child development. The chapter also illustrates some variants advocated in recent years by neobehaviorists (*liberal* behaviorists) who have sought to bring the movement into closer proximity with the data of present-day cognitive psychology.

A derivative of behaviorism that rose to prominence in the 1960s and 1970s is *social learning theory,* which includes a present-day version called *contextualism.* In contrast to Watsonian behaviorism, social learning theory does recognize cognitive activity, even while emphasizing the analysis of overt behavior. Precepts and investigative methods of social learning theory and contextualism are traced in Chapter Nine.

But before starting our detailed inspection of these matters, it is useful to recognize that there is considerable confusion about how to characterize conceptual schemes referred to as *behaviorism.* For example, some writers have distinguished between S-R and S-O-R behaviorists (Woodworth, 1929). The S-R designation has been applied to psychologists who focus on observable stimuli (S) and on a person's subsequent response (R), without suggesting what might be happening inside the person between the S and the R. Both Watson and Skinner have often been identified as S-R theorists. In contrast, the S-O-R symbol designates psychologists who are willing to speculate about what occurs within the organism (O) that transposes a stimulus into a response. Different theorists refer to the O function in different ways. Some call it *intervening variables,* some call it *thinking* or *cognitive activity,* and others call it *information processing.* It is possible to assign social learning theorists, contextualists, and certain types of neobehaviorists to the S-O-R camp.

However, objections have been raised about the validity of both the S-R and S-O-R formulas. One complaint is that: "Stimulus-response psychologies lead us to expect that given a stimulus, we might predict the response, and that given a response, we might retrodict the stimulus. . . . This formulation treats acts and feelings as mechanical responses to stimuli, and it treats persons as robots or penny-in-the-slot machines" (Lee, 1988, pp. 151–152). So, according to this observation, children should not be pictured simply as response machines that act only when stimulated by environmental forces. Rather children should be seen as initiators of their own behavior, ones who draw on stimuli from the environment (E). In that event, it might be more reasonable to posit a relationship of $O \rightarrow E \rightarrow O \rightarrow R$. Or, as another possibility, the interaction of O and E to produce R might be pictured as $O \leftrightarrow E = R$. In effect, these conflicting proposals indicate that there is a large measure of disagreement among psychologists about such matters.

A second source of confusion is the abundance of adjectives attached to the word *behaviorism* to distinguish one version from another. As early as the 1920s, A. A. Roback, an early student of behaviorism, identified ten classes and seventeen subclasses of behaviorism that he divided into four general groupings:

> structural behaviorism (focusing on the mechanics of organisms), functional behaviorism (focusing on the relationship between an organism and its environment), psychobehaviorism (allowing consciousness and introspection a role in psychology along with behaviorism), and nominal behaviorism (encompassing theorists such as McDougall who called themselves behaviorists but whose theories included little of Watson's original behavioristic platform) (Logue, 1985, p. 177).

In recent times, different conceptions of behaviorism have borne such varied designations as *original, classical, standard, strict, extreme, methodological, metaphysical, modified, radical, liberal, operant, eclectic, social, paradigmatic, purposive, cognitive, sane, subjective, true,* and *interbehaviorist* (Lee 1988, p. 81; Logue, 1985, pp. 176–177). Not only is there a multiplicity of such terms, but one author frequently invests a given term with meanings different from those employed by another. Consequently, when reading the professional literature, we do well to inspect with care the details of each author's writings about behaviorism to determine exactly what he or she intends.

The reason Skinner's version of behaviorism is featured in Chapter Eight is that he is the best known behaviorist of the past half century. He created operant behaviorism and "has more fully and more explicitly explored the implications of a contingency-oriented psychology than any other psychologist" (Lee, 1988, p. 79). And A. C. Catania and S. Harnad (1988, p. 3) state that: "Of all contemporary psychologists, B. F. Skinner is perhaps the most honored and the most maligned, the most widely recognized and the most misrepresented, the most cited and the most misunderstood."

Part Four closes with a perspective that addresses the question: What research methods are associated with different theories, and what are the strengths and limitations of such methods? In answer, the perspective proposes how different theorists' research methods can be influenced by considerations of control, reality, precision, reproducibility, significance, and feasibility.

CHAPTER EIGHT

Skinner's Operant Conditioning

By the time his career ended in 1990, no American research psychologist was better known than Burrhus Frederic Skinner (1904–1990). The public fame of this Harvard professor resulted from his skillful and often controversial application of his learning theory to the solution of practical educational, personal adjustment, and social problems. In the mid-1950s he refined and popularized such learning devices as teaching machines and programmed textbooks (Skinner, 1972). In the late 1960s the behavior modification approach to therapy for disturbed people drew heavily on Skinnerian doctrine. In the 1970s his book *Beyond Freedom and Dignity* (1971) recommended a plan for social control through operant conditioning that he contended would produce an increasingly peaceful, orderly, cooperative, and efficient society. His theory also has clear implications for the field of child development.

In this chapter I trace the outlines of Skinner's system and describe the principal ways the system can be applied to the understanding of child growth and behavior. Later in the chapter I discuss the work of Sidney W. Bijou and Donald M. Baer, who have been leaders among child psychologists in applying Skinnerian concepts to the analysis of child development. Finally, I note some newer departures to illustrate a variety of behaviorist perspectives that have appeared in recent times.

THE NATURE OF OPERANT CONDITIONING

The seeds of Skinner's behaviorism can be traced back to Pavlov's dog. In the early twentieth century the Russian physiologist Ivan Petrovich Pavlov

(1849–1936) demonstrated what has become known as *classical conditioning*. He placed meat powder (called an *unconditioned stimulus*) on a dog's tongue, which caused the dog to automatically salivate (called the *unconditioned response*). Then, on a series of subsequent occasions (called *trials*) Pavlov sounded a bell at the same time he gave the food (the meat powder) to the dog. When the food was accompanied by the bell enough times, he found that he could withhold the food and the bell's sound itself would cause the dog to salivate. The bell was now the *conditioned stimulus* that brought about the *conditioned response* of salivating. Classical conditioning, then—which often is called *respondent conditioning*—consists of substituting a new stimulus for an old one by presenting the two at the same time, or nearly the same time, then dropping the old stimulus and allowing the new one to bring about the original response. Pavlov's work inaugurated the era of *S-R* or *stimulus-response* psychology.

American behaviorists adopted the S-R concept as the appropriate model for explaining human behavior without having to speculate about what was possibly going on inside an organism's central nervous system. It was no longer necessary to imagine such things as mind or soul to account for the way people acted. By observing what sorts of stimuli elicited what sorts of responses, psychologists could explain what makes people behave as they do.

One problem that early behaviorists met was that they often could not identify accurately what stimulus was bringing about the responses they observed. Hence they were forced to assume the operation of stimuli they actually could not locate. In the 1930s Skinner suggested a solution to this common problem. He proposed that there was not one kind of conditioning but two. One was the classical S-R relationship demonstrated by Pavlov. The other, and by far the more frequent in human behavior, Skinner labeled *operant* or *instrumental conditioning*. Instead of the behavior being drawn out or elicited by a stimulus, the behavior (response) was simply *emitted* or expressed without any observable stimulus evoking it.

For example, a pigeon in a cage just naturally does pigeon-like things—walking about and pecking. A baby in a cradle just makes natural baby movements—wiggling its arms and legs in a random way. In Skinner's opinion, it is not important to identify the stimulus that started the pecking and the arm and leg movements. Rather, if we are to understand why behavior occurs, it is far more important to inspect the *consequences* of these movements, for the consequences are what come to control actions. The term *consequences* here refers to whether the pigeon's or infant's movements bring satisfaction to the organism. If the pigeon is hungry and happens to peck a plastic lever that drops food pellets into the cage, then this consequence of the food's satisfying the hunger drive may strengthen the tendency for the pigeon to peck the lever again the next time it is hungry and is in the same cage. After the pigeon has had enough trials at this task, it gradually will become more efficient; that is, it will gradually eliminate the previous random walking and pecking at other things and will peck the lever directly when hungry. So we say the pigeon has *learned* lever pecking, and this learning has been caused or controlled by the consequences of fulfilling the hunger need.

It is Skinner's contention that all or nearly all behavior is a result of either respondent (classical) or operant conditioning, with by far the larger part of human behavior being operant as the child increases in age. If the consequences are rewarding, the actions will more likely be repeated the next time the individual is in a similar situation. If the consequences are either painful or simply useless, the actions will less likely be repeated in the future. Rewarding consequences strengthen tendencies to act; nonrewarding consequences weaken tendencies to act the same way again, so eventually the nonrewarding acts will be dropped or *extinguished* entirely.

This is the general idea of classical (respondent) and operant conditioning. However, in this introduction the theory has been oversimplified, and I have used terms that Skinner and his followers would find imprecise and perhaps misleading. For instance, Skinnerians do not approve of such terms as *hunger need* if such terms require that we assume something inside a person that we cannot observe. They also object to such words as *reward* when its use assumes a feeling state that cannot readily be identified and that is considered to be the cause of some sort of behavior. However, I used these terms, just as Skinner himself used them, because they are familiar and explain the issues more easily than if I had started off with only behaviorist definitions. However, at this point I will begin using more standard behaviorist wording in order to delineate the key features of Skinnerian theory.

To begin, I should point out that Skinner on occasion has denied that he has constructed a theory (Skinner, 1972, pp. 69–71). He claims to be more an empiricist, collecting observable facts of behavior and summarizing them in terms of principles. He proposes that he simply tells it as it is. However, in the broad way that *theory* was defined in Chapter One, his formulations do indeed qualify as theory, as his other writings would attest (Skinner, 1974, pp. 18–20).

He created the concept of *operant* or *instrumental* conditioning to focus prime attention on the importance of consequences in controlling the acts that immediately preceded them. In other words, the act is the operator (operant) or instrument that brings about the consequence.

Types of Consequences

What most people think of as a reward is called a *reinforcer* by behaviorists. A consequence is a *positive reinforcer* if it causes the act to increase in the future when a similar situation arises. For example, if a hungry infant is fed right after he happens to hit a rattle in his crib, the tendency for him to hit the rattle next time he is hungry is increased. This means that feeding has positively reinforced rattle hitting. Likewise, if an affection-hungry school girl picks papers up from around her desk and thus is given a hug by her teacher and told, "You're a great helper, Jenny," then the tendency for Jenny to pick up papers in the future is strengthened. The hug and kind words have positively reinforced the act of tidying up.

Sometimes a child's acts stop an unpleasant condition. For instance, the second-grade teacher is screaming at the children to get into their seats and keep quiet. The unpleasant screaming stops as soon as the children are all in their seats. So the act of sitting down has been instrumental in stopping the unpleasant harangue. The pleasant state of quiet is, for the children, a *negative reinforcer* for sitting down. In effect, a consequence of an action is called a negative reinforcer if the action has caused some unpleasant (*aversive,* in behaviorist terms) condition to stop. Next time the teacher starts ranting at the class, the children can be expected to sit down more promptly because sitting down produced the happy state of quiet the first time.

That is, both positive and negative reinforcement are rewarding. Both increase the likelihood that the child will repeat the same act in similar future circumstances. It is positive reinforcement if it starts a pleasant consequence. It is negative reinforcement if it stops an unpleasant consequence, such as noise or criticism.

A third sort of consequence is *punishment.* Consequences are called punishing or aversive if they reduce the tendency for the child to behave the same way in the future. Punishment, as any parent or teacher knows, is supposed to discourage acts of the same sort on later occasions. Punishment can involve either imposing something unpleasant (spanking, requiring extra homework) or removing something pleasant (taking away privileges).

But punishment is not the only way to eliminate undesired acts. Another way is simply not to reinforce the acts. If a child crosses his eyes in school to get attention but no one pays any attention to this antic, the eye crossing can be expected to stop for it has failed to achieve the desired consequences. In brief, *extinction* of the behavior occurs.

Studies by some behaviorists in the past have caused them to conclude that punishment only temporarily suppresses the expression of undesired behaviors; it does not eliminate or extinguish them. These investigators have claimed that when the punishing agent is not present, the undesired behaviors occur again. However, other analyses of the influence of punishment have caused some learning theorists to disagree that punishment is merely a temporary suppressor. They have concluded instead that punishment can be as effective as nonreinforcement in extinguishing undesired acts (Hilgard & Bower, 1975, pp. 223–225).

The foregoing elements, then, represent the basic framework of operant conditioning. If consequences of acts are reinforcing, then the acts will be learned and will appear again when the child is in similar situations. These reinforced actions become habits and form a pattern of behavior that might be called the child's style of life or personality. Consequences that are unrewarding—either punishing or simply nonreinforcing—result in behaviors being dropped from the child's repertoire of actions.

Skinner's Notion of Learning

In the discussion so far I have used the word *learning* to refer to a child's coming to the point of habitually showing a particular behavior when in a given situation. However, there is really a more precise way to view learning from the standpoint of operant conditioning. You may recall that in the operant type of conditioning, the focus is not on how we get the child to display a behavior in the first place but on what happens to that behavior as the result of the consequences that follow it. From this perspective, learning is not seen as the process of the child's first displaying the behavior but rather as the process of her displaying it consistently, that is, of her responding at a high rate of frequency when in similar stimulus situations. For example, if a nine-year-old girl comes home from playing with neighborhood friends only one time in ten when her mother calls, "Time to come in, Karin," then we would say that Karin has not learned very well to come when called. Her rate of response is only 10 percent. We do not mean Karin is ignorant of how to return home when her mother calls; her occasional correct response shows that the excepted behavior is in her repertoire. But in saying she has not learned very well, we mean she does not respond consistently in this stimulus situation. However, her mother can increase Karin's rate of responding (help her better learn to come when called) by manipulating the consequences. Or, in behaviorist terms, she can rearrange the *reinforcement schedule* to increase her daughter's tendency to come when summoned.

Skinner has made particularly useful contributions to the analysis of the effect on behavior of different kinds of reinforcement schedules. For example, the effects on performance differ when *continuous reinforcement* (rewarding every time the desired act occurs) is used rather than *intermittent reinforcement* (rewarding only certain times the act occurs). Furthermore, different schedules of intermittent reinforcement yield different results. A *fixed-ratio* schedule (such as rewarding every third or every fifth response) has a different effect from a *fixed-interval* schedule (rewarding a response after every two minutes or every five minutes). These sorts of schedules, combined with a variety of others, can produce an array of different behavior results (Hilgard & Bower, 1975, pp. 216–217). For example, when an eight-year-old pupil is in the early stages of learning to raise his hand to speak in class rather than to shout out his opinion, he can profitably be rewarded on each occasion that he raises his hand. But after the habit has been well established, intermittent reward will probably serve to maintain the habit against extinction better than continuous reinforcement.

We can summarize Skinner's viewpoint by saying that from his behaviorist perspective child development is a process of the growing individual's learning increasingly complex and refined ways of acting as a result of the consequences that have followed the behavior she or he has attempted. The role of parents and teachers is therefore twofold: (1) to get children to try desirable acts and (2) to arrange consequences of children's acts so that desirable behavior is reinforced and undesirable behavior is extinguished through nonreinforcement or punishment.

CONDITIONED REINFORCEMENT AND CHAINING

One charge frequently aimed at the operant-conditioning model is that the theory is oversimplified. While critics admit that operant conditioning might account for certain simple acts, they claim it cannot explain complex skills or creative thinking. However, Skinner has proposed several mechanisms that he believes readily account for any sort of behavior that people exhibit, whether the actions are—as nonbehaviorists might say—mental or physical.

The first mechanism is described in the principle of *conditioned reinforcement:* A consequence (called a *stimulus*) that is not originally a reinforcing one can become reinforcing through repeated association with a consequence that is already reinforcing (Keller & Schoenfeld, 1950, p. 232). In other words, if a mother comes to feed her infant son each time he is hungry, and the consequences of the feeding is that it satisfies the infant's hunger, then after enough repetitions of this act the appearance of mother herself—even without food—becomes reinforcing or satisfying. Mother now has the power of being a reinforcer. She has become a *con-*

ditioned or a *secondary* reinforcer. Her appearance and the associated acts that accompanied the original feeding—her smiling and saying, "What a good boy"—can now be used to reinforce or teach other behaviors. For instance, when the growing infant happens to say "mah" during his babblings, the mother's smile and her comment, "What a smart boy—now say Mama," serve to reinforce the utterance of "mah." Consequently, the chance of the child's uttering "mah" again in the mother's presence is increased.

Not only does a growing child soon build up a significant store of conditioned reinforcements that can serve as rewards for actions, but many of these secondary reinforcers become generalized to other actions. That is, the reinforcer not only strengthens its original act but, by being associated with many actions, comes to strengthen any with which it is connected. For adolescents, money is a strong generalized reinforcer and can be used to strengthen or reward all sorts of behavior. For both younger and older children, such phrases as "good girl" and "that's the way to do it" become generalized reinforcers, attached to many behaviors.

F. S. Keller and W. N. Schoenfeld have summarized in the following way the two principles that govern these examples:

> Once established, a secondary reinforcement is independent and non-specific; it not only will strengthen the same response which produced the original reinforcement, but will also condition a new and unrelated response. Moreover, it will do so even in the presence of a different motive.
>
> Through generalization, many stimuli besides the one correlated with reinforcement acquire reinforcing value—positive or negative (1950, p. 260).

Two other conditioning functions that help explain complex behavior are *shaping* and *chaining*. *Shaping* consists of first reinforcing any gross approximation that the child achieves of a desired refined act. Then, after the gross form of the behavior has been well established, it can be shaped by gradual steps into the ultimate refined form by requiring better and better approximations before reinforcement is provided. For instance, in teaching a child to bat a ball, we will first offer praise for her swinging the bat, whether or not she hits the ball. As her swing improves, we no longer praise just any swing, but only those that hit the ball. When she can hit the ball nearly every time, we limit our praise to her hitting the ball into the field in front of her, and we do not praise foul balls that bounce to the side or to the rear. This process of gradually placing more precise limits on the kinds of acts that are reinforced continues, enabling the child to shape her batting skill till she can hit the ball in more precise directions and to specified distances. In a similar fashion, shaping helps expand and refine children's verbal behavior as their utterances are altered by the positive and negative reactions of people with whom they interact.

Chaining enables a person to hook together a sequence of small, individual conditioned acts to compose a complex skill. The process of chaining begins at the final end of the chain rather than at the beginning. Each preceding link of the chain is hooked on by associating it with the link that has already been established through reinforcement. For instance, consider the complex skill known as "having good table manners." We start with a child who yearns for both food and parental approval. Over a sequence of days the child is permitted to eat and is told, "That's fine" and "You're doing a good job" when he uses a fork rather than his fingers for lifting small pieces of meat to his mouth. When the pattern of using the fork is established, we add a new requirement. The child must use a knife and fork to cut large pieces of meat into smaller pieces before he is permitted to eat or is complimented for his actions. When he has learned these two links—eating with the fork after cutting up the pieces—we impose a new requirement, that of tucking a napkin into his shirt before he cuts up the meat, picks up pieces with the fork, eats, and is complimented. By such a process an extended set of habits or conditioned links can be formed into a complicated skill.

In summary, the simple mechanism of reinforcement not only accounts for specific simple acts, but the processes of secondary reinforcement, stimulus generalization, shaping (response discrimination), and chaining can account for all sorts of complex activities, in the opinion of behaviorists. And, they say, it is not necessary for us to fashion these processes consciously; they occur as natural behavior in everyone.

THE SCOPE OF SKINNER'S THEORY

In at least three important ways, Skinner's theory can be called broad in scope. First, it is not limited to any cultural setting; it purports to explain development in all societies. Second, its principles apply to all age levels, from the prenatal period to death. Third, it claims to explain all varieties of behavior—physical, mental, social, emotional. Although the first two claims have not attracted much criticism, the third has been the center of an extended debate, so it warrants close attention.

As noted earlier, behaviorism was originally a reaction against *mentalism*. It was a reaction against saying that human action was caused by ideas or feelings that arose in an unobservable place called *mind* or *soul*. Furthermore, behaviorism was a reaction against mentalists' research methods, which consisted largely of introspection, of a philosopher pondering about the nature of his own thoughts and emotions and then proposing elements or functions of the mind that he thought produced or controlled the thoughts and emotions.

Early behaviorists like Watson and Max Meyer claimed that if psychology is truly to become a science, it must focus solely on objective, publicly witnessed information. Such things as thoughts, mind, and feelings should have no place in this proposed science of human behavior. However, critics of behaviorism said that it is nonsense to deny the existence of such obvious phenomena as thoughts and feelings simply because these things are not directly seen by people outside the skin of the person who is doing the thinking and feeling. In sum, over the past half century behaviorists, including Skinner, have been charged with proposing a simplistic, mindless psychology. But Skinner, while admitting the charges are valid criticisms of early behaviorists, denies that they apply to him. In order to distinguish himself from the others, he has created two labels: (1) *methodological behaviorism* to identify those who would ignore the existence of thoughts and feelings and (2) *radical behaviorism* to identify his own position, which recognizes thoughts and feelings as normal "covert acts" and accepts introspection as a legitimate mode of inquiry (Skinner, 1974, pp. 13–18).

According to Skinner, the sin of mentalism—as practiced by Freud, Piaget, and many others—has been to focus exclusively on mental events. This focus has distracted their attention away from an analysis of the external environment's consequences that are the elements, he says, that can really account for why people act as they do. But in censuring the mentalists, Skinner has not uncritically embraced the methodological-behaviorist position of Watson and, more recently, of J. R. Kantor. Rather, Skinner has criticized methodological behaviorism for committing the opposite error:

> By dealing exclusively with external antecedent events, it turned away from self-observation and self-knowledge. Radical behaviorism restores some kind of balance. It does not insist upon truth by agreement and can therefore consider events taking place in the private world within the skin. It does not call these events unobservable, and it does not dismiss them as subjective. It simply questions the nature of the object observed and the reliability of the observations (1974, pp. 16–17).

So Skinner accepts thoughts and feelings, but he believes that people's techniques for investigating them are not well developed or very trustworthy. Consequently, he finds it best to depend heavily on an analysis of environmental conditions and people's observable reactions in order to understand a person's genetic and environmental history. He finds it of no explanatory help to create such words as *mind* or *consciousness* to account for a person's inner life. He contends (1974, p. 17) that "what is felt or introspectively observed is not some nonphysical world of consciousness, mind, or mental life but the observer's own body." In other words, Skinner has not divided the person into the traditional opposing aspects of physical and mental. He considers the individual to be an integrated unit. Some actions are observed by people outside the individual's skin (overt behavior) and others are observed only by the individual through introspection (covert behavior).

HEREDITY VERSUS ENVIRONMENT

Behaviorists traditionally have been criticized for underestimating the role of heredity in development. However, Skinner has reacted to such criticism by again distinguishing between the viewpoint of methodological behaviorists and his own. Several decades ago, Watson claimed he could take any healthy infant and raise it to become whatever he chose—doctor, lawyer, artist, beggarman, thief. However, Skinner (1974, p. 221) has dismissed this claim by calling it a "careless remark" and has proposed instead what he considers a more balanced view of the relative contributions of genetic endowment and environmental influences.

To understand Skinner's own position, we should first recognize that he believes the basic drive behind all behavior, human as well as nonhuman, is to survive. All actions are designed to promote the survival of both the individual and the species. Humans, like other species, inherit biological potentials that serve in some ways to enhance and in other ways to limit the chance of surviving in different environments. The potentials that a person inherits have been determined over past eons of time by the survival of the fittest, Darwin's natural selection. People with those traits that promoted survival lived on to produce offspring with these same high-survival characteristics. People lacking such traits died early, so their strains were not reproduced.

For purposes of analysis, it is useful to divide inherited characteristics into two types, although in actual practice the two merge into each other. The first type is well suited to stable environments, and the second to variable, unpredictable environments. That is, some environmental conditions—conditions of climate or the nature of predators and diseases, for example—are relatively permanent over time. In these environments that are stable over a period of centuries, a species can directly inherit traits that arm it for survival, traits like a heavy, white fur coat to match the arctic snow color and instincts or reflexes that give ample warning of approaching predators. But frequently, environmental conditions cannot be directly predicted. Conditions change from year to year, even from day to day. In such settings it is not helpful to inherit a specific, limited reflex or instinct. Rather, it is better to inherit the ability to change behavior on the basis of the environment's reaction. In other words, a species can inherit learning capacity, the ability to profit from the consequences of behavior. This is the second sort of inheritance and the one that Skinner considers the most important thing that humans derive from their genetic endowment. Humans' high level of intelligence or adaptability results from an unusually sensitive genetic potential for operant conditioning.

When Skinner has been pressed to tell exactly which behaviors or personality traits he believes people inherit and which he thinks they learn, he has refrained from identifying specific items, for he claims that not enough research has been done to give clear answers. But he has stated that many of the things that other theorists, such as Gesell and Freud, attribute to heredity are actually learned through conditioning. Skinner concludes that:

> Genetic causes sometimes become a kind of dumping ground: any aspect of behavior which at the moment escapes analysis in terms of contingencies of reinforcement is likely to be assigned to genetic endownment, and we are likely to accept the explanation because we are so accustomed to going no further than a stage of the organism (1974, p. 44).

Skinner, then, would not place himself at either extreme in the nature–nurture controversy. And he rejects the methodological behaviorists' contention that human personality is completely malleable, ready to be formed into whatever pattern the controllers of reinforcement desire. In his novel about a utopian community, *Walden Two* (1948), Skinner described a society in which all children have a highly similar environment until age 10 since they are all raised together in communal centers over the first decade of their lives rather than in individual families. Yet even with this common environment, the children living in Walden Two display a range of intelligence "almost as great as in the population at large. This seems to be true of other abilities and skills as well" (Skinner, 1948, p. 104). In effect, Skinner has proposed that genetic endowment accounts for a significant amount of the variation among children. He is not a thoroughgoing environmentalist. Nevertheless, he appears to assign a more important role to environmental forces than do the other theorists studied so far in this book.

THE STAGES OF CHILD REARING

In several previous chapters we have seen that theories of development are sometimes divided into *stage* and *nonstage* models. A stage model typically pictures the growth of the child as a series of distinct steps or phases. At around a particular age, the child changes noticeably from being one sort of person into being another sort. Then, for some time, the child retains the characteristics of this second sort until once more she or he makes a noticeable change and reaches a new level or phase of growth.

Contrasting with this conception of sudden change from one phase to another is the nonstage model that pictures growth as a very gradual process. Changes occur in miniscule amounts. It is true that in both stage and nonstage theories the child at age 6 will be obviously different from the way she looked and acted at age 3. But to nonstage theorists she has not arrived at 6 by any sudden leaps or insights. Instead, age 6 is just an accumulation of very slight alterations since age 3.

Generally, stage theories have been proposed by investigators who say heredity plays the greater role in development, whereas nonstage models have been devised by those who give more credit to the environment. This linking of stages with hereditarians and gradual growth with environmentalists is not a logical necessity. Gradual growth could reasonably be attributed to a genetic time schedule, and stages might be accounted for by sudden major changes in environmental forces. However, the observed linking has been the dominant trend, and Skinner's theory fits the pattern by being a nonstage model.

Skinner sees development as a continuous, incremental sequence of specific conditioned acts. It is not that he is unable to conceive of behavior being studied in terms of age or the passage of time, "as in the development of a child's verbal behavior or his problem-solving strategies or in the sequence of stages through which a person passes on his way from infancy to maturity" (Skinner, 1972, pp. 567–573). But he feels that (1) it is more accurate to view the developmental steps as very small ones and (2) it is unprofitable to focus only on *what* happens at a particular stage and to ignore the question of *why* it occurs. In other words, he is critical not only of picturing growth as major jumps followed by lengthy plateaus, but also of the developmentalists', or what he refers to as *structuralists'*, failing to explain why these changes occur, other than to state that the cause is an assumed internal maturation whose timing follows a genetic clock. Skinner's interest has been in the management or control of development, not in just describing what it looks like when it takes place.

So in his writings, Skinner makes almost no point of describing the characteristics of children at different age levels. Despite this, he has given some prominent attention to stages, but his stages have been *phases of the environmental treatment of the child,* treatment designed to produce optimal development. In short, he prescribes ways to treat children at different age levels to promote their happiness and well-being. To explain what these prescriptions are, I draw upon two of Skinner's publications, which were issued in the middle of his academic career. The first is an article from a

1945 *Ladies Home Journal* describing an air-conditioned, sanitary box in which he and his wife raised their infant daughter (Skinner, 1972, pp. 567–573). The second is the novel *Walden Two* (Skinner, 1948), and particularly the series of chapters detailing child-care methods in the utopian community. I will use child rearing in Walden Two as the focus of the discussion.

Ideal Child Rearing

In the psychologist's ideal child-rearing system, boys and girls are not raised by their individual families but are brought up in communal care centers till they reach puberty. At around age 13, adolescents, individually or in pairs, set up their own living quarters in the apartment complex that houses the adults in the mythical rural American town called Walden Two.

The first two decades of life in Walden Two are divided into five child-raising stages: (1) a lower-nursery stage for infants from birth to age 1, (2) an upper-nursery stage for those ages 1 and 2, (3) a middle-childhood phase for ages 3–6, (4) later childhood for ages 7–13, and (5) adolescence after age 13.

The basic philosophy during this entire two-decade span is that it is important to fulfill children's needs as quickly and as completely as possible in their earliest years. Then, very gradually, the demands and annoyances of normal life are introduced at a scientifically controlled rate that ensures that children can master them without acquiring negative feelings. This system of *behavioral engineering* or controlled operant conditioning is designed to encourage "the productive and strengthening emotions—love and joy. . . . But sorrow and hate—and the high-voltage excitements of anger, fear, and rage—are out of proportion with the needs of modern life, and they're wasteful and dangerous." In Walden Two such emotions, along with jealousy and envy, which "breed unhappiness," are almost unknown (Skinner, 1948, p. 83).

This pattern of providing an initially easy environment that becomes more and more difficult as children acquire the ability to adjust is intended to yield the reward of "escape from the petty emotions which eat the heart out of the unprepared." Children raised in Waldon Two not only get the satisfaction of pleasant social relations, they also become far more efficient workers "because they can stick to a job without suffering the aches and pains which soon beset most of us. They get new horizons, for they are spared the emotions characteristic of frustration and failure" (Skinner, 1948, pp. 90–91).

This is the general strategy of child rearing. During the first five years after birth adults see that no important need goes unsatisfied, so the child begins life practically free of anxiety and frustration. But eventually, through the mastery of gradually increasing frustrations, youths in Walden Two experience "the heartache and the thousand natural shocks that flesh is heir to" (Skinner, 1948, p. 93).

With this overall plan in mind, let us now consider some of the ways Walden Two's adults engineer the environment to produce such admirable results.

Birth to Age 1   Infants in Walden Two do not stay at home with their mothers but are collected together in the "lower nursery," each baby in an air-conditioned, enclosed crib like the "baby box" in which the Skinners raised their second daughter for the first year of her life. The purpose of the box is to furnish the infant with a healthful climate, free from the confinement of clothes and blankets and from dust and germs. The baby, clad only in a diaper, lies or sits or crawls about on an easily cleaned plastic mattress, plays with rattles and toys hung from the ceiling of the box, and gazes at the passersby through the large glass window that forms one side of the enclosed crib. The walls of the box are insulated from noise and temperature changes. A shade lowered over the window when the baby is asleep prevents light from disturbing the infant's naps.

After Skinner's own daughter, Deborah, had been in such a box for eleven months, he reported that because of the box's filtered air:

> The baby's eyes, ears, and nostrils remain fresh and clean. A weekly bath is enough, provided the face and diaper region are frequently washed. . . . She has always enjoyed deep and extended sleep, and her feeding and eliminative habits have been extraordinarily regular. . . . Although there have been colds in the family, . . . the baby has completely escaped. She has never had a diaper rash. . . .
>
> One of the commonest objections [of friends] was that we were going to raise a "softie" who would be unprepared for the real world. But instead of becoming hypersensitive, our baby has acquired a surprisingly serene tolerance for annoyances. She is not bothered by the clothes she wears at playtime, she is not frightened by loud or sudden noises, she is not frustrated by toys out of reach. . . . A tolerance for any annoyance can be built up by administering it in controlled dosages, rather than in the usual accidental way. Certainly there is no reason to annoy the child throughout the whole of its infancy, merely to prepare it for later childhood (Skinner, 1972, pp. 570–572).

In Walden Two the parents come each day or so to see the baby, to take it from the box and play with it a while. But this personal attention and display of affection are offered not only by the parents but also by the men and women who are in charge of the nursery. The purpose of sharing the responsibility for infants is to enable a child to imitate numerous desirable models who combine to form "a sort of essential happy adult. He can avoid the idiosyncrasies of a single parent" (Skinner, 1948, p. 119).

Ages 1 and 2   When children are around one year old in Walden Two, they move from their individual cubicles in the lower nursery to the upper nursery. This advanced nursery is composed of several small playrooms furnished with child-size equipment, a dressing room with a locker for each child, and small air-conditioned sleeping rooms. Clad only in diapers, children sleep on easily cleaned plastic mattresses. At playtime they are either naked or in training pants.

Child-raising practices continue to be guided by the principles followed in the lower nursery. Children's needs are met as soon and as completely as possible, with the result that the young child still knows nothing of frustration, anxiety, or fear. This does not mean, however, that the child has no experiences that might bring about frustration. It means, instead, that the behavioral engineers who schedule the child-raising program introduce potentially discouraging experiences "as carefully as we introduce any other emotional situation beginning at about six months" (Skinner, 1948, p. 100). For example, some of the toys children are given are designed to build perseverance.

The personnel of the nursery is balanced between men and women so as to "eliminate all the Freudian problems which arise from the asymmetrical relation to the female parent" (Skinner, 1948, p. 120).

Ages 3 to 6, Middle Childhood   From the standpoint of sleeping accommodations, this period is divided into two segments. At ages 3 and 4 each child is given responsibility for her own cot in a dormitory, and she is introduced to wearing regular clothing. At ages 5 and 6 children move into a complex of alcoves, each furnished like a regular room and holding three or four children with their beds and personal belongings. They are expected to gradually assume increased responsibility for the upkeep of their quarters. A careful schedule of conditioning in ethical behavior is conducted so that the foundations of ethical conduct are virtually complete by age 6.

Ages 7 to 13, Later Childhood   At age 7 children move from the alcoves into a complex of small rooms, each room designed for two children. At frequent intervals roommates are changed so children learn to live with different sorts of age-mates. They no longer eat in a dining room for children but use the adults' cafeteria.

It is impossible to distinguish formal from informal education in Walden Two since children are being taught by designed conditioning schedules wherever they are—in their living quarters, on the playground, and in the community's workshops, laboratories, studios, reading rooms, and fields. Early in their lives, children are given work to do, so they come to have a personal stake in contributing to the community.

Walden Two's behavioral engineers claim that their education system is far superior to that of the typical town because teachers do not waste time duplicating home training or changing the cultural and intellectual habits that children might have acquired outside of school.

From the child's first months after birth, the community depends on his natural curiosity and natural needs to motivate him to learn. The behavioral engineers appeal to humans' "drive to control the environment. . . . We don't need to motivate by creating spurious needs. . . . Promising paradise or threatening hellfire is, we assumed, generally admitted to be unproductive" (Skinner, 1948, pp. 87, 101–102).

The education system has no grade levels since "everyone knows that talents and abilities don't develop at the same rate in different children" (Skinner, 1948, p. 97). Pupils are encouraged to progress as rapidly as they like in any field, and they are not expected to waste time in a classroom being bored by activities they have outgrown. No subjects like English or social studies or science are taught. Rather, children are taught techniques of learning and thinking. Then they are provided chances to learn geography, literature, the sciences, and the like by themselves, based on the firm foundation they have received in ways of thinking: logic, statistics, scientific method, psychology, and mathematics. Children who do not appear to have an aptitude for learning a particular skill or type of knowledge are not required to do so. In other words, Walden Two's educators do not "waste time teaching the unteachable" (Skinner, 1948, p. 97).

Age 13 and Beyond, Adolescence   As the child passes puberty and becomes sexually potent, Walden Two does not require that he or she postpone mature forms of sexual gratification until age 20 or older. Instead, the adolescent finds "an immediate and satisfying expression of his natural impulses . . . very different from the secrecy and shame which most of us recall in connection with sex at some time or other" (Skinner, 1948, p. 111). When teenagers fall in love, they become engaged, at which time they consult the Manager of Marriages. He examines their interests, school records, and health status. If there are major discrepancies between the couple in intellectual abilities or temperament, they are advised not to marry or, at least, to postpone marriage for a while. But those who do seem well matched are encouraged to marry and begin having children when they are still age 15 or 16. This early satisfaction of sexual needs, combined with young people's early and gradual introduction to the world of work, makes the period of adolescence "brief and painless."

As for their living accommodations, the young teenagers move, at least temporarily, into rooms in the adult apartment complex, where they usually live in pairs. At the time of marriage, or whenever else he or she chooses, the individual can participate in building a larger room for himself or herself or can refurbish an existing room that has become available.

In effect, during the latter teens the youth gradually achieves adult status without the extended period of stress that adolescence in American society has ostensibly involved.

BIJOU AND BAER'S ADDITIONS TO RADICAL BEHAVIORISM

Perhaps the best known of the child development theorists adhering closely to a Skinnerian behaviorist viewpoint have been Sidney W. Bijou and Donald M. Baer. A significant contribution of these two authors has been their adopting three developmental periods suggested by J. R. Kantor (1959) and their illustrating in detail how traditional behaviorism can account for the changes observed in children at each level of growth. The labels attached to the three successive stages have been *universal, basic,* and *societal.*

The *universal stage,* which extends from the prenatal months until symbolic behavior or language becomes prominent at around age 2, derives its name from the fact that the growth of infants in all societies is much alike during these first years. Although the infant interacts with the environment and thus is influenced by the consequences of his or her actions, the greater determinant of behavior at this time is the child's maturing biological nature. So environmental stimuli play a very limited role in controlling the infant's "simple but self-preserving respondents" and in guiding the development of other behaviors related to "maintaining the biological necessities of life" (Bijou & Baer, 1965, pp. 2–3). The causes of similarities among children in all societies at this stage are primarily the basic biological similarities of the human species, which are the focus of attention in infancy. But, in addition, the social and physical environments are much the same from one culture to another, "not only because of the similarity in limitations imposed by extreme biological immaturity but also because of the extensive uniformity in infant-caring practices" (Bijou & Baer, 1965, p. 179).

The *basic* or second stage of development covers the years between about age 2 and ages 5 or 6. By now the child's biological development is sufficiently stable to meet her basic needs so she is more effective in interacting with the environment and can devote more energy to developing psychological behaviors. The patterns of action acquired during these preschool years depend heavily on the sort of social environment the child's family provides, although part of the child's characteristics are still determined by her biological structure, which results from her genetic inheritance.

During the basic stage, the personality structure is formed through the kinds of opportunities and contingencies the child's parents and other family members habitually provide. In these years the child's basic discriminations and forms of behavior are acquired.

The *societal stage* or third period of development begins around the time the child enters the primary grades and continues throughout the years of schooling. During this period, a myriad of influences from his culture serve to alter and expand the basic pattern of action or personality structure that was fabricated through biological inheritance and the nurturing practices of his family.

In sum, Bijou and Baer demonstrate how respondent and operant conditioning principles can account for the similarities and differences among children at three successive stages of growth.

Responses to Criticism

In addition to applying radical behaviorism to the interpretation of stages of development, Bijou has responded to critics who charge that behaviorism as a learning theory can neither account for child development in general nor explain the causes behind development. He has also answered those who claim that radical behaviorism views the child as only a passive organism and that practical applications of conditioning can harm children.

In reply to the first of these criticisms, Bijou states that while the radical behaviorism model is yet incomplete and therefore is still "on the way to becoming a mature theory," it is nevertheless a "comprehensive approach, including all the essential components of a system" (Bijou, 1979, p. 4). Specifically, modern behaviorism

1. Is founded on a clearly stated philosophy "that the subject matter of psychology is the continuous interaction between a behaving organism and physical and social events that can be observed objectively. . . . Therefore, reductionism, or the analysis of psycho-

logical interactions in terms of biological, physical, or chemical processes, is rejected totally" (Bijou, 1979, p. 4).

2. Is a *general* theory whose basic tenets account for (a) the strengthening or weakening of relationships between the child and her environment, (b) changes in abilities and skills, (c) a child's pattern of remembering and forgetting, (d) the transfer of learning from one situation to another, and (e) motivation, emotion, and conflict.

3. Has an established research methodology.

4. Has a precise method for translating basic research into practical applications.

Critics have also claimed that radical behaviorism does not adequately explain the causes underlying children's actions because it fails to identify the events of the past that have contributed to the child's present personality. In reply, Bijou contends that behaviorists are not oblivious to the child's developmental history. However, what is important about this history is not the past events themselves but rather the way such events have shaped the child's skills and attitudes that exist today. Since behaviorists believe that looking to the past cannot inform them accurately of what residue past events have left in the child's present life, they choose instead to observe the child systematically today in order to determine what the present-day consequences are of the child's "interactional history; that is, we learn what the specific events in his or her functional environment mean to him or her" (Bijou, 1979, pp. 5–6).

A further charge frequently leveled at behaviorists is that they view children as passive objects manipulated by environmental forces, objects that "must be stimulated. Hence . . . the person is not seen as playing an active, contributory role in his or her own development" (R. M. Lerner, 1976, p. 279). Bijou says this criticism may be true of Watson's original methodological behaviorism but not of radical behaviorism. The modern behaviorist believes that in every interaction with the environment, the child contributes her own responses and internal stimuli, which have been determined by her genetic structure and personal history. Furthermore, as the child develops, she responds increasingly to stimuli and environmental factors she herself has produced, so that she is engaging in active self-management. But this does not mean the child's behavior is directed toward some inherent goal, such as the goal of self-actualization in humanistic theory (Chapter Thirteen) or of formal operational thought in Piaget's model of cognitive development (Chapter Ten) (Bijou, 1979, pp. 7–8).

Behavior Management

In recent years one of the most popular applications of behaviorism has been in the use of operant conditioning for *behavior management* or *behavior modification.* Such conditioning has been employed by parents for socializing their children, by teachers seeking to control pupils' classroom behavior, and by therapists attempting to alter clients' undesirable habits and phobias. However, objections have been raised in a number of quarters on the grounds that these practices are manipulative, violate human rights, and often harm those who are the objects of the conditioning. Bijou has replied that the principles involved are certainly not inhumane but, rather, are simply the normal ones underlying all behavior, human and nonhuman alike. Therefore utilizing the principles consciously and systematically is not an act of malice or exploitation but is just good sense, for it increases the efficiency in the behavior management that parents, teachers, and therapists all normally attempt. As for potential harm that may result, Bijou states that "this is true for the practical application of any scientific finding when the applier is not adequately trained to the task" (Bijou, 1979, p. 9).

Finally, critics have claimed that behaviorism is useful for analyzing only the simplest stimulus-response learning but fails to account for the complexities of children's language development, problem solving, and creativity. Bijou's answer is that radical behaviorism is yet a new science, still incomplete, but one that displays great potential for explaining all of these phenomena in terms of observable interactions of children with their environment.

ENHANCED BEHAVIORISM

Although the proportion of psychologists in the behaviorism camp has dwindled since the 1950s, the people currently allied with the movement include a goodly number of spirited innovators dedicated to refining and extending the theory. Their contributions may be in book form or in such behaviorist-oriented journals as *Behaviorism* (started in 1972) and *Journal of Experimental Analysis of Behavior,* as well as in less parochial periodicals, such as *The Journal of Mind and Behavior* and *American Psychologist.* The following three examples illustrate something of the range of topics represented by these contributions.

Multiple-Term Contingencies

In her book, *Beyond Behaviorism,* V. L. Lee (1988, pp. 61–62) explains that:

A contingency is an if-then relation between behavior and an end result. . . . If you exceed the speed limit, your chance of getting a ticket increases; if you talk, you hear your own voice; . . . [so] the behavior is required if the end result is to occur. A causal relation is at the heart of the contingency, in the sense that the behavior makes a difference. It produces something that *would not* otherwise occur or prevents something that *would* otherwise occur. . . . Radical behaviorism, the philosophy of operant psychology, assumes that many acts are shaped and maintained by contingencies of which we are not aware. It assumes that the contingencies of which we are aware constitute only a subset of the total number of contingencies.

Lee portrays every *action* in life as an if-then contingency (*behavior* → *consequence* or *means* → *end*), thereby making such contingencies the basic units of operant behaviorism and, for that matter, of all psychology as a science. "A psychology of action . . . [implies] that in conducting our lives we pursue ends and vary the means to those ends, whether consciously or not" (1988, p. 151). From such a perspective, an individual's complete psychological life is comprised of the entire collection of contingencies found in that person's repertoire of behavior. Child development becomes the process of children accumulating an ever-growing assemblage of actions, that is, of *means* → *end* units.

One of the criticisms of behaviorism has been that it has oversimplified the analysis of people's activity by drawing so much of its evidence from laboratory experiments with nonhuman subjects—white rats, pigeons, and the like. When the generalizations about contingencies derived in such settings are then applied to predicting human behavior, the predictions have often proven faulty. In diagnosing these problem cases, certain behaviorists have proposed that the difficulty lies in the limited number of terms included in the contingency statement. For example, a two-term contingency statement includes only a description of (1) the behavior and (2) the consequence. A two-term statement usually works for certain kinds of events: "If you brush your teeth with peppermint toothpaste, you get a peppermint taste" (Lee, 1988, p. 61). But even in such a simple example as this, the two-term contingency statement fails if there is something wrong with your taste buds. As a solution, M. Sidman (1986) has joined others in proposing that multiple-term contingencies need to be adopted to account more accurately for many kinds of behavior. A three-term contingency could be a statement that includes one environmental condition, a behavior, and a consequence: "If a police car is driving behind your car when you exceed the speed limit, your chance of getting a ticket increases." A four-term contingency could consist of a behavior, two environmental conditions, and an outcome: "If you vigorously exercise when the atmospheric temperature is over 100 degrees and the humidity is over 90 percent, your chances of suffering heat prostration are increased." Such a statement can be turned into a five-term contingency if such a personal characteristic as age is added to the formula: "People over age 70 are more likely than people under age 40 to suffer heat prostration if they exercise vigorously when the temperature is over 100 and the humidity over 90."

Clearly this notion that events result from a combination of causal factors is hardly new. A belief in multiple causation is implied every time someone describes such a factor as atmospheric temperature as "a necessary but not sufficient cause." In like manner, a child's being raised in a poverty neighborhood cannot be considered *the* cause of membership in a youth gang but, rather, only one of a number of contributing conditions. So the point of mentioning multiple-term contingencies here is not to suggest that it is a novel concept. My purpose is to illustrate the way some behaviorists have responded to the criticism that they have been simplistic in depicting causal relations. By applying the concept of multiple-term contingencies, they are able to add precision to explanations of why different people act as they do in different situations.

Egoistic and Altruistic Acts and Character Traits

John B. Watson would have considered the study of such constructs as *character traits* to be far outside the realm of true psychology. Yet the study of unviewable traits is not unusual within the ranks of present-day behaviorists. For instance, in the journal *Behaviorism*, E. Sober (1989) offers a philosophical analysis of *egoism* and *altruism* as motivators of human behavior. Sober first grants that some people's characters are more egoistic (self-serving) and other people's more altruistic (other-serving), but then he concludes that no one's behavior toward others is driven solely by a single trait—egoism or altruism. Instead, any act—whether judged egoistic or altruistic—is governed by a combination of the individual's preferences, especially by the extent to which, in each particular situation, self-interest and others' interests are mutually supporting or are in conflict. (*Mutual support* means an action simultaneously promotes one's own welfare and that of others; *conflict* means an action sacrifices either one's own needs or the needs of others.) Under mutual support conditions, we cannot judge whether an individual's character is egoistic or altruistic, since the same act fulfills the needs of both the actor and the recipients. So it is only under conflict conditions that we can judge whether a person's character is more egoistic or altruistic. In effect, not every situation provides the opportunity to decide whether the actor has a more or less altruistic character. "Indeed, it is a possibility not to be dismissed lightly that altruists seldom act altruistically. This is not to say that they act selfishly. Rather, the point is that altruists may seldom find themselves in . . . choice situations" which require that they sacrifice their own welfare for the good of others (Sober, 1989, p. 101).

And like Sober, a variety of other behaviorists of various stripes have been including cognitivist concepts in their analyses of people's actions.

Compatible Perspectives

When behaviorists and cognitive psychologists have written about each other, they have typically adopted a pugilistic approach, bashing members of the opposite camp with charges of engaging in specious logic, failing to make accurate predictions, or practicing unsound methods of data collection and analysis. Although such bouts still take place in the professional literature (L. Miller, 1988; Moore, 1990; Skinner, 1984, 1985; Stemmer, 1989), there is also an increasing number of articles recognizing virtue in both behaviorist and cognitivist positions. This attitude of tolerance is exemplified in R. Schnaitier's (1987) claim that mental models do not represent alternatives to behaviorist explanations but, rather, fill a different and complementary explanatory niche to that of behaviorism. His point is that behaviorism and cognitivism do not address the same thing. The object of behaviorism, he contends, is to establish the relation between behavior and the context of its occurrence. In contrast, the object of cognitivism is to establish the design of the internal machinery through which functioning organisms are capable of behaving in context.

In somewhat the same manner, M. Mishkin and T. Appenzeller (1987) reconcile the putative differences between behaviorist and cognitivist interpretations of habits, learning, and behavior by suggesting that learning may be built on two quite different systems—one of them the source of noncognitive habits (behaviorism) and the other the source of cognitive memory (mentalism).

In a different vein, R. A. Kleinginna and A. M. Kleinginna (1988) have concluded from their historical review of experimental psychology that experimenters operating from behaviorist, functionalist, and cognitive perspectives have been broadening their areas of study and recognizing commonalities rather than differences among their theoretical positions and research findings.

The question of commonalities has led to an animated debate over the suggestion that present-day cognitive psychology is not a new paradigm but merely a disguised version of behaviorism (Chaplin, 1987; Martindale, 1987). Academicians also continue to argue over A. C. Catania's proposal of a *synthetic behaviorism* that combines the language and practice of behaviorists and cognitivists in a manner intended to resolve long-standing differences (Paniagua, 1986).

In short, the practice of modern-day behaviorism includes a growing diversity of attempts to achieve a rapprochement with the cognitive models that have come to dominate the field of child development in recent decades.

PRACTICAL APPLICATIONS

Behaviorism in all its modern varieties has yielded a substantial body of practical implications for child raising, education, and therapy.

Skinner's model served as the foundation for the programmed text-books and teaching machines that achieved their greatest popularity in the late 1950s and early 1960s. Skinner advocated the preparation of *linear learning programs* consisting of logically ordered small steps of information presented to the learner, who is required to respond at each step (filling in an answer in an incomplete sentence). The learner then receives immediate feedback about how accurate his answer—and thereby his learning—has been at that point. It was Skinner's intention to have the steps arranged so gradually and logically that the learner would be correct nearly every time he answered, with the resultant reinforcement (feedback) strengthening the permanence of each stimulus-response learning bond. Principles from this early model of programmed instruction are observed today in many of the *learning packages* being developed for the microcomputers that are playing a rapidly expanding role in classroom and home instruction. In addition, the international *mastery-learning* instructional movement has drawn on Skinnerian principles for portions of its methodology (Block & Anderson, 1975; Keller & Sherman, 1974).

In the mid-1980s, Skinner rebuked American educators for what he labeled "The shame of American education." He argued that students could learn twice as much as they currently learned with the same amount of time and effort. He proposed that such a goal could be achieved if (1) the aims of education were clarified, (2) each student was permitted to advance at his or her own pace, and (3) the problem of motivation was solved with programmed instructional materials. In Skinner's opinion, much of the fault for the schools' instructional inefficiency lay in the cognitive psychology which, he contended, was taught in the nation's teacher-preparation institutions. He would replace cognitive theory with operant-conditioning technology, thereby equipping teachers to provide more efficient instruction (Skinner, 1984).

Skinner's theory has also contributed in a major way to the behavior modification techniques described in Chapter Nine, with the effectiveness of such procedures being demonstrated by a growing quantity of empirical research (Kazdin, 1981, pp. 34–57). For example, findings in studies of preschool, elementary school, and special-class pupils "have indicated that when a teacher pays any kind of attention to unruly conduct, such behavior tends to increase (reinforcement); when she directs her attention to desirable personal-social behavior (reinforcement) and totally ignores undesirable behavior, that behavior tends to decrease (extinction)" (Bijou, 1985).

Behaviorism's practical applications in education and therapy have achieved international scope with the establishment of such organizations as the Association for the Advancement of Behavior Therapy and the International Association of Behavior Analysis. Behavioral courses and service programs have been introduced in such diverse nations as the United States, Britain, Brazil, West Germany, Peru, Australia, Colombia, and New Zealand.

As a final item of practical application, I should note that people who have heard of Skinner's baby box often ask, "Whatever happened to the infant daughter who spent the first months of her life in an Air-Crib?" To satisfy such curiosity, M. Forbes and F. Block (1990, p. 247) report that when Deborah Skinner grew to adulthood, she became a "successful artist, married to a political scientist. . . . Skinner's older daughter, Julie, who was not raised in an Air-Crib, . . . graduated from Radcliffe and later received a doctorate in psychology . . . , [then became] a professor of educational psychology at Indiana University and married a sociologist. Julie raised both her daughters in Air-Cribs."

SKINNER'S OPERANT CONDITIONING: AN ASSESSMENT

I feel that Skinner deserves high scores on most of the criteria proposed in Chapter One.

Skinner's model is clearly described (item 2), enjoying the advantage over mentalist theories of not including in its elements such nonobservable, internal items as ego or conscience, items whose characteristics are difficult to depict to other people.

As attested by *Walden Two* and the programmed learning and behavior modification programs that educators and therapists have adopted in recent years, Skinner's theory offers very detailed guidance for child-rearing practices (item 4).

Since the Skinnerian model is founded on empirical studies of overt behavior, and the mechanisms that account for behavior are rather simple, the theory has the qualities of internal consistency (item 5) and falsifiability (item 7). It has also led to a great deal of research and practical application (item 8). It has helped lead to the extensions of behaviorism found in this chapter and Chapter Nine and to the applications mentioned earlier in the realms of programmed instruction and behavior modification practices.

However, strong criticisms have been raised about the theory's being overly simple, unrealistically economical (item 6). This ostensible over-simplification has caused critics to question how adequately the theory reflects the real world of children (item 1) and how well it explains the past and predicts the future (item 3). In particular, Skinner has been charged with extending conclusions derived from animal experiments—primarily with pigeons and rats—to humans, without accounting properly for differences of intellectual quality among the species. For example, Noam Chomsky (1967), as a leader in the field of psycholinguistics, has argued that Skinner has been imprecise in analyzing such commonsense terms as

Skinner's Theory

How well do I think the theory meets the standards?

The Standards	Very Well	Moderately Well	Very Poorly
1. Reflects the real world of children		X	
2. Is clearly understandable	X		
3. Explains the past and predicts the future		X	
4. Guides child rearing	X		
5. Is internally consistent	X		
6. Is economical		X	
7. Is falsifiable	X		
8. Stimulates new discoveries	X		
9. Is self-satisfying		X	

want, like, and *plan* into operant-conditioning elements. Furthermore, Chomsky has assailed Skinner's assumption that children simply repeat the words or phrases they hear, that is, repeat the ones that have brought reinforcement. Chomsky claims that children formulate for themselves, through unseen mental processes, a deeper grammar that undergirds the meaning of the surface appearance of their sentences. This deep grammer structure enables children to recognize the equivalent meanings of utterances that are dissimilar in their surface structure *(The girl ate the cake* or *The cake was eaten by the girl* or *The cake was gone, for the girl had eaten it).*

Widespread dissatisfaction has also been expressed over Skinner's explanation of creativity. Many psychologists who admit that reinforcement, nonreinforcement, and punishment can affect whether a person retains or drops a given behavior also feel that Skinner avoids the problem of how the behavior got started in the first place. Where does a new or unique behavior come from? Is it proper just to call the pigeon's marching and pecking about the cage *random behavior* without accounting for why the pigeon marches and pecks rather than skates and coughs? How does a brilliant symphony or novel or scientific theory arise? Any psychologist who gives more credit to unobservable thinking behavior—to cognitive activity—can claim that Skinner's few principles of conditioning fail to offer an adequate explanation of innovative or creative acts.

In addition to the foregoing technical objections to radical behaviorism, other critics have, on humane or religious grounds, reacted against Skinner's views. Such criticism is based on a feeling that "it just doesn't seem right" that life operates on the basis of Skinnerian principles. D. B. Stevick, speaking from a Christian perspective, concluded about *Walden Two* that:

> Behavioral engineering rules out the risk and the achievement of freedom, love, self-giving, commitment, self-discipline, loyalty, memory, creativity, and hope. The significance of politics, the integrity of art, the warmth and support of human intimacy—all are lost. . . . The most precious thing about man is his humanity. Walden Two commends its deliberate abandonment (1968, p. 28).

In response to such a charge, Skinner would probably reply that, like it or not, radical behaviorism simply describes the truth about why people act as they do.

If we were to add an *adaptability* criterion to our nine assessment standards, it might read like this: "A theory is better if it permits adjustments in its structure so as to accommodate for widely recognized problems that the theory failed to resolve in its original form." Critics of radical behaviorism might then rank Skinner's model low on adaptability for what they regard as the inflexibility of Skinner and other doctrinaire operant behaviorists. M. J. Mahoney (1989, p. 1374) has suggested that:

> radical or orthodox behaviorism may have lost much of its hold on scientific psychology in large part because of its dogmatic objectivism and scientist intolerance, an intolerance that has become increasingly more evident as that hold has dissipated. . . . However, I hasten to add that this assertion applies only to orthodox (radical) behaviorism and not to the more common liberal versions of behavior therapy or to the varieties of . . . behaviorism that encourage creativity and innovation in experimental methods and conceptual models.

Because I believe there is substantial truth in these criticisms, yet feel that the theory has significant virtues, I have marked it near the center on items 1 and 3, then somewhat above the center on item 6. In terms of its overall self-satisfying quality (item 9), I have rated the theory at the "moderately well" position.

FOR FURTHER READING

Skinner, B. F. (1972) *Cumulative Record: A Selection of Papers,* 3d ed. New York: Appleton-Century-Crofts. Representative articles from various stages of Skinner's early career.

Skinner, B. F. (1974) *About Behaviorism.* New York: Knopf. This is an up-to-date, highly readable overview of radical behaviorism.

Skinner, B. F. (1987) *Upon Further Reflection.* Englewood Cliffs, N.J.: Prentice-Hall. A selection of fourteen succinctly written papers published between 1981 and 1986 in which Skinner seeks to clarify issues that he felt his critics misunderstood or misinterpreted in his previous writings. The articles reflect three aspects of Skinner's professional life, those of the philosopher of science, the experimentalist, and the utopian visionary.

For Bijou and Baer's overall scheme, see:

Bijou, S. W., and D. M. Baer. (1961) *Child Development: Vol. I. A Systematic and Empirical Theory.* New York: Appleton-Century-Crofts.

For a detailed analysis of the first stage of development, see:

Bijou, S. W., and D. M. Baer. (1965) *Child Development II: Universal Stage of Infancy.* New York: Appleton-Century-Crofts.

A detailed account of the second stage appears in:

Bijou, S. W. (1976) *Child Development: The Basic Stage of Early Childhood.* Englewood Cliffs, N.J.: Prentice-Hall.

CHAPTER NINE

Social Learning Theory and Contextualism

The reason social learning theory is paired with behaviorism in Part Four is that each of them assigns a key role to environmental consequences—especially to reinforcement—in determining the personality characteristics people acquire. Behaviorism can thus be considered at least a partial progenitor of social learning models. The comparisons between the social learning perspective and Skinner's operant behaviorism offered in the following pages are intended to highlight likenesses and differences between the two. The psychologist most often mentioned for contributions to social learning theory is Albert Bandura. Hence his version of the model is featured in the following description, as supplemented by reference to the work of Julian B. Rotter, another pioneer in the field.

The word *contextualism* in relation to human development theories rose in popularity in the late 1970s and throughout the 1980s. R. M. Lerner (1986, p. 26) has explained that:

> In contextualism, developmental changes occur as a consequence of reciprocal (bi-directional) relations between the active organism and the active context. Just as the context changes the individual, the individual changes the context. As such, by acting to change a source of their own development—by being both products and producers of their contexts—individuals affect their own development.

Some writers see contextualism as a derivative of social learning theory or of some other established model, such as Roger W. Barker's ecological psychology (Chapter Fourteen) or K. F. Riegel's dialectical theory (1975). In contrast, others regard social learning theory as only one variant of an overarching metatheoretical contextualism viewpoint (Zimmerman, 1983). In any event, the term *social learning theory* predates *contextualism* in popular use, so I address the two in that order in the following presentation.

BANDURA'S CONCEPTION OF SOCIAL LEARNING

Social learning theory gets its name from the emphasis it places on social variables as determinants of behavior and personality. It proposes to remedy an overdependence of earlier behaviorism on principles derived mostly from studies of animal learning and of human learning in one-person experiments. Social learning theorists attempt to correct this earlier bias by basing many of their principles on studies of the interaction of two or more people.

The social learning movement has sought to offer both (1) a balanced synthesis of mentalism (known today as *cognitive psychology*) and the principles of behavior modification and (2) an analysis of social influences on human development. In the mid-1970s, E. R. Hilgard and G. H. Bower (1975, p. 599) called this movement "a selective distillation of what is probably a 'consensus' position of moderation on many issues of importance to any theory of learning and behavior modification."

Although Albert Bandura (born 1925), a Stanford University psychologist, shares many basic convictions with behaviorists, he disagrees with traditional S-R theorists on the role of imitation in personality development. Among the areas in which Bandura's position differs from that of such radical behaviorists as Skinner, four are of particular importance: (1) the way a child acquires a new behavior that the child has never attempted before (a phenomenon Skinnerians have difficulty explaining), (2) the key steps involved in the process of learning from models, (3) the way that consequences (reinforcement, punishment) influence future actions, and (4) the development of complex behaviors.

The Origin of New Behavior

According to a commonly held S-R view, a child learns such things as language by first babbling a variety of sounds and then having certain of these sounds rewarded by people around her because the sounds approximate words they use. When the child happens to say *dah* or *ee* or *kee,* she is rewarded with smiles and caresses since the sounds have been uttered in the presence of *daddy, eating,* and *kitty.* When such events occur on several occasions, the sounds become conditioned to the objects they represent in the language of that particular culture. Although such a lucky coincidence between sounds and objects might account for children acquiring some simple words, Bandura and other social learning advocates find it inconceivable that this fortuitous process produces the thousands of words and the complex syntax and grammar that the child has mastered by the time she enters school.

In contrast, social learning theorists propose that most of a child's learning comes from his actively *imitating* or *modeling* what he sees and hears other people say and do. Bandura uses the word *modeling*—along with such terms as *observational learning* and *vicarious learning*—to mean that the child adds to his repertoire of actions by seeing or hearing someone else perform the behavior rather than by overtly carrying out the behavior himself (Bandura, 1969, pp. 118–120). So in the social learning theorists' opinion, children's new actions are not simply spontaneous and random hit-or-miss behaviors, with the hits being learned because they are reinforced. Instead, children seek to reproduce what they observe. In some cases this is *one-trial learning*. The first attempt is perfect. In other cases, the first attempt only approximates the desired action, and so requires *shaping* through more refined attempts before the child achieves a level of behavior considered satisfactory by the reinforcing agents in his environment.

Some theorists agree with the importance of imitation but feel that the process only operates when the child's attempts are directly reinforced as she reproduces an observed action. However, Bandura and other social learning investigators have produced evidence to support the belief that a child will also learn when the reinforcement is only vicarious. When six-year-old James observes six-year-old Henry being rewarded for saying "please" in order to get something he wants from the teacher, James learns to say "please" in similar circumstances.

People who have spent much time around children are not likely to consider this idea that children imitate others to be a discovery of cosmic dimensions. It seems to be pretty much common sense. Parents, teachers, coaches, and police commonly use principles of modeling to instruct children in how to add a new learning to their array of skills and knowledge. This sort of instruction is reflected in such phrases as "Try it this way" or "Let me show you" or "I'll tell you how to do it" or "Just read the directions." But more controversial and less obvious than these aspects of imitation is the role of *incidental learning*.

The issue of incidental learning has long been a topic of debate among learning theorists. The question at the center of the debate is this: Can a person learn something he sees or hears if this thing does not fulfill a need he is currently seeking to satisfy or if he is not rewarded for learning it? Many theorists say the answer is no. They claim that a person learns only those things that meet a need he is currently seeking to satisfy. Other things in the environment that are not pertinent to fulfilling the present need are passed by and not learned. And many theorists claim that reinforcement or reward is required for learning. Without reinforcement, either direct or vicarious, the child does not acquire a new skill or knowledge. (See the summary of latent-learning studies in Hilgard & Bower, 1975, pp. 134–136.)

However, Bandura and other social learning advocates have conducted experiments that suggest that the answer to the incidental-learning question is yes, at least in some cases. Children who are not seeking to satisfy any apparent need and who are not rewarded by a current happening may actually learn from the experience, storing in memory the results of their incidental observation for use at some later, appropriate time. According to Bandura, the error made by psychologists who do not admit to such incidental learning has been their confusing learning with performance. Since children who were not reinforced for a given act in experiments did not perform the act, it was assumed that without reinforcement, vicarious or direct, there had been no learning. But Bandura's evidence has supported the belief that people do not overtly display many things they have learned from a model if these things do not appear to yield sufficient rewards in the situation at hand. In other words, social learning theorists assume that for a given life situation, each of us has a series of possible reactions we might display. We have several answers we might give to the question being posed. However, in this multiple-choice situation, all answers are not equally plausible. Some seem better than others, and those better answers are the only ones we exhibit publicly, so other people do not realize that we have learned additional possible answers as well.

Bandura, then, contends that children do not just happen to hit on a new sort of behavior that is then reinforced; instead, he says, children acquire new behaviors by observing models in their environment. But what about the child's *creating* a novel behavior that she has not even seen before? How does this come about? Again, radical behaviorists seem to consider such novel acts accidental or built up in some way from small links of behaviors already carried out. But the social learning theorist of Bandura's persuasion accounts for novel acts by concluding that:

> When exposed to diverse models, observers rarely pattern their behavior exclusively after a single source, nor do they adopt all the attributes even of preferred models. Rather, observers combine aspects of various models into new amalgams that differ from the individual sources. . . . Different observers adopt different combinations of characteristics (Bandura, 1977, p. 48).

So from the social learning viewpoint, novel behavior results from the child's combining different segments of various behaviors he has observed in other people, with the observation including both direct witnessing of events and such indirect modes of securing examples as reading or hearing about ideas and actions.

The Process of Learning from Models

How observational learning takes place is far from completely understood. However, some of the conditions that influence it have been identified. According to Bandura, the main reason a child learns from seeing or hearing a model is that the information she thereby acquires helps her decide how the observed behavior might help or hinder her in fulfilling her needs on some future occasion. This information is stored in the memory in symbolic form, as images or as verbal symbols, for future reference.

This process of learning from models consists of five main functions: (1) paying *attention*, (2) *coding* for memory, (3) *retaining* in memory, and (4) *carrying out motor actions*—and all four of these steps require (5) *motivation* (Bandura, 1977, pp. 22–29).

First, when a child observes a model, the child must *attend to the pertinent clues* in the stimulus situation and ignore the aspects of the model and the environment that are incidental and don't affect the performance that the child seeks to learn. The child's failure to perform the behavior properly later, especially if the behavior has been complex, is often due to his misdirecting his attention at the time the model was observed. Teachers frequently try to prevent this error by eliminating as many of the irrelevant stimuli from the setting as possible and by verbally directing the child's attention to those aspects of the model's performance that are the most important.

A second requirement for imitative learning is that the child accurately record in memory a *visual image* or *semantic code* for the act she has witnessed. Without an adequate coding system, the child fails to store what she has seen or heard. There are obvious developmental trends in the ability to profit from models. Older children learn more readily from witnessing others' performances than do younger children. This superiority of older children is due in large part to their more advanced ability to use symbols. Bandura points out (1977, p. 30) that the infant's use of modeling is confined mainly to instantaneous imitation. The very young child will imitate the adult's gesture or word immediately instead of reproducing it after a period of time. But as the child grows up and has more experience in associating words or images with objects and events, she can store these symbols in order to recall and reproduce the events after increasingly extended periods of time. In effect, the development of language and of schemes for coding observations enhances the child's ability to profit from models. Not only must the observations be coded for memory (the input portion), but the codes must be suitable for transforming the perceptions into overt actions (the output portion). Otherwise the child ends up with useless knowledge, symbols that have been stored but cannot be retrieved in a form that leads to action.

A third factor influencing whether the knowledge will be available when needed is that of *memory permanence*. Although the operation of memory is still poorly understood by psychologists, one thing is clear— memories fade or disappear with time. Therefore much that children learn from observing models is forgotten, so that such learning is no longer available when the child needs it to solve some problem in life (Bandura, 1969, p. 202). Such memory-aiding techniques as rehearsal (review or practice) and attaching multiple codes to an event (associating a variety of interlinked words or images with the event) serve to keep the stored information at a level that makes it readily retrieved when needed.

A fourth factor influencing the success of learning from models is that of *reproducing* the observed motor activities accurately. It is not enough that the observer get the *idea* of the actions to perform or that he code and store the idea adequately, it is also necessary for him to get the motor behavior, the muscular *feel* of the behavior. He usually cannot do this perfectly on the first trial. Thus he needs a number of trials in which he approximates the behavior and then receives feedback from this experience to correct the deviations from the ideal that his earlier attempts have involved. It should be apparent that developmental trends in learning efficiency are partially a result of the older child's greater muscular strength and control in comparison to that of the younger child. Even if the younger child could attend properly to the cues of the observed performance and could encode the observations mentally as images or verbal symbols, the younger child still would not perform the modeled activities as well because his muscular development is not as advanced as the older child's.

The fifth requirement in the process of learning from models is that the learner be *motivated* to carry through the several steps of the process. In the behaviorist tradition, this motivational function has been embedded in the crucial role of the *consequences of behavior*. Since the interpretation that Bandura and other present-day social learning theorists place on the function of consequences differs from that of radical behaviorists like Skinner, we need to pay special attention to this aspect of the learning process.

The Role of Consequences

According to Skinner's theory of operant conditioning, in a given stimulus situation a person has a series of likely responses she might give. Which response will actually be given depends upon the comparative strengths of the competing responses in the individual's repertoire of responses. In addition, the strength of a potential response depends on how often that response has been reinforced in the past when the individual has been in a similar situation, that is, when she has faced what she considers a similar problem. In the opinion of radical behaviorists, this strengthening of response tendencies through reinforcement is automatic. When a person's actions are reinforced or rewarded, it is not necessary for her consciously to tell herself, "That worked out well, so I'll try it again in the future." Instead, the strengthening of the response simply comes about without the need for the individual to assess the effect of her behavior. Furthermore, the typical adherent of operant conditioning believes that in order for this automatic strengthening to be most effective, the consequence (reinforcement or reward) must occur as soon as possible after the act so that the two become intimately connected or "conditioned."

However, Bandura disagrees with this interpretation of how consequences influence subsequent behavior.

> Although the issue is not yet completely resolved, there is little evidence that reinforcers function as automatic shapers of human conduct. . . . A vast amount of evidence lends validity to the view that reinforcement serves principally as an informative and motivational operation rather than as a mechanical response strengthener (Bandura, 1977, p. 21).

By *informative* Bandura means that the consequences, rewarding or punishing, tell the child under what circumstances it would seem wise to try a particular behavior in the future. In other words, the consequences improve the child's prediction of whether a given act will likely lead to pleasant or unpleasant outcomes on a later occasion. Bandura does not believe, as radical behaviorists do, that a consequence exerts its influence in reverse chronology, strengthening the behavior that preceded the rewarding consequence. Rather, he contends that the consequence exerts its influence into the future by giving the child information about what effects he can expect if he later acts that same way in a similar stimulus circumstance. By adopting such an interpretation, Bandura feels that he places himself in a better position to account for children learning from models than are the radical behaviorists who propose that consequences automatically reinforce the preceding actions that the individual carried out.

That is, Bandura points out that the child can learn from observing others as well as from behaving himself, since watching others can give him the same information he gets from his own behavior consequences if he attends to the significant elements of the observed action.

When Bandura speaks of the *motivational* role of consequences, he means that children will more likely try to learn modeled behavior if they value the consequences the behavior seems to produce. If a pupil yearns for the teacher's approval and observes that the teacher gives such approval to children who spell well, then she is motivated to pay attention to the week's spelling words and to rehearse them so they are well stored in memory.

In summary, then, Bandura does not believe that consequences reinforce responses automatically and strengthen the response that immediately preceded the consequences. Instead, he sees consequences as *regulators* of future behavior—they regulate by means of giving the individual information about likely future consequences and by motivating her to act in one way rather than another in order to obtain the results she seeks.

Complex Behaviors

Not only do Bandura's ideas about modeling differ from those of radical or methodological behaviorists, but his beliefs about how complex behaviors are acquired differ as well. Contrary to more traditional behaviorists, he does not believe a child develops complex behaviors by first imitating one small element of the observed pattern and then gradually building up the entire pattern through a step-by-step accrual of successive elements. Rather, he says that:

> Patterns of behaviors are typically acquired in large segments or in their entirety rather than through a slow, gradual process based on differential reinforcement. Following demonstrations by a model, or (though to a lesser extent) following verbal descriptions of desired behavior, the learner generally reproduces more or less the entire response pattern, even though he may perform no overt response, and consequently receive no reinforcement, throughout the demonstration period (Bandura & Walters, 1963, p. 106).

However, once the new behavior has been comprehended through observation, the likelihood that it will be displayed in the child's personality is governed chiefly by schedules of reinforcement and punishment.

A final aspect of imitation learning that is important in Bandura's system is *the nature of the models.* Experimental studies support the commonsense notion of hero worship in the following ways: (1) Children are more likely to model their own behavior after the actions of people they regard as prestigious than after actions of people who are not highly regarded. (2) Children are more likely to adopt behavior patterns from models of their own sex than from the opposite sex. (3) Models who receive rewards, such as money, fame, high socioeconomic status, are more often copied than ones who do not. (4) People who are punished for their behavior tend not to be imitated. (5) Children are more influenced by models they perceive to be similar to themselves, such as in age or social status, than by models they see as being quite different from themselves (Bandura & Walters, 1963, pp. 10–11, 50, 84, 94–100).

In summary, imitation is viewed by Bandura as a major device in children's social development, for through the observation of models, children add new options to their repertoire of possible behaviors. Furthermore, models help children decide under what circumstances they can most profitably put these new options into practice.

From Bandura's social learning perspective we can conceive of child development as a process (1) of the child's gradually expanding his repertoire of answers or possible actions by means of both observing others and trying the actions himself and (2) of the child's using information from the observed consequences to guide future decisions about when one response will be more appropriate than another to fulfill needs and attain rewards. Like Skinner, Bandura does not separate development into a series of stages, but he considers the process of cognitive and social growth to be one of gradual accrual of an ever widening array of response possibilities for increasingly differentiated stimulus situations.

With Bandura's views of the importance of observational learning in mind, let us turn to a currently popular application of social learning theory in the treatment of deviant behavior.

Normality and Deviance

In putting his model of development to practical use, Bandura has centered attention on psychotherapy and the correction of antisocial behavior. His technique of treating deviance does not take the form of curing mental disorders or of alleviating the underlying causes of mental disease, as has been the case in traditional psychiatric practice. Instead, he has rejected the medical concept of deviance, the concept that the person exhibiting the undesired behavior is sick and that this mental condition must be treated to make him well. In place of this belief about curing illness, Bandura advocates what has been termed *behavior modification,* because he is convinced that an act that "is harmful to the individual or departs widely from accepted social and ethical norms" is not symptomatic of some disease but is simply "a way that the individual has learned to cope with environmental and self-imposed demands. Treatment then becomes mainly a problem in social learning rather than one in the medical domain" (Bandura, 1969, p. 10).

In keeping with this viewpoint, Bandura would treat a child who displays undesirable social behavior by manipulating the consequences of the child's acts so that the child finds it more rewarding to adopt more acceptable behavior than to continue in the currently unacceptable pattern. By extrapolating principles from Bandura's discussion, the process of carrying out behavior modification can be summarized in four basic steps:

1. Identify the specific behavior you wish to have the child substitute for the presently unacceptable behavior.

2. Arrange for the child to try out this new, desirable behavior. There are several ways this can be done: simply wait for it to occur spontaneously, provide a model, verbally explain what the desired behavior is, shape it through gradual approximations, or use several of these techniques.

3. Determine what sorts of consequences will be strongly reinforcing or rewarding to the child and what sorts will be punishing.

4. Manipulate consequences so that the desired behavior, when it appears, will yield greater reinforcement than does the undesirable behavior. In other words, arrange a schedule of reinforcement and/or punishment that will make it profitable for the child to give up the old behavior in favor of the new.

Although this process is easy to outline, it is often difficult to carry out in practice. However, such behavior modification is conceived by social learning theorists to be the most effective means possible of correcting a child's deviant acts.

Critics of behavior modification have charged that it is a naive, superficial approach to psychotherapy or personality improvement. They claim that seeking directly to change the child's overt actions fails to get at the underlying cause. Such criticism is based on the view that overt behaviors, such as thumb sucking, temper tantrums, or stealing, are just surface symptoms of an underlying disorder buried deep in the personality, probably in the unconscious. Bandura, in reacting to such charges, says that both psychodynamic and social learning theorists are seeking underlying causes. However, the two camps differ in where they believe these causes lie.

Psychoanalysts propose that the causes are repressed conflicts left over in the unconscious from the child's failing to solve the conflicts faced during earlier psychosexual stages of development. Therefore the therapist digs into the patient's psyche to identify which events in the past produced the conflicts and then seeks to help the patient consciously relive these events and put them into a mentally healthy perspective. Such analysis, say the psychodynamic therapists, frees the patient from her symptoms of deviance, and the personality disorder is cured.

In contrast to this psychodynamic view, social learning therapists hunt for "underlying causes" in the child's present environment. For the social learning theorist, the term *cause* refers to the satisfying consequences that the child's deviant behavior continues to bring him. The child's regrettable behavior persists because it pays off or because he does not know any other way to behave that will bring him more satisfactory consequences. The task of the therapist, then, becomes that of carrying out the four steps of behavior modification.

In both psychodynamic and social learning theories it is possible to "simply treat the symptom" without getting at the "real cause." However, the meaning of this phrase is quite different under the two theories. With the typical psychodynamic approach, "simply treating the symptom" usually means punishing or rewarding the child so she will stop sucking her thumb in school or will stop stealing objects from her classmates' desks. Or it could mean giving the child a posthypnotic suggestion to avoid thumb sucking or stealing. However, in the psychodynamic view, such treatment only suppresses the particular symptom on which the treatment has focused. And because the underlying causes—repressed conflicts—have not been touched, other symptoms will arise.

In social learning theory "simply treating the symptom" is a phrase interpreted to mean that the therapist has been too narrow in her perception of the number of different situations in which the child's deviant response is used. For instance, a ten-year-old boy throws temper tantrums at home, around the neighborhood, in the classroom, and on the playground when things do not go his way. According to social learning theorists as well as other behaviorists, this pattern of action is maintained because people ultimately yield to the boy's demands in order to "avoid all that fuss." To solve the problem, the teacher may seek to eliminate the tantrums in class (1) by not reinforcing them, (2) by helping the boy observe models who use such techniques as reasoning or discussion instead of tantrums to get their way, and (3) by rewarding the boy's attempts to use these more mature techniques. However, while the undesirable behavior may be reduced in school, it may persist at home, around the neighborhood, and on the playground because the consequences in these out-of-class settings have not been altered. Critics of the behaviorists' reinforcement and punishment approach may charge that the classroom treatment of the problem was just getting at the symptoms but not the cause. But the social learning theorist can reply that if the consequences in all four environments—classroom, home, neighborhood, and playground—were altered, the tantrums would disappear entirely, and the problem would be cured.

However, another difficulty may arise to cause Freudians and their psychodynamic colleagues to continue to criticize the behaviorists' approach. It is possible that the tantrums will disappear in all settings, but the new behavior that is substituted may also be deviant. For example, the boy, when he fails to get his way by tantrums, may withdraw from the classroom group and sit brooding. The psychodynamic therapist can now claim that this is simply *symptom substitution,* that one sort of deviance has replaced another because the real unconscious cause was not unearthed and resolved. The social learning therapist will disagree. He will likely say that for any given stimulus situation the ten-year-old has learned a hierarchy of possible responses. The most powerful of these at the top of his hierarchy of appropriateness has been the temper tantrum. If the consequences are altered so such behavior does not pay off for the child, then he can be expected to turn to the next most promising option in his strata of habits. By *promising* I mean that response that he estimates will bring the most satisfying results in such stimulus situations. Often this second most likely response is also considered undesirable by the important people in his life. So if withdrawal and brooding is the second choice among his options, the social behavior problem is not solved. He is still labeled a problem child.

According to social learning theorists, this is not a problem of symptom substitution, however; it is a problem of the child's having a response hierarchy whose most promising options (that is, promising in the boy's estimation) are all undesirable ones for the society in which he lives. Therapy does not consist of hunting for an unconscious cause. Rather, it consists of helping the boy learn a new, socially approved behavior that is so rewarding that it takes priority over all of the undesirable responses in his repertoire of likely reactions to frustration, both in school and out (Bandura, 1969, pp. 48–52).

As implied, Bandura subscribes to a *reference-group* interpretation of normality and deviance. A child is normal or abnormal only in terms of how her behavior compares to the behavior of other members of a designated group. This reference group might be Catholics, American ten-year-olds, upper-class children, Central Elementary School fifth graders, or any other group. It should be apparent that a child might be considered normal when compared to one group but deviant when compared to another. Hence, when the question of normality arises, it is important to identify the reference group to be used in answering the question.

This matter of reference groups is important not only for determining normality or deviance in a child's development but also for understanding why attempts at behavior modification may fail. Consider a junior high school boy who steals money and equipment from his classmates and from the teacher. School authorities consider this behavior undesirable, so they seek to change it by altering its consequences. They punish the boy by keeping him after school, and they offer him special privileges if he will go for a period of one month without stealing anything. But he continues to steal, and this puzzles the teacher and principal, for it is apparently contrary to social learning principles. But, in the eyes of the social learning theorist, they have simply failed to realize that the boy is still being reinforced for stealing. He persists in his deviant act because he continues to be rewarded by his own preferred reference group, by his gang of delinquent peers whose approval he values more than that of school authorities. Consequently, deviant behavior cannot be understood or altered without our recognizing that various groups' norms are often in conflict with each other and that the rewards dispensed by one group are more influential than those dispensed by another because the child values the first group more. This means that we need to identify which reference groups or individuals serve as the most valued ones in the child's life.

Finally, social learning theory discourages the application of such traditional psychiatric labels as *neurosis* and *psychopathic personality* to children exhibiting antisocial behavior. These children are not considered diseased or mentally deranged. The cause of their deviance, whether it appears to be harmful to themselves or to be contrary to social norms, is not to be found by use of special medical terms or principles. Instead, social learning theorists contend that "a single set of social learning principles can account for the development of both prosocial and deviant behavior and for modifications of behavior toward greater conformity or greater deviation" (Bandura & Walters, 1963, p. 221). Thus treatment of the child consists of altering the consequences the environment provides for the undesired behavior. It does not consist of searching in the depths of the child's psyche for psychosexual or psychosocial conflicts.

Conscience and Self-Control

In social learning theory a child's conscience or moral values are not inborn. The infant arrives in the world amoral. Then, by the same modeling and conditioning principles that produce all of her other beliefs, she gradually acquires her values and a capacity for self-control and self-direction. In other words, her character is learned, not inherited.

Investigations cited by Bandura support his contention that the development of self-control or conscience is heavily influenced by the models children observe and by patterns of direct reinforcement that they encounter, such as disciplinary measures used by parents and teachers. The degree to which a child will resist temptations has been most readily affected in experimental situations by how immediately the model in the situation is rewarded or punished. The characteristics of the model also influence how likely it is that the child will adopt the modeled self-control or lack of it, with the greatest influence exerted by models who are capable, successful, and prestigious.

The timing of reward and punishment is also important. Bandura suggests that many parents mold a child's conscience—meaning his guilt feelings or self-punishing tendencies—more successfully by withholding privileges than by applying aversive stimuli such as a spanking or isolation. He believes that the frequent superiority of withholding or withdrawing positive reinforcers over applying aversive measures is to a great extent the result of timing. Typically, the parent withholds the reinforcer until the child expresses guilt or some self-punishment response. Then the privilege or desired object is restored to the child. But "parents on most occasions administer aversive stimuli some time after a deviation has occurred and fail to make its termination contingent on the child's expressing self-punitive responses" (Bandura & Walters, 1963, p. 221). As a result of the postponed punishment and the indefiniteness of the time to remove the punishment, the child is less likely to adopt the self-control standards the parent desires. Studies have also suggested that the withholding of privileges serves most effectively to develop the child's self-control if the agents who withhold the rewards and subsequently reinstate them are warm, affectionate people rather than unaffectionate people or people who hold a grudge (Bandura & Walters, 1963, pp. 197–199).

PRACTICAL APPLICATIONS OF BANDURA'S MODEL

I have already described basic steps in the behavior modification process as practiced today in many schools and clinics. And the sorts of educational applications described in Chapter Eight for radical behaviorism apply as well to ones deriving from Bandura's theory. But the practical use of Bandura's proposal and similar social learning schemes goes well beyond applications of operant conditioning. For instance, the following studies represent only a handful of more than two hundred reported in *Psychological Abstracts* for the years 1983–1990:

1. The treatment of adolescents' problems of acquired immune deficiency syndrome (AIDS) (Flora & Thoresen, 1988), delinquency (Hawkins & Weis, 1985), pregnancy (Hagenhoff et al., 1987), learning disabilities (Gresham & Elliott, 1989), bulimia (Love et al., 1985), cigarette smoking (Krohn et al., 1985), marijuana use (Akers & Cochran, 1985), alcohol use (Brook & Brook, 1985), and drunk driving (DiBlasio, 1988).

2. The analysis of Dutch children's health-related behavioral intentions (de Vries, Dijkstra, & Kuhlman, 1988), children's aggression in Zapotec Indian communities (Fry, 1988), aggressive behavior in German schools (Petermann, 1987), ways to combat American children's use of illicit drugs (Bush & Iannotti, 1985), middle-childhood social skills in Jerusalem (S. R. Rose, 1987), the development of American children's prosocial skills (Batson et al., 1987), sex role identification among Soviet preschoolers (Kolominskly & Meltsas, 1985), and the switch from homosexuality to heterosexuality among boys in the Sambia tribe of Papua New Guinea (J. D. Baldwin & Baldwin, 1989).

ASSESSING BANDURA'S SOCIAL LEARNING THEORY

Like Skinner's presentation of operant behaviorism, I find Bandura's description of social learning theory easy to understand, falsifiable, internally consistent, and directly applicable to child rearing. Furthermore, as the above list of applications suggests, Bandura's theory has stimulated a large quantity of empirical studies and thus deserves high marks for its fertility.

Compared to Skinner's radical behaviorism, social learning theories are not as subject to the charge of devaluing mental activity. And unlike Skinner, social learning theorists have accorded a prominent place to the function of imitation in personality development. They have also conducted their research on people, particularly on children, rather than on animals, thus avoiding the criticism directed at Skinner that he has drawn simplistic conclusions about human development by founding many of his principles on conditioning experiments with pigeons and rats. For all of these reasons, I would rate social learning theorists higher than Skinner on how well they reflect the real world of children and explain the past and predict the future.

I would also give social learning theory a higher rating on economy of explanation (item 6) because Bandura's version appears to suffer less from the criticism of being overparsimonious than does Skinner's behaviorism.

Bandura's Theory

How well do I think the theory meets the standards?

The Standards	Very Well	Moderately Well	Very Poorly
1. Reflects the real world of children	X		
2. Is clearly understandable	X		
3. Explains the past and predicts the future	X		
4. Guides child rearing	X		
5. Is internally consistent	X		
6. Is economical	X		
7. Is falsifiable	X		
8. Stimulates new discoveries	X		
9. Is self-satisfying	X		

Despite this array of strengths, social learning theory has not been universally adopted by people concerned with explaining children's development. Parents and teachers who seek information about what children are like at different age levels receive no aid from the social learning model, for it describes *how* children learn rather than *what they are like* at different stages of their lives. In addition, developmentalists who see a child's genetic endowment and the influence of internal maturation as prime factors behind child growth may also find fault with social learning theorists' slighting of hereditary influences on development.

Finally, all behaviorist approaches, social learning theory included, have been criticized for giving too little recognition to how children think and feel about themselves. Developing children, critics have claimed, are not just animated mechanisms to be programmed to suit the desires of the agents that control their environments. Rather, in the opinion of humanistic critics (Chapter Thirteen), children are unique personalities with hopes and plans and feelings that make up the essence of their humanness. Behavioristic approaches appear to overlook this matter.

While social learning theory has not satisfactorily answered all the questions about development posed by other theorists, parents, and teachers, it has come perhaps the closest of any theory to describing how children acquire the learned, rather than the inherited, aspects of their personalities. An appraisal offered by Hilgard and Bower in the mid-1970s seems equally appropriate today:

> Social learning theory provides the best integrative summary of what modern learning theory has to contribute to solutions of practical problems. It also provides a compatible framework within which to place information-processing theories of language comprehension, memory, imagery, and problem solving. . . . For such reasons, social learning theory would appear to be the "consensus" theoretical framework within which much of learning research (especially on humans) will evolve in the next decade (1975, p. 605).

In regard to its overall self-satisfying quality (item 9), I would rate social learning theory higher than Skinner's behaviorism.

ROTTER'S SOCIAL LEARNING VIEWS

Julian B. Rotter is an American psychologist whose book *Social Learning and Clinical Psychology* (1954) outlined a view of personality development that drew on concepts from such diverse sources as Alfred Adler's "individual psychology," Kurt Lewin's field theory, and the works of behaviorists Edward L. Thorndike, E. C. Tolman, and Clark Hull (Rotter, 1982, pp. 1–2).

Adler was a Viennese psychiatrist who worked closely with Sigmund Freud until they parted ways in 1912 over key theoretical disagreements. In particular, Adler deposed the sexual drive as the central motivating force behind human behavior and substituted in its place the belief that a deep-seated feeling of inferiority constantly stimulates the child to seek security and a sense of significance. Furthermore, as Rudolph Dreikurs explains:

> The leading idea of the Individual Psychology of Alfred Adler is found in his recognition of the importance of human society, not only for the development of the individual character, but also for the orientation of every single action and emotion in the life of a human being (1950, p. 1).

Lewin, a German psychologist who emigrated to the United States to teach at the University of Iowa and the Massachusetts Institute of Technology, focused attention on the way a multitude of environmental and biological factors in an individual's life combine to form a field of influence that determines the person's thought and action at any particular moment.

Thorndike was a Columbia University professor who proposed a series of "psychological laws" that govern how learning takes place. Tolman, a University of California psychologist, devised a theory of learning that pictured children's behavior as always goal-directed—as always designed to achieve an objective. Furthermore, in Tolman's opinion, children's experience with the world enables them to create cognitive maps of reality so that most important products of the learning process are the mental maps that guide an individual's future pursuit of goals. Hull was a Yale University professor who offered a precise way of determining how consequences affect behavior during the learning process.

Rotter drew from the foregoing ideas in formulating his own theory. Although his scheme has been less popular than Bandura's, it still continues to exert a minor influence on studies of development and psychotherapy (Burke, 1983; Love et al., 1985). Something of the flavor of Rotter's model can be suggested by his ideas about reinforcement, needs, and expectancies.

The most basic building block in Rotter's theory is the concept of reinforcement as derived from Thorndike's "law of effect," which describes the influence that consequences of a behavior will exert on future behavior in similar circumstances.

A second foundational precept relates to needs. Rotter proposes that the infant is first motivated to action by physiological needs—hunger, thirst, warmth, release of bodily wastes, and others. As the satisfaction of these basic needs becomes associated (through classical conditioning) with such caretakers as parents, the infant develops *learned needs* called *psychological needs* or *acquired goals*. These include goals of pleasing others, of engaging in amicable social relations, of adopting others' characteristics and values, and the like. As the child's social interactions accumulate, psychological needs become powerful motivators on their own, no longer dependent on their physiological antecedents. And because the child's psychological needs are generated out of the particular social interactions in which that child engages, psychological needs can differ from one culture to another, one family to another, and one child to another (Rotter, 1982, pp. 58–61).

Reinforcement creates within children's personalities a series of *expectancies* about what kinds of future behaviors will likely result in rewards and in punishments. Children's experiences thus help define for them the degree to which their intentional actions will produce the outcomes they desire. If they can accurately predict how their actions will influence results, their belief that they are in control of their fate is strengthened (the expectancy that they have internal control of reinforcement). However, if their experience suggests that they cannot govern the outcome by the way they act, then they attribute the control of their fate to external factors (luck, chance, others' power). The extensive psychological literature on *locus of control* over the past two decades is founded on such an expectancies conception of development.

In summary, human development from Rotter's perspective consists of the child's gradually acquiring goals (psychological needs), skills, and expectancies that depend on the experiences (behaviors and their reinforcement consequences) provided by that child's particular social environment. The child's personality at any given time is composed of these goals, skills, and expectancies.

The way Rotter's model guides such practical activities as psychotherapy is reflected in the following proposals:

> The problem of psychotherapy is seen as a learning situation in which the function of the therapist is to help the patient accomplish planned changes in his observable behavior and thinking. Since patients come into therapy with many different motives [acquired goals], different values placed on particular kinds of reinforcements, different expectancies for possible sources of gratification, different limits on skill, and different higher level learning skills, conditions for optimal learning will likewise vary considerably from patient to patient. . . . Consequently, there is no special technique which can be applied to all cases, and differences in therapists must eventually be systematically related to patient differences to obtain maximally efficient results (Rotter, 1982, pp. 256–257).

With the principal characteristics of two social learning theories now sketched, we next consider what kinds of models can properly be subsumed under the rubric *contextualism*.

THE NATURE OF CONTEXTUALISM

The core concept of the recent contextualism movement is really nothing new. It is the assumption that human development is a process of interaction between (1) the child as a psychobiological organism and (2) the child's sociophysical environment. Hence the virtue of contextualism is to be found in the presumed sophisticated, balanced view of person and context transactions that the movement espouses rather than in any novelty of the basic idea itself. Bandura (1978, p. 344) has certainly reflected a contextualist perspective in saying that "psychological functioning involves a continuous reciprocal interaction between behavioral, cognitive, and environmental influences." B. J. Zimmerman's (1983) overview of contextualism paradigms features Bandura's version of social learning theory as a prime example of a contextualist approach. And Rotter's (1982, p. 5) theory likewise qualifies as contextualist when he contends that "The unit of investigation for the study of personality is the interaction of the individual and his or her meaningful environment."

The term *contextualism,* in effect, does not identify any specific model of development but, rather, represents a point of view that can be exemplified by diverse models. Two additional theories that can conveniently be sheltered under the contextualism umbrella are ones proposed by Klaus Riegel and Jaan Valsiner. Their models' principal features are sketched briefly in the following pages to illustrate ways that contextualist theories may be alike and ways they may differ from each other.

Riegel's Dialectical Theory

The concept *dialectic,* as proposed by the German philosopher Georg Wilhelm Friedrich Hegel (1770–1831), refers to an interpretive method in which an assertable proposition (the *thesis*) is necessarily opposed by a second equally reasonable but apparently contradictory proposition (the *antithesis*), with their mutual contradiction subsequently resolved at a higher level of truth by a third proposition (the *synthesis*). Consider this simple application of Hegelian dialectic to the study of child development. Imagine that a researcher spends several hours with each of ten three-year-olds, trying to teach them how to read a page of a beginner's story book. None of the ten succeeds with the task, thereby leading the investigator to propose that "Three-year-olds are not intellectually mature enough to learn to read" *(thesis)*. However, when a friend asks to have her three-year-old daughter try the task, the girl, after a good deal of effort, haltingly reads the page. This leads to an observation that conflicts with the thesis: "A three-year-old did learn to read" *(antithesis)*. To reconcile this pair of contradictory conclusions, the researcher revises the orginal propositions to form the following synthesis: "Most three-year-olds are not mature enough intellectually to learn to read (at least by the method I used), but a few can learn to read; apparently one reason for this is that chronological age is only a rough correlate (a surrogate variable) of children's evolving reading aptitude, meaning that an estimate of a child's reading readiness cannot accurately be based just on chronological age." Hegel considered this thesis-antithesis-synthesis pattern to be the perpetual law of thought.

In a dramatic political and economic adaptation of Hegel's formula, the German social activist Karl Marx (1818–1883) applied the dialectic scheme to explain societal evolution. In Marx's *dialectical materialism,* he proposed that the production and consumption of the world's products (materials) under capitalism resulted in a dialectic conflict between owners of industry and their workers, a conflict that could be resolved only by socialist revolution.

Recently, Klaus F. Riegel has applied Hegel's general dialectical formula to explain the process of human development (1972, 1975, 1976, 1979). To begin, Riegel proposes that the events in children's lives that contribute to development are best studied along four dimensions labeled the *inner-biological,* the *individual-psychological,* the *cultural-sociological,* and the *outer-phsysical.*

> A dialectic interpretation of development is based on the recognition that the interactions among these progressions of events are not always coordinated and synchronized. Whenever these interactions are out of step or contradictory, a conflict or crisis is said to exist. In a dialectic conception it is the discordance and tension of these contradictory interactions [Hegel's thesis/antithesis] that become the source of new development, more specifically, of leaps in development. Through the development of coordinating and integrative actions and thoughts, synchrony will be established and thereby, progress achieved [Hegel's synthesis]. Yet even as synchrony is attained, new discrepancies emerge and, in doing so, produce a continuous flux of contradictions and developmental change (Riegel, 1976, p. 350).

Riegel suggests that dialectical discordances can occur within one dimension or between two or more. For example, along the inner-biological progression, an eleven-year-old girl can experience her first menstruation period, the menarche, and at the same time may contract tonsillitis. Hence, there is a conflict between two aspects of the inner-biological dimension in that she must adjust to two distressing biological events, with the infected tonsils adding to the discomfort of the menarche and further disturbing her physiological harmony. In addition, the menarche is an event inconsistent with girl's existing self-concept, so that inner-biological change precipitates disorder in her individual-psychological self. At the same time, the attitudes of her society (cultural-sociological) toward the menarche also can affect her in ways she has not yet experienced, therein requiring revisions in her customary social conduct (such as using sanitary pads and perhaps avoiding other girls when in the school lavatory). Thus, disturbance has occurred across three dimensions as a result of the original inner-biological change. The girl now faces the developmental task of working out a suitable synthesis of the discordant elements. So in Riegel's system the process of growing up is composed of changes in one dimension that produce conflicts in other dimensions, necessitating a new synthesis of the four dimensions if development is to proceed satisfactorily.

By placing the thesis-antithesis-synthesis formula at the center of his theory, Riegel laid the foundation for criticizing an aspect of Piaget's theory of cognitive growth.

> The concepts of conflicts and contradictions ought to receive at least as much attention as the stabilizing concepts [in Piagetian theory] of solutions and agreements. Instead of directing all our attention toward the question of how problems are solved and answers are given, at least equal emphasis should be devoted to the issue of how problems are created and questions are raised (Riegel, 1976, pp. 349–350).

Riegel also admonished traditional psychologists for emphasizing fixed entities in development—traits, capacities, abilities, skills, and underlying motivating drives. He contended that the emphasis, instead, should be on children's concrete interactions during activities of daily life within which dialectic operations continually take place. "A dialectic theory of development regards the individual as being in a continuous process of change brought about through the successive interactions of concrete events over time" (Riegel, 1976, p. 394).

Such a conviction bears important implications for research methodology. For example, Riegel cited people's everyday dialogues as prime examples of short-term dialectic exchanges that contribute to increments of development. In successful dialogues, each participant expresses a view of the topic, listens to the other's reply, then responds to the reply, and so on. The resulting chain of exchanges can represent an orderly linkage of questions, answers, contradictions, and subsequent syntheses to form a pattern of ideas not recognized by either speaker prior to their meeting. A step in intellectual development has taken place. Group discussions and interactive social games can perform the same function. Therefore, in regard to investigative goals and methods, Riegel has chided linguists and psychologists for concentrating their analyses on formal descriptions or idealized systems of language and on the elements of such systems (words, morphemes, letters, phonemes). In his opinion, progress would be better served if researchers stressed the social aspects of language, especially the communication and the construction of meaning that occur in dialogues (Riegel, 1976, p. 376).

Riegel has also identified research procedures devised in recent years to trace longer-term dialectical interactions. For instance, studies of cohorts of children growing up during different eras have shown that differences

in social environments between one era and another can be more significant causes of certain child attributes than are the maturational factors
cited in the past as determinants of children's characteristics (Riegel, 1976,
p. 362). In effect, Riegel has pointed out the need for revised research
methods if investigations are to be conducted within his dialectical, contextualist paradigm.

In assessing Riegel's dialectical model, I will offer two observations.
First, I think his scheme does indeed exemplify contextualism since it
pictures the process of development as progressing through interactions
among four dimensions, with the cultural-sociological and the outer-
physical dimensions assuming strong roles in the process. Furthermore,
Riegel has advocated research methods that depend on real life contexts—
in situ environments—for generating data.

But, as a second observation, I question the practical usefulness of his
quartet of dimensions. Although the four appear to offer a logical way to
categorize aspects of development, they do not seem as helpful as a number
of other analytical schemes (such as analyzing development in terms of
interactions among genetic, developmental-history, and present-environ-
ment forces). One difficulty with Riegel's model is the problem of distinguishing clearly which dimension is being represented by a particular
event or influence in the child's life. For instance, in our illustration of the
girl entering puberty, we can ask whether her contracting tonsillitis qualifies as a sociological-cultural event (she was exposed to the germs in a social
setting), as an outer-physical event (the setting in which she was infected),
or as an inner-biological event (antibodies in her bloodstream combat the
streptococcus bacteria). In other words, while it is easy enough to create
illustrations that demonstrate the idea of the four dimensions and their
interactions (as with our eleven-year-old), investigating specific people's
lives in order to distinguish among the dimensions and to chart their
transactions is quite a different matter. Getting agreement among investigators about how to analyze individual cases in a profitable way would
seem to be most difficult.

To conclude, in its present state of development, the dialectical model's imprecision stands as a barrier to the theory's usefulness in guiding
child rearing and in equipping evaluators to judge the theory's internal
consistency, falsifiability, and fertility. A search of the journal literature in
psychology throughout the 1980s indicates that Riegel's theory has stimulated little or no empirical research or practical applications. Thus, up till
now, Riegel's scheme has served more adequately for pointing out shortcomings of other theories—such as Piaget's—than for charting programs
of research or of educational and child-raising practices.

Valsiner's Cultural-Historical Theory

The reason Jaan Valsiner's theory belongs under the contextualist banner is that it is "built up within the individual-socioecological frame of reference, whereas the majority of psychological theories are constructed from the perspective of the inter-individual reference system" (1987, p. 230). That is, Valsiner does not focus on internal traits of the child (abilities, attitudes, cognitive styles). Instead, he concentrates on interactions between the child and the environment that produce those ostensibly enduring traits. And instead of emphasizing an imagined stable order of development, he stresses the dynamic, shifting aspects of growth processes. Furthermore, rather than centering attention of likenesses between children and on the uniformity within a given child, he argues that the general rule in development—both from one child to another and within the same child—is "variability of behavior and thinking" (1987, p. 230). Therefore changes in each child's unique environments interact with changes in the child, so that generalizations or "laws of development" that are intended to apply to an entire group of children (five-year-old girls, seventh-grade boys) are of little value because "every individual developing child is an organism interrelated with his environment, and is thus lawful in himself" (Valsiner, 1987, p. 230).

In Valsiner's comments about how closely his views match other people's perspectives, he contends that the foregoing assumptions on which his theory is founded are contrary to the beliefs of laypersons and of "the majority of child psychologists (who have followed the laypersons' common sense)" (1987, p. 230). Consequently, he would anticipate that most people might consider his scheme both radical and unreasonable.

At the core of his theory is the proposal (1) that children's range of experience is defined by the environments they inhabit minute by minute and day by day and (2) that the nature of these environments is to a great extent controlled by children's caregivers—parents, siblings, babysitters, teachers, and the like. Children's psychophysical development is governed principally by what they learn in such settings and by how their health and physical well-being are influenced by their surroundings. And because the succession of environments traversed by one child is so different from that experienced by another, there will be marked dissimilarities in the two children's development. A girl growing up on a Chinese junk in Hong Kong harbor becomes a very different person than a girl raised in an affluent San Francisco suburb. The environments faced by a Hindu boy in a mountain village of Bali are dramatically different from those encountered by a black boy in a South African mining town. Valsiner's attention to such contrasts accounts for his stressing variability over similarity among children in their development.

Although the complexities of his model cannot be detailed in the brief treatment given here, his concept of three *zones* can be described to reflect the theory's dominant tack. First is the *zone of free movement* (ZFM). This zone represents the set of items available to influence a child's actions in a particular environmental setting at a given time. The term *items* in this context refers to the areas of the environment, objects (including humans) in that setting, and ways the child can interact with those objects. According to Valsiner (1987, pp. 231–232), "the structure of ZFM is dynamic; given the change in goals or conditions, the boundaries of ZFM are constantly being reorganized. That reorganization may be initiated by either the child or caregivers, or by all of them at the same time."

The kinds of experiences a ZFM provides for a child are limited by the caregivers, who fence off those realms of action they consider unsuitable for the young one's development. Parents can prohibit children from playing with certain companions and can monitor the television programs children see and the books they read. For historical reasons, societies can differ from each other in how liberally they define the ZFM that children are permitted. For instance, a greater diversity of ZFM options is available in Britain's present-day multicultural society than in Saudi Arabia's highly cohesive Muslim culture.

Valsiner's second zone concept is the *zone of promoted action* (ZPA), which represents those modes of action that caregivers encourage or demand within the zone of free movement. Cultures and individual families vary in how restrictively they delineate what constitutes proper or acceptable action in the successive contexts a child moves through day after day. The most controllable situation of parent-child interaction occurs when the zone of free action is very narrow (permitting the child to act in only one way) and that zone is coterminus with the zone of promoted action. The decision-making role of parents is much simplified in such a society since they merely need to urge their children to act in that single permissible way.

A very different child development situation results when the zone of free movement is extremely broad and the zone of promoted action is very narrow, in fact, almost imperceptible. Under such conditions, both the culture and the particular parents allow children great freedom for developing themselves. Many options for action are available to the child in a given context, with little or no guidance offered by caregivers regarding which option might yield the most desirable long-term results. The rationale behind such parental behavior often derives from the conviction that children grow up best if they follow their "natural bent": "When left to their own devices, children know what's good for them." In other cases, the young are permitted great freedom of choice simply out of parental neglect; caregivers are distracted by their own interests and pay little or no attention to child-raising responsibilities.

The last of Valsiner's three zones stems from L. S. Vygotsky's theory (Chapter Eleven). It is the *zone of proximal development* (ZPD), defined as "the set of actions that the child can perform when helped by another person, but which are not yet available to the child in his individual acting" (Valsiner, 1987, p. 233). In other words, by working together with a caregiver, the child is able to carry out activities that are just beyond her own independent abilities.

In Valsiner's opinion, postulating the three zones and analyzing permutations of their interactions enables one to derive insightful interpretations of a variety of child development phenomena—permissive parenting, abusive parenting, methods of instruction, goal setting, rules of behavior, stages of development, and more.

The historical-cultural factors that are assigned a central role in Valsiner's scheme operate at several levels. At the broadest level, people within a given society share in common influential *physical settings* (buildings, mountains, oceans, deserts), *items of material culture* (houses, tents, autos, camels, books, television receivers), *customs* (eating habits, modes of greeting, education, religious ceremonies), *bodies of knowledge* (scientific, social, religious, artistic), and *values* (moral, monetary, aesthetic). The patterning of these cultural elements in a given society is a product of the society's particular historical evolution. And the way that Valsiner's zones of free movement, of promoted action, and of proximal development are delineated for child-raising purposes is governed to a great extent by the particular society's shared cultural characteristics. The society in general, therefore, designates certain right and wrong ways to rear the young.

Just as the cultural traits of a society are rooted in that society's history, so also are the cultural characteristics of parents and teachers rooted in the history of their own upbringing within such a society. "The setting of goals by people who organize child/environment relationships is canalized by their cultural background" (Valsiner, 1987, p. 1143). Yet these personal histories include not only cultural factors common to nearly everyone but also additional factors (or variants of common factors) somewhat unique to their individual families, schools, churches, and companions. The caregiver's developmental history (as constructed from the general culture and subgroup or family culture) influences the way he or she defines the three context zones featured in Valsiner's model.

Finally, the growing child is daily accumulating a history that affects what that child can become in the years ahead. In other words, at any point in the child's development, the accumulation of past experiences in the form of stored knowledge, skills, and attitudes helps define (1) the child's perception of the three context zones and (2) the manner in which the child will react to the way caregivers manage the zones.

Now consider the matter of research from Valsiner's perspective. It is apparent that his theory places demands on the investigator that cannot be met by many of developmental psychology's traditional instruments and methods, such as ability and achievement tests, laboratory experiments, and statistical treatments of group data. Such techniques are hardly appropriate for tracing the developmental effects on a particular child of environments that are in a periodic state of flux. Consequently, the researcher who seeks to comprehend child-environment transactions from the viewpoint of Valsiner's contextualism is like a portrait painter whose model refuses to sit still, whose background scenery is apt to change without warning, and who finds uninvited newcomers intruding onto the set. Therefore more suitable investigative methods for contextual analysis are those of (1) observing caregivers and children in their daily interactions (with such observations recorded on videotape or audiotape), (2) interviewing caregivers and children about how they have interacted during past encounters, and (3) interviewing people and searching historical accounts for information about the society's customs that affect caregiver-child transactions. Detailed examples of such approaches have been included in Valsiner's recent works (1987, 1988a).

In assessing Valsiner's theory, I note that its scope is limited to clarifying only those aspects of development strongly affected by the way caregivers structure children's surroundings. However, as Valsiner points out, such a limitation still leaves a great range of phenomena to which the theory can apply since so much of children's behavior is influenced by the contexts in which it occurs and the form of those contexts is strongly affected by cultural tradition (Valsiner, 1987, pp. 236–237).

In regard to the realistic quality of the model, I find that it convincingly reflects the actual world of children. It is also easily comprehended, is internally consistent, and appears economical. Although the theory offers no direct guidance for child rearing, it does provide a way caregivers can analyze the zones (freedom of movement, promoted action, proximal development) that caregivers create to form the environments within which children develop. In regard to its analytical potential, the theory is better prepared to explain the past than to predict the future since the configurations of the environments that a child will later encounter are usually highly complex and not readily discerned ahead of time. This quality of partial indeterminacy of future environments is what causes Valsiner to describe his scheme as an open system, one whose end products cannot be forecast with much accuracy. In regard to its fertility, the model is of such recent vintage that its potential for stimulating empirical studies

cannot yet be judged. Overall, I believe Valsiner's contextualist theory
satisfactorily performs the function for which it was intended—that of
providing a perspective for interpreting how children's environments are
arranged by caregivers who themselves are products of a particular society's cultural history.

As a closing note, I should mention that Valsiner's developmental
psychology is a telling example of his own contextual background. During
the 1970s he completed his higher education at Tartu University in the
Soviet republic of Estonia. In 1980 he left his homeland to spend six
months in Western Europe at Justus Liebig University in Germany, then
immigrated to the United States, first accepting an appointment in developmental studies at the University of Minnesota, then transferring to
the University of North Carolina (1987, pp. ix–x). His contextualist model
of development displays elements linked to theorists who have worked in
each of these locations. For example, his scheme is strongly imbued with
the traditional Soviet concern for ways cultural-historical factors influence
development within social contexts. He has also drawn on Kurt Lewin's
notions about how the child's *psychological field* changes from one event in
life to another so that

> the developing child and his caregivers are viewed as being engaged in
> constant negotiation and renegotiation processes involving different
> "boundaries" in their relationships with one another and the environ-
> ment at large. The boundary conditions define (and redefine) the struc-
> tured nature of the child-environment relationships, which (following
> Vygotsky's key idea of internalization of external experience) is gradual-
> ly carried over from the realm of child's (externally constrained) actions
> on the environment into his internally constrained thinking, feeling, and
> programming of actions (Valsiner, 1987, p. 231).

In addition, Valsiner's theory stresses the child's very active engage-
ment in the process of growing up, a stress that he credits to the American
James Mark Baldwin (1861–1934), the Swiss Jean Piaget (1896–1980), and
the Russian Lev Vygotsky (1896–1934).

In closing, I would suggest that when you meet ecological theory in
Chapter Fourteen you will recognize that Valsiner's contextualist model
could fit into that chapter as reasonably as it has in Chapter Nine.

FOR FURTHER READING

Bandura, A. (1969) *Principles of Behavior Modification*. New York: Holt, Rinehart &
   Winston.

Bandura, A. (1977) *Social Learning Theory.* Englewood Cliffs, N.J.: Prentice-Hall.

Reigel, K. F. (1979) *Foundations of Dialectical Psychology.* New York: Academic Press.

Rotter, J. B. (1982) *The Development and Application of Social Learning Theory.* New York: Praeger.

Valsiner, J. (1987) *Culture and the Development of Children's Action.* Chicester, England: Wiley.

JUDGING THE APPROPRIATENESS OF RESEARCH METHODS

What research methods are associated with different theories, and what are the strengths and limitations of such methods?

The aim of this perspective is (1) to identify symbiotic relationships between theory and research methodology and (2) to illustrate significant characteristics of research methods that affect how adequately any particular theory explains child development.

INTERDEPENDENCE OF THEORY AND RESEARCH METHODS

A symbiotic relationship obtains between a theory and the investigative techniques used both to generate and to validate the theory. For instance, Heider's commonsense attribution model was initially founded on ordinary people's comments about why folks act the way they do in everyday life. Then, after Heider created his model for analyzing such comments, hypotheses derived from the theory could be tested by means of additional observations of commonsense situations so as to validate, refine, and extend the scheme.

In contrast, Skinner's theory originated in experiments with animals in laboratory settings, experiments designed to reveal how manipulating animals' environments influenced the habits they acquired. From his observations, Skinner concluded that animals' behavior could be explained and predicted in terms of the kinds of consequences that followed their actions. And because his pigeons and rats were unable to communicate verbally, the experimenter could not depend on testimonials from his subjects about their thinking processes. Nor, indeed, did Skinner consider testimonials or introspection necessary because he was satisfied that his analyses of the connection between actions and their consequences explained the causes of behavior very nicely. When he then applied his theory to people, he assumed that (1) the basic principles of learning in animals fit humans as well and (2) the investigative methods he had developed with animals were, with certain revisions, also proper to use with people.

Humanistic psychologists, in a spirit quite the opposite of Skinnerian behaviorists, have created their notions of development from people's expressions about how they feel about themselves, about other people, and about their hopes for the future. As a result, humanists pay as much attention—or even more—to individuals' revelations about their private thoughts and feelings as to the individuals' overt actions.

In effect, the kinds of original data or observations from which a theory is created strongly affect the focus and scope of the theory. In turn, the model the theorist builds from such data will tend to delineate the methods of investigation to be used for testing, refining, and extending the theory.

STRENGTHS AND LIMITATIONS OF POPULAR RESEARCH METHODS

It is important to recognize that the self-serving reciprocity between theory and method can lead to incomplete or distorted interpretations of child development. It is likewise important to realize that no investigative method is perfect in itself. Each displays strengths and limitations that influence the adequacy of any theory to which that method is closely bound. The nature of such limitations can be demonstrated by considering where different research methods are typically located along dimensions of *control, reality, precision, reproducibility, significance,* and *feasibility*.

Control

The dimension labeled *control* refers to how well a researcher can assess or measure the variables that are involved in human development. A basic assumption underlying this dimension is that changes in child growth are the result of a variety of factors, not just one. Hence an important challenge investigators face is that of identifying which factors are involved and how to measure the amount of influence that each factor exerts on development.

A high level of control is achieved when the researcher conducts an experiment in which all but one causal factor are held constant, or else the remaining factors cancel each other out so that only one factor is allowed to vary. Sometimes two or three factors are permitted to vary, and then the researcher uses multivariate statistics to judge the amount of influence each factor has exerted on development. For instance, a popular way to attempt control in heredity–environment studies is to use pairs of monozygotic twins (twins born from the same fertilized ovum), so that their genetic inheritance is ostensibly identical. That is, genetic inheritance is assumed to be constant and environments are allowed to vary (some twins have been raised together in the same family, while others have been separated and grow up in different families). Conclusions are then drawn about the relative influence of heredity and environment on selected aspects of development—personality traits, cognitive ability, physical agility, or the like.

Another common approach to control involves placing children in a laboratory situation in which some environmental factors are held constant while others are varied systematically. The ones that are varied are often called *treatments*. For example, imagine that we wish to study how well children can learn different techniques for memorizing vocabulary words in a foreign language. The techniques will be rehearsal (say the words over and over), association (link new words to other words already in memory), and visual imaging (picture the words' graphic form). We also want to know how such a skill is influenced by age. To conduct our experiment, we decide to use children from three age groups—ages 4, 6, and 8—so we can estimate how memory ability changes with the passing years. Within each age group, an equal number of children will be randomly assigned to each of the three treatments—rehearsal, association, and visual imaging. By ensuring that the assignment of children is random, we are attempting to rule out the influence of extraneous variables—ones other than age and type of treatment—that might influence the final results. With a reasonably large number of children in each treatment group (perhaps a hundred or more), we feel rather safe in assuming that, because our assignments of children to the three treatments are random, such factors as level of intelligence, previous experience with a foreign language, and study habits are distributed about the same in one group as in the others. Consequently, these extraneous variables will not be the cause of one group succeeding better than another on the final memory scores.

Behaviorists have been particularly dedicated to controlled experiments. And when pigeons or white rats are used as subjects of research on development, even greater control can be wielded over the variables than is true when children are the subjects. Both the heredity and environment of animals can be manipulated with a good deal of precision, so the researcher can feel quite confident that the results derived from the studies reflect the influence of the one or two factors that were permitted to change.

At the opposite end of the control scale from laboratory experiments are the methods used by contextualists (Chapter Nine), ecologists (Chapter Fourteen), and ethologists (Chapter Fifteen), who typically study children in their natural settings. Such researchers may immerse themselves in the daily life of the people they are studying, thus becoming *participant-observers* who seek to disturb normal events as little as possible. Since they cannot actively control variables, the investigators carefully record events over an extended period of time in an effort to estimate which variables have been most influential in effecting the observed outcomes.

Because laboratory researchers' control techniques are designed to rule out or equalize extraneous variables, advocates of this approach tend to assume that "Other things being equal, this one variable is the cause of the developmental change." In response, ecologists and ethologists are apt to reply, "But that's the point—other things are never *equal;* other things must be taken into account." In short, critics of traditional laboratory studies charge that experimental control is bought at the expense of facets of life that are significant for understanding child development. And this brings us to the reality dimension.

Reality

The reality criterion concerns how well the research methods reflect the way development actually occurs under natural conditions. The term *natural* in this context means the way children develop without special intervention, such as without the researcher's applying "unnatural" controls.

The danger of ignoring reality is what interested P. Mounoud when he wrote:

> If we look critically at the experimental situations which have been devised over the past few decades, we will notice that they present extreme simplifications and impoverishments of reality. Striving to be more experimental, they turn out to be more and more fragmentary. This does not imply any opposition on my part to strict experimental approaches, but we should be conscious of their limitations as well as of their advantages. Above all, it is necessary to place studies of specific problems within broader contexts (1986, pp. 41–42).

A. L. Brown voiced the same complaint when she observed that attitudes toward research methods in child development have changed in recent times:

> Initial forays [in experimental developmental psychology] were . . . adapted from animal laboratories. . . . But children were notoriously

unreliable accomplices; the variability in their data suggested perversity rather than compliance. . . . The best situation in which to study very early memory development is in a natural context in which the child is likely to understand the task and be motivated to perform it. Young children's performance on laboratory tasks is often markedly inferior to their performance in a game setting. . . . Mental acts occur in living contexts, and . . . the minimum unit of analysis must be the operations performed by an individual in context (1979, pp. 248–250).

In a similar vein, critics of Freud have questioned how well psychoanalytic theory reflects reality when its picture of child development is founded on neurotic patients' recollections of their childhood as revealed in dreams and free-association remarks that are interpreted symbolically by a dedicated adherent of the theory.

Thus the conundrum posed for researchers is: How can we get high levels of both control and reality? No one yet appears to have solved this puzzle, so that any particular investigative method represents some compromise between control and reality. Researchers continue to hunt for ways to wed the pair more compatibly.

Precision

Linked to both control and reality is the matter of *precision,* meaning how accurately aspects of development can be assessed, compared, and contrasted. The battle of precision frequently is waged with an arsenal of such words as *quantitative* versus *qualitative, statistical* versus *narrative, sampling error, critical ratio, interrater reliability, time sampling, scaling, error of measurement,* and more.

One debate among proponents of different theories concerns the desirability of quantitative versus qualitative research methods. Quantitative methods emphasize changes in *amounts* as children develop—in the numbers of words three-year-olds know, in how many mathematics problems high school sophomores answer correctly, in the percentage of six-year-olds who can read a simple book, and the like. Qualitative methods, on the other hand, emphasize changes in *focus, structure,* or *complexity* as children grow up—in how children perceive the opposite sex before and after puberty, how well they grasp the concept of *fair play,* how adequately they understand other people's points of view, and such.

Strong advocates of precision typically like to have research results cast in numerical form. The more specific the numbers, the better. Reporting "63 percent" is better than reporting "most" or "the majority"—and "63.07 percent" is better yet. Research techniques that yield quantitative results are more often associated with such theoretical schemes as behaviorism and social learning theory than with humanistic psychology and psychoanalysis. It is difficult for a humanist to see how a child's self-concept and dreams of the future can meaningfully be cast in numerical form. Likewise, a psychoanalytic interpretation of the images of racing cars and tunnels in a teenager's dream does not easily lend itself to quantification. From the perspective of humanists and psychoanalysts, precision is obtained by careful observation, detailed recording, and clear descriptions of events—not by numbers.

Often a theory's investigative methods focus on both qualitative and quantitative changes. Piaget, whose early publications contained reports that were almost exclusively qualitative, later added quantification in response to critics' complaints that he had failed to report the proportion of children at different age levels who displayed various modes of thinking. While researchers on both sides of the quantitative–qualitative fence continue to argue for the superiority of their approach, in my mind there is little need to pit one camp against the other. Both quantitative and qualitative reports are needed. Each serves a valuable function in the explanation of child development. The issue, then, becomes one of determining what combination of the two furnishes the clearest picture of how and why children grow up as they do.

Reproducibility

Since theories of development are expected to apply to all children (or at least to all children within a particular culture or type), the evidence on which a theory is founded should be *reproducible*. For example, if a theorist studies one child and concludes that a particular combination of vitamins accounts for the child's improvement in problem-solving skill, then we should be able to reproduce this phenomenon with other children. Feeding the same mixture of vitamins to others and then assessing for improvement in problem solving enables us to discover whether the theorist's proposal applies to all children and thus is a general rule of child development rather than something unique to a single child. Experimental methods commonly used by behaviorists, certain social learning theorists, Piaget (Chapter Ten), Vygotsky (Chapter Eleven), and information-processing advocates result in high ratings on the reproducibility criterion. But such is often not the case with humanistic (Chapter Thirteen), ecological (Chapter Fourteen), and ethological (Chapter Fifteen) theorists. For humanists, the difficulty of reproducing a postulated relationship arises from their emphasis on the uniqueness of each individual's personality and from their dependence on a research methodology of introspection and self-report whose results vary from one person to the next. Contextualists, ecologists, and ethologists may consider it impossible to reproduce a significant event in a child's life if they believe that no combination of environmental and hereditary factors ever completely occurs the same way twice. Thus the best they can do is draw their estimates of theoretical relationships from reoccurrences of natural events that only approximate the original occurrence on which they based their proposals.

Hence the problem of reproducibility is closely linked to matters of control and reality. The more factors that are controlled, the easier it should be to reproduce a posited relationship between cause and effect. At the same time, the more that factors are controlled, the more the research method may distort the natural conditions of daily life.

Significance

The question of *significance* is at stake when people respond to a research outcome with "Who cares?" or "So what?" or "What makes you think the results of this study are significant?" K. P. Hillner, from the vantage point of a humanist, had this issue in mind when he complained that:

> Even though methodology merely is a means to a certain end in every system of psychology, traditional behavioristic experimental psychology tends to lose sight of this fact and treats methodology as an end in itself. A specific research problem is chosen because it is amenable to a well-accepted/documented experimental technique, not because it is relevant for unraveling [human] nature or serves as a significant contribution to the psychological literature. One could never accuse a humanist of being guilty of confusing means with ends: The sole criterion of the humanist in choosing research projects is meaningfulness. A given study is undertaken because it is psychologically relevant and pertains to the human issues and concerns, as defined by the humanistic psychologist. For the humanist, the degree of objectivity or validity afforded by a given research technique is purely a secondary matter (1984, pp. 259–260).

It is often said that the most crucial step in conducting research is that of framing the question the research is to answer. This initial research question, in effect, determines how significant the results of the investigation can be. Hillner's claim, then, is that behaviorists too often have been guided by "What can I learn about child development by using well-established experimental techniques?" rather than by such a query as "What do I most need to learn about child development in order to enhance children's growth and happiness?" Behaviorists, certain social learning theorists, and information-processing advocates reply to such a charge with two counter arguments. First, they deny that the questions they ask are unimportant for explaining development. Second, they contend that investigative techniques that depend heavily on people's naive opinions and introspection and that fail to control for a host of variables are unlikely to produce believable answers for even "the most significant" questions. Thus the issue of significance is connected to matters of control, reality, precision, and reproducibility.

It is apparent that different people value different types of information about development and thus assign different levels of significance to different research methods. Parents who are concerned with daily child-rearing decisions (as in behavior modification) will assign greater significance to research methods that yield answers to immediate child-raising questions than they will to methods (psychoanalytic) that answer questions about factors in a child's distant past that may have influenced early personality development.

But no matter what questions researchers designate as most significant, their efforts to apply investigative methods that furnish convincing answers to their questions are usually restricted by considerations of feasibility.

Feasibility

The *feasibility* dimension concerns the practicality of an investigative method. Frequently researchers first conceive of a study as if ideal conditions existed. Then, as they inspect the circumstances they must face in actually carrying out the study, they retreat from the ideal to the practical by revising their project to accommodate for the constraints imposed by their real life situation. Four of the most common constraints are those of time, funds, complexity, and the welfare of the children who are expected to participate in the research.

Consider the matter of time in cases of longitudinal versus cross-sectional research. In longitudinal research, an investigator traces the growth of the same group of children over a period of several years. Such an approach not only provides data about children at successive age levels but also permits the investigator to identify particular patterns of development of individual children in the group. However, researchers are often unable or unwilling to dedicate eight or ten or more years to a single study, especially when they run the risk of not being able to locate all of the original members of the group as the years pass and families move away. Furthermore, a large percentage of the people conducting developmental studies are graduate students doing research for their master's or doctoral degree. Rarely can they afford the time required for conducting longitudinal investigations. Hence they substitute a cross-sectional design by simultaneously studying children of different age groups, perhaps comparing children of ages 3, 6, 9, and 12 in order to draw inferences about developmental changes. However, cross-sectional studies can furnish information only about how groups differ *on the average*. Such studies cannot tell how individual children change over the years, nor can they tell whether today's three-year-old group would actually score the same as today's twelve-year-old group if the three-year-olds could be tested nine years in the future.

Time is also a constraint when an investigator needs schoolchildren as subjects. School personnel and parents are usually unwilling to jeopardize pupils' progress with their schoolwork by their spending many hours in a child development experiment. A further time limitation relates to children's attention span. Young children cannot tolerate lengthy experimental sessions without tiring and becoming bored.

Limitations of funds is a further important restriction on research methods. Financial demands mount with each increase in the equipment needed, the time and personnel required, the number of children to be studied, the distances to be traveled, the complexity of data analysis, and more.

Complexity, as a third form of constraint, refers to how complicated the research design, the data gathering, and the data analysis will be. Very often the methodology that theoretically should yield the most valuable results is far too intricate and convoluted to be implemented in the real world, so the initial ideal plan must be replaced by a simpler one when the research is actually carried out.

A fourth restriction has become more apparent in recent years in the United States and in similar nations where government agencies have become increasingly sensitive to protecting the welfare of the children who are the subjects of research. Typically, regulations for guarding the rights of children obligate researchers to furnish evidence that the investigation they are about to launch will keep the children's identities anonymous, will not damage the children physically or psychologically, and will yield information sufficiently valuable to society to warrant any bother or distress that the subjects might experience. In the main, these regulations represent quite sensible protective measures. However, in some cases regulations have been imposed by pressure groups for political rather than humanitarian reasons and are so restrictive that they rule out the possibility of conducting studies that are both (1) of marked value for understanding child development and (2) very unlikely to jeopardize children's welfare (Strazicich, 1988). In short, regulations—whether reasonable or unreasonable—significantly influence the research methods that can feasibly be adopted.

Conclusion

In summarizing, I would emphasize that understanding why any theory of development has assumed its particular form requires an appreciation of the interdependence among (1) the research methods and data on which the theory was originally built, (2) the subsequent investigative methods that derive from the key questions generated by the theory, and (3) how the theory's research methodology has been influenced by considerations of control, reality, precision, reproducibility, significance, and feasibility.

THE GROWTH OF THOUGHT AND LANGUAGE

A search for patterns of development in children's cognitive and verbal skills and for the mechanisms that bring these patterns about

The two chapters in Part Five treat a pair of cognitive development theories that have attracted a host of adherents over the past several decades. The theories are (1) Jean Piaget's psychology of the child and (2) Soviet development models, particularly as guided by Lev Semenovich Vygotsky. The title of this part—The Growth of Thought and Language— is not meant to suggest that other theories described in this volume have ignored mental development or verbal communication. Rather, the title simply highlights the fact that a major emphasis in the Piagetian and Soviet models has been the growth of children's cognitive and verbal abilities.

Jean Piaget (1896–1980) was a Swiss who has often been acclaimed the most influential researcher in the field of child development in the twentieth century. He gained this distinction for proposing a novel model of children's mental development, a model founded on a great quantity of ingenious research on children from the time of birth into adolescence. Beginning in 1921 and continuing for nearly sixty years, he published hundreds of journal articles and books on all sorts of questions related to children's thought processes: how dreams and play evolve, how symbols develop, how moral judgment grows, how perceptions change, how intelligence improves, how numbers are conceived, how physical events occur, and many more. The diverse topics on which Piaget wrote are all connected to his basic model of intellectual growth. The view of Piaget offered in Chapter Ten focuses on the most fundamental elements of that model.

The second theoretical persuasion examined (Chapter Eleven) is one that has dominated developmental psychology in the Soviet Union for more than six decades. The Soviet perspective has been included for two main reasons. First, it illustrates a development theory that, out of political necessity, conformed to the tenets of the Marxist sociopolitical philosophy on which the Soviet state was founded. Second, Soviet developmentalists have displayed noteworthy inventiveness in research methodology and analysis while producing a great quantity of empirical studies on childhood and adolescence.

In terms of chronology, the two chapters make a fitting pair, since Piaget and Vygotsky pursued their initial investigations of child development and contructed their basic systems during the same decade, the 1920s. However, their subsequent careers were markedly different. Vygotsky died in 1934, and his works were suppressed until years later, when their release to the world led to the high status they enjoy today. In contrast, Piaget was able to continue his investigations from the 1920s until his death in 1980, a sixty-year career that made him the most famous child development theorist of all time.

Both Piaget's and Vygotsky's systems qualify as stage theories by virtue of their picturing the child as passing from one distinctive phase of cognitive and language development into another. However, some critics have doubted the validity of the stages they proposed, and others have even questioned the whole idea of stages. To delineate key facets of this debate, Perspective D, at the end of Part Five, focuses on the likely future of stage theories.

CHAPTER TEN

Piaget's Cognitive Development Theory

Jean Piaget (1896–1980) was a precocious boy who, in his teens, had already developed an intense interest in biology, particularly in the biological bases of knowledge. By age 21 he had earned a doctorate at the university in his hometown of Neuchatel, Switzerland, and had published more than two dozen professional papers on biological studies, most of them concerning mollusks. This early specialization in biology had a lasting influence on his conceptions of the development of the mind.

Upon finishing his doctorate, he shifted his attention to psychology, which he studied in Swiss psychological clinics and at the Sorbonne in Paris. While in Paris (1919–1921), Piaget worked on standardizing tests of children's abilities in the laboratory school of the French expert on intelligence measurement, Alfred Binet. During this time Piaget was not as interested in whether children got the test items correct as he was in the thinking processes that led children to produce the answers they gave, especially the incorrect answers. This interest set the focus for his research during the rest of his career.

Although Piaget is commonly referred to as a child psychologist, the research task he set for himself was that of a *genetic epistemologist*. This means that the central question guiding his investigations was not, What are children like? but, How does knowledge develop in humans? Or more precisely, How does the relationship between the *knower* and the *known* change with the passing of time? So the term *genetic* (meaning the genesis or the mode of development) and *epistemology* (the theory of knowledge) does indeed describe the field of his endeavors. Children of different age levels just happened to be the instruments by which his investigations in this field were carried out.

In the following review of Piaget's work, we will consider: (1) his methods of research, (2) his conception of knowledge, (3) his conception of the process by which children's knowledge grows, (4) his definition of the stages of intellectual growth, (5) four of his key concepts, (6) the practical applications of his theory in education, (7) research challenges, and, finally, (8) an assessment of his theory.

PIAGET'S CLINICAL METHOD

While working at Binet's test-construction laboratory, Piaget devised the basic technique of studying children that would become the mainstay of his methodology during the next fifty years. His approach, known as a *clinical method,* involved a researcher posing problems for children and then observing how the children went about finding a solution. For children who had not yet reached puberty, the problems usually involved objects the child could see and manipulate, such as two lumps of clay that could be formed into different shapes or two glasses of water of different sizes. By the time the child could use language at age 3 or 4, the experimenter asked questions about solutions to the problems being posed. During the adolescent years, children were more often given verbal problems and asked how they arrived at their solution.

Unlike some other experimenters, Piaget did not limit himself to asking each child a preconceived set of questions. Rather, after beginning an interview with a standard question or two, he felt free to create, on the spot, additional questions designed to probe the thought processes that produced the child's initial answer. Piaget defended this deviation from a single, standard set of questions by explaining that all children do not interpret a given question in the same way. Thus the experimenter probes the child's understanding and may then cast the problem in a different form to help ensure that the problem situation is the same for each child, even though the working of it may not be identical each time (Phillips, 1975, pp. 4–5).

A typical interview is illustrated in the following passage in which eight-year-old Per is being questioned about some flowers—primulas and other varieties—that the woman interviewer placed before the child. The interviewer's purpose was to discover how Per classifies objects into a general set (flowers) and into subsets within the general set (primulas, violets, tulips). At the point we enter the discussion, Per has already devised three levels of classes: yellow primulas, primulas, and flowers (adapted from Inhelder & Piaget, 1964, p. 107).

Interviewer: Can one put a primula in the box of flowers (without changing the label)?

Per: Yes, a primula is also a flower.
Inteviewer: Can I put one of these flowers (a tulip) in the box of primulas?
Per: Yes, it's a flower like the primula.

When the experimenter does so, Per changes her mind and puts it back with the other flowers.

Interviewer: Can one make a bigger bunch with all the flowers or with all the primulas?
Per: It's the same thing, primulas are flowers, aren't they?
Interviewer: Suppose I pick all the primulas, will there be any flowers left?
Per: Oh, yes, there will still be violets, tulips, and other flowers.
Interviewer: Well, suppose I pick all the flowers, will there be any primulas left?
Per: No, primulas are flowers, you're picking them too.
Interviewer: Are there more flowers or more primulas?
Per: The same number, primulas are flowers.
Interviewer: Count the primulas.
Per: Four
Interviewer: And the flowers?
Per: Seven.
Interviewer: Are they the same number?
Per (*astonished*): The flowers are more.

In effect, then, Piaget's research methodology consisted of his first observing children's reactions to their surroundings. Then, on the basis of these observations, he composed hypotheses about the sorts of biological and mental structures that underlie their reactions. Finally, he cast the hypotheses in the form of problems or questions that he posed to children in order to reveal their thinking processes and thus test the hypotheses. Over the years he produced many problem situations that were subsequently used by researchers in many parts of the world to investigate matters that Piaget studied, as well as other aspects of development.

PIAGET'S CONCEPTION OF KNOWLEDGE

A useful step toward understanding Piaget's theory is to learn how he defined *knowledge* because his conception differs from most popular beliefs. We can perhaps best see this difference by beginning with a review of four commonsense ideas about knowledge and how it is acquired.

First, common sense holds that knowledge is a body of information or beliefs a person has acquired, either through instruction or through direct experience with the world. This idea of a collection of information is reflected in such everyday phrases as "She's a storehouse of knowledge" and "I wish I had all his knowledge."

Second, it is also a commonsense conviction that a person's knowledge is a fairly faithful representation of what the person has been taught or has witnessed. It is assumed that if two people, both with good eyesight, observe an event from the same vantage point, their knowledge of the event will be essentially identical. The great dependence on witnesses in court cases is founded on this conviction.

Third, common sense indicates that our storehouse of knowledge is increased as we add item upon item from our daily experiences. That is, we take in bits of information and pile them onto the proper heap in the storehouse, with each heap related to a different aspect of life.

Fourth, common sense tells us that whenever we need to recall an item of knowledge from the storehouse of memory, the item can be recovered in essentially the same condition as it was when first acquired. Of course, some details of the item may now be a bit vague, but if we can recall the item at all, it will be basically in its original form.

How did Piaget's views differ from such commonsense notions? To begin, he did not agree that knowledge is a body of acquired information or a state of possessing such information. Instead, he conceived of knowledge as a *process*. To *know* something means to *act* on that thing, with the action being either physical or mental or both. The two-year-old child's knowledge of a ball consists of his picking it up, pressing it with his fingers, tossing it, and observing it bounce away. As children grow up, they gain more experience with such direct, physical knowing, and they mature internally so that they are increasingly freed from having to carry out direct physical behavior in order to know something. They become able to produce mental images and *symbols* (words, mathematical figures) that represent objects and relationships. Hence the older child's knowledge increasingly becomes mental activity. She "thinks about" things by carrying out *interiorized actions* on symbolic objects (Piaget, Apostel, & Mandelbrot, 1957, pp. 44–45). So to Piaget, knowledge was a process or repertoire of actions rather than an inventory of stored information.

Piaget also disagreed with the commonsense idea of *perception*, that is, with the way objects or events are recorded in the child's mind. In Piaget's opinion, the child does not take in a picture of objective reality. Instead, as the child perceives or takes in the world, the picture is biased by the condition of the child's perceptual mechanism. If we adopt the analogy of viewing the world through glass, then in the Piagetian model the child does not record events through a clear window. Rather, he views events through a colored lens that is given its present focus and tint by both (1) the child's past experiences and (2) his current stage of internal maturation. The way that two children know (act on) the same object will not be identical, for the lens of one will have a somewhat different focus and tint than the other's.

But if knowledge is a process of acting on percepts rather than a collection of information, then what is *memory* and how does it operate? Piaget agreed that the results of a person's past actions can be stored as memories to be retrieved when needed. He also agreed that the quantity of memories increases with maturation and experience. But he did not believe that the act of remembering is simply a matter of summoning images of past events from memory and placing them in the showcase of consciousness so that, like museum pieces, they can be viewed in their passive, original condition. Rather, retrieving stored vestiges of the past, which he labeled *active memory,* is "interiorized recitation" or "a reconstitution of the past" (Piaget, 1946, pp. 5, 261). Remembering is a reenacting of the original process of knowing. However, it cannot simply be a repetition of the original knowing because the child's mind has subsequently been altered by additional experiences and further internal maturation. So the interiorized recitation or rehearsal of the stored event is, as it were, now performed on a somewhat altered mental stage according to revised stage directions.

To summarize, in Piaget's system, knowledge is a process of acting— physically and/or mentally—on objects, images, and symbols that the child's perceptual lens has cast into patterns that are somewhat familiar to her or him. The objects are found in the world of direct experience, while the images and symbols can be derived not only from the "real world" but from memory as well.

One way to conceive of mental growth or the development of intelligence is to picture it as a constant effort on the part of the child to expand and refine her knowledge, her repertoire of mental actions. Or, in different terms, "All knowledge is continually in a course of development and of passing from a state of lesser knowledge to one which is more complete and effective" (Piaget, 1972, p. 5).

This idea that a child's knowledge improves with age is hardly a noteworthy discovery. Everyone knows that already. But what everyone does not know is the specific ways knowledge changes, at what times it changes, and for what likely reasons. These are the things Piaget provided. Table 10.1 illustrates five categories of behavior he treated. In the description, I am using the verbs *recognizing* and *constructing* as synonyms, believing that the more passive *recognizing* is the familiar way people refer to such mental behavior but that *constructing* more accurately reflects Piaget's conception of knowledge as a process of active production on the child's part.

These, then, are some of the directions of intellectual development that Piaget's theory depicts and explains (Piaget & Inhelder, 1969). Our

Table 10.1 Growth in Sample Aspects of Knowledge: Infancy to Adolescence

From Infancy	Through Early and Middle Childhood	To Adolescence
Egocentrism versus Objectivity Not distinguishing between self and the environment	Partially distinguishing between self and the environment	Clearly differentiating self from objects of the environment
Object Permanence (Conservation) Not recognizing (not constructing) the permanence of objects whose location is changed	Recognizing (constructing) object permanence when location is changed, but failing to recognize (to construct) which characteristics of objects are unchanged (or are conserved) when objects are transformed	Recognizing (constructing) which aspects of objects are unchanged (are conserved) when the objects are transformed
Symbolic Functioning Not recognizing (not constructing) that one thing can represent something else	Recognizing (constructing) symbolization through such acts of imitation as gesture, play, drawing, and oral echoing	Recognizing (constructing) complex written and spoken symbols and signs

Internalization of Action Adapting to the environment solely by physical acts	Beginning to act internally on objects (manipulate them mentally) while observing them	Accomplishing faster, more complete adaptation by internally (mentally) manipulating objects of the environment, their classifications, and their relationships
Classes and Relationships Not recognizing (not constructing) classifications of objects or relationships among objects	Recognizing (constructing) classes and relationships among objects that are directly touched, seen, or heard	Not only recognizing (constructing) classifications of and relationships among objects directly perceived but also (1) of imagined objects and events and (2) of classification and relationship systems themselves

next task is to identify the mechanisms that, in Piaget's opinion, bring about these kinds of development.

THE MECHANISMS OF DEVELOPMENT

The purpose of all behavior or all thought, according to Piaget's system, is to enable the organism—the child—to adapt to the environment in ever more satisfactory ways. Piaget called the techniques of adaptation *schemes* or, in older translations of his writings from the original French, *schemas* or *schemata*. A scheme or technique of adjustment can be biological or mental or both. In Piaget's words:

> A scheme is the structure or organization of actions as they are trans-
> ferred or generalized by repetition in similar or analogous circumstances
> (Piaget & Inhelder, 1969, p. 4).

The *grasping* movement of the infant's hand is such a scheme, a physical organization of actions that the infant can generalize to grasp a bottle, a rattle, or the edge of the crib. On the intellectual level, an adolescent's concept of a *series* is also a scheme, a mental organization of actions. He can apply it in constructing a series of numbers, arranging a series of sweaters according to shades of color, or arranging a series of young girls by height or attractiveness.

A scheme can be very simple, such as the action pattern involved by a child putting her thumb into her mouth. Or it can be complex, comprising physical and mental subschemes, as in the chain of acts required for starting a car and driving it down the street or in the mental chain needed for solving quadratic equations.

Schemes always include accompanying feeling tones. When Piaget talked of *affective schemes,* he did not mean schemes distinct from mental structures but "simply the affective aspect of schemes which are otherwise also intellectual" (Piaget, 1962, p. 207).

The newborn's schemes are very limited in number, consisting of reflex action patterns—sucking, crying out, sneezing, flexing limbs, and the like. But as the days pass, other sensorimotor actions build out of these beginnings. Then, still within the first year of life, identifiable intellectual schemes evolve and over the following years multiply enormously. Thus, when we conceptualize child development in terms of schemes, we should picture it as the child's acquiring ever greater quantities of schemes that become interlinked in ever more sophisticated patterns.

How does this process of evolving schemes come about? To understand the process, we need to learn the meanings Piaget assigned to the words *assimilation* and *accommodation*. To help explain these matters, I would liken schemes to musical themes or tunes, for tunes are organizations of sounds just as schemes are organizations of sensorimotor and mental actions.

The Function of Assimilation

At every point in his life, the child's adaptation to the environment in order to satisfy his needs is accomplished by means of schemes. The child's repertoire of schemes at any given time is like a collection of melodies he already knows. When he faces the problem of satisfying needs, he inspects the environment to perceive how its apparent structure seems to fit schemes currently in his armory. It's as if he listens to the sounds coming from his surroundings to determine if they match, or nearly match, a tune he knows. When he finds what he considers a good match, he has achieved his adaptation. When the infant in the crib drops her doll onto the floor, she inspects the scene to decide if the conditions of her problem match any scheme or strategy in her repertoire of solutions. A twelve-year-old boy assigned to draw a map of the route from home to school must likewise search his available action structures to find ones appropriate to the task. A high school student listening to her English teacher lecture about the plot structure in *Hamlet* must incorporate the ideas from the lecture into suitable schemes already in her mind if she is to comprehend, or mentally construct, the meanings intended by the teacher.

This process of matching environmental stimuli to existing mental patterns is not simply a matter of ingesting objective reality from the world. Rather, the child reshapes the events of the world somewhat to fit the pattern of his or her existing schemes. It's as if the child hears several tones, and decides that they sound enough like a familiar melody to indeed be that melody.

Piaget applied the label *assimilation* to this process of taking in or understanding events of the world by matching the perceived features of those events to one's existing schemes. As Piaget put it: "To assimilate an object to a schema means conferring to that object one or several meanings" (Piaget, Jonckheere, & Mandelbrot, 1958, p. 59).

The Function of Accommodation

However, often the perceived structure of events does not readily fit the child's available schemes, even with some perceptual bending or shaping of that structure. When this occurs, one of two consequences can be expected. The first is that the event is not assimilated at all. It is ignored or passed by, like a person's rejecting several sounds as meaningless noise instead of recognizing them as a familiar tune. The encounter with the environment simply does not register on the child. Such is the case when a father tries to teach his young son to draw with proper visual perspective but finally concludes, "He can't do it at all. He just doesn't catch on."

The second possible consequence of a poor match between the perceived environment and available schemes is not outright rejection but dissatisfaction and continued efforts to achieve a match.

> New objects which present themselves to consciousness do not have their own qualities which can be isolated . . . they are vague, nebulous, because unassimilable, and thus they create a discomfort from which there emerges sooner or later a new differentiation of the schemas of assimilation (Piaget, 1963, p. 141).

So it is that schemes, under pressures from perceived realities of the environment, are altered in form or multiplied to accommodate for the lack of an adequate match. In effect, a tune from the child's existing store of melodies is revised to become a variation of the original theme, a variation that better fits the sounds of the world. Piaget used the term *accommodation* to identify this process of altering existing schemes to permit the assimilation of events that otherwise would be incomprehensible.

Since no new event is perfectly identical with those past events that were used in the formation of schemes, there is always some degree of mismatch of schemes with new events. But this is cared for by the balancing counterplay between assimilation and accommodation, which are two of the basic innate acts Piaget called *functional invariants*. Assimilation reshapes the environmental input to fit existing schemes, whereas accommodation revises or adds to the schemes to readjust for environmental features that cannot conveniently be ignored or distorted.

Just as adaptation to the world is achieved by the functions of assimilation and accommodation, so within the child's biological-mental self a process of *organization* operates to ensure that all schemes are properly interrelated, properly adjusted to each other to form an integrated person.

> It is sufficiently well known that every intellectual operation is always related to all the others and that its own elements are controlled by the same law. Every schema is thus coordinated with all the other schemata and itself constitutes a totality with differentiated parts. Every act of intelligence presupposes a system of mutual implications and interconnected meanings (Piaget, 1963, p. 7).

Therefore a child's development, according to Piagetian theory, seems somewhat like a progressively complex symphony. Its multiple melodies are the schemes formed from the balanced counterpoint of assimilation against accommodation. And the interweaving of themes produces a coordinated whole.

All these matters can be summarized in three quotations from Piaget:

> The filtering or modification of the input is called *assimilation;* the modification of internal schemas to fit reality is called *accommodation* (Piaget & Inhelder, 1969, p. 6).

> Adaptation is an equilibrium between assimilation and accommodation (Piaget, 1963, p. 6).

> The "accord of thought with things" (adaptation) and the "accord of thought with itself" (organization) express this dual functional invariant of adaptation and organization. These two aspects of thought are indissociable: It is by adapting to things that thought organizes itself and it is by organizing itself that it structures things (Piaget, 1963, p. 8).

Four Causal Factors

We next face the question of what factors or forces determine how this adaptation-organization system will operate in a given child's development. What causes a child to acquire her particular schemes and at what times in her growing up? How does environment as compared to heredity influence the kinds and rate of scheme formation?

In responding to such questions, Piaget proposed four underlying causal factors: (1) heredity (internal maturation), (2) physical experience with the world of objects, (3) social transmission (education), and (4) equilibrium.

1. Heredity   In the continuing debate among developmentalists over the roles of nature and nurture, Piaget has been classified by most writers as an interactionist, and certainly he considered himself so. He did not accord either heredity or environment greater power in determining development. Instead, he saw each playing a distinct and necessary part to complement the part of the other.

What role did Piaget see nature playing? He said that not only does heredity provide the newborn with the initial equipment to cope with problems she or he will meet in the world, but heredity also establishes a time schedule for new development possibilities to open up at periodic points throughout the child's growing years. This is the internal-maturation factor in heredity. It functions rather like a legislative body, which from time to time passes a new act of *enabling* legislation. Each such act, or maturational change, creates possibilities for new schemes to be created that could not have been generated earlier, but this action neither requires nor guarantees that the potential schemes will materialize. The extent to which the potentialities are actually realized is determined by the sorts of experiences the child has with his or her environment. So internal maturation is a necessary but not sufficient condition for development to proceed.

Much of the practical use of Piaget's findings for educators and parents lies in his identification of approximate age levels at which the maturation needed for developing particular schemes or intellectual operations occurs. If suitable maturation has not yet taken place, it is futile to try to teach the child a particular skill. The probable reason the father failed to teach his young son proper visual perspective was that the maturation necessary for developing the required schemes had not yet occurred.

Piaget (1973, p. 27) viewed as folly the efforts of some psychologists to dissociate the effect of heredity from that of the heredity–environment amalgam in seeking to decide which of the two is more important for development: "If a maturation effect intervenes everywhere, it remains dissociable from the effects of the exercise of learning or of experience."

2. Physical Experience   It is essential to recognize that Piaget, unlike most theorists, separated the child's trafficking with the environment into two varieties: (a) direct and generally unguided experience with objects in the world—called *physical experience*—and (b) the guided transmission of knowledge, that is, education in a broad sense—called *social transmission*. We will consider direct experience first, for it is the type on which Piaget has focused the greater part of his attention.

In this case, the child directly manipulates, observes, listens to, and smells objects to see what occurs when they are acted upon. From such investigations the child generates a logic or knowledge of the properties of things and how they work. Piaget stressed that it is not observation of the passive objects themselves that develops the child's logic or intelligence, but the set of conclusions the child draws from those actions that bring about events and influence objects. So simply seeing a feather or brick or lump of clay is not enough for intellectual development to take place. Such development depends on the *experience* derived when physically or mentally participating in such events as the following:

A chicken feather and a metal bolt are simultaneously dropped from the same height.

A brick is put into a bucket full of water, and a pine block the size of the brick is put into a second bucket of water.

Three lumps of clay are rolled into shapes: the first into a ball, the second into a sausage, the third into a long snake.

The child tries to cut a board—first with scissors, next with a knife, and then with a saw.

These sorts of experiences contribute to the aspect of intellectual development that Piaget (1973, p. 2) called *spontaneous* or *psychological:* "the development of the intelligence itself—what the child learns by himself, what none can teach him and he must discover alone."

Although physical experience with the action of objects is essential to mental growth, by itself it is, like maturation, insufficient to bring about development.

3. Social Transmission This is education in a broad sense—the transmission of knowledge to the child from without. Like the first two factors, this one is important but is insufficient by itself to effect mental growth, for it depends upon both maturation and direct experience to prepare the schemes that permit assimilation of what parents, the school, and the general social milieu seek to teach the child. This factor contributes what Piaget called the *psychosocial* aspect of cognitive development (1973, p. 2).

4. Equilibrium This last force is the one that maintains a balance among the other three, fitting the maturational, direct experience, and social transmission influences together harmoniously. Piaget (1973, p. 29) felt the need for such a factor because "a whole play of regulation and of compensation is required to result in a coherence."

In summary, then, the sorts of knowledge the child acquires in terms of mental schemes, and the time at which they are acquired, depend upon such factors as maturation, physical experience, social transmission, and equilibrium. These factors regulate the stages of cognitive growth through which, in Piaget's system, all children normally develop. It is to this series of levels or stages that we now turn.

LEVELS AND STAGES OF DEVELOPMENT

As noted in Chapter 2, one of the traditional issues in the field of child development is whether growth proceeds continuously—by imperceptibly small increments—or advances by stages. And if a theorist proposes that it does indeed move by stages, then what criteria does she or he apply in identifying a stage?

Piaget, like apparently all developmentalists, recognized that from day to day, growth is continuous, with no major leaps ahead from one day to the next and no extended plateaus of dormancy in growth. At the same time, when he viewed the entire span of the growth years, Piaget was able to distinguish breaks in the process. These breaks suggested to him that the child has at each such point completed one phase of development and is now engaged in a further one.

To say that Piaget proposed *a* series of developmental stages would be oversimplifying his work. Actually, he identified a number of different series, each related to a different aspect of personality or mental life. For example, one series concerns steps in understanding physical causality (1930), another the steps in imitation and play (1951), still another in the conception of moral principles and justice (1948), and others in understanding number (1952), space (1956), and movement (1969). But underlying these and other specific series of stages there appears to be a basic set that provides the framework for overall sensorimotor-intellectual development. Let's look at this underlying set.

There is some confusion in the writings of Piaget and his followers about how many major stages, and their constituent substages, best reflect the growth process. Some authors picture three major levels, others four, and some even five. In the following discussion I have cast the scheme into one of its most familiar forms, with four major levels or periods, each divided into subperiods designated as stages. In this fourfold division, the levels are called (1) the sensorimotor period, (2) the preoperational thought period, (3) the concrete operations period, and (4) the formal operations period. As we trace the child's progress through the stages, we will see her grow from being (a) an entirely self-centered infant with no realistic knowledge of her environment to become (b) an adolescent who employs logic and language with facility to intellectually manipulate the environment and thus comprehend, ever more realistically, how the world functions.

Although age designations are attached to each of the four periods in the following discussion, they should be regarded as only approximations, as rough averages, for as Piaget pointed out:

> They are not stages which can be given a constant chronological date. On the contrary, the ages can vary from one society to another. . . . But there is a constant order of succession . . . that is, in order to reach a certain stage, previous steps must be taken. The prestructures . . . which make for further advance must be constructed.
>
> Thus we reach a hierarchy of (mental) structures which are built in a certain order of integration and . . . appear at senescence to disintegrate in the reverse order (1973, pp. 10–11).

Level 1: The Sensorimotor Period (Birth to Age 2)

During the first two years, infants are unable to verbalize very well any thoughts they may have, so it is necessary to estimate their intellectual growth by the manner in which they sense (see, hear, feel, taste, smell) their environment and by the manner in which they subsequently act upon it (motor behavior). Piaget's observations of children in this age period enabled him to distinguish six stages through which they develop (Piaget & Inhelder, 1969, pp. 4–12).

The first stage (0–1 month) features the baby's adapting to his environment by means of his inherited, ready-to-operate, unlearned *reflexes*. It is by reflex activity that the baby sucks, cries, breathes, coughs, urinates, defecates, and makes gross bodily movements.

The second stage (1–4 months) is marked by the infant's gradually acquiring adaptive actions as the result of experience. During the first stage there was no distinction between the functions of assimilation and accommodation. But during the second, assimilation and accommodation can be distinguished as the infant starts to alter her sensorimotor action patterns (her schemes) on the basis of the responses of her environment. "For instance, when the child systematically sucks his thumb, no longer due to chance contacts but through coordination between hand and mouth, this may be called acquired accommodation" (Piaget, 1963, p. 48).

During this second stage the child engages in a great deal of repetitive activity, such as grasping and letting go of something over and over again. These actions, labeled *primary circular reactions,* were interpreted by Piaget as evidence that learning new associations or acquiring knowledge is not accomplished by the environment's imposing them on the child's mind. Rather, as noted in our earlier discussion of Piaget's concept of knowledge, intellectual development even during the sensorimotor period involves understandings "discovered and even created in the course of the child's own searchings" (Piaget, 1963, p. 55). So the repetitious activity of the infant is purposive, designed either to preserve or rediscover an act or skill. In other words, it functions as practice.

The third stage (4–8 months) marks the beginning of the infant's distinguishing between self and outside objects. It also marks the start of intentional acts, of consciously acting to attain a goal. The intention, however, is of a transitional type. The child does not foresee a goal, then attempt an act designed to achieve the goal. That sort of "true" intention comes at the fourth stage. But during the third stage the child will repeat an act that he happens to have performed with satisfaction. The primary circular reactions of the second stage were not movements designed to produce a particular result in the environment; they were simply self-centered acts showing no apparent awareness of an environment. However, at this third stage, the repetitive behavior that occurs—the *secondary circular reactions*—suggests a beginning awareness of the environment, for the acts seem directed toward reproducing a result that, by chance, has just been effected. For example, when the infant happens to hit a rattle hanging within reach in his crib, he may enjoy the sound. Then by gradually moving his hands and occasionally hitting the rattle, he begins to distinguish between his hand, the rattle, and other objects, so he comes purposely to grasp or hit the rattle directly and not by chance.

The fourth stage (8–12 months) signifies the emergence of clear acts of intelligence. The infant anticipates people and objects. She searches for objects that are out of sight, thus showing that objects have now attained a quality of permanence for her. Prior to this time, if a toy was moved from one location to another, she apparently felt that it had dissolved into the nothingness around her and that a new toy had appeared from the nothingness at the second location, even though the toy had been shifted from the first spot to the second within the baby's presence. Along with this initial step in recognizing qualities of permanence of objects, the infant also begins to comprehend cause and effect, that certain acts will bring about predicted results. Consequently, she can conceive of an end result ahead of time, then fashion an act to bring the result about. Her behavior now can be called truly intentional and thus qualifies as the beginning of *practical intelligence,* which consists of envisioning goals or desired ends and then employing existing schemes as means for achieving the ends (Piaget & Inhelder, 1969, pp. 10–11).

The fifth stage (12–18 months) involves the child in *tertiary circular reactions.* Recall that primary circular reactions (1–4 months) were events repeated over and over simply to preserve them, a kind of practice. Secondary circular reactions (4–8 months) were the purposive repetition of acts the infant found satisfying the first time, and so chose to repeat again and again, even in new settings—a kind of application of known means to new situations. In contrast, tertiary reactions are not exact repetitions of the original act. Rather, they consist of reproducing the original event in modified form—a kind of variation on the original theme. The one-year-old, according to Piaget (1963, p. 266), tries, "through a sort of experimentation, to find out in which respect the object or the event is new. In other words, he will not only submit to but even provoke new results instead of being satisfied merely to reproduce them once they have been revealed fortuitously."

Prior to the fifth period, acts of intelligence involved only an application of existing schemes to new situations, that is, assimilating new events into already acquired schemes by attending only to the features of the object or event that were similar to existing schemes. But now, in the fifth period, the child pays greater heed to the ways the new object or event differs from his present mental constructs, and he employs the process of accommodation to differentiate existing schemes and construct more suitable new ones. So tertiary circular reactions involve "reproductory assimilation with differentiated and intentional accommodation" (Piaget, 1950, p. 104).

The sort of "discovery of new means through active experimentation" (Piaget, 1963, p. 267) that marks this fifth stage was illustrated by Piaget with the case of a child who, sitting on the floor, seeks a toy that is out of reach. During his grasping, he pulls the edge of the small rug on which the toy lies, an act that is either an accident or a substitute for getting the toy. When he notices how his tug on the rug made the toy move toward him, he then intentionally pulls the rug as the instrument for obtaining the object (Piaget & Inhelder, 1969, p. 11).

Object Relations   Up to this point in our discussion of mental growth stages, I have implied but not addressed directly one of the most important dimensions of development in Piaget's system. It is that of *object relations,* meaning the way the child conceives of herself in relation to the objects of the world as well as the way she sees the objects' relationships to each other. In the beginning, the infant's universe is centered entirely on her own body and actions. There are no objects but only a world of what Piaget called "unsubstantial tableaux" that vaguely appear and then dissolve, never to reappear, or else they come back in some altered form (Piaget & Inhelder, 1969, p. 14). Nor is there a single space and time within which sensations of sight, sound, touch, temperature, taste, and smell are coordinated. Being lifted into mother's arms and fed is, in Piaget's estimation, sensed by the baby as separate impressions of postural change, pressures on various parts of the body, the touch of the lips to the nipple, voice sounds, shifting light patterns, and the ingesting of milk—none of which has any connection with the others. When the infant's mental organization of the universe is so unstructured, she does not—indeed could not—conceive of cause and effect relationships among objects. Even during the advance of infancy, as she begins to differentiate objects from herself and invest them with some permanence in time and space, her conception of cause remains egocentric: Nothing happens in the world except as a result of her own wishes and actions. But by gradual steps over the coming years she recognizes more accurately objective causality in the world.

In summary, an important perspective from which to view child development is that of object relations. Among researchers, Piaget is particularly noted for his contributions in tracing developmental changes in children's conceptions of the permanence of objects, the objects' positions in space and time, and causal relations among them. In our continuing discussion of mental stages, this should become readily apparent.

At the sixth and final stage (18–24 months) of the sensorimotor period, the child no longer has to experiment with objects themselves to solve problems, but can represent them mentally and can cognitively combine and manipulate them. In effect, he is now mentally inventive. For example, a child at this stage sees a toy outside his playpen out of reach. He also sees a stick within arm's reach. He decides that he can use the stick as a tool for pulling the toy to the playpen, and he then uses the stick for this purpose. Prior to the sixth stage he might have gotten the toy if the stick had already been in his hand and he had groped for some time and happened to touch the toy. But he would not have preplanned the act by mentally combining the stick and the toy's distance before picking the stick up. Attainment of this new inventiveness makes intelligence now "capable of entering the framework of language to be transformed, with the aid of the social group, into reflective intelligence" (Piaget, 1963, p. 356).

Level 2: The Preoperational Thought Period (about Age 2 to Age 7)

In our review of this level of preoperational thought, we need to understand what Piaget meant by *operations*. Such understanding will make clear what sort of "operational thought" this level 2 thinking precedes, that is, what sort it prepares the child to perform at a later level of growth.

Operations, in Piaget's system, are ways of manipulating objects in relation to each other, such as arranging them in a series according to size or putting them in classes according to color. If the objects are actually before us, like actual colored blocks or ponies, the manipulations we perform on them, either by physically moving them or by observing how we might move them, are called *concrete operations*. We will meet these operations when we come to the third major period of development, which follows the preoperational level. When concrete operations are transposed into verbal propositions about the relationships that exist or might exist among objects, and these propositions are mentally manipulated, the intellectual actions are called *formal operations* (Piaget, 1969, p. 206). These we will meet at the fourth level of intellectual growth.

An operation, however, is not just any manipulation of objects. Indeed, as the term *preoperational thought* indicates, the mental activities of most children under age 7 do not yet qualify as operational. To be classified as operations, actions must be internalizable, reversible, and coordinated into systems that have laws that apply to the entire system and not just to the single operation itself. As Piaget explained, operations:

> are actions, since they are carried out on objects before being performed on symbols. They are internalizable, since they can also be carried out in thought without losing their original character of actions. They are

reversible as against simple actions which are irreversible. . . . Finally, since operations do not exist in isolation, they are connected in the form of structured wholes (1972, p. 8).

The characteristics of operations should become clear when we review the third and fourth periods of intellectual growth, for then we will discuss in some detail illustrations of children displaying operational thinking. For the present we will review the preoperational thought period knowing that it leads to children's performing concrete and formal operations.

This preoperational period can be divided into two stages. The first extends from age 2 to about 4 and is characterized by egocentric use of language and heavy dependence on perception in problem solving. The second lasts from about age 5 to around 7 and is marked by more social or communicative speech and greater dependence on intuitive thinking rather than just on perception.

Before inspecting these two stages in detail, we need to be aware of the great importance Piaget attributed to language in the development of intelligence during this period. Language, he said, performs three roles: (1) It enables the child to communicate with other people, thus opening the opportunity for socialization of action; (2) it enables the child to internalize words in the form of thoughts and a system of signs; and most important, (3) it internalizes action so the child does not have to depend on manipulating things physically to solve problems. Instead, she can represent them by mental images with which she conducts experiments. She becomes less bound by time and space. She can increasingly imagine things that are out of sight, far distant, and in the past. She can experiment with these things in different mental combinations far quicker than she could manipulate them physically.

Egocentric Speech   During the years 2–4, the child learns an increasing variety of words. He begins to talk a lot, and the talk is two varieties. Some of his talk is *social communication*—asking parents to reach a toy he cannot get, telling his sister he wants the doll back, or telling mother he wants to go to the toilet.

But a far larger proportion of the child's talking and listening is *egocentric,* a running oral commentary that accompanies what the child is doing at the moment and is not intended to communicate anything to anyone else. Since this kind of talk often appears in social situations, such as in a group of children at play, it can at first glance be mistaken for social communication. However, on closer inspection it becomes apparent that everyone is talking to herself or himself without listening to the others. For this reason, Piaget labeled such speech *collective monologues.* An important

causal factor behind this discourse, in Piaget's opinion, is the child's lingering self-centeredness. The child still views life from her own perspective
and has difficulty seeing things from the perspectives of others. Hence she
does not try to comprehend what others say so she can respond from the
viewpoint they express.

To check this hypothesis, Piaget observed preoperational children in
situations requiring them to explain something to another child, and then
noted, from the other child's behavior, how well the explanation or directions had been understood. The observations revealed a systematic
egocentricity in the sense that the child giving directions had great difficulty adopting the other's viewpoint, so as to cast the explanation in a form
readily comprehended from the second child's perspective (Piaget & Inhelder, 1969, pp. 120–122).

While children's growing language skills aid their mental development, they do not free reasoning abilities from the influence of immediate
perception. Children of age 2 through 4 or 5 base their problem solving
heavily on what they see or hear directly rather than on what they recall
about objects and events. What they perceive about an object is what
dominates their conclusions, not what they conceive about the object based
on memories of the object's permanent characteristics. Children at this age
suffer from the limitations of what Piaget called *centration*. Presented with a
visual stimulus, a child centers on one aspect and believes that this aspect
completely characterizes the stimulus. The child cannot consider two dimensions, such as height and width, at the same time. For instance, if there
is the same amount of water in two glasses of identical size and shape, the
four-year-old will agree that both contain the same amount of water. But if
the child sees the water from one glass poured into a taller and thinner
glass, he will center on the height dimension only and conclude that the
taller glass contains more water. It may be apparent that centration is not
the only factor involved in the child's error of judgment. Other characteristics of immature logic also contribute to the error. For example, the
preoperational child fails as well to comprehend the principle of *compensation*, that is, that the dimensions of an object can operate in coordination so
that one dimension compensates for another. The greater width of the
original glass compensates for its lack of height.

Intuitive Thought   By the time the child reaches age 5 or 6 or so, she enters
the stage Piaget labeled *intuitive thought.* It is a transition period between
depending solely on perception and depending on truly logical thinking.
An experiment with beads illustrates the characteristics of such transitional
thinking. Six red beads are lined up on a table, and the child is told to put
as many blue beads on the table as there are red ones. At age 4 or 5 the

typical child makes a row of blue beads about the same length as the red row, without bothering to make sure there are six blue ones. But a child a year or two older lines up six blue beads opposite the red ones, thus displaying progress toward recognizing equivalent quantities. But there are still shortcomings in his logic, for if the experimenter then spreads out the red beads to form a longer line, the six-year-old thinks the number of red and blue beads is no longer equivalent (Figure 10.1). He is still unduly influenced by perception of line length rather than the logic of quantity. In the terminology used by Piaget, the child has not recognized that the number of beads has been *conserved* or is *invariant* even though the length of the two lines has been altered (Piaget, 1950, p. 132).

Another Piagetian experiment also illustrates the transitional—between dependence on perception (on how things look) and on logic (on what principles govern their operation)—nature of the child's thinking during this stage of intuitive understanding. Three beads—one red, one blue, one yellow—are on a string that passes through a cardboard tube (Figure 10.2). A child is asked to observe the order of the beads before they are slipped into the cardboard tube where they cannot be seen. Then the child is asked to predict the order in which the beads will emerge from the other end of the tube. All children can predict correctly. But if asked to tell in what order they will emerge if poured back out through the same end

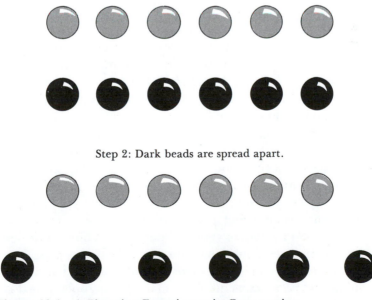

Step 1: Beads lined up in pairs.

Step 2: Dark beads are spread apart.

Figure 10.1   A Piagetian Experiment in Conservation

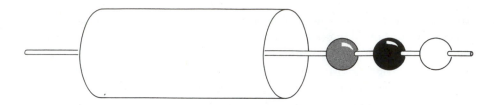

Figure 10.2   Piaget's Beads and Tube Task

they entered, the child under age 4 or 5 will be confused. She fails to see that they will emerge in the opposite sequence if they are backed out of the tube. Furthermore, while the beads are in the tube, if the apparatus is turned 180 degrees and the child is asked the order in which the beads will emerge, the child from about age 4 to about age 7 will fail to see that half a turn will change the order to emergence from red-blue-yellow to yellow-blue-red. She then is given a chance to try it and see what happens. Intuitively she comes to recognize what the half turn will do. By experimenting further, she finally admits that if given two half turns, the order of emergence will be the same as it was originally. She intuitively gets the idea, yet still does not understand the principle that an even number of half turns keeps the emergence as it was originally, but an odd number reverses the order of emergence. This is shown by the fact that even after the experiments, the child is no better able to predict the effect of three half turns than she was originally (Piaget, 1950, pp. 135–136).

In short, the intuitive stage marks a movement toward greater *decentration*. The child is better able to see more than one factor at a time that influences an event. He is on the verge of a major advance in logical thought.

To summarize, children make several important growth gains during the preoperational thought level between ages 2 and 7. They acquire facility in spoken language as a tool for communicating with others and for helping themselves think aloud. By age 7 their communicative language greatly increases as collective monologues decrease. They also gain skill in solving problems intuitively when the objects involved in the problems are in front of them. They become less self-centered in that they recognize that objects have an existence and permanence of their own that does not depend on the child's wishes or actions. Specifically, children recognize the permanence of an object's substance when its location or shape is changed. Water poured from a bowl into a tall glass is still water. A ball of clay rolled into a sausage shape remains the same clay. But preoperational children are still in the process of transition toward decentering, for they do not yet recognize that volume, weight, and mass are also conserved in the acts of pouring and rolling. Even though they have made great advances by age 7 in comprehending how the universe of things operates, they are still strongly dependent on perception (how events seem to the eye) rather than on logic (what principles govern events).

Level 3: The Concrete Operations Period (about Age 7 to Age 11)

At the concrete operations stage, children become capable of performing operations that are directly related to objects. In the formal operations period, which comes later, they will learn to perform operations on verbally stated hypotheses and propositions that are not limited to particular objects (Piaget & Inhelder, 1969, p. 100). The term *concrete* does not mean children must see or touch actual objects as they work through a problem. Rather, "concrete" means that the problems involve identifiable objects that are either directly perceived or imagined. In the later formal operations period children are able to move ahead to deal with problems that do not concern particular objects. To illustrate this difference, we can consider the following two items, the first suitable for the concrete operations child, the second for the more advanced formal operations child or adolescent:

Concrete: If Alice has two apples and Caroline gives her three more, how many apples will Alice have altogether?

Formal: Imagine that there are two quantities which together make up a whole. If we increase the first quantity but the whole remains the same, what has happened to the second quantity?

It may be apparent that even though children do not need to see the objects in order to carry out the operations, in the early transitional phase toward learning and mastering such operations, they will be aided by viewing the actual objects or pictures of them.

In the earlier brief introduction to the term *operations,* I defined it but did not illustrate its several characteristics. I will do so now. Piaget said that for an action of the child to qualify as an operation, it had to be internalizable, reversible, and coordinated into overall systems. Furthermore, operations are not unique to an individual child but are common to all people of the same intelligence level. Finally, an operation assists the child not only in his private reasoning but also in his "cognitive exchanges," which bring together information and combine it in various ways (Piaget, 1953, p. 8; Piaget & Inhelder, 1969, pp. 96–97).

By *internalizable* Piaget meant the actions can be carried out in thought "without losing their original character of actions" (1953, p. 8).

By *reversible* he meant they can be readily inverted into their opposite. For example, two groups of apples that have been combined (added together) to form a whole group can easily be reduced (subtracted from the whole) to their original status. Hence adding is an operation. In contrast, Piaget said, writing from left to right is only a simple action and not an operation, for it cannot be inverted into writing from right to left without the child's having to develop an entirely new set of actions (1953, p. 8).

Reversible transformations may be of two varieties: *inversions,* where $+A$ is reversed by $-A$ (addition reversed by subtraction, multiplication reversed by division) and *reciprocity,* where $A < B$ is reciprocated by $B > A$ (the width of the bowl of water compensates for its lack of height, and the height of the glass of water compensates for its lack of width). When an object is moved or transformed in some way, in a transformation that qualifies as operatory, not everything about the system changes. Some features remain constant. As we have seen, Piaget gave the label *conservation* to this feature of constancy or invariance of objects. So we can say that a child's scheme or idea of a permanent object consists of that combination of features of the object that do not change when the object is moved or acted on. How adequately the child's scheme matches that of adult logic or "reality" can be judged if we assess which aspects of objects the child believes have been conserved during the transformation. Many of the problem situations Piaget contrived for children to solve are designed to test children's notions of conservation. And his investigations have shown that the particular aspects a child sees as being conserved depend on the child's age, or more accurately, on the child's developmental level.

For example, when two lumps of clay the same size and shape are shown to a child and then one lump is rolled into a sausage form, the child of age 7 or 8 discovers that the substance has been conserved. But not until age 9 or 10 does she discover that the weight has been conserved as well. And not until age 11 or 12 does she discover the conservation of volume that occurs when an object is immersed in water and the displacement measured (Piaget & Inhelder, 1969, p. 99).

Thus during the concrete operations period, from age 7 to around 11 or so, children gradually discover more of the properties of objects and transformations and master mental operations that can be applied to their concrete world.

The concrete operations child not only gains greater command of the notions of conservation and reversibility but also becomes capable of decentering his attention, of recognizing the way two or more dimensions of an event interact to produce a given result. He no longer centers his attention solely on the height of the water glass or only on its width but considers both dimensions simultaneously and recognizes their interaction. When presented with twelve wooden beads (nine red, three white), the child no longer will say there are more red beads than wooden beads when asked to compare red ones with wooden ones. At the concrete operations level he now recognizes that color and construction material are two different classifications, and he is not stuck by centering on only color or material. He also can now order things in a series according to a stated criterion, such as size or number.

Whereas the preoperational child focused on the static beginning state and final state of an object in a transformation, the concrete operations child can comprehend the transformation as a process. For example, typical preoperational children at age 3 or 4 think there is more clay in five small balls than in the original large ball from which the five were made. Even when the transformation, and its reverse of recombining the five into one, is performed before their eyes, three- and four-year-olds still say that the five contain more clay than the one. But by age 6 or 8, children agree that the quantity remains the same in the change from one to five balls and back again.

The egocentrism that caused the younger child to see things only from her own viewpoint changes as the older child achieves the aspects of cognitive growth mentioned above and as her increased facility with language leads to greater socialization. The child in the concrete operations period now has a more objective view of the universe and better understands how others see things.

Children's concepts of causation also mature during this period. For instance, a comparison of a child aged 6 years and 8 months and a child aged 10 years and 3 months illustrates the development of the concept of displacement of volume. The experiment involves dropping a small stone into a container of water (Piaget, 1930, pp. 169–172).

When the experimenter asks the six-year-old what will happen if the stone is dropped into the water, the child says the water will rise *"because it is heavy in the water."* The experimenter says, "You see the pebble hanging on this thread: if I put it in the water as far as this (half-way), will it make the water rise?" *"No, because it is not heavy enough."*

In contrast, the ten-year-old says the water will rise *"because the pebble takes up space."* The experimenter asks, "If I put this wood in, what will happen?" *"It will lie on the water."* "And what will the water do?" *"It will rise because the wood also takes up space."* "Which is the heavier, this pebble (small) or this wood (large)?" *"The pebble."* "Which will make the water rise the most?" *"The pebble takes up less space, it will make the water rise less."*

So the child arrives at the early teen years with increased skill in accounting for the cause of physical events and is ready to solve not only problems that involve objects, but also problems concerning hypotheses and propositions about relationships.

Level 4: The Formal Operations Period (about Age 11 to Age 15)

In adolescence children are no longer limited by what they directly see or hear, nor are they restricted to the problem at hand. They can now imagine the conditions of a problem—past, present, or future—and develop hypotheses about what might logically occur under different combinations of factors. For example, if we begin a problem with "Imagine that water in the river ran up hill . . .," children younger than 12 will claim that the subsequent problem cannot be solved because water does not run up hill. But by the close of the formal operations period teenagers can accept the hypothetical condition of upward flow and can apply it in solving the posed problem.

Another of Piaget's favorite examples further illustrates the difference between the concrete operations child and the one who has attained formal operations ability. This is a problem involving *transitivity,* meaning that a relationship between two elements or objects is carried over to other elements logically related to the first two. For example, the child has solved the problem of transitivity if he recognizes that when $A = B$ and $B = C$, then $A = C$. Or if $A < B$ and $B < C$, then $A < C$. So the question posed to the child is this: "Edith is fairer than Susan; Edith is darker than Lily; who is the darkest of the three?" Piaget (1950, p. 149) found that before age 12 children rarely could solve this. Instead, they engaged in such reasoning as: "Edith and Susan are fair, Edith and Lily are dark, therefore Lily is darkest, Susan is the fairest, and Edith is in between." However, the adolescent in his midteens can solve the problem accurately, for he comprehends the transitivity it involves.

Prior to early and middle adolescence, therefore, children are still bound by their perceptions. But during the formal operations period they are able to engage in *"pure* thought which is independent of action" that they see or carry out themselves (Piaget, 1950, 149). Adolescents can hypothesize and draw deductions from the hypotheses. They can understand general theories and can combine them to solve assumed problems. In effect, by age 15, the framework of the average youth's thinking has evolved into its mature state. The types of thought of which the adult is capable are now all within the youth's repertoire of mental functions.

Does this mean, then, that there is no intellectual growth beyond mid-adolescence in Piaget's model of the mind? No, it does not. It means that the framework of thought is complete, but the framework is not all filled in. Further experiences during the years of youth and adulthood fill in the outline with additional, more complex schemes or greater knowledge, so the adult *does* know more than the adolescent. However, the adolescent is capable of all the forms of logic that the adult commands.

According to Piaget, the most obvious distinction between adolescent and adult thought is the greater lingering egocentrism displayed by adolescents. The teenage youth, with her newly acquired skills of logical thought, is an idealist who expects the world to be logical. She fails to recognize or accept the reality that people do not operate solely on the basis of logic, and she becomes a reformer and critic of the older generation, foreseeing a glorious future in which she and her peers will right today's wrongs. In Piaget's opinion, this egocentrism and idealism is rendered more realistic and social by the youth's entering the occupational world or by her taking on serious professional training.

> The adolescent becomes an adult when he undertakes a real job. It is then that he is transformed from an idealistic reformer into an achiever. In other words, the job leads thinking away from the dangers of formalism back into reality (Inhelder & Piaget, 1958, p. 346).

This move from adolescence into adulthood, then, completes the sequence of stages through which the intellect develops during the first two decades of life.

Piaget's notion of periods of development was not limited to the set of general intelligence stages described above. He also identified minor sets of stages for special aspects of cognitive growth. For example, his pioneering studies of moral development led him to distinguish three phases in children's conception of lying. Below age 5 or 6, children equated lying with saying something naughty, that is, with saying something forbidden by adults. Around ages 5 to 7, children could distinguish between an intentional falsehood and an unintentional error, but they still applied the word *lie* to each of these sorts of acts. Not until age 10 or 11 did most children accurately define lying as intentionally giving a false statement (Piaget, 1948, pp. 139–144).

FOUR CONCEPTS: A CLOSER LOOK

The foregoing introduction to Piaget's system serves as a backdrop to a more detailed examination of four concepts mentioned earlier, those of genetic epistemology, stages or periods of development, functional invariants, and equilibrium.

Genetic Epistemology

At the beginning of this chapter genetic epistemology was defined as the study of changes in the relationship between the knower and the known with the passing of time. I noted as well that Piaget's investigations of children's cognitive development were stimulated by his interest in clarifying issues of genetic epistemology rather than by his desire to catalogue ways children at different age levels think about the world around them. And because this epistemological intention led to Piaget's publishing findings about how children's minds operate, some people have inferred that genetic epistemology and Piaget's proposals are one and the same. To correct this impression, Jacques Vonéche, who occupies the Piaget professorial chair at the University of Geneva, has suggested that the general discipline of genetic epistemology should be:

> disembarrassed from the unhappy fusion it has undergone, in recent times, with Piaget's specific attempt to orient that discipline along certain lines. . . . [Furthermore] besides limiting genetic epistemology to the sole attempts of Jean Piaget, there is another confusion generally made by philosophers and scientists alike, that of fusing Piaget's epistemology with his psychology. Numerous examples can be given of people who sincerely think that genetic epistemology is the title Piaget bestowed upon his theory of intellectual development in human ontogeny, although it should have seemed unlikely that a person of Piaget's considerable historical erudition and critical acumen would conflate individual developmental psychology with genetic epistemology (1985).

Piaget's approach represents only one of a variety of solutions scholars have attempted for studying "the mechanisms of the growth of knowledge" ever since James Mark Baldwin coined the term *genetic epistemology* in 1906 (Baldwin, 1906, 1908, 1911). And as Vonéche has implied, *genetic epistemology* and *genetic psychology* are not the same thing, even though there is a connection between them. Genetic psychology can be defined as the study of how the intelligence or the behavior of a typical member of a species changes over a lifetime. However, genetic epistemology involves not only this question of how intelligence develops but also such philosophical issues as the nature of being (ontology), the way knowledge should be defined, and the kind of evidence admissible for establishing the validity of knowledge.

The theory we have reviewed in the foregoing pages has been Piaget's psychology of cognitive development, not his complete version of genetic epistemology. However, it is useful to note ways in which certain of his assumptions about epistemology influenced his research methods and theoretical conclusions. For example, Piaget did not assume, as philosophical solipsists do, that the "real world" is simply what the individual's experience tells him is real. Rather, Piaget assumed that there is a "real world" outside of the individual "knower"; as children develop they achieve an increasingly accurate match between what is most adults' conception of a real world and the child's own conception. And, as noted earlier, Piaget also defined knowledge in a particular way—as physically or mentally acting on things, rather than as a fund of beliefs shared by members of a given society or as an individual's own storehouse of information. Furthermore, Piaget held that evidence obtained by the methods of modern science constitutes genetic epistemology's proper way of knowing. Finally, he viewed genetic epistemology as an interdisciplinary undertaking in which developmental psychologists participated with other scientists.

> The first rule of genetic epistemology is therefore one of collaboration. Since its problem is to study how knowledge grows, it is a matter then, in each particular question, of having the cooperation of psychologists who study the development as such, of logicians who formalize the stages or states of momentary equilibrium of this development, and of scientific specialists who show interest in the domain in question [such as physics, biology, sociology]. Naturally we must add mathematicians, who assure the connection between logic and the field in question, and cyberneticians, who assure the connection between psychology and logic (Piaget, 1972, p. 8).

Stages of Development

Among scholars of Piagetian theory, the terms *stages, steps, levels, periods,* and *phases* of development are sometimes employed interchangeably. Or, as found earlier in this chapter, a major plateau in development may be called a *level* or *phase* and a subplateau called a *step* or *stage* or *substage*. But whatever the term used, the idea behind all such designations is that children's development is marked by times of noticeable change that are interspersed with times of stability.

Although all stage theorists agree that stages involve alternating times of change and of stability, few believe that change and stability is the *only* quality that defines a stage theory. Instead, most theorists propose additional factors they believe a growth pattern should exhibit in order to qualify its stable times as *stages*. As for Piaget, he contended that stages should have five further qualities—they must be universal, invariant in sequence, tranforming and irreversible, gradually evolved, and ultimately in equilibrium.

1. *Universality.* The quality of universality means that stages are the same for all members of the species. A pattern of behavior that is found only in some children does not qualify as a stage. The pattern must be found in all children.

2. *Invariant Sequence.* In Piaget's view, as well as in the opinion of most developmentalists, sets of behaviors do not compose a hierarchy of stages unless everyone goes through the sets in exactly the same sequence. For example, if some children exhibited formal operational thinking directly after the sensorimotor phase, whereas other children moved from sensorimotor to preoperational thought, then Piaget's sets of sensorimotor, preoperational, and formal operational thinking would not be stages. All children must pass through all the stage gates in the same order.

3. *Transformation and Irreversibility.* When children enter a new stage, they not only interpret all future experiences through the lens of the new stage, but problems solved in the past by the methods of the previous stage are all now tranformed, seen through the conceptual lens of the new stage. In effect, the child who has thoroughly progressed into formal operational thinking will seldom if ever go back to thinking in concrete or preoperational terms. This means that the naivete of early childhood is "spoiled" by progress into the more sophisticated thought of middle childhood. In short, stage progression is irreversible. For instance, after children in the concrete operations stage discover the principle of compensation (that the width of a glass bowl compensates for its lack of height, enabling the bowl to hold as much water as does a tall glass), they no longer limit their attention to only one dimension of containers whenever they are asked about the quantities and weights of a substance that might fit into various containers. With this discovery, children are never again amazed by the kinds of results that surprised them at an earlier age when they saw liquid poured from one vessel into another of a different shape.

4. *Gradual Evolution.* Elevation to a new level or stage does not occur all of a sudden, or even within a period of a month, a few months,

or a year. Instead, in Piaget's system movement to a new stage occurs gradually, a bit here and a bit there until finally enough of a child's behavior exhibits the traits of the new stage to say that the transformation to the next level is complete. For example, children do not grasp the conservation of substance, quantity, mass, or volume of objects all at the same time but accomplish it only over a period of years.

5. *Equilibrium.* Once a child consolidates his thinking patterns into a coherent way of acting in the world, this new stage of cognitive development is said to have reached a state of stability and balance. The stage is now in equilibrium.

Piagetian stage theory does not require that children pass through the stages at the same speed nor that all children eventually reach the highest level. Piaget expected individual differences in the rate of progress, and he noted that some children would fall short of the formal operations level or, in the case of severe mental retardation, might not even get past the sensorimotor or preoperational levels.

However, while the five attributes of stages may seem clear at a conceptual level, some of them have posed awkward problems about child nature as observed in daily life. For example, when a child's thought processes about a variety of aspects of her life are compared, it is clear that there is considerable unevenness in the kinds of thinking she exhibits in solving different types of problems. For example, in mathematics it is typical for children to conceive of the conservation of number and length before that of area and volume. And the differences in the stages of children's thought processes in one domain, such as mathematics, and another, such as that of moral reasoning, are even greater. This brings up the question of whether the general stages of mental growth Piaget postulated really do form a valid description of how children's thinking develops. Perhaps there are only special stages for different aspects of life that cannot legitimately be compounded into a single general system.

One way that Piaget accounted for this lack of coordination of children's thinking processes was the notion of gradual evolution, described under item 4. He gave the term *horizontal décalage* to the apparent lag in a child's applying in all aspects of life a mode of thinking that Piaget proposed was characteristic of a single stage. For example, during the concrete-operations phase of development, when children see a ball of plasticine clay divided to become five smaller balls, they do not simultaneously discover that both the substance and the weight have been conserved as the number of balls has changed from one to five. Instead, children comprehend the conservation of substance (clay remains clay) at an earlier age than they comprehend that the weight also remains unchanged. In effect, there is some horizontal *décalage* (meaning *displacement*) between the time a child applies a new stage of thinking to one facet of life and the time she applies that same stage to other facets. However, we may ask: Does labeling this phenomenon *horizontal décalage* really explain the apparent unevenness in the way children apply a particular level of thought to different aspects of life, including different subject-matter areas in school? We will examine this further in the assessment of the theory at the end of the chapter.

Piaget called *vertical décalage* a child's applying increasingly complex modes of thought to the same phenomenon or problem in life. For example, in the beads-and-tube task pictured earlier, a kindergarten child may physically reverse the tube and thereby be able to tell the order in which the colored beads will emerge from the tube, although she cannot explain why she knows. In contrast, a primary-grade child not only can predict the order of the beads without physically turning the tube but also can explain how her mental image of the tube has enabled her to solve the problem. Subsequently, a youth who has achieved formal-operations thought patterns can even explain the abstract principle which enables her to accurately predict the order of the beads, no matter how many times the tube is turned. Thus *vertical décalage* refers to the displacement of one mode of thought by a sequence of more sophisticated modes as the child matures. Although the notion of horizontal décalage seems somewhat at odds with Piaget's theory of broadly encompassing stages of mental development, the idea of vertical décalage fits quite logically into his stage model.

Functional Invariants

It is apparent that Piaget's model accounts for the ways in which children's thought structures vary from one stage of development to the next. He also points out that, as children grow up, their schemes change by increasing in number, in precision, and in interconnections. But not everything about development changes as the years pass. Certain aspects continue unaltered over the entire life span. Piaget called these aspects *functional invariants* to signify not only that they are stable but also that they are *processes* or *functions* rather than structures.

Two such functions are *adaptation* and *organization*. Throughout life, people adapt to their environment and reorganize their schemes in ways that promote survival. Three other invariant functions—*assimilation, accommodation,* and *equilibrium*—serve as the chief instruments for promoting adaptation and organization. The lifetime process of adapting and organizing consists of a never-ending cycle of assimilation, of accommodation, and of the achievement of a temporary state of equilibrium which is soon disturbed by events that stimulate further assimilation, which starts the cycle over again.

Among these invariants, the one whose meaning seems most elusive is equilibrium, so let's inspect it in more detail.

Equilibrium

At least part of the reason people have difficulty comprehending *equilibrium*, or the companion term *equilibration*, is that Piaget seems to have used it to mean different things at different times. In general, *equilibration* seems to mean a process of movement toward a state of *equilibrium* or of balance, a state in which an organism remains until conditions upset the balance. In this sense, "a state of equilibrium is not a state of final rest, but constitutes a new point of departure" (Piaget in Battro, 1973, p. 57). However, these rather gross meanings seem insufficient to clarify Piaget's diverse applications of the term; as the following excerpts from English translations of his publications suggest.

> [We may] (a) conceive of equilibrium as characterized by *maximum* entropy, (b) or as due to the intervention of coordinations which introduce from outside an order diminishing the entropy, (c) or else as due to a sequence of "strategies" of which each one will be oriented by the results of the preceding one up to the moment when the actions become reversible through the very coordination of these preceding strategies that would have been freed from the earlier historic process in order to reach equilibrium.

> Equilibrium [is the] place of specific junction between the possible and the real.

> The structures can be interpreted as . . . the result of an autonomous process of equilibration.

> The best equilibrated states . . . correspond to a maximum of activities and a maximum of opening up of exchanges.

> The system is in equilibrium when the operations of which the subject is capable constitute a structure such that the operations can unfold in two directions (either by strict inversion or negation, or by reciprocity). It is therefore because the totality of possible operations constitutes a system of potential transformations which compensate each other—and which compensate each other as far as obeying the laws of reversibility—that the system is in equilibrium.

> We shall say that a structure has . . . a permanent equilibrium if, when the initial field C is modified to C' the substructure of the elements

corresponding to *C* conserves the same equilibrium as before (Piaget in Battro, 1973, pp. 49, 56–58).

In addition, Piaget modified his basic conception of equilibrium by attaching to it such adjectives as *momentary, semipermanent, permanent,* and *operational.* However, these adjectives seem to have been of limited help to his reading audience.

P. H. Miller (1983, pp. 75–76) has attempted to clarify Piaget's usage by proposing that Piaget differentiated the use of equilibrium according to at least three spans of time: (1) the moment-to-moment encounters a child has with the environment as the child attempts to master the encounters by assimilating, accommodating, and finally achieving the state of satisfactory resolution called equilibrium; (2) the final step in a child's moving gradually out of one stage and establishing himself securely in the next higher stage; and (3) the process of achieving ever better adaptation and organization over the entire series of growth periods, birth through adolescence.

Finally, there are frequent passages in which equilibration seems to mean the unexplainable coordinating power that makes all parts of the developmental system work together in harmony.

EDUCATIONAL APPLICATIONS OF THE THEORY

During the past three decades Piaget's writings have exerted a growing influence on the conduct of education in many parts of the world. Piaget himself pointed out the educational implications of his model. To illustrate some of these implications, we will inspect the Piagetian model's application to questions of: (1) the choice of learning objectives, (2) curriculum sequencing, (3) grade placement of topics, (4) the assessment of children's intellectual functioning, and (5) teaching methodology.

The Choice of Learning Objectives

As educators have selected learning goals for pupils to pursue, they usually have based their choices on tradition or on analyses of what children need to learn in order to succeed in the culture in which they are growing up.

The word *tradition* in this context refers to the curriculum of the past. That is, members of the adult generation recall what they were taught in school and assume that this same pattern of facts, concepts, skills, and values will be equally proper for the coming generation of children. This might be called the conservative approach to selecting objectives since it emphasizes the conservation or retention of traditional goals.

The phrase *analyses of what children need to learn in order to succeed* identifies the practice of educators who inspect present-day society and predict changes that will likely occur in that society over the coming decades. On the basis of such analyses, they estimate the knowledge, skills, and values that will best equip the growing child or youth to become a happy, constructive member of that society. This could be called the *personal-social adjustment* approach to establishing objectives, for it emphasizes the achievement of objectives that enable the individual to fulfill personal needs within a culture that is continually evolving. A curriculum produced by such a process of analysis can be expected to retain some of the goals of the past, but it also will offer new objectives that result from changes in the society.

There is also a third tack, which derives from Piagetian theory and might be called the *cognitive development* approach. To understand the main focus of this approach, we need to consider once again (1) the distinction Piaget made between *spontaneous* or *psychological* development and *psychosocial* development and (2) his ideas about the interaction of nature and nurture.

As explained earlier, several factors determine when a child will develop through the levels of sensorimotor reactions, of concrete operations, and of formal operations. The first factor is the internal maturation of the neural system. The time at which the maturational steps needed for a given level of cognitive functioning occur is established by nature, by the child's genetic time schedule. But the developmental potential that this maturation provides cannot be realized unless the child obtains suitable direct experiences in life, experiences that bring the potential to fruition. Piaget called these unguided experiences (the second factor) *psychological* or *spontaneous* development. The third factor is that of more formal instruction, the sort that goes on in school. It needs to be preceded by the first two, maturation and psychological development, if it is to be successful. Piaget called this third factor *psychosocial* development.

This Piagetian view of intellectual growth is the foundation for the cognitive development approach to selecting instructional goals. From such a perspective, the central goal of the school is not to teach particular facts and concepts, nor is it to teach solutions to personal and social adjustment problems. Instead, the purpose of schooling is to promote the optimal development of thinking skills appropriate to each level of growth. As a result of such schooling, by the time the child reaches adolescence she should be able to efficiently apply formal operational thinking in understanding life and in solving whatever problems she faces. In such a curriculum the child does indeed learn facts and concepts. However, these are not selected for any inherent value they might have but rather for their worth in fostering the development of the particular level of cognitive growth that the child is currently working toward.

Curriculum Sequencing

Piagetian theory not only furnishes a vantage point from which to select objectives, it suggests as well the sequence in which these objectives and their associated learning tasks should appear in the curriculum. For example, in reasoning about scientific and mathematical phenomena, children at the preoperational level can consider only one dimension at a time, such as only the height or only the width of an object. At the concrete operations level they can comprehend the interaction of two dimensions, such as height and width, simultaneously. Not until they reach the formal operations level can they consider the interaction of more than two variables. A similar sequence has been identified in the realm of moral or ethical judgments.

> At the egocentric stage in the logic of feeling, the self becomes the single dimension around which feelings and social interaction revolve. The second, sociocentric stage corresponds to concrete operations, in interacting with peer-group norms as the other dimension. The allocentric stage is multidimensional like formal operations: the individual can construe himself as a dimension in a matrix, including abstract principles and social norms as other dimensions (Biggs, 1976, p. 157).

A further example of a sequence is that of understanding the conservation aspects of physical objects. The child's comprehension moves from that of understanding the conservation of the quantity of substance (the space an object appears to take up) to that of the weight of the substance and then to that of the density of the substance.

These sequences, along with a variety of other more specific ones, can suggest to curriculum developers a psychologically sound order in which to confront children with different learning tasks. In the traditional school curriculum, children are often expected to acquire concepts of mass, weight, volume, space, time, causality, geometry, speed, and movement in a sequence that is at odds with the child's natural pattern of comprehending such concepts (Elkind, 1976, p. 196). A curriculum plan founded on Piagetian theory and empirical studies would seek to correct such incoordination between development and school learning activities.

Grade Placement of Topics

Piaget's results also suggest at what general age level each step in a given sequence is likely to occur. For instance, understanding of conservation of substance seems to come around age 7 for most children, of weight around age 9, and of volume around age 11 or 12 (J. L. Phillips, 1975, p. 100).

These age points are similar, but not identical, from one child to another and from one ethnic or socioeconomic group to another. Differences among children in the age at which they achieve a particular new level are apparently due to differences in those primary causal factors that Piaget said underlie development: the genetic time schedule for internal maturation, self-directed experience with the world, and instruction or training. Some children are genetically equipped to advance earlier than others. Some have better opportunities to engage in profitable direct experiences and to receive more useful instruction. What these differences in influence mean for curriculum developers is that some flexibility is needed in the grade placement of learning goals founded on Piagetian theory. Not every child will be ready at the same time to accomplish the next step in a cognitive development sequence. However, the general placement of a given objective in the school's grade hierarchy can be estimated. Curriculum developers know whether a particular cognitive skill is more suitable for the preschool years than the primary grades (1 through 3) or for the upper elementary grades (4 through 6). They also know whether a particular understanding is more likely achieved in the junior high (grades 7 through 9) than the senior high years (10 through 12).

As already noted, Piaget, besides outlining the stages of development described earlier for general cognitive development, also identified within the general structure a variety of separate sequences, such as one for the understanding of number, another for causality, a third for conservation of physical aspects, a fourth for moral reasoning, and so on. Although the pattern of one such sequence is much like the pattern of another, the timing of steps within different sequences does not always coincide. In other words, there is some unevenness in progress between sequences.

This lack of coordination between sequences can be illustrated by noting that the logic children use to explain their moral or ethical judgments usually lags a couple of years behind the level of logic they use to explain physical phenomena. It is not yet known whether this lag is due entirely to the greater amount of experience and instruction children have with physical events as compared to moral issues or whether some maturational factor also contributes its influence. Piaget's most frequent collaborator, Barbel Inhelder, believed:

> The general succession of stages seems to be confirmed by all authors, but the relationship between different tasks and substructures, apparently requiring the same mental structure, is still far from adequately explored; what is more, the experimental findings on this point are difficult to interpret (1968, p. vii).

However, the implications of such a finding for curriculum developers seem clear. It is not sufficient to use only Piaget's *general* developmental stages as guides to the placement of learning activities in the school's grade structure. Rather, it is important to assign activities according to the various types of sequences that are involved. For example, activities to promote a given level of moral judgment should be assigned a grade or two later in the school program than activities to promote a similar level of mathematics and science knowledge.

It is possible, though, to use the same general topic or problem situation at both a lower and an upper grade level. For instance, E. A. Peel, a British educational psychologist (1976, p. 181), recommended that a spiral plan for teaching both physical science and social science can be adopted for adolescents. In such a program, students in an upper secondary grade can return to topics they studied three or four years earlier. The virture of this approach from a Piagetian viewpoint is that the pupils are thereby not simply reviewing or repeating their earlier experience since during the intervening years the *quality* of the students' intelligence has changed. Whereas a child at the beginning of the secondary school could offer only partial and single explanations of a phenomenon, the youth in high school is able to apply "a greater conceptual repertoire and more mature form of intellectual enquiry" (Peel, 1976, p. 181) to the same phenomenon. In effect, the second time the youth studies the topic she or he does so by means of a new, more complex cognitive lens—in other words, a more complex schema.

The Assessment of Intellectual Functioning

Piagetians are critical of the use of traditional intelligence tests for estimating children's cognitive development and readiness for another step in a learning sequence. Their chief complaint is that the typical intelligence test determines whether the child can give a correct answer to questions; it does not reveal the child's thinking processes. Thus the test fails to indicate a pupil's current level of cognitive development. As a result, Piagetians prefer to base their judgments of children's cognitive styles on: (1) how children solve the problems posed in the tasks Piaget used in his research studies and (2) teachers' observations of the level of children's reasoning during the regular activities of the classroom (Elkind, 1976, pp. 171–194).

Dissatisfaction with standard intelligence tests has stimulated a pair of researchers at the University of Montreal, Monique Laurendeau and Adrien Pinard, to devise a new scale of mental development, a test that represents "an attempt to combine the advantages of Piaget's method (thoroughness and flexibility of questioning) with those of traditional psychometric methods (standardization of questioning)" (J. L. Phillips, 1975,

p. 162). Unlike such tests as the Stanford-Binet or Wechsler Intelligence Scale for Children, the Montreal scale does not involve each child's being asked to answer exactly the same questions. Instead, the way a child responds to one question influences the nature of the succeeding questions the child is asked. Furthermore, the tester is not only interested in the number of right answers the child gives, but is equally interested in "wrong" answers since they too are valuable in revealing the child's mode of thinking. In sum, the Montreal project represents an extension of Piagetian theory into the realm of formal intelligence testing.

Teaching Methodology

A common way to conceive of teaching methodology within a Piagetian-based curriculum is to define the two most basic responsibilities of the teacher as those of:

1. Diagnosing the current stage of a child's development in the various growth sequences the curriculum is designed to promote, and

2. Offering learning activities that challenge the child to advance to the next higher step of the particular type of sensorimotor cognitive development that the sequence involves.

In other words, the teacher is not viewed as being a fount of knowledge from which the pupils are expected to fill their minds. Nor is the teacher's job simply that of a pleasant clerk who displays equipment and materials in the classroom and then stands back while children explore the objects on their own. Instead, the teacher is expected to achieve a proper balance between actively guiding or directing children's thinking patterns and providing opportunities for children to explore by themselves.

Not all educators have come up with exactly the same picture of teacher behavior for achieving this balance between active guidance and passive permission. H. G. Furth and W. Wachs, who describe their experimental Piagetian-type school in their book *Thinking Goes to School* (1975), recommend that the teacher offer a sequence of activities that will enable pupils to achieve their next developmental steps efficiently. The activities give a structure or direction to pupils' work, but each child is free to pursue each activity in his own manner or is free not to participate in the activity at all if he so chooses.

> The teacher in our school knows that he can do no more than provide the occasion and leave the child free to use it well. He can coach and facilitate and encourage; but in the final analysis it is the child himself who initiates intellectual growth (Furth & Wachs, 1975, p. 46).

A somewhat different version of the teacher's role within a Piagetian-based curriculum is given by D. Elkind (1976), who identified three modes of learning, each featuring a different combination of the assimilation and accommodation processes.

The first mode Elkind called *operative learning*. It is most prominent when the child's intelligence "is actively engaged by the materials she is interacting with" (Elkind, 1976, p. 113). Working with the materials, the child may face contradictions in the way she supposes they will respond, and the contradictions will force her to abstract new understandings from her actions on the materials.

> Operative learning, in addition to facilitating the development of mental operations, also gives rise to *practical intelligence*. Practical intelligence consists of the operations and knowledge the child requires to get about in the everyday world. Much of it . . . is unconscious (Elkind, 1976, p. 114).

The second mode Elkind called *figurative learning*. It involves the child acquiring "aspects of reality" that cannot be reconstructed or rediscovered by the child on his own but "must be largely copied" (Elkind, 1976, p. 114). Perhaps the prime example of this mode is the learning of language—the vocabulary, syntax, pronunciation, and gesture that make the speech of one culture different from that of another. For such aspects of reality, the teacher adopts a more active instructional role, more "teaching" in its traditional sense.

The third mode is *connotative learning*. It is the "conscious conceptualization of one's own mental processes, what has been called *reflective intelligence*." It is most prominent during the years of adolescence (Elkind, 1976, pp. 115–116). "Connotative learning is expressly concerned with the construction of meanings, with establishing connections between concepts and figurative symbols. It is no less than the child's efforts to make sense out of her world" (Elkind, 1976, p. 116).

In promoting operative learning, the teacher may bring objects—a bird, a telescope, a toy boat—to the classroom and may pose questions that stimulate pupils to discover aspects of the item. However, to a great extent the pupils are left on their own to explore the objects. For the figurative mode, the teacher furnishes models and gives demonstrations and explanations, such as showing how to carry out arithmetic computation efficiently or how to use phonics to discover the pronunciation of new words met in a reading passage. With connotative learning, the teacher still encourages pupils to make discoveries and use the communication skills they have acquired, but the "teacher's most important role in connotative learning is to help children do work of the quality that they are really capable of doing" (Elkind, 1976, p. 231). In other words, the teacher stimulates them to produce to the best of their ability.

Whether teachers adopt a Furth and Wachs version or an Elkind version of a Piagetian-based instructional style, they need to carry out their teaching in a setting that is conducive to a substantial amount of small-group and individual activities. Tables, desks, and chairs need to be movable. Different interest centers around the classroom need to be available for use by pupils who are at a given developmental level and can most profitably pursue activities and use materials suited to promoting progress to the next level.

In summary, Piaget's theory and his empirical research findings suggest guidelines about how children's sensorimotor-cognitive development can best be nurtured.

PIAGET'S THEORY: AN ASSESSMENT

By the 1990s, the status of Piaget's model had reached a phase that occurs in the life of nearly every influential model in developmental psychology. A typical theory's life span begins when the scheme is newly formulated, then announced publicly in a journal or book. Initially this innovative proposal has a difficult time gaining widespread acceptance since most developmentalists already subscribe to some existing model. However, as the new theory's proponents extol its virtues to a growing audience, and as empirical investigations and applications of the proposal multiply, the throng of believers increases. Subsequently, when the theory reaches the apex of its prominence, it is placed under critical surveillance by professionals in the field who test its hypotheses and scrutinize its logic. Any weaknesses found in the clarity of the theory's definitions or in its ability to explain and predict can undermine people's faith in its worth. A subsequent decline in the theory's status is accompanied by the appearance of other scholars' ways of explaining growth and behavior. Such has been the fate of Piagetian theory as its popularity among developmentalists has waned in recent years. C. J. Brainerd (1983, p. vi) states that the early 1980s witnessed:

> a rapid decline in the influence of orthodox Piagetian theory, a fact that is now acknowledged by Piagetians and non-Piagetians alike. Until the mid-1970s, Piaget's ideas dominated the landscape the way Freudian thinking once ruled abnormal psychology. Since then, however, the picture has changed dramatically. Empirical and conceptual objections to the theory have become so numerous that it can no longer be regarded as a positive force in mainstream cognitive developmental

research, though its influence remains profound in cognate fields such as education and sociology.

Other observers, while admitting to shortcomings of Piaget's formulations, have been more positive than Brainerd in recognizing the Swiss theorist's contributions. R. Case (1985, p. 24) has concluded that:

> Piaget played the same role for intellectual development as Darwin had played for the development of the species. He gathered a vast fund of empirical data on the intellectual behavior of the human organism over time. He developed and integrated a number of previously existing notions within a framework that not only explained the existing data, but led to the discovery of a wide variety of new data. Finally, he provided a view of mankind the significance of which transcended the particular discipline and data from which it was derived, and which was of great social significance.

Some of the reasons for the recent decline in the popularity of Piagetian theory are described in the following paragraphs in which the nine standards of judgment from Chapter One provide the framework for evaluating Piaget's contributions.

In regard of the theory's fertility (item 8—stimulates new discoveries), Piaget's work deserves a top rating. As E. R. Hilgard and G. H. Bower (1975, p. 327) have remarked: "One of the great problems that have beset psychology as a science is that there are so few discoveries of genuinely new phenomena. . . . Consequently, it is worth noting that the facts of conservation, as pointed out by Piaget and his associates, represent one of the genuine 'discoveries' within his experimental observations."

Not only did Piaget conduct pioneering studies in multiple facets of cognitive development, but his work stimulated thousands of other investigators to expand and refine his notions. For the years 1983–1990, *Psychological Abstracts* listed 721 journal articles that concerned Piaget's work, with 104 of them focusing particularly on the structure and use of the theory itself. Rather frequently, follow-up studies have cast doubt on certain of Piaget's conclusions, thereby inspiring critics to offer alternatives to the traditional Piagetian model. Thus, in recent decades, a substantial body of neo-Piagetian or post-Piagetian literature has evolved (Bruner, 1964; Case, 1985; Dason, 1977; Pascual-Leone, 1976; Scholnick, 1983; Valsiner, 1987; Zimmerman, 1983). As an example, Klaus Riegel (1973, pp. 346–370), who styled his own theory of development as *dialectical*, criticized Piaget for ending the stages of intellectual growth with the formal operations period of adolescence. Riegel accepted the Piagetian stages as being reasonable as far as they went, but he proposed a dialectical scheme of his own whereby one set of psychological forces struggled against other sets to produce development beyond the middle teen years. In short, no other developmental psychologist has ever inspired as much discussion and empirical research as Piaget has.

Piaget's model has also been judged internally consistent and parsimonious (standards 5 and 6). Case (1985, pp. 23–24) maintains that the model's basic elements represent "a sophisticated, coherent, and tightly interrelated system. . . . Given the great diversity of phenomena for which it accounted, it utilized remarkably few constructs and postulates."

As for reflecting the real world of children (item 1), the theory gains strength from the host of empirical studies on which the author based his speculation. Nevertheless, in several respects it falls short of accurately reflecting reality. The first shortcoming concerns individual differences

Piaget's Theory

How well do I think the theory meets the standards?

The Standards	Very Well	Moderately Well	Very Poorly
1. Reflects the real world of children		X	
2. Is clearly understandable		X	
3. Explains the past and predicts the future		X	
4. Guides child rearing		X	
5. Is internally consistent	X		
6. Is economical	X		
7. Is falsifiable		X	
8. Stimulates new discoveries	X		
9. Is self-satisfying		X	

among children. Piaget's great emphasis was on what the average child does. It is true that Piaget did recognize some diversity in rate of development, and he suggested that the social milieu within which a child is reared will affect this rate. But he did not offer any careful analysis of how different factors or agents in the social setting influence the attainment of the wide variety of differences in cognitive functions that children exhibit. As B. J. Zimmerman (1983, p. 4) has noted, "Piaget gave little attention to the effect of the social dimensions of the environment—the individual and collective behavior of other people—on children's reasoning. The concepts that he studied were generally nonsocial in nature (e.g., space, number, time, conservation, and mathematics) and thus were less likely to be contextually dynamic."

In judging how readily Piaget's work can be understood (item 2), I have marked the theory just slightly above the middle. A variety of notions proposed by Piaget seem rather easy to comprehend, at least on the surface. That seems to be the case for the concepts of assimilation, accommodation, and conservation; for the general nature of levels through which children develop; and for the proposal that the sequence of levels is the same for all children. However, this clarity can dissipate when readers seek precise meanings for *cognitive structure,* for how equilibration functions, and for the apparent inconsistency between the concepts of *stage,* and *horizontal décalage.* Brainerd (1983, p. ix) complains that:

> conflicting interpretations abound and, more important, we do not know how to set about measuring the relevant variables. For some years, it was fashionable to suppose that Piagetian constructs, like the ideas of quantum physicists, were merely difficult for the average mind to comprehend and that careful study of the theory would dispel the conceptual fog. As this has not happened, a more plausible hypothesis is that the theory is intrinsically opaque.

Although I find much of Piaget easy enough to understand, I must agree with Brainerd's concern, since I have difficulty comprehending certain key aspects of Piagetian thought. For instance, I find an unsatisfying circularity in some of Piaget's explanations, as when he suggested in publication *A* that equilibrium explains reversibility ("The equilibrium finally reached between assimilation and accommodation explains then the reversibility of the operational grouping.") and in publication *B* that reversibility explains equilibrium ("Equilibrium will thus be defined by reversibility.") (Piaget in Battro, 1973, pp. 56–57).

As for the scheme's value in explaining the past and predicting the future (item 3), it does rather well both (1) for the sorts of cognitive behavior on which the model focuses and (2) for the average child. Piaget claimed that the sequence of the changes plotted in his stages of mental growth is invariant from one child or one society to another. Empirical investigations conducted in many nations support this claim (Dason, 1977; Piaget, 1973, p. 7; Sigel & Hooper, 1968). He further noted that the rate of passage through stages may vary by as much as two years between the average children of one culture and those of another (Piaget, 1973, pp. 25–27). So he predicted accurately the types and sequence of cognitive behaviors children can be expected to exhibit, but he did not furnish adequate explanations of deviations from the average.

In terms of guidance for child rearing (item 4), the theory has proven of great interest to educators, who have been making increasing use of Piaget's description of developmental stages to determine the sequence and grade placement of cognitive skills to be learned, particularly skills in mathematics and the physical sciences. Educators are also using Piagetian tests—the problems from his clinical method—both for assessing children's developmental status and for providing them with opportunities to try the thought processes represented in the developmental stages of the theory (Furth & Wachs, 1975; Tronick & Greenfield, 1973; Piaget, 1970b). In addition, a sequence of annual conferences for members of the helping professions resulted in a series of publications describing applications of Piagetian theory to pediatrics and social work (Magary, Poulsen, Levinson, & Taylor, 1977; Poulsen & Luben, 1979). Thus the Piagetian model offers a good deal of guidance for child rearing in cognitive areas.

The model does not, however, furnish guidance for treating a variety of other problems that confront parents, teachers, pediatricians, and social workers. The problems I refer to are ones reflected in such phrases as *poor self-concept, lack of friends, easily frustrated, too heavily influenced by undesirable peers,* and *lacks significant goals or purpose in life.* For coping with such matters, Piaget is of little help. But, as he frequently pointed out, his area of concern was genetic epistemology; and the above problems are not central to that concern. In assessing the theory on item 4, I balanced the foregoing positive points against the negative and rated the scheme between "very" and "moderately well."

Next, how falsifiable is the theory (item 7)? Many aspects of Piaget's model are in forms that make determining their validity very testable. Such is true of the developmental stages, both their sequence and their age placement. However, several of the concepts at the core of the theory are not, I believe, susceptible to confirmation or disconfirmation. Included are the concepts of schemes, assimilation, and accommodation. I see no way of testing their validity. Hence I balanced the many falsifiable aspects of the Piagetian model against the apparently few that must be accepted on faith and marked item 7 somewhat above the center.

Finally, I find the theory to be overall quite satisfying (item 9). Despite the reservations mentioned above, I am convinced that the greater part of Piaget's writings is valuable and accurate. After studying his works, I feel that I understand the development of children's thinking processes far better than before. And as a consequence, I believe I can work more effectively with children and youths. I feel the theory rates a high mark.

FOR FURTHER READING

Piaget, J., and B. Inhelder. (1969) *The Psychology of the Child.* New York: Basic Books. Although any of the books listed under Piaget's name in the bibliography at the end of this volume offers useful insights into his many-sided theorizing, this volume by Piaget and his long-time colleague, Inhelder, is particularly helpful in reviewing not only the principal aspects of basic cognitive development but also the associated social and affective interactions, including moral feelings and judgments.

Battro, A. M. (1973) *Piaget: Dictionary of Terms.* New York: Pergamon Press. People who have had difficulty with the meaning Piaget intended for the specialized terms he used will find this book useful. Battro lists Piagetian terms alphabetically and then under each he gives one or more definitions in the form of quotes from Piaget's writings.

Campbell, S. F. (1976) *Piaget Sampler.* New York: Wiley. An autobiography by Piaget (covering the years 1896–1966) appears as Chapter 10 in this potpourri of articles by the theorist.

Many books published in recent years have been designed to offer a condensed version of Piagetian theory, ones more readily understandable than Piaget's original writings. The following two small volumes, one by Phillips and the other by Sigel and Cocking, are among the more readable and up-to-date books of this type.

Phillips, J. L., Jr. (1975) *The Origins of Intellect: Piaget's Theory,* 2d ed. San Francisco: Freeman.

Sigel, I. E., and R. R. Cocking. (1977) *Cognitive Development from Childhood to Adolescence: A Constructivist Perspective.* New York: Holt, Rinehart & Winston.

CHAPTER ELEVEN

Vygotsky and the Soviet Tradition

During the years following the Russian revolution near the close of World War I, psychologists under the new Soviet Union government struggled with the problem of devising a theory of human development compatible with the Marxist political tenets on which the new state was founded. By the mid-1920s the most successful solution to this problem was that created by Lev Semenovich Vygotsky (1896–1934), a teacher of literature whose first research as a young scholar between 1915 and 1922 focused on artistic creation (Vygotsky, 1971). In 1924 Vygotsky began serious work in the areas of developmental psychology, education, and psychopathology, pursuing these interests at a highly productive pace until he died of tuberculosis in 1934 at the age of 38.

Although his career as a psychologist was brief, Vygotsky earned high regard in the Soviet Union for establishing an acceptable sociopolitical foundation for much psychological investigation. He did this by casting in suitable research form "the Marxist-Leninist thesis that all fundamental human cognitive activities take shape in a matrix of social history and form the products of sociohistorical development" (Luria, 1976, p. v).

In other words, according to this doctrine, the intellectual skills or patterns of thinking that a person displays are not primarily determined by innate factors, that is, inherited intelligence or mental abilities. Instead, patterns and levels of thinking are products of the activities practiced in the social institutions of the culture in which the individual grows up. In keeping with this thesis,

It follows that practical thinking will predominate in societies that are characterized by practical manipulations of objects and more "abstract" forms of "theoretical" activity in technological societies will induce more abstract, theoretical thinking. The parallel between individual and social development produces a strong proclivity to interpret all behavioral differences in developmental terms (Luria, 1976, p. xiv).

From this viewpoint, the history of the society in which a child is reared, and the child's own developmental history in terms of her experiences in that society, are both extremely important in fashioning the ways the child will be able to think. Furthermore, advanced modes of thought—conceptual thinking—must be transmitted to the child by means of words, so language becomes a crucial tool for deciding how children learn to think.

It was in an atmosphere of these assumptions that Vygotsky wrote *Thought and Language* shortly before his death. In 1936, two years after its publication, the volume was suppressed in the Soviet Union because of disputes within the nation's psychological community. But when the disputes ended, the book was distributed once again. However, it wasn't translated into English until 1962, so it is only since then that Vygotsky's theory has become widely understood and discussed in English-speaking countries. During the 1970s further works by Vygotsky and his followers were translated into English, providing ample evidence of his talent as a theoretician and practitioner who was skilled in applying research findings to the improvement of child rearing and schooling (Cole, 1977; Luria, 1976; Valsiner, 1988b; Vygotsky, 1978).

This chapter is divided into six sections: (1) a description of key influences on Vygotsky's theory, including the linkage between Marxist social philosophy and Vygotsky's view of child development, (2) an example of Vygotsky's applying his theory to explain the growth of thought and language, (3) a series of generalizations he proposed about child development, (4) a brief review of principal trends in Soviet developmental psychology from the 1920s into the 1980s, (5) practical applications of Vygotsky's model, and (6) an assessment of the theory.

The chapter focuses on Vygotsky's theorizing, not simply because he was the chief architect of Soviet developmental psychology in the early years of the Communist regime, but because his proposals contribute to discussions in contemporary psychology. The late Alexander R. Luria (1902–1977), a world-renowned Soviet developmentalist, before his death wrote that:

> Vygotsky was a genius. After more than half a century in science I am unable to name another person who even approaches his incredible analytic ability and foresight. All of my work has been no more than the working out of the psychological theory which he constructed (Vygotsky, 1978, dust jacket).

KEY INFLUENCES ON VYGOTSKY'S THEORY

Three characteristics that marked Vygotsky's work were: (1) a sincere dedication to Marxist social philosophy and a conviction that psychological development was intimately linked to the tenets of that philosophy, (2) a thorough acquaintance with the work of leading European and American psychologists of his day and of earlier decades, and (3) great ingenuity in devising methods for studying children and for interpreting the data his methods produced.

Marxism and Vygotsky's Theory

When two German political philosophers, Karl Marx (1818–1882) and Friedrich Engels (1820–1895), in 1847 published their vision of societies evolving toward utopian communism, they founded their proposal on three core assumptions: (1) activity generates thinking, (2) development advances by dialectical exchanges, and (3) development is a historical process within cultural contexts.

1. Marx postulated that people's acting within particular social environments accounts for both (1) the differences in privilege and role among subgroups in society and (2) the particular contents of individuals' minds and modes of thinking. He proposed that people's consciousness (attitudes, conception of reality, psychophysical skills) is constructed from the production and distribution activities in which they engage. Marx stated that:

    > In the social production of their life, men enter into definite relations that are indispensable and independent of their will, relations of production which correspond to a definite stage of development of their material productive forces. . . . The mode of production of material life conditions the social, political, and intellectual life process in general. It is not the consciousness of men that determines their existence, but, on the contrary, their social existence that determines their consciousness (Marx, 1859, p. 389).

    Vygotsky concurred with this conviction, so his theory of development pictures children engaging in activities and, from this engagement, constructing the contents of their minds. Thus thinking does not initially create action; instead, action creates thought. Mental development is the process of children internalizing the results of their transactions with their environment.

2. Marx contended that societies develop through a process of resolving dialectic confrontations. As noted in Chapter Nine, Hegel's

dialectical formula for logical thought consisted of an assertion (thesis), its opposite (antithesis), and the resolution of the thesis-antithesis conflict by means of a revised conclusion (synthesis). Marx adopted the dialectical concept to account for the development of societies. As a social system for producing and distributing materials (such as a feudalistic agricultural society with its landlords and serfs) became well established (thesis), advances in technology (industrial revolution) precipitated conflicts within that system (antithesis). The conflicts could only be resolved by that social structure's transformation into a new one (capitalism). Once capitalism became established, further conflicts arose to render it unsuitable, with the proper resolution in Marx's view being a transformation of the sociopolitical-economic system into one of communal ownership of the production and distribution of goods. Among the several dialectical confrontations that would be involved in such societal development, the one that Marx featured in his theory of dialectical materialism was the struggle between social classes.

Vygotsky applied the dialectical formula to child development by proposing that as children go about the activities of their lives, their established ways of doing things (thesis) don't always work because these ways fail to accommodate to the conditions of the current situation (antithesis). Hence children must devise new problem-solving methods that satisfy those conditions (synthesis). Child development, therefore, consists of an endless stream of dialectical conflicts and resolutions, with the resolutions then internalized to form the child's increasingly sophisticated physical and psychological knowledge. This knowledge then becomes the set of theses (understandings, skills, expectations) with which the child approaches the next of life's activities.

3. Marx conceived of societal development as a process of evolution. Because of technological advances, societies developed from a feudal to a capitalistic and ultimately to a socialistic form of material production and consumption. As he contended in *The Communist Manifesto*, "All property relations in the past have continually been subject to historical change consequent upon the change in historical conditions" (Marx, 1847, p. 231). Thus a society's history is a chronology of purposeful change (development). The phrase "history in the making" refers to the dialectical exchanges occurring at any particular time. By analyzing such change processes, we come to understand how the society devel-

ops. The culture (way of life) of a given society at any point in time is not only a product of the society's past history but is also the contextual foundation for future development.

Vygotsky adopted such a cultural-historical viewpoint when he formulated his child development model. Understanding how and why children develop as they do requires that we understand the nature of the culture's historical background because the environments that children inhabit confront children with opportunities and demands unique to that culture. Furthermore, the history of the child's own ontogenetic development (the succession of the child's past dialectic confrontations) determines how the child is prepared to resolve upcoming problem situations.

In summary, Vygotsky's theory of human development represented a synthesis of assumptions that fit nicely into the Marxist theory on which Soviet society was constructed.

Vygotsky and the International Psychological Community

A factor of particular importance to the progress of Vygotsky's work was his intimate knowledge of current and past psychological events in Western Europe and North America.

> In contrast to Vygotsky's outright rejection of American and Russian behaviouristic thinking, his positive contribution to psychology was clearly rooted in the continental-European psychology of his time. German Gestalt psychology . . . had a strong influence. . . . Kurt Lewin's field theory surfaces in appropriate places in Vygotsky's writings. . . . He develops further on Binet's work on memory [and] criticizes and follows Piaget. . . . [He] was likewise open to the important ideas that Freud and other psychoanalytic thinkers had explicated (Valsiner, 1988b, p. 121).

To understand something of the climate for psychology in Vygotsky's time, we need to recall two antithetical views of human thought that were prominent in the early twentieth century.

The first was a traditional view of the mind that grew out of the faculty psychology of past centuries. Psychologists in the late nineteenth and early twentieth centuries studied mind and its functions by means of introspection. A person carefully looked into his or her own mind to analyze the working of perception, thought, memory, feelings, and the like.

The second movement was in direct opposition to the first. It represented an effort to be scientific and objective about the study of humans, just as physics, chemistry, and biology were objective sciences. As described in Chapter Eight, the movement in America was known as behaviorism, for its leaders proposed that the proper study of humans involved observable behavior as measured and recorded by scientists rather than by the people being observed. In effect, the staunchest behaviorists of Vygotsky's day had eliminated mind and its functions in favor of analyzing only observable acts.

Vygotsky saw shortcomings in both of these schools of theory. He did not trust introspection as a secure methodological base on which to found scientific psychological theory. And as for behaviorists' rejecting mind, he wrote:

> In that psychology ignores the problem of consciousness, it blocks itself off from access to the investigation of complicated problems of human behavior, and the elimination of consciousness from the sphere of scientific psychology has as its major consequence the retention of all the dualism (mind versus body) and spiritualism of earlier subjective psychology (1962, p. vi).

Vygotsky's Research Techniques

Given Vygotsky's basic assumptions (activity generates thought, and development results from dialectical exchanges in historical-cultural contexts), he now needed suitable methods for conducting empirical research. But he recognized that the standard investigative methods of stimulus-response psychologists were poorly suited to studying children's in-process mental development. He could not expect to discover children's ongoing thought processes simply by presenting the children with a stimulus (a test question) and then noting how closely their responses matched the correct answer. Such a method would show only whether the child gave the desired response. Instead, what Vygotsky wanted to know was the pattern of events operating in children's actions and thoughts as they grappled with a task and, in the midst of grappling, effected a change in their own mental development. So the child's procedure in constructing an answer was what interested Vygotsky, not whether the answer was right. During his search for suitable investigative techniques, he spoke admiringly of Piaget's *clinical method,* which he felt was far closer to the mark than traditional S-R methods. But for his own empirical studies he placed children in problem-solving situations of his own creation (Valsiner, 1988b, pp. 128–140).

The *double-stimulation method* that Vygotsky devised drew on ideas from P. Janet's psychiatric practice in France and W. Köhler's Gestalt experiments with apes in Germany. The method involves placing a child in a problem-solving setting that contains a collection of objects that form a complex pattern of stimuli. Some of the objects have been purposely selected by the experimenter, while others are incidental parts of the experimental situation. The child has a goal to achieve. The goal is either overtly defined by the researcher or simply inferred by the child from the nature of the context. The child's task is to figure out how to attain the goal by means of the objects in the setting. The term *double stimulation* refers to two sorts of stimuli to which the child can attend in performing the task—stimulus objects and stimulus means. The child is expected to inspect (be stimulated by) the objects at hand and thereby conceive of ways (stimulus means) the objects might be used to achieve the goal. The experimenter's aim is to discover how the child acts and thinks during this event. To achieve such understanding, the researcher tracks the course of the child's actions and listens to the child's remarks that accompany the actions. From the sequence of actions and the child's commentary, the experimenter draws inferences about what sort of intellectual development has occurred during the problem-solving incident. The following segment of a double-stimulation experiment is one I devised to illustrate a research setting and a set of child behaviors that could typify such an investigative approach (Valsiner, 1988b, pp. 134–140).

The same situation was posed on separate occasions to six-year-old Justin and to his eight-year-old cousin, Courtney. The task was a simulated problem introduced to Justin in the following manner:

Investigator: The mother of a six-year-old boy told him, "We're going on a trip this weekend, and we can't leave the cat home alone. So we have to take him over to Aunt Martha's in the cat box. The cat's now in the kitchen. Would you please go there and put him in the box. But be careful. If he thinks we're going to take him to Aunt Martha's, he'll try to get away." Now, Justin, here's a picture of the kitchen. Look at the things in the room and tell me what you think the boy should do to get the cat into the box. (See Figure 11.1.)

Justin: (Studies the picture for a moment, then points to the dish on the rug.) I'd put this milk in the box, and the cat would go in the box to drink the milk.

Investigator: All right. But what if the cat tried to run away while you were doing that? Is there anything you could do when you first come into the room?

Justin: I'd close the window and door. And then I'd put the milk in the box.

Investigator: That sounds good. But suppose there wasn't any milk in the dish. What could you do then?

Justin: I'd put cat food in the dish, and the cat would smell it and go in to eat.

Investigator: Where would you get the cat food?

Justin: (Points to the right-hand cupboard.) I'd get it out of there.

Investigator: Look around the kitchen and see if there's anyplace else to get cat food.

Justin: (Studies the picture, points to the box labeled Cat Food and slowly reads aloud.) Cat food. (He smiles and nods.) In there. That's cat food.

Justin's cousin, Courtney, is later faced with the same task, but the main character in her anecdote is an eight-year-old girl. Courtney responds to the assignment in this fashion:

Courtney: I'd grab the cat and put him in the box and close the door.

Investigator: Okay. But when you first enter the kitchen, is there anything you might do to make sure the cat doesn't get away before you grab him?

Courtney: I'd close the window and door.

Investigator: Could you think of any way to get the cat into the box without grabbing him?

Courtney: There's a box of cat food. I'd put some cat food in the cat box, and when the cat goes in to eat, I'd close the door.

We can now speculate about the nature of the two children's thought patterns as they dealt with the problem of getting the cat into the box. At the outset, neither child was at a loss for a solution. That is, both were

Figure 11.1 A Drawing Used in a Double-Stimulation Approach

prompt in suggesting a reasoned means of boxing the cat. And while neither child spontaneously considered the likelihood that the animal might escape from the room before their solution was put into operation, once that possibility was proposed by the investigator, both children immediately suggested closing the window and door. Since both children had cats in their own homes, their own experiences undoubtedly influenced their proposed solutions. For example, when Justin was asked where he would find cat food, he pointed to a kitchen cupboard, which was where the cat food was stored in his own home. The two children's physical size may also have affected their initial solution. Courtney was considerably larger than Justin and thus may have had more success in grabbing cats than had Justin.

We can also speculate about what the two children may have learned during the problem-solving incident. It is worth noting that when Justin was asked where he would find cat food, he pointed to the cupboard rather than to the box of cat food. Only when he was prompted to inspect the picture more closely did he read the "Cat Food" label. This behavior can be viewed against Justin's acquaintance with reading. He was currently in first grade, where he read simple primers quite adequately, though with studied effort. In his experience, reading was apparently something done in story books rather than a tool used for solving everyday problems. Hence he depended on his own past knowledge of cupboards rather than on the labels in the picture to guide his search for cat food. In contrast, third-grader Courtney immediately pointed to the "Cat Food" label when asked how she might entice the animal into the carrying case. She appeared to use reading as an instrument of daily problem solving.

When the children later told their parents about the event, both said they would first close the door and window and then they would put the cat in the carrying case. Justin added that he could get cat food out of a box on the floor. Thus it seems likely that each may have learned something new during the activity.

It is instructive to recognize how Vygotsky's approach to research differs from two other experimental models commonly used in child study. One of these models is the S-R variety. The child is furnished a stimulus, and the child's response is then recorded. All sorts of test situations assume this form, including tests to measure intelligence, academic achievement, physical agility, values, attitudes, and more. Surveys that employ questionnaires or interviews are also of the S-R variety. Although these techniques can reveal what the respondent apparently knows or believes at that moment, they tell nothing about how such knowledge and beliefs develop.

A second common experimental design, in its simplest form, consists of a pretest, a treatment, and a posttest. For example, in the area of arithmetic instruction, if we want to discover whether children become more accurate if they learn to subtract whole numbers by an equal-additions method rather than a decomposition method, we can:

1. *Pretest* a large group of children on their subtraction ability, particularly their skill in subtracting quantities that involve carrying.

2. Divide the large group into two subgroups, so that the pattern of pretest scores of one subgroup match the pattern of the other subgroup, thereby making the groups equal in skill at the outset.

3. *Provide different treatments* by teaching one subgroup by the equal-additions method and the other by the decomposition method.

4. *Posttest* both groups to discover what difference each treatment has made in the children's subtraction skills.

While such an approach may help us decide which method of instruction is—on the average—more effective, it tells us nothing about how different children think while they do subtraction, or how their thinking developed during the treatment sessions, or why they got some problems right and others wrong. In the pretest–treatment–posttest design, the *dependent variable* is the posttest score, for it ostensibly has been determined by what occurred during the treatment. The dependent variable is thus the *consequence* of the child's experience. The magnitude of the posttest score in relation to the pretest score is thus of primary interest to the experimenter. However, such is not the case with either Vygotsky's double-stimulus approach or Piaget's clinical method. For them, the dependent variable or consequence of the experiment is found in the record of the child's series of actions and running commentary. The results of their investigations are qualitative, not quantitative. In the opinion of such developmentalists as Vygotsky and Piaget, inferences about the ongoing development of a child's acts and thoughts during a problem-solving session cannot be cast meaningfully into numbers, then summarized as averages, interpreted by means of analyses of variance, and the like.

It is important to note that Vygotsky's methods were not limited to experiments in which the researcher traced the child's pattern of thinking while that thinking was developing. Like Piaget, Vygotsky and other Soviet psychologists also frequently studied children's current mental skills and beliefs, then estimated what kinds of developmental experiences must have contributed to such beliefs.

In assessing the worth of Vygotsky's efforts, J. Valsiner (1988b, p. 140) has proposed that:

Vygotsky's major contribution to developmental psychology lies in his efforts to provide the discipline with a methodological strategy that would afford the empirical study of developmental phenomena. . . . It involves the empirical analysis of the process of development, either "on-line" (i.e., through analyzing the dynamics of subjects' solving of the experimental problem within the setting and resources given), or "off-line" (as in the case of [after-the-fact] efforts to analyze the developmental process of already existing phenomena using the available information).

THE DEVELOPMENT OF THOUGHT AND LANGUAGE

A more detailed review of one of Vygotsky's principal interests illustrates how he used newly created objective methods for studying cognition and speech, methods that did not depend on the introspection or "spiritualism" that he had ridiculed.

His investigations were designed to determine which of three possibilities best represented the developmental relationship between thought and language. Was thought identical with language, as Watsonian behaviorists claimed when they said thinking is just silent speaking? Or was thought independent of language, complete in itself, as many introspectionists seemed to believe, with language simply serving as the tool for communicating thought to others—just as a camera is an instrument for communicating visual images? Or, as a third possibility, were thought and language separate functions that could commingle and in so doing modify each other?

To arrive at an answer, Vygotsky (1) analyzed a host of studies of thought and language conducted by psychologists and anthropologists from numerous countries and (2) devised his own investigations of thought and speech as found among children, adolescents, and adults in the Soviet Union. He cast his interpretations of these findings as three sets of conclusions about child development. The first set concerned the development of conceptual thought, the second the development of speech, and the third the connection between the first two. The nature of these conclusions is the subject of the rest of this section. However, we will consider the three sets in reverse order, beginning with Vygotsky's general views on the relationship between the development of thought and the development of language (*language* in this case meaning *speech*).

In general, Vygotsky concluded that the child's thought and speech begin as separate functions with no necessary connection between them. They are like two circles that do not touch. One circle represents nonverbal thought, the other nonconceptual speech. As the child begins to grow up, the circles meet and overlap (Figure 11.2). The juncture of the two represents *verbal thought,* meaning that the child has now begun to acquire concepts that bear word labels. A *concept* here means an abstraction, an idea that does not represent a particular object but rather some common characteristic shared by—or some relationship among—diverse objects.

The two circles never completely overlap. Even though the common portion becomes more prominent as the child develops (particularly in a highly literate cultural setting), there always remains some nonverbal thought and some nonconceptual speech. An example of nonverbal thought in the adult is her skillful use of tools. An example of nonconcep-

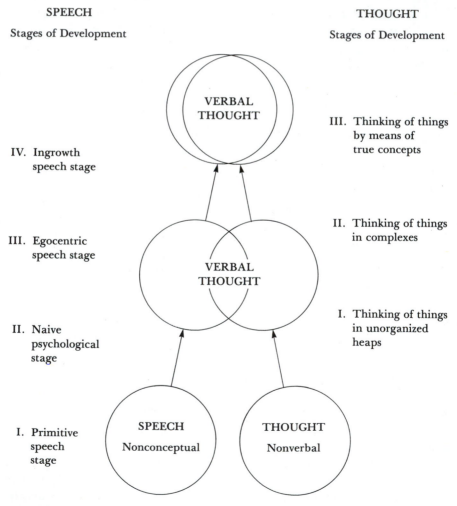

SPEECH

Stages of Development

IV. Ingrowth speech stage

III. Egocentric speech stage

II. Naive psychological stage

I. Primitive speech stage

THOUGHT

Stages of Development

III. Thinking of things by means of true concepts

II. Thinking of things in complexes

I. Thinking of things in unorganized heaps

VERBAL THOUGHT

VERBAL THOUGHT

SPEECH
Nonconceptual

THOUGHT
Nonverbal

Figure 11.2   Vygotsky's View of Speech and Thought Development tual speech is her singing an old song or reciting a poem or repeating a memorized telephone number. These repetitions by rote are "mental activity" but are not of the conceptual variety that Vygotsky identifies as verbal thought.

Figure 11.2 shows Vigorsky's general idea of the thought—language relationship during a child's development, but the actual coordination between the two circles is probably far more complex. Vygotsky admitted that the pattern of their interaction was not yet clear. But he did contend that:

> Progress in thought and progress in speech are not parallel. Their two growth curves cross and recross. They may straighten out and run side by side, even merge for a time, but they always diverge again. This applies to both phylogeny and ontogeny (1962, p. 33).

Vygotsky disagreed with theorists who said that children, as a result of internal maturation, can achieve skill in advanced conceptual thought on their own, distinct from what they are taught. While admitting the necessary role of internal maturation in development, Vygotsky believed that children's informal and formal education through the medium of language strongly influences the level of conceptual thinking they reach. If the language climate within which children grow up (direct speech, mass communication media) is dominated by simplistic or "primitive" language, then the children will think only simplistically or primitively. But if the language environment contains varied and complex concepts, then children will learn to think in varied and complex ways, given that their initial biological equipment (sense organs, central nervous system) is not impaired.

In extending the scope of his theorizing beyond children's development, he suggested that the stages through which a child's thought and language evolve are likely the same as those through which humanity's has evolved over eons of time. Thus studying children's ontogenetic development not only helps us understand the child's thought and speech but also serves as the most practical method for estimating the phylogenetic development of our species.

These are the general features of Vygotsky's theory. The model is not a completed theory, with all details filled in and each proposal buttressed with a mass of empirical evidence. Rather, as Jerome S. Bruner (Vygotsky, 1962, p. viii) has written, the book *Thought and Language* "is more programmatic than systematic." It's as if Vygotsky had found only parts of the thought–speech puzzle by the time he wrote the volume, and his theory or "program" represented his assumption that when the rest of the parts were eventually discovered, the final assemblage would take on the general configuration he had outlined in his proposal.

Stages in Speech Development

Vygotsky's studies led him to conclude that speech development proceeds through the same four stages and is governed by the same laws as those relating to other mental operations that employ signs, that is, such other operations as counting and memorizing with the aid of mnemonic devices (Vygotsky, 1962, pp. 46–47).

He called the first of these four stages the *primitive* or *natural stage*. This first period, which represents the time before the circle of language overlaps the circle of conscious thought, lasts from birth until about age 2 in Vygotsky's opinion. The stage is characterized by three nonintellectual speech functions. First are sounds representing *emotional release*—crying with pain or frustration, cooing or babbling with contentment. Next, as early as the second month after birth, these emotional noises are joined by sounds that can be interpreted as *social reactions* to other people's voices or appearance. The noises of social contact include laughter and a variety of inarticulate sounds. The third type of thoughtless speech consists of the child's first words, which are *substitutes for objects and desires*. These are words learned by conditioning, by parents and siblings matching the words frequently to objects, just as some animals can be conditioned to recognize words as labels for things.

Around age 2 the primitive stage ends and the second period begins, that of *naive psychology*. The child discovers that words can have a symbolic function, and he displays this discovery by frequently asking what things are called. He no longer is simply conditioned by others to label objects and actions, but actively seeks this information himself. As a result, his vocabulary increases at a great rate. With the advent of the naive stage, the circles of language and thought begin to merge.

During this second period the child exhibits the beginnings of practical intelligence by recognizing characteristics of her surroundings and by starting to use tools, that is, starting to use objects as means to accomplish desired ends. However, her language is considered naive because she uses grammatical structures properly without recognizing the underlying functions they serve.

The experience the child gains using language in relation to the objects of the world subsequently enables the child to move to a third level, the stage of *egocentric speech*. This kind of talk makes up a large proportion of the preschool and kindergarten child's speech, particularly that occurring in play situations. It takes the form of a running monologue that accompanies the child's activities, whether he works alone or beside others. It requires no response from anyone because it is not directed at anyone but the speaker. This commonly observed phenomenon has been interpreted in various ways by different investigators. Some have viewed egocentric speech as a "running accompaniment" or tune that merely parallels the child's thought and activity as he plays. But Vygotsky arrived at a different conclusion. He saw egocentric speech as an important new tool of thought. Not only does the child think to speak, but what he says to himself influences what he then will think, so the two interact to produce together conceptual or verbal thought.

To test this hypothesis, Vygotsky arranged for problems to arise during the play-work activities of young children. For example, a pencil for the drawing task would be missing or the paper would be too small or too large. The investigators then observed that the amount of egocentric talk on these occasions was double that observed when children did not face such problems (Vygotsky, 1962, pp. 16–17). This Vygotsky interpreted as evidence that egocentrc speech is not just a release of tension or an expressive accompaniment to activity but is also a significant tool "of thought in the proper sense—in seeking and planning the solution of a problem" (1962, p. 16).

Nor did Vygotsky agree that egocentric speech simply died out after age 7 or so. Rather, he saw the decline of egocentric speech as a signal of the onset of the fourth stage in his developmental hierarchy, the *ingrowth stage*. The child learns to manipulate language in her head in the form of soundless speech, thinking by means of logical memory that employs inner signs for solving problems. Throughout the rest of her life, the individual will use both inner speech and outer speech as tools in conceptual or verbal thought.

In summary, children's speech grows through four stages between the time of birth and the years of primary school, age 7 or 8. The process begins with nonintellectual or "thoughtless" speech and develops via naive and egocentric language into inner speech that is inextricably interwoven with conceptual thinking. Now that we have traced development from the vantage point of speech, we will trace the development of verbal thinking from the vantage point of thought.

Stages in Conceptual Thought Development

Vygotsky's method of studying the development of conceptual thought involved two steps: (1) devising a test that would reveal the process a person follows when faced with the necessity to create a concept and administering the test to children, adolescents, and adults and then (2) comparing the developmental hierarchy revealed in this testing with reports from other psychologists who had longitudinally followed the conceptual growth of individual children from one year to another. The purpose of this comparison was to determine whether the differences observed in testing cross sections of people of different ages accurately reflected the changes in thought processes that occur in the individual as he or she matures.

To begin we will briefly look at the testing instrument Vygotsky created (now known as the Vygotsky blocks), for it reveals something of his research ingenuity. One of the sticky problems faced in testing children's concept-formation process is that of finding concepts for them to generate in the testing situation that we are sure they did not already know. In particular, we want to ensure they have mastered the concept and have not simply memorized a word that suggests they know the concept when they actually do not.

Vygotsky solved this problem by constructing a set of twenty-two wooden blocks of different colors, shapes, heights and sizes (*size* meaning overall horizontal area). These characteristics vary in such a manner that no two blocks are alike in all ways. On the bottom surface of each block is written one of four nonsense words: *lag, bik, mur, cev.* Irrespective of the blocks' color or shape, *lag* appears on all tall, large blocks; *bik* on all flat, large ones; *mur* on tall, small ones; and *cev* on short, small ones. Each testing session begins with the examiner spreading the blocks before the child in a random mixture, then turning up a sample block and showing the child the name on the bottom. The child is asked to pick out all the blocks he thinks are the same kind, that is, ones that bear the same name. When the child has done so, the examiner turns up one of the selected blocks he knows is wrong and shows the child that it does not bear the correct word. The child is asked to try again. This process is repeated over and over until the child solves the problem. The solution, of course, requires that the child recognize that the word represents a concept composed of two of the dimensions of the blocks—both height and horizontal size. Since there is no single word in normal language representing this combined concept, the child cannot have known or rote memorized it prior to the testing session (Vygotsky, 1962, pp. 56–57).

Throughout the testing session the examiner carefully watches the combinations the child chooses each time, for the nature of each combination reflects the strategy of thought in which the child has engaged. Using the block problem with several hundred subjects of different ages enabled Vygotsky to identify a hierarchy of three major stages children pass through in achieving true conceptual thought between the preschool years and middle adolescence. Within each stage, children also traverse a series of subphases.

Conceptual thinking is really a mode of organizing one's environment by abstracting and labeling a quality shared by two or more phenomena. The major steps in children's intellectually organizing perceived phenomena are (I) clustering things into unorganized heaps, then (II) putting things together in complexes, and, as puberty arrives, (III) beginning to think in genuine concepts. But even when the adolescent achieves the ability to think conceptually, she does not entirely abandon the two earlier forms of thought; they merely subside in frequency and reappear on certain occasions.

The three major stages and the subphases, based upon children's and adolescents' solutions to the Vygotsky-blocks problem, are as follows (Vygotsky, 1962, pp. 58–81):

Stage I   Thinking in *unorganized congeries* or heaps. During this period the child puts things in groups (and may assign the group a label) on the basis of what are only chance links in the child's perception.

> *Subphase I-A: Trial-and-error grouping.* The groups are created at random, blind guess.

> *Subphase I-B: Visual-field organization.* The child applies a grouping label to a collection of things that happen to appear together in space and time.

> *Subphase I-C: Reformed heaps.* The child first produces groupings on the basis of either guess or visual-field organization, then in dissatisfaction tries to reform the heaps by shifting elements in them around, but the items are still not alike in any inherent way.

Stage II   Thinking in *complexes*. Individual objects are united in the child's mind not only by subjective impressions but also by bonds that actually exist among the objects. This is a step away from egocentric thinking and in the direction of objectivity. In a complex, the bonds between components are *concrete* and *factual* to some degree rather than abstract and logical. Five types of complexes succeed one another during this stage of thought.

> *Subphase II-A: Associative* complexes. These are based on any bond the child notices, such as color, shape, or nearness of objects to each other.

> *Subphase II-B: Collection* complexes. Items are grouped by contrast rather than by similarity. For example, one block of each color may be put in a group and given a label. (At a dinner table, a knife, fork, spoon, plate, cup, and saucer would make up a set of a collection variety.)

> *Subphase II-C: Chain* complexes. These involve a consecutive joining of individual items with a meaningful bond necessary only between one

link and the next (as in the game of dominoes). A *large* green block may be linked to a *large red* block, then a *red* small *round* one followed by a *round* yellow middle-sized one.

Subphase II-D: Diffuse complexes. These are groupings in which there is a fluidity in the attribute that unites the individual elements. The child may put triangles together, then add a trapezoid to the group because the trapezoid's points remind the child of a triangle's points.

Subphase II-E: Pseudoconcept complexes. These at first view appear to be groupings based on true conceptual thinking. But when the label the child has applied is challenged, he shows he is unable to rationalize the grouping condition adequately. If he has put all red blocks together and the experimenter turns two blocks over to show they do not bear the same name (one is *mur* and the other *bik*), the child is unable to give up his first basis for grouping and to seek a different one, a different characteristic that unites the objects. Pseudoconceptual thinking represents a transition from thinking in complexes to thinking in true concepts.

Vygotsky made an important distinction between pseudoconcepts and true concepts: True conceptual thinking requires that the child spontaneously group objects on the basis of abstract characteristics that she perceives and not simply apply ready-made labels that she has been taught to use with other, common groupings. Vygotsky explained this phenomenon, which causes many adults to mistakenly assume that young children think conceptually, in this way:

> Pseudoconcepts predominate over all other complexes in the preschool child's thinking for the simple reason that in real life, complexes corresponding to word meanings are not spontaneously developed by the child: The lines along which a complex develops are predetermined by the meaning a given word already has in the language of adults (1962, p. 67).

Stage III   Thinking in *concepts*. On the threshold of this final major stage, we will pause and inspect two paths of thought development—*synthesizing* and *analyzing*—that have now converged to make conceptual thinking possible.

The first path was through the sequence of complexes. The main function involved in such complex thinking was the *drawing together* or synthesizing of phenomena that share common aspects. The second path leading to conceptual thinking followed the process of *separating* or analyzing phenomena by singling out or abstracting elements from them. In

Vygotsky's opinion these two processes, uniting and separating, arise from different sources in the child's development. We have already traced the path of drawing together or synthesizing. We will now move back to find the beginnings of the other, that of abstracting or analyzing.

In his experiments, Vygotsky located the beginnings of abstracting at the point where children identified ways in which objects were *maximally similar,* that is, alike in as many ways as possible. For example, they pick two blocks that are both tall *and* yellow or both short *and* green. But since such pairs of blocks also differ in shape or horizontal size, the child's abstracting process is somewhat in error. However, at this age the child overlooks the discrepancies and overemphasizes the similarities he first identified.

At the next stage of abstraction, the child identifies a *single characteristic* by which to group objects, selecting only green blocks or only tall ones. Vygotsky called these single-characteristic selections *potential concepts.*

The child then takes the final step into conceptual thinking when she makes a new synthesis of accurately abstracted traits, a synthesis that is stable and convincing in her mind, and this synthesis "becomes the main instrument of thought" (Vygotsky, 1962, p. 78). The child—by now an early adolescent—views things in terms of her synthesized and analyzed concepts. But even among adolescents conceptual thinking is somewhat unstable, being more consistent in concrete situations that have objects present than in solely verbal situations. Furthermore, there is no sharp break between one sort of thought and another. As the child begins to achieve conceptual thought, her thinking in complexes continues, although it diminishes in frequency. A person, even as an adult, is never "purely" a conceptual thinker.

Throughout this process of mental development, language has served as a significant tool or mediator for thinking activity. The intellectual operation of forming concepts, according to Vygotsky (1962, p. 81), "is guided by the use of words as the means of actively centering attention, of abstracting certain traits, synthesizing them, and symbolizing them by a sign."

As mentioned earlier, after Vygotsky conducted his experiments with the blocks and identified his hierarchy of mental acts leading to true concept formation, he studied the literature on children's linguistic development, on the thought processes of primitive peoples, and on the nature of languages as such. The comparison of his own experimental results with those from the professional literature convinced him that the stages he had identified were essentially an accurate description of the development of conceptual thought. He apparently felt that a significant portion of the thought-and-language puzzle had been solved.

KEY GENERALIZATIONS
ABOUT DEVELOPMENT

Vygotsky also produced a variety of other insights that illustrate other facets of development. The following selections reflect some of these beliefs. Each selection in a sense describes a direction that development takes, since each is cast in a form that pictures the way the condition of the young child changes as the child grows toward adolescence.

Structures and Functions

At each level of development, the child's manner of interacting with the world is determined by the particular *structures* of the personality at that time. A given structure equips the child to function in a particular way. By *function*, Vygotsky appeared to mean the way the child interpreted the world and responded. The first structures displayed by the newborn and young child Vygotsky termed *elementary*. They are seated in the conditioned and unconditioned reflexes, in the basic biological nature of the individual, and their functions "are totally and directly determined by stimulation from the environment" (Vygotsky, 1978, p. 39).

As the child grows up, he periodically arrives at new stages at which new structures are built, thereby creating potentials for new functions. Vygotsky termed these *higher structures*, ones that emerge in the process of cultural development and utilize signs (language) and tools. Whereas the elementary functions consist of the child's reacting directly to stimuli from the environment, for "higher functions, the central feature is self-generated stimulation, that is, the creation and use of artificial stimuli which become the immediate causes of behavior" (Vygotsky, 1978, p. 39). The older child, then, "thinks up" things to do and employs language and tools in pursuit of need fulfillment.

Vygotsky proposed that as a child moves from a more elementary to a higher structure, the process at each step of development involves the same sequence of events. "The initial stage is followed by that first structure's destruction, reconstruction, and transition to structures of the higher type. . . . Higher psychological functions are not superimposed as a second story over the elementary processes; they represent new psychological systems" (Vygotsky, 1978, p. 124). Note that Piaget (Chapter Ten) held similar views.

Memory

In keeping with his lower and higher levels of structure and function, Vygotsky defined two separate types of memory. The lower type, corresponding to elementary structures, he called *natural memory*. This sort dominates the intellectual behavior of both young children and nonliterate peoples. Natural memory consists of a person's retaining mental images of actual experiences and objects. Such "memory traces" resemble pictures and sounds in the mind, revealed in studies of young children's eidetic or photographic records of events. Natural memory is the most basic form of cognition, "the definitive characteristic of the early stages" of mental development (Vygotsky, 1978, p. 51).

In contrast to natural memory is the abstract variety that evolves as the child gains command over signs that form language. Objects and events can be symbolized as words and figures, and these symbols can themselves be manipulated to form new meanings. The older child develops concepts by abstracting a common quality from various events and by comprehending principles that represent relations among the concepts. For the adolescent, remembering is not simply the recall of images. As Luria (1976, p. 11) explained, "although the young child thinks by remembering, an adolescent remembers by thinking." An adolescent girl's "memory is so 'logicalized' that remembering is reduced to establishing and finding logical relations; recognizing consists in discovering that element which the task indicates has to be found" (Vygotsky, 1978, p. 51).

Perception

As the child develops, her perception progresses from a natural form to higher forms that are mediated by language. The preverbal infant seems to perceive only immediately present visual and aural fields. Then, as language is gradually acquired, the child gains more control over what she attends to and how she perceives it. Vygotsky concluded that the chief function of speech for the young child is that of applying labels to things, thereby singling out the object from its background for attention and imposing some of her own structure on the natural sensory field. At the same time, the child accompanies her first words with expressive gestures, ostensibly compensating with gesture for her shortcomings in communicating with language.

At a more advanced stage of development, speech functions as an instrument for synthesizing and thereby producing more complex forms of perception. Speech frees the child from the immediate visual field.

> The independent elements in a visual field are simultaneously perceived; in this sense, *visual perception is integral*. Speech, on the other hand, requires sequential processing. Each element is separately labeled and then connected in a sentence structure, *making speech essentially analytical* (Vygotsky, 1978, p. 33).

In summary, then, these examples of the theorist's beliefs about elementary and higher functions, about memory, and about perception illustrate his deep conviction that acquisition of tool use and language is essential for the development of higher cognitive processes. And in keeping with his Marxist views about the significance of the social environment for development, he saw the language environment—the *culture*—in which a child is raised as being crucial in determining the direction and extent of the individual's intellectual growth. The history of that particular culture and the history of the individual child's experience in that culture mold the child's cognitive abilities.

CENTRAL CONCERNS IN SOVIET DEVELOPMENTAL THEORY: 1920s–1980s

In pointing out the chief interests of Soviet developmentalists during the past seven decades, V. V. Davidov (1985) emphasized the crucial role played by activity at each stage of child development. An *activity* is a person's goal-oriented, genuinely industrious interaction with the world, with the product of this activity becoming transformed in the structure of the individual's intellect. More specifically, as a child engages in a type of social interaction with others in his or her culture, this activity is accompanied by signs or language that represent the activity. The signs or language are then internalized by the child so that the internalization alters the psychic structures that, in turn, produce new psychic functions by which the child interacts with the world.

At the base of such a theory is the concept of a hierarchy of types of activities, with a dominant or *leading activity* at the top of the hierarchy at each stage of development. Thus each period of human development is motivated by a particular leading activity. The change from one leading activity brings about a change in the person's perception of life and signifies the transition from one stage to the next. A leading activity is marked by three features: (1) it is the chief factor establishing a given period in the child's psychological development, (2) it is within the field of this activity that particular psychic functions emerge, and (3) the climax of the activity forms the foundation for the next leading activity.

Thus successive leading activities signify the focus of development over the passing years and become a series of developmental stages. The best-known version of this series was described by Vygotsky and D. B. Elkonin (Davidov, 1985; Elkonin in Cole, 1977, pp. 538–563). It consists of six levels:

1. *Intuitive and emotional contact between child and adults (birth to age 1).*
   The basic types of development produced by this contact include feeling a need for interacting with other people, expressing emo-

tional attitudes toward them, learning to grasp things, and displaying a variety of perceptual actions.

2. *Object-manipulation activity (early preschool years, ages 1–3).* Children
    adopt socially accepted ways of handling things, and through
    interaction with adults they develop speech and visual-perception
    thinking (memory images).

3. *Playing-games activity (later preschool years, ages 3–7).** Children en-
    gage in symbolic activities and creative play. They now have some
    comprehension of how to cooperate together in group endeavors.

4. *Learning activity (elementary school years, ages 7–11).* Children devel-
    op theoretical approaches to the world of things, a function that
    involves their considering objective laws of reality and beginning
    to comprehend psychological preconditions for abstract theoreti-
    cal thought (intentional mental operations, mental schemes for
    problem solving, reflective thinking).

5. *Social-communications activity (early adolescence, ages 11–15).* Adoles-
    cents gain skills in initiating types of communication needed for
    solving life's problems, in understanding other people's motives,
    and in consciously submitting to group norms.

6. *Vocational-learning activity (later adolescence, ages 15–17).* Older
    adolescents develop new cognitive and vocational interests, grasp
    elements of research work, and attempt life projects.

The transition from one stage of development to another disrupts the
stability of the child's ways of thinking and interacting with the world and
produces *crises* as the child struggles with the prerequisites for the next
activity that is to occupy the leading role. Thus development is composed
of cycles of stability interspersed with transitional crises.

Davidov (1985) identified five major concerns that are increasingly
engaging the attention of Soviet developmental psychologists: (1) elucidating the basic concepts of development concerning humans in general and
specific ways individuals' intellects evolve, (2) creating a complete theory of
intellectual development incorporating the leading activities of the successive stages of child growth, (3) discovering how the historical development of a society relates to its members' intellectual development, (4)
determining methods for studying critical periods over the entire life span
of development, and (5) studying intellectual development in middle-aged
and elderly people.

*Traditionally Soviet children have started elementary school at age 7, some of them having been in
preschool programs for two or three years.

PRACTICAL APPLICATIONS

In a society whose entire apparatus—scientific, organizational, artistic, educational, social, athletic—is designed to promote such sociopolitical goals as those of Marxist-Leninism, developmental psychologists are necessarily practical people who focus their theories on the solution of problems in the society. Vygotsky and his fellow developmentalists accepted this responsibility with apparent enthusiasm as they applied their studies to aiding the physically and mentally handicapped, spreading literacy throughout the third largest population in the world, improving instructional methods in the schools, raising the level of intellectual functioning of disadvantaged groups in the society (Luria, 1976), and promoting better child-rearing practices in general.

In formulating the theoretical foundations for these practical undertakings, Vygotsky and his colleagues often departed from the dominant views of European and American psychologists. An example from Vygotsky's writings illustrates one of these departures. The issue is that of learning readiness. That is, how does a teacher or parent know when a child is capable of learning to perform a given intellectual function or task? This determination traditionally has been based on aptitude and intelligence test scores. The child's developmental level is determined on the basis of how adequately she or he answers the question or solves the problems posed by the test. Or Piagetian tasks have been used to reveal the present mode of the child's mental functioning. Ostensibly this assessment informs the educator of the base on which instruction might build. If the child's test performance shows that he has mastered the level of thought necessary for a given type of learning, then those learning activities are appropriate for that child at that point. However, if the child's intellectual development appears insufficient for pursuing the proposed learning task, then the task should be postponed until a later date.

However, Vygotsky disagreed with this line of logic and proposed instead that two developmental levels were important for determining whether a given sort of learning could profitably be attempted. The first and lower level, which he called the *actual developmental level,* was the one established by the tests or Piagetian tasks. It showed the stage of development that had already been completed. But Vygotsky contended that this level was not a good indicator of how well a child can learn new material with some hints or help from an instructor. Besides the development that has been completed, there is development that is currently evolving, and this sort of learning potential is not adequately revealed by traditional tests. Rather, it is revealed during the process of teaching a child, by observations of how the child's intellect functions in relation to hints or leading questions or suggestions from a sensitive instructor. Studies conducted by Vygotsky and his associates supported this contention and motivated him to identify a second developmental level that extends above the actual level. He called this the *zone of proximal development*.

> [The zone] is the distance between the actual developmental level as determined by independent problem solving and the level of potential development as determined through problem solving under adult guidance or in collaboration with more capable peers.

> The zone of proximal development defines those functions that have not yet matured but are in the process of maturation, functions that will mature tomorrow but are currently in an embryonic state. These functions could be termed the "buds" or "flowers" of development rather than the "fruits" of development. The actual developmental level characterizes mental development retrospectively, while the zone of proximal development characterizes mental development prospectively (Vygotsky, 1978, pp. 86–87).

Such a notion of learning readiness, when applied to practical teaching situations, significantly influences the teacher's decision about what kinds of learning activities to provide and how to decide whether children are capable of profiting from them. For example, a teacher who knows the sequence in which the zones of proximal development evolve in the field of mathematics can predict the next mathematical skill that a child should be capable of mastering. Equipped with this knowledge, the teacher can design learning activities for the child that will stimulate the early fruition of that skill.

VYGOTSKY'S THEORY: AN ASSESSMENT

As in previous chapters, the nine standards of appraisal from Chapter One provide the framework for evaluating Vygotsky's theory.

Vygotsky's theorizing warrants a rather high mark for how well it reflects the real world of children (item 1). His speculations were founded on the results of experiments with children of various ages, and he sought to check his conclusions with other studies from various nations. I would have rated item 1 even higher if his theory had been further supported with data from studies specifically designed to test his hypotheses (1) by experimental methods in addition to those using such devices as the Vygotsky blocks and (2) with children from more varied cultural environments.

The theory is clearly described (item 2), particularly in its English-language form, which profits from the translators' organizational improvements.

The theory explains the past and predicts the future (item 3) of verbal-thought development for children in general. However, it does not (at least in the form described in *Thought and Language*) provide a means for analyzing the influence of causal factors in a child's life so that the individual child's progress toward conceptual thought can be explained or predicted. Thus I have given it only a moderate rating on item 3.

Implications for child-rearing practices (item 4) in the form of suggestions for teaching scientific concepts have been included in Vygotsky's writings. But as in the case of item 3, I feel the theory's usefulness as a guide to child rearing is limited by the failure to specify how causal factors combine in an individual child's life to determine his or her particular

Vygotsky's Theory

How well do I think the theory meets the standards?

The Standards	Very Well	Moderately Well	Very Poorly
1. Reflects the real world of children		X	
2. Is clearly understandable	X		
3. Explains the past and predicts the future		X	
4. Guides child rearing		X	
5. Is internally consistent	X		
6. Is economical		X	
7. Is falsifiable	X		
8. Stimulates new discoveries	X		
9. Is self-satisfying		X	

intellectual development. Thus I have rated the theory as moderate on item 4.

I have not located any internal inconsistencies in Vygotsky's model (item 5), and it appears economical (item 6) in that complex theoretical mechanisms are not used to account for phenomena that might be equally well explained by less complex ones. I feel, however, that more elements and a better explanation of their interactions are needed to account for the results he obtained with his block experiments. The theory as it appears in *Thought and Language* is more programmatic than complete and systematic. At the time of Vygotsky's death it was necessarily still in skeletal form. My mark near the center for item 6, therefore, represents my opinion that the theory was somewhat overly economical, barren in detail.

In terms of falsifiability (item 7), I believe all of Vygotsky's hypotheses and proposals, as well as his actual stages of growth, can be tested experimentally to determine whether they are supportable in fact.

As stimulators of new discoveries (item 8), Vygotsky's theoretical proposals are apparently highly regarded in the Soviet Union (Luria, 1976, pp. v, 11–12; Vygotsky, 1962, pp. ix–x). And since his work has been published in the West, it has set off new speculations and investigations that are appearing at an increasing rate outside the Soviet Union. Over the nineteen-year period 1964–1982, *Psychological Abstracts* listed only 34 journal articles that drew on Vygotsky's work. In contrast, over the eight-year span 1983–1990, more than 120 such studies were cited from publications both inside and outside the Soviet Union. Thus I have rated Vygotsky's work high on item 8.

Overall, I find Vygotsky's theory of thought and language and his innovative research methods quite satisfying (item 9).

FOR FURTHER READING

Vygotsky, L. S. (1978) in M. Cole, V. John-Steiner, S. Scribner, and E. Souberman (eds.), *Mind in Society*. Cambridge, Mass.: Harvard University Press.

Vygotsky, L. S. (1962) *Thought and Language*. Cambridge, Mass.: M.I.T. Press.

For Soviet psychological investigations utilizing Vygotsky's proposal that cognitive development as reflected in speech is heavily influenced by the child's sociohistorical bakground, see:

Cole, M. (ed.) (1977) *Soviet Developmental Psychology*. White Plains, N.Y.: Sharpe.

Luria, A. R. (1976) *Cognitive Development: Its Cultural and Social Foundations*. Cambridge, Mass.: Harvard University Press.

Luria, A. R., and F. Yudovich. (1971) *Speech and the Development of Mental Processes in the Child*. Harmondsworth, England: Penguin.

For Piaget's reaction to Vygotsky's criticism of an early version of Piagetian theory, see:

Piaget, J. (1962) *Comments on Vygotsky's Critical Remarks Concerning the Language and Thought of the Child and Judgment and Reasoning in the Child*. Cambridge, Mass.: M.I.T. Press, 16 pages.

For a detailed, highly readable chronicle of the evolution of Soviet developmental psychology, including Vygotsky's role in that pageant, see:

Valsiner, J. (1988b) *Developmental Psychology in the Soviet Union*. Bloomington: Indiana University Press.

ESTIMATING THE FUTURE OF STAGE THEORIES

What are characteristics of recent stage theories, and what might be expected of stage theories in the years ahead?

Three of the ways in which theorists have traditionally charted the course of development are: (1) in terms of a direction, that is, tracing how development progresses from an initial condition to a final condition; (2) as processes of growth; and (3) as a hierarchy of stages. Some writers have adopted only one of these perspectives. Others have combined two or all three.

Kurt Lewin (1889–1947) and Heinz Werner (1890–1964) are examples of authors who depicted development in the first of these ways. Each proposed a set of dimensions along which, according to their analyses, development naturally advances. Their dimensions, stated as growth principles, were in most cases remarkably alike, even when the labels they applied to the principles were dissimilar (Barker, Dembo, & Lewin, 1943, pp. 441–442; Werner, 1961).

To illustrate, let's consider three of the dimensions on which they agreed. Their first principle held that the child develops from a simple to an increasingly complex organism in terms of perceptual ability, thought processes, language, social interaction, physical skills, and the like. For Lewin, this was the principle of *differentiation*. For Werner, it was progression from the *syncretic* (global, general, indistinct) to the *discrete* (diverse, numerous, varied). A second principle centered on the gradually improving coordination among the various aspects of the child's differentiating self. Lewin's term for this was *organized independence* while Werner's was *articulation*. The two authors also agreed that the growing child becomes ever more *realistic*, in the sense of being able to distinguish between (a) what might be or what we wish to be or what we imagine could be and (b) what things really are.

In contrast, other theorists have portrayed development in terms of growth processes. Such is true of behaviorists and social learning proponents, as well as the information-processing advocates, ecological psychologists, and ethologists whom we meet in later chapters. For supporters of a growth-process perspective, the emphasis is not so much on the direction of development as it is on the operations that produce developmental change. Among radical behaviorists, these operations are reflected in such terms as *operant conditioning, reinforcement, shaping,* and *chaining.* Social learning theorists add such processes as *modeling, attending,* and *coding for memory.* Process-oriented theorists are often referred to as *functionalists* since they focus on the functions of the environment in promoting development.

Our third option for describing development is to characterize growth as a series of stages. Examples are the phases of development proposed by Gesell, Havighurst, Freud, Erikson, Piaget, and the Soviets. The purpose of this perspective is to carry the analysis of stage theories a step further by (1) describing key features of some recently proposed models and (2) estimating what might be expected of stage theories in the future.

FOUR RECENTLY PROPOSED STAGE THEORIES

Periodically an author produces a new stage theory, but more often than not, the proposal is not entirely new. Instead, it's a variation of some existing model. Such is the case with the first three theories described below. All three are direct responses to Piaget's model. They reflect their creators' attempts to correct ostensible shortcomings of Piaget's scheme. The last of the theories is a different matter. Not only is it a reaction against what its creator considers to be inadequacies of Piaget's and Freud's models, but it also represents an effort to match phases of human development to Christian historical eras. The four theories are labeled *recent* because all appeared in print during the 1980s.

As a preparation for inspecting these models, we can profitably consider the matter of what constitutes a *structure* and a *stage.* Although not everyone in the field of child development agrees on how *structure* should be defined, I imagine that most would find the following statement fairly acceptable: *A cognitive structure is an interpretive framework that an individual applies in giving meaning to stimuli from the environment.* Robbie Case (1986, p. 58) has defined such structures as "order-imposing devices with which children come equipped at birth" and then change in a predictable pattern with increasing age. Children's intellectual development can then be seen as progressive alterations in their cognitive structures—in the mental templates they use for comprehending their world. K. W. Fisher and R. L. Canfield (1986) have pointed out that changes in structures can be brought about in more than one way, for example, by intense emotional encounters (religious conversion, child abuse), by vivid learning experiences (producing insight), and by maturational advances in the child's nervous system. The last of these—maturation governed chiefly by the child's inherited genetic timing system—is the type of structural change usually referred to as *developmental*. It is the kind of structural change common to all children, and it forms the basis for stage theories of child development. Stage theorists typically are labeled *structuralists* because of their stress on how development depends so heavily on the genetically governed physical and mental structures through which the organism interprets events in the environment.

As in the case of structure, there has been—and continues to be—considerable disagreement about the meaning of *stage* (Levin, 1986). But, for present purposes, the following meaning will suffice as a starting point: *A new stage of cognitive development has been reached when there has been a marked change in cognitive structures that bear on varied domains of thought, when the nature of the change is similar for children of relatively the same age, and when the new structures will continue in use for some time.* In other words, a fairly abrupt change in structures is followed by a *plateau*—by an extended period of time when no dramatic alterations occur. The term *domains* in this context refers to such areas as language use, mathematical functions, the explanation of physical events, self-concept, and the like. Ways that such a general notion of stage can be rendered less simplistic and more precise is illustrated in the four theories described below.

In the following presentation, the topics addressed under each theory include events that occasioned the theory's creation and its distinctive features.

Case's Four-Stage Scheme

In the mid-1980s, Robbie Case (1985) at the Ontario Institute for Studies in Education published a new version of cognitive development theory grounded in extensive empirical research. In constructing his model, he drew a portion of his concepts and investigative methods from several progenitors, principally J. M. Baldwin (1895), J. Piaget (1963), J. S. Bruner (1964), J. Pascual-Leone (1976), and D. Klahr and J. G. Wallace (1976). Case's stated purpose in devising this new departure was to resolve some of the difficulties encountered in the models proposed by these predecessors.

His stage structure in its gross features is similar to, and generally supportive of, Piaget's scheme of sensorimotor, preoperational, concrete operational, and formal operational periods. However, Case designated the upper three stages with labels he felt more accurately described the sorts of mental processes exemplified in children's thinking from early childhood through adolescence. As shown in Figure D.1, he substituted the term *relational* for Piaget's *preoperational,* the term *dimensional* for *concrete operational,* and *vectorial* for *formal operational.*

Case found much to commend in Piaget's detailed analysis of the phase of mental growth from birth to about age 18 months, and he agreed that the term *sensorimotor* accurately reflected the infant's intellectual functions. But he disagreed that the succeeding phase of early childhood (around age 2 months to about age 5) should be called *preoperational,* as if it were simply a preparation for the following stage (ages 5–11). "The period from 2 to 5 years of age is not just a precursor of concrete operational development. It is a distinct stage of its own, with its own sequence of operative structures and its own final operational system" (1985, p. 116). In applying the label *relational* to this period, Case suggested that from around age 2 until children enter kindergarten, they develop mental skills of comprehending relations between observed phenomena in their lives, such as in recognizing ways that different animals are similar to each other.

According to his analysis, the next period (ages 5–11) is distinguished by children's ability to mentally manipulate phenomena that can be aligned along dimensions—including such polar dimensions as hot–cold, far–near, more–less, long–short, high–low, frequent–seldom, old–young, and others. Hence the term *dimensional* replaced Piaget's *concrete operational.*

Next, Case concluded that a more accurate descriptive word, *vectorial,* should replace *formal operational* in order to signify the ability of children beyond age 11 to explain or predict what will result from the interactions of two or more dimensions. For example, vectorial thought processes are required for predicting how a balance beam will respond to the interaction of *varied weights* at *varied distances* along the beam arms. In its playground form, this problem is encountered with a teeter-totter or seesaw. The matter of judging the interaction of weight and distance can be rendered quite complex when precise estimates of weights and distances, along with certain unknown quantities, are required. Case proposed that within this fourth stage "children are no longer focusing on either of . . . two dimensions separately. Rather, they are focusing on a more abstract dimension: the vector that results from [the dimensions'] opposition" (1985, p. 108).

A key feature of Case's theory is the proposal that within each stage there is a sequence of subphases *(substages)* that advance the child's thought processes from less sophisticated to more sophisticated modes of operation. These substages, common to all four major stages, are entitled (0) *operational consolidation,* (1) *unifocal coordination,* (2) *bifocal coordination,* and (3) *elaborated coordination.* As suggested in Figure D.1, at the operational con-

VECTORIAL STAGE
+3 Elaborated Coordination 15-18 years
+2 Bifocal Coordination 13-15 years
+1 Unifocal Coordination 11-13 years
0. Operational Consolidation 9-11 years

DIMENSIONAL STAGE
+3 Elaborated Coordination 9-11 years
+2 Bifocal Coordination 7-9 years
+1 Unifocal Coordination 5-7 years
0. Operational Consolidation 3.5—5 years

RELATIONAL STAGE
+3 Elaborated Coordination 3.5—5 years
+2 Bifocal Coordination 2—3.5 years
+1 Unifocal Coordination 1.5—2 years
0. Operational Consolidation 12-18 months

SENSORIMOTOR STAGE
+3 Elaborated Coordination 12-18 months
+2 Bifocal Coordination 8-12 months
+1 Unifocal Coordination 4-8 months
0. Operational Consolidation 0-4 months

Figure D.1 Case's Stages of Mental Development (Adapted from, Case, 1985, p. 413) solidation phase the child is essentially integrating in a secure form the accomplishments of the previous stage rather than acquiring a significantly new style of thinking. For this reason, Case numbered the first phase 0. In contrast, the subsequent three substages represent added mental skills and thus are assigned numbers 1, 2, and 3. At the unifocal coordination substage, the child is able to center attention on a variety of individual factors, but can only focus on one such factor at a time to solve a problem—one sensorimotor movement at ages 4 to 8 months, one relationship at ages 1.5 to 2 years, one dimension at ages 5 to 7 years, and one interaction of contrasting dimensions (vectorial) at ages 11 to 13 years. However, with additional maturation and experience, children advance to a bifocal coordination substage where they can direct attention at two different factors to solve a problem—two sensorimotor movements at ages 8 to 12 months, two relationships at ages 2 to 3.5 years, two dimensions at ages 7 to 9 years, and two interactions of contrasting dimensions (vectorial) at ages 13 to 15 years. In like manner, at the final elaborated coordination level of a major stage, children can coordinate two or more factors in a sophisticated way to solve a problem.

Although space limitations prohibit my demonstrating each of the stage progressions in detail, an example from the dimensional stage may suffice to illustrate how children's thinking typically advances (Siegler, 1976). Children ages 3.5 through 10 years were shown a balance beam with four pegs at equal intervals on either side of the fulcrum, along with a stack of doughnut-shaped weights that could be slipped onto the pegs (Figure D.2). The task was to predict how the beam would behave if the weights were arranged in various quantities and at various distances along the beam. Children operating at the unifocal coordination substage (ages 5–7) approached this problem by concentrating their attention on the dimension of weight, with their focus on the number of separate weights. Their

Figure D.2   Balance Beam for Testing School-Age Children's Reasoning Patterns [Adapted from Case, 1985, p. 104. Originally appeared in "Three Aspects of Cognitive Development" by R. S. Siegler, in *Cognitive Psychology*, Vol. 4, pp. 481–520 (1976).]

strategy involved counting the number of weights on each side, noting which side had the larger number, and choosing that side as the one that would go down when the beam was free to move.

At the next substage (bifocal coordination, ages 7–9), children could solve the problem by coordinating two dimensions: (a) noting which side had the greater number of weights, (b) noting the side that had weight at a greater distance, and (c) concluding that if the weights were about equal, the side with the greater distance would go down; otherwise, the side with the greater weight would go down. At the third substage (elaborated coordination, ages 9–11), children appeared to use addition and subtraction to solve problems involving more complex combinations of weights and distances than could be managed by children still operating at substages 1 and 2.

> The addition strategy is quite simple. Children merely add the number of weight and distance units on each side, and pick the one with the greater total value as the one which will go down. The subtraction strategy is more complicated, but follows the same basic logic. Children first compute the difference between the two weights, and the difference between the two distances. They then base their decision on the dimension with the greater difference. For example, if the weights are 2 and 8, and the distances are 4 and 3, they pick the side with the greater weight to go down, because the difference along this dimension is greater than that along the distance dimension (Case, 1985, p. 106).

Not only has Case used his model for charting children's reasoning about inanimate objects but also for interpreting children's language development and the way they think about people's social interactions. The model is thus conceived to be a general theory of intelligence, applicable to a variety of aspects of mental development.

In a number of ways Case's scheme has advanced development theory by accounting for phenomena that were not adequately explained by earlier models. For instance, as noted in Chapter Ten, the fact that children conceive of the conservation of substance, quantity, weight, and mass at different ages rather than simultaneously casts in question the existence of a single qualitatively distinct mode of thinking (concrete operational) covering the entire range of elementary-school years. The term *horizontal décalage* serves as a label for such inconsistency but not as an explanation. However, Case's notion of substages within each major stage permits him to rationalize the inconsistency. That is, in the early unifocal coordination phase of a stage (ages 5–7), the child focuses on separate factors (such as dimensions of height, width, weight, mass), each of which may develop at a different time. Only by the third substage (elaborated coordination) do all of these separate insights become integrated into a general, qualitatively distinct mode of thought governing a broad spectrum of mental activities.

In conclusion, while the above summary identifies a few central elements in Case's scheme, it is far too brief to reveal the tightly knit logic that renders the theory internally consistent, understandable, and generally falsifiable. And the quantity of empirical evidence on which it is founded suggests that the scheme accurately reflects the real world of childhood. Finally, Case appears judicious in recognizing limitations in what he has accomplished. He wonders whether his postulated set of horizontal structures (his subphase and stage characteristics) is the best model of children's mentation. Other puzzles that he considers not yet solved are ones of short-term-memory storage space, the number of cognitive transitions that take place during the preschool years, and the relationships between children's emotional and cognitive development as well as between their procedural and declarative knowledge (Case, 1985, pp. 420–424).

Fisher's Skill Development Theory

Kurt W. Fisher, a professor of psychology at the University of Denver, has proposed a *skill theory* that "treats cognitive development as the construction of hierarchically ordered collections of specific skills" (1980, p. 477). Because explaining Fisher's model in its complete form would require a great many pages, the brief version I offer here is admittedly bare bones. I shall describe only a few of the main features of his proposal, only enough to suggest his general approach to the problems he seeks to solve.

At the outset, Fisher acknowledged virtues in both Piaget's and Skinner's work, as well as in proposals of information-processing psychologists and skill learning theorists. However, he felt that Piaget placed too much emphasis on children's internal maturation and neglected environmental contexts while Skinner did just the opposite. Therefore Fisher developed a model intended to represent an evenly balanced interaction between nature and nurture:

> The skills in the theory are always defined jointly by organism and environment. Consequently, the skills are characterized by structures that have properties like those described by organism-oriented psychologists and that simultaneously are subject to the functional laws outlined by environmentally oriented psychologists (K. W. Fisher, 1980, pp. 478–479).

The skills on which the theory focuses are those techniques children acquire for acting on their world. Such acting can be motor (observable physical movements), perceptual (constructing meanings for what is observed), or mental (manipulating percepts and concepts). Thus Fisher's skills are analogous to Piaget's schemes and Skinner's operants. Like Piaget and Case, Fisher has pictured development as proceeding from the simplest sensorimotor acts in infancy to the manipulation of abstract systems in early adulthood. But rather than describing such development as a progression through a series of stages, Fisher has chosen to depict it as movement through ten levels that are subsumed under three tiers (Table D.1).

As shown in Table D.1, within each tier, cognitive development advances through four types of levels—single sets, mappings, systems, and systems of systems. A *set* in Fisher's usage means "a source of variations that the person can control" by physically or mentally acting on things (K. W. Fisher, 1980, p. 486). A set on the sensorimotor tier is very simple, such as the infant's reaching actions *(variations)*. Sets on the higher tiers are more complex, such as a child's conception (mental representation) of the

Table D.1   Fisher's Levels of Cognitive Skills Development

Cognitive Tiers and Levels	Age of First Development
Tier 1: Sensorimotor	
Level 1: Single sensorimotor sets	Several months after birth
Level 2: Sensorimotor mappings	Middle of first year
Level 3: Sensorimotor systems	End of first year, start of second year
Level 4: Systems of sensorimotor systems	Early preschool years
Tier 2: Representational	
Level 4: Single representational sets	Early preschool years
Level 5: Representational mappings	Late preschool years
Level 6: Representational systems	Grade school years
Level 7: Systems of representational systems	Early high school years
Tier 3: Abstract	
Level 7: Single abstract sets	Early high school years
Level 8: Abstract mappings	Late high school years
Level 9: Abstract systems	Early adulthood
Level 10: Systems of abstract systems	

Table adapted from K. W. Fisher, 1980, pp. 479, 522.

kinds of actions (variations) suitable for playing the role of doctor or of mother *(thing)*.

The first level on a tier involves single sets. This means that the child can act on (perceive, conceive, think about) a set by itself but not one set in relation to another. The very young infant may follow with her eyes the motion of a toy passed across her crib, and she may also be able to reach and grasp, but she does not connect the seeing and the reaching so as to catch the toy. The means–end combination of seeing and reaching to grasp the toy occurs at the second level, that of *mapping* (connecting) one set onto another. For the older child, mapping may occur when the child, in imaginative play, integrates the doctor role with the role of mother—the doctor converses with the mother about the treatment of the patient (a doll).

At level 3, the child can relate not only one, but two aspects of each action that forms a system. On the sensorimotor tier, the toddler can recognize the distance and speed of a moving toy and adjust her reaching motion to catch it. The older child, playing doctor, may coordinate different aspects of the medical role with different aspects of the mother's role to produce a more complex form of play. Finally, at level 4, the child relates one system to another. For instance, at the sensorimotor level, the child understands that any "object is in fact the focus of a number of different sensory-motor systems; that is, every object can be made to . . . produce many types of actions. The ability to understand objects in this way (as independent agents of action) first develops at level 4" (K. W. Fisher, 1980, p. 493).

As shown in Table D.1, the fourth level in each tier serves as the foundation of the next higher tier. The child's being able to perceive relations between two systems of sensorimotor actions—sights, sounds, touch sensations, movements—is the first step in the ability to represent mentally such single attributes as weight, length, and width. Then in the latter preschool years, children are able to correlate (map) two such attributes of things. During their time in the elementary grades, their ability to conceive of these attributes as operating in systems progresses, so that: "With only level 6 skills, the person can understand most of the individual kinds of conservation that Piaget and his colleagues have documented . . . but cannot integrate those separate conservations into an abstract concept of conservation" (K. W. Fisher, 1980, p. 495). Such integration begins to occur at level 7, where "In an abstract set, the person abstracts an intangible attribute that characterizes broad categories of objects, events, or people" (K. W. Fisher, 1980, pp. 494–495). Then, as a high school youth and young adult, the individual develops growing sophistication in mapping one abstract set onto another, conceiving of abstract sets as systems and as interrelating systems. Youths who have advanced to level 10 can now meaningfully discuss such matters as: (1) the effect of gravity on the ocean tides, the movement of the planets, and space travel, (2) the relation of supply to demand in capitalist and communist economic systems, (3) the relation of the surface grammatical structure of languages to their deep structure, and (4) theories of child development.

Fisher's substituting the word *tier* for *stage* was apparently motivated by a desire to preclude readers' bringing existing notions of *stage* to his model. In contrast to a traditional Piagetian idea of stages, Fisher's levels and tiers involve a good deal of flexibility. Whereas the genetic human nature common to all children furnishes a basic maturational time schedule that conveys all children through the same general tiers and levels, each child's unique environmental experiences and particular genetic structure leads to differences among children in skills they acquire, in when they gain the skills, and, to some extent, in what order. For example, the pattern of two children's development can vary because of their different learning opportunities, the instructional methods they experienced, and the emotional environment in which their learning took place. Thus it should not be surprising that a child may display different levels of skill in reading, calculating, drawing pictures, operating a computer, and/or speaking a foreign language.

Not only do children's learning histories result in different levels of development of different sets of skills, but the context in which a given skill is displayed can influence the level a child exhibits on a particular occasion. Fisher has applied the term *environmental support* in reference to how much the context may guide the child toward utilizing a skill at one level rather than at another. Take the example of a teacher who is providing primary grade children the opportunity to engage in creative dramatics by playing a medical doctor. The teacher would provide a high level of environmental support by demonstrating (with such objects as a stethoscope, thermometer, or doll) a doctor treating a patient and then allowing the children to play as they wish. In contrast, a low level of environmental support would involve simply furnishing the objects and suggesting that "you might want to play a doctor" without providing any demonstration. In experiments of this type, Fisher found that children age 7.5 typically showed in their free play a functional level 4 under the low-support condition but level 5 in the high-support context (K. W. Fisher & Canfield, 1986, pp. 252–255).

In summary, then, Fisher has built into his theory several ways to account for the unevenness of children's development across skills (Piaget's *horizontal décalage* problem) and for the varied paths of cognitive skill development that are sometimes found in empirical investigations.

A further way Fisher has adjusted his theory to empirical findings is by proposing five transformation rules that specify how a skill is converted into a new, more advanced skill. The five rules are "the heart of the mechanism for predicting specific sequences of development" (K. W. Fisher, 1980, p. 497). He has labeled them *intercoordination, compounding, focusing, substitution,* and *differentiation.* The first two rules designate how existing skills are combined to produce new ones. Intercoordination identifies combinations that produce development from one level to the next (macrodevelopment), while compounding identifies combinations that result in small increments of development within a level (microdevelopment). Focusing and substitution identify smaller microdevelopmental steps than does compounding. Specifically, focusing accounts for "moment-to-moment shifts from one skill to another, and substitution designates certain cases of generalization of a skill" (K. W. Fisher, 1980, p. 497). The last rule, differentiation, identifies how sets of skills may become divided into subsets while the other four transformations are taking place. Although Fisher does not believe that his five rules cover all the factors governing skill development, he contends that applying the five can furnish better predictions of cognitive growth than have previous theories.

In assessing this skill development model, I would give nearly the same sort of ratings as I proposed for Case's theory. Fisher's carefully reasoned presentation of his theory makes it appear internally consistent and disconfirmable. His explanation is well illustrated with empirical studies of children's reasoning skills. His incorporating children's learning histories, emotional conditions, and the notion of environmental support appear to furnish reasonable interpretations of empirical findings not adequately explained by classical Piagetian theory. I found the major features of the theory understandable. However, a number of details seemed unclear. For example, I did not know precisely how to distinguish one set or system from another in aspects of life that were not specifically illustrated in Fisher's explanation. The exact criteria to use in making such distinctions in a diversity of life situations appears to need clarification. But overall, this recent stage theory (or *tier* theory) appears to be an advance over Piaget's scheme—a move in the right direction.

Mounoud's System of Coding Capacities

Pierre Mounoud is a professor in the Faculty of Psychology and Educational Sciences at the University of Geneva in Switzerland. While still following Piaget's general lead in formulating stages of development, Mounoud has revised Piaget's conception in several respects—in how to name the stages, how much time is spent in a stage, what subphases occur within a stage, and what the child *constructs* while advancing through a stage. The names of the stages and the age levels at which they occur in Mounoud's model are shown in Table D.2.

Mounoud has retained the notion of four major stages but has re-named the last three to represent more accurately his notion of their essence. To grasp this point, we need first to understand what Mounoud believes children construct at each stage of development.

> Piaget's psychogenetic theory regarding the construction of structures appears to me to be extremely vulnerable to criticism. From my point of view, what the child constructs are not structures but *representations or internal organizations of contents*. The child arrives at them by means of structures, which I feel are more economically considered as preformed. Now it is possible to reinterpret the process of reflective abstraction as a *process of construction of representations* and no longer as a process of construction of logical structures (internalization of general coordina-tions of action) (Mounoud, 1986, p. 51).

In other words, Mounoud chooses to regard the general sensorimotor and mental lenses through which children interpret their world as already existing in the child's nature and evolving by means of a genetically set

Table D.2   Mounoud's Stages of Cognitive and Motor Development

Stages	Child's Internal Representations	Type of Organization
Birth	Sensorial representations (preformed) linked with pre-formed structures + new coding capacities (the per-ceptual code)	Sensorimotor organization (preformed)
18–24 months	Perceptual representations (constructed) +new coding capacities (the conceptual code)	Perceptuomotor organization (constructed)
9–11 years	Conceptual representations (constructed) +new coding capacities (the semiotic code)	Conceptuomotor organization (constructed)
16–18 years	Semiotic representations (constructed)	Semioticomotor organization (constructed)

Table adapted from Mounoud, 1986, p. 52.

timing system. He does not accept the notion that the child constructs these general capacities or viewpoints during the process of growing up. Instead, these preformed, evolving structures periodically equip children with new capacities for coding their experiences with the environment. Infants gradually develop coding abilities limited to what is directly perceived: "How it looks and how it sounds and how it feels is what it means." So in Mounoud's system, what the child constructs during these early years are not basic sensorimotor structures (the basic lenses) but, rather, psychomotor records (representations) of the child's encounters with the environment (internal organizations of contents).

During the preschool years (ages 2–8), the child's perceptual capacities are well developed so that environmental encounters are interpreted (internal representations are constructed) in terms of their appearance, sound, and touch. In other words, children internalize perceptuomotor organizations of the world. At the same time, children are beginning to develop new coding capacities, ones based not just on how things look, but on logical properties of things—on concepts rather than merely on percepts. The process of development during these years carries children fully to the next major stage of how they code their experiences, that of conceptual thought (ages 9–15). Their mental organizations of the world are now chiefly in terms of concepts. And it is during this third stage that they gradually develop a new way to represent the content of their world, that of abstract symbols and signs (semioticomotor organization), a capacity that can be fully achieved by ages 16 or 18.

It should now be apparent that in Piaget's system of four stages (sensorimotor, preoperational, concrete operational, formal operational), the beginning of the upper three stages occurs considerably earlier than in Mounoud's system. This difference can be explained by Mounoud's assumption regarding the process of development within a stage. He proposes that within each stage there occur two levels of behavioral organization or of object elaboration that represent "two qualitatively distinct levels of organization of exchange between subject and environment. These two levels would characterize an *invariant developmental sequence* which defines the internal dynamics of each stage" (Mounoud, 1986, p. 51).

On the first level within a stage, the child's newly evolved coding capacities equip the child to produce what Mounoud calls "the first revolution" in organizing the child's interactions with the environment. This revolution consists of the child's analyzing actions and objects into constituent parts in order to form new elementary representations that are "partial, local, and juxtaposed" rather than integrated and interrelated. This segmenting of experiences "comes to an end with the integration of these elementary representations into *new or global representations* which are momentarily rigid and nondecomposable, nonsegmentable. The second revolution consists precisely in the decomposition of these total representations into parts or units in such a way as to establish relationships between their components" (Mounoud, 1986, p. 53).

In summary, within each stage, the child's encounters with the environment elicit an innate, evolving general capacity for segmenting a whole into abstract units and then reforming the units into new, more sophisticated patterns of how to represent the world (Mounoud, 1986, p. 45). This second, reformulating revolution occurs near the middle of a stage and is consolidated over the months or years prior to the next stage. Thus, within the perceptuomotor stage, this second revolution appears around age 6, when the child enters school and now has the coding capacity to learn reading, writing, calculating, and the conservation of weight, mass, and number. Consequently, Mounoud's second revolution during the perceptuomotor stage coincides with the beginning of Piaget's concrete operations stage.

In the nature–nurture debate, Mounoud admits that his model credits genetic forces with greater influence on development than environmental factors: "This conception ascribes a more important role to the process of neural maturation and the biological substrates of behavior which determine the origin of the steps in this developmental sequence. The maturation of the neural system itself depends on the nature of the interactions of the organism with the environment but in a nonspecific way, these interactions at the most being able to accelerate or slow down the process" (Mounoud, 1986, p. 55).

My assessment of Mounoud's scheme is much the same as for Case's and Fisher's theories. I find his line of logic reasonable, his explanation understandable, his hyphotheses testable, and his contentions convincingly illustrated with empirical studies. His model offers abundant research possibilities, as there are numerous details yet to be clarified and hypotheses to be tested in situations other than those from which Mounoud generated his scheme.

We turn now from the three neo-Piagetian theories to one derived from an entirely different tradition.

A Fundamentalist Christian Theory

A defining precept of any fundamentalist religious tradition is that ultimate truth resides in the denomination's divinely revealed doctrine. Consequently, evidence about the nature of human development is to be found in the sect's scriptures, not in empirical investigations. This means that hermeneutics, as the science of scriptural interpretation, provides the proper methodology for extracting a theory of development from the sacred writings. In a variety of present-day societies (industrialized as well as agricultural), membership in fundamentalist religious bodies is widespread, thereby providing a vast audience of adherents seeking the truth about how children develop—or, more to the point—how children should develop. As a result, many modern-day religious leaders feel obliged to meet their parishioners' need by providing both theory and practical advice about development. This obligation has become particularly acute during the twentieth century as increasing numbers of secular models of development have appeared to challenge religious dogma.

One example of recent doctrine-based models is a theory issued by P. A. Captain under the title *Eight Stages of Christian Growth* (1984). His expressed motive was to dispel the confusion he sensed among Christians who had unsuccessfully sought to "integrate secular psychological theories with Biblical principles. . . . My goal is to discover the truth about man as revealed to us by God" (Captain, 1984, p. x). Two assumptions undergirding Captain's proposal are: (1) each human's life span comprises stages that parallel eight major eras in the Bible's chronicle (ontogeny recapitulates biblical history) and (2) at each stage a particular human need seeks fulfillment and a particular personality characteristic or emotion is emphasized. (The author adopted his idea of a hierarchy of human needs from Maslow, whom we shall meet in Chapter Thirteen.) The resulting biblical stage

Table D.3   Biblical stages of human development

Biblical Era	Biblical Stage of Development	Hierarchy of Basic Needs	Age Range
Garden of Eden	Innocence		Prenatal
Adam to Noah	Nurturance	Security (to be special)	0–2
Noah to Moses	Obedience	Liberty (to be free)	2–6
Moses to Prophets	Behavior	Competence (to be successful)	6–12
Prophets to Christ	Motive	Acceptance (to be liked)	12–20
God the Son	Meaning	Commitment (to have a cause)	20–30
God the Holy Spirit	Love	Intimacy (to be close)	25–45
God the Father	Fruit	Value (to be remembered)	40–

Table adapted from Captain, 1984, pp. 12, 18.

structure is shown in Table D.3. Captain's proposed developmental levels are labeled *biblical stages* because he based them on prominent events and characters of the Christian Bible.

The strength of Captain's theory is that it furnishes fundamentalist Christians a conception of development grounded in sacred scripture. However, for me the author's line of reasoning requires investments of faith and quirks of logic that I find difficult to tolerate. In addition, the model's source material and foundational assumptions render it inaccessible to empirical testing, unlikely to stimulate new discoveries, and highly questionable as a depiction of the real world of childhood and adolescence.

A LIKELY FUTURE FOR STAGE THEORIES

A number of writers in recent decades have forecast, or at least implied, the demise of stage theories on the grounds that the theories' predictions too often fail to match the picture of child development revealed in empirical studies (Case, 1986, pp. 59–61; Klahr & Wallace, 1976). However, as illustrated by Case, Fisher, Mounoud, and a number of other authors (Bruner, 1964; Halford, 1982; Pascual-Leone, 1976), revised versions of stage theory are alive and thriving in the realm of developmental psychology. To characterize this collection of new schemes, I. Levin (1986, p. viii) has noted that they "all agree with major features of the Piagetian structure-based stage model but liberate it from certain constraints so as to make it fit the current state of the art."

Case (1986) has suggested that a key feature of recent progress in stage theorizing has been increased dialogue among proponents of the three traditional views of development—one emphasizing process (the empiricists), another emphasizing structures (the rationalists), and a third emphasizing historical and cultural factors (the social contextualists). In other words, theorists operating from each of these three basic world views have increasingly sought to incorporate features of the other two perspectives into their own models. Consequently, stage proponents have attempted to account for the day-by-day processes that contribute to development and for the contexts in which development occurs. As a result, they draw such conclusions as that offered by K. W. Fisher and R. L. Canfield:

> Stage and structure do not appear to be monolithic, unitary, fixed characteristics of a child. Instead, they seem to be dynamic, variable properties of the child-in-a-context. Different children show different stages in a given context, and different contexts produce different stages in the same child. To deal with the ambiguity of stage and structure, investigators need to use methods that allow them to detect variations in

stage and to expand their range of observations to include likely sources of such variation. These sources include not only the age and learning history of the child, but also factors that specifically relate to short-term variations in stage such as degree of environmental support and task complexity, and factors that are likely to produce long-term individual differences in developmental sequences such as emotional experiences and strategies of approaching tasks (K. W. Fisher & Canfield, 1986, p. 259).

The future is likely to witness more of this cross-fertilization, so that some investigations of unsettled issues

will lead to interesting discoveries about children's cognitive development. [In contrast, other issues that arise] will probably have the fate of many thought-provoking problems in the past, and either lead to a blind alley or simply become too boring to the community at large. However, the basic questions of how and what develops, [as] concealed behind the concepts of stage and structure, are still the crux of our domain (Levin, 1986, p. xix).

In effect, stage theories, in some form, seem destined to be with us forever.

PART SIX

COMPUTER ANALOGUES
AND THE SELF

A search for the way children gain skill in processing information and for how a child's innermost self develops

The pair of theories analyzed in Part Six are distinctly different from each other, but not necessarily incompatible. While both are primarily products of the past three decades, they differ dramatically in their philosophical underpinnings, their investigative methods, the aspects of child nature that their proponents consider most important, and the precision of their conceptual structures.

The first of the pair is information-processing theory (Chapter Twelve). The principal exemplar on which the theory has been built is the electronic computer, an analogue chosen on the assumption that advanced forms of computers carry out many of the same functions as the human brain. Thus we might presume that attempts to simulate all sorts of human thought processes with computers could be a fruitful way of discovering the nature of human mental operations and of how such operations develop during childhood and adolescence. Investigative techniques typically employed by information-processing advocates have included (1) the creation of computer programs intended to replicate human mental functions and (2) the analysis of how people apparently carry out steps of human thought that form an information-processing chain—(a) receiving sensations from the environment, (b) interpreting these sensations, (c) storing the results of the interpretation in long-term memory, and (d) retrieving the contents of memory when they are needed for acting on the environment.

The second of our theories is humanistic psychology (Chapter Thirteen), characterized by K. P. Hillner as a conception of development that focuses on the person, personality, ego, self, the essence of one's being and existence. Humanism is concerned with such psychological phenomena as creativity, love, self-regard, growth, autonomy, identity, responsibility, and adjustment. As a remedial or interventionist endeavor, humanism amounts to a psychotherapeutic process that strives to make the individual understand himself/herself better and be more aware, independent, open, integrated, and stable (1984, p. 238).

Because the essence of humanistic psychology is found in individuals' unique views of themselves in relation to their world, research methods that involve measurements and observations of a person by outsiders are of far less interest than individuals' feelings about themselves. Likewise, drawing generalizations about groups (normative-descriptive studies) and making comparisons of one person with another are of little or no use to humanists.

As for theoretical precision, information-processing models are more detailed and specific than humanistic views, whose misty dimensions are often rather difficult to make out. Information-processing theory is readily communicated through verbal descriptions, diagrams, equations, and computer programs. In contrast, humanistic views involve a large measure of emotions and self-perceptions that are not easily conveyed through words, graphs, statistics, or formulas.

By saying that these two very different perspectives on development are not necessarily incompatible, I am suggesting that it is possible to include a concept of *self* as one component of long-term memory in an information-processing model.

Perspective E, at the close of Part Six, addresses matters of causation as they relate to theories presented in this book. The issue, when stated as a question, becomes: In different theories of child development, what is meant by *cause*?

CHAPTER TWELVE

Information-Processing Theory

As a way of explaining children's behavior, information-processing theory attempts to picture what happens between (1) the moment a child receives impressions from the environment through the senses (mainly through the eyes and ears) and (2) the moment the child visibly responds with such behaviors as speaking, writing, manipulating a toy, catching a ball, or the like. This process has often been compared to the operation of an electronic computer. Data are entered into the computer *(input)*, manipulated within the machine *(throughput)*, and then the results are printed on paper or displayed on a television screen *(output)*. While we can directly witness the first and third steps (input and output), the middle step—the internal operation of the computer—is unseen. Unless we open the computer and have the skill to analyze the inner works while they function, the computer remains a mystery and we must be satisfied with theorizing about what may be going on inside.

The problem of analysis is essentially the same when we view children from an information-processing perspective. Only the input stimuli (observed environment) and the output behavior (observed actions) can be directly witnessed by people outside the child. We are left to speculate about the throughput segment of the process. And although the child can, by introspection, witness this segment and report the way he believes he "thinks," there is a host of evidence to suggest that such introspection leads to incomplete and faulty descriptions. Not only is the immature child's interpretation of his or her thinking process inadequate, adults' analyses of their mental operations appear incomplete and faulty as well because thinking is a highly complex activity whose elements are not readily apparent in our consciousness.

Information-processing theorists speculate about the nature of the throughput portion of the sequence. (This is the portion that, over the decades, has been identified by diverse terms: *mind, self, personality, the inner child, the organism,* and *the mysterious black box.*) They attempt to specify the components of the child's internal mechanisms for manipulating information and to delineate how these components interact to produce the child's behavior.

So far, I have spoken of information-processing theory in the singular, as if it were one unified model consisting of a single set of agreed-upon characteristics. However, this is hardly the case. Within the well-populated camp of information-processing theorists, debates abound about the types of components that compose a person's processing system and about how the components interact. Developmental psychologists Robert Kail and Jeffrey Bisanz (1982, p. 47) propose that information processing, at least in its present state, should properly be dubbed a framework, not a theory, since within this framework are a multitude of different theories that have been created over the past two decades or so. While it is beyond the scope of this chapter to review all these versions, we can look at some of the widely agreed-upon components and can identify the key issues that are debated.

As noted in earlier chapters, among people who write about human development theories it is customary to speak of the earliest forms of a theoretical proposal as *standard* or *classical* models and then append some other adjective (*neo* or *post* or *revised*) to subsequent varieties as a means of differentiating among the successive versions. Such has been the case with information-processing theory. The pioneering schemes created in the 1960s and early 1970s are now labeled *standard, early,* or *classical* to distinguish them from types introduced more recently (Pylyshyn, 1989). In this chapter, we first look at a typical classical model that illustrates an early version of information-processing theory. Subsequently we inspect recent reformations of the information-processing paradigm.

Information-processing theories frequently imply that people of all age levels treat information the same way. In other words, the developmental dimension is often overlooked. But because our concern throughout this book is with children, our discussion includes material about how information may be processed differently at various stages of children's growth. The topics are presented in the following sequence: (1) the interacting components of classical information processing, (2) modes of investigation, (3) reformations of classical models, (4) information processing and development, (5) practical applications, and (6) a summary assessment.

CLASSICAL COMPONENTS OF THE INFORMATION-PROCESSING SYSTEM

The general notion of people functioning as processors of information is nothing new. Historical accounts show that from ancient times people have speculated about how they receive information from the environment, how they think about and remember this information, and how they reach a decision and act on it. What is new is that recent investigations have added greater precision to describing the likely parts of the processing system and their ways of operating.

As typically conceived today, the human processing system consists of four principal elements: (1) *sense organs,* such as eyes, ears, taste buds, pressure and pain nerves in the skin, and others, which receive impressions from the environment, (2) *short-term memory* or working memory, which holds a very limited amount of information for a short period of time, (3) *long-term memory,* which stores large amounts of information perhaps indefinitely, and (4) *muscle systems* energized by nerve impulses to perform all of the motor acts people carry out, such as reading, speaking, running, assembling machines, and the rest. The system also involves functions or processes within each element and the interactions among these elements.

At first glance it might appear that the system operates in the sequence listed above: Sensations from the environment are entered into short-term memory where they are interpreted (perceived), then moved into long-term memory where they are stored until needed for action, at which time they are retrieved to determine what motor acts, if any, to perform. However, because such a sequence is much too simple to account for the way people actually think and behave, theorists have proposed more complex models comprising networks of interaction, with various kinds of information passing instantaneously back and forth among the elements rather than simply traveling in one direction along a single track from the sense organs' input to the muscles' output. The following description is one version of such a processing network.

This version is a model I have assembled from the work of various theorists in order to offer a relatively simple illustration of what can be involved in information-processing explanations of human thinking.* I will illustrate the system with an imagined problem-solving situation faced by an eighteen-year-old who is trying to decide which route to take to a city 300 kilometers away. But before tracing the way the eighteen-year-old would process information according to the theory, I need to describe

*See Anderson, 1983; Broadbent, 1958; Kail & Bisanz, 1982; Klahr & Wallace, 1976; Newell & Simon, 1972; Uttal, 1981.

the system in terms of each component's: (1) function, (2) type of contents, (3) capacity or quantity of contents, (4) processing time, and (5) interactions with other components. The hypothetical system is displayed schematically in Figure 12.1.

The Senses

The open region at the far left in Figure 12.1 represents the world outside the person. The large box enclosed by the black line is the person. The individual's intercourse with the environment is mediated by (1) the sense organs as input channels or "windows to the world" and (2) the muscle systems as output channels or actors on the world.

To simplify the explanation, Figure 12.1 shows only three sense modalities—eyes, ears, and the pressure receptors under the skin that people commonly call touch or the tactile sense. Although the organs for detecting smell, taste, temperature, pain, and body position are not pictured, remember that they also feed environmental information into the system.

Each sense organ is obviously a very specialized instrument, attuned to just one kind of stimulation from the environment—the eyes receive only a narrow segment of the wide spectrum of light waves, the ears a narrow range of sound waves, and the tactile receptors only a portion of the impulses that impinge on the skin. Thus, while the sense organs gather information from the environment, they do so in a highly selective way, filtering out far more of the world's potential information than they allow to enter the human processing system.

Short-Term Memory

Stimuli collected by the sense organs are initially processed in what different theorists have variously called *short-term memory, primary memory, active memory,* or *working memory.* Some writers use these terms as synonyms; some make distinctions among them. For example, R. L. Klatzky (1980, p. 87) divides short-term memory into two functions: (1) that of storage, meaning the retention of recognized impressions for a brief time, and (2) that of working memory, meaning "ongoing cognitive activities—for instance, meaningful elaboration of words, symbol manipulation such as that involved in mental arithmetic, and reasoning."

Sensory Memory   In the version of the traditional information-processing approach offered in these pages, short-term memory consists of three stages. The first, *sensory memory,* is apparently located in the sense organ itself and is a stage of momentary image retention. Sensory memory is an

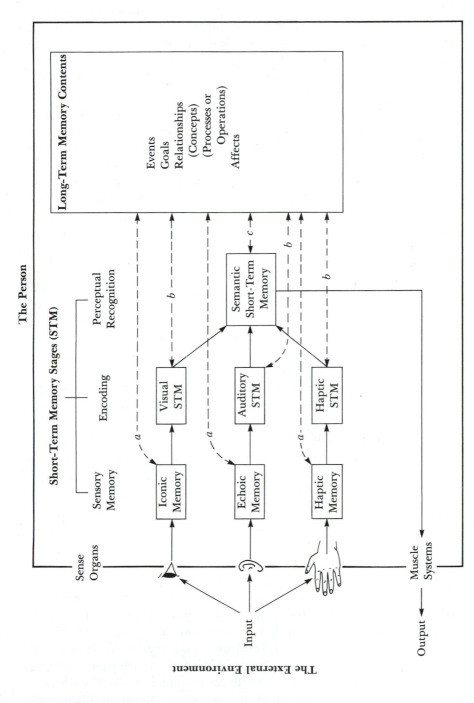

Figure 12.1 One Classical Version of the Human Information-Processing System

unselective form of memory for everything that strikes the particular organ within the range of its receptiveness. The eye's sensory memory holds all receivable light impulses striking the eye, the ear's holds all receivable sound waves striking the ear, and the pressure receptor's holds all tactile sensations on the skin.

Labels applied to memory at this early stage reflect the notion that information is still in a relatively "original" form—*iconic memory* for visual images, *echoic memory* for auditory impressions, and *tactile* or *haptic memory* for touch sensations. The storage of this information is only momentary, perhaps no longer than half a second for visual stimuli before the impression dissipates. Auditory information apparently can last as long as one to two seconds before decaying (Klahr & Wallace, 1976, p. 174). During this momentary retention of stimuli impressions, an interchange occurs between sensory memory and long-term memory (indicated by the lines labeled *a* in Figure 12.1). To clarify the nature of this interchange, we need to take a brief look at the contents of long-term memory.

In this version of information processing, long-term memory is the storage location of ideas or *mental constructions* derived from the person's past experiences. This collection of ideas is the person's *knowledge base*. At each of the three stages of short-term memory, an interchange or transaction (*a*, *b*, and *c* in Figure 12.1) takes place between the particular short-term stage and long-term memory. The transaction both (1) informs pertinent portions of long-term memory of the nature of the information received at that juncture and (2) permits long-term memory to tell that particular short-term stage which aspects of the stimuli to filter out and which to send along to the next stage. We assume that interchange *a* results in sensory memory identifying certain gross characteristics of the stimuli—such as distinguishing figure from ground—and sending the resulting crudely defined information to the next step along the pathway. An example of distinguishing figure from ground could be separating the outline of a nearby person from the pattern of colors produced by the foliage and buildings behind the person. In the auditory mode it could be separating the sound of a voice from the background sounds of birds chirping, leaves rustling, and a truck rumbling by.

Encoding   The second stage is that of *encoding* or recasting the sensory-memory information into a form that can be used at the third stage. This notion of *encoding* reflects a key assumption made in information-processing theory—that sense impressions are not manipulated or stored in memory in their original form. Instead, impressions are translated into codes, into symbols or *representations* suitable for manipulation by the nervous system. At this second stage of our model, such encoding is accomplished through transaction *b* with long-term memory, in which instructions are issued by long-term memory for how the stimulus information from stage 1 should be symbolized for use at stage 3. As shown in Figure 12.1, stage 2 short-term memory is still divided according to the sense modalities in which the stimuli were originally received. Visual, auditory, and haptic memories are still separated from each other. Stage 2 memory is assumed to last only a brief time and to be of very limited capacity, unable to hold much information, with auditory capacity perhaps greater than visual capacity (Broadbent, 1970).

Semantic Memory   The third stage is called *semantic* short-term memory because at this point the coded materials from the three channels of stage 2 are combined and compared to selected contents of long-term memory to yield meaning (transaction *c*). Stage 3, in effect, is that of *perceptual recognition,* where the person identifies the information for what it represents in terms of her memory (long term) of past experiences. In conscious thought, this is the "Aha!" juncture at which she discovers "So that's what it is!"

Studies of how much information people are able to keep immediately in mind—that is, to maintain in semantic short-term memory—firmly suggest that the average adult can hold seven "chunks" of information at one time, although some people can manage as many as nine chunks while others can manage no more than five or six (G. A. Miller, 1956). A *chunk* can be defined as "a portion of a person's knowledge base that is always activated and deactivated as a unit" (Kail & Bisanz, 1982, p. 59). A chunk may be either simple, such as a specific person's name, or it can be complex, such as the concept *television-receiver's-tuning-system* that may, in a single phrase, represent an electronic engineer's entire knowledge of the network of elements that comprise the tuning mechanism of a television receiver.

In speaking of seven chunks, it's important to recognize a distinction between immediate *memory* and immediate *consciousness*. Experiments conducted by S. Sternberg (1969) have suggested that while an individual can immediately recall seven chunks of information, the amount he or she is consciously using in a given instant is more likely to be a single unit or chunk.

Long-Term Memory

I am assuming that long-term memory has two principal functions: (1) directing the operation of the entire information-processing system and (2) storing coded material derived from the person's past experiences. While short-term memory has very limited capacity, long-term memory can apparently accommodate infinite amounts of material. And, as implied in their names, short-term memory retains material very briefly, while long-term memory may retain material indefinitely.

In this version of information processing, I am proposing that coded material stored in memory is of several sorts—single events or episodes, goals, relationships (including concepts and processes), and affects. A *single event* is the memory trace about a specific person or object from a particular incident in the past. E. Tulving (1972) labeled this sort of memory *episodic* to indicate that it is a kind of knowledge specific to a given context, that is, knowledge of how things appeared and when they happened. He contrasted episodic knowledge with what he called *semantic* memories, which consist of more generalized instruments of thought, such as concepts and processes that are not limited to one place or time.

A *goal* is something the individual seeks to accomplish. Goals are the motivational components of information processing. They energize the individual to focus attention on particular facets of the environment and to draw from long-term memory particular contents for interpreting sense impressions.

A *relationship* is a connection between one item in memory and another. Relationships may be of various types. One of the most important is that of concepts, with *concept* being defined as an abstraction of specified characteristics that are shared by individual people, objects, or incidents from the past. Typically a label is attached to the abstraction. For example, *square, red, weather, weaponry, religious,* and *theory* are concept labels. Another relationship is the comparison of one concept with another. For example, the relationship between the concepts *square* and *circle* is defined by the ways in which square and circle are both alike and unalike. (While I define concepts as relationships, some writers prefer to categorize concepts as *associations* rather than relationships and to reserve the term *relationship* for the usages below.)

Some relationships can be called causal because the individual assumes that one concept is the producer of another—as when the idea of heat under a pan of water produces the idea of boiled water. Many causal relationships are complex, with more than one prior condition (the assumed cause) combining to produce a resulting condition (the assumed effect). The idea of how long it will take water to boil can be conditioned by ideas of the amount of water, the water's original temperature, the degree of heat, the heat source, the shape of the pan, atmospheric pressure, and more.

A *process* is a kind of procedural knowledge—a series of steps performed to accomplish some end. Examples of processes are the series of operations required for multiplying 27 by 64, for defining *hypothesis,* for diagraming a sentence, for reading a map, and for driving a car.

Affects are emotions, as suggested by such words as *anger, pity, affection, frustration, attraction,* and *disappointment.* In long-term memory some type of affect or emotional tone is often associated with events, goals, and relationships.

The Structure of Long-Term Memory Of particular interest to information-processing theorists is the anatomy of long-term memory. What are the structural components of memory and how are they interlinked? One popular suggestion is that long-term memory is organized something like a fishnet, with each node or intersection where the strands are knotted together representing an individual memory trace, such as an event or concept. The multiple strands extending out from the node are the links to other nodes; that is, the strands lead to other events or concepts that the person associates with the memory trace at the original node. The links between some nodes are stronger than between others, meaning that communication across the strong linkages is more frequent and more rapid than between weak linkages. In other words, strong links represent close associations between memories, whereas weak links represent distant associations, ones more difficult to conceive. Obviously such a memory network is infinitely more complex than a simple fishnet in order to account for the intricacies of human thought (Anderson, 1983).

Let us look again at the interactions between long-term memory and the three stages of short-term memory. One of the most important interactions is that of matching the stimuli received from the environment with the contents of long-term memory. In particular, perceptual recognition results when the newly coded material from short-term stage 3 matches identical or similar coded material in the long-term memory network. In this theory, the person "understands" the sensory input or "sees what it means" by accomplishing a satisfactory match. In other words, the person assigns a "meaning" from long-term memory to each new recognizable sensory encounter with the environment.

I am suggesting as well that active decision making and problem solving are carried out through transactions between semantic short-term memory and long-term memory. Not only is information from the environment entered into semantic short-term memory, but material from long-term memory (incidents, goals, relationships, affects) is also inserted into semantic short-term memory and used there. Since short-term memory has such a limited capacity, it is necessary during problem solving for the contents of short-term memory to be constantly changing. Thus there is a great flow of extremely rapid transactions going on all the time, producing the "stream of consciousness" of the person's awareness.

Influences on Long-Term Memory   The source of most, if not all, of the contents of long-term memory is the person's earlier experiences. This is hardly a surprise, for it accords with the commonsense notion that what people remember is what they have learned in the past. But not so apparent is the discovery from experimental studies that the material entered into memory may be distorted during the encoding and storing activities, that is, during the *memory-construction* process. People who hear or read a series of sentences relating to an incident do not simply memorize the sentences. Instead, they tend to abstract the main ideas conveyed in the sentences, and they store this abstracted or more economical version in long-term memory, often omitting some of the original details or the exact phrasing of the incident. Furthermore, ideas already in memory about a given topic will influence how coded traces of a new experience are constructed and stored. For example, hearing about possible dishonesty in public office may well be interpreted and stored differently if the incident is said to involve George Washington or Abraham Lincoln than if it is said to involve some other president whose reputation is less admirable. In effect, new information tends to be coded and stored in ways that make it accord with logic, with one's emotions, and with the contents of one's current knowledge system.

In addition, the coded traces of experiences—called *representations*— may not reside in the long-term state in their original condition but, rather, may be revised in various ways. With the passing of time, or at the moment the memory is retrieved, the memory may be altered by new experiences that have entered the knowledge system since the original memory was recorded, thereby causing one's recollection to differ from the originally stored representation. The new experiences may have distorted the original memory by casting doubt on its logic, by making it more elaborate, by simplifying it so as to fit a stereotyped pattern, or by coloring it with emotions of pleasure or distaste (Dooling & Christiaansen, 1977; Klatzky, 1980, pp. 301–305; Loftus, 1975).

The combined short-term and long-term memory components make up the human knowledge system. Kail and Bisanz concluded that:

> Despite discrepancies among various theories, most theorists generally agree on the general properties of the human knowledge system. (A) There are, theoretically, no limits on the quantity of knowledge that can be stored. (B) Knowledge is not lost; "forgetting" reflects an inability to access knowledge. (C) Most knowledge can be accessed by multiple routes and multiple cues, reflecting the fact that knowledge is rich in

interconnecting links. (D) Knowledge is characterized by a weak form of *cognitive economy:* not all of one's knowledge about concept X need be associated directly with X. . . . Instead, some of this knowledge is available only indirectly, via inference. (E) A process can operate on itself as well on other representations and processes (1982, p. 50).

The System's Behavioral Output

After having described short-term and long-term memory, let's look at the final link in the information-processing chain, that of behavioral output, such as speaking to a classmate, climbing stairs, stepping on the car's brake pedal, writing a homework assignment, and the like. Each decision made in semantic short-term memory elicits from long-term memory coded directions for activating the appropriate muscles. These coded directions are transmitted through the efferent nerve system to the proper muscle locations to perform the behavior. The action completes the information-processing cycle.

Although overt action has thus been described as the final link in the processing chain, it should be apparent that overt action does not have to occur in order for cognitive development to take place. As our own introspection informs us, we can record events in memory, acquire new concepts, and attach different emotions to memories simply by "thinking things over" or "coming to a conclusion" or "changing our mind" without displaying this in an observable act. However, eventually such development will be reflected in the ways we act on the world.

The Central Phenomena—Attention, Perception, and Memory

As perhaps can be inferred from the foregoing discussion, information-processing theories are designed particularly to explain relationships among a trio of phenomena of traditional interest in psychology, those of attention, perception, and memory.

In regard to *attention,* theorists have attempted to account for several factors studied by psychologists for more than a century, from the time of William James and even earlier (James, 1890, pp. 402–404). James and others observed that attention is a purposeful operation, so that people actively seek stimuli rather than only passively record impressions imposed on them by the environment. Furthermore, people seek selectively. They focus on certain items for conscious analysis while ignoring others. Such selectivity is necessary because the human attention-directing mechanism has limited capacity and apparently can operate on only one item at a time rather than on several simultaneously. To account for such observations as these, theorists have proposed that the information-processing mechanism includes (1) filters to keep the system from being overloaded and (2) special storage provisions, as suggested at the initial stages of short-term memory, to extend the time available for extracting information from relatively short-lived inputs (Horton & Turnage, 1976, p. 205). Theorists have also proposed cycles of interaction between short-term and long-term memory in order to explain how a person's goals help filter stimuli and how an individual assigns meaning to impressions received from the sense organs.

The phenomenon of *perception,* in which the act of attention is imbedded, typically involves all the steps of the information-processing chain from the environmental stimuli through the stage of semantic short-term memory of Figure 12.1. Different theorists have proposed different stages in the process of perception, with some offering more stages and some fewer than the ones in the version we are using here. Some theorists have hypothesized that the most significant stage in perception occurs at the sense organ itself—at the eye, the ear, or skin. Others have proposed that the most significant stage is in the brain at the semantic-memory level. In short, a variety of theories of perception exist, with no one of them yet earning general acceptance within the information-processing community (Uttal, 1981, pp. 986–987).

As for *memory,* some writers have sought to explain its complex operations by hypothesizing the existence of such subdivisions as short-term and long-term memory and by identifying a variety of factors affecting the storage and retrieval of information. Others have rejected the notion of such components as short- and long-term memory and speak instead of different depths or levels of processing (Craik & Lockhart, 1972). In effect, there continues to be a diversity of notions about how memory operates.

An Example of the System in Operation

To illustrate how our sample theory can be used to interpret everyday behavior, let's apply the theory's elements to analyze our fictitious eighteen-year-old's trip to a city 300 kilometers away.

As the young woman walks through the business district of her home town, her long-term memory alerts the three stages of her short-term memory to her general goal—to take the trip—as well as to the steps of a process or *strategy* for achieving the goal. This strategy, constructed from her experiences in past years and stored in long-term memory, consists of (1) locating a map of the area, (2) identifying on the map alternative routes to the city, and (3) comparing the desirability of the various routes by testing the alternatives against a series of criteria, including those of distance to travel, road conditions, amount of traffic, safety, attractiveness of the scenery, and others. As she strolls along the street under the influence of this "mental set," she scans the environment for sources of road maps. Her visual attention is caught by a travel agency sign on a store window. For this girl at this moment, that particular sign is a "salient stimulus" in the environment because it matches one of the relationships she has stored in long-term memory (travel agency = maps and road information). Her decision to enter the agency (a decision reached in semantic short-term memory) evokes from long-term memory sequences of operations that cause her efferent nerve system to order the muscular movements that allow her to walk into the shop.

Another process now drawn from long-term into short-term memory starts her scanning the walls to locate sensory stimuli to match the concept of *road map* whose defining features, stored in long-term memory, have now been entered into her short-term memory. By the time she scans halfway across the back wall, she finds the desired match. This accomplishment evokes from long-term memory a process that directs her muscles to transport her to the wall to pick up the map. Next, her inspection of the map is guided by a map-analysis process that has just been transferred into short-term memory from long-term memory. The map-analysis process or strategy, constructed in the past from her experiences in reading maps, is composed of a series of steps that include locating the map legend that defines symbols for types of roads, distances, directions of the compass, and cities and towns. As an aid in visually following the alternative routes on the map, the girl adds another modality by tracing each route with her right index finger. At the same time she listens to an employee of the travel agency answer the question she has asked about traffic conditions on the different routes. She is, in effect, simultaneously receiving visual, haptic, and auditory input that is being encoded into semantic short-term memory where it will contribute to her decision about which route to follow.

At this point we leave the young woman, on the assumption that this brief and admittedly simplified analysis has illustrated how incidents from everyday life can be interpreted with one version of the information-processing perspective. We are now prepared to consider the principal methods of inquiry that have led to such theorizing.

MODES OF INVESTIGATION

Classical information-processing theorists have been employing two modes of investigation for generating and refining their proposals.

The first mode involves using human subjects in experiments designed to answer questions about such matters as how patterns of reflected light stimulate receptor nerves in the eyes, what number of chunks of information can be accommodated in short-term memory, and how material from short-term memory is encoded for storage in long-term memory.

The second mode, which utilizes information from the first mode's experiments, involves employing electronic computers to simulate human mental operations. Theorists working in this rapidly growing field of *artificial intelligence* propose that if they can program a computer to produce the same sorts of solutions to problems that a human would produce, they will have taken a significant step toward understanding human thought processes. In making such a proposal, they are assuming that if a computer program is given the same problem-solving input as a human and the computer produces the same output as the human, then the program may well contain the same sorts of components and processing steps as those operating in the human nervous system.

In applying this same line of logic to explaining children's intellectual development, psychologists face two tasks: (1) devising a series of computer programs so that each program accurately simulates children's thinking processes at a particular stage of mental growth and (2) explaining the means by which the program at one stage can be transformed into the next program in the series. So far, theorists designing computer programs to represent children's thinking processes have been more successful with the first of these tasks than with the second. For example, D. Klahr and J. G. Wallace (1976) managed to prepare what they judged to be rather satisfactory computer simulations of Piagetian preoperational and concrete operations substages for the task areas of class inclusion, conservation, and transitivity. However, the two investigators admitted to being far less successful in fashioning an adequate explanation of how a child makes the transition from preoperational to concrete operations thinking. They decided that more experimentation was needed.

With this overview of classical information-processing models as a foundation, we next consider revisions of such theory that are intended to solve problems encountered with the classical versions.

MODIFICATIONS OF CLASSICAL THEORY

Most critics of information-processing models have not faulted the standard theory for being entirely wrong-headed but, rather, for being incomplete and thereby distorting the picture of human development. My purpose in this section is to describe (a) refinements of classical information-processing theory proposed since the mid-1970s and (b) further conditions of human experience that need to be recognized in future models if they are adequately to account for cognitive development. The discussion is organized around two questions: (1) What revisions of the original information-processing model have appeared in recent times? (2) What suggestions for the improvement of information-processing theory can be derived from comparing computers and humans?

Recent Refinements of Classical Theory

B. J. Zimmerman (1983, p. 3) has illustrated one form of disenchantment with early cybernetic (electronic computer) models by noting that "Neisser's 1967 book, *Cognitive Psychology,* was a widely read, generally sympathetic description of the cybernetic version of information processing. However, in his 1976 text, significantly entitled *Cognition and Reality,* Neisser renounced the utility of cybernetic models of human thought because of their limited capacity to describe the complex reciprocal relationship between people and their proximal environment." Thus, to render information-processing theory sensitive to different environmental conditions, revised models need to portray contexts far more precisely than the general provision of "The External Environment" in Figure 12.1.

Further shortcomings of classical theory have been cited by M. H. Ashcraft (1989, p. 64) in relation to the following seven current themes of cognitive psychology. Each theme in some way will either alter the patterning of the cognitive functions pictured in Figure 12.1 or will require an elaboration of how those functions operate.

1. *Attention.* Whereas the phenomenon of attention was not entirely ignored in standard models, critics charged that its importance was not adequately recognized in most early versions of the theory. That is, the key role of attention in the transfer of information from sensory memory to short-term working memory and attention's essential function in any conscious or partly conscious mental operation need to be featured more prominently.

2. *The Conscious to Automatic Dimension.* An analysis of the amount of conscious effort needed to perform a given mental act suggests that mental processes can be aligned along a scale ranging from *highly conscious* at one end to *entirely automatic* or nonconscious at the other. Actions that are simple and have been practiced frequently become automatic, in the sense that no intentional effort is required to carry them out. For example, when people are first learning to drive a car, they need to concentrate on each movement in the sequence of sensorimotor acts that lead from turning on the ignition to finally guiding the auto through traffic. For the experienced driver, this series of decisions becomes essentially nonconscious. If an information-processing theory is to be com-

plete, it needs to include such a conscious-to-automatic dimension among its features.

3. *Serial and Parallel Processing.* When a person is learning something new or working on a complex problem, information is apparently processed serially, that is, step after step. But in the case of well-practiced, simpler tasks, two or more acts may be carried out in parallel, as in the case of a motorist listening to the radio or talking with a companion while driving down the highway. Classical models of information processing tended to picture all cognitive and motor activity as serial.

4. *Data-Driven versus Conceptually Driven Processes.* In earlier chapters we met both empiricists and structuralists. Empiricists (Skinner, contextualists) propose that what we come to understand is determined primarily by the environment, that is, by the nature of the events people witness. Such a process of understanding can be labeled *data driven.* In contrast, structuralists (Piaget, Case, Mounoud) emphasize the importance of people's mental templates in fashioning the understandings derived from environmental encounters; people impose meanings on events they witness, so their understandings are *conceptually driven.* Ashcraft proposes that both of these processes operate in the cognitive system, with the particular relationship between a stimulus and the person's memory structures determining which of the processes dominates at a given moment.

    Whereas data-driven processes are assisted very little, if at all, by already-known information, conceptually driven processes are those that rely heavily on such information. Thus, a conceptually driven process uses the information already in memory, and whatever expectations are present in the situation, to perform the task; data-driven processes use only the stimulus information (Ashcraft, 1989, p. 64).

    Information-processing theories can profitably incorporate this data-driven versus conceptually driven dimension among their components.

5. *Knowledge Representation.* As noted earlier, an issue still far from being resolved is the question of how knowledge is stored in long-term memory. Various answers to this question continue to be offered by different theorists without a consensus being achieved. One conception is Tulving's (1972) division of memories into episodic and semantic knowledge. Another is J. R. Anderson's

(1983) division of mental storage into *declarative memory* (events, facts, concepts—the nature of things) and *production memory* (procedural knowledge, operations—how to do things). It seems clear that any adequate version of information processing needs to include some such conception of knowledge representation.

6. *Tacit Knowledge and Inference.* Another matter given too little attention in early models is the issue of how a person's tacit knowledge (the backlog of information already available in long-term memory) leads to inferences that embellish the meaning derived from environmental stimuli. That is, an explanation of how people's systems of tacit knowledge and inference operate to determine their understandings can usefully be inserted into versions of information processing.

7. *Metacognition.* The final item in Ashcraft's list is metacognition— our self-awareness and monitoring of how our cognitive system operates. This factor was essentially overlooked in much of the early theorizing about information processing.

With Ashcraft's seven updated features in mind, we can now consider two ways they can be used to elucidate the nature of children's cognitive development. First, they can alter the method of diagraming an information-processing model. Second, they can be applied in our estimating the manner in which children's cognitive processes develop over the years.

Diagraming Additional Components

The task of recasting information-processing models into an refurbished graphic form requires a somewhat different approach than that used in Figure 12.1. One way this might be attempted is shown in Figure 12.2. The first obvious feature of this approach is that a single static diagram is insufficient to illustrate a system that varies in relation to different environmental contexts, different points along a conscious–automatic dimension, and different patterns of tacit knowledge. At least two diagrams are needed to suggest how such variables can affect cognitive processes. Even more diagrams that picture additional combinations of the variables would be even better. The two diagrams in Figure 12.2 can properly be accompanied by the following kind of explanation in order to clarify the conditions that distinguish incident A from incident B:

> Four-year-old Daphne is taken by her father for her first visit to the zoo, where they buy popcorn that Daphne munches as they walk from one exhibit to another. *(Incident A)* At the giraffes' enclosure, Daphne stops

INCIDENT A

INCIDENT B

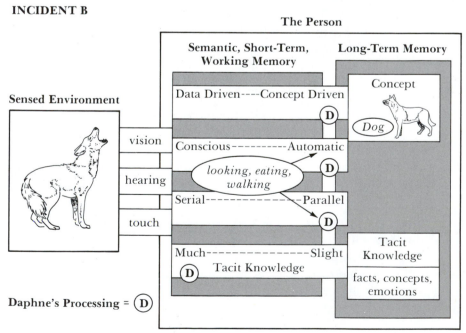

Figure 12.2 A Version of a Child's Information-Processing System During a Visit to the Zoo

eating popcorn to stand and stare at a mother giraffe and her offspring. Daphne asks, "What's that thing?" Her father explains, "It's a giraffe — from Africa." The girl inspects the tall animal from head to foot. Her father asks, "Didn't you ever see one in a picture book?" Daphne shakes her head and continues staring. *(Incident B)* Later, as she and her father come to an enclosure labeled *Coyote,* Daphne glances at the two animals standing beside a tree and comments between bites of popcorn, "Like Ranger." Ranger is the name of the German shepherd dog that lives across the street from Daphne's home. This time, rather than stopping to stare at the animals, Daphne continues walking and consuming popcorn.

To interpret the child's behavior in terms of Figure 12.2, we can speculate that the processing of the giraffe encounter (incident A) was strongly data driven, required much conscious attention, was serial (Daphne stopped eating and walking as she inspected the giraffes), and was unembellished by tacit knowledge because Daphne had no readily applicable concept in memory to apply to such a towering, long-necked, mottled creature. In contrast, the coyote encounter (incident B) was more conceptually driven (Daphne had a readily available concept into which the stimulus fit), was more automatic (required little conscious attention because the animal seemed so familiar), was bolstered by tacit knowledge (her experience with Ranger's characteristics), and thus enabled Daphne to engage in parallel processing (she could simultaneously perceive the animal and continue walking and eating popcorn). Therefore, compared to the graphic model in Figure 12.1, the revised form of diagraming of Figure 12.2 more adequately reflects the way differences in environmental stimuli can influence how information is processed.

Child Development and the Seven Themes

Ashcraft's themes can also be used for answering the question, As children grow up, what is it that develops? In response, we can suggest that development from infancy through adolescence is marked by an increase in the proportion of mental and psychomotor operations that are (1) automatic rather than conscious, (2) processed in parallel rather than serially, and (3) conceptually driven rather than data driven. Furthermore, as the years advance, (4) children's tacit knowledge expands so they can draw increasingly complex and accurate inferences, (5) their metacognition skills become more elaborate, and (6) knowledge in long-term memory is represented in more refined, complicated patterns. Children also (7) gain greater conscious control over directing their attention.

Computers and People Compared

In addition to Ashcraft's themes, other pertinent features of information-processing models can be identified by comparing characteristics of computers and of humans. Such an exercise can help suggest (1) what cautions should be observed in interpreting human cognition in terms of computer operations and (2) what changes in computer hardware and software might more adequately simulate the ways children think.

One simple way such comparisons can be pursued is shown in Table 12.1, which contrasts present-day computers and humans on a series of characteristics. While it is apparent that computers and people can be compared along far more dimensions than those listed in Table 12.1, for our present purpose these twelve characteristics should suffice. The twelve are ones that seem to me particularly significant from the viewpoint of basing a theory of children's cognition on a cybernetic model.

Researchers in the field of artificial intelligence use such comparisons as the above in their efforts to produce computer simulations that more adequately mirror human thinking. Hence, as advances in these efforts are achieved, information-processing theories that rely on a cybernetic design can be expected to represent human thought more adequately. But even before more sophisticated computers are created, child development theorists who are guided by computer designs when creating models of children's cognitive functions can properly extend their theories beyond the confines of existing computer designs in order to accommodate for such differences between machines and people as shown in Table 12.1.

Perhaps the most dramatic shortcoming of existing cybernetic models as analogues of child thought is found in the final item in the table—*Operating Condition over the Unit's Lifetime.* Cybernetic models fail to show how sensorimotor and cognitive abilities systematically change with the passing of time. In effect, computer simulations—at least at present—are not developmental. Thus more than just the elements contained in cybernetic models is required for theories of child development so as to account for the advances from infancy through adolescence in the characteristics depicted in Table 12.1. That is, extensions beyond computer designs are needed to explain changes in children's sources of stimulation, mobility, standardization (extent of individual differences), memory, sources of processing "programs," and the rest.

In summary, then, comparing computers and humans can be useful for identifying (1) human characteristics that designers of computers can seek to simulate in their cybernetic models and (2) ways that human development theories based on cybernetic analogues need to be extended to reconcile the differences between computers and people.

Table 12.1 Comparison of Computers and People

The Computer	*The Person*
Source of Stimulation	
Waits for environmental input.	Searches the environment for input and also has input imposed by the environment.
Mobility	
Is stationary, cannot move itself except when built in a movable robot form, and even then the flexibility and adaptability of its movements are quite limited.	Is self-moving (auto-mobile), can view environments from various perspectives; movements are highly flexible and adaptable.
Level of Standardization	
Highly standardized. Within a given type of computer, the structure and function of all members of that type are essentially identical. The influence of typical environmental conditions (temperature, length of use, skills of the operator) on the function of the computer is quite limited. Thus knowing the traits of one member of that type permits highly reliable predictions about the operation of any other member. A computer's operation is highly similar in different contexts.	Standardization is limited to those characteristics that comprise "human nature" at any stage of development. Such human nature permits marked variability in how one member of the species functions compared to another member. Even monozygotic twins, who start off with identical genetic potential, soon differ from each other as a consequence of varying environmental forces in their lives. Thus knowing the characteristics of one member of the species permits no more than gross, somewhat unreliable predictions of specific characteristics of another member, even when the two members are the same chronological age. And a given individual's functions often vary from one context to another.
Condition of Memory	
Static, stationary, retains input in precisely the state it was received.	Active, alters stored material as the result of new input, of alterations in the biological structure, and of the passage of time.
Nature of Programs for Processing Data	
Stable—programs remain in the same form in which they were originally prepared. Except in	Active—processing continually reconstructs "programs" in relation to input and to biological altera-

(continued)

Table 12.1   (*continued*)

The Computer	*The Person*
rare cases, programs must be changed by an outside operator.	tions in the organism. Person can be instructed by others in ways to alter programs. Person can also discover how to alter own programs.

Damageability

Can be damaged by accidents or wearing out of building materials so that memory is lost or processing goes awry.	Can be damaged by accidents or wearing out of "building materials" so that memory is lost or processing goes awry.

Maintenance of Structure

Can monitor the condition of many of its own functions and can report when certain components or functions go wrong. Usually cannot repair itself.	Can monitor the condition of many of its own functions and can report when certain components or functions go wrong. Often can repair self, though the repair process may require that certain usual functions cannot be performed for some period of time.

Maintenance of Operating Efficiency

Stops operating when capacity is overtaxed, but is not subject to boredom, lack of motivation, fatigue, and emotional disturbance.	Stops operating when capacity is overtaxed, and is highly subject to boredom, lack of motivation, fatigue, and emotional disturbance.

Scope or Range of Functions

Confined to a limited set of programs. Compared to humans, deficient in potential for creating novel solutions.	Extends to a far greater variety of "programs" than are available in present-day computers, particularly ones involving creativity in literature, science, social science, and the arts.

Processing Speed

Faster than people in performing routine computations and in storing large quantities of data in long-term memory.	Slower than computers in performing such functions as computing and storing large quantities of data in long-term memory.

Processing Complexity

Far more accurate than people in combining, comparing, calculating, summarizing, and reporting results for large quantities of data of a kind readily manipulated by rules of logic.	Far more competent than computers in manipulating variables that have not been clearly defined or predicted ahead of time and whose weightings (degrees of importance for arriving at a solution) have not been specified. (These

Table 12.1 (*continued*)

The Computer	The Person
	cognitive functions are sometimes referred to as intuiting, estimating, guessing, imagining, and envisioning.).
Operating Condition over the Unit's Lifetime	
Essentially constant, barring relatively rare breakdowns of the machine's hardware components or faults that humans have built into software, either unintentionally (programming errors) or intentionally (viruses).	Very inefficient at the beginning. Efficiency typically improves markedly over the first two or three decades, then is likely to decrease for some functions and remain constant or gradually increase for others over the next three decades or so, and finally during the sixth and seventh decades will deteriorate in varied degrees for different individuals.

INFORMATION PROCESSING AND DEVELOPMENT

By conducting experiments with children at different age levels and by devising additional computer simulations, investigators in recent years have been furnishing a rapidly growing quantity of data about changes that occur in human information processing as people advance in age. Let's now look at examples of the kinds of data resulting from such studies. We begin by focusing (1) on sensory intake and short-term memory, (2) on long-term memory, and (3) on interactions between components of short-term and long-term memory.

Sensory Intake and Short-Term Memory

One notable difference between the infant and the older child concerns elements in the environment to which children attend.

A strong environmental characteristic for attracting attention is that of *novelty,* of things out of the ordinary. The infant, with such a limited store of experience with the world, can be expected to find novelty in events that are quite usual to the more experienced older child. Thus the younger child pays attention to events the older child ignores because such events are so ordinary for the older one.

> We see in the behavior of the developing infant that many aspects of attention . . . involve largely automatic reactions to rather simple characteristics. That is, the early responses of infants can be accounted for by assuming the infant is automatically "captured" by sensory input to a greater degree than is an older child or an adult. As the infant develops through childhood to adulthood, he seems to be less and less a "captive" of sensory stimulation and more and more a "capturer" of sensory input (Horton & Turnage, 1976, p. 203).

In brief, the growing child increasingly sets his or her own goals and then purposely seeks out situations in which to invest attention in order to achieve the goals. J. F. Mackworth divided this process of the development of attention into three main stages. At the first stage the very young infant focuses on patterns or objects in his visual and auditory environment, attending to them frequently and at great length, since

> His task at this time is to construct internal models of the environment, and everything that he sees is new. Throughout life he will continue to construct such models, but as he grows older his attention is devoted more to comparing new experiences with already stored models. Since the neonate has no such stored models, he must spend a great deal of time on assimilating the stimulus, and therefore he shows little or no habituation (1976, p. 145).

The second of Mackworth's major stages extends from around age 1 until 4 or 5. It consists of the child's beginning to show acquaintance with, or *habituation* to, patterns she has seen or heard before and to select for study those patterns that exhibit novelty. However, at this stage the child may center attention chiefly on a few features on which to base a decision and may overlook other features that would contribute to a more accurate judgment about the significance of the observation. E. Vurpillot (1976, p. 231) noted that the young child's responses to what he observes are often fluctuating and contradictory from one moment to the next "because he focuses his attention first on one detail, then on another. . . . Thus, his greatest weakness lies in an absence of coordination between all the cues he is capable of perceiving and the rules he is capable of using."

At the third stage, the older child or adolescent achieves better cognitive control over attention. She is not so hasty as the young one and can search a display until she acquires all the needed information. She is also better at selecting important details, at altering judgment on the basis of feedback, at abstracting a rule from a sequence of events, and at changing the rule if necessary.

In addition to the matter of how children's ways of attending change with time, another developmental factor in the early phase of processing appears to be the capacity of short-term memory. In discussing the model pictured in Figure 12.1, I proposed that semantic short-term memory in the average adult can accommodate seven chunks of information. Or, stated another way, the average adult has an *apprehension span* of seven chunks, a capacity that apparently was not present at birth but, instead, evolved during the years of childhood. According to some studies, at eighteen months the average child's span is one chunk, a capacity that by age 5 appears to have increased to four chunks, then to five chunks a year or so later, and finally to seven by adolescence. Such changes in short-term memory capacity could help account for the differences in children's thinking and acting at different age levels. For example, observations of children between ages 1 and 2 show that they commonly employ a single word to represent a set of ideas (the phenomenon of *holophrasis*) an older child would describe in several words. Whereas the six-year-old might say, "Mother's bringing the cake out now," the eighteen-month-old is likely to say only "mom" or "cay" in the same situation. S. Farnham-Kiggory (1972, p. 62) speculated that "the one chunk span of the eighteen-month-old may be the basic factor in his production of holophrases."

However, not only the number of chunks a child can accommodate but other factors as well contribute to the improved operation of short-term memory with increasing age. One such factor is the structure of the chunks. A chunk that is a concept—such as *transportation*—carries a broader range of meaning by encompassing more of the world's phenomena than does a chunk that represents only a single event or fact—such as *mother's blue dress*. A chunk that represents an entire operation or process, such as the sequence of steps involved in mounting a bicycle and riding it along a winding path, is more encompassing than a chunk that represents only the licking of a postage stamp. Thus, according to one explanation of the contents of short-term memory, a chain consisting of actions that have been practiced so thoroughly that they come to compose an automatic process can be considered a single chunk since when the first action or idea in the chain appears in short-term memory it can trigger the rest of the sequence without the individual having to apprehend—that is, intentionally have to "think about"—the subsequent links in the process. And when an entire chain can be represented as a single chunk, the remaining spaces in short-term memory are available for other chunks of information. According to the theory, this greater complexity of the chunks in the older child's repertoire of memories helps her short-term memory function more efficiently than the younger child's.

The capacity of a child's processing system may also influence what the child attends to in the environment. Infants are attracted by simpler stimuli, such as simpler geometric forms, than are older children because, perhaps, infants lack the capacity to manage complex forms in immediate memory. However, the issue of whether, and how much, the capacity of short-term memory increases with age is neither simple nor settled. Certain investigators have proposed that older children's superiority to younger ones in performance that depends on memory does not result from any larger short-term capacity but rather from the older child's greater fund of knowledge in long-term memory and from his greater facility in using such mnemonic strategies as rehearsal and the clustering of items to be remembered (Chi, 1976, p. 559).

Development of Long-Term Memory

While changes in the sense organs and in short-term memory account for a portion of the age differences in information processing, by far the largest part of the differences is caused by changes in long-term memory. The changes are apparently of two general types: (1) alterations in the nerve structures as determined by genetically timed growth processes and (2) changes in the knowledge base or contents of memory as the result of experience. It is likely that these two types are not independent but that they interact. In other words, the gradual maturation of nerve tissues and changes in their patterning provide increasing potential for the individual to profit from interactions with the environment. And, in turn, as time passes, the kinds of memories or knowledge the person accumulates as a result of experiences may hasten or retard the maturation of the electrochemical structures of the nervous system.

Perhaps the most obvious developmental difference between the older and younger child's knowledge base is the quantity of contents stored there, available for interpreting environmental stimuli and for problem solving. The typical older child has compiled a greater number of memory traces (nodes) of events and relationships as the result of more years of experience and a more mature nervous system.

Besides having a greater fund of items in their knowledge base, older children have a greater number of associations between the items or nodes than do younger ones. For example, the typical older child recognizes more ways that the concepts *bucket, string, food, sea,* and *tuna* can be connected than does the younger child. In a sense, the young child's knowledge base is like a small, very loosely woven fabric, knit with only a few strands of memory traces and with the simplest of stitches. In contrast, the adolescent's long-term memory is more like a widespread fabric of intricately interwoven strands forming complex patterns. And it is both the number of items and their patterning of connections that determine how complex a chunk of knowledge will be when it is summoned for action into semantic short-term memory. For instance, a chunk identified by the label *arithmetic* encompasses a great number of items linked in complex patterns in the knowledge base of the typical adolescent, but the chunk *arithmetic* has far fewer items with simple links in the long-term memory of a typical six-year-old.

Furthermore, the processes (sequences of steps for accomplishing a goal) that a child has available in his knowledge base increase in both number and sophistication with advancing age. For instance, if children are asked to memorize a telephone number or a list of street names, the younger ones are likely to depend on only one strategy, such as *rehearsal* (saying the number or list over and over). However, as J. H. Flavell (1977, p. 195) has noted, "rehearsal is by no means the most effective mnemonic strategy available to a sophisticated and resourceful information processor." Adolescents will not only rehearse the items but will *cluster* or *group* them according to some common factor, such as their ordinal or alphabetical sequence. Adolescents may also intentionally *associate* the items with others already in memory, such as comparing the phone number to their own phone number or to a similar number from history, for example, 1492 or 1776 or 1945.

Besides the increase in the variety of mnemonic techniques used, the way a given technique is used also changes as children grow older. For instance, in rehearsing a sequence of items to recall later, children in the lower primary school grades will repeat each new item several times, but they usually do not connect that item with others during the rehearsal process. In contrast, adolescents cluster the items to be memorized into groups, attaching each new item of the sequence to a group, and then practice the group as a whole. In effect, older children are more conscious of their rehearsal technique and more actively fashion their approach in ways that improve the storage and later recall of the information (Ornstein & Naus, 1978). Their superior ability to recall material may thus be caused to a great extent by their imposing some kind of organization on the material when it is first met, whereas younger children do not tend to impose organization.

> Until the age of 7 or 8, children do not ordinarily elaborate and transform stimuli that are to be recalled later. Older children, 11 or 12 years of age, begin to rearrange items and construct additional relationships spontaneously, as adults commonly do (Paris, 1978, p. 153).

Furthermore, older children more readily recognize when a process learned in one setting will be suitable to apply in a different setting.

> There . . . appears to be an identifiable transitional stage during which the child can use a strategy under certain conditions or can learn to use it during a relatively brief training session. However, the strategy is not

used spontaneously nor does it show the characteristics of durability or generality. . . . It appears that learning, whether it be through spontaneous experience, informal education, or formal training, is critical in the development of the use of strategies (Hagen, Jongeward, Jr., & Kail, Jr., 1975, p. 73).

In summary, children's mnemonic strategies are not present in long-term memory at birth nor do they automatically appear full-blown at particular times of life; rather they are acquired through experience. The question of whether—and when—they are acquired appears to depend on both the maturity of the child's nervous system and the child's particular foundation of experiences from which to construct the strategies.

Interactions of System Components

As diagramed in Figures 12.1 and 12.2, the human information-processing system includes a constant series of transactions between the contents of long-term memory and the stages of short-term memory. Likewise, the stages of short-term memory constantly interact with each other. The complexity of these interactions is one of the most important factors that render theorizing about information processing so difficult. This assumed complexity can be illustrated by the *verbal-loop hypothesis,* which is an explanation of the changes in children's memory skills with the passing years. In the earlier explanation of Figure 12.1, I proposed that incoming sensations are not perceived or stored in their original form but instead are translated into some sort of code for perception and storage. This encoding likely involves different stages of translation and appears to vary according to the developmental level of a person's cognitive system. In particular, encoding appears related to a person's level of verbal ability, that is, the person's facility in using words. For instance, experiments in which people were asked to reproduce visual forms or to write digits they heard suggest that people perform this task by first translating the visual forms and digit sounds into words and then drawing the forms and digits under the guidance of the verbal descriptions they had stored in memory (Kaufman, 1974, p. 533). The path from input to output was mediated by a *verbal loop* in the middle. If this hypothesis is true, then it may help explain the superiority of older children over younger ones in reproducing visual and auditory stimuli—the older children have greater verbal facility for coding stimuli into words. But while the verbal-loop notion offers some insight into information processing, it is admittedly a crude and very incomplete explanation of the complex relationships that account for people's perceiving and storing and recalling information.

Another facet of the interaction of long-term and short-term memory is speed. Studies of information processing suggest that even when younger and older children both use the same mental procedures in problem solving, the older ones do so more rapidly. The reason is perhaps that the older child's longer experience with the steps of a strategy equips her to manipulate messages through the components of the system with greater facility than can the younger child.

Finally, we may summarize the main developmental characteristics of the human information-processing system by concluding that as age increases, processing increases in speed, in complexity, and in the integration of the system's parts. Furthermore, the data stored in long-term memory grow in quantity, variety, and complexity.

PRACTICAL APPLICATIONS

The most obvious applications of information-processing theory occur in teaching, where the information-processing perspective is helpful in two major ways.

First, information-processing models alert instructors to the stages by which children ingest information from the environment, commit it to memory, and retrieve it to solve problems. By understanding this sequence, a teacher can provide experiences that give learners practice with each stage. Teachers can also help children analyze their own acts of perceiving, storing, and recalling so that they gain greater conscious control over each stage of the process. For instance, children can be taught such memory-enhancing strategies as rehearsal, grouping items, key-word associations, acronyms and rhymes as mnemonic devices, and multiple associations. In other words, teachers can help children's metaperception and metamemory, helping them "learn how to learn."

The second application is one I have found particularly valuable, that of using the model as a guide to the diagnosis and treatment of children's learning difficulties. Diagnosis involves first identifying how each component of the model can be assessed through tests, observing the child in learning situations, and interviewing the child. These assessment techniques are used to determine how efficiently each component of the child's information-processing system is operating so that the location of the cause of the child's learning problem may be discovered. Are the child's sense organs faulty, causing either poor eyesight or distorted hearing? Is the child motivated to attend to learning stimuli; that is, does he have the goal of attending to learning stimuli? Was the stimulus encoded inaccurately or not recorded at all during the exchange between short-term and long-term memory (perhaps accounting for the reading disorder of dyslexia or the quantitative-comprehension disorder of dyscalculia)? Or was the stimulus perceived accurately but not stored in a manner that permits ready retrieval, so that when the child needs to recall the memory he cannot? Or have all of the foregoing steps been performed adequately, but a faulty system of sending messages to the muscles has prevented the child from accurately expressing in behavior the results of his learning, as is apparently the case with at least some children who suffer from cerebral palsy?

Once a decision is reached about which components in the system, or which relationships between components, are at fault then methods designed for treating those specific faults are applied. The methods may consist of special training procedures, medical interventions, or both (Thomas, 1989c).

In addition, research studies describing the pace at which various components of the information-processing system develop let parents and teachers know what sorts of learning children can reasonably be expected to exhibit at different stages of growth. For example, studies of this sort already suggest at what age children typically can learn a particular mnemonic technique, such as that of creating key words to associate with items to be learned. A growing number of research reports also illustrate ways of teaching such mnemonic techniques and of assessing how well children master them (Ashcraft, 1989, pp. 684–685; Brown & DeLoache, 1978; Chi, 1976; Hagen, Jongeward, Jr., & Kail, Jr., 1975).

INFORMATION-PROCESSING THEORY: AN ASSESSMENT

Once again, my assessment is guided by the nine criteria introduced in Chapter One.

I have rated the theory high on item 1 (the real world of children) because the information-processing model is founded on a growing body of empirical research with children, and computer simulations of child thought and behavior utilize such research for devising the relationships that make up the computer programs.

I have rated the model rather high on clarity (item 2) because those who write about information processing usually are careful to define their terms and illustrate their definitions with examples from research studies or observations of children. Nevertheless, there are a number of matters that are not clear. Yet the fault, I believe, lies not so much in the theorists' lack of skill in explicating what they believe as in the complexity of the problems they are attempting to solve. They typically admit that they have yet to find satisfactory solutions for numbers of the issues they face. So, to the extent that they have been unable to formulate adequate explanations of observed phenomena, their theorizing necessarily remains unclear. Examples of difficult areas are those of the structure and function of short- and long-term memory, of the process for encoding stimuli sensations, and of the way a person's goals arise to direct attention to selected aspects of the environment.

The theory appears to explain the past and predict the future (item 3) for the elements of child development on which its components focus—the sense organs, attention and perception, and operations of memory. When the present status of these components is assessed, the information-processing theorist is able to propose what has happened in children's past to account for the components' present status. Research studies performed under the guidance of information-processing models provide an expanding pool of information about the development of the sense organs, perception, and memory. As a consequence, predictions about children's

Information-Processing Theory

How well do I think the theory meets the standards?

The Standards	Very Well	Moderately Well	Very Poorly
1. Reflects the real world of children	X		
2. Is clearly understandable		X	
3. Explains the past and predicts the future		X	
4. Guides child rearing	X		
5. Is internally consistent	X		
6. Is economical	X		
7. Is falsifiable		X	
8. Stimulates new discoveries	X		
9. Is self-satisfying		X	

future status in relation to these elements can be made with increasing confidence. It is true, however, that predictions about the "average" child of a given age continue to be more reliable than predictions about any particular child. Before more precise judgments can be made about the future of individual children's information-processing systems, more evidence is needed about the causes of children's individual differences in their information-processing components.

I have rated the model high as a guide to child rearing because the results of empirical research provide specific suggestions about what to expect of children at different age levels and about how to promote the development of the information-processing components. Parents and teachers can draw on a growing body of information about care of the eyes and ears, about directing children's attention toward constructive activities, and about strategies for improving memory and for retrieving stored information.

I have not located internal inconsistencies in the versions of information-processing theory I have inspected, so I gave the model a high rating on item 5. Likewise, the components and their interactions as proposed by various theorists have not appeared unduly elaborate to account for the data they intend to explain, so a high rating for economy (item 6) seems warranted as well.

To a great degree both the proposed elements of the information-processing system and the interactions among the elements seem testable, at least potentially (item 7). Some concepts—such as those of short- and long-term memory and the components of each of these hypothetical functions—have not yet been specified precisely enough to determine very well how the concepts can be isolated and their interactions measured, but progress toward this end is being made in empirical studies, particularly with the aid of computer technology. As a consequence, the future of achieving the operational specificity needed for testing the truth of the theory seems to me very promising.

A high rating for the theory's ability to stimulate new discoveries (item 8) appears justified on the basis of the growing quantity of research related to the senses, to the encoding of stimuli from the environment, to the process of memorizing, to problems in the retrieval of stored information, to the mechanisms that guide the muscles to act, and to computer simulations of information-processing functions.

All things considered, I find the information-processing model very satisfactory (item 9). For me, it provides a convincing, integrated structure within which to explain such disparate phenomena as environmental stimuli, the operation of the sense organs, attention and perception, memory, and observable behavior. I rated it somewhat below the maximum "very well" level because only recently have versions of the theory addressed the ways different environments influence mental processes and the relationship between conscious and unconscious mental operations. Furthermore, theorists have not focused sufficient attention on such issues as the role of the emotions and the underlying forces that produce a person's goals. These matters I believe need to be formally incorporated into the theory if it is to provide a balanced conception of thought and behavior.

FOR FURTHER READING

Ashcraft, M. H. (1989) *Human Memory and Cognition*. Glenview, Ill.: Scott, Foresman. Ashcraft's detailed description of information-processing theory, of diverse viewpoints, and of empirical studies is thorough and written in a most engaging style.

Posner, M. I. (ed.). (1989) *Foundations of Cognitive Science*. Cambridge, Mass.: MIT Press. An in-depth description of "the mind as a symbol processor" and "intelligence from the perspective of computation."

Classical versions of information-processing theory from a child development perspective are described in the following sources.

Flavell, J. H. (1977) *Cognitive Development*. Englewood Cliffs, N. J.: Prentice-Hall.

Kail, R., and J. Bisanz. (1982) "Information Processing and Cognitive Development," in H. W. Reese and L. P. Lipsett (eds.), *Advances in Child Development and Behavior*, Vol. 17. New York: Academic Press.

Klahr, D., and J. G. Wallace. (1976) *Cognitive Development: An Information-Processing View*. Hillsdale, N. J.: Erlbaum.

Miller, P. H. (1983) *Theories of Developmental Psychology*. San Francisco: W. H. Freeman, Chap. 4.

CHAPTER THIRTEEN

Humanistic Perspectives

The realm of present-day humanistic psychology can be pictured as two circles, with the smaller inside a larger. The smaller one represents a publicly declared movement launched in America in 1962 with the formation of the Association of Humanistic Psychology (AHP), and the initial publication of the *Journal of Humanistic Psychology*. The larger, surrounding domain includes not only the inner-circle people who subscribe to the association's tenets, but also other theorists who differ in certain respects from members of the inner coterie. While there actually is no precise borderline separating inhabitants of the inner domain from those in the surrounding territory, for purposes of discussion it is convenient to distinguish between the two. The humanistic version of development offered in this chapter reflects convictions of theorists from both the inner circle and the outer realm. Other versions of a humanistic approach, from both the inner and outer domains, can be found in the writings of Gordon W. Allport (1968), Arthur W. Combs and Donald Snygg (1959), Earl C. Kelley (1962), Rollo May (Reeves, 1977), Frederick S. Perls (1951), Carl Rogers (1961, 1973), and other authors who write for such publications as the *Journal of Humanistic Psychology, The Humanistic Psychologist, Journal of Phenomenological Psychology, Review of Existential Psychology and Psychiatry,* and *Self and Society.*

Humanists, in contrast to behaviorists' practice of analyzing people from the outside, analyze them from the inside. Introspection becomes the chief investigative technique, for humanistic psychologists believe that the quintessence of an individual is found not in her overt acts but in her

400

thoughts and feelings about her personal experience. This inward view of personality has appeared over the centuries in numerous versions, each bearing its own name—humanism, existentialism, phenomenology, mysticism, and others. Philosophers of a humanist persuasion have stressed a belief in each person's possessing a free will that permits him or her to make choices and display creative powers as an individual. One variety of this viewpoint, developed in nineteenth-century Europe under the name *existentialism*, proposed that the reality of life resides in each individual's interpretation of his personal existence. Existentialists have emphasized the importance of a person's fully experiencing each moment of life. In a similar manner, *phenomenologists* have proposed that the "truth" about life is found in experiencing rather than in objective descriptions of people's behavior as measured and tested by the techniques of natural science. A mid-twentieth-century variant of phenomenology appeared in a book entitled *Individual Psychology* by two U.S. psychologists, Combs and Snygg, who accorded prime attention to the *phenomenal self,* meaning the personally recognized "I" or "me."

Humanistic psychologists in their research methodology "do not claim to be 'objective.' They are intent on the discovery of methods within the highly subjective interchange of a relationship which will garner 'personal knowledge' of another human being" (Buhler & Allen, 1972, p. 24). As a result of this viewpoint, other psychologists who regard experimental methods as the best source of information about child growth often believe that humanistic approaches do not qualify as proper theories of development. However, under the broad definition of *theory* adopted in this book, humanistic views can form theories of development, for they furnish answers to most of the questions posed about development in Chapter Two. The humanistic theory described in this chapter is a composite version built mainly around beliefs extracted from the writings of Abraham Maslow, Charlotte Buhler, and Alvin R. Mahrer, with the first two authors representing the inner circle of humanistic psychologists and the third representing a position that differs in several ways from the beliefs of the inner group.

The following discussion opens with (1) a brief introduction to the humanistic movement that arose in the 1960s. The presentation then continues with humanistic perspectives on (2) the original nature of the child, (3) the importance of needs and goals, (4) the nature of the self, (5) directions and stages of development, (6) healthy growth, disease, and deviance, and (7) nature and nurture. The chapter closes with (8) practical applications of such a theory and (9) an assessment of the humanistic approach.

THE ROOTS OF MODERN-DAY HUMANISTIC PSYCHOLOGY

The movement represented by the creators of the Association of Humanistic Psychology (AHP) in the early 1960s was primarily an attempt to focus attention on the growth of *self*. At the same time, it was a reaction against two current streams of psychological thought and thus was dubbed "a third force" in psychology by a Brandeis University professor, Abraham Maslow (1908–1970).

The two theoretical positions that humanistic psychology rejected were behaviorism and psychoanalysis. Behaviorism was accused of reducing individuals to a system of observable acts and thereby missing such human aspects as people's values, feelings, hopes for the future, choices, and creativity. Behaviorists were charged with neglecting to picture the human being as a unitary person in pursuit of goals and ideals (Maslow, 1968, 1970). Freudian psychoanalysis was accused of adopting a negative model of humanity, of espousing a morbid emphasis on neurotic behavior and of failing to define the nature and the path of positive, healthy personality development.

Humanistic psychology, as reflected in the association's tenets, is marked by:

1. A centering of attention on the experiencing *person*, and thus a focus on *experience* as the primary phenomenon in the study of man. Both theoretical explanations and overt behavior are considered secondary to experience itself and to its meaning to the person.

2. An emphasis on such distinctively *human qualities* as choice, creativity, valuation, and self-realization, as opposed to thinking about human beings in mechanistic and reductionist terms.

3. An allegiance to *meaningfulness* in the selection of problems for study and of research procedures and an opposition to a primary emphasis on objectivity at the expense of significance.

4. An ultimate *concern with and valuing of the dignity and worth of man* and an interest in the *development of the potential inherent in every person*. Central in this view is the person as he discovers his own being and relates to other persons and to social groups (the AHP brochure).

In effect, humanistic theorists propose a positive, optimistic picture of humans and believe that life "is to be lived subjectively, as it takes place."

Ideas arising within the humanistic movement have not been molded into one system, nor do the beliefs of one theorist always agree with those of others, as this chapter demonstrates. Furthermore, humanistic theory is not specifically a child development theory, for most of its materials focus on adults or speak about the life span in general without distinguishing very clearly between one age period and another. However, from the writings of certain humanistic psychologists it is possible to derive answers to many questions about child development.

Three theorists whose works are particularly useful as sources of such answers are Abraham Maslow, Charlotte Buhler (1893–1974), and Alvin R. Mahrer (born 1927). Maslow was first trained in experimental psychology and psychoanalysis, but he concluded that both of these traditions failed to give proper attention to what he considered the essence of human personality, that is, to a person's sense of *self* and to the immediate experiencing of life. Buhler was a well-known European psychologist who made her first contributions to the child development literature in Austria before establishing her home in the United States. Mahrer, now a professor of psychology at the University of Ottawa in Canada, was raised in the United States by Czech-immigrant parents. He earned a doctorate at Ohio State University before entering private practice as a psychoanalytic therapist, and then gradually moved away from psychoanalysis to an existential-humanistic position, which he refers to as *experiential psychotherapy*. His book *Experiencing: A Humanistic Theory of Psychology and Psychiatry* (1978) offers extensive proposals about the process of development. As will be illustrated, Mahrer's views in several respects differ from those of Maslow and Buhler. Mahrer admits that he "cannot feel very much at home with the typical humanistic psychologists."

THE ORIGINAL NATURE OF THE CHILD

In most versions of humanistic theory the biologically determined inner nature of the human consists of basic needs, emotions, and capacities that are either neutral or positively good. Such "bad" characteristics as destructiveness, cruelty, and malice are not innate, according to Maslow (1968, pp. 3–4), but are "violent reactions *against* frustration of our intrinsic needs, emotions, and capacities. . . . Since this inner nature is good or neutral rather than bad, it is best to bring it out and to encourage it rather than to suppress it. If it is permitted to guide our life, we grow healthy, fruitful and happy."

Therefore the goal of guiding child development is to foster the expression of the child's inner nature. This task is difficult because the inner essence of the child's personality is not very hardy but, rather, is delicate and easily damaged by unfavorable experiences. Suppressing or distorting the expression of the inner nature causes some degree of sickness, bodily ailment, or behavior deviation that sometimes shows up immediately but other times may surface months or years after the maltreatment. Nevertheless, even when the inner essence is suppressed, it continues to live in the depths of the unconscious, always striving for expression or, in Maslow's language, for *actualization.*

Although Buhler and many other humanistic theorists would agree with Maslow's conception of the child's original nature, Mahrer has offered a different proposal. He claims that it is a *humanist* rather than a *humanistic* belief that "the infant has a basic nature which is inherently free, spontaneous, creative, loving, active, striving, actualizing" (Mahrer, 1978, p. 634). As an alternative to such a notion of inherent human nature, Mahrer has proposed what he regards as a true humanistic concept of the initial state of infancy, a state he labels *primitive personality.* The primitive personality is not simply something inside the newborn but rather is composed of (1) the physical characteristics and inner potentials of the infant, (2) the parents' convictions of what an infant should be like, and (3) the relationships that exist between the infant and parents as a result of the parents' ideas of how to treat such an infant (Mahrer, 1978, p. 619). The interaction of these internal and external forces, Mahrer contends, determines what the infant experiences, so the interaction is properly identified as the *primitive personality* or original state of the child.

In summary, the dominant conception among humanistic theorists—and humanists—is that the child's original nature is one of positive striving to actualize an inner essence that is good and constructive. But there are other theorists, such as Mahrer, who also identify themselves as humanistic but who subscribe to a somewhat different view of the initial condition of the child.

HUMAN NEEDS AND GOALS

A key concept to which humanistic psychologists subscribe is that human behavior is motivated primarily by the individual's seeking to fulfill a series of needs. However, not all theorists use the word *needs* to label the internal force they believe drives people to thought and action. Some theorists prefer such terms as *wishes, drives, goals, impulses,* or *potentials* (Mahrer, 1978, pp. 20–23).

To differentiate a humanistic view from the concept of needs in other theories, Maslow distinguished two types. The first he called *deficiency needs.* Examples of this variety are the needs for food, for drink, for a comfortable temperature, for safety from bodily harm, for close love relationships, for respect, and for prestige. He proposed that deficiency needs can be recognized by five objectively observed characteristics of the person and by two subjectively experienced feelings. Objectively, a need for something exists if (1) its absence breeds illness, (2) its presence prevents illness, (3) its restoration cures illness, (4) under certain free choice situations, it is preferred by the deprived person over other satisfactions, and (5) it is found to be inactive, low, or functionally absent in the healthy person. Subjectively, a deficiency need is felt as (6) a conscious or unconscious yearning and desire and (7) a lack or deficiency (Maslow, 1968, p. 22).

Beyond these deficiency needs, which are included in other theories of child development, humanistic psychologists postulate a second cluster called *growth* or *self-actualization* needs. Theorists have had far more trouble in specifying this second group than in identifying deficiencies. Maslow admitted that:

> Growth, individuation, autonomy, self-actualization, self-development, productiveness, self-realization, are all crudely synonymous, designating a vaguely perceived area rather than a sharply defined concept. . . . We just don't know enough about growth yet to be able to define it well (1968, p. 24).

But in an initial attempt at a general definition, Maslow proposed that the self-actualizing need is a striving to realize one's potentials, capacities, and talents; it is a seeking to fulfill a mission or destiny or vocation; it can be a fuller knowledge and acceptance of one's own personality and "an unceasing trend toward unity, integration, or synergy within the person" (Maslow, 1968, p. 26).

The highest stage of growth in humans, then, is the achievement of such self-actualization. Commenting on this highest stage, Buhler and M. Allen (1972, p. 45) have said, "All humanistic psychologists see the goal of life as that of using it to accomplish something in which one believes."

The human needs in Maslow's system, then, form a hierarchy ranging from the most basic physiological deficiency needs at the foundation to the self-actualization needs at the apex. Maslow proposed that the lower needs must be filled before the upper-level needs receive attention. In descending order from the apex, they can be placed in five clusters (Maslow, 1970, pp. 80–89):

1. *Self-actualization need:* doing what one, *individually,* is fitted for: "What a man *can* be, he *must* be. He must be true to his own nature."

2. *Esteem needs:* for self-respect and self-esteem and for the esteem of others.

3. *Belongingness and love needs:* for family, friends, lover; affection, rootedness, intimacy.

4. *Safety needs:* for security and stability, for freedom from fear, anxiety, and chaos. This includes a need for structure, law, and limits.

5. *Physiological needs:* for air, food, drink, rest, fulfilling the appetites, and for achieving balance or homeostasis within the body.

THE NATURE OF THE SELF

One conviction that all humanistic psychologists hold in common is the importance of the *self* as the central concern in human development. Although the term *self* appears frequently in humanistic literature, it is not always described in the same way by different writers or even in the same way at all times by a single writer.

Arthur Combs and Donald Snygg (1959, p. 124) proposed that the *phenomenal self* "is not a mere conglomeration or addition of isolated concepts of self, but a patterned interrelationship or Gestalt of all these. It is the individual as he seems from his own vantage point."

Rollo May called the self "the organizing function within the individual . . . by means of which one human being can relate to another; consciousness of one's identity . . . as a thinking-intuiting-feeling and acting unity; . . . not merely the sum of 'roles,' but the capacity by which one *knows* he plays these roles; it is the center from which one sees and is aware of these 'sides' of himself" (quoted in Reeves, 1977, pp. 286–287).

Gordon Allport (1961, p. 110) described the self as a "kind of core in our being. And yet it is not a constant core. Sometimes the core expands and seems to take command of all our behavior and consciousness, sometimes it seems to go completely offstage, leaving us with no awareness whatsoever of self."

Frederick Perls called the self the integrator, the synthetic unity, and "the artist of life." And while it is "only a small factor in the total organism/ environment interaction, . . . it plays the crucial role of finding and making the meanings that we grow by." It is the "system of contacts [with the environment] at any moment" and is "flexibly various, for it varies with the dominant organic needs and the pressing environmental stimuli; it is the system of responses; it diminishes in sleep when there is less need to respond" (Perls, Hefferline, and Goodman, 1951, p. 235).

Although these descriptions view the self as being entirely conscious, such theorists as Earl Kelley include unconscious functions as well:

The self consists of an organization of accumulated experience over a whole lifetime. It is easy to see, therefore, that a great deal of the self has been relegated to the unconscious, or has been "forgotten." This does not mean that these early expriences have been lost. It merely means that they cannot readily be brought into consciousness (1962, p. 9).

Both Maslow and Buhler, like many other humanistic theorists, accept the principal agents that Freud defined as composing the personality or mind: id, ego, and superego. They also accept the various Freudian instincts, impulses, and defenses, as well as the primary process (seeking immediate pleasure) and the secondary process (the ego's recognizing the real world and fulfilling the id's demands in the light of reality). But for the humanistic psychologist these separate and often conflicting agents and tendencies become increasingly integrated into a compatible unity—into the *essential self*—as the person matures. Thus the individual who is fulfilling all of her or his needs, basic as well as self-actualizing ones, is marked by a smooth working together or *synergy* of the composite elements of personality (Buhler & Massarik, 1968, p. 19).

Likewise, humanistic psychologists often subscribe to the levels of consciousness postulated by Freud, even if they do not always include the unconscious level in their concept of the essential self. They feel that much of human behavior arises from unconscious motives and that "those portions of ourselves that we reject and repress out of fear and shame do not go out of existence" (Maslow, 1971, p. 158) but go underground into the unconscious. However, humanistic writers strongly disagree with Freud's idea that the contents of the unconscious are principally—if not entirely— antisocial, that is, selfish and resistant to moral values. They believe that the contents also include the roots of creativeness, joy, and goodness.

In humanistic belief, conscience differs somewhat from the punitive Freudian superego whose contents derive exclusively from the rules and expectations imposed by the environment, particularly expectations imposed by parents. Maslow proposed that in addition to values that the child ingests from people around her, her conscience also has a genetic source, a kind of intrinsic feeling or knowledge of the right thing to do. This faint voice has its beginnings in the ancient nature of humans and is linked to the instincts of lower forms of life. It is an inner knowledge of one's true self. Maslow said that intrinsic guilt arises when an individual senses he has betrayed his own inner nature and has deviated from the path of self-actualization.

In Maslow's view, intrinsic guilt is a most desirable thing for it warns the child that she is straying from her true destiny. On the other hand, guilt based on unreasonable expectations from the environment is frequently nonconstructive and detracts from the pursuit of one's identity and self-fulfillment.

A question of continuing debate among humanists is whether the self is an entity or a collection of separate selves, each of which comes into play under particular conditions. P. D. Ouspensky suggested that:

> The principal mistake we make about ourselves is that we consider ourselves one; we always speak about ourselves as "I" and we suppose that we refer to the same thing all the time. . . . We do not know that we have not one "I," but many different "I's," connected with our feelings and desires, and have no controlling "I." These "I's" change all the time; one suppresses another, one replaces another, and all this struggle makes up our inner life (1957, p. 3).

In recent years this notion of multiple selves has been expressed in its most popular form by the psychiatrist Eric Berne in such books as *Games People Play* (1967) and *What Do You Say after You Say Hello?* (1972). In Berne's theory, the three selves that contend for attention on different occasions are those expressing (1) vestiges of the person as a young "child," (2) an internal representation of the person's "parent," (3) and the person as a rational "adult."

In summary, then, despite some lack of consensus about the exact features of the self, all humanistic theorists consider the self the focal object of human development.

THE DIRECTIONS AND STAGES OF DEVELOPMENT

As noted earlier, humanistic psychology was not created as a child psychology. It was devised by theorists concerned mainly with helping adults achieve better personal and social adjustment or, in more positive terms, achieve greater self-actualization. Hence the attention of most humanistic psychologists has focused on childhood only in incidental ways. Our picture of the direction of development and stages of growth in childhood must therefore be gleaned from passing comments. In effect, humanistic psychology, as outlined by its best-known proponents, has not been organized as a system of phases of childhood and adolescence as correlated with chronological ages. To some degree Mahrer is an exception, for he has identified what he calls a sequence of *plateaus* in the development of self. This hierarchy of plateaus represents the closest approximation in humanistic theory to the stages of growth identified in such development models as those of Piaget, Freud, Gesell, and Havighurst.

Despite this lack of precisely defined growth steps for the first two decades of life in most humanistic theories, Maslow and Buhler have identified at least two general levels of change, those of *childhood* and *adolescence*. In discussing these levels, Buhler distinguishes biological from psychological development. From a biological standpoint, she divided the first twenty-five years of life at age 15. During childhood, ages 0 to 15, there is progressive physical growth without reproductive ability. During adolescence or youth, ages 15 to 25, there is continued growth following the onset of reproductive ability (Buhler & Massarik, 1968, p. 14).

Psychological development can also be viewed as two general segments, childhood and adolescence, but the distinctions are not nearly as clear as in the biological realm. Psychologically, the child grows toward self-actualization, toward achieving clearer goals in life and better integration of needs and values. This development of *self* is somewhat correlated with biological growth, in that the very young child is not very self-actualized. Time and experience are required for the child to achieve greater self-realization and synergy. But time alone is not enough. Just becoming older does not assure self-actualization. There are many adolescents and adults who still have not achieved psychological maturity. So the passing of childhood and the arrival of adolescence provides *opportunities for becoming* mature, but such maturing is not automatic.

Buhler concluded that the first appearance of a self-conscious ego occurs when the young child is between ages 2 and 4. During this time "I want" behavior is prominent as "the child begins to discover his own self and the possibility of giving himself a direction of his own" (Buhler & Massarik, 1968, pp. 30–31). The way a child expresses this self-consciousness varies greatly from one child to another, with such individuality being both genetic and environmental in origin. "The child with creative potential begins his first attempts toward self-realization when he is between 2 and 4 years" (Buhler & Massarik, 1968, p. 32).

Motivational Trends

Throughout the next eight or ten years the child's personality gradually evolves until the arrival of marked psychological change around age 10 to 12 or so. At this time, according to Buhler, several *motivational trends* appear, trends that extend into the future and mark the child's individuality in rather permanent ways.

One trend concerns a *constructive-destructive* dimension that involves the person's basic attitude toward life, an attitude that is becoming well set during this period of development. The attitude either can be one of building up positive human relationships and optimistic plans for the future, or it can be one of tearing down relationships by attacking others and despairing of the future. Which of these tendencies is dominant is most clearly evidenced in the way children interact with their parents, particularly in the way conflicts between child and parent are either resolved or expanded.

A second trend relates to *achievement motivation.* The extent to which a child will strive to achieve in her adult life and the form of this achievement will show up most clearly after puberty.

Beliefs and values that are based on more than blind acceptance develop in the early adolescent years, along with *love* and other *commitments* to a cause or to other people. Buhler said that the voluntarily chosen bonds of intimacy and commitment in a mutually shared sex and love relationship may result in "the ecstatic experience of unity . . . one of the most, if not *the* most, essential aims of the maturing person." Maslow called this feeling of unity one of the individual's *peak experiences* (Buhler & Massarik, 1968, p. 37). (The term *peak experiences,* frequently found in humanistic literature, identifies the most wonderful experience or experiences of your life, happiest moments, ecstatic moments, moments of rapture [Maslow in R. Wuthnow, 1978, p. 57]. The attainment of increasing numbers of peak experiences is, from a humanistic perspective, an important goal of human development.)

But even with adolescents' new concern for personally adopted values and immediate ambitions, they usually have only vague and tentative life goals. Rarely do they view life as an entirety, as a complete span of years with possibilities of an integration of all its aspects. "It is the exceptional youth who asks what life is all about" (Buhler & Massarik, 1968, p. 42).

Like Buhler, other writers in the humanistic vein consider adolescence to be a time of increased awareness and searching in the realm of values, goals, and commitment for something considered worthwhile. It is also a time of significant confusion. In this sense, the typical humanistic psychologist would agree with Erikson's notion that adolescence is experienced as an identity crisis. Maslow commented that the uncertainty of many adults in the United States about their own values has led many young people to live not by clear adult values but by "adolescent values, which of course are immature, ignorant, and heavily determined by confused adolescent needs" (Maslow, 1968, p. 206).

In summary, while most humanistic psychologists recognize at least prepuberal childhood and postpuberal adolescence as separate stages in personality development, they do not define substages within these periods, nor do they discuss even these two broad periods in any systematic way. Instead, they give only incidental attention to any idea of growth stages being correlated with age.

A Hierarchy of Plateaus

As mentioned earlier, Mahrer has proposed a sequence of five *plateaus* of personality growth and has linked the sequence to age levels, albeit in a rather vague manner. To contrast his system with the typical sets of growth periods postulated in other theories, Mahrer "sets aside the whole framework of biosocial, biopsychological stages of development" since he contends that "there are no intrinsic forces moving the child from one plateau to another, no biological factors, no built-in developmental sequences, no neurophysiological or hereditary or cultural lines of development" (1978, pp. 788, 790). Instead, he proposes that "people are responsible for an individual's staying on one plateau or moving to another. Those people may include the individual himself, his family, the groups in which he lives, significant strangers" (1978, p. 788)

The hierarchy of plateaus begins after birth with the *primitive personality*, which is the condition of the child encompassed within a *primitive field*. This primitive psychological field is created by parents and others in the child's environment who have a concept of what the infant should be like and who base their treatment of the infant on that concept. During this period the child has no sense of self but is dependent for her identity on the way others act toward her. "What I am is a function of how others see me" (Mahrer, 1978, p. 791). Whether the child advances out of this early condition and onto the next plateau depends on how she is treated by the people in charge of her welfare. If not treated constructively, she could remain a primitive personality all her life, forever relying on the external world as a mirror of her identity.

With proper nurturing, the individual advances to the second plateau, where a sense of self is born. Mahrer estimates that for some people this occurs in early childhood, but for most it happens during middle childhood between ages 6 and 12. For still others it does not appear until adolescence or adulthood, or perhaps never. He further proposes that this second state is not achieved suddenly but occurs "in bits and pieces, little juttings and bursts" (1978, p. 799).

On the third plateau the child becomes an active seeker, a constructor of experience, employing his growing potentials to select activities and to organize his world so that particular kinds of experiences occur. Instead of being manipulated by his environment, he actively fashions and utilizes his surroundings for his own purposes.

While the third period witnesses the individual initially developing skills or "operating potentials," on the fourth plateau new and more sophisticated skills are devised, ones that enable the person to experience life in greater depth and complexity.

The fifth, optimal state of being is that of self-integration and self-actualization, a plateau "beyond normal, mature, adjusted, healthy . . . achieved by a very small proportion of individuals. . . . Our concept is like that of a yogi, an individual who has attained the goal of yoga. . . . the union of self with the supreme reality or universal self" (Mahrer, 1978, p. 833).

Mahrer pictures the plateaus as representing a sequence of three struggles, first to acquire selfhood or personal identity during infancy and early childhood, next to preserve one's identity against the pressures of a changing environment, and finally to "lose selfhood" in ultimate self-actualization.

In conclusion, some developmental periods can be extracted from the works of a few humanistic authors. However, humanistic writers generally do not offer a *growth-stage* theory, but rather a *growth-directions* theory, meaning that a person grows gradually out of being one kind of individual toward being a different kind. But, to recognize whether a child is indeed developing in a proper direction, we need a definition of the desired end product or the desired goal that development is to pursue. Maslow defined this *direction of healthy growth* in two ways, one general and the other more specific.

As a general definition, he said that people are motivated in their development toward "ongoing actualization of potentials, capacities and talents, as fulfillment of mission—or call it fate, destiny, or vocation—as a fuller knowledge of, and acceptance of, the person's own intrinsic nature, as an unceasing trend toward unity, integration or synergy within the person" (Maslow, 1968, p. 25).

But many people found this definition unduly vague, so he provided a more specific description of the end condition of healthy development by specifying a series of traits displayed by a self-actualized person. Such a paragon of excellence exhibits (Maslow, 1968, p. 26):

1. Superior perception of reality

2. Increased acceptance of self, of others, and of nature

3. Increased spontaneity

4. Increased problem solving

5. Increased autonomy, and resistance to enculturation

6. Increased detachment and desire for privacy

7. Greater freshness of appreciation, and richness of emotional reaction

8. Higher frequency of peak experiences

9. Increased identification with the human species

10. Changed (the clinician would say, improved) interpersonal relations

11. More democratic character structure

12. Greatly increased creativeness

13. Certain changes in the value system

Other humanistic theorists besides Maslow have proposed their own set of directions in which development should proceed. For example, Combs (1962, pp. 53–62) has contended that the truly adequate personality (1) both gives love to others and feels loved by them, (2) is open to new experiences, (3) closely identifies with others so that she treats them in a highly responsible, trustworthy fashion, and (4) has a "rich and available perceptual field," meaning that she is well enough informed about the world to clearly understand events in which she is enmeshed.

Carl Rogers (1973, p. 12) pictured proper development as proceeding from rigidity toward flexibility, from static living toward "process living," from dependence toward autonomy, from being predictable toward an "unpredictable creativity," and from defensiveness toward self-acceptance.

HEALTHY GROWTH AND DEVIANCE

In place of the terms *normal* and *abnormal,* Maslow spoke of *health* and *illness* or of *mature* and *immature* development. For example, he distinguished between two sorts of immaturity, *chronological* and *unhealthy.* Chronological immaturity is found in the child as he grows up; it is expected, even necessary, for it consists of the healthy process of developing from a state of weakness, ignorance, and lack of direction to an adult state of self-fulfillment. But when the same sorts of symptoms are found in the adult, they are considered unhealthy, for by adulthood the individual should have become strong, wise, well integrated, and clear in his values and goals.

Deviance—that is, being different from others or failing to fit the norms—is not regarded as necessarily unhealthy. Indeed, being deviant in terms of expressing one's own talents and of following the guidance of one's unique inner gyroscope was viewed by Maslow as essential to achieving self-actualization. If a person adopts the typical behavior or norms of a culture that blocks the expression of her inner nature or personality core, then she is not considered to be normal in the sense of developing properly or in a healthy pattern. Instead, she is regarded in Maslow's system as being immature and unhealthy, for "the main source of illness (although not the only one) is seen as frustrations (of the basic needs, . . . of idiosyncratic potentials, of expression of the self, and of the tendency of the person to grow in his own style and at his own pace) especially in the early years of life" (Maslow, 1968, pp. 193–194).

So it is not deviance from the common or typical behavior of a society that is viewed with disapproval in the humanistic model; it is deviance from one's potential. A child who does not "fit in" to his culture or who "stands against the crowd" is a psychologically healthy child by humanistic standards if that culture is a bad one. And by *bad* Maslow meant a culture that is growth-inhibiting rather than growth-fostering. "The 'better' culture gratifies all basic human needs and permits self-actualization. The 'poorer' cultures do not" (Maslow, 1968, p. 211).

NATURE AND NURTURE

The general humanistic position on heredity–environment issues is that the infant is born with inherited potentials—for growth and for self-fulfillment by pursuing constructive missions—but that these potentials will not flower at all unless they are properly nurtured by the people with whom the child interacts during the growing years. As the discussion of Maslow's views has already suggested, he assigned heredity a strong role in personality development. The essence of the sort of person a child should become is established in the genetic structure as a unique *self* composed of latent talents and interests. The environment then determines how adequately this idiosyncratic self or identity unfolds or becomes actualized. So while humanistic theorists recognize the significance of innate potentials as the seeds of personality, they still place great emphasis on the function of the social environment in producing the actual personality the growing child displays. The self "is built almost entirely, if not entirely, in relationship to others. While the newborn babe has the equipment for the development of the self, there is ample evidence to show that nothing resembling a self can be built in the absence of others" (E. C. Kelley, 1962, p. 9). "People discover their self concepts from the kinds of experiences they have had with life—not from telling, but from experience" (Combs, 1962, p. 84).

PRACTICAL APPLICATIONS

Although the most extensive applications of humanistic psychology have been therapeutic and consciousness-raising activities for adults, a substantial body of literature has been produced as well on child-rearing practices and on schooling and therapy during the first two decades of life. Such child-focused literature can be divided into two types. The first consists of general guidelines and warnings about raising children. The second consists of specific activities for promoting humanistic goals of development.

Examples of general guidelines are such observations as:

> A high quality of maternal love and care . . . seem to prepare the child for emotional contacts with other people and to supply enough confidence to encourage the exploration of new situations. . . . Among the greatest benefits of psychoanalysis is the fact that it has disclosed the damaging consequences of extreme parental demands and discipline. . . . On the whole, it may be assumed that warmth and permissiveness facilitate the growth of sociable, yet independent children, and that parental hostility has debilitating effects (Buhler & Massarik, 1968, pp. 174–178).

> Once the infant puts forth a rudimentary nubbin [of individuality], parental figures can develop that behavior by [an] . . . integrative relationship that is expressed in warmth, love, closeness, acceptance. . . . To relate disintegratively is to relate with fear and hate, depression and anger, meaninglessness and menace to the behavior bit put forth by the infant (Mahrer, 1978, pp. 698–699).

> Anytime a pupil's actions suggest that he can profit from expressing and comprehending (emotionally as well as intellectually) his feelings, the teacher should use methods suitable for promoting such expression and comprehension (Thomas & Brubaker, 1971, p. 260).

> We know only too well that a parent cannot make his children into anything. Children make themselves into something. The best we can do and frequently the most effect we can have is by serving as something to react against if the child presses too hard. . . . Schools should be helping children to look within themselves, and from this self-knowledge derive a set of values, . . . spontaneity and . . . naturalness" (Maslow, 1971, pp. 169, 185–186).

Maslow's faith in the correctness of the child's natural inclinations caused him to recommend a *permissive regime,* meaning that parents should begin meeting the child's needs directly and with as little frustration as possible in early infancy. But as the child acquires greater strength and experience, adults should gradually cease gratifying his needs directly. They should now arrange the child's environment so he can gratify his own needs and make his own choices, for "he 'knows' better than anyone else what is good for him" (Maslow, 1968, p. 198).

The intention of Maslow's educational scheme is not to prevent the developing child from ever experiencing frustration, pain, or danger. But, with a good foundation in the early years of safety, love, and respect, the child should increasingly be allowed to face difficulties that enable her to acquire frustration tolerance. Part of self-realization comes as the older child and the youth learn about their strengths and limitations and learn ways to extend their abilities by overcoming difficulties, "by straining . . . to the utmost, by meeting challenge and hardship, even by failing" (Maslow, 1968, p. 200). Curiously, this general pattern of child raising—except for the desirability of failing—sounds much like the pattern found in Skinner's *Walden Two,* illustrating the observation that children may be treated in similar ways from quite different theoretical viewpoints.

Some humanistic writers have gone beyond offering general suggestions and have described specific activities for implementing their suggestions. For example, Mahrer (1978, pp. 766–771) has proposed a regimen for promoting an infant's development out of the condition of primitive personality into an initial sense of self. The routine to be carried out with the six- to nine-month-old child consists of the adult playing with the baby for thirty minutes to an hour each day. However, it is the infant, not the adult, who determines the direction of the play. The adult's role is first to furnish *effectance-promoting objects* that the child can touch, grasp, squeeze, shape, mouth, crumple, push, throw, hit, release, roll, take apart, open, and close. The objects should also make noise, have odors, and be different colors. And all the objects should be started, stopped, and manipulated by the baby himself, not by the adult. With such equipment at hand, the adult's task is to remain within *interactive distance* of the infant, meaning that the adult's face is within 2 feet of the child. The baby is then allowed to initiate his own behavior, with the adult focusing attention on and commenting about what the baby is doing, being careful all the while not to interfere with or redirect the infant's activity.

For school-age children and youths, a variety of other writers have proposed specific learning activities. These can be illustrated by examples from *confluent education,* which is a variant of the humanistic movement that emphasizes a confluence or compatible flowing together of the cognitive and emotional aspects of experience. For instance, to help children investigate their feelings about communicating with others under unusual circumstances, one set of activities consists of pupils dividing into pairs. Each pair first sit back to back to converse with each other orally, then sit facing each other to communicate only with their eyes, and finally—with eyes closed—to communicate only with their hands. To foster greater "self-awareness and other-awareness," each child is next asked to "close his eyes and with his hands explore his own face very slowly and get in touch with the various textures and parts of his face" and then to explore the face of his partner (G. I. Brown, 1971, pp. 29–32). An opportunity to investigate feelings of trust and distrust is provided by the *blind walk,* which involves one of the pair of children being blindfolded and then led by her partner around the classroom and other areas of the school. An additional activity to promote self-awareness has been labeled a *fantasy body trip.* Students close their eyes, assume comfortable positions, and "move into themselves" by concentrating on different parts of the body, with each student "beginning with his toes, moving gradually up to his head, experiencing any sensations he might feel emanating from that part of the body" (G. I. Brown, 1971, p. 35).

Numerous additional activities devised by proponents of humanistic development demonstrate ways to plumb the experiences of loneliness, affection, responsibility, anxiety, faithfulness, prejudice, social acceptance and rejection, confidence, insecurity, emotional dependence and independence, and more. Over the past three decades an increasing number of such activities have been included in elementary and secondary school curricula and in nonformal educational programs.

HUMANISTIC THEORY: AN ASSESSMENT

Three of the greatest strengths of the humanistic approach are its attention to children's feelings and values as part of their real world (item 1), its concern for the individual's hopes and plans for the future (item 3), and its application of a humanistic view to child raising (item 4).

I agree with humanistic psychologists that the world that is most significant to the child or adolescent is the one she feels that she is experiencing at the moment. This attention to the phenomenal self seems to be a proper counterbalance to the heavy dependence on objectively observed actions of behaviorist views. The typical humanistic theory seeks to devise general principles that underlie different facets of growth, not just one aspect such as cognitive development. However, by concerning itself only with general principles, it has failed to trace the specific ways one aspect, such as langue usage, develops in comparison to the ways other aspects, such as physical agility, grow. Hence I have rated humanistic psychology high on item 1 but not at the top.

Some critics have faulted present-day humanistic theory for ostensibly limiting its focus to a limited segment of society, so they would rank the theory low on item 1 for being only relevant to those who "have" (i.e., achieved sufficient economic wealth) and completely irrelevant to those who are the "have-nots" (i.e., in Maslow's terms, 1968, those too busy concerning themselves with lower-level needs rather than higher-level needs such as self-actualization). Herein lies the contradiction in the practice of contemporary "humanistic" psychology—a contradiction which must be resolved in order for "humanistic" psychology to evolve into a truly *humanistic* psychology (Buss, 1976, p. 258).

The humanistic approach is notable for recognizing the influence on development of the child's hopes, expectations, and plans for the future, which are facets of experience neglected in many other theories. I have sought to recognize this contribution by a relatively strong rating on item 3.

That rating would have been higher if the manner in which humanistic theory explains the past were more precise.

Two general principles of child rearing that humanistic theorists appear to support are that (1) the adult should seek to perceive life from the emotional and cognitive perspectives of the child and, through such empathy, should treat the child in ways that show respect for and understanding of the child's phenomenal self, and (2) the adult should respect the child's right to be an individual with interests, talents, and emotions of her own. I am convinced that these principles are desirable guides in child raising, so I have rated the humanistic approach high on item 4. But again, the rating is not at the top of the scale, for I believe humanistic theory lacks the specificity that parents and teachers look for in their search for ways to treat the growing child. However, a lack of precise directives to parents is perhaps a necessary part of any theory that emphasizes the unique character of each child.

On other dimensions, I have judged that humanistic theory doesn't fare so well. One problem is its lack of clarity (item 2). Humanistic writers describe their ideas in terms that can carry quite different meanings for different readers. When you speak of your *peak experiences,* of your *self-realization,* of *authenticity* and *synergism,* and of your *identity,* how am I to know whether I have experienced the same things that cause you to use these words? Likewise, when I seek inner guidance in making a decision, how do I know which of my impulses represents my *true* inner self, the one that directs me toward self-actualization, and which impulses represent values I have learned from my environment, values that may conflict with my innate essence or calling?

Further puzzles have arisen from seemingly self-contradictory principles offered by humanistic writers. For example, Maslow wrote that "for self-actualizing people, there is a strong tendency for selfishness and unselfishness to fuse into a higher, superordinate unity" (1968, p. 207).

In addition, Maslow's system proposes that children are immature because they are at lower levels in the needs-fulfillment hierarchy and at lower levels on the scales of maturity. Yet he stated that "the highest maturity is discovered to include a childlike quality" (1968, p. 207). If such is true, then how it operates requires a clearer explanation than the existing humanistic literature seems to provide.

In effect, one of the very strengths of humanistic theory, its insistence on the importance of unique personal experiences, leads also to one of its serious weaknesses—its imprecision in communicating the essence of one person's experience to another.

The same personal or existential quality of humanistic thought also contributes to the theory's lack of falsifiability (item 7). The difficulty here

Humanistic Theory

How well do I think the theory meets the standards?

The Standards	Very Well	Moderately Well	Very Poorly
1. Reflects the real world of children	X		
2. Is clearly understandable			X
3. Explains the past and predicts the future		X	
4. Guides child rearing	X		
5. Is internally consistent			?
6. Is economical			?
7. Is falsifiable			X
8. Stimulates new discoveries		X	
9. Is self-satisfying		X	

rests to a great degree in humanistic theorists' preference for using introspection as their principal investigative technique. Although Maslow accepted the objective, scientific modes of studying people that have evolved over the past century or so, he criticized the adoption of behaviorism and of logical positivism as the exclusive, or even as the preferred, mode of understanding human development. He claimed that such approaches to studying the growing child result only in verbal, analytic, conceptual rationality and ignore the more significant aspects of personality—the hopes, feelings, fears, and ambitions of the experiencing self. For example, in discussing motivation, Maslow stated that:

> The original criterion of motivation and the one that is still used by all human beings except behavioral psychologists is the subjective one. I am

motivated when I feel a desire or want or yearning or wish or lack. No objectively observable state has yet been found that correlates decently with these subjective reports, i.e., no behavioral definition of motivation has yet been found.

Now of course we ought to keep on seeking for objective correlates or indicators of subjective states. . . . But until we find [them] we ought not make believe that we have. Nor ought we neglect the subjective data that we do have (1968, p. 22).

Not only does humanistic theory draw upon self-reports, but it accords a key position to nonlogical, or even illogical, intuitive impressions or feelings, which it claims are so often expressions of the true inner self.

If our hope is to describe the world fully, a place is necessary for preverbal ineffable, metaphorical, primary process, concrete experience, intuitive, and esthetic types of cognition, for there are certain aspects of reality which can be cognized in no other way (Maslow, 1968, p. 208).

This attitude about the proper sources of evidence about personality development influences the humanistic view of the way the theory is validated. In earlier chapters I noted that behavioristic theories depend upon the experimental or field-study testing of hypotheses as the appropriate way to determine whether the theory or some part of it is true. But humanistic psychologists trust their own feelings and logic more than many sorts of objective data to validate their theory. To most if not all humanistic psychologists, it appears to be enough to contend that "I know that's the way things are because it makes sense and feels right to me." But such a testimonial would less likely satisfy a behaviorist, a Piagetian, or a psychoanalyst.

In terms of the theory's internal consistency (item 5) and economy of explanation (item 6), I have placed question marks in the lower reaches of the appraisal scales. My puzzlement regarding these matters is occasioned by a lack of precision in the definition of terms and of the relationships among variables. I find myself unable to make a careful estimate of internal consistency and economy of explanation when I fail to understand the elements of the system adequately. To a considerable extent, humanistic writing appears cast in unscientific, literary language. Rhetoric and obvious enthusiasm do not, I feel, sufficiently make up for what seems to be a structural imprecision in the theory.

During the past three decades or so, humanistic views have gained wide public attention and have influenced the way teachers, parents, social workers, and others perceive children (G. I. Brown, 1971; Fantini & Weinstein, 1968; Leff, 1978). However, this success in attracting people's interest in perceiving children in ostensibly more "humane" ways has not led to a significant number of new discoveries about children. It is true that such proposals as Maslow's hierarchy of needs have been innovative. But in many instances, the matters of which humanistic writers speak have been matters that people of earlier times sensed intuitively, and the humanistic theorists' contribution has been to stimulate the rediscovery of these insights about self, about feelings, and about hopes for the future. As a case in point, humanistic literature includes frequent allusions to concepts from Eastern religions, especially to Hindu and Buddhist notions (Muzika, 1990; Tart, 1990). In more than three hundred articles bearing on humanistic psychology in the standard psychological journal literature for the period 1974–1990, the objects of discussion were adults or people in general. Attention was rarely directed at development during childhood, and even then the mention was chiefly incidental. If you search through current child development textbooks, you will find very few new items of knowledge about child growth contributed by theorists and researchers using humanistic approaches. Hence I have marked the theory in the lower ranges of item 8. My purpose in giving such a rating is not to downgrade the importance of the humanistic persuasion but only to note that humanistic psychology has not stimulated significant amounts of new information or innovative perspectives on child development.

Humanistic theory, then, appeals most to people who place a high degree of trust in their intuitive sense of what is true about the development of one's self. The theory is less convincing to people who require a tightly reasoned, logical model whose elements can be verified through experimental or observational approaches. However, humanistic theorists do not claim to have produced a finished, close-knit theory of child development. Instead, they see their proposals as constituting only a beginning toward a model of human nature "as a total, single, comprehensive system of psychology" (Maslow, 1968, p. 189). And they also believe that their approach, with its emphasis on the experiencing self, holds more promise for revealing the essence of human personality than do such systems as psychoanalysis and behaviorism. I find it moderately self-satisfying (item 9).

FOR FURTHER READING

Buhler, C., and M. Allen. (1972) *Introduction to Humanistic Psychology.* Monterey, Calif.: Brooks/Cole.

Mahrer, A. R. (1978) *Experiencing: A Humanistic Theory of Psychology and Psychiatry.* New York: Brunner/Mazel.

Maslow, A. H. (1968) *Toward a Psychology of Being.* New York: Van Nostrand Reinhold.

Maslow, A. H. (1970) *Motivation and Personality,* 2d ed. New York: Harper & Row.

SPEAKING OF CAUSE

In theories of child development, what is meant by *cause?*

A prime purpose of all theories of human development is to account for why people grow up the way they do. In other words, theories represent speculation about what causes people to evolve from a single cell in the mother's womb into a newborn infant and subsequently into a child, an adolescent, and an adult who displays a configuration of features unique to that individual.

The purpose of the following perspective is to identify a variety of meanings that philosophers and scientists have assigned to the term *cause* and to suggest which of these meanings have been implied in the theories described in Chapters Three through Fifteen. The first part considers the usefulness of identifying causes and the second describes diverse meanings of cause.

THE USEFULNESS OF IDENTIFYING CAUSES

At the outset, it may be helpful to compare a commonsense view of cause with a contrasting view espoused in recent times in the physical sciences.

Common sense would agree with the proposal of the early American theologian Johnathan Edwards (1703–1758) that "nothing ever comes to pass without a cause" and with the contention of Dutch philosopher Baruch Spinoza (1632–1677) that "Nothing exists from whose nature some effect does not follow" (D. Lerner, 1965, p. 2). In other words, events don't "just happen"—rather, one thing produces another. Parents' engaging in a sexual act causes a child to be born nine months later. A three-year-old's knocking a tea cup off the kitchen table onto the floor causes the cup to shatter. That is, common sense holds that life's reality is reflected in the phrase "all events have causes."

In contrast to this belief is the view expressed by such thinkers as Bertrand Russell (1872–1970), the English philosopher of science who observed early in this century that "The Law of Causality . . . is a relic of a bygone age, surviving like the [British] monarchy, only because it is erroneously supposed to do no harm" (D. Lerner, 1965, p. 5). In keeping with Russell's conviction,

> Many influential scientists and philosophers have argued that the notion of cause plays a diminishing role in modern science, especially in the more advanced branches of it, such as mathematical physics, and that the notion is . . . a primitive, anthropomorphic interpretation of the various changes occurring in the world. It is beyond serious doubt that the term "cause" rarely if ever appears in the research papers or treatises currently published in the natural sciences, and the odds are heavily against any mention in any book on theoretical physics (Nagel, 1965, pp. 11–12).

What such scientists substitute for traditional cause-and-effect relationships is simply a statement of the probability that two or more conditions or events occur together. They speak of *functional relationships* between the two conditions, such as, "Whenever water is present and the air temperature at sea level is changed from 90 degrees above 0 Celsius to 105 degrees above 0, the water vaporizes 100 percent of the time." Or "In 50 percent of fatal auto accidents, alcohol was found in the blood of at least one of the drivers, so it is probable that in half of future accidents one or both drivers will have alcohol in their blood." That is, they claim that such probability statements suffice for predicting events without the need to speculate that one of the variables has caused the change in the other variable, or that a third factor has caused the changes in the original two. Although the reason the variables are correlated is unexplained, the fact that they interact in a consistent manner enables us to predict changes in one by knowing what changes are occurring in the other.

However, critics suggest that people who subscribe to this *noncausality* position are not settling the sticky question of cause; they are merely avoiding it (D. Lerner, 1965, p. 7). And observing physicists outside of the laboratory would imply that they conduct their daily lives on the conviction that there are such things as identifiable causes, so that events are not simply baffling correlations. Consequently, the physicist will turn the television set to a different channel when he fears that the sex and violence on the present channel may have a "bad influence" on his five-year-old daughter.

It appears to me that the noncausality trend in certain sectors of modern science might well be the result of theorists' puzzlement over (1) the multiplicity of ways causation can be interpreted, (2) the great complexity of the factors involved in cause, and (3) the difficulty—or perhaps impossibility—of identifying an *ultimate* or *final* cause. In any event, for purposes of the present perspective, I am assuming that there are such things as causes behind the way children develop and that the kinds of cause posited in one theory can differ from the kinds posited in another. In the practical world of child rearing, it is obviously useful to identify causes underlying development because then attempts can be made to manipulate causal factors to optimize favorable types of development and remedy those types deemed undesirable.

DEVELOPMENT THEORIES AND THEIR PERSPECTIVES ON CAUSATION

The following review of viewpoints of cause is organized under three topics—varieties of causal factors, the chronological location of cause, and nature's plan. Each topic is illustrated with examples from theories reviewed in this book.

Varieties of Causal Factors

Perhaps the most obvious differences in theorists' views of causality is in (1) the types of causal factors they posit, (2) the relative strengths of the different types, (3) the manner in which the types interact, and (4) the importance of various types at different times in a child's life.

Types of Factors A convenient way to think of types is in terms of principal causal factors and of the subfactors subsumed under them. For instance, the most commonly cited broad types of cause are *heredity* and *environment*. Then under each of these, constituent subtypes can be listed. Under *heredity,* particular gene combinations might be postulated as responsible for different kinds of development—physical, cognitive, emotional, or the like. Then within each kind, more specific gene patterns might be proposed. Hence, within the cognitive domain, different sets of genes could be presumed to account for the development of such abilities as verbal reasoning, quantitative reasoning, spatial relations, musical talent, and others. In a similar fashion, *environment* might be dissected into causal components—home and family, school, peers, mass communication media, and more. These components might be decomposed into even more detailed subtypes, such as, within the home-and-family category, the influence of each parent and each sibling might be analyzed separately.

   In summary, a significant way theories differ is in the patterning of general and specific causal factors proposed to account for children's development. For example, the version of commonsense attribution theory described in Chapter Five was divided into three general types of cause— characteristics of the self, characteristics of the environment, and such indeterminate influences as supernatural intervention and luck. And under each of these general categories, constituent subfactors were listed. In Havighurst's model, developmental tasks arise from three sources—the child's biological structure, the society's demands, and the personal values of the individual. Piaget proposed four general causal variables that contribute to the individual's survival—heredity, the child's physical experience, social transmission (people instructing the child), and equilibration. In Skinner's operant conditioning, a single type of causal factor—the nature of the consequences that follow the child's actions—is considered sufficient to explain development. In a similar way, each of the other theories offers its own propositions about general and specific sources of cause.

Strength of Factors   A second way theorists differ is in the amount of influence they assume that each factor exerts on development. Gesell attributed far more power to genetic factors than to environmental influences. Piaget credited heredity with more influence than did Vygotsky. Skinner, social learning theorists, and ecologists assume that environmental factors are dominantly responsible for shaping children's growth.

Patterns of Interaction   The manner in which causal factors relate to each other also varies from one theory to another. Piaget described a sequence of three steps by which causal elements played their roles. He contended that a genetic timing plan first established the sequence of neural development that equipped children to learn different cognitive skills. Next, children developed cognitive structures through their unguided encounters with the environment. Only after unguided experiences prepared the cognitive structures could instruction profitably take place.

The essence of information-processing theory lies in its system of interactions among the individual's sensori-cognitive-motor elements and selected aspects of the environment.

From a humanistic perspective, Maslow stated that *needs,* as causal forces, operated in a hierarchical fashion, with basic physical needs demanding fulfillment before self-realization needs could be pursued.

In Riegel's dialectical theory, the pattern of interaction that plays itself over and over during the process of development consists of this sequence: a presently existing condition of the child (thesis) encounters a contradictory life situation (antithesis) that stimulates the child to revise the existing condition in a way that resolves the contradiction (synthesis).

Factors Related to Phases of Growth   Theorists often assume that the significance of a given factor will differ from one period of development to another. In psychoanalytic theory, the influence of parents on the child's psychosexual development is more important during the early years of childhood (oral, anal, early genital periods) than during adolescence (mature genital period), when peer influence increases. In Erikson's system of psychosocial stages, parents play a more crucial role during the child's trust-mistrust and autonomy-doubt crises (ages 0–3) than during the industry-inferiority crisis (ages 7–12) when school becomes an increasingly potent influence. Likewise, in the scheme of stages proposed by Vygotsky and Elkonin, the *leading activity* that becomes a key causal factor within a growth stage will differ from one stage to another. For instance, the leading activity for ages 3 to 7 is game playing, whereas at ages 15 to 17 the activity is vocational learning.

To conclude, the foregoing examples suggest that one useful way to compare the ways different theories account for development is to analyze the theories in terms of (1) the general and specific types of causal factors proposed, (2) the presumed strength of each factor in affecting development, (3) the manner in which the factors are believed to interact, and (4) the relative importance of different factors at successive age levels.

The Chronological Location of Cause

An entirely different way to perceive causes is in terms of their chronological location—in the past, the present, or the future.

Looking to the Past   Psychoanalytic theory, in its psychotherapeutic form, focuses on causes in the past, particularly on those distressing experiences in an individual's childhood that were repressed and, since that time, have seethed unresolved in the unconsious, precipitating physical or psychological disorders that now require the attention of a psychoanalyst. Therapy involves identifying events from the past responsible for present disorders so they can be relived vicariously in a way that places them in an acceptable, realistic perspective. A cause residing in the past is also the concern of developmental-task adherents when they contend that the reason children may be having difficulty with a task at their present stage of growth is that they failed to complete an earlier task.

When theorists conduct a retrospective search for cause, they are often assuming that causes are linked together in cumulative chain of cause and effect relationships that recede endlessly into the past. This historical mode of reasoning has been called a *genetic* explanation since it involves "the use of statements of initial conditions that require mention of sequentially ordered events occurring at different times" (Nagel, 1965, p. 17). How such a chain may be formed can be illustrated by the following line of reasoning:

> A six-year-old girl is judged to be shy because her father has so often criticized the child for not achieving up to the father's expectations. The father's high expectations, in turn, are the result of his growing up with eleven siblings in a family that was constantly in financial distress; and in order to work his way out of his family's poverty condition, he developed the habit of setting high standards of productivity for himself and of working hard to achieve them. Now that he is financially well to do and has children of his own, his lasting fear of poverty causes him to set high standards of performance for his offspring as well. The reason for the father's poverty-ridden childhood was that his own parents had been poorly educated peasants from Europe who had immigrated to the United States when their ancestral farmland had been inherited by their older siblings, so they had no source of income.

And in like manner we could continue to trace back over the centuries the linkages of cause and effect that we assume have contributed to the shyness of our present-day six-year-old. Each cause produces an effect, and that effect itself becomes a cause of a subsequent effect. However, to do a proper job of it, we would need to identify not just one cause behind each effect but, rather, to cite a network of causal factors that converged to produce each effect. By engaging in such a mode of reasoning, we have adopted a historical approach to explain development. This attempt to move progressively back into the past is what philosophers have labeled the *infinite regression*—there seems to be no beginning to the chain of cause and effect relationships. One solution to this problem has been to adopt a theological position and identify the *first cause* or *final cause* as God, Allah, the Cosmic Soul, the Great All-Knowing, or the like. Such a solution is offered by the familiar proposal of a final cause in the opening phrases of the Judeo/Christian/Islamic scriptures: "In the beginning, God created the heaven and the earth. . . . And God said, Let us make man in our image, after our likeness" (Genesis, verses 1, 26). Or, we could eschew a theological explanation and, instead, cite the secular scientists' first cause, the *big bang*. But this hardly settles the question of the *ultimate* cause, since we still need to account for what caused God or the big bang. Commonsense explanations often involve some version of genetic explanation, with people often arriving at the ultimate cause rather quickly. After proposing one or two links to the past, they conclude that the cause was "God's will" or "nature's way."

A historical approach to causality is often used in accounting for the ostensible *national character* displayed by a particular social group, such as the Slovaks, Scots, Arabs, or Malays. Ways that members of the group are alike are seen as resulting from a common developmental history that can be estimated by tracing cause and effect forces in the group's past. And Darwinian theory represents a historical endeavor to explain the origin and characteristics of all species.

Looking at the Present   Contextualist and ecological theorists, rather than looking at the past, stress present conditions as the causes of present behavior. Kurt Lewin, as a founding father of contextualist perspectives, proposed that an individual's thoughts and actions at any one time are the result of the entire configuration of forces within that person's current life space. The term *life space* refers to all internal (physiological, mental) and external (environmental) factors that affect the person consciously or unconsciously at the moment. These forces can include events of the past. However, it is not the past events themselves but, rather, the current residue in memory that influences present behavior (Lewin, 1942, p. 217). Hence it is not important to resurrect the past. Instead, we need to identify present environmental and internal conditions (including memories) that currently affect the person.

Looking to the Future   Humanistic psychology illustrates a theoretical position that locates cause in the future. Humanists pay particular heed to how a person's ambitions, hopes, dreams, and expectations for the months and years ahead influence development. The notion that children are goal directed and actively pursue self-realization is used by humanistic theorists to help account for why the young develop as they do.

And while the above discussion has separated the retrospective, the immediate present, and the prospective views of cause, it should be apparent that a given theory may reflect two or three of these perspectives. Psychoanalysts do not completely ignore the present, nor do humanists concentrate entirely on the future. Piaget and Vygotsky concerned themselves with both the past and the present. Nevertheless, even when theorists include more than one chronological location, they still differ in regard to which location they emphasize in explaining cause.

Nature's Plan

The phrase *nature's plan* identifies a belief that the pattern of children's development follows a predetermined program built into the species' gene structure. Growing up is simply the gradual unfolding of that plan. This belief is a form of teleological explanation—that development is a revelation of nature's purpose and design. As noted in Chapter Seven, Erikson labeled this plan *the epigenetic principle*. Gesell and his colleagues have been strong advocates of a teleological position. And neo-Darwinism is the form of nature's plan in which sociobiologists and other varieties of ethologists (Chapter Fifteen) anchor their theories of development.

CONCLUSION

Statements about child development are of three major varieties— descriptive, prescriptive, and explanatory. Descriptive statements tell what children are like at any given time and how they change from one time to another. Description is based on observations, measurements, and children's introspective testimonials about what they think and how they feel. Prescriptive statements tell what children should be like and are based on the ideals or set of values held by the person offering the prescription. Explanatory statements are estimates about what causal factors account for the ways children develop. The present perspective has focused on explanatory statements. I have suggested that the task of understanding the conception of cause represented in a particular theory can be profitably pursued by identifying (1) the types of general and detailed causal factors that the theorist delineates or implies, as well as the strength and interaction of these factors as different periods of children's development, and (2) the chronological emphasis implied in causal attributions—emphasis on the past, present, or future. Furthermore, identifying the assumptions that a theorist may make about "nature's plan" can also prove enlightening.

ENVIRONMENTS AND GENETIC PLANS

A search for patterns of environmental influence and for the biological templates of human nature

The two varieties of theory described in Part Seven have been devised in recent times as correctives to what their creators have claimed to be simplistic or distorted features of existing models.

The first of the pair, ecological psychology (Chapter Fourteen), is intended to remedy *intraindividual stage theorists'* neglect of the complex ways environments influence children's development. People espousing ecological models accuse such theorists as Sigmund Freud and Jean Piaget (or at least accuse interpreters of Piaget) of explaining "development either by reference to elementaristic traits or systemic mechanisms which are supposed to locate strictly inside the organism. . . . Very often psychologists who use this [framework] model their thinking along the lines of traditional genetics, posit the existence of psychological analogues of genes that are supposed to cause temporal unfolding of predetermined developmental sequences of phenomena" (Valsiner, 1987, p. 46). Thus ecological theorists, rather than looking chiefly inside the individual to answer the "why" of development, focus primary attention on the environments the child inhabits—or, perhaps more to the point, they attend to the interactions of the individual with those environments (the individual–ecological frame of reference). Chapter Fourteen briefly reviews the evolution of ecological theory in the Kurt Lewin–Roger Barker line, then provides a more detailed description of Urie Bronfenbrenner's (1979) ecological model.

The second general type of theory in Part Seven is offered in Chapter Fifteen under the title Ethology and Sociobiology. Ethologists, in contrast to ecologists, seek to remedy what they consider to be the neglect of human biological inheritance in explanations of why children develop as they do.

In the opening paragraphs of his book *Human Ethology* (1989), Irenäus Eibl-Eibesfeldt reproaches sociologists, psychology's behaviorists, and anthropology's cultural relativists for assigning no role to inherited biological tendencies in the development of human communication skills, social behavior, ethics, and aesthetics. In depicting the state of these three social science disciplines prior to the mid-twentieth century, Eibl-Eibesfeldt argues that:

> The possibility that some aspects of behavior might, through phylogenetic adaptation, be genetically programmed was not even considered. . . . As late as the 1970s, the majority of behaviorists and sociologists viewed humans as primarily passive beings subject to the formative influences of their surroundings. . . . Parallel to the development of behaviorism in psychology there developed in anthropology a pronounced cultural relativism according to which culture is a construct on which the laws of biology have no influence. . . . The decisive impetus for revising this extreme environmental approach came from behavioral biology (ethology). . . . [In the 1930s and 1940s, the pioneers of ethology] Lorenz and Tinbergen demonstrated that phylogenetic adaptations determine behavior in well-defined ways. . . . By introducing the dimension of phylogeny into the science of behavior, their work incorporated Charles Darwin's findings (1989, pp. ix–x).

Eibl-Eibesfeldt's reference to Darwin raises the issue of the relationship between phylogeny and ontogeny in child development. Phylogenetic theories are designed to answer the question, By what process has the human race—species *Homo sapiens*—developed in comparison to the process by which other species have developed? Ontogenetic theories, on the other hand, are intended to answer the question, By what process does an individual human change from the moment of biological conception until the time of death?

The two most popular present-day phylogenetic theories are Darwin's and the biblical account to which fundamentalist Jews, Christians, and Muslims typically subscribe. The biblical version holds that God created the first humans, Adam and Eve, on a particular day several thousand years ago, completing these initial ancestors of the human race in a form that has remained essentially the same in all their descendants down to the present day. Darwin, in contrast, proposed that all living things trace their origins back to a common simple organism. Since that time millions of years in the past, certain descendants of the earliest organisms have become more complex and differentiated as a result of both genetic mutations and the extent to which the mutants' characteristics have equipped them to survive changes in environmental conditions. Ethologists are much concerned about the way such phylogenetic development has produced different species, and are particularly concerned about the ways genetic composition makes members of a given species alike. In other words, ethologists are especially interested in understanding children's *human nature*—what one child has in common with all other children. On the basis of this understanding, the ethologist is subsequently interested in knowing the way such a phylogenetically developed nature contributes to ontogeny—that is, contributes to the individual child's development through transactions with his or her daily surroundings.

In summary, both ecologists and ethologists are much interested in environments. However, the focus of their interests differs. Ecologists are most concerned with how the patterning of a child's daily environments influence that child's development. Ethologists, on the other hand, are more concerned with the way environments of the species' past (phylogenetic environments) have fashioned those inherited genetic structures that serve as templates for the propensities, potentials, and limitations that govern how children can behave and what they can learn from their present environments.

The perspective that closes Part Seven is entitled "Charting Trends of the Times." It is designed to answer the question of what major shifts have occurred over time in the popularity of the thirteen principal theories described in Chapters Three through Fifteen.

CHAPTER FOURTEEN

Ecological Psychology

Urie Bronfenbrenner (born 1917) credits his own childhood environment with directing his attention to the crucial role children's social and physical settings play in fashioning their development.

> It was my good fortune to have been brought up on the premises of a state institution for those who were then called "the feebleminded," where my father was a neuropathologist. Along with his medical degree, he had a Ph.D. in zoology, and he was a field naturalist at heart. The institution's grounds offered a rich biological and social terrain for his observant eye (Bronfenbrenner, 1979, p. xi).

From such a vantage point, young Bronfenbrenner learned how plants' and animals' surroundings affect their growth as well as how the social and physical environment of an institution can influence the development of its residents. Specifically, he noted that the social behavior, personalities, and tested intelligence of people held at the institution changed in relation to the social situations in which they were placed. This early introduction to the influence of environments on the developmental fate of living things had a strong effect on Bronfenbrenner's later career as a developmental psychologist at Cornell University. Much of his academic life there was dedicated to cross-cultural research in such diverse locations as Nova Scotia, the Soviet Union, China, Eastern and Western Europe, Israel, and the United States. As a result of his observations, he concluded that:

> Seen in different contexts, human nature, which I had previously thought of as a singular noun, became plural and pluralistic; for the

different environments were producing discernible differences, not only across but also within societies, in talent, temperament, human relations, and particularly in the ways in which the culture, or subculture, brought up its next generation (1979, p. xiii).

He also recognized that the environments in which children live are so multifarious and intertwined that the task of understanding their effect on children is extremely demanding. To simplify and systematize this task, he devised the ecological theory of development whose principal features are described in this chapter. But before we concentrate on Bronfenbrenner's scheme, we may profit from recognizing some of the events in the realm of ecological psychology that preceded and paralleled his work.

BACKGROUNDS OF ECOLOGICAL PSYCHOLOGY

An important ancestor of ecological theory is Gestalt psychology, which evolved as a significant movement in Germany during the early decades of the twentieth century. Gestalt views became disseminated in America during the 1920s and the 1930s when such prominent figures as Kurt Koffka (1886–1941), Kurt Lewin (1890–1947), Heinz Werner (1890–1964), and Fritz Heider (1897–1988) immigrated to the United States to accept university posts. Gestalt theory, when applied to child development, conceives of the child as a whole, integrated organism. The word *Gestalt* in the German language means "configuration," thus reflecting the holistic viewpoint typical of European theorists in many scientific fields, in contrast to the British associationism from which behaviorism partially derived. *Associationism* represents a tradition that conceives of development as proceeding by small, additive increments that gradually accumulate to form the personality or to comprise the child's repertoire of acts. But to the holistic or field theorist, a new stimulus or experience does not simply add a new element to a child's store of actions or knowledge, leaving the previous elements undisturbed. Instead, every significant new experience can alter the relationship of many or all of the existing elements that have made up the personality to this point, so the patterning of the child's entire individuality is influenced.

The holistic or field-theory concept of development is sometimes explained by the use of an example from astronomy. Assume that a new planet the size of Saturn is added to the solar system between Earth and Mars. This addition does not simply place a new speck of light in the sky of earthlings and martians. Rather, its gravitational pull influences the paths of all the planets in the solar system, having more effect on the closer bodies than on the distant ones. So with the entire pattern of the solar framework altered, the system itself becomes something new. In psychology, holistic or Gestalt theorists propose that a similar effect occurs in the development of a child's personality each time the child encounters impressive new experiences or each time an internal physiological change is triggered by the individual's genetic structure.

What is now known as *ecological* or *environmental* psychology owes part of its evolutionary background to the work of Lewin and his colleagues during the 1930s and 1940s, principally at the University of Iowa. Lewin labeled his Gestalt perspective *topological psychology*, a term adopted from the field of mathematics where *topology* is a type of geometry that gives attention to the relationships among spaces, especially to the distance between one space and another and to the barriers between the two. He coined the term *life space* to encompass all of the facts that influence a child's behavior at a given time. As mentioned earlier, in this system a *fact* is not an objectively verifiable observation from the "real world." Instead, a fact is any element within the child's psychological environment that affects that individual's behavior or thought; this includes forces of which the child is unaware as well as elements the child accepts as real or true.

In 1947, the year Lewin died, two of his co-workers, Roger W. Barker and H. F. Wright, accepted academic appointments at the University of Kansas, where they gave topological psychology a particularly strong environmental bent by concentrating on the role of environmental forces in a child's life space (Barker, 1978). They noted that in biology the term *ecology* refers to the interrelationship between a plant or animal and its environment, so they borrowed the term to describe their way of studying how children's surroundings affect behavior and development.

Barker (1968) noted that traditional psychology showed ways in which people differed from each other but failed to trace the great variations in thought, feeling, and action that an individual child experiences during a typical day. Furthermore, according to Barker, a large proportion of the variation within a single child's life can be accounted for by the environments or *behavior settings* through which that child commonly moves. In effect, ecological theorists contend that we can account for a great deal of a child's behavior if we know her current environment. For example, we can predict that if a typical teenager is in church, she will not be shouting, but if she is at a basketball game she will shout loud and long. If she is walking to the drug store, we can predict that she will not be walking in line, but if she is marching in the school band during the Fourth of July parade, she will be carefully keeping in line and in step with her companions.

To move ecological theory beyond these commonsense observations, Barker and his colleagues identified a variety of components of behavior settings so that the nature of a child's significant surroundings could be analyzed more systematically. For instance, they proposed that a behavior setting (such as a history class or a dinner party) is comprised of two main elements: (1) the typical ways people act (called *standing patterns of behavior*) and (2) the *milieu,* which is made up of two components. The first component is *physical things*—desks and wall maps in history class, the dining table and silverware at the dinner party. The second is *time boundaries*—a forty-five-minute class period, a two-hour dinner party. The milieu is said to be circumjacent to (that is, it encompasses) the behavior of the people in the setting. Such terms were created to help ecological analysts organize their observations of the environments in which children grow up. One of the Kansas group's most detailed investigations focused on the effect school size exerts on students' development (Barker & Gump, 1964; Barker et al., 1970). The group accurately predicted that students of smaller high schools engage in a wider variety of activities, assume more responsibility, hold more extracurricular positions of importance, and are more highly motivated to take active part in voluntary activities than is the case with students in larger schools (Ross, 1985).

One important branch of environmental psychology focuses on issues of particular concern to community planners, architects, and social service agencies. The issues relate to questions of how human behavior is affected by urban crowding, inner-city decay, suburban growth, sparsely settled rural regions, resource availability, institutional size, and the like. Attempts to understand the influence of physical settings on people's lives have spawned a variety of theories. For instance, an *information-overload* model holds that people have a limited capacity to process information, so when excessive stimulation from the environment occurs, they ignore peripheral inputs in order to give adequate attention to primary tasks. "The result is that responses to these peripheral nonsocial or social stimuli are minimal or nonexistent" (J. D. Fisher, Bell, & Baum, 1984, p. 83). An *understimulation* theory proposes that monotonous environmental stimulation causes boredom and less reason for people to take action. A *behavior-constraint* model suggests that when children feel they have lost control over their environment, they behave in ways they think will recover their control and freedom of action.

Among investigators toiling in this domain are developmentalists seeking to discover valid generalizations about the interactions of specific types of physical settings on child growth and adjustment. J. F. Wohlwill and W. van Vliet's book, *Habitats for Children* (1985), illustrates this type of inquiry. For instance, van Vliet derived the following generalizations from reviewing studies of the role of housing type, household density, and neighborhood density on children's peer interactions and social adjustment:

Neighborhood density may be conceptualized as a factor contributing to the field of opportunities for interactions with peers. Such interactions may be either socially desirable or deviant. Except possibly for situations of extreme crowding or isolation, the acceptability of children's social relations does not appear to be related to the conditions of neighborhood density under which they come about. . . . Research findings do not demonstrate convincingly that high neighborhood densities contribute to maladjusted behavior. . . . Some studies suggest that, in suburbs, children's interactions with peers are less frequent and less spontaneous and fewer times revolve around common interests than is the case in city environments. In these investigations neighborhood density has not been singled out for study as a variable which may, in part, be responsible for these differences (van Vliet, 1985, p. 194).

Developmentalists have proposed a variety of approaches to understanding environmental influences in children's lives. One of the most systematic of these schemes is the one created by Bronfenbrenner, which we will now inspect in some detail.

BRONFENBRENNER'S ECOLOGICAL THEORY

To begin, Bronfenbrenner defines the ecology of human development as:

the scientific study of the progressive, mutual accommodation between an active, growing human being and the changing properties of the immediate settings in which the developing person lives, as this process is affected by relations between those settings, and by the larger contexts in which the settings are embedded (Bronfenbrenner, 1979, p. 21).

In Figures 14.1 and 14.2, I have sought to diagram the relationships that Bronfenbrenner has posited among the elements of his definition.

The model's most basic unit of analysis is the *microsystem*—"a pattern of activities, roles, and interpersonal relations experienced by the developing person in a given setting with particular physical and material characteristics" (Bronfenbrenner, 1979, p. 22). Figure 14.1 pictures three typical settings for such microsystems—school, home, and peer group locations. (Barker would label these locations *behavior settings* [1968; Schoggen, 1989].) A crucial conviction in Bronfenbrenner's scheme is that the influence of a behavior setting on a child's development is not exerted by the "objective" or "real life" nature of the activities, roles, and interpersonal relations seen there. Rather, the influence derives from the child's perception or interpretation of these factors. Bronfenbrenner agrees with Lewin's early proposal that: (1) the phenomenological (internally interpreted or experienced) environment dominates the real environment in guiding

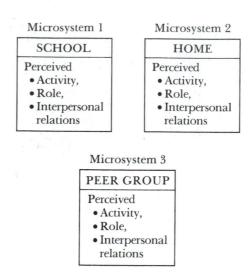

Microsystem 1

SCHOOL

Perceived
  • Activity,
  • Role,
  • Interpersonal
    relations

Microsystem 2

HOME

Perceived
  • Activity,
  • Role,
  • Interpersonal
    relations

Microsystem 3

PEER GROUP

Perceived
  • Activity,
  • Role,
  • Interpersonal
    relations

Figure 14.1   Children's Microsystems of Experience

behavior, (2) it is folly to try to understand a child's action solely from the objective qualities of an environment without learning what those qualities mean for the child in that setting, (3) it is important to discover how the objects, people, and events in the situation affect the child's motivations, and (4) it is essential to recognize the influence on behavior of "unreal" elements that arise from the child's imagination, fantasy, and idiosyncratic interpretations (Bronfenbrenner, 1979, pp. 24–25).

An analyst is best equipped to comprehend a child's behavior by learning how the child perceives the activities, roles, and interpersonal relations displayed in that setting. The term *activities* refers to what people are doing. *Roles* are the actions expected of people holding a position in society, such as the position of parent, infant, sibling, teacher, friend, coach, or the like. *Interpersonal relations* are the ways people treat each other, as shown by what they say and do as a result of their being together. Bronfenbrenner adopted the term *microsystems* to reflect his conviction that behavior settings provide the smallest unit of analysis (micro) and that the three most significant components of a setting (activities, roles, and interpersonal relations) form a Gestalt or interacting behavior field (system) in which a change in one component could affect the entire configuration and produce a new meaning for the child. An obvious methodological problem faced in the analysis of a microsystem arises from the fact that the components are often in flux, as determined by shifts in the ongoing activities and by readjustments occurring in the participants' roles and relations. An analyst of the microsystem is thus obliged to aim at a moving target.

The task of understanding children's behavior in a microsystem is further complicated by three phases of influence outside the immediate behavior setting. Bronfenbrenner applies the label *mesosystem* to the first phase beyond the microsystem, as symbolized by the configuration within the second largest box in Figure 14.2.

> A mesosystem comprises the interrelations among two or more settings in which the developing person actively participates (such as, for a child, the relations among home, school, and neighborhood peer group; an adult, among family, work, and social life) (Bronfenbrenner, 1979, p. 25).

As the double-pointed arrows suggest, the pattern of interrelationships among microsystems can influence the child's perceptions and

Figure 14.2 Embedded Systems of Children's Environmental Experiences behavior within any of the settings in which the child is presently located. For instance, children's experiences in the classroom on any given day are typically affected by their impressions of the attitudes of their parents and their peers.

Bronfenbrenner applied the label *exosystem* to the next phase outside the mesosystem.

> An exosystem refers to one or more settings that do not involve the developing person as an active participant, but in which events occur that affect, or are affected by, what happens in the setting containing the developing person (Bronfenbrenner, 1979, p. 25).

The three illustrative exosystems in Figure 14.2 are the workplaces of the child's parents, school board decisions that affect the child, and an older sister's network of companions. If the parents' workplaces are nearby rather than hundreds of miles distant, then parents will have more time to spend with the child. If the child is a slow learner and the school board decides to "mainstream" slow learners into regular classes rather than providing such pupils with special instructional help, then the child's progress in school can be affected. In addition, the child's development can be somewhat different if an older sister's companions engage in activities that draw her away from home much of the time so she rarely is available to "baby sit" her younger sibling.

Finally, the source of influence most remote from the children's immediate experience is the array of attitudes, practices, and convictions shared throughout society at large. This *macrosystem* is composed of the *cultural milieu*, which is represented in Figure 14.2 by the large box encompassing the microsystems, mesosystem, and exosystems of the child's environment.

A question may now be asked about what implications this model holds for researchers and others (parents, teachers, social workers, club leaders) who try to understand children's development. First, the model suggests which aspects of the child's environment should be the principal foci of data gathering. These aspects include:

1. The behavior setting of the child's immediate microsystem (e.g., the school playground during recess)

2. The activities, roles, and interpersonal relations of the primary participants in that setting (e.g., the playground supervisor and the boys and girls on two competing soccer teams)

3. The mesosystem—the influences of other microsystems on the child's perceptions in this setting (e.g., the child's recollection of

recent soccer games and what parents might say if the child performs well or poorly in this game)

4. The exosystems (e.g., the school's "sports committee" that es-
    tablished the rules for such games, and the length of the recess
    period as determined by the school's time schedule)

5. The cultural milieu (e.g., the expectations widely held in the soci-
    ety about such matters as abiding by the rules, being "a good
    winner and a good loser," placing the team's welfare above one's
    own welfare, and obeying people in authority)

Second, the model's use of the term *systems* implies that an analyst not
only should gather evidence about the foregoing five components, but also
about the transactions among them. The analysis of transactions can profitably involve decisions about (a) which elements apparently have influenced
which others, (b) the nature of this influence (what did A cause B to do),
(c) to what extent was the influence reciprocal (did B also alter A's performance or characteristics), and (d) which of the elements appeared
to exert the most powerful effects (was element C's influence great but
D's negligible).

It is obviously impossible to chart moment-to-moment alterations in
the model's complex of components and their interactions. Thus, to render
the task of analysis feasible, it is necessary for an investigator to select
occasions for taking ecological "snapshots" or for making summaries of
ecological events. These occasions should be chosen for their likely significant effect on the child's long-term abilities and attitudes. To aid with this
decision about when a new snapshot is warranted, Bronfenbrenner has
suggested the notion of *ecological transition,* meaning a shift that occurs
whenever the child's position in the ecological environment is significantly
altered due to a change in role, setting, or both. We might infer that there
can be major and minor transitions. Major ones include the newborn's
coming home from the hospital, the child's learning to walk and talk
around age 18 months, entering nursery school at age 3, starting the
primary grades at age 6, going to summer camp, moving with the family to
a new city, and witnessing the parents' divorce (Bronfenbrenner, 1979, pp.
26–27). Minor transitions can involve less dramatic changes that, nevertheless, leave some residue of attitudes or skills that contribute to long-term
development. A minor transition might occur with a girl's membership in a
high school choir, with a nine-year-old's having a grandmother live in the
home for six months, and with a teenager's developing acne. The task of
the researcher becomes one of charting the child's ecology before and after
the transition point and noting both (1) the factors that apparently have

precipitated the transition and (2) the effects the transition produced on the child.

> I shall argue that every ecological transition is both a consequence and an instigator of developmental processes. . . . [Thus] from the viewpoint of research, every ecological transition constitutes, in effect, a ready-made experiment of nature with a built-in, before-after design in which each subject can serve as his own control. In sum, an ecological transition sets the stage both for the occurrence and the systematic study of developmental phenomena (Bronfenbrenner, 1979, p. 17).

A critical feature of research methodology in Bronfenbrenner's scheme is what he calls *ecological validity*, meaning "the extent to which the environment experienced by the subjects in a scientific investigation has the properties it is supposed or assumed to have by the investigator" (Bronfenbrenner, 1979, p. 29). His emphasis on ecological validity derives from a concern that too often research on children is conducted in laboratories or other unique settings, and then broadly inclusive generalizations are drawn about development without regard for how children's interpretations—their phenomenological perceptions—are affected by the different configurations of different environments. Several lessons about research methods are suggested by this notion of ecological validity. First, reports of research should describe the study's influential environmental variables, and investigators should limit their conclusions to ones applicable to children who experience life within similar ecological domains. Second, the focus of analysis should be the children's perceptions of the environment rather than the environment's "objective" characteristics. Thus the research methods need to be ones that reveal children's phenomonological interpretations, instead of ones that merely identify observable characteristics of the setting. But the task of accurately eliciting children's perceptions is far more difficult than that of simply describing the setting. Such a job can most adequately be performed by investigators who themselves are intimately acquainted with the culture and thus able to discern the nuances of language and the undercurrent of attitudes embedded in children's responses. Derek Freeman (1983), in his caustic criticism of Margaret Mead's *Coming of Age in Samoa* (1968), faulted her for drawing erroneous conclusions about Samoan adolescent girls' development because of Mead's failure to comprehend the Samoan cultural milieu and her approaching the research task with the aim of "proving" a hypothesis rather than of understanding the significance of Samoan adolescents' remarks from the perspective of the Samoan macrosystem.) Bronfenbrenner and his co-workers have admitted that existing research techniques are still inadequate for achieving the desired ecological validity. He sees the task of creating such techniques as an item developmentalists need to include on their future agenda.

An additional consideration in Bronfenbrenner's scheme is the concept of *developmental validity*. In order for an observed change in a child's perceptions or activities in one setting to qualify as developmentally valid, that change must be shown to carry over to other behavior settings and other times. In effect, changes that are unique to a given time and place and fail to appear in other ecological settings are not credited as developmental since they fail to exert a lasting effect on the child's attitudes or skills.

In addition to identifying the components of his theory, Bronfenbrenner has spelled out in considerable detail the way research can be conducted from the perspective of the model. In his analysis, he describes studies that can be conducted in either laboratory situations or such natural settings as children's institutions (fondling homes, children's hospitals), child-care centers, and nursery schools. However, "well-designed ecological experiments are, as yet, not easy to find. I have therefore had to invent some examples where they did not exist. Moreover, in many instances there was a dearth not only of relevant research but also of relevant research ideas. Accordingly, [this discussion offers] . . . even more proposed hypotheses than proposed investigations" (Bronfenbrenner, 1979, p. 42). In short, the theory's potential for generating widespread, fruitful research still remains to be demonstrated.

PRACTICAL APPLICATIONS

Ecological theory appears to hold considerable promise for guiding child rearing, educational practices, social work, and child therapy as soon as more adequate appraisal techniques are created and an expanding range of empirical investigations produce a growing fund of convincing generalizations about relationships within the theory's four levels of systems (micro, meso, exo, and macro).

The focus of Bronfenbrenner's theory is on children's interpretations of their surroundings rather than on the objective characteristics of those surroundings. Thus practical applications must involve methods of effecting constructive changes in children's perceptions of their environments. Such perceptions could be improved by one or more of the following methods: (1) changing the damaging components of an environment (a microsystem), (2) transporting children out of unsuitable environments and into favorable ones, (3) assigning to other microcosms the child-raising responsibilities that are not being performed adequately in a current microcosm (changing the mesosystem), or (4) altering children's perceptions of those environments that they must continue to inhabit. To illustrate, consider the situation of a boy whose development is deemed to suffer from his living with neglectful parents. The neglect takes the form of the parents' failing to teach the boy appropriate social behavior, failing to offer him affection and emotional support, and blaming him for being an unsatisfactory son. Such neglect is judged to contribute to the boy's unsuitable behavior in microsystems outside the home (the school, the Scout troop, the neighborhood peer group) where he is rude to peers and adults, resists assuming responsibility, and seeks attention by bragging and criticizing others. Attempts to alter these characteristics could include (1) changing the parents' child-rearing practices through counseling, (2) placing the boy in a boarding school, (3) having school personnel and the Scout leader teach proper social behavior and furnish emotional support, and (4) counseling with the boy to alter his perception of his home life, thereby equipping him to accept his parents for what they are, to stop blaming himself for the way his parents treat him, and to adopt people outside the family as models to emulate.

In summary, the ability of Bronfenbrenner's type of theory to produce practical applications depends on the success with which ecological investigative techniques reveal where within the four levels of systems (micro, meso, exo, macro) counterproductive components are operating. Then steps can be taken to change those components in ways that constructively alter the child's perception of environments in relation to self.

ECOLOGICAL THEORY: AN ASSESSMENT

In rating Bronfenbrenner's model, I have qualified my judgments on several of the nine standards with the symbol P signifying *potential*. This is because the details required for translating the theory into practice do not appear well worked out as yet. I do find Bronfenbrenner's basic argument convincing (though hardly novel)—that the environmental forces he identifies significantly influence children's development. I believe he is correct in both (1) alerting us not to neglect these forces and (2) proposing a heuristic scheme for categorizing the multitudinous forces into four interlocking systems. What is now needed is a set of more precise guidelines than the author has so far provided to render the model operational (item 2—clarity). As a way of illustrating only three of the numerous aspects of the theory that call for more detail, imagine that we wish to study a thirteen-year-old girl's development from the perspective of the ecological model. Then we face such questions as:

1. *Discriminating among microsystems.* How do we decide where one microsystem leaves off and another begins in the following epi-

sode—the girl walks to school with companions, is joined by additional companions, accompanies them into a video store for a few minutes, then continues with the group to school where she chats with a teacher before entering class? Perhaps more important, how can we determine if this series of incidents exerts a significant enough effect on the girl's development to warrant our bothering to seek her interpretation of the events?

2. *Identifying roles.* If we define a microsystem by its physical setting during a period of time (Tuesday's seventh-grade forty-five minute math class), which roles should we identify for people in that setting when some of the people may be evincing more than one role or may shift from one role to another? For instance, our thirteen-year-old assumes the role of learner as the teacher explains a new math function, the role of monitor when she passes out rulers and compasses to her classmates, the role of tutor when she helps a boy with a difficult problem, and that of student representative when she requests on behalf of the others that the teacher not assign homework the night of the championship basketball game. Should each of these roles be identified in our study? If not, what criteria should we use for choosing those roles that are to be depicted?

3. *Assessing the strength of system components.* Implicit in the theory is the assumption that some elements of the model will exert greater influence on the child's perceptions and behavior than will others. Although Bronfenbrenner has proposed some general principles for judging the relative power of elements or subsystems, the way one would make this judgment in a specific case is still unclear. In the case of our thirteen-year-old girl, how do we estimate the degree to which such exosystems as the girl's parents, her television viewing habits, or her study of "the democratic process" in history class has caused her to represent the group in requesting that homework not be assigned?

My intention in citing these ambiguous and clouded features of ecological theory is not to suggest that the model lacks potential value. Rather, my purpose is simply to explain why I have employed two symbols, X and P, in rating the theory. I have used X to indicate what I judge to be the theory's present status on the nine assessment standards and then have placed a P on several of the scales to suggest the potential the theory might hold if the current imprecision of its key features can be rectified. Bronfenbrenner himself has been frank in recognizing that his model is still in an early formative stage, particularly in regard to the details of devising suitable investigative techniques and applications to child rearing and education. Thus, because his version of ecological psychology is so new in the developmental marketplace, there is as yet a paucity of empirical examples to illustrate its applications or to test its hypotheses. Even the number of hypotheses that might be tested is as of yet quite small. Therefore, compared with such theories as Freud's, Piaget's, Vygotsky's, Skinner's, and Bandura's, his ecological model is still very much a baby, so its contributions to developmental psychology—whatever they may be—lie necessarily in the future.

In terms of the theory's present, actual status, I have given the highest ratings for its internal consistency and economy (items 5 and 6). That is, the model's components do not appear to conflict with each other, nor do they seem unduly elaborate as a means of accounting for the phenomena they are intended to explain.

I have given the lowest rating to item 7 because the theory presently is on such a high level of abstraction. Only when specific hypotheses are spelled out for particular aspects of the model can empirical tests be applied to confirm or disconfirm those aspects. I have also rated the theory low for its value in explaining the past and predicting the future (item 3) because of the problems of imprecision illustrated in my example of the thirteen-year-old girl. If past development is to be convincingly explained and future development predicted, there need to be precise ways of (a) identifying the strengths of significant components in each system (micro, meso, exo, macro), and (b) plotting the interactions among components and systems. Such precision is apparently not yet available for Bronfenbrenner's scheme. And the adequacy of the theory for guiding child rearing (item 4) is governed by its ability to explain and predict.

My rating of item 8 (stimulates new discoveries) between *moderate* and *poor* recognizes (a) on the plus side, the new insights Bronfenbrenner arrived at in the process of creating his scheme, and (b) on the minus side, the fact that the theory is still in its infancy, not widely adopted by other researchers for empirical investigation nor yet subjected to extensive critiques that might lead to additional novel insights by means of comparisons with existing data and models.

I have estimated that the model is moderately good in terms of clarity (item 2). While I find the basic structure of the model easy to understand, I am left puzzled about a variety of the theory's more specific aspects, as suggested in the illustration of the thirteen-year-old. As for reflecting the real world of children (item 1), my own experience suggests that the environmental factors featured in the model all seem to be significant forces in fashioning children's development. But once again, the lack of sufficient detail and precision in how the components interrelate to pro-

Bronfenbrenner's Theory

How well do I think the theory meets the standards?

The Standards	Very Well	Moderately Well	Very Poorly
1. Reflects the real world of children	P*	X†	
2. Is clearly understandable	P	X	
3. Explains the past and predicts the future	P		X
4. Guides child rearing	P		X
5. Is internally consistent	X		
6. Is economical	X		
7. Is falsifiable	P		X
8. Stimulates new discoveries	P		X
9. Is self-satisfying	P	X	

P* = Potential status   X† = Present, actual status

duce the development that a particular child exhibits causes me to rank the theory as being only moderately realistic.

As the locations of the *P* ratings on the chart suggest, if the issues of precision can be resolved, I think Bronfenbrenner's proposal might serve as a most valuable instrument for explaining and predicting the role of environments in children's development. In the theory's present state, I find it moderately satisfying (item 9).

FOR FURTHER READING

Barker, R. (ed.). (1978) *Habitats, Environments, and Human Behavior.* San Francisco: Jossey-Bass. Descriptions of nineteen studies conducted by Barker and his associates between 1947 and 1972 at the Midwest Psychological Field Station, University of Kansas.

Bronfenbrenner, U. (1979) *The Ecology of Human Development.* Cambridge, Mass.: Harvard University Press. An elucidation of Bronfenbrenner's four-level environmental systems model, with examples of its application, especially in early childhood.

Schoggen, P. (1989) *Behavior Settings.* Stanford, Calif.: Stanford University Press. A revised, updated, and extended version of Roger Barker's 1968 volume, *Ecological Psychology.*

CHAPTER FIFTEEN

Ethology and Sociobiology

Ethology, in its most general sense, is the study of the behavior of animals (including humans), especially as that behavior occurs in natural environments. *Sociobiology,* as a subcategory of ethology, is the study of the biological bases of the ways members of a species act toward each other and toward members of other species.

Although ethology traces its historical roots back to Charles Darwin (1809–1882) and other naturalists of the nineteenth century, its modern version is of rather recent origin, beginning with the animal studies of two Europeans shortly before World War II. The two—Austrian Konrad Z. Lorenz (1903–1989) and Dutch Nikolaas Tinbergen (born 1907)—were awarded the Nobel Prize in physiology in 1973, the year that Lorenz assumed the directorship of the Department for Animal Sociology in the Austrian Academy of Science. Tinbergen spent most of his professorial life at Oxford University in England. Lorenz (1977) is perhaps best known for describing the phenomenon of *imprinting,* which is the propensity of a newborn animal to attach itself emotionally to the first being it encounters as a nurturing guardian, such as the mother. This imprinting attachment was demonstrated by Lorenz when goslings followed him as their nurturing guardian. Tinbergen (1973) is recognized for directing his work toward answering four questions he considered essential for a proper understanding of behavior (Hinde, 1983, p. 28): What causes this behavior? How did it develop? What is its biological function? How did it evolve?

From the 1930s well into the 1960s, ethologists were chiefly zoologists whose work centered almost exclusively on nonhuman species. However, by the latter 1960s, increased communication between ethologists and psychologists led to the application of ethological concepts and research methods to humans, particularly to children. A leader in this effort was John Bowlby, a London psychoanalyst who studied the emotional bonding of a newborn child to a nurturing adult (1969, 1980). Throughout the 1970s and 1980s, the adoption of ethological approaches for understanding child development grew at an accelerating pace, and even greater advances are expected in the 1990s.

It is not proper to speak of ethology as *a theory* or to think of ethologists as all subscribing to a unified conceptual system from which particular hypotheses are derived. Rather, ethology is more accurately defined as a set of "orienting attitudes" shared by those who engage in comparative animal studies. Such attitudes derive in large part from Darwin's theory of evolution and from the research techniques on which his theory was founded. R. A. Hinde (1983, p. 29) has noted that the early ethologists, in keeping with Darwin's model and investigative techniques, were convinced:

> that the description and classification of behaviour is a necessary preliminary to its analysis; that the behaviour of an animal cannot be properly studied without some knowledge of the environment to which its species has become adapted in evolution; and that questions about the evolution and biological function of behaviour are, in principle, as valid and important as those about its immediate causation (and, it may be added, development).

It is thus impossible to understand ethologists' viewpoint unless we first recognize assumptions they hold in common. So in the following discussion I will review in an elementary fashion a number of those beliefs, asking your forbearance if the review is unduly reminiscent of a class in high school biology.

A FOUNDATION OF NEO-DARWINISM

At the outset it is important to establish the definitions of two terms: *species* and *population*. A *species* is a collection of individual organisms capable of interbreeding under natural conditions. The phrase *natural conditions* is an essential part of this definition for it requires that we establish separate species categories for two organisms that can be induced to mate under experimental conditions but that do not interbreed in a natural setting. Hence lions and tigers form two separate species, even though they can be successfully interbred in captivity (Wilson, 1975, pp. 8–9).

A *population* is a set of organisms of the same species occupying a clearly delimited geographical area at the same time. Thus a single hill of ants is not an entire population—a population in this case is all the colonies of ants of the same species in that particular area. Or a population can comprise all the indigenous people living in a cluster of interlinked islands of the South Seas.

With these definitions of species and population in mind, let's turn to five propositions that our theorists appear to subscribe to as underlying assumptions.

1. *Species reproduction.* For humans, as well as for all other species that require two parents as the source of reproduction, a new member of the species is conceived when a sperm cell from the male combines with an ovum from the female. This combination produces a new cell that immediately divides. The resulting pair of cells also divide, and this process of dividing to produce increasing numbers of cells continues over and over. Each step in the sequence creates cells of slightly different properties, cells capable of specialized functions, until finally they represent a fully constructed new member of the species, including such variegated, coordinated parts as heart and spleen, throat and lungs, skin and hair, eyes and brain.

2. *The genetic plan.* The architectural design for this new fish or fowl or human is provided by thousands of genes carried by chromosomes contained in the sperm cell of the father and in the ovum of the mother. In humans the chromosomes total forty-six, with twenty-three contributed by the female and twenty-three by the male.

   The inherited genes determine both (1) the border limits within which development normally can occur and (2) potentialities for variation within these limits. By *border limits* I mean the identifying features of the species, the common elements that all normal individuals in the species share. As a simple example, humans normally are born with two eyes in front of the head, one on each side of the upper bridge of the nose. In contrast, rabbits and frogs are normally born with eyes farther to the side of the head. By *potentialities for variation* I mean that within these limits particular gene combinations determine some variation of the general characteristic. So eye color and acuity of sight can vary from one normal child to another, depending on the specific mix of genes received.

   The connection between a gene and a given characteristic—such as skin color, intelligence, or competitiveness—is not a simple one. A chromosome does not merely contain a skin color gene or competitiveness gene that by itself determines the hue of the person's skin or the degree of competitiveness. Rather, the inherited foundation of such characteristics is determined by a number of genes located at various places among the chromosomes. Within the same family, one child will inherit a different mix of genes than his siblings, except in the case of identical (monozygotic) twins. Hence it is obviously not only the variations in the environment that cause differences among children in the same family, but also variations in the combination of genes received by each child.

3. *The network of species.* Ethologists subscribe to Darwin's proposition that none of the species, human or otherwise, is a separate creation, unrelated to the others. Rather, all species are links in a network of living things. The network extends from the simplest one-celled organisms—or from even more primitive stages of matter—to the most advanced species, that of the human being.

4. *The natural purpose.* If there is a natural purpose to life, a goal toward which all living things are driven by their nature, then that is *survival*. In its most basic sense, this is not the survival of the individual organism, since all individuals die. Nor is it even the survival of the species, for species are eliminated or altered with the passing of time. Rather, the basic aim seems to be the survival of the genes, which are the carriers of life itself (Wilson, 1975, pp. 3–4).

5. *Natural selection.* Living things obviously do not develop in a vacuum. They develop in environments that can vary in temperature, humidity, oxygen content, food supply, type of predator, and the like. Only those species survive and thrive that are well suited to changes that occur in their environments. Those poorly suited to environmental changes die off. This is the process of natural selection, the survival of the fittest. Such a point of view, refined since Darwin published his theory of evolution in 1859, is the new Darwinism that undergirds much of the work conducted today on the biological origins of human behavior, and thus is the foundation for the origins of child development.

ETHOLOGY'S PLACE IN THE STUDY OF CHILDREN

Since most ethological studies have been conducted on nonhuman species, the question is often asked, Why use studies of animals to elucidate the development of humans? Why not simply study humans directly? A typical answer is that provided by Hinde in *Biological Bases of Human Social Behaviour:*

> Understanding human behaviour involves problems infinitely more difficult than landing a man on the moon or unravelling the structure of complex molecules. . . . If we are to tackle them, we must use every source of evidence available to us. Studies of animals are one such source. Sometimes such studies are useful to the extent that animals resemble man, and sometimes they help just because animals are different and permit the study of issues in a simplified, isolated, or exaggerated form. They may assist us in understanding the behaviour of man not only through factual comparison between animal and man, but also by helping us to refine the categories and concepts used in the description and explanation of behaviour and social structure. But the use of animals involves dangers: it is so easy to make rash generalizations, to slip from firm fact to flight of fancy, to select examples to fit preconceptions. Studies of animals must therefore be used circumspectly, and the limitations of their usefulness specified (1974, p. xiii).

The following sketch of ethologists' contributions to the field of child development is presented in two parts: (1) propositions from animal investigations that may profitably guide the study of children and (2) fruitful research methods.

RELEVANT PROPOSITIONS FROM ETHOLOGY

Substantive contributions that ethology may offer the field of child development can be illustrated in the form of six propositions related to the concepts of bonding, altruism, social intelligence, dominance and submission, temporary social separation, and sensitive periods. A *proposition,* as the term is used here, is a generalization from the study of animals that may apply as well to humans and, as such, may explain some aspect of child development.

Proposition 1: Bonding. In the earliest hours and days of life a strong mutual emotional attachment or bond occurs between the newborn and an immediate nurturing adult. This bond tends to continue over the following years, even in the face of harsh treatment of the child by the adult.

No newborn creature from species in the upper levels of the animal kingdom is able to fend for itself. In order to survive, all neonates require the aid of at least one nurturing adult until they mature enough to find their own food and shelter and to protect themselves from predators, illness, and accident. An early mutual emotional attachment helps ensure that a specific adult assumes the responsibility for each newborn and that the newborn identifies a particular adult as the one to whom she has a right to turn in time of need. This attachment increases the likelihood that the newborn will survive and will later produce offspring of her own. As interpreted from the perspective of Darwinian theory, within each animal species those genetic lineages that have fostered a strong reciprocal emotional bond between an offspring and a parent at the outset of the newborn's life have survived better than genetic lines that have not. As a consequence, over succeeding generations the gene strains that have fostered bonding have become widespread throughout the species, making bonding a "natural" developmental characteristic of the species.

The notion of early parent-offspring bonding, first generated from observations of nonhumans, stimulated Bowlby (1969, 1980) to try to determine whether the generalization about bonding was also true for humans. Following Bowlby's lead, M. H. Klaus and J. H. Kennell (1976) have shown that there appears to be a critically sensitive period for bonding during the first few hours following birth. During this period, readiness to establish emotional attachment seems particularly strong. Comparisons between a group of mothers who had close contact with their newborns during the first few hours and a group who did not showed that the close-contact mothers in subsequent months displayed more fondling behavior and eye contact with their infants than did the other group of mothers. Bowlby's research and similar evidence have since affected infant-care routines in hospitals by influencing growing numbers of hospital personnel to have mothers spend more time with their babies in the hours and days immediately after birth.

The bonding example illustrates the process through which ethology can influence child-raising practices. First, a generalization about development is drawn from observations of nonhuman species. Next, the generalization is tested out in laboratory experiments and field studies of humans. If the generalization appears supported by the research on humans, then child development specialists recommend child-rearing techniques that incorporate the new knowledge.

Proposition 2: Short-term separation of infants from their mothers can result in long-term effects on the psychological development of the infants.

This principle was initially proposed by such investigators as Bowlby (1951) and R. A. Spitz (1950) on the basis of observations of human mother-infant separation in such settings as fondling homes and hospitals. However, confounding factors in these real life settings prevented researchers from drawing clear conclusions about the conditions determining the apparent effects. Since it would be inhumane to manipulate mother-infant relationships in controlled experiments in order to control various factors, a number of ethologists took on the task of performing experiments with nonhuman species, such as rhesus and macaque monkeys (Hinde, 1983; Hinde & McGinnis, 1977).

The studies showed that the symptoms displayed by primate infants were similar to those observed in human babies separated from their mothers—initial active protest and distress followed by depression, decreased movement, and reduced play activity. However, the avoidance of the mother upon reunion that is frequently seen in children was seldom observed in primates. The primate experiments have suggested that the effects of separation on infants can be influenced by such variables as the mother-infant relationships before and after separation, alternative sources of mothering during the separation, and the infant's sex, age, peer relationships, and more (Hinde, 1983, p. 73).

The primate experiments are deemed useful for the study of child development in at least three ways: (1) the nonverbal responses to separation that are similar in human and monkey infants may not require explanations at a high level of complexity, (2) variables observed in primate relationships may warrant closer attention as possible sources of influence in human mother-child relationships, and (3) results of the primate studies may serve as material for generating and testing theories about the nature of early attachment in human development.

Proposition 3: A specified event in an individual's life produces a stronger effect on development if it occurs at a particular time than if it occurred earlier or later than that time. Or, stated differently, a given result can be produced more readily during a particular time period than at either an earlier or later period.

This proposition comes in both rigid and flexible versions. The rigid version is the *critical-period* principle, and the flexible version the *sensitive-period* principle. The critical-period proposal holds that unless an environmental event happens during a strictly delimited time frame in an organism's development, the effect that event could produce will not occur. Lorenz is credited with popularizing the notion of critical periods after he observed that the young of many bird species will react to a moving object in the way they would react to a parent, provided the object is displayed within a period extending from a few hours after birth to a few hours or days later (Hinde, 1983, p. 41). Since Lorenz considered this period unchangeable, he labeled it *critical.* "However, it soon became apparent that the limits of the period were not irrevocably fixed by inherent developmental processes . . . and that imprinting was not irreversible. . . . The term sensitive period, thus, became more popular" (Hinde, 1983, p. 41).

The sensitive-period proposal, in effect, is more lenient. It holds that a particular result is more readily produced during a certain time frame than would be true earlier or later. It does not imply that the period is precisely defined by chronological age or that similar results cannot be produced later. Studies of primates, in particular, have suggested relationships between time periods and attachment and the learning of various skills. The term *readiness* has been commonly used to reflect the concept of sensitive periods for learning in humans. A comparison of both the similarities and differences between human and nonhuman subjects in their sensitive periods has proven useful in the understanding and application of the idea of readiness in child rearing and education.

Proposition 4: Altruism. The greater the genetic similarity between two individuals, such as two children, the greater the degree of altruism they will display toward each other.

This proposition is an extension to humans of a kinship theory that zoologists have recently built from studies of altruistic (self-sacrificing) behavior among insects—ants, bees, wasps, and termites—that differ in the extent of their sociality (Alexander & Sherman, 1977; Hamilton, 1964; Trivers & Hare, 1976; Wilson, 1975).

In this kinship theory, an act is called "altruistic" if it benefits another organism while harming the organism performing the act. And to make *benefit* and *harm* easy to measure objectively, benefit and harm are assessed in terms of the reproductive success of an organism, that is, the organism's success in producing its own offspring. An act is thus altruistic if it harms the individual's chances of producing its own offspring while aiding another organism in producing and maintaining its own. At this point the line of reasoning will not make sense unless we recall that within neo-Darwinism the goal of nature is not the survival of the individual but the survival of the genetic line. And in some cases in which organisms are struggling against difficult environmental circumstances, a self-sacrificing act will better ensure that the organism's genetic line, as carried by a close relative of the individual, will prosper than if each individual behaved entirely selfishly without regard for the welfare of others. When the males of the tribe array themselves in the front line of defense against dangerous predators, each of them is reducing his chances of personal survival and reproductive success more than if he tried to escape on his own, leaving the females and young at the mercy of the predators. But his cooperative, altruistic act helps maximize the chance that the large proportion of his genes, which are also carried by the close relatives he is defending, will survive through future generations.

This general line of logic suggests why natural selection over the centuries has encouraged the development of altruistic behavior by promoting the survival and reproduction of genes particularly conducive to such acts. However, in such a general form, the logic does not help us specify the conditions under which an altruistic act rather than a selfish act can be expected. And it is here that zoologists' recent work on kinship theory may offer some help. Scientists have now devised formulas for estimating under what conditions natural selection will favor genes conducive to altruistic acts. The formulas include two main factors: (1) the degree of genetic relatedness of the two organisms concerned (that is, the proportion of genes common to the two individuals) and (2) the comparative cost and benefit to the organism carrying out the act and to the recipient of the act. As R. L. Trivers and H. Hare have put it:

> For natural selection to favor an altruistic act directed at a relative, the benefit of the act times the altruist's r (degree of relatedness) to the relative must be greater than the cost of the act (1976, p. 249).

In other words, the theory proposes that, through the evolutionary process, genes have been selected that encourage an organism to engage in more self-sacrificing behavior for the benefit of close relatives than for distant relatives. But in all instances, altruism has limits. The individual will bear a higher personal cost for the sake of closely related individuals, but when the cost becomes so high that it exceeds the product of (a) the benefit to the relative times (b) the degree of relatedness, then the actor can be expected to behave selfishly rather than altruistically.

Such, then, is the general direction of reasoning and the beginnings of specifying conditions in kinship theory as based on and tested in altruistic-versus-selfish behavior among social insects. But what might all this have to do with child development? It provides some hypotheses about the bases and conditions of altruism in humans. It suggests some lines of inquiry for investigating such hypotheses as proposition 4, the hypothesis that natural selection for the human species has operated in such a way as to genetically predispose children to display more altruism toward others who are closely related to them than toward people more distantly related. The proposition implies such research questions as the following:

1. To what extent do children exhibit self-sacrificing behavior toward members of their family because the children have been taught to do so, and to what extent is such behvaior a result of genetic predisposition?

2. A common ideal of social democracy is to have children treat other people on the basis of each person's individual behavior rather than a person's membership in some subgroup of society (a family, tribal, religious, ethnic, or socioeconomic subgroup). Does this mean that in order to achieve the ideal, those people in charge of child rearing must counteract a natural (genetically based) propensity of children to behave more altruistically toward people who are closely related to them than toward people with whom they have fewer genes in common?

Proposition 5: Social Intelligence. The majority of problems people face in daily living are ones involving interactions with other people. The ability to solve these problems can be labeled "social intelligence." Such ability is not accurately assessed by means of traditional intelligence tests but, rather, requires different appraisal techniques, ones that directly confront the individual with social-interaction problems.

Throughout the twentieth century, the most popular way of formally appraising a person's problem-solving ability has been by means of intelligence tests that consist of oral or printed questions. This line of appraisal began in France with the work of Alfred Binet during the first decade of the century, and the tradition continues strong today. However, a number of critics, including Jean Piaget, have charged that such tests tell only whether a respondent gives an acceptable answer; they do not reveal the thought processes involved in arriving at the answer. Hence Piaget and others have created different techniques for assessing human mental abilities, techniques that involve a tester posing problem situations for a child and then observing how the child's thought processes operate as she or he seeks a solution.

But studies by ethologists have called into question the suitability of both traditional intelligence measures and Piaget's problem-solving tasks. The question has arisen from ethologists' observations of animals during the animals' daily living routines in their natural habitats. What constitutes intelligent behavior in such real life social environments may be rather different from the things measured by typical intelligence tests. In particular, the kinds of problems that appear on intelligence tests are seldom ones involving decisions about how to act in social situations, nor does the contrived laboratory setting in which intelligence tests are typically administered include the same sorts of forces that can affect people's decisions in social settings. So ethological studies have helped alert psychologists to the limitations of both Binet-type and Piaget-type measures of intelligence, thus stimulating the search for better ways of formally assessing children's development in solving problems met in the social intercourse of real life.

Proposition 6: Dominance/Submission. A genetic line best survives if individuals from the line's gene pool are organized socially in such a way that the most capable members are in positions of leadership and control, while members who are less powerful, less inventive, or less talented accept subservient positions.

This proposition derives from neo-Darwinism via the following line of logic. The *gene pool* of a population consists of all varieties of genes possessed by the members of that population. Each new member of the population is constructed from one particular combination of genes from that pool. This means that not all members born into the population have the same characteristics, nor are all combinations of genes that compose individuals equally suited for promoting survival. Furthermore, the genetic line thrives best when individuals of the species do not live isolated from each other, solving the problems of survival alone. Instead, the lineage thrives when its members are organized as a social system that exhibits a division of labor and power, and the inherited differences among individuals in the system equip members better for some roles than for others. As the generations pass, the greater the effectiveness of the social system in fostering survival, the greater will be the survival rate of those members who carry genes that fit them well for that system. That is, more of the fittest members will survive and pass on their socially suitable genes to future generations. Through this process, newborns of the species are increasingly equipped with genetic tendencies that in the past have supported the social organization that has become the norm for the given species, whether it be ants, sharks, bees, baboons, or dogs.

Among the range of social characteristics that ethologists trace to such genetic foundations is the dominant/submissive behavior noted among animals in the upper reaches of the evolutionary system, particularly among primates. The dominance/submission hierarchy is defined in animal societies by the way power and privilege are apportioned among the members, especially in matters of access to mates, to food, to desirable resting spots, and the like. Some animals rather readily assume submissive roles, displaying their submission by such ritualistic postures as rolling onto their backs and exposing their bellies or lowering their heads and cowering. Others do not so easily submit but, instead, challenge their rivals for positions of dominance. Yet, once the less powerful are intimidated by threats or defeated in combat, they accept a subservient role, permitting the group to get on with daily living under stable social conditions.

Studies of dominance/submission patterns in animals have stimulated similar studies with children. As a consequence, a growing body of knowledge has accrued about the unstated rules children follow for regulating relationships in childhood groups and about the effectiveness of the adjustment strategies they attempt, such as physical attack and defense, teasing, name-calling and casting insults, verbal threats, escape, gifts of appeasement, weeping, joining forces with peers to gain strength in numbers, and so on. Such studies have shown that in the early stages of a group's formation, as at the beginning of the school year, conflicts are frequent until dominant members prove themselves and the losers in the struggle accept positions lower in the social hierarchy. Thereupon, conflicts diminish dramatically and the work of the group moves ahead more peaceably (Savin-Williams, 1976; Sherif, 1966; Strayer & Strayer, 1976).

The above list of six propositions is intended to be merely illustrative, certainly not definitive. Other propositions derived from ethology that prove of aid in understanding child development are those bearing on (1) communication and sign stimuli that affect social relationships (smiling, eye movements, frowning, posturing, emitted sounds), (2) adaptiveness to new environmental conditions, (3) parent-child relationships, (4) displays of affection, (5) aggression, (6) experiences early in life, (7) self-regulatory mechanisms, (8) aesthetic responses, and (9) moral behavior (Eibl-Eibesfeldt, 1989; Hinde, 1983; Wilson, 1978). Books have also been written comparing humans with other species in terms of play (Mueller-Schwarze, 1978), infanticide (Hausfater & Hrdy, 1984), and maternal influences on early behavior (Bell & Smotherman, 1980).

In summary, explanations of child development from an ethologist's perspective place particular emphasis on biological forces (derived during the evolution of the species) as determiners of tendencies for behavior. For instance, a Harvard University ethologist, Edward O. Wilson, writing on human nature, states his conviction that genetic factors play a dominant role in determining what an individual can learn:

> The learning potential of each species appears to be fully programmed by the structure of its brain, the sequence of release of its hormones, and, ultimately, its genes. Each animal species is "prepared" to learn certain stimuli, barred from learning others, and neutral with respect to still others. . . . So the human brain is not a tabula rasa, a clean slate on which experience draws intricate pictures with lines and dots. It is more accurately described as an autonomous decision-making instrument, an alert scanner of the environment that approaches certain kinds of

choices and not others in the first place, then innately leans toward one option as opposed to others and urges the body into action according to a flexible schedule that shifts automatically and gradually from infancy into old age (1978; pp. 67, 69).

FRUITFUL RESEARCH METHODS

Because animals rather than people have been the traditional subjects of ethological investigations, such devices as interviews, questionnaires, diaries, recordings of conversations, and paper and pencil tests have necessarily been unsuitable for ethologists' data-gathering purposes. Instead, the basic tool in ethological research has been careful observation of the appearance and actions of individuals and groups within precisely described environments. Because ethologists have concentrated so intently on the use of observation, they have managed to develop observational techniques into a sophisticated array of procedures that might profitably be adopted in the study of children, especially in the study of infants and young children whose verbal abilities are limited.

The following brief examples illustrate (1) basic steps usually followed in observational studies, (2) some alternatives within these steps, and (3) the embellishment of the ethnologists' tools with other methods when studies focus on children rather than on nonhuman species.

Basic Steps in Observational Research

Typical phases in conducting ethological studies are as follows (Eibl-Eibesfeldt, 1989, pp. 107–112);

1. *Observing* the subjects' appearance and behavior, preferably in their natural habitats rather than under contrived laboratory conditions, since behavior can vary with the environment in which it is carried out.

2. *Recording* the results of the observation. This can take diverse forms, depending on the sorts of questions the investigator is seeking to answer, on the subjects' characteristics, on the physical and social setting, on the time available, on the equipment used (handwritten notes, videocamera, audio-recording equipment), and on the investigator's skills. The resulting record or behavioral inventory is typically called an *ethogram*.

3. Organizing the observations into *categories*. The selection of categories is governed by the particular problem or question the researcher is seeking to clarify.

Categorization is often based on function; . . . our knowledge of function is often founded on intuition. Functional categories of this kind include greeting, courting, comforting, or appeasing. If such category names are used, they must be precisely defined and their function also verified. . . . A greeting consists of several behavioral patterns such as head nodding, smiling, rapid raising of the eyebrows, and more (Eibl-Eibesfeldt, 1989, p. 108).

4. In a subsequent step of synthesis, individual categories of behavior can be connected to represent *behavior patterns*. One common approach to combining subunits is to interpret them as steps in a subject's strategy for reaching a goal, such as a sequence of behavior units involved in finding a lost object, playing a game, or preparing a meal.

5. *Broader ranging generalizations* can be derived when selected behavior patterns are compared for their likenesses and differences. For instance, in a study of mother-child relations, a series of behavior patterns from observations of a particular mother interacting with her child on various occasions can be analyzed to determine what is common across occasions and what varies by occasion. At a broader level of abstraction, a collection of behavior patterns from observations of a number of mothers and their children in the same community can be compared to provide generalizations about similarities and differences within that group. At still higher levels of generalization, conclusions about mother-child relations for one community can be compared with those from other communities, one ethnic group can be compared with another, and, ultimately, one species can be compared with others.

Options among Observation Techniques

The first step in the above sequence will be used to demonstrate that a variety of alternatives are available under each of the steps. Eight modes of observing are identified along with suggestions about the function each serves (Hinde, 1983, pp. 37–38).

1. *Spontaneous sampling (ad libitum sampling).* The observer notes everything possible that comes to her attention or that interests her. This is the most typical initial form of observation carried out in natural history studies. As a form of observational "browsing," it furnishes a record of the most conspicuous events. It then needs to be followed by more precisely directed observations.

2. *Sociometric charting.* This technique involves filling out a matrix or charting social interactions to reveal the relative social positions of individuals within a group of two or more children. In one form of matrix completion, the names of the individuals in the setting can be listed across the top (columns) and down the side (rows) of a chart. Then interactions between pairs of individuals can be tallied in the cell that is the intersection of the two individuals' names. The number of tallies in a cell indicates the frequency of the pair's interactions, while special tally symbols are used to indicate such relationships as dominance and submission or friendliness and antagonism. Sociometric maps can also be constructed to display the amount, direction, and quality of participation of different children in the group (Thomas, 1960).

3. *Focal individual sampling.* All behavior of one individual during a specific period of time is recorded in detail. Responses of others to that individual may also be noted. Such information is valuable in studies of the pace and variety of a child's activities, permitting comparisons among children as well as across situations in which the child participates.

4. *Sampling all instances of selected behavior types.* This method is useful for revealing the frequency, length, quality, nature of participants, and consequences of such forms of child behavior as arguing during games, settling a dispute in the classroom, or planning a small group project. Such a mode of observation is suitable when the events are easily seen and do not move too fast to be recorded adequately.

5. *Sequence sampling.* The purpose with this approach is to trace the series of actions that comprise a given behavior pattern. The recording begins with the initial act of a behavior episode, such as when a baby cries or when a six-year-old starts to prepare her own lunch. Recording of each subsequent step in the sequence continues until the episode is over. Results of sequence sampling enable the investigator to compare different children's modes of addressing the same kind of life situation, or comparisons can be made of the same child's modes over time, that is, from one developmental stage to another.

6. *One–zero sampling.* This is a somewhat crude but easily conducted form of recording observations. It consists of the investigator making a tally mark each time the target behavior occurs, such as each time a child asks a question in class, each time a baby is asleep,

or each time a parent disciplines an eight-year-old. Although one–zero sampling is useful for determining how often a given behavior appears, it fails to show either the length of time involved in each occurrence or the quality or consequences of the behavior.

7. *Time sampling* (also known as *instantaneous sampling*). During a predetermined time interval, an investigator records every act carried out by a child. For example, in a nursery school, a researcher may observe a particular child at three five-minute time periods during the morning. Time sampling is particularly useful for estimating the percentage of time children spend in rather common activities.

8. *Multiple-scan sampling*. This is an extended form of time sampling in which the observer records all the behaviors of one individual in a group for a specified time interval, then does the same for another individual, continuing in this fashion until all members of the group have been observed. The sequence may then be started over with the initial child and continued through the cycle of group members. Such a method is appropriate when time sampling for a single child is inadequate for revealing the behavior shown (since it fails to reflect the group's influence) and when the researcher wants information about a number of children during that same time period.

It should be apparent that variations and combinations of these eight approaches can expand even further the investigator's observational tools to suit diverse research goals and behavior settings.

Amplifying Methods for the Study of Children

As ethologists have increasingly turned their attention from nonhuman species to people, they have added further techniques to their customary observation methods.

First, they distinguish between *distanced observation* and *participatory observation*. In distanced observation, the investigator is an outsider who views, but not does not enter, the effective environment of the subjects being studied. Claims made for distanced observation are that it enhances objectivity and avoids contaminating the naturalness of the subjects' behavior with the observer's influence. Participatory observation, on the other hand, involves the investigator intentionally interacting with the subjects. Claims made for its value are that the role of participant equips the researcher with opportunities to learn subjects' motives, attitudes, and conceptions that are either difficult or impossible to discover from a distanced vantage point (Eibl-Eibesfeldt, 1989, pp. 107–108).

It is apparent that distanced observation is the dominant, traditional approach in ethology since participation with nonhuman species is relatively rare and of a low level of usefulness. The type of participation with nonhuman species that yields the greatest information is customarily that which involves people interacting with domesticated pets—usually dogs and cats, but also primates, pigs, horses, and the like. The most common form of participant observation in ethological studies of humans occurs when a researcher, investigating child development in an unfamilar culture, lives with the people of that culture for an extended period of time in an effort to understand customs and attitudes that typically underlie their behavior.

To supplement their distanced and participatory observations of child development, ethologists have increasingly adopted such devices as interviews, questionnaires, attitude surveys, projective methods (ink-blot tests, picture-story tests), aptitude tests, and achievement tests. As a consequence, the ethologist's repertoire of investigative techniques has become very extensive indeed.

PRACTICAL APPLICATIONS AND RESEARCH CHALLENGES

I have combined applications and research challenges here because the practical applications of ethology to child development take the form of suggestions for research studies. The purpose of such studies is to discover the extent to which generalizations derived from observing nonhuman species can validly be applied to interpreting children's growth and behavior. In addition to the propositions from ethology mentioned above, let's consider several more in the form of questions that demonstrate the broad range of child development research topics that can be generated from ethological theory.

E. D. Wilson (1978, p. 99) has written, "Are human beings innately aggressive? . . . The answer . . . is yes." But in disagreement with Wilson, there are those who contend that aggressivity, although widespread, is the result of living conditions that precipitate conflict and competition and is not the result of an inborn human tendency. From this difference of opinion a variety of research questions can be evoked. For instance, in what ways can children's environments be arranged to eliminate aggressive behavior at successive stages of growth? And if aggressivity cannot be eliminated, what child-rearing practices can be used to channel it into constructive acts (ones aiding other people in fulfilling their needs) rather than destructive acts (ones frustrating others' need-fulfillment attempts)? To what extent do models of aggression the child observes in the family, in school, and on television influence the amount and type of aggression the child exhibits at different age levels?

Wilson (1978, p. 128) has further observed, "Women as a group are less assertive and physically aggressive." Is this true of children of all ages? Or is it simply that boys and girls are equally assertive but use different techniques for expressing assertiveness? And if this is so, to what extent are the differences innate and to what extent the result of cultural influences? More precisely, how can child-rearing practices alter possible sex differences in assertiveness?

As for sexual behavior, to what extent are preferences for heterosexual versus homosexual activities inborn? How do different models of sexual behavior in a child's environment influence the child's sex preferences and activities at different age levels? In terms of vocations, are there certain roles for which females are innately better suited than males, and vice versa?

To what extent are a child's competitive/cooperative and introversive/extroversive actions a result of a genetic tendency to behave in such a manner? How much room is there for environmental forces at different age levels to alter the course of such traits or tendencies?

Is there any truth in beliefs of the past that antisocial acts of children and youths are based, at least partly, on "a bad blood line" or "bad seed"? Or, in more modern parlance, are there actually "psychopathic personalities," meaning people whose underlying genetic endowment so predisposes them to antisocial acts that efforts to teach them prosocial behavior are destined to fail?

How much are children from a given population (such as an inbred tribal or ethnic group) genetically predestined to display one pattern of social behavior (such as a tendency to settle disputes by reasoning) than another (a tendency to settle disputes by physical violence)?

These questions and far more that derive from ethological investigations provide an extensive source of research opportunities for the field of child development.

ETHOLOGICAL THEORY: AN ASSESSMENT

In explaining my reasons for the ratings on the accompanying chart, I begin with items awarded high marks and then consider ones with lower ratings.

Item 1, concerning how closely the theory reflects the real world, is divided into two subscales, the first focusing on ethologists' main source of data—nonhuman species—and the second focusing on the chief subject of this book—children. I rated ethological theory high on item 1a because each concept in the major ethologists' writings is profusely illustrated with examples from field studies of a broad variety of species. However, many sociologists and social psychologists would probably give item 1a a lower rating because they believe ethologists credit genes with too great a role in determining individuals' psychological characteristics and groups' social patterns. Although ethologists do not ignore the place of learning in personal traits and social organization, they do see genetic structure as setting narrower boundary lines within which learning can take place than many social scientists would likely accept. The strong genetic preference exhibited by typical ethologists is reflected in Wilson's contention that what evolves in human development is a set of genetically based capacities to learn certain things rather than others with a certain degree of ease:

> Pavlov was simply wrong when he postulated that "any natural phenom-
> enon chosen at will may be converted into conditioned stimuli." Only
> small parts of the brain represent a tabula rasa; this is true even for
> human beings. The remainder is more like an exposed negative, waiting
> to be dipped into developer fluid (1975, p. 156).

While ethologists may be criticized for taking a position toward the hereditarian camp in nature–nurture controversies, when more data have been compiled it may turn out that they are correct, or nearly so. In any event, I have given them the benefit of such doubts in marking item 1a on the basis of the wide range of field studies with which they have buttressed their theoretical generalizations and principles of development.

In judging the theory's clarity (item 2), internal consistency (item 5), and economy of explanation (item 6), I have concluded that the main books and articles on ethology available to the public are clearly written and contain ample illustrative descriptions of behavior among many species (see, for example, Eibl-Eibesfeldt, 1975; Hinde, 1974; Lorenz, 1977; Wilson, 1975, 1978). Likewise, neo-Darwinism as expressed in ethological theories does not seem encumbered with more concepts than the minimum needed to explain the phenomena ethologists discuss.

Items 3 and 7 (explains past and predicts future; is falsifiable) can conveniently be considered together for they share a common weakness. The weakness is that ethological theory, at its present stage of development, is composed of a set of broad concepts and principles intended to explain the evolution of all psychological and social behavior in all species; but as yet the theory is not sufficiently detailed and precise to produce an unequivocal description of any population's past development or future evolution. The theory does not provide the information needed to judge

Ethological Theory

How well do I think the theory meets the standards?

The Standards	Very Well	Moderately Well	Very Poorly
1. Reflects the real world of:			
1a. Nonhuman species	X		
1b. Children		X	
2. Is clearly understandable	X		
3. Explains the past and predicts the future		X	
4. Guides child rearing			X
5. Is internally consistent	X		
6. Is economical	X		
7. Is falsifiable		X	
8. Stimulates new discoveries	Potential P		Actual X
9. Is self-satisfying		X	

specifically the genetically set limits or potentialities for various aspects of human development. Nor does the theory elucidate the way different environmental influences complement the genetic pattern to produce the characteristics individual humans display at various stages of growth. Ethology is still at the stage of a natural history, with theorists observing social behavior in one or two species, proposing concepts that could explain such behavior, then extending the application of these concepts by "logical reasoning" to other species without rigorously testing the validity of this extension. As Wilson has pointed out in discussing the subrealm of ethology known as sociobiology:

> The greatest snare in sociobiological reasoning is the ease with which it is conducted. Whereas the physical sciences deal with precise results that are usually difficult to explain, sociobiology has imprecise results that can be too easily explained by many different schemes (1975, p. 28).

The cure for this shortcoming, Wilson says, lies in adopting methods of "strong inference." This means deriving alternative hypotheses from the theory, creating crucial experiments or field observations that will reveal which of the competing hypotheses is the most tenable, and then accepting or revising the theory's concepts in light of these test results (Wilson, 1975, p. 28). Until ethological models reach this stage of methodology, they will continue to be nonfalsifiable and will furnish inconclusive explanations of past and future.

The ratings on items 1b and 4 (children's real world and guidance for child rearing) are only moderate (1b) or somewhat below moderate (4) since most ethological studies have not dealt directly with children's lives. Bowlby's work (1969, 1973, 1980) in the 1950s and 1960s provided the most specific early applications of ethological theory to child development. Such applications have become far more extensive in recent times, as attested by the writings of N. G. Blurton Jones (1972), P. K. Smith and K. J. Connolly (1980), Hinde (1974, 1983), and Eibl-Ebesfeldt (1989).

On item 8, I have marked ethological theory for both its actual and its potential value in stimulating new discoveries. As demonstrated in the discussion of research challenges, ethological theory has great potential for stimulating new discoveries in child development. However, so far the direct applications of ethological findings to child development research have been quite limited.

For the final assessment standard—how satisfying ethological theory is from a child development perspective—I have marked ethology in the moderate range to reflect a counterbalancing between (1) the strengths of the theorists' line of reasoning about species in general and (2) a lack of conclusiveness that surfaces when they apply this reasoning to explain complex human behavior. In particular, I would like the kind of detailed extension of the theory that would account for why children develop psychologically and socially the way they do during the first two decades of life.

FOR FURTHER READING

Eibl-Eibesfeldt, I. (1989) *Human Ethology.* New York: Aldine de Gruyter. This textbook, written by the current president of the International Society for Human Ethology, addresses basic concepts and methods of ethology, social behavior, communication, ontogeny (including various development theories), humans in their habitats (ecology), ethology's contribution to aesthetics, and biology's contributions to ethics.

Hinde, R. A. (1987) *Individuals, Relationships, and Culture: Links between Ethology and the Social Sciences*. New York: Cambridge University Press. In analyzing the relationship between biology and human socioculture, Hinde proposes that "Sociocultural structure is the product of brains that were shaped by selection acting in the empirical world of actual behavior." Understanding the dialectical interchanges between humans' biological structure and their environment so as to produce individuals' cultural characteristics "requires both a psychological analysis of the ways in which the sociocultural structure is formed by the propensities of the human mind, and a sociological analysis of the ways in which individuals, internalizing the symbols of the culture, come to experience the culture as part of themselves and themselves as part of the culture" (p. 145).

CHARTING TRENDS OF THE TIMES

What major shifts have occurred over time in the popularity of various theories of child development?

Writing this perspective is a risky venture—like a trek through a badly lit cave, inviting slips and bumps every step of the way. The attempted trick is to trace the popularity over the past eighty years of the major theories reviewed in this book so as to show how enthusiastically each theory has been embraced by two sorts of groups, *professionals* and *the concerned public.*

The data base for such speculation is not very solid. It would satisfy no one's standards of adequate sampling. My three sources of information have been (1) comments found in books and journal articles about the status of different theories over time; (2) published reviews of the contents of psychology textbooks, of the incidence of journal articles, and of the membership in professional organizations to reveal which theories are most in vogue at different times; and (3) my own observations during an academic career spanning the last fifty-two years of the eighty-year period. That half century began in 1939 when, as an undergraduate, I enrolled in a psychology course entitled "The Science of Human Behavior" and was taught synapses and conditioning. In graduate school I learned of normative studies and Gesell, of Gestaltists, of Freud, and of further varieties of behaviorism (Hull, Hilgard, Tolman, Dollard, Miller). As a college instructor in 1949, I was situated in a psychology department whose personnel made the department 60 percent psychoanalytic, 10 percent Lewinian, and 30 percent eclectic. Since those days my work has directed me through Piaget, Vygotsky, humanistic and existential perspectives, cybernetics, Oriental religions, ecological psychology, ethology, and into the many-faceted *cognitive revolution* that currently dominates theorizing about child development.

My admitting to such aberrant sampling should make it clear that the intention of this perspective is not to disclose *truth* about shifts in the popularity of theories. Rather, the purpose is to estimate *trends* and thereby provoke thought and discussion. The charts throughout the perspective, and their accompanying rationales, are my guesses. Readers are invited to argue the matter and alter the trend lines in ways they believe more adequately approximate the actual state of affairs.

In each chart the pair of trend lines are labeled *professionals* and *the public*. The definition of *professionals* may vary from one theory to another, but generally it identifies people who have academic degrees in psychology, education, social work, medicine, or related disciplines. Such people are engaged in occupations that involve teaching in institutions of higher learning, conducting research, writing journal articles and books, or providing psychotherapeutic, instructional, and social services to the populace. People included under *the public* are not necessarily the entire *general public*. Instead, they are nonprofessionals who are likely to have a good chance to know about the theory under discussion. Such people might be called *the concerned* or *informed public*. As will be seen, those who qualify as members of the concerned public may differ from one theory to another.

In the charts, the word *popularity* means "acceptance of" and not just "knowledge about." A person may know a good deal about Watson's behaviorism without considering his proposal an acceptable theory of child development. Thus the trend lines in the charts identify the estimated quantity of a theory's advocates or disciples, including those partial disciples who are unwilling to endorse all features of a theory.

The unit of measurement of the vertical axis of the charts is quite inexact, ranging only from a vague *high popularity* at the top to a vague *low popularity* at the bottom. Hence the general pattern of each trend curve, not the exact height for any given year, is the important matter. The heights of the curves are certainly arguable.

So, with this a multitude of caveats as a foundation, we move ahead to estimating trends of the times.

ESTIMATES OF THEORY TRENDS

The thirteen models of development reviewed below are presented in the following order: normative-descriptive studies, developmental-task theory, commonsense attribution theory, Freud's psychoanalysis, Erikson's psychosocial model, Skinner's behaviorism, social learning theory, Piaget's scheme, Soviet theory, information-processing theory, humanistic approaches, ecological psychology, and ethology.

Normative-Descriptive Studies

In Chapter Three, normative-descriptive studies were represented by the work of Gesell and his colleagues. Such studies describe the status of a group of children or adolescents on one or more dimensions or character-istics, such as height, physical agility, reading skill, aggressive versus sub-missive behavior, moral values, self-confidence, and hundreds more. The researchers who conduct such studies usually report the group's average performance and the amount of variability among members of the group. The performances of different age groups are often compared in order to reflect an average pace of children's development.

In the graph below, *professionals* are people who conduct research on child development or use research results in their teaching and clinical practice. The ascending slope of the professionals' line represents the rapid growth in normative-descriptive studies over the first half of the twentieth century. The descending slope for recent decades is not intended to sug-gest that the number of descriptive studies has declined. Rather, it is meant to show that descriptive research that is not interpreted in terms of theory has been far less welcome in recent decades than it was earlier in the century. What is typically required today is a theoretical setting within which descriptive material is analyzed in terms of hypotheses tested, theoretical links explored, or new explanations generated. In other words, empirical material (description) *plus* theory is now the expectation among most professionals.

The public in this chart refers principally to concerned parents, teach-ers, club leaders, social workers, authors of newspaper and magazine articles, and advertisers of products that appeal to child audiences. I have drawn the public line to reflect my belief that interest in descriptive in-formation over the first half of the century rose at the rate such material

Popularity of Normative-Descriptive Studies

was produced and used by professionals. Subsequently, interest among this public in descriptive norms has, I believe, remained at a high level. Child development trade books, along with introductory college textbooks on development, are usually heavy laden with normative-descriptive contents.

Developmental-Task Theory

As noted in Chapter Four, the developmental-task perspective evolved chiefly from the work of leaders in the progressive education movement of the 1930s and 1940s. The rapid upsurge of interest on the part of *professionals* (instructors in courses on child development, curriculum developers, classroom teachers) occurred in the early 1950s as a consequence of such publications as C. Tryon and J. Lilienthal's (1950) chapter in a yearbook of the Association for Supervision and Curriculum Development and R. J. Havighurst's *Human Development and Education* (1953). Since then the developmental-task approach continues to be recognized by professionals as a useful notion, but the role assigned to it for interpreting child development has diminished. The model's usefulness in stimulating research has been minimal.

The public in this graph refers to college undergraduates who take courses in human development and to members of the general public who read trade books on child rearing and education.

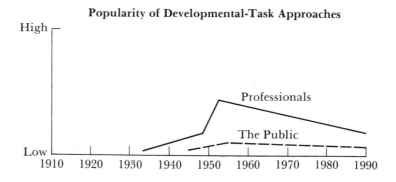

Commonsense Attribution Theory

The public in the graph below is meant to be the *general population*. The straight line across the top of the chart is intended to suggest that naive or commonsense psychology underlies most people's interpretation of child development and behavior. I am assuming that the popularity of commonsense theory remains constant over time. I am also assuming that new ideas from psychologists' theories and empirical studies that are widely disseminated and are accepted within the society become incorporated into people's commonsense theory.

The line representing *professionals* in the chart refers to developmentalists who create theories and who write and teach about development. The line has been drawn to suggest that such professionals always accept a certain level of commonsense theory, but they differ from the general public in that they also include formal theoretical notions in their own belief system that are not generally understood or accepted by the general public. My purpose in suggesting a rise in the level of commonsense notions among professionals after the 1950s is to suggest the influence on formal theorizing of certain commonsense ideas in recent decades. For example, the declining popularity of behaviorism after the midcentury was due in part to a reintroduction into development research of the commonsense idea that child development theory should be founded on studies of children (instead of animals) in their real life settings (instead of in laboratories). Furthermore, the decreased popularity of Freudian theory was due in part to the commonsense belief that development theory is more validly derived from the direct study of a normal range of children than from listening to neurotic adults recalling their childhood. Social learning, contextual, ecological, and human ethology models have incorporated such commonsense ideas into their methodologies. A recent illustration of a theorist advocating greater dependence on naive theory is V. L. Lee's (1988) urging developmentalists to recognize the value of concepts found in people's ordinary talk.

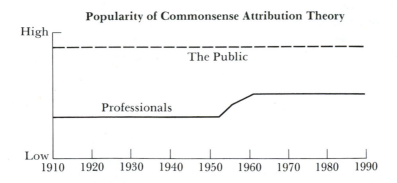

Popularity of Commonsense Attribution Theory

Freud's Psychoanalytic Theory

By 1900, when he published his *Interpretation of Dreams,* Sigmund Freud's work was already becoming well known among psychiatrists and psychologists in Europe. But it was only after Freud accepted G. Stanley Hall's invitation to appear at the anniversary celebration of Clark University in

Massachusetts in 1905 that most professionals (psychiatrists, psychologists, educators, social workers) and the general public in America were introduced to psychoanalytic theory. During the 1920s and 1930s, Freud's growing array of publications were translated from the original German into English, and articles reflecting Freud's revolutionary views gained a ready audience in America, both among professionals and among members of the reading public. Freudian concepts (unconscious motives, infantile sexuality, ego, repression, regression, projection) entered the everyday parlance of informed Americans. Slips of the tongue and dreams were now considered to be disguised forms of shameful memories that slinked past the mind's censor into consciousness. By the 1940s, psychoanalytic therapy had become the dominant mode of treatment for neuroses, and advice in books about child-raising practices reflected a clear strain of psychoanalytic theory.

During the years of its greatest popularity, the psychoanalytic movement spawned alternative versions know as neo-Freudian proposals. Prominent among neo-Freudian theorists in America were Karen Horney (1885–1952), Harry Stack Sullivan (1892–1949), and Eric Fromm (1900–1980). All three agreed that Freud had failed to recognize the great influence that people's social environments exerted on their personality development. Therefore, in the place of Freud's conception of child development being dominated by biological drives, they substituted the proposal that human personality is more a product of cultural shaping than of biological determinism. Sullivan, for example, equated psychiatry with social psychology, and he described his own interpersonal theory of psychiatry as the study of people's social interactions. However, the two theorists who exerted the greatest influence on child development were Anna Freud and Erik Erikson. Such disciples helped sustain interest in psychoanalytic theory following Sigmund Freud's death in 1939 by extending their realm of investigations beyond the traditional analytic session. For example:

1. Anthropological investigations were made of the symbols, rituals, and child-rearing practices of primitive societies.
2. Laboratory experimentation was conducted, primarily animal studies of regression and fixation.
3. Tests, especially those of the projective personality variety [Rorschach ink blots, word-association lists], were used to externalize the content of the psychodynamics of the normal human [child, adolescent, and] adult (Hillner, 1984, p. 215).

However, since the 1950s, adherents of traditional psychoanalytic theory have declined among psychotherapists, researchers, writers and teachers about child development, and early childhood educators. Social learning models and other cognitive theories founded on the study of normal children have come to dominate the field. Yet an active corps of faithful professionals continue to publish their interpretations and research in several psychoanalytically oriented journals.

In the chart, I have drawn *the public* line below that of the *professionals* throughout the eighty-year period to reflect my impression that the American public that became aware of Freudian theory never accepted the psychoanalytic model as willingly as had the professionals. But, as noted earlier, a variety of Freudian concepts have by now become a part of the informed public's commonsense theory. For this reason, I have indicated with the public trend line a modest but sustained Freudian influence on public thought at the opening of the 1990s.

Erikson's Psychosocial Theory

Although Erikson had already made significant contributions to the field of human development from the 1930s through the 1950s, a comprehensive description of his theoretical position did not appear until 1959 (Erikson, 1959). Hence, in the graph, the charting of his influence on theories of child development begins only at the close of the 1950s. Thereafter, the popularity of his psychosocial model grew rapidly, sustained by a steady flow of books elaborating on his proposal.

Theorists and practitioners who have profited from Erikson's work include those who have extended his theory, those who have sought to verify his concepts, and those who have applied his model in psychotherapy or in explaining people's behavior. Examples of extensions are Logan's "A Reconceptualization of Erikson's Theory: The Repetition of Existential and Instrumental Themes" (1986) and Franz and White's "Individuation and Attachment in Personality Development: Extending Erikson's Theory" (1985). Verification studies have included Gray, Ispa, and Thornburg's "Erikson Psychosocial Stage Inventory: A Factor Analysis" (1988) and Ochse and Plug's "Cross-Cultural Investigation of the Validity of Erikson's Theory of Personality Development" (1986). Practical applications are illustrated in Hamachek's "The Self's Development and Ego Growth: Conceptual Analysis and Implications for Counselors" (1985) and Rose's "The Design of Atmosphere: Ego-Nurture and Psychic Change in Residential Treatment" (1988).

The *professionals* in the graph are researchers and instructors who teach child development courses as well as psychotherapists and social workers who deal with children and their parents. The *public* consists of college students in child development courses and members of the general public who read about development in magazines and books on child rearing. In the chart, I have suggested that the popularity of Erikson's views has diminished somewhat since the 1970s, as a variety of newer theories of children's social development have attracted the interest of both professionals and the informed public.

Popularity of Erikson's Psychosocial Theory

Skinnerian Behaviorism

In their review of American psychology from the beginning of the twentieth century, W. Kessen and E. D. Cahan (1986) have pictured the years 1913 to 1930 as a doctrinaire period when behaviorism and the measurement of intelligence were the central issues. From 1930 to 1952, the versions of behaviorism provided by Clark L. Hull and B. F. Skinner were dominant. But since the mid-1950s, cognitive theories have commanded the largest following among professionals in the field.

To appraise the present-day status of behaviorism, P. A. Lamal (1989) inspected the theory's popularity in 1988, the year that marked the seventy-fifth anniversary of J. B. Watson's (1913) "Psychology as the Behaviorist Views It," the fiftieth anniversary of Skinner's (1938) *The Behavior of Organisms,* and the twentieth anniversary of the *Journal of Applied Behavioral Analysis.* Lamal reported that in 1987, when there were 95,000 members and affiliates of the American Psychological Association, only 2 percent of them were identified with the behaviorist division of the society. That same year, in a listing of 406 job openings for psychologists, less than 7 percent called for behaviorists, and most of those were for work with the retarded and developmentally disabled. In the 1988 U.S. federal funding of research on AIDS (acquired immune deficiency syndrome), less than 2 percent was for an explicitly behavioral approach to the problem. From such data, and from more of a similar nature, Lamal (1988, pp. 530–531) concluded: "It is clear that the discipline of psychology is not influenced [at present] by behaviorism." His inspection of current books in the fields of literature and the arts led him to observe: "Here we find that if behaviorism is not ignored, it is vilified" (p. 532).

In the graph below, the term *professionals* refers to college instructors in the social sciences and education, researchers, schoolteachers, psychotherapists, and practitioners who work with the mentally handicapped. *The public* in this context is comprised of people interested in learning practical techniques for guiding their children's development in socially desirable directions. By drawing *the public* line so far below the *professionals,* I am suggesting that even in the heyday of behaviorism in academic circles, concerned parents and teachers apparently depended on an eclectic mixture of theory to guide their child-rearing practices. The mixture would seem to contain a small portion of operant conditioning and a large measure of common sense and normative-descriptive information, as typified in the advice offered by Dr. Benjamin Spock in his books about child care, which sold more than 30 million copies between 1945 and 1985 (Spock & Rothenberg, 1985).

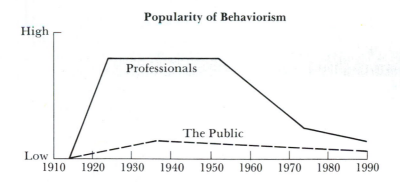

Social Learning Theory

Robert B. Cairns (1983, p. 334) has tracked the growth of social learning models from a set of antecedents through three generations of theory evolution. The antecedents he identifies during the period 1900 to 1938 include behaviorist learning theories, psychoanalysis, Baldwin's and Piaget's cognitive development schemes, and Lewin's field theory. In the first generation of social learning models (1938–1960) he places Skinner's operant conditioning along with the proposals of four Yale University professors—John Dollard, Neal Miller, Robert Sears, and J. W. Whiting—who translated key psychoanalytic concepts into learning-theory hypotheses that could be tested experimentally. Julian B. Rotter's work also belongs in this period. A prominent characteristic of the first generation is the attention theorists directed to the way the consequences of a child's actions in a particular social setting affect the child's behavior in similar settings on future occasions. Cairns's second generation features (1) Albert Bandura, with his emphasis on the way children acquire behaviors by imitating people they observe, and (2) behavior analysts S. W. Bijou and D. M. Baer, whose concept of *reciprocal reinforcement* proposes that not only does a mother's actions reinforce her child's behavior but the child's acts also reinforce the mother's behavior. As for the third generation (the 1970s and 1980s), Cairns observes that the models he associates with this most recent period "are not as readily defined. Perhaps it is too early to expect a clear delineation of positions, or, equally likely, the trend is toward less encompassing but more precise explanations of specific phenomena" (p. 334). Within the third generation he has located three sorts of theory. First is *transactional analysis,* which he identifies as the study of "how the activities of the 'other' individual synchronize, facilitate, inhibit, or redirect the course" of the social interchange between two people (p. 15). Second is *social-cognitive reinterpretation,* which concerns "how the actions of others are interpreted, how children perceive the roles of other persons, how social stereotypes are formed, [and] how the cognitive stage of the child influences his social behaviors" (p. 351). Third are *social-environmental structure* models, as illustrated in the work of such theorists as Urie Bronfenbrenner. In effect, social learning schemes are a variegated lot, suggesting a diversity of directions in which future theorizing can turn.

The chart starts with Cairns's first generation and carries the social learning models well into the third generation. The term *professionals* here

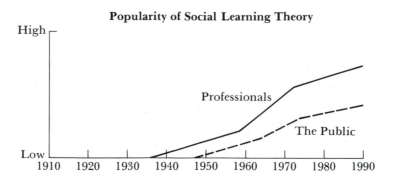

Popularity of Social Learning Theory

encompasses researchers and instructors in the field of child development as well as behavior therapists in child-guidance clinics, social agencies, and schools. *The public* includes college students taking courses in development and members of the general public who read about modern movements in psychology.

Piagetian Theory

In the chart, the lines representing trends in Piagetian theory refer solely to America. If Europe were included, the popularity of Piaget's work would be shown as far higher from the 1920s through the 1950s. As R. M. Lerner (1986, pp. 22–23) has noted:

> Piaget's theory of the development of cognition was known in America in the 1920s. Yet because of the "clinical" nature of his research methods, his nonstatistical style of data analysis, and the abstract constructs he was concerned with—all of which ran counter to predominant trends in the United States—his theory and research were not given much attention until the late 1950s. . . . [Then] the Swiss scientist Piaget was rediscovered, and it can fairly be said that concern with the abstract and conceptual ideas of his theory came to dominate developmental psychology throughout the 1960s. In fact, his influence continues . . . both as a result of further substantiation of his ideas and by promoting discussions of alternative theoretical conceptualizations.

Popularity of Piagetian Theory

The *professionals* in the chart are college instructors in the fields of development and education, child development researchers, and those educators who base curricula and instuctional practices on child development theory and empirical results. *The public* is comprised of college students studying development as well as parents and of members of the general public who read trade books and magazine articles on child rearing.

Soviet Theory à la Vygotsky

As in the case of Piaget, the trends in the Vygotsky chart refer to his theory's popularity in America. As I mentioned in Chapter Eleven, Vygotsky's work, though received enthusiastically in the 1920s in the Soviet Union, was subsequently suppressed over the next two decades for political reasons. It did not reach audiences in Western Europe and America until his writings were released by Soviet authorities and English translations of his work and that of his colleagues were published in the 1960s and 1970s (Luria, 1976; Vygotsky, 1962, 1963, 1978). Since then, Soviet theory has continued to rise in esteem among *professionals* (Americans who teach about child development, conduct research, and apply development theories to educational practice). *The public* in the chart is composed of college students in child development and teacher-education classes and members of the general public who read trade books and magazine articles about child development.

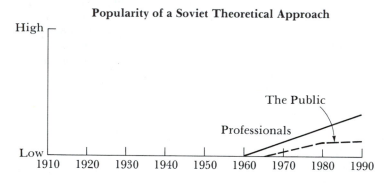

Information-Processing Theory

As a theory of child development, information processing traces its origins to a 1958 article by A. Newell, J. C. Shaw, and H. A. Simon entitled "Elements of a Theory of Human Problem Solving." Subsequently, as such investigators as D. Klahr and J. G. Wallace (1976) created detailed computer programs to test the elements of the theory, more members of the academic community joined the growing number of information-processing enthusiasts. At the same time, critics such as U. Neisser issued warnings about the shortcomings of the early versions of cognitive development based on computer simulations of thought and on laboratory experiments: "If cognitive psychology commits itself too thoroughly to this model, there may be trouble ahead. Lacking in ecological validity, indifferent to culture, even missing some of the main features of perception and memory as they occur in ordinary life, such a psychology could become a narrow and uninteresting specialized field" (Neisser, 1976, p. 7).

This recognition of the limitations in the original information-processing models led to a measure of disenchantment with their potential and stimulated theorists to integrate elements of information processing with other versions of cognitive psychology—including contextualism—to produce the more recent forms described in Chapter Twelve (Case, 1985, pp. 43–51).

The *professionals* in the chart are primarily psychology instructors and researchers in institutions of higher learning. *The public* is comprised chiefly of college students in the fields of psychology and education and of schoolteachers, therapists, and members of the general public who follow events in the realm of psychology.

Popularity of Information-Processing Theory

Humanistic Perspectives

Humanistic conceptions of development existed in the ancient past and are likely to continue into the distant future. For centuries, the search for *self* and for methods of achieving higher states of personal existence have assumed prominent roles in major religions, such as Christian mysticism, Islamic Sufism, Hindu Yoga, and Zen Buddhism. In addition, many varieties of mystical practices have not been attached to traditional religions.

Recent decades have witnessed the ascension and subsequent decline of the more formal, scientifically oriented humanistic perspectives reviewed in Chapter Thirteen. The leaders of this movement were already well-established academicians and therapists when, in the latter 1950s and early 1960s, they formally banded together. They were united by the belief that the true nature of humans—the experienced *self* and an optimistic potential for personal fulfillment—was missing in behaviorism and traditional psychoanalysis. As noted in Chapter Thirteen, this group included such respected psychologists as Abraham Maslow, Carl Rogers, and Charlotte Buhler. The social climate of the 1960s, with America's involvement in the unpopular Vietnam War, quickly drew into the humanistic movement a host of young people searching for "more authentic" personal experience than they found in mainstream society. The humanistic movement thus attracted a mixed bag of academicians and youthful "free souls." This mixture caused certain of the academicians to distance themselves from the movement's openly displayed organizations and practices. Such was the case of Henry Murray, a Harvard professor whose landmark *Explorations in Personality* (1938) and Thematic Apperception Test had exerted so much influence on the field of personality theory. M. B. Smith, in a memorial following Murray's death in 1988, wrote:

> Murray's version of secular humanism was the worldview of a whole person, of a thoughtful, imaginative person, of a magnanimous, self-respecting person. It was the view of a psychologist who saw human potentiality and actuality in their complex multivalence, who combined a sense of the mystic and nonrational with a keen and steady eye for tough realities that contemporary culture conspires to help most people ignore or misconstrue. . . . The vaunted lauching of humanistic psychology as a Third Force could hardly have been very special or newsworthy for Harry Murray. All along he had been *doing* humanistic psychology of an imaginative, solid, and well-considered kind. But he shared no common ground with the countercultural, antiscientific version of the humanistic movement that followed (1990, p. 12).

In 1987, A. Giorgi wrote a retrospective analysis of the past three decades of the humanistic movement. His was an attempt to account for "What went wrong?" and for why "humanistic psychology, even to its adherents, has not lived up to the hopes and expectations it kindled at its beginnings" (Giorgi, 1987, p. 6). He noted that by the mid-1980s hardly 1 percent of the members of the American Psychological Association belonged to Division 32, the humanistic subgroup. And psychologists of an openly humanistic bent were far less common in university posts than they had been a quarter century earlier. Giorgi cited several reasons for the descent of humanistic psychology: (1) it has never shed its image of being no more than a protest movement associated with the 1960s countercul- ture, (2) it has produced only a smattering of research that would satisfy typical canons of scientific investigation, and (3) it has failed to offer acceptable innovative research approaches for investigating the areas that humanistic psychology has properly opened for study—"values, personal growth, peace, peak-experiences, the relationship of psychology and cul- ture, psychology and cowardice, honesty, foresight, relations with com- munities, creativity, play, mystic experiences and so on" (Giorgi, 1987, p. 12). Giorgi summarized his observations by saying "that I see the crisis of humanistic psychology as being the same as that for psychology: the prob- lem of what it means to have an authentic psychology of the human person" (p. 19).

The chart recognizes the continuation of humanistic schemes from past centuries and, at the same time, features the versions of humanistic (including existential and phenomenological) theory and practice that emerged in the 1960s. In the chart, the *professionals* who have made it their business to disseminate humanistic beliefs do not necessarily hold academic degrees or teach in traditional institutions of higher learning. A substantial number qualify as experts on the basis of their attendance at workshops, retreats, and training sessions conducted by proponents of their particular brand of humanistic conviction. They then assume positions within those same organizations or else set up their own programs for guiding people into elevated levels of personal experience and self-fulfillment.

The public represented in the chart is composed primarily of young people between the ages of 15 and 30. During the 1960s and into the 1970s, many were involved in the peace and free-speech movements. Many joined communes, conducted rallies protesting the actions of government and university authorities, dressed as "hippies," engaged in meditation, used psychedelic drugs to achieve extraordinary mental states, and/or practiced "free love." A smaller proportion of this public was composed of middle-aged aficionados attracted by the opportunities for self-expression offered by a humanistic view of life. I have estimated that the enthusiasm for humanistic practice has been greater and has lasted longer among *the public* (the now middle-aged who were youths in the 1960s and early 1970s) than among *professionals,* particularly among professionals in academic posts or those who serve as school psychologists or therapists in child-guidance clinics.

Popularity of Humanistic Perspectives

Ecological Theory

As noted in Chapter Fourteen, significant attention to the ecological settings in which children grow up was featured in Kurt Lewin's field theory and in his concept of *life space* from the latter 1920s into the 1940s. At the end of the 1940s and into the 1950s, the term *ecological psychology* was applied by a Lewin disciple, Roger Barker, to studies he and his colleagues conducted on the effect of children's environments on their behavior. These studies generated the modicum of interest in ecological forces represented by the *professionals* line in the chart between the latter 1940s and the mid-1970s. The rapid upsurge in professionals' interest in children's habitats during the 1980s can be documented by the popularity in the professional literature of the views of U. Bronfenbrenner, R. M. Lerner, K. F. Riegel, J. Valsiner, and others.

The term *professionals* in the chart refers to academicians who teach and write about child development and to such practitioners as counseling psychologists, school psychologists, the personnel of child-guidance centers, and social workers. *The public* refers to college students in child development classes and to parents who keep abreast of books, magazine articles, and television programs that feature pioneering work in child development.

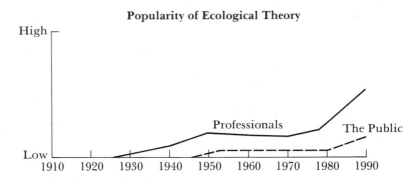

Popularity of Ecological Theory

Ethology and Sociobiology

Although Darwinism has exerted a long-standing influence on theories of child development, its current presence in human ethology and sociobiology is of recent origin, in the latter 1950s with the work of J. Bowlby and his colleagues. Since that time, publications in the field have grown at an increasing pace as biologists and psychologists who traditionally focused attention on the behavior of animal species have been directly studying the manifestations of human genetic potentials within diverse habitats (Eibl-Eibesfeldt, 1989; Hinde, 1987). Although *professionals* (those who teach and write about child development) have begun to incorporate ethological theory into their offerings, a review of textbooks and journals in the field of child development suggests that the amount of attention to human ethology is as yet rather meager. For this reason, I have drawn the *professionals* line at a low level in the chart. And because the amount of information about ethology and sociobiology in child development publications available to parents is quite limited, I have drawn *the public* line even lower.

A FINAL OBSERVATION

To summarize general trends, I would suggest that recent times have witnessed far greater attention to (1) how environmental contexts affect development, (2) how the structures and operations of the mind influence the way encounters with environments influence development, and (3) how children's genetic endowment provides a maturational foundation for development. Theorists have also been offering increasingly sophisticated versions of developmental stages in order to remedy shortcomings identified in the conceptions of stages proposed by Piaget, Vygotsky, and the like.

Finally, a possible danger in tracing trends in the popularity of theories is that doing so may imply that people choose only one of the available models as their own belief system and reject all elements of the remaining options. But that is apparently more the exception than the rule. Most people—professionals and members of the public alike—seem to compound their set of convictions from elements of more than one theory. It is true that a person may emphasize one model over another, thereby appearing to be a Piagetian or Eriksonian or contextualist. But closer inspection will usually show that such people have been eclectic, adapting aspects of various models to form a convincing scheme.

THEORY CENTERED IN VALUES— MORAL DEVELOPMENT

A search for the ways children's and youths' moral reasoning and moral behavior evolve

All of the theories reviewed so far in this book have been *broad-scale models,* in the sense that all have addressed physical and mental development in general or cognitive development in general. In contrast, the two theories inspected in Part Eight concern a limited aspect of child development, that of moral reasoning and behavior. My purpose in confining this final section of the book to such a topic is twofold.

First, I wish to illustrate how a theory can be devised to focus on a restricted aspect of child life. For this purpose, I have chosen the most popular view of moral development of the past three decades, Lawrence Kohlberg's stage model of moral reasoning (Chapter Sixteen). If more general theories, such as Piaget's or Vygotsky's or Bronfenbrenner's can be dubbed *macrotheories,* then Kohlberg's scheme can qualify as a *minitheory* because of its concentration on a restricted facet of children's lives. Other facets on which developmental minitheories have focused include play, fantasy life, creativity, skill at analyzing physical phenomena, mathematical reasoning, oral language ability, reading skill, self-esteem, and more. Minitheories have also been proposed to explain the development of different aspects of children's cognitive functions—visual perception, auditory perception, haptic perception, working memory, long-term memory, eye and hand coordination, and the like. In fact, there are dozens upon dozens of minitheories designed to account for all sorts of limited facets of human behavior. Some developmentalists believe that creating these models of restricted scope is a more profitable endeavor than are efforts to devise macrotheories intended to account for every aspect of development on the basis of a relatively few components and their interactions. Minitheories, they argue, are apt to have greater explanatory and predictive power because they are obligated to account for a narrower range of variables than are the all-encompassing macrotheories.

My second purpose in Part Eight is to demonstrate directly how a new theory can be constructed from elements of existing ones. The way new theories draw on the work of their predecessors has already been demonstrated in earlier chapters, but only incidentally. In some cases, an earlier theorist has been credited with a good idea that is now incorporated into another author's model. Piaget profited from Baldwin's ideas about parallels between linguistic and nonlinguistic development, Bandura built on Skinner's notions of reinforcing consequences, Bronfenbrenner drew on Lewin's concept of life space, and Valsiner benefited from Vygotsky's historical-cultural scheme. In other cases, a new theory represents a reaction against what its author considers to be objectionable elements of earlier models, as happened when Maslow formulated his humanistic scheme to remedy unacceptable aspects of behaviorism and psychoanalysis. Thus theorists may draw upon either positive or negative features of existing models.

This matter of the cumulative effect of successive theories is first illustrated in Part Eight with Kolhberg's work, which incorporates key concepts from such intellectual forbears as Piaget, the German philosopher Immanuel Kant (1724–1804), the American philosopher John Dewey (1859–1952), and others. But a more dramatic demonstration is the proposal described in Chapter Seventeen. To account for the contents of that chapter, I should first explain that in recent years I have been exploring the realm of moral development in some detail, motivated by a desire to synthesize a model that might clarify aspects of development that seem inadequately explained by existing proposals (Thomas, 1986, 1988, 1989a, 1989b). The results of this attempt are sketched in Chapter Seventeen under the title "An Integrated Theory of Moral Development." The word *integrated* refers to my adapting features of other theories of development in an effort to account for how children evolve their moral convictions and apply those convictions in their daily behavior.

DELINEATING THE MORAL DOMAIN

As a preparation for inspecting the contents of Chapters Sixteen and Seventeen, it will be helpful to consider ways of defining the domain on which the two theories focus, that is, the moral domain. To do this, we can begin with a more general term, *value,* of which *moral* is a subcategory.

In Chapter One, I proposed that *facts are objective information*—observations or measurements that are publicly verifiable. In contrast, *values* are opinions about the desirability or propriety or goodness of something. The "something" may be a person, an object, a place, an event, an idea, a kind of behavior, or the like. Statements of fact tell what exists, in what amount, and perhaps in what relation to other facts. Statements of value tell whether something is good or bad, well done or poorly done, suitable or unsuitable. Our focus in Part Eight is on values, not facts, although many of the values discussed will involve the use of facts.

The word *moral* as intended in the following chapters is only one subitem under the general term *value*. Many values do not qualify as moral ones. For instance, there are *aesthetic values* that involve judgments offered from an artistic viewpoint. Aesthetic values, when applied to a flower garden, a poem, a painting, or a dance performance, are reflected in such phrases as "pleasing to the eye" or "nicely turned metaphor" or "delightfully innovative." Another category is that of *technical* or *functional values*. These focus on how efficiently something operates or on how well its parts coordinate. People are applying functional values when they complain about an erratic washing machine or about government inefficiency. *Economic values* concern how much profit or loss an investment yields. *Prudential values* guide a person's social relations and her use of time and energy so as to yield the greatest benefits. A girl finds it prudent not to tell her teacher that the teacher's breath smells sour, and a boy finds it imprudent to wander away to play ball after his father asked him to mow the lawn.

What, then, are *moral values*? Although at first glance this might seem like an easy question to answer, closer inspection shows it to be a matter of considerable disagreement. For example, Piaget (1948, p. 1) wrote that "All morality consists in a system of rules, and the essence of all morality is to be sought for in the respect which the individual acquires for these rules." In contrast, Kohlberg (1976) proposed that the moral domain is one concerning issues of justice. He contended that at different age levels, children's and adolescents' moral judgments are founded on different conceptions of justice, with the highest and most worthy level based on principles of universal equal rights among all people and the overriding value of human life.

M. Siegel (1982) also sees a sense of justice, which he terms a sense of *fairness*, as the culmination of children's general moral development. This sense, he suggests, "involves an ability to consider consistently and without contradiction the interests and intentions of others, to act bearing these in mind and without the guidance of a superior authority, and to generalize fully this behavior in all relevant situations" (Siegel, 1982, p. 2). In Siegel's opinion, a sense of fairness is not simply an intuitive or emotional sense of right but, rather, is a conscious, intentional decision about how to act: "Fairness is a rational attribute not reducible to mechanistic processes. Actions taken without cognition cannot be considered moral" (Siegel, 1982, p. 5).

E. Turiel (1980) has contended that such investigations as Piaget's and Kohlberg's studies have improperly mixed moral concepts with social conventions. To Turiel (1980, pp. 71–72), moral issues are limited to ones that concern *justice,* a term he limits to acts that could cause physical or psychological harm to others, violate people's rights, or affect the general welfare. Social conventions, on the other hand, "constitute shared knowledge of uniformities in social interactions and are determined by the social system in which they are formed," with examples being conventional modes of dress, forms of greeting, and rules of games. In Turiel's view, social conventions can be changed by consent of the members of the group without seriously affecting people's welfare, whereas moral precepts cannot.

In contrast, E. Maccoby (1968, p. 229), from a social learning viewpoint, has differed with Piaget, Kohlberg, and Turiel by broadly describing moral values as beliefs "shared in a social group about what is good or right." Likewise, she has described moral action as "behavior a group defines as good or right and for which the social group administers social sanctions." Thus, under Maccoby's definition, Turiel's social conventions could qualify along with justice as matters of morality, so long as the members of the group agreed. The viewpoint espoused by Maccoby has been called *cultural relativism* or *social relativism* in contrast to the *universality* standard represented by Kohlberg's proposal that morality consists of equal-handed justice among all social groups, no matter what the personal notions of morality may be among the group members. A further extension of the relativistic position is *individualistic relativism,* which accords each person the right to define the moral domain in whatever ways suits his or her preferences.

A still different conception of morality is expressed by C. Gilligan (1982, 1988), who argues that males and females base their conceptions of moral matters on separate assumptions that derive from the different roles the two sexes have traditionally been assigned in their societies. She proposes that in virtually all cultures women's central activity has been in child care, whereas men have been charged with administering the society and its productive facilities. These assignments have left females in a dependent, subservient role to men. As a consequence, according to Gilligan (1982, p. 19), a woman's conception of morality that arises from caring for other people "centers around the understanding of responsibility and relationships, just as the [male's] conception of morality as fairness ties moral development to the understanding of rights and rules."

While the foregoing display of ways to define the moral domain falls short of exhausting the options, it should be sufficient to indicate that the issue of how best to portray the realm of moral development continues to be a matter of lively debate. It is therefore useful, when inspecting a theory, to know how the particular theorist has defined the realm. The definitions assumed by the theorists whose work is described in Chapters Sixteen and Seventeen are given early in those chapters.

THE LAST ISSUE

Part Eight closes with the book's final perspective, one that suggests how the essence of a theory might be expressed in the form of a concise figure of speech. This perspective has been left to the last so it might summarize the contents of the entire volume in the form of a series of metaphors, one for each prominent theory described in the book.

CHAPTER SIXTEEN

Kohlberg's Moral Development Model

Lawrence Kohlberg (1927–1987) was a Harvard University psychologist and professor of education whose research for his doctoral degree in 1958 at the University of Chicago focused on the moral reasoning skills of a group of boys aged 10 to 16 (Kohlberg, 1958). This early work formed the basis of a career that made him the most widely discussed developmentalist in the field of morality of the past three decades.

We begin our inspection of Kohlberg's model by considering the characteristics he believed distinguished moral judgments from other types of value decisions:

> Unlike judgments of prudence or aesthetics, moral judgments tend to be universal, inclusive, consistent, and based on objective, impersonal, or ideal grounds (Kohlberg, 1968b, p. 490).

Thus, according to Kohlberg, it is not a moral judgment when a girl says to her companion, "She's so sensitive about her looks that if you tell her to fix her hair differently and to wear different clothes, she'll never want to be around you again, so just don't talk about such things when you're with her." This is only a prudential judgment, for it is not universal (does not apply to all social situations), nor is it based on impersonal or ideal grounds. In contrast, it is a moral judgment when a girl says, "They should outlaw capital punishment because no one has a right to take another person's life under any circumstances." This judgment is universal, applies in all situations, and is founded on ideal convictions. By Kohlberg's defining the nature of moral judgments in such a manner, it is clear that he was not a cultural relativist. He would apply his definition of moral judgments equally to all societies under all conditions.

In his theory, Kohlberg traced the steps by which children grow toward making "truly moral judgments." The steps "represent a progressive disentangling or differentiation of moral values and judgments from other types of values and judgments" (Kohlberg, 1968b, p. 410). Children who are successful in advancing to the highest stage of moral judgment by the time they become adolescents are ones who base their appraisals of moral issues on concepts of justice. In Kohlberg's view, this means that such young people ground their opinions on the *rights of the individual,* and they judge an act wrong if it violates those rights. Kohlberg further contended that a right in this sense is founded on *equality* and *reciprocity,* so that people are equal in terms of exchange (or contract) and of reward for merit. *Justice* implies that the law is impartial and applies to all equally in its maintenance of the rights of the individual (Kohlberg, 1967, pp. 173, 176).

I'll explain how Kohlberg saw children growing toward the position of basing moral judgments on concepts of justice by first describing (1) the theory's focus and (2) its research methodology. Then I'll (3) delineate the moral growth stages, (4) describe how Kohlberg saw children's natures interacting with their environments to determine their stage of moral development, (5) point out several important characteristics of the moral growth stages, (6) note what Kohlberg's beliefs imply for moral education, and (7) assess the model in terms of criteria described in Chapter One.

THE THEORY'S FOCUS

Moral development is usually viewed as one aspect of socialization, with *socialization* meaning the process by which children learn to conform to the expectations of the culture in which they grow up. In the case of moral values, children not only learn to conform, they also *internalize* these standards and thereby accept the standards as correct and as representing their own personal values. A value is considered to be internalized and not just imposed by outsiders when the child conforms in situations (1) that tempt her to transgress and (2) that afford slight chance of her behavior being discovered, punished, or rewarded.

People who have sought to trace the development of morality in children have typically focused on one or more of three aspects of personality: *observed behavior, feelings of guilt,* or *the basis for a moral judgment.*

In the case of *observed behavior,* the question asked by the investigator is, Does the child display greater honesty or integrity or a sense of justice as he grows older? Extensive studies of honesty in children and youths have yielded either inconclusive or negative answers to this question (Hart-shorne & May, 1928–1930). Rather than basing their response to tempta-tion only on a growing internal sense of honesty, children and adolescents appear more often to base their actions on prudential judgments (How likely is it that I will be caught?) or on social pressures (Will the group disapprove?). Thus Kohlberg rejected observed behavior as a profitable criterion for moral development.

A second approach to the study of rule internalization focuses on how the *emotion of guilt* grows as the years advance. This emotion refers to the self-critical and self-punishing acts of anxiety and regret that follow transgression of a rule or cultural standard. Here the assumption is that the child obeys in order to avoid feeling guilty. Kohlberg (1968b, p. 484) said this assumption underlies the concept of conscience in psychoanalysis and in learning theories. He concluded that even though studies of children through projective techniques show a sudden upsurge in such guilt feelings in the years prior to puberty, projective techniques have not been able to predict consistently whether children really will resist temptation. Hence his own theory is not founded on charting the emotion of guilt over the years of childhood and youth. Instead, his work has centered on a third approach, that of tracing the *bases of the child's judgments of moral issues.*

In investigating the *judgmental* side of moral development, the ques-tion becomes, Has the child internalized a moral standard, and can she justify that standard to herself and to others? Such an approach was used in the early 1930s by Piaget and has since been refined by other scholars, with Kohlberg being the most prominent researcher in the field during the past three decades. In Kohlberg's opinion the issue is not whether the child acts honestly or whether she feels guilty about transgressing the rules. Instead, the moral development issue is the judgmental basis the child uses for assessing moral behavior.

KOHLBERG'S RESEARCH METHODS

The studies on which Kohlberg's theoretical proposals are founded consist of describing to children a series of incidents, each involving a moral dilemma. Each child is then asked which solution would be the best or proper one for each dilemma and why that solution would be better than others. For example, here is a typical Kohlberg incident, the one known as the Heinz problem.

> Mrs. Heinz was near death from a special type of cancer. The doctors
> thought one kind of drug might save her. The druggist who made the
> medicine she needed was selling it for ten times the amount that it cost

him to make it. The sick woman's husband, Heinz, did not have enough money for the medicine, so he went to borrow the money from everyone he knew, but he could collect only about half of what the druggist was charging. Heinz told the druggist his wife was dying and asked him to sell him the medicine cheaper or to let him pay later, but the druggist refused. The druggist said he discovered the drug and he was going to make money from it. So Heinz got desperate and later broke into the drugstore to steal the drug for his wife. The question then is: Should the husband have tried to steal the drug? Why or why not? (Adapted from Kohlberg, 1971, p. 156.)

Responses to such moral dilemmas are then analyzed by Kohlberg and his colleagues to determine which of six developmental stages of moral judgment are reflected in the child's or youth's answers. The task of analyzing and grading children's answers does not involve simply comparing an objective answer sheet to children's responses. Rather, the grading scheme requires training and involves some measure of subjective judgment on the part of the analyst.

Kohlberg began using his moral incidents with a sample of seventy-five young American adolescents in the mid-1950s, and he subsequently tested the same subjects as they grew into adulthood in order to discover the pattern of changes in judgments that might have occurred with the passing years. Furthermore, he and his co-workers tried to discover what influence cultural factors have on the growth of moral judgments. To accomplish this, they used the test incidents with both middle-class and lower-class adolescents in the United States and with youths in such diverse locations as Mexico, Thailand, kibbutz communities in Israel, a primitive Malaysian village, Turkey, Taiwan, and others. On the basis of these studies, Kohlberg concluded that the stages of moral development he identified are universal—found in all cultures—but that the percentage of youths of different age levels who are at a given stage will vary from one society to another. The nature of these variations will be discussed after I explain the characteristics of the stages.

THE LEVELS AND STAGES OF MORAL GROWTH

In Kohlberg's system, growing up in moral judgment consists of advancing through three levels of development, from a *premoral* or *preconventional* level to one that involves conforming to *society's conventions* and finally to a top level that transcends convention and is based on personal, *self-accepted moral principles*. This top level is sometimes called *postconventional* or *autonomous*. Each level contains two stages, as defined in Table 16.1.

Table 16.1   Description of Moral Judgment Stages

I. *Preconventional Level (Premoral Level).* A person follows society's rules of right and wrong but in terms of the physical or hedonistic consequences (punishment, reward, exchange of favors) and in view of the power of the authority who imposes the rules.

> **Stage 1.** *Punishment and obedience orientation.* Whether an action is good or bad depends on whether it results in punishment or reward. If the individual is going to get punished for it, it's bad so he shouldn't do it. If he won't get punished, he can do it, regardless of the human meaning or value of the act.

> **Stage 2.** *Naive instrumental orientation.* Proper action instrumentally satisfies the individual's needs and occasionally the needs of others. As in the marketplace, human relations are based on getting a fair return for one's investment. Reciprocity or fairness involves "you scratch my back and I'll scratch yours," but not out of loyalty, gratitude, or justice.

II. *Conventional Level.* A person conforms to the expectations of her family, group, or nation. She actively supports and justifies the existing social order.

> **Stage 3.** *Good-boy, nice-girl orientation.* A person acts in ways that please or help others and are approved by them. For the first time, the individual's intention becomes important ("she means well"). Approval is earned by being "nice."

> **Stage 4.** *Law-and-order orientation.* A person is doing the right thing when he does his duty, shows respect for authority, and maintains the existing social order for its own sake.

III. *Postconventional, Principled, or Autonomous Level.* A person tries to identify universal moral values that are valid, regardless of what authority or group subscribes to the values and despite the individual's own connection or lack of connection with such authorities or groups.

> **Stage 5.** *Social-contract orientation.* This usually involves legalistic and utilitarian overtones. Moral behavior is defined in terms of general individual rights and according to standards that have been critically examined and to which the whole society has given its consent. This is the "official" morality of the American Constitution and the American government. There is a clear recognition that personal values and opinions are relative, and thus there are procedures for reaching consensus and for changing laws for social utility reasons (rather than freezing laws because they are inviolate, as under stage 4's law-and-order orientation).

> **Stage 6.** *Universal ethical principle orientation.* A person's moral judgments are based on universal principles of justice, on the reciprocity and equality of human rights, and on respect for the dignity of humans as individual persons. *Right* is defined by the individual's conscience in accord with self-chosen, general ethical convictions.

Recast and simplified from Kohlberg, 1967, p. 171.

Besides identifying six steps or stages, Kohlberg described thirty or more aspects of life about which people make moral judgments. A person will reveal his dominant stage of moral judgment each time he expresses opinions about any of these aspects. It was Kohlberg's conviction, based on administering his moral judgment incidents to children and youths, that there is a high correlation between a person's stage in regard to one aspect and his stage in regard to others. For example, a young woman's judgment about the value of human life, about telling the truth, and about people's duties and obligations will all tend to reveal the same level of moral development.

The thirty or more aspects of life are divided into three varieties: (1) modes of judgment of obligation and value, (2) elements of obligation and value, and (3) issues or social institutions about which judgments are made. The principal aspects falling within each of these categories are universal, for they are found in all cultures according to Kohlberg. Here is one version of the aspects:

Modes of Judgment of Obligation and Value: Judgments of (a) right, (b) having a right, (c) duty or obligation, (d) responsibility, (e) praise or blame, (f) punishment or reward, and (g) nonmoral value or goodness. Also (h) justification and explanation.

Elements of Obligation and Value: (a) prudence (consequences desirable or undesirable to *oneself*), (b) social welfare (consequences desirable or undesirable to *others*), (c) love, (d) respect, (e) justice as liberty, (f) justice as equality, and (g) justice as reciprocity and contract.

Issues or Institutions: (a) social norms, (b) personal conscience, (c) roles and issues of affection, (d) roles and issues of authority and democracy (division of labor between roles related to social control), (e) civil liberties (rights to liberty and equality as humans, citizens, or members of groups), (f) justice of actions apart from fixed rights (trust, reciprocity, contract in actions of one person), (g) punitive justice, (h) life, (i) property, (j) truth, and (k) sex (1971, p. 166).

To show how one of these aspects can be interpreted in terms of the stages, consider a moral judgment incident focusing on the issue of life (item *h* in the issues list) and see how three boys reacted to the incident. The event posed to the boys involved a doctor who had to decide whether to "mercy kill" a woman requesting death because she was suffering intense pain.

13-year-old boy: "Maybe it would be good to put her out of her pain, she'd be better off that way. But the husband wouldn't want it, it's not like an animal. If a pet dies you can get along without it—it isn't something you really need. Well, you can get a new wife, but it's not really the same." (Scored as stage 2—the value of life is instrumental to satisfying the needs of its possessor or others.)

16-year-old boy: "No, he shouldn't [kill her]. The husband loves her and wants to see her. He couldn't want her to die sooner, he loves her too much." (Scored as stage 3—the value of life is based on empathy and affection of family members toward its possessor.)

16-year-old boy: "The doctor wouldn't have the right to take a life, no human has the right. He can't create life, he shouldn't destroy it." (Scored as stage 4—life is sacred according to a categorical or religious order of rights and duties.) (Kohlberg, 1967, pp. 174–175.)

To summarize, note that Kohlberg's six stages represent a movement from lower levels of moral decision, where moral decisions are entangled with other value judgments and the rules are changed as the facts in the case change, to higher levels that separate moral values (justice and reciprocity) from other sorts and that utilize universal principles that apply to anyone in any situation. To illustrate this movement from the particular to the universal rule, consider three of the stages as they relate to the value of life. At stage 1, only important people's lives are valued, at stage 3 only family members', but at stage 6 all life is valued morally equally (Kohlberg, 1971, p. 185).

THE INTERACTION OF NATURE AND NURTURE

In response to the question of which moral stages a given child will pass through and when she or he will do it, Kohlberg adopted an interactionist position. He did not believe a child's moral stages are produced entirely by genetic inheritance or entirely by factors in the environment. Rather, he proposed that four principal factors interact to determine how high in the six-stage hierarchy a person will progress and when he or she will arrive at each stage. The first factor, and the one with the greatest genetic or inherited component, is the individual's *level of logical reasoning* as identified in Piaget's cognitive growth system. The second, a personal factor that probably has both genetic and environmental elements, is the child's desire or *motivation,* sometimes referred to as the child's *needs.* The remaining two factors are entirely environmental: (1) the child's opportunities to learn *social roles* and (2) the *form of justice* in the social institutions with which the child is familiar. To understand how these factors interact, we need to inspect each in more detail.

The Level of Cognitive and Logical Development

In the realm of children's logical thinking, Kohlberg identified himself as a disciple of Piaget. First, he was convinced that it is the child's nature to pass through the cognitive development stages identified by Piaget. He further believed that the achievement of a particular cognitive level in Piaget's scheme is a necessary prerequisite of the child's achieving a particular moral reasoning stage.

To substantiate his belief, Kohlberg administered both Piagetian logical thinking tasks and his own moral-incident tests to the same group of subjects. He discovered that children who did not succeed on a given level of Piaget's tasks almost never showed the moral reasoning level that paralleled the Piagetian tasks. In contrast, children who were in the upper levels of moral reasoning could almost always complete the parallel and the lower-level Piagetian tasks. Consequently, Kohlberg concluded that the sort of logical thinking represented by Piaget's hierarchy forms the necessary foundation for the kinds of moral reasoning measured by his own moral-decision situations. This logical thinking component, then, is the maturational or "natural growth" factor—and perhaps the most powerful of the four factors that Kohlberg believed determine a child's level of moral reasoning.

If the child's cognitive stage were the only component of moral judgment, then as soon as the child reached a given cognitive level, her moral judgments would likewise be at the same level. But such is not the case. There is often a gap between the two, with moral reasoning lagging behind cognitive skill in various degrees. The cause of this lag, according to Kohlberg, is the condition of the other three factors that interact with mental maturity.

The Factor of Will or Desire

While it is always in our own interests to reason at the highest level of which we are capable, it may not be in our best interests to make moral judgments at the highest level. Some people who are capable of judging morally at stage 6 may not do so because they do not wish to end up as martyrs as did Socrates, Lincoln, and Martin Luther King, Jr. So a youth may have the concepts of stages 5 or 6 but not use them habitually because they do not seem worth the trouble or the risk in his particular social setting. Thus a portion of the slippage between cognitive level and moral stage may be accounted for by the operation of a girl's or boy's emotions, desires, or "will power." However, Kohlberg felt that this factor of *will* plays only a minor part in determining judgment stages. The other three factors in the quartet of influences are far more important (Kohlberg, 1971, pp. 188–190).

Social Role-Taking

Kohlberg agreed with many social psychologists that children become socialized by learning to take the roles of people around them. As children interact with others, they imagine themselves in the others' shoes and see life from others' perspectives. Children also learn to see themselves as others see them. Hence *role-taking* or identifying and empathizing with other people enables the child to become an effective social being.

Within the broad sphere of socialization, the development of the more specific area of moral judgment "is based on sympathy for others, as well as on the notion that the moral judge must adopt the perspective of the 'impartial spectator' or the 'generalized other'" (Kohlberg, 1971, p. 190). How well a child learns to adopt others' roles depends to a great extent on the conditions of her social environment. Some environments encourage role-taking and thus hasten children's advance up the moral judgment hierarchy. Other environments limit opportunities to learn role-taking and thus slow children's advances in moral growth and may prevent them from ever reaching stages 4 or 5.

Kohlberg suggested that it is this difference in role-taking opportunities among cultures or social-class levels that apparently accounts for the marked differences in moral judgment development among societies and between middle and lower socioeconomic classes within a society.

> In four different cultures, middle-class children were found to be more advanced in moral judgment than matched lower-class children. This was not because the middle-class children heavily favored a certain type of thought which corresponded to the prevailing middle-class pattern. Instead, middle-class and working-class children seemed to move through the same sequences, but the middle-class children seemed to move faster and farther (1971, p. 190).

Other studies by Kohlberg's group have shown that popular children who participated a great deal with their peers were far more advanced in moral judgment than unpopular or nonparticipating children. At least part of the cause of this difference seems to be differences in role-taking opportunities in the children's families. Greater role adoption was promoted by families that encouraged sharing in decisions, awarded responsibility to the child, pointed out consequences of action to others, communicated within the family group, and exhibited emotional warmth.

Some people have assumed that the most crucial of these home elements for furthering moral development is the degree to which the atmosphere is warm, loving, and identification-inducing. However, Kohlberg said this is not so. Apparently some minimum level of warmth in her personal contacts with others is necessary for a child or adolescent to feel she is an accepted participant in the social circle. However, what is far more important is that the environment furnish many role-taking opportunities, not that the child receive maximum affection from the group (Kohlberg, 1971, p. 191).

The Justice Structure

The fourth variable that contributes to the growth of moral judgment is the justice structure of the social groups or institutions with which the child interacts. Such social entities include the family, the neighborhood gang or play group, the school, the church, the community, the nation, and those media that provide vicarious opportunities for role-taking—television, radio, books, magazines, and the like.

At all stages of moral development, the individual has some sort of concern for the welfare of others. But only by stage 5 is this concern based on what Kohlberg regarded as principles of true justice, those of *equality* and *reciprocity*. The principle of equality means that we "treat every man's claim equally, regardless of the man" (Kohlberg, 1967, p. 169). The principle of reciprocity means equality of exchange. It means "punishment for something bad, reward for something good, and contractual exchange" or fulfilling one's bargain.

Within a given society the groups or institutions with which the growing child is intimately involved vary in their justice structures. A public school that the child is forced to attend under compulsory education laws is different from a university that the youth attends voluntarily. A neighborhood play group is different from a reformatory. A Girl Scout troop differs from a family. A family dominated by an autocratic father differs from one in which children are encouraged to make decisions, take responsibility, and be rewarded in accordance with how they carry out their self-imposed commitments.

In effect, Kohlberg proposed that children who participate in social groups that operate on a high level of equality and reciprocity will move to higher levels of moral judgment than children whose main participation is in groups that have lower sorts of justice structures.

So the dominant level of moral judgment a child or youth uses results from the interaction of four determinants: her level of cognitive and logical maturation, her will or desire, her opportunities for role-taking, and the dominant modes of justice in the main social groups of which she is a part.

THE THREE CHARACTERISTICS OF THE STAGES

A large proportion of modern social scientists as well as the "culturally enlightened" laity are what Kohlberg labeled *ethical relativists*. They believe that moral principles vary from one culture to another and that there is no logical way to explain or reconcile these differences among cultures. Such a line of thought can easily lead to the conviction that one culture's moral values are as good as another's since each culture has as much right to its own value system as does any other culture. On the basis of this assumption, we would conclude that a person is morally developed or well adjusted when he abides by the dominant values of his society. But it is not necessary for an ethical relativist to stop the extension of this line of logic at the societal level. If he chooses, he can carry it on to individuals within a society. In such a case, he can conclude that it is each individual's right to adopt his own code of ethics, since there is no logical way to judge one person's code better than another's. (Of course, it is clear that extending ethical relativism to the individual will have important consequences for the individual's fate because if he deviates markedly from the group's norms he can be dubbed odd or possibly locked up by the dominant group as a criminal or lunatic.)

However, Kohlberg was not an ethical relativist. He contended that moral development does not depend on the particular society's dominant ideas of justice. Instead, he said that the developmental stages he identified are universal, integrated, and invariant.

By *universal* he meant that he believed the stages are true of all societies. Originally Kohlberg believed that in every culture there are people at all six stages. But more recently he questioned whether stage 6 is ever actually achieved (Colby, Kohlberg, Gibbs, & Lieberman, 1983, p. 5). It is true, however, that the dominant moral stage for the society as a whole, or for a given age level, will differ from one culture to another. One culture may operate mostly on stage 2 reasoning, another on stage 4 reasoning. But this does not mean that the patterns of moral thought are quite different in the two cultures. Rather, the discrepancies result from the children in one society advancing up the six-stage hierarchy at a different rate than the children in the other society. The differences in rate might be due partially to genetic differences between the two groups but more likely result from differences in the role-taking opportunities and justice structures of the two cultures. Kohlberg said that the same stages of moral reasoning are found in all societies, although the number of persons at each stage may differ, as illustrated in Figure 16.1. The graphs compare the moral judgments of boys in middle-class U.S. and Mexican communities with those in an isolated village in Turkey. The age levels charted are 10, 13, and 16. As the graphs indicate, by age 16 some boys in each of the cultures were at each of the six levels of moral growth. However, a larger percentage of U.S. and Mexican boys than of Turkish boys were at higher stages at each age level.

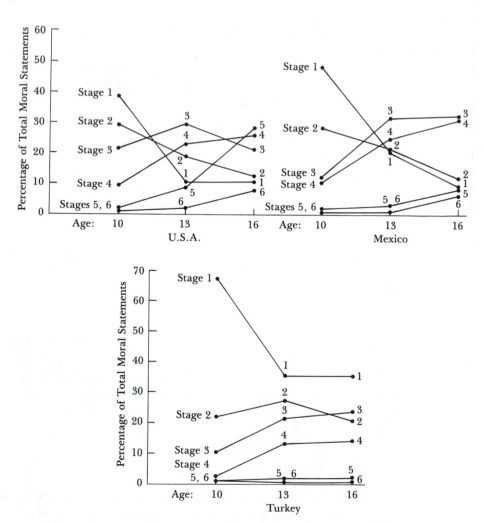

Figure 16.1 Boys' Moral Judgments in Three Societies (Kohlberg & Kramer, 1969, p. 104)

By *integrated* Kohlberg meant that in various aspects of life a person's moral decisions will reflect a similar level of development. It would be rare indeed for a person to operate at stage 1 when judging honesty, at stage 3 when judging freedom, and stage 6 when judging responsibility. Rather, judgments in all realms will tend to cluster around the same level—around 1 and 2, around 3 and 4, or the like.

By *invariant* Kohlberg meant that a youth cannot skip a stage or two while advancing to a higher level. People must pass through each stage in sequence. A key reason for this invariance, in Kohlberg's opinion, is that each successive stage consists of components of the prior stage plus a new component or two.

These principles of universality, integration, and invariance, and the four proposed determinants of moral growth, have important implications for how Kohlberg's theory can be put to practical use.

PRACTICAL APPLICATIONS: FASHIONING A PROGRAM OF MORAL EDUCATION

If Kohlberg's theory is correct, what should be the form of moral education? Before applying our foregoing discussion to answering this question, we need to consider one more concept that Kohlberg adopted from Piaget's theory of cognitive development, that of *equilibration* or of seeking equibrium. In Piaget's system, a child continues to be satisfied with simplistic, unsophisticated answers to questions of relationships among things until (1) she reaches a particular age of internal maturation and (2) has engaged in enough activites related to the question. At this point she begins to feel dissatisfied and a bit disordered, for she feels an incongruence between her existing schemes (or conception of reality) and a newly perceived reality. This dissonance throws her out of cognitive equilibrium and serves as a motive to "change her mind" or to accommodate in order to set things right—in order to attain equilibrium once more.

Kohlberg applied this same principle of equilibration to growth in moral judgment. When the child is cognitively mature enough and has had enough role-taking experiences in relation to groups that have suitable justice structures, then he can be stimulated toward upward movement in the moral judgment stages by being confronted with problems of moral conflict. In other words, moral education properly consists of confronting the child or adolescent with moral dilemmas at the same time that the child is maturationally and socially ready to take a step ahead.

With this use of equilibration in mind, let's now review the components of a moral education system as conceived within Kohlberg's scheme. First, the goal of moral education is not to inculcate a particular set of values that are dominant or at least common in a given society. Instead, the goal is to stimulate the child's growth through the six stages that are considered universally valid for all cultures. The teacher's expectation for where the child or youth should be in moral growth at a particular time is governed by the teacher's recognition of the level of a child's cognitive development (per Piaget) and of the opportunities the child enjoys to adopt roles in social groups. The expectation is also influenced by the sorts of justice found in the groups in which the child participates and by the child's motivation—that is, will it seem worthwhile to the child to think at a higher moral level?

The methodology the teacher adopts consists primarily of posing moral decision problems for the students and having various students give their arguments to support their decisions. In this process, some students will argue from the viewpoint of a higher stage than will others. Or the teacher may argue from a higher stage. This conflict of arguments is intended to produce a feeling of disequilibrium in young people who are approaching the threshold of a new stage, so that the basis for their thinking begins to change and they are hoisted to the new level.

In summary, Kohlberg objected to a pair of commonly practiced systems of moral education: (1) the "thoughtless system of moralizing by individual teachers and principals when children deviate from minor administrative regulations" and (2) "the effort to inculcate the majority values, particularly as reflected in vague stereotypes about moral character" (Kohlberg, 1967, p. 169). In place of these he recommended a system that stimulates "the 'natural' development of the individual child's own moral judgment and of the capacities allowing him to use his own moral judgment to control his behavior." The purpose is to aid the child "to take the next step in a direction toward which he is already tending, rather than imposing an alien pattern on him" (Kohlberg, 1967, p. 169).

A further application of Kohlberg's theory takes the form of *the just community*. This term was created by Kohlberg to identify the practice of using the daily moral dilemmas faced in school as the subject of students' study of moral decision making. The just-community approach was tried out in an alternative school that operated under the aegis of a larger "regular" high school. The sixty or so students enrolled in the alternative school were ones who had had difficulty meeting the academic and social behavior standards of the regular high school, so they provided a particularly good test of the just-community approach. Kohlberg's group guided the staff and students of the alternative school in establishing a system of democratic governance in which students and teachers would "overcome their reliance on traditional authority patterns" and "learn to democratically share the responsibility for decision making" (Hersh, Miller, & Fielding, 1980, p. 151). Events during the school day that involved stealing, missing classes, use of drugs, and the like became discussed issues, with students and faculty members having an equal voice in how to resolve the issues. Instituting and operating such a system proved to be complex, time consuming, and in a constant state of negotiation.

Clearly, the idea of teachers sharing power and responsibility with students for the conduct of a classroom or school is not new. It goes back at least to the early decades of this country, led by John Dewey's contention that education is not just a preparation for life but, rather, education is life. What is novel about Kohlberg's just community is the linking of his stages of moral development to the operation of such a system. In other words, discussions about moral issues that are faced in the conduct of the school are directed toward raising moral decisions to

> the highest level of moral reasoning available to its student members. That is not to say at a principled [stage 5 or 6] level, for no students in this school have developed beyond stage 4, and most reason at stage 3 level. The staff's task is not to impose higher-stage reasoning but to offer the soundest reasoning students are capable of understanding and to continually encourage students to exercise the best of their moral reasoning in arriving at communal decisions. When that is achieved, and when students stand behind their decisions and enforce them, the school can be said to be operating as a just community (Hersh, Miller, & Fielding, 1980, p. 154).

Staff members involved in this just-community project reported that it did increase students' skills resolving moral conflicts by peaceful, reasoned means. Power's (1988) review of subsequent just-community projects in other places led him to conclude that Kohlberg's approach succeeded in establishing school cultures conducive to the development of socio-moral reasoning and action. However, Hersh, Miller, and Fielding (1980, p. 158) have cautioned that, "Because our schools are so oriented toward 'measurable' growth, teachers may find it frustrating to embrace a model that involves long-term learning (often up to five years) and is difficult to measure precisely."

KOHLBERG'S THEORY: AN ASSESSMENT

When Kohlberg's model of moral deveopment is appraised according to the standards proposed in Chapter One, his theory shows up well in several respects.

The theory provides both for explaining children's past moral judgment behavior and for predicting their future behavior (item 3). Not only does it permit predictions for the average child, but by proposing four interacting determinants of moral judgment development, it offers the

Kohlberg's Theory

How well do I think the theory meets the standards?

The Standards	Very Well	Moderately Well	Very Poorly
1. Reflects the real world of children		X	
2. Is clearly understandable		X	
3. Explains the past and predicts the future	X		
4. Guides child rearing	X		
5. Is internally consistent	X		
6. Is economical	X		
7. Is falsifiable	X		
8. Stimulates new discoveries	X		
9. Is self-satisfying		X	

possibility of doing so for individuals as well (if proper measures of the four variables and their interaction are made available).

The moral education scheme Kohlberg founded on his theory offers clear guidance for child rearing (item 4). Likewise, the theory appears to be internally consistent (item 5) and economical (item 6). It has also stimulated a variety of new investigations and discoveries, particularly in the way moral judgment develops in different cultures (item 8). Kohlberg has been credited with opening a number of new perspectives on moral growth and for doing "some very hard and very unfashionable thinking on moral thought" along with "producing evidence that should force psychologists to take the cognitive aspects of morality seriously as an important influence on behavior" (Alston, 1971, p. 284). In the standard psychological journal literature for 1974 to 1990, more than 220 investigations bearing on

Kohlberg's theory were reported, with the total number spread rather evenly over the seventeen-year period. Thus his work has been a source of continuing interest among researchers and educators.

On the scale of clarity (item 2), the theory deserves a mixed score. On the positive side are the many specific examples Kohlberg cited from children's moral dilemma responses that clarify terms and differentiate one stage from another. Such phrases as *instrumental relativist orientation* and *social-contract legalistic orientation* are illustrated with examples from children's responses. However, in the opinions of informed scholars in the field, other key terms have not been distinguished clearly. R. S. Peters (1971, pp. 246–248) has taken Kohlberg to task for being vague and unsophisticated in comparing *character traits* (honesty, courage, determination) unfavorably with *principles* (a sense of *justice*). A similar criticism has been directed at Kohlberg's distinctions between the *form* and *content* of moral reasoning in a given culture. Kohlberg said that the content of moral judgments may vary from culture to culture, but the more basic form of judgments does not. Yet, when these two concepts are analyzed in detail, it appears that Kohlberg failed to produce adequate criteria for differentiating between them.

On item 1, Kohlberg can be credited with basing his model on data drawn from a variety of real children. However, there is a question about how realistic he was in the scope of moral decisions that he analyzed. The theory is founded on evidence collected from having children and youths offer solutions to moral dilemma incidents posed to them. Since Kohlberg wanted to make the respondents think hard in order to test their reasoning, he necessarily posed incidents that had no obvious solutions in terms of the dominant standards of a child's culture. However, as W. P. Alston (1971, p. 284) has pointed out, these represent only a minor portion of the daily moral decisions a person makes. Thus, according to Alston, Kohlberg's methodology has necessarily caused him to ignore the host of judgments young people make by *habit*. Habitual judgments are easy ones because the reward and punishment system of the culture has fashioned the individual's "character" so that the solution to such moral issues is obvious and no alternative solutions can compete successfully with the habitual one. Alston believes that this lack in Kohlberg's research method distorted the theorist's view of the significance of habit or "character traits" and of emotion in determining moral thought and behavior.

This questionable representativeness of Kohlberg's moral incidents seems to have resulted from the unsystematic manner in which he selected his original dilemmas. For his doctoral research in the 1950s, he created nine moral dilemmas to which his youthful subjects were asked to respond. Since that time, these same nine incidents have been used for nearly all of the studies conducted by Kohlberg and his followers. Four of the incidents involve people taking others' property without permission, three concern people being tempted to inform on others, one involves the mercy killing of a terminal cancer patient, and one a soldier's sacrificing himself for the sake of his military unit. On the basis of respondents' reactions to these incidents (or more frequently, to only a few of the incidents), investigators have drawn conclusions about the stage of the respondents' moral reasoning. However, even a casual review of life's moral situations indicates that this selection of dilemmas is hardly representative of the decisions most people face. In effect, a sound system for choosing dilemmas has not been provided by the Kohlberg group (Thomas, 1989b). This shortcoming has caused me to mark item 1 as no higher than the moderately well level.

Finally, Kohlberg has been criticized for proclaiming the principle of justice the sole occupant of the highest stage of moral thought without having sufficient cause to label it more worthy than several other virtues that might have been selected—for example, sympathy, concern for others, courage, integrity, or autonomy. As Peters has written, Kohlberg's findings

> are of unquestionable importance, but there is a grave danger that they may become exalted into a general theory of moral development. Any such general theory presupposes a general ethical theory, and Kohlberg himself surely would be the first to admit that he had done little to develop the details of such a general ethical theory. Yet without such a theory the notion of "moral development" is pretty unsubstantial (1971, pp. 263–264).

So Kohlberg's theory, like the rest we have considered, has drawn both praise and criticism. But whatever its shortcomings, it remains the most stimulating and potentially fertile model of children's moral growth in current psychological and philosophical circles. For this reason, I have rated it as quite self-satisfying overall (item 9).

FOR FURTHER READING

Colby, A., L. Kohlberg, J. Gibbs, and M. Lieberman. (1983) *A Longitudinal Study of Moral Judgment.* Monographs of the Society for Research in Child Development, Serial No. 200, Vol. 48, Nos. 1–2. Chicago: Society for Research in Child Development.

Kohlberg, L. (1967) "Moral and Religious Education in the Public Schools: A Developmental View," in Theodore R. Sizer, *Religion and Public Education.* Boston: Houghton Mifflin.

Kohlberg, L. (1984) *The Psychology of Moral Development.* San Francisco: Harper & Row.

CHAPTER SEVENTEEN

An Integrated Theory of Moral Development

Over the past few years my interest in theories has centered particularly on models of moral development (Thomas, 1986, 1988, 1989a, 1989b). The pursuit of this interest has prompted me to assemble components from a variety of development theories to form a composite model that I call *an integrated theory of moral development*. The view of the model offered in the following pages is a much abbreviated version of a book-length description of the theory that will appear in a forthcoming volume of the same title as this chapter.

As the contents of the chapter illustrate, the scheme offered here has been fashioned from elements of the models described earlier in the book, particularly from the role of consequences in behaviorism and social learning theory, Freud's levels of consciousness, neo-Piagetian conceptions of developmental stages, ecological psychology's concern for environments, and Kohlberg's use of moral dilemmas. The entire scheme is set within an information-processing framework. I have also added components of my own that seem necessary for explaining how children's moral values develop and are applied in moral decision situations.

The topics that comprise the chapter are presented in the following order: (1) problems with existing theories, (2) foundational definitions, (3) principal features of the model, (4) foundational components, (5) long-term memory, (6) the nature of environments, (7) functions of working memory, (8) stages of moral development, and (9) an assessment of the theory.

PROBLEMS WITH EXISTING THEORIES

This scheme is designed to cope with an array of problems that seem inadequately resolved in available descriptions of moral development.

The first problem is one that A. L. Brown (1979, p. 235) claims is a shortcoming of many developmental models: "at best they provide a description of the stages or states of development but they cannot account for the transformations that lead to growth." Such is the case of Piaget's and Kohlberg's proposals. Both Piaget and Kohlberg offer some general processes (assimilation, accommodation) or conditions (neural maturation, opportunities to adopt roles) that affect moral development, but neither of them describes the way daily events effect changes in moral reasoning.

A second problem derives from the imprecise conception of moral values that existing theories provide. For instance, they fail to account for why such a principle as "thou shalt not kill" is typically applied differently in different contexts.

A third difficulty is the discrepancy between people's apparent moral values and their behavior in moral decision situations. Why do people sometimes—perhaps rather often—fail to act in keeping with their stated moral principles?

Another objection, intimately linked to all three of the foregoing difficulties, is that the analysis of environments in the development of both moral reasoning and moral behavior is inadequate in existing theories.

A fifth concern is the imprecise way that most theories depict the architecture of the mind. In particular, they fail to address the role apparently played by different levels of consciousness in people's moral thought and action.

The theory outlined in this chapter is a response to these challenges.

FOUNDATIONAL DEFINITIONS AND ASSUMPTIONS

Throughout the chapter, the term *moral development* refers to *changes in the system by which people make moral decisions.* The theory, in effect, intends to explain how and why the moral aspects of the mind change with the passing of time.

As noted in the introduction to Part Eight, not everyone subscribes to the same definition of the moral domain. However, the model offered in this chapter is not dependent on a particular definition of *moral.* It can accommodate nearly any popular conception of moral. It can be used with Piaget's conception of moral development as "learning the rules," Kohlberg's notion of advancing toward "contractual, even-handed justice," Gilligan's proposed "compassionate caring," or Maccoby's "cultural relativism."

One important assumption undergirding the model is that no moral values are innate. A newborn infant has not inherited a sense of right and wrong. The child does not innately know what behavior is morally good or morally bad. In other words, moral rules are learned in the process of growing up.

A second key assumption is that the child does inherit a potential for self-punishment and self-reward, that is, a capacity to feel guilty and ashamed and to feel self-satisfied and proud. This is the capacity to develop a conscience. However, the contents of the conscience—that is, exactly what events make the child feel guilty or proud—are not innate but are learned.

With these introductory ground rules in hand, we turn now to the structure of the theory.

PRINCIPAL FEATURES OF THE MODEL

Figure 17.1 offers a graphic representation of the model. Key characteristics of environments are listed on the left side and key features of the person on the right. At the bottom of the person-rectangle are foundational components that derive from the individual's genetic inheritance and current biological state. The main genetic factors are (1) ability capacities, such as intellectual and physical potentials, and (2) the rate at which these capacities mature during childhood and adolescence. A person's current biological state is influenced not only by these genetic factors but also by nutrition, disease, and accident.

The foundational components support an information-processing network comprised of the senses, working memory, long-term memory, and the neuromuscular system that acts on the world. Among the most important features of this network are the components of long-term memory, where the results of moral development reside. A person's current moral state is represented by the patterning of these components at any given time.

The environmental structure at the left is conceived to serve the three functions of determining (1) the opportunities a person will have to encounter moral decision situations, (2) the environmental cues that the individual believes should influence moral decisions, and (3) the kinds of consequences the person will experience from his or her actions in moral situations. The role played by these three factors in the life of a growing child is determined chiefly by the people who control the child's experiences. These people serve as fabricators of the environments the child encounters and thereby they exert a crucial influence on the child's moral development.

The following detailed description of the model begins with the foundational components, then continues with long-term memory, the nature of environments, working memory, and acting on the world.

518

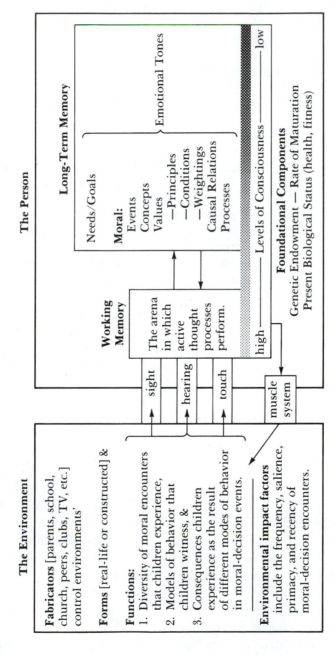

Figure 17.1 A Moral Development Model

FOUNDATIONAL COMPONENTS

Four principles of human development that seem universally accepted are that (1) genetic endowment defines a range of potential intellectual ability within which environmental influences can operate to produce the actual intellectual skills people display in their lives, (2) such genetic endowment can differ from one person to another, so that one individual's potential will differ from another's, (3) the flowering of genetic potential evolves gradually over the first two decades of life, and (4) the maturation rate of this flowering can differ from one person to another. These principles reflect basic constraints operating at any juncture of a child's life to affect how adequately the child can understand moral issues and the consequences to be expected from different responses to moral situations. In effect, these genetically seated conditions are the essential building blocks on which moral development is necessarily based. Such genetic factors are the primary determinants of the successive moral development stages postulated by both Piaget and Kohlberg. We can propose that moral education efforts that disregard such principles are bound to fail.

Another foundational factor is the physiological state of the individual as a result of nutrition, illness, or accident. The term *nutrition* in this context refers to any substance that a person ingests. I am assuming that the growing child's nutritional state can affect how adequately the child derives moral "lessons" from the environment, stores these lessons in long-term memory, and uses them in making moral decisions. An adolescent under the influence of mind-altering drugs is not likely to respond to moral decision situations in the same manner as one who is on a nutritionally balanced diet. As E. R. Hilgard (1949) once observed, the superego is soluble in alcohol. Furthermore, chemical imbalances or illnesses that influence the nervous system can affect what the child is able to learn as well as how emotions alter moral decisions, particularly such emotions as depression, rage, guilt, and fear.

THE NATURE OF LONG-TERM MEMORY

For purposes of moral development, the principal components of long-term memory are conceived to be (1) needs and goals, (2) records of events, (3) concepts, (4) moral values, (5) causal relations, and (6) processes.

Needs/Drives, and Goals

I believe children are need-fulfilling organisms that use the environment to satisfy needs. In other words, the child's actions are motivated by the twofold goal of (1) identifying objects and activities in the environment that will fulfill needs and (2) developing skills and strategies for obtaining the objects and activities. From a psychoanalytic perspective, this search of the environment for objects that will satisfy needs is the function of the ego that Freud labeled the *secondary process.*

The child's need system takes the form of a hierarchy, with each higher stratum being instrumental in meeting the more basic needs on the tiers below. The all-encompassing need at the base is that of ensuring the survival and perpetuation of the human genetic line, as proposed by such sociobiologists as E. O. Wilson (1978). On the next higher stratum is the need for the individual to survive—self-preservation. On the third level are basic needs that promote such self-preservation—needs for food, drink, warmth, harm avoidance, comprehending the environment, and others. Above this level are the more specific ways that each of these third-level needs can be fulfilled. Some types of food are better than others for sustaining health and energy, some types of drink more suitable, some ways of maintaining optimum body temperature more adequate, and so on. The term *goal* in the present context refers to the types of objects or activities the child identifies as appropriate for meeting a particular need or cluster of needs.

Some people prefer to call the forces that motivate human action *drives* rather than *needs.* The two terms are like the opposite sides of a coin—two facets of the same thing. Whereas *need* suggests a lack the child is attempting to satisfy, *drive* can suggest stored-up energy the child is seeking to expend by investing it in particular objects and activities. Thus the hunger drive represents the need for food and the curiosity drive the need to comprehend the environment.

From the perspective of moral development, needs are important in at least two ways. First, in certain cultural settings, a need itself can be morally controversial. The most obvious case is the need for sexual expression, which in some religious sects has been viewed as inherently immoral, both in thought and deed. Second, and far more significant because of its all-pervasive nature, is the matter of the methods a child adopts for fulfilling a need. Some methods are considered moral and others immoral. Much of the process of socialization during childhood is directed at teaching children to become moral beings by adopting approved techniques of meeting their needs and by rejecting unacceptable techniques. Socialization in this sense is moral education.

Events

A portion of children's memories is comprised of past events in which they participated, as either actors or observers. These are what E. Tulving

(1972) called *episodic* memories. The events of significance here are the ones interpreted as involving moral matters—a parent scolding the child for lying about who took the cookies, a Sunday school lesson about the Ten Commandments, an argument on the playground about breaking rules, a TV program in which a girl is raped, a newspaper account of an army invading a neighboring country, and the like. Memories of events are the raw materials from which the next four components of long-term memory are constructed—concepts, moral values, causal relations, and processes.

Concepts

In the present context, a *concept* is defined as a characteristic common to, and abstracted from, a variety of facts or events or other concepts, with a label attached to the concept so it can be consciously communicated in speech and writing and can be readily manipulated during thought. The label is typically a single word or a short phrase. Examples of concepts significant in moral development are *cheating, honesty, exploitation, altruism, felony, fair play, injustice, philanthropy, child abuse, compassion, hardheartedness,* and *kindness.* The process of moral education includes teaching children meanings for such concepts so they know what sorts of behavior and values are implied when those terms are used.

Moral Values

The contents and applications of the *moral values* component in Figure 17.1 are characterized by four key factors—principles, conditions, weightings, and emotional tones (Thomas, 1989b).

Moral Principles   At the core of each value is a *moral principle* in the form of an unembellished statement of what is right or, in its reciprocal form, what is wrong. Table 17.1 illustrates several such principles. The ones selected for inclusion in the table are common to many cultures.

Conditions   In any moral decision, the application of a moral principle is affected by a series of *conditions.* The presumption here is that rarely if ever is any moral principle applied unconditionally to every life situation to which that principle can apply. In effect, the way a principle is used in order to arrive at a moral decision depends on certain circumstances in the particular case at hand. Here are four typical conditions:

1. *Age.* While the age of the individuals involved in a moral situation is often a consideration in people's moral judgments, it is not really age itself but, rather, some other characteristic that is highly corre-

Table 17.1   A Sampling of Moral Principles

Virtues to Be Encouraged	*Transgressions to Be Avoided*
Regard for human life: Everyone should protect others from harm and should seek to enhance others' physical and mental well-being.	*Disregard for human life:* No one should exploit or harm others, either physically or psychologically.
Honesty: Everyone should tell the truth.	*Deceit:* No one should try to deceive others by lying or by deviously withholding the truth.
Self-determination: All of us, within our levels of ability, should be permitted to decide on the way we will live our lives, provided that (a) we do not unduly intrude on others' rights to lead their lives and (b) we bear our fair share of responsibility in caring for our own welfare and for that of the group.	*Exploitation:* No one should be forced to yield to the demands of others in ways that decrease the individual's self-perceived welfare, provided that the individual bears a fair share of responsibility in caring for his or her own welfare and the welfare of the group.
Respect for property: Everyone should protect others' right to hold and use property to which they have proper or legal claim.	*Stealing and vandalism:* No one should take or use others' property without their permission. No one should damage others' property.
Contractual integrity: People who have freely agreed, in either written or oral form, to perform an action should faithfully carry out that commitment.	*Contractual unreliability:* People should never avoid performing actions that they have freely agreed to carry out.
Compassion, altruism: Everyone should exhibit sympathy for, and offer aid to, people who suffer misfortune.	*Disdain, coldheartedness:* No one should ignore or scorn people who suffer misfortune.

lated with age (such as *knowledge of right and wrong* or *logical reasoning ability*). A three-year-old who does not tell the truth is usually judged differently than a nineteen-year-old who is not truthful.

2. *Intention.* Whether an act is deemed moral or immoral often depends on the answer to the question, "Why did he do it? What was he trying to accomplish?" Intention frequently is regarded as a

defining characteristic of moral behavior, in that intention distinguishes acts involving morality from acts that result from mistakes, accidents, and chance.

3. *Relationships among participants.* Typical relationships are those within a family (parent/child, brother/sister), between age groups (adults/adolescents), between the sexes, between ethnic or religious groups, and between social roles (police officer/thief). Perhaps the most dramatic illustration of the effect of this relationship variable appears during wartime, when moral principles applied to one's own country are distinctly different from those applied to the enemy's.

4. *Seriousness of consequences.* The severity of the consequences of a moral incident for recipients of the act as well as for the perpetrators can affect judgments about the moral status of the incident. For example, depending on the conditions, sexual intercourse may be judged in one case a mere peccadillo and in another case a mortal sin.

Other conditions that often affect people's judgments of moral incidents are the participants' degree of self-control (mental disorder, physical ability, and such), awareness of likely consequences, ethnic status, socioeconomic status, marital situation, and the legal status of an act.

In summary, conditions are contextual factors that qualify the application of moral principles in specific situations. A person discovers which conditions to apply by scanning the particular environment in which a decision is called for.

Weightings   The third distinguishing feature of moral values is a *weighting factor.* Certain principles are accorded more importance than others in people's moral judgements. For instance, in the case of a conflict between the principle "protecting human life" and the principle "telling the truth," an individual can regard the value of life more highly than the value of truthfulness and therefore arrive at a decision that gives greater weight to life than to truth telling. Likewise, conditions can vary in their importance. In a decision that requires a choice between "intention" and "relationship between the participants," an individual can consider a parent-child relationship more important than intention in arriving at a moral judgment.

Emotional Tone   Moral values, and their application in specific situations, are assumed to be accompanied by *affect,* that is, by feelings reflected in such terms as *guilt, pride, fear, confidence, hate, love, depression, joy*, and the like. The emotional tone of a given moral incident is often complex, involving a combination or succession of different emotions. Also, emotions can vary in intensity from weak to strong.

The emotional qualities of a moral event are significant in that they can affect a participant's willingness and ability to take particular actions. Emotions therefore have a motivating effect, inducing a person to adopt actions that will increase positive feelings and decrease negative ones. In other words, a child's *conscience* or *superego* is represented in the present theory as a linkage between moral values and positive (rewarding) or negative (punishing) emotions. These linkages are assumed to result from children's experiences with the world, so that over time children accrue a growing array of internalized rewarding and punishing emotions that influence how they feel and behave when faced with moral decisions.

Emotions can also influence how rational participants' behavior will be and how well they can foresee the consequences of their present actions. Furthermore, the emotional states of observers of moral incidents or of people who learn of past incidents (as in the case of a jury in a court trial) can also affect those individual's moral judgments. As suggested by the diagram in Figure 17.1, an emotional tone is not only attached to moral values but to the other components of long-term memory as well.

In summary, the process of making moral decisions is assumed to involve a complex kind of mental algebra whose formulas are comprised of particular combinations of principles and conditions, their weightings, and accompanying emotions. The specific variables that will be manipulated in carrying out such computations during a given moral encounter is determined by (1) the current patterning of the contents of an individual's moral values (including emotions) and (2) that person's perception of which elements in the present environmental context are relevant to those contents. How such a process may operate is suggested below. But before we inspect the process, we need to understand the postulated role of causal relations.

Causal Relations

A *causal relation* is an *if-then* belief that a person holds. Such beliefs can be either *descriptive* or *prescriptive*. A descriptive or explanatory relation is an if-then conviction about what consequences actually will result in real life situations if certain conditions obtain. For instance, "If the police catch that girl stealing jewelry from the store, she'll end up in jail." Or, "If I give money to feed hungry people and then if sometime later I need help, some kind person will also probably help me."

In contrast, a prescriptive causal relation represents a correlation that a person believes *should* obtain in life, whether or not it commonly does. For example, a prescriptive relation proposed by the Chinese philosopher Confucius is: "If there are ways that you do not wish to be treated, then do not treat others in those ways" (Waley, 1938). Or, as Jesus Christ later voiced the same basic notion in his Golden Rule: "All things whatsoever ye would that men should do to you, do ye even so to them" (St. Matthew, 7:12). Prescriptive causal relations, then, are convictions about the way people should act in moral situations. Frequently, if not always, a descriptive relation (an if-then event that actually will occur) is implied in a prescriptive relation (what one should do). Thus Confucius, as a social philosopher, suggested that if his precept was followed, then individuals would be happy and their family, community, and nation would prosper. Christ, as a theologian, suggested that people who adopted his advice could expect a blissful afterlife with God in heaven: "In my Father's house are many mansions. . . . I go to prepare a place for you" (St. John, 14:2).

Causal relations are crucial elements undergirding moral behavior, for they represent what individuals expect will result from their actions. If they think the consequences of a given act will be contrary to their welfare, they will avoid that act and choose an alternative that they expect will bring more adequate need fulfillment. Thus causal relations link behaviors to consequences. Much of moral education involves teaching children about such relations.

Processes of Moral Development

The term *processes* refers to patterns of mental operations involved in thinking about moral matters. There appear to be a number of major processes, with minor subprocesses or subroutines often embedded within them. The following example, which focuses on the function of making a moral decision, illustrates the notion of processes as intended in this theory. Other hypothesized processes that could serve equally well as examples are ones that involve: (1) learning a moral concept, (2) recalling a moral event, (3) establishing a causal relation, (4) assigning a value to an event, (5) associating conditions with a moral principle, or (6) attaching an emotional tone to a moral value. I am assuming that processes are stored in long-term memory and are drawn into working memory at the time they are needed.

But before inspecting the posited decision-making process, we should recognize the significance of the *levels of consciousness* dimension in Figure 17.1. I am assuming that all of the contents of long-term memory can be at different levels of availability to consciousness. The individual, at the stage of working memory, may be quite aware of some contents and quite unaware of others; yet both the lucidly conscious and the concealed and unconscious contents are presumed to affect moral thought and behavior. Thus the process described in the following examples is presumed to function at different levels of awareness when brought into working memory. I am also assuming that as children grow up, their awareness of their needs and goals, past events, concepts, values, and processes grows in amount and complexity. This awareness of how one's moral development processes operate might be dubbed *metaprocessing*. An implicit aim of moral education is to render moral components of the mind more conscious and thus more rational.

Figure 17.2 pictures a circuit or loop of eight steps representing a process of making a decision in a moral situation. Such an operation includes not only the manner of arriving at a decision but also the way the consequences of the decision affect the contents of long-term memory (Thomas, 1986, pp. 352–353).

Step 1.   By means of the senses of sight and hearing, a schoolgirl's working memory encounters an event in the environment that she interprets as involving morality, because the incident fits the definition of *moral* in the moral values component of her long-term memory. (A boy has copied answers from the girl's test paper, but when the teacher accuses him of cheating, the boy denies that he copied.)

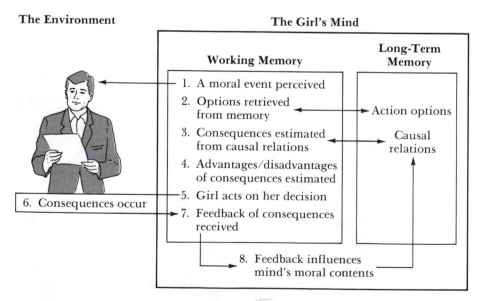

Figure 17.2   A Decision-Making Process

Step 2. The girl's working memory extracts events and concepts from her long-term memory that inform her of what actions she might take in this situation. (She could tell the teacher that the boy did indeed copy, she could attack the boy physically after class, she could keep quiet about the whole affair, she could tell her classmates about the incident, she could make an anonymous phone call to the boy's parents, or she could take any of a number of other such actions that come to mind.)

Step 3. From the causal relations in her long-term memory that seem pertinent to such events and concepts, the girl predicts what consequences will likely result from the alternative actions she could take.

Step 4. Weighing (in working memory) the advantages and disadvantages of the various expected consequences, she decides how to act in order to maximize (in terms of need fulfillment) the advantages and minimize the disadvantages.

Step 5. She acts on her decision. (She does not tell the teacher, but after class she tells her classmates.)

Step 6. Following her action, consequences occur. (The classmates tease the boy on the playground, they tell pupils from other classes about the incident, and one classmate leaves an anonymous note about the matter on the teacher's desk. The boy then threatens the girl: "I'll get you for this.")

Step 7. The girl receives feedback regarding the consequences, informing her about the accuracy of her prediction of consequences at step 3. (She hears her classmates tease the boy, the teacher asks her if the accusation in the anonymous note is true, and she's threatened. In terms of her expectations at step 3, she's not surprised that her classmates tease the boy, but she is astonished that someone wrote the note the teacher asks her about. Furthermore, she did not expect the boy to threaten her.)

Step 8. The feedback influences the contents of long-term memory. To the extent that the actual consequences confirm her prediction at step 3, the feedback strengthens the patterning of the original contents—those memories of events and causal relations and the emotions associated with them. (In Piagetian terms, this is *assimilation*.) But to the extent that the prediction of consequences proves to be in error, the feedback alters the original contents by generating changes in the mind's pattern of events and causal relations (Piaget's *accommodation*).

In summary, the decision-making process, when carried through in overt action, serves moral development by strengthening the existing contents of long-term memory whenever expectations are confirmed by consequences. But whenever expectations are not confirmed, the process serves moral development by "changing the person's mind" in the sense of revising existing contents to render them more accurate, complex, and sophisticated as reflectors of reality. (Such an interpretation of development obviously draws heavily on behaviorism and social learning theory.)

It may be useful at this juncture to recall the definition of moral development intended throughout this chapter. *Moral development* refers to *changes in the system by which people make moral decisions.* That system is comprised of the structure and contents of long-term memory as described above. *Development* means changes in the system through interactions between internal neural maturation (determined chiefly by a genetic timing mechanism) and environmental encounters (which furnish learning opportunities that either strengthen or alter the existing contents of the mind).

Early in this chapter I mentioned Brown's (1979, p. 235) complaint that many developmental models "provide a description of the stages or states of development but they cannot account for the transformations that lead to growth." I believe that the integrated theory's conception of processes helps account for those transformations by postulating what apparently occurs as children's day-by-day encounters with moral events fashion the contents of their long-term memory.

THE NATURE OF ENVIRONMENTS

As suggested on the left side of Figure 17.1, environments can profitably be analyzed in terms of four characteristics—their fabricators, functions, forms, and impact factors. I believe that when we identify permutations of these aspects, we go a long way toward accounting for the way that children's encounters with different environments can influence those children's moral development.

Fabricators

The word *fabricators* refers to the people and institutions in the society that establish which environmental events children will experience. It seems apparent that during the early years of the child's life, the most important fabricators are parents. They determine the kinds of moral situations the young will face within the family, and they can control such outside influences as the child's companions, television programs, and story books. During middle childhood, while members of the family continue to be important agents for delineating the kinds of moral events children witness, the school, neighborhood, and church serve to expand the range of people and media that determine the nature of children's exposure to moral events. For instance, the incidents witnessed by boys and girls growing up in an inner-city ghetto can differ markedly from those seen by children in an affluent suburb or a small farming community.

Fabricators not only affect the kinds of moral incidents children meet but also help shape the interpretations children draw about the incidents. In particular, a fabricator influences the values children assign to incidents when the fabricator proposes answers for such questions as: Was the behavior of the participants in that event right or wrong? Should the participants be praised or condemned, rewarded or punished? And why?

In summary, people and institutions can control the kinds of moral situations a child meets and can influence the values the child applies when interpreting those situations. Because fabricators can differ markedly in the amount of control they maintain over the sorts of encounters and values children experience, children can be expected to differ from one another in the moral contents of their minds.

Functions

For purposes of moral development, environments can be seen as serving three principal functions—they define the scope or range of moral events that children have a chance to experience, they furnish models of how people can act in moral decision situations, and they suggest the consequences that will likely follow different kinds of moral behavior.

Forms

The forms of environments in which children encounter moral matters can be divided into two general types—real life and constructed. Real life environments are ones met naturally in the routine of living. They have not been created by someone for either teaching or testing children. Constructed environments, on the other hand, are ones devised to promote or to assess children's moral development.

Constructed environments can vary in the degree to which they approximate real life environments. This point can be illustrated by our aligning examples of moral instruction along a scale ranging from highly abstract at one end to highly realistic at the other. An example at the highly abstract end would be a teacher's telling pupils to be honest, loyal, just, and compassionate and then expecting the children to display such traits in daily life. In effect, exhorting the young to memorize the biblical Ten Commandments or the Boy Scout Law is a highly abstract environmental encounter.

A less abstract form is an anecdote that embodies a moral lesson. The parables of the Christian Bible and incidents from the lives of mythical or actual heroes (Sir Galahad, Joan of Arc, Abraham Lincoln, Martin Luther King, Jr.) are instances of this type of constructed environment. So also are the moral dilemmas posed by Piaget and Kohlberg for assessing the stage of children's moral development. Such anecdotes, in contrast to abstract concepts of honesty and justice, are able to promote all three functions of environments listed above — provide opportunities for children to encounter an extended range of moral issues, offer models of behavior that children can imitate, and suggest consequences to expect from different types of behavior in moral situations.

At a point closer to the real life end of the scale are the more detailed accounts of moral matters found in such reading matter as novels and biographies that picture people engaged in a series of moral decisions. These extended narratives are able to depict moral matters within more complex settings than can a brief anecdote.

Reality can be approached even more closely when moral events are portrayed on the stage or in motion pictures and television programs. Unlike novels and biographies, which require considerable imagination on the part of readers, dramatic presentations can approximate the sights and sounds that real life environments involve.

An additional aspect of reality can be achieved when children and youths engage in sociodramas that require that they interact with other players to resolve moral issues. Role playing has the advantage of obligating participants to generate spontaneous responses to other people's actions, an important characteristic of real life events that is missing in novels and dramas. Role playing can also evoke emotions similar to those experienced in real life environments.

Implicit throughout the foregoing discussion is the conviction that the closer a constructed environment approximates real life conditions, (1) the more accurately children's minds (their moral development) will represent real life moral decisions and (2) the more accurate will be the picture of children's moral development that researchers derive from constructed environments that are used as evaluation instruments.

Impact Factors

The phrase *impact factors* refers to conditions that affect how, and to what degree, environmental encounters will influence the moral contents of a child's mind. Such factors are apparently quite numerous. The ones described below have been selected for the purpose of illustration and are not a definitive list.

Perhaps the most obvious factors are those found in traditional principles of learning as proposed by educational psychologists, such as those of *frequency, salience, primacy,* and *recency.*

The *frequency principle* proposes that many repetitions of the same type of environmental encounter will exert a greater influence on moral development than will few repetitions. Witnessing forty television programs featuring sexual abuse will have a different effect on the contents of a child's mind than will two such programs, as social learning theory would suggest.

Salience refers to how intrusive, demanding, startling, or surprising something in the environment appears to be. The novelty of an environment often renders it highly salient.

In studies of certain forms of learning, the earliest items learned *(primacy)* as well as the latest ones *(recency)* are more readily recalled than are events in between. For moral development, we can propose that environmental encounters early in a child's life can have a particularly lasting effect on the contents of the child's mind if, at the time of those encounters, the child is mature enough to assimilate the significance of the events. Likewise, we can postulate that recent events assume particular significance in affecting the moral contents because they are still likely to be "fresh in mind," undiluted by intervening events and less subject to the fading of memory that so often occurs with passing time.

With the foregoing conceptions of long-term memory and environments as a background, we turn now to working memory, which is the hypothesized place in which transactions between the mind and environment take place.

WORKING MEMORY

Working memory is considered to be the arena of active thought, the stage on which the processes of interacting with the world and of manipulating the contents of long-term memory are being performed at any given moment.

The phrase *interacting with the world* means engaging in transactions with the environment. One example would be a girl deciding whether to snitch on her teenage brother whom she has seen smoking marijuana. Another would be a student in a sociology class trying to understand the distinction between *misdemeanor* and *felony*.

The phrase *manipulating contents of long-term memory* refers to a child's thinking about matters that are drawn entirely from long-term memory rather than from the outside environment. The child already has in long-term memory all the raw materials—events, concepts, causal relations, values—required for pondering moral matters. Much of creative thought and all dreaming are of this nature. Such thinking involves rearranging materials selected from memory into new patterns. This type of manipulation takes place when a person tries to answer such questions as: If I had to choose between saving a classmate from a fire and, in the process, getting badly burned myself, what should I do? Or, what are some of the consequences that could likely result from my writing anonymous threatening letters to the school principal?

An essential assumption made about working memory is that it can operate at more than one level of consciousness. In our earlier discussion, this matter of levels of consciousness was given only passing mention. But because degrees of consciousness play such an important role in moral development, it is appropriate at this point to inspect the matter in greater detail. The phenomenon of consciousness, as intended here, is represented as a scale ranging from highly conscious to deeply unconscious. The scale is comprised of one major dimension and an accompanying minor dimension. The major dimension is labeled *ease of recall* and the minor *precision of recall*.

Ease is measured in terms of response time. The shorter the interval between the intention to recall a memory and the actual recall, the more conscious the memory, and vice versa. A person's quickly recalling a memory without the need of prompting or clues is an example from the highly conscious end of the scale. Recollection that takes more time or requires prompts to bring it about is closer to the middle. Items that cannot be retrieved at all, even with extended effort, time, and cues, are from the deeply unconscious sector.

Precision is measured in terms of detail and accuracy. The more detailed and accurate the recalled memory, the more highly conscious it is considered to be, and vice versa.

Operationally, a person is credited with *recall* whenever he or she expresses the retrieved material in verbal, graphic, or mathematical form. Although people may claim introspective recall ("I remember it now, but I can't quite put it into words"), they are not credited with retrieval unless they can express it in some public form, even if it takes the form of selecting the correct answer from a series of displayed options.

As noted earlier, I am presuming that much of the mental activity that bears on moral matters operates subliminally; that is, it occurs below the threshold of consciousness. Accepting this presumption can help explain why investigators have found the task of appraising children's moral development so troublesome. Children often cannot explain why they made a particular moral decision because they are not conscious of the factors that produced the decision.

STAGES OF MORAL DEVELOPMENT

A final aspect of the theory not portrayed in Figure 17.1 is that of development stages. Investigations of young people's moral reasoning (as tested with moral dilemma anecdotes) and of their real life moral behavior have often revealed two sorts of inconsistency. First is the Piagetian phenomenon of *horizontal décalage*—children may reason at one level (one stage) in certain situations and at a different level (another stage) in other situations. Second, their moral behavior may be inconsistent with what one would expect on the basis of the highest stage of moral reasoning they have displayed in their responses to hypothetical moral dilemmas.

In the present theory, the notion of stagewise development differs from traditional conceptions. A traditional view assumes that once children advance to a higher stage, they don a new set of mental spectacles that cast their world in a new light, and they henceforth abandon the previous stage's modes of interpreting life. In contrast, what I am proposing is that while children do, indeed, advance to new levels of cognitive skill, they do not abandon modes of perception held before. Instead, they retain the earlier modes in their perceptual repertoire for use on suitable occasions. Thus a *stage* in this sense means acquiring a significantly new ability to interpret events, but without the loss of existing tendencies or abilities. Stagewise development is therefore defined as *the progressive accumulation of options*—of adding new arrows to the cognitive quiver.

Such a view of stages enables us to make sense of apparent inconsistencies between children's "highest moral reasoning stage" and certain of their behaviors in real life situations. We assume that when faced with real life decisions, children (1) inspect the context to see how its characteristics match the moral values patterns (principles and their conditions) in their long-term memory and (2) select those behaviors that their causal-relations memories suggest will yield the greatest benefits in need fulfillment. Such a process of inspection and selection may lead them to choose an action based on their "highest moral reasoning stage" or it may lead them to choose a behavior from an earlier stage. Under this conception of progressive accumulation of options, the determinant of moral behavior is not the child's highest moral reasoning level but, rather, it is the inspection-and-selection process that guides the child's choice from the entire stockpile of interpretation-and-action options.

I believe that one of the neo-Piagetian solutions to the horizontal décalage problem is also of use in accounting for stages. Thus I would include either Case's or Fisher's proposal (see Perspective D at the end of Part Five) as an element of this integrated theory's account of development stages.

This, then, completes our tour of the integrated moral development model, and we are ready to evaluate it.

AN ASSESSMENT OF THE THEORY

In view of my vested interest in this model, I can hardly claim to be objective in its assessment. But to keep the pattern of chapters consistent, I will rate this scheme on the nine assessment dimensions, then leave it to you to correct those ratings that seem unduly self-serving. Two symbols, P and X, have been employed in the appraisal—P = potential and X = actual. Those items whose status seem to require a history of empirical research for judging the *actual* condition have been rated here only on *potential* because the empirical evidence is not yet available. Items that can be judged on the basis of a line of logic without the need for empirical results have been given an *actual* rating.

In regard to item 1, I believe the model shows good potential for reflecting the real world of children, particularly because it (1) provides for the analysis of how different environmental conditions (fabricators, functions, forms, impact factors) help account for differences among children in their moral development and (2) provides for the influence of nonconscious factors in moral thought and action.

My rating the model moderately well for its understandability (item 2) is based principally on the reactions of university students who have read this chapter and discussed it in class. I did not give item 2 a top rating because the students and I have both been dissatisfied with the imprecision of certain aspects of the theory. In particular, we are not at all comfortable with the lack of detail about the way working memory interacts with long-term memory, about the role of unconscious factors in moral decisions, and about how different memories achieve their particular levels of consciousness. Furthermore, ways that needs or drives from long-term memory guide the child's search of the environment and ways that aspects of the environment become sufficiently salient to demand the child's attention are not explained satisfactorily. These shortcomings and similar ones prevent the theory from deserving a rating above moderately well.

I have marked the theory potentially high on explaining the past and predicting the future (item 3) because I believe its components more adequately provide for the factors that affect children's moral developments than do existing theories. For example, such proposals as Piaget's, Kohlberg's, and Gilligan's have not been very successful (1) in accounting for why a child may make one type of moral decision in one situation and a different type in another and (2) in explaining why children's moral behavior is often at odds with their moral reasoning. This integrated theory can, I believe, go a long way toward explaining such matters. My reasons are as follows.

First, from the perspective of the integrated theory, we would not be at all surprised to find children varying their moral principles from one situation to the next. Indeed, we would expect children to adjust their moral principles in relation to (1) how the conditions linked to their moral principles match the conditions observed in their present environmental encounter and (2) the relative weighting they give to moral principles that may be in conflict (honesty versus loyalty) in that particular context. If we learn the influential conditions that a child attaches to different principles, and if we can estimate the relative importance that two principles have for the child in the present context, we are prepared to explain the child's decision and to hazard predictions about similar environmental encounters in the future.

Second, the theory has several ways to account for apparent discrepancies between children's moral reasoning and their moral behavior. First, the most popular way of evaluating children's mode of moral reasoning has been that of posing brief anecdotes about moral decision incidents—moral dilemmas—and asking the young to judge whether the decisions made by the participants in the anecdotes were morally right or wrong and why. Such anecdotes differ in several important ways from real life moral action. They are *constructed environments* that fail to include many of the potential conditions that children consider when they make real life decisions. In other words, the anecdotes have been cleaned of cues that may be significant in children's moral value systems. Then, such researchers as Piaget and Kohlberg have used a very limited number of hypothetical incidents on which to base wide-ranging generalizations. (In the case of Kohlberg, the number has been no more than nine, and usually fewer.) And there appears to be no evidence that such a selection of moral dilemmas adequately samples the broad range of moral situations children face in life (Thomas, 1989b). In addition, children who respond to hypothetical dilemmas do not need to bear the consequences of their decisions as they do in real life. In short, we should not expect accurate predictions of what behavior will occur in diverse real life moral incidents when such predictions derive from children's answers to a few hypothetical anecdotes and when children need not suffer the consequences of their decisions. Therefore the integrated theory suggests that more adequate assessment techniques should be employed for judging the state of children's moral values and behavior. Such techniques should accommodate (1) a diversity of moral principles and their conditions that comprise the moral value component of the child's long-term memory, (2) weightings given to different principles and conditions, (3) the multiple cues in different environmental contexts that can be pertinent to the conditions children link to their moral principles, and (4) the actual consequences children can experience in real life moral situations.

On item 4—potential for guiding child rearing—I rated the integrated theory rather high because it (1) identifies four significant environ-

An Integrated Theory of Moral Development

How well do I think the theory meets the standards?

The Standards	Very Well	Moderately Well	Very Poorly
1. Reflects the real world of children	P*		
2. Is clearly understandable		X†	
3. Explains the past and predicts the future	P		
4. Guides child rearing	P		
5. Is internally consistent		X	
6. Is economical	X		
7. Is falsifiable	P		
8. Stimulates new discoveries	P		
9. Is self-satisfying		P	

P* = Potential status   X† = Present, actual status

mental variables that can be manipulated to influence children's moral experiences and (2) alerts adults to the complex patterns that children's moral values system can assume. I also judged the theory rather high on internal consistency (item 5) and economy (item 6). Furthermore, I believe it has the potential for generating a host of hypotheses that are testable, thereby qualifying it for being falsifiable (item 7) and fertile (item 8). However, a major problem in terms of falsifiability is posed by the notion of levels of consciousness. The difficulty researchers have experienced over the decades in trying to fathom the nature of nonconscious mental events suggests that the task of delineating the levels-of-consciousness feature of this theory may perhaps be intractable.

Finally, I find the proposed scheme fairly self-satisfying. It has helped me answer questions that I felt were not answered adequately by other theories I've studied. Yet this proposal still leaves important issues unanswered or unclear. So, it's back to the drawing board, then on to empirical investigations.

DEPICTING THEORIES IN THE GUISE OF METAPHORS

What analogies are most useful for representing the central themes of theories of development?

At the most general level of analysis, authors often adopt a metaphor or simile as a poetic aid for conveying the essential nature of a theory. They typically liken the theory to some phenomenon familiar to most readers. Robbie Case (1985, pp. 57–59) has illustrated this practice in reference to a number of well-known models of development. He proposes that J. H. Baldwin (1895), by drawing heavily on Darwin's views, portrayed the growing child as "an organism whose intellectual development recapitulates that of the species from which it has evolved." Piaget's child is a "young scientist, who constructs successively more powerful logico-mathematical tools." In Vygotsky's scheme, young children are social beings whose intellectual processes are tools acquired from their special historical and cultural settings. Classical information-processing theory portrays the child as a complex computer "capable of modifying the programmes with which it has been endowed, in a fashion that is responsive to the environment in which it finds itself." To characterize his own theory, Case envisions the child as a traveler through life, a problem solver motivated by natural desires whose realization is blocked by natural barriers; fortunately, the child has the capacity to refine and recombine innate procedures so as to overcome the barriers.

In a manner similar to Case's, I now propose metaphors to represent the other theories described in earlier chapters. I begin with Gesell, who viewed the child as a genetically programmed biological oscillator that switches between good and bad phases of growth on an annual schedule.

Havighurst pictured children as laborers performing a sequence of tasks. The tasks they face at successive periods of life are assigned to them by their evolving biological nature, by their physical environment, and by the demands of their cultural settings.

From the viewpoint of commonsense theory, children are pilgrims wending their way through life. How readily they advance toward their destination depends on how well their growing array of abilities *(can do)* and the strength of their willpower *(try to)* equip them to overcome the obstacles *(task difficulty)* they meet along the way.

Freud's child is a sexually driven, hedonistic being, which, when confronted with society's restrictions, reluctantly curbs its direct pleasure seeking by disguising its motives behind defense mechanisms. Erikson's child, while basically the same as Freud's, additionally faces the problem at each stage of growth of resolving the conflict between that stage's pair of dialectical tendencies.

Operant behaviorism pictures the child as a reacting robot that gradually develops habitual ways of responding to various environmental circumstances. Which actions will become habitual is determined by the kinds of consequences that occur after the robot has tried acting in several different ways in a given situation. Ways of acting that produce greater reward become habits. Ways that produce less reward or result in punishment are dropped from the robot's active repertoire of reponses.

Social learning theory portrays children both as actors and as members of the audience in the daily dramas that make up life's social experiences. Actors participating in such dramas learn—for future reference—the consequences they can expect from playing particular roles in different social settings. Members of the audience learn these same consequences from witnessing the plays.

According to Riegel's dialectical theory, the child is an arbitrator, continually negotiating the resolution of contradictory biological, psychological, and environmental forces. The accumulation of experience derived from this procession of negotiations equips the child with a growing supply of skills that render the child more adept at producing future resolutions.

Valsiner's model, like Vygotsky's, depicts young children as social beings who construct their intellectual skills from the tasks they perform in their particular historical and cultural settings.

In Captain's fundamentalist Christian theory, human development mirrors the biblical chronicle, with seven stages of the life span symbolizing seven eras from the Old and New Testaments.

From the perspective of humanistic theory, children are explorers, with each one in search of two sorts of treasure: (1) a unique personal identity or individuality called *self* and (2) activities that promote need fulfillment, particularly activities that create an exhalted feeling of euphoria known as a *peak experience*. Although the search can yield many gems along the way, the quest is never completed but, rather, is always in a state of *becoming*.

Bronfenbrenner's ecological model depicts children as peripatetic translators who are constantly interpreting the meaning of every environmental setting they pass through. Each meaning results from a combination of (1) the interpreter's direct experiences and (2) opinions imposed by outside agencies (exosystems) and by the general culture (the macrosystem).

Ethological theory portrays the child as an organism whose species characteristics have been fashioned over eons of time by mutations in genetic structure, determining the species' ability to adjust to changing environments. The human organism's adjustment is often achieved by the organism altering the environment to make it more suitable for survival. The most important of the organism's genetic traits is its ability to profit from experience. Among all the species, humans have the greatest capacity to learn.

In Kolhberg's scheme, the child is a magistrate who, with the passing of time, increasingly adopts more socially oriented, rather than self-oriented, principles for distinguishing right from wrong moral behavior.

Finally, in my integrated theory of moral development, children are like architects and builders, continually reconstructing the patterns of their moral values. The process of reconstruction is governed by (1) the history of the child's cognitive and moral development up to the present time, (2) the level of maturation of the child's nervous sytem, and (3) the nature of the moral events that the child currently encounters in the routine of daily living.

Such, then, is one version of metaphors intended to epitomize the theories met in this book.

REFERENCES

Adler, A. (1930) "Individual Psychology," in C. Murchinson (ed.), *Psychologies of 1930.* Worchester, Mass.: Clark University Press.

Akers, R. L., and J. K. Cochran. (1985) "Adolescent Marijuana Use: A Test of Three Theories of Deviant Behavior." *Deviant Behavior,* Vol. 6, No. 4, pp. 323–346.

Alexander, R. D., and P. W. Sherman. (1977) "Local Mate Competition and Parental Investment in Social Insects." *Science,* Vol. 196, No. 4289, pp. 494–500.

Allport, G. W. (1961) *Pattern and Growth in Personality.* New York: Holt, Rinehart & Winston.

Allport, G. W. (1968) *The Person in Psychology: Selected Essays.* Boston: Beacon.

Alston, W. P. (1971) "Comments on Kohlberg's 'From Is to Ought,' " in T. Mischel (ed.), *Cognitive Development and Epistemology.* New York: Academic Press.

Ames, L. B., and C. C. Haber. (1990) *Your Eight Year Old.* New York: Dell.

Ames, L. B., and F. L. Ilg. (1976) *Your Four Year Old.* New York: Dell.

Anastasi, A. (1958) "Heredity, Environment, and the Question 'How?' " *Psychological Review,* Vol. 65, No. 4, pp. 197–208.

Anderson, J. R. (1983) *The Architecture of Cognition.* Cambridge, Mass.: Harvard University Press.

Anthony, E. J. (1986) "The Contributions of Child Psychoanalysis to Psychoanalysis," *Psychoanalytic Study of the Child,* Vol. 41, pp. 61–87.

Archard, D. (1984) *Consciousness and the Unconscious.* La Salle, Ill.: Open Court.

Ashcraft, M. H. (1989) *Human Memory and Cognition.* Glenview, Ill.: Scott, Foresman.

Baldwin, A. L. (1967) *Theories of Child Development.* New York: Wiley.

Baldwin, J. D., and J. I. Baldwin. (1989) "The Socialization of Homosexuality and Heterosexuality in a Non-Western Society." *Archives of Sexual Behavior,* Vol. 19, No. 1, pp. 13–29.

Baldwin, J. M. (1895) *The Development of the Child and of the Race.* New York: Macmillan. Reprint. Clifton, N. J.: Augustus M. Kelley, 1968.

Baldwin, J. M. (1906, 1908, 1911) *Thoughts and Things or Genetic Logic.* 3 Vols. New York: Macmillan.

Bandura, A. (1969) *Principles of Behavior Modification.* New York: Holt, Rinehart & Winston.

Bandura, A. (1977) *Social Learning Theory.* Englewood Cliffs, N. J.: Prentice-Hall.

Bandura, A. (1978) "The Self System in Reciprocal Determinism." *American Psychologist,* Vol. 33, pp. 344–358.

Bandura, A., and R. H. Walters. (1963) *Social Learning and Personality Development.* New York: Holt, Rinehart & Winston.

Barker, R. G. (1968) *Ecological Psychology: Concepts and Methods for Studying the Environment of Human Behavior.* Stanford, Calif.: Stanford University Press.

Barker, R. G. (ed.). (1978) *Habitats, Environments, and Human Behavior.* San Francisco: Jossey-Bass.

Barker, R. G., T. Dembo, and K. Lewin. (1943) "Frustration and Regression," in R. G. Barker, J. S. Kounin, and H. F. Wright (eds.), *Child Behavior and Development.* New York: McGraw-Hill.

Barker, R. G., and P. V. Gump. (1964) *Big School, Small School.* Stanford, Calif.: Stanford University Press.

Barker, R. G., et al. (1970) "The Ecological Environment: Student Participation in Non-Class Settings," in M. B. Miles and W. W. Charters, Jr. (eds.), *Learning in Social Settings.* Boston: Allyn & Bacon.

Battro, A. M. (1973) *Piaget: Dictionary of Terms.* New York: Pergamon Press.

Batson, C. D., J. Fultz, P. A. Schoenrade, and A. Paduano. (1987) "Critical Self-Reflection and Self-Perceived Altruism: When Self-Reward Fails." *Journal of Personality and Social Psychology,* Vol. 53, No. 3, pp. 594–602.

Bell, R. W., and W. P. Smotherman (eds.). (1980) *Maternal Influences and Early Behavior.* New York: Spectrum.

Bernard, H. W. (1970) *Human Development in Western Culture.* Boston: Allyn & Bacon.

Berne, E. (1967) *Games People Play.* New York: Grove Press.

Berne, E. (1972) *What Do You Say after You Say Hello?* New York: Grove Press.

Biggs, J. B. (1976) "Schooling and Moral Development," in V. P. Varma and P. Williams (eds.), *Piaget, Psychology, and Education.* Itasca, Ill.: F. E. Peacock.

Bijou, S. W. (1976) *Child Development: The Basic Stage of Early Childhood.* Englewood Cliffs, N. J.: Prentice-Hall.

Bijou, S. W. (1979) "Some Clarifications on the Meaning of a Behavior Analysis of Child Development." *Psychological Record,* Vol. 29, No. 1, pp. 3–13.

Bijou, S. W. (1985) "Behaviorism: History and Educational Applications," in T. Husén and T. N. Postlethwaite (eds.), *International Encyclopedia of Education* (Vol. 1. Oxford, England: Pergamon Press, pp. 444–451.

Bijou, S. W., and D. M. Baer. (1961) *Child Development.* Vol I: *A Systematic and Empirical Theory.* New York: Appleton-Century-Crofts.

Bijou, S. W., and D. M. Baer. (1965) *Child Development.* Vol. II: *Universal Stage of Infancy.* New York: Appleton-Century-Crofts.

Bijou, S. W., and D. M. Baer. (1967) "Operant Methods in Child Behavior and Development," in S. W. Bijou and D. M. Baer (eds.), *Child Development: Readings in Experimental Analysis.* New York: Appleton-Century-Crofts.

Block, J. H., and L. W. Anderson. (1975) *Mastery Learning in Classroom Instruction.* New York: Macmillan.

Blurton Jones, N. G. (ed.) (1972) *Ethological Studies of Child Behaviour.* Cambridge, England: Cambridge University Press.

Boring, E. G. (1963) *The Physical Dimensions of Consciousness.* New York: Dover.

Bowlby, J. (1951) *Maternal Care and Mental Health.* London: HMSO.

Bowlby, J. (1969) *Attachment and Loss.* Vol. 1. *Attachment.* New York: Basic Books.

Bowlby, J. (1973) *Attachment and Loss.* Vol. 2. *Separation: Anxiety and Anger.* New York: Basic Books.

Bowlby, J. (1980) *Attachment and Loss.* Vol. 3. *Loss.* New York: Basic Books.

Brainerd, C. J. (ed.) (1983) *Recent Advances in Cognitive-Developmental Theory.* New York: Springer-Verlag.

Bricker, D. D. (1986) *Early Education of At-risk and Handicapped Infants, Toddlers, and Preschool Children.* Glenview, Ill.: Scott, Foresman.

Broadbent, D. E. (1958) *Perception and Communication.* New York: Macmillan.

Broadbent, D. E. (1970) "Psychological Aspects of Short-Term and Long-Term Memory." *Proceedings of the Royal Society* (London), Series B, Vol. 175, pp. 333–350.

Bronfenbrenner, U. (1979) *The Ecology of Human Development.* Cambridge, Mass.: Harvard University Press.

Brook, D. W., and J. S. Brook. (1985) "Adolescent Alcohol Use." *Alcohol and Alcoholism,* Vol. 20, No. 3, pp. 259–262.

Brown, A. L. (1979) "Theories of Memory and the Problems of Development: Activity, Growth, and Knowledge," in L. S. Cermak and F. I. M. Craik (eds.), *Levels of Processing in Human Memory.* Hillsdale, N. J.: Erlbaum, pp. 225–258.

Brown, A. L., and J. S. DeLoache. (1978) "Skills, Plans, and Self-Regulation," in R. Siegler (ed.), *Children's Thinking: What Develops.* New York: Wiley.

Brown, G. I. (1971) *Human Teaching for Human Learning: An Introduction to Confluent Education.* New York: Viking Press.

Bruner, J. S. (1964) "The Course of Cognitive Growth." *American Psychologist,* Vol. 19, No. 1, pp. 1–15.

Buhler, C., and M. Allen. (1972) *Introduction to Humanistic Psychology.* Monterey, Calif.: Brooks/Cole.

Buhler, C., and F. Massarik (eds.). (1968) *The Course of Human Life.* New York: Springer.

Bullough, V. I. (1981) "Age at Menarche: A Misunderstanding." *Science,* Vol. 213, No. 4505, pp. 365–366.

Burke, J. P. (1983) "Rapprochement of Rotter's Social Learning Theory with Self-Esteem Constructs." *Social Behavior and Personality,* Vol. 11, No. 1, pp. 81–91.

Burks, B. S. (1928) "The Relative Influence of Nature and Nurture upon Mental Development," in *Nature and Nurture.* Part I: *Their Influence upon Intelligence.* 27th Yearbook of the National Society for the Study of Education. Bloomington, Ill.: Public School Publishing.

Bush, P. J., and R. J. Iannotti. (1985) "The Development of Children's Health Orientations and Behaviors: Lessons for Substance Use Prevention." *National Institute on Drug Abuse Research Monograph Series,* No. 56, pp. 45–74.

Buss, A. R. (1976) "Development of Dialectics and Development of Humanistic Psychology." *Human Development,* Vol. 19, No. 4, pp. 248–260.

Cairns, R. B. (1977) "Sociobiology: A New Synthesis or an Old Cleavage?" *Contemporary Psychology,* Vol. 22, No. 1, pp. 1–3.

Cairns, R. B. (1983) *Social Development: The Origins and Plasticity of Interchanges.* San Francisco: W. H. Freeman.

California State Penal Code. (1975) Sacramento: State of California, Title I, Sec. 26.

Campbell, S. F. (1976) *Piaget Sampler.* New York: Wiley.

Captain, P. A. (1984) *Eight Stages of Christian Growth.* Englewood Cliffs, N. J.: Prentice-Hall.

Case, R. (1985) *Intellectual Development, Birth to Adulthood.* Orlando, Fla.: Academic Press.

Case, R. (1986) "The New Stage Theories in Intellectual Development: Why We Need Them; What They Assert," in M. Perlmutter (ed.), *Perspectives for Intellectual Development.* Hillsdale, N. J.: Erlbaum, pp. 57–96.

Catania, A. C., and S. Harnad (eds.). (1988) *The Selection of Behavior: The Operant Behaviorism of B. F. Skinner: Comments and Consequences.* New York: Cambridge University Press.

Chaplin, W. F. (1987) "On the Thoughtfulness of Cognitive Psychologists." *Journal of Mind and Behavior,* Vol. 8, No. 2, pp. 269–279.

Chapman, A. J., and H. C. Foot (eds.) (1976) *Humour and Laughter: Research and Applications.* London: Wiley.

Chi, M. T. H. (1976) "Short-Term Memory Limitations in Children: Capacity or Processing Deficits?" *Memory and Cognition,* Vol. 4, No. 5, pp. 559–572.

Chilman, C. S. (1983) *Adolescent Sexuality in a Changing American Society,* 2d ed. New York: Wiley.

Chomsky, N. (1967) "Review of Skinner's Verbal Behavior," in L. A. Jakobovits and M. S. Morn (eds.), *Readings in the Philosophy of Language.* Englewood Cliffs, N. J.: Prentice-Hall.

Colby, A., L. Kohlberg, J. Gibbs, and M. Lieberman. (1983) *A Longitudinal Study of Moral Development.* Monographs of the Society for Research in Child Development, Serial No. 200, Vol. 48, Nos. 1–2.

Cole, J. E., and C. Levine. (1987) "A Formulation of Cole's Theory of Ego Identity Formation." *Developmental Review,* Vol. 7, No. 4, pp. 273–325.

Cole, M. (ed.). (1977) *Soviet Developmental Psychology.* White Plains, N. Y.: Sharpe.

Coles, R. (1970) *Erik H. Erikson: The Growth of His Work.* Boston: Little, Brown.

Combs, A. W. (1962) "A Perceptual View of the Adequate Personality," in A. W. Combs, E. C. Kelley, A. H. Maslow, and C. R. Rogers (eds.), *Perceiving, Behaving, Becoming.* Washington, D. C.: Association for Supervision and Curriculum Development.

Combs, A. W. (1975) "Humanistic Goals of Education," in D. A. Read and S. B. Simon (eds.), *Humanistic Education Sourcebook.* Englewood Cliffs, N. J.: Prentice-Hall.

Combs, A. W., and D. Snygg. (1959) *Individual Behavior.* New York: Harper & Row.

Craik, F. I. M., and R. S. Lockhart. (1972) "Levels of Processing: A Framework for

Memory Research." *Journal of Verbal Learning and Verbal Behavior*, Vol. 11, pp. 671–684.

Dangelo, D. A. (1989) "Developmental Tasks in Literature for Adolescents — Has the Adolescent Female Protagonist Changed?" *Child Study Journal*, Vol. 19, No. 3, pp. 219–238.

Dason, P. R. (ed.) (1977) *Piagetian Psychology, Cross-Cultural Contributions*. New York: Gardner.

Davidov, V. V. (1985) "Soviet Theories of Human Development," in T. Husén and T. N. Postlethwaite (eds.), *International Encyclopedia of Education*, Vol. 8. Oxford, England: Pergamon, pp. 4721–4727.

Deutsch, J. M. (1943) "The Development of Children's Concepts of Causal Relations," in R. G. Barker, J. S. Kounin, and H. F. Wright (eds.), *Child Behavior and Development*. New York: McGraw-Hill.

de Vries, H., M. Dijkstra, and P. Kuhlman. (1988) "Self-Efficacy: The Third Factor Besides Attitude and Subjective Norm as a Predictor of Behavioural Intentions." *Health Education Research*, Vol. 3, No. 3, pp. 273–282.

DiBlasio, F. A. (1988) "Predriving Riders and Drinking Drivers." *Journal of Studies on Alcohol*, Vol. 49, No. 1, pp. 11–15.

Dollard, J., and N. E. Miller. (1950) *Personality and Psychotherapy*. New York: McGraw-Hill.

Dooling, D. J., and R. E. Christiaansen. (1977) "Episodic and Semantic Aspects of Memory for Prose." *Journal of Experimental Psychology: Human Learning and Memory*, Vol. 3, No. 4, pp. 428–436.

Dreikurs, R. R. (1950) *Fundamentals of Adlerian Psychology*. New York: Greenberg.

Drum, P. A. (1990) "Language Acquisition and Human Development," in R. M. Thomas (ed.), *The Encyclopedia of Human Development and Education*. Oxford, England: Pergamon, pp. 269–275.

Dunstan, J. I. (1961) *Protestantism*. New York: Braziller.

Durkin, D. (1976) *Teaching Young Children to Read*, 2d ed. Boston: Allyn & Bacon.

Dusek, J., O. B. Carter, and G. Levy. (1986) "The Relationship Between Identity Development and Self-Esteem during the Late Adolescent Years: Sex Differences." *Journal of Adolescent Research*, Vol. 1, No. 3, pp. 251–265.

Duvall, E. M. (1971) *Family Development*. Philadelphia: Lippincott.

Eibl-Eibesfeldt, I. (1975) *Ethology: The Biology of Behavior*, 2d ed. New York: Holt, Rinehart & Winston.

Eibl-Eibesfeldt, I. (1989) *Human Ethology*. New York: Aldine de Gruyter.

Elkind, D. (1976) *Child Development and Education*. New York: Oxford University Press.

Ellenberger, H. (1970) *The Discovery of the Unconscious*. New York: Basic Books.

Erikson, E. H. (1958) *Young Man Luther: A Study in Psychoanalysis and History*. New York: Norton.

Erikson, E. H. (1959) *Identity and the Life Cycle in Psychological Issues* (monograph). Vol. 1, No. 1. New York: International Universities Press.

Erikson, E. H. (1963) *Childhood and Society*, 2d ed. New York: Norton.

Erikson, E. H. (1964) *Insight and Responsibility*. New York: Norton.

Erikson, E. H. (1968) *Identity: Youth and Crisis*. New York: Norton.

Erikson, E. H. (1969) *Gandhi's Truth*. New York: Norton.

Erikson, E. H. (1975) *Life History and the Historical Movement*. New York: Norton.

Erikson, E. H. (1977) *Toys and Reasons*. New York: Norton.

Erikson, E. H. (1982) *The Life Cycle Completed*. New York: Norton.

Fantini, M., and G. Weinstein. (1968) *Toward a Contact Curriculum*. New York: Anti-Defamation League of B'nai B'rith.

Farnham-Diggory, S. (1972) *Information Processing in Children*. New York: Academic Press.

Fisher, J. D., P. A. Bell, and A. Baum. (1984) *Environmental Psychology*, 2d ed. New York: Holt, Rinehart & Winston.

Fisher, K. W. (1980) "A Theory of Cognitive Development: The Control and Construction of Hierarchies of Skills." *Psychological Review*, Vol. 87, No. 6, pp. 477–531.

Fisher, K. W., and R. L. Canfield. (1986) "The Ambiguity of Stage and Structure in Behavior: Person and Environment in the Development of Psychological Structures," in I. Levin (ed.), *Stage and Structure: Reopening the Debate*. Norwood, N. J.: Ablex.

Flavell, J. H. (1977) *Cognitive Development*. Englewood Cliffs, N. J.: Prentice-Hall.

Flexner, S. B., and L. C. Hauck. (1987) *The Random House Dictionary of the English Language*, 2d ed. New York: Random House.

Flora, J. A., and C. E. Thoresen. (1988) "Reducing the Risk of AIDS in Adolescents." *American Psychologist*, Vol. 43, No. 11, pp. 965–970.

Fodor, J. A. (1983) *The Modularity of Mind*. Cambridge, Mass.: MIT Press.

Forbes, M., and F. Bloch. (1990) *What Happened to Their Kids? Children of the Rich and Famous*. New York: Simon and Schuster.

Franz, C. E., and K. M. White. (1985) "Individuation and Attachment in Personality Development: Extending Erikson's Theory." *Journal of Personality*, Vol. 53, No. 2, pp. 224–256.

Freeman, D. (1983) *Margaret Mead and Samoa: The Making and Unmaking of an Anthropological Myth*. Cambridge, Mass.: Harvard University Press.

Frenkel-Brunswik, E. (1954) *Psychoanalysis and the Unity of Science. Proceedings of the Academy of Arts and Sciences*, Vol. 80.

Freud, A. (1974) *The Writings of Anna Freud*. 5 Vols. New York: International Universities Press.

Freud, S. (1900) "The Interpretation of Dreams," in J. Strachey (ed.), *The Standard Edition of the Complete Psychological Works of Sigmund Freud*. Vol. 4. London: Hogarth, 1953, pp. 1–338.

Freud, S. (1910) "Five Lectures on Psychoanalysis," in J. Strachey (ed.), *The Standard Edition of the Complete Psychological Works of Sigmund Freud*. Vol. 11. London: Hogarth, 1957, pp. 3–56.

Freud, S. (1915a) "Repression," in J. Strachey (ed.), *The Standard Edition of the*

Complete Psychological Works of Sigmund Freud. Vol. 14. London: Hogarth, 1957, pp. 141–185.

Freud, S. (1915b) "The Unconscious," in J. Strachey (ed.), *The Standard Edition of the Complete Psychological Works of Sigmund Freud.* Vol. 14. London: Hogarth, 1957, pp. 159–215.

Freud, S. (1917) "Introductory Lectures on Psychoanalysis, Part III," in J. Strachey (ed.), *The Standard Edition of the Complete Psychological Works of Sigmund Freud.* Vol. 16. London: Hogarth, 1957, pp. 243–482.

Freud, S. (1920) "Beyond the Pleasure Principle," in J. Rickman (ed.), *A General Selection from the Works of Sigmund Freud.* New York: Liveright, 1957, pp. 141–168.

Freud, S. (1923) *The Ego and the Id.* London: Hogarth, 1974.

Freud, S (1933) *New Introductory Lectures on Psychoanalysis.* New York: Norton.

Freud, S. (1938) *An Outline of Psychoanalysis.* London: Hogarth, 1973.

Freud, S. (1964) *The Standard Edition of the Complete Psychological Works of Sigmund Freud.* 30 Vols. James Strachey (trans. and ed.). London: Hogarth.

Fry, D. P. (1988) "Intercommunity Differences in Aggression among Zapotec Children." *Child Development,* Vol. 59, No. 4, pp. 1008–1019.

Fuchs, R. (1988) "Culminating Effects of Success and Failure in the Course of Learning Projects within the Frame of Developmental Tasks." *Psychologische Beitrage,* Vol. 30, No. 3, pp. 322–343.

Fuller, R. C. (1986) *Americans and the Unconscious.* New York: Oxford University Press.

Furstenburg, F. (1981) "Implicating the Family: Teenage Parenthood and Kinship Involvement," in T. Ooms (ed.), *Teenage Pregnancy in Family Context.* Philadelphia: Temple University Press, pp. 131–164.

Furth, H. G., and W. Wachs. (1975) *Thinking Goes to School.* New York: Oxford University Press.

Gardner, A. (1983) *Frames of Mind.* New York: Basic Books

Gesell, A., and F. L. Ilg. (1949) *Child Development: An Introduction to the Study of Human Growth.* New York: Harper & Row.

Gesell, A., F. L. Ilg, L. B. Ames, and G. E. Bullis. (1977) *The Child from Five to Ten.* New York: Harper & Row.

Gilligan, C. (1982) *In a Different Voice.* Cambridge, Mass.: Harvard University Press.

Gilligan, C., J. V. Ward, and J. M. Taylor (eds.). (1988) *Mapping the Moral Domain.* Cambridge, Mass.: Harvard University Press.

Giorgi, A. (1987) "The Crisis of Humanistic Psychology." *The Humanistic Psychologist,* Vol. 15, No. 1, pp. 5–20.

Godin, A. (1971) "Some Developmental Tasks in Christian Education," in M. P. Strommen (ed.), *Research in Religious Development.* New York: Hawthorne Books.

Gray, M. M., J. M. Ispa, and K. R. Thornburg. (1986) "Erikson Psychosocial Stage Inventory: A Factor Analysis." *Educational and Psychological Measurement,* Vol. 46, No. 4, pp. 979–983.

Gresham, F. M., and S. N. Elliott. (1989) "Social Skills Deficits as a Primary Learning Disability." *Journal of Learning Disabilities*, Vol. 22, No. 2, pp. 120–124.

Hagen, J. W., R. H. Jongeward, Jr., and R. V. Kail, Jr. (1975) "Cognitive Perspectives on the Development of Memory," in H. W. Reese and L. P. Lipsitt (eds.), *Advances in Child Development and Behavior*. Vol. 10. New York: Academic Press.

Hagenhoff, C., A. Lowe, M. F. Hovell, and D. Rugg. (1987) "Prevention of the Teenage Pregnancy Epidemic: A Social Learning Theory Approach." *Education and Treatment of Children*, Vol. 10, No. 1, pp. 67–83.

Halford, G. S. (1982) *The Development of Thought*. Hillsdale, N. J.: Erlbaum.

Hall, C. S. (1954) *A Primer of Freudian Psychology*. Yonkers, N. Y.: World Book.

Hall, C. S., and G. Lindzey. (1970, 1978) *Theories of Personality*, 2d, 3d eds. New York: Wiley.

Hall, G. S. (1891) "The Contents of Children's Minds on Entering School." *Pedagogical Seminar*, Vol. 1, No. 2, pp. 139–173.

Hall, G. S. (1904) *Adolescence*. 2 Vols. New York: Appleton-Century-Crofts.

Hamachek, D. E. (1985) "The Self's Development and Ego Growth: Conceptual Analysis and Implications for Counselors." *Journal of Counseling and Development*, Vol. 64, No. 2, pp. 136–142.

Hamill, P. V. V. (1977) *NCHS Growth Curves for Children*. (Vital and Health Statistics, Series 11, No. 165. Data from the National Health Survey). Washington, D. C.: US Government Printing Office.

Hamilton, W. D. (1964) "The Genetical Evolution of Social Behavior." *Journal of Theoretical Biology*, Vol. 7, No. 1, pp. 1–52.

Harris, M. L., and C. H. Harris. (1971) "A Factor Analytic Interpretation Strategy." *Educational and Psychological Measurement*, Vol. 31, No. 3, pp. 589–606.

Hartmann, H. (1959) "Psychoanalysis as a Scientific Theory," in S. Hook (ed.), *Psychoanalysis, Scientific Method, and Philosophy*. New York: New York University Press.

Hartshorne, H., and M. A. May. (1928–1930) *Studies in the Nature of Character*. 3 Vols. New York: Macmillan.

Hausfater, G., and S. B. Hrdy (eds.). (1984) *Infanticide*. New York: Aldine.

Havinghurst, R. J. (1953) *Human Development and Education*. New York: Longmans, Green.

Hawkins, J. D., and J. G. Weis. (1985) "The Social Development Model: An Integrated Approach to Delinquency Prevention." *Journal of Primary Prevention*, Vol. 6, No. 2, pp. 73–97.

Hebb, D. O. (1970) "A Return to Jensen and His Social Critics." *American Psychologist*, Vol. 25, No. 6, p. 568.

Heider, F. (1958) *The Psychology of Interpersonal Relations*. New York: Wiley.

Hersh, R. H., J. P. Miller, and G. D. Fielding. (1980) *Models of Moral Education*. New York: Longman.

Hilgard, E. R. (1949) "Human Motives and the Concept of the Self." *American Psychologist*, Vol. 4, No. 9, pp. 374–382.

Hilgard, E. R. (1952) "Experimental Approaches to Psychoanalysis," in E. Pumpian-Mindlin (ed.), *Psychoanalysis as a Science.* Stanford, Calif.: Stanford University Press.

Hilgard, E. R., and G. H. Bower. (1975) *Theories of Learning,* 4th ed. Englewood Cliffs, N. J.: Prentice-Hall.

Hillner, K. P. (1984) *History and Systems of Modern Psychology.* New York: Gardner.

Hinde, R. A. (1974) *Biological Bases of Human Social Behavior.* New York: McGraw-Hill.

Hinde, R. A. (1983) "Ethology and Child Development," in M. M. Haith and J. J. Campos (eds.), *Handbook of Child Psychology.* Vol. II: *Infancy and Developmental Psychobiology.* New York: Wiley, pp. 27–93.

Hinde, R. A. (1987) *Individuals, Relationships, and Culture: Links between Ethology and the Social Sciences.* New York: Cambridge University Press.

Hinde, R. A., and L. McGinnis. (1977) "Some Factors Influencing the Effects of Temporary Mother-Infant Separation—Some Experiments with Rhesus Monkeys." *Psychological Medicine,* Vol. 7, No. 2, pp. 197–212.

Hirsch, J. (1970) "Behaviour-Genetic Analysis and Its Biosocial Consequences." *Seminars in Psychiatry,* Vol. 2, pp. 89–105.

Hogan, J. D., and M. A. Vahey. (1984) "Modern Classics in Child Development: Authors and Publications." *Journal of Psychology,* Vol. 116, No. 1, pp. 35–38.

Holt, R. F. (1989) *Freud Reappraised: A Fresh Look at Psychoanalytic Theory.* New York: Guilford.

Hook, S. (1959) "Science and Mythology in Psychoanalysis," in S. Hook (ed.), *Psychoanalysis, Scientific Method, and Philosophy.* New York: New York University Press.

Horton, D. L., and T. W. Turnage. (1976) *Human Learning.* Englewood Cliffs, N. J.: Prentice-Hall.

Hurlock, E. G. (1968) *Developmental Psychology,* 3d ed. New York: McGraw-Hill.

Ilg, F. L., and L. B. Ames. (1955) *The Gesell Institute's Child Behavior.* New York: Dell.

Ilg, F. L., L. B. Ames, and M. D. Baker. (1981) *Child Behavior.* New York: Harper & Row.

Inhelder, B. (1968) "Forward," in I. E. Sigel and F. H. Hooper (eds.), *Logical Thinking in Children.* New York: Holt, Rinehart & Winston.

Inhelder, B., and J. Piaget. (1958) *The Growth of Logical Thinking from Childhood to Adolescence.* New York: Basic Books.

Inhelder, B., and J. Piaget. (1964) *The Early Growth of Logic in the Child.* London: Routledge & Kegan Paul.

Ittyerah, M., and A. Samarapungavan. (1989) "The Performance of Congenitally Blind Children in Cognitive Developmental Tasks." *British Journal of Developmental Psychology,* Vol. 7, No. 2, pp. 129–139.

James, W. (1890) *The Principles of Psychology.* New York: Holt, Rinehart & Winston.

Jensen, A. R. (1969) "How Much Can We Boost IQ and Scholastic Achievement?" *Harvard Educational Review,* Vol. 39, No. 1, pp. 1–123.

Jensen, A. R. (1973) *Educability and Group Differences.* New York: Harper & Row.

Johnston, L. D., P. M. O'Malley, and J. G. Bachman. (1986) *Drug Use among American High School Students, College Students, and Other Young Adults: National Trends through 1985*. Rockville, Md.: US National Institute on Drug Abuse.

Jones, E. (1961) *The Life and Works of Sigmund Freud*. New York: Basic Books.

Jones, E. E., and K. E. Davis. (1965) "From Acts to Dispositions: The Attribution Process in Person Perception," in L. Berkowitz (ed.), *Advances in Experimental Social Psychology*. Vol. 2. New York: Academic Press.

Jones, E. E., D. E. Kanouse, H. H. Kelley, R. E. Nisbett, S. Valins, and B. Weiner. (1971) *Attribution: Perceiving the Causes of Behavior*. Morristown, N. J.: General Learning Press.

Jones, E. E., and R. E. Nisbett. (1971) *The Actor and the Observer: Divergent Perceptions of the Causes of Behavior*. Morristown, N. J.: General Learning Press.

Jung, C. G. (1953) "On Psychical Energy," in *Collected Works*. Vol. VIII. New York: Pantheon.

Kail, R., and J. Bisanz. (1982) "Information Processing and Cognitive Development," in H. W. Reese and L. P. Lipsitt (eds.), *Advances in Child Development and Behavior*. Vol. 17. New York: Academic Press.

Kail, R., and J. W. Pellegrino. (1985) *Human Intelligence: Perspectives and Prospects*. New York: W. H. Freeman.

Kantor, J. R. (1959) *Interbehavioral Psychology,* 2d rev. ed. Bloomington, Ind.: Principia.

Kaufman, L. (1974) *Sight and Mind*. New York: Oxford University Press.

Kazdin, A. E. (1978) *History of Behavior Modification: Experimental Foundations of Contemporary Research*. Baltimore, Md.: University Park Press.

Kazdin, A. E. (1981) "Behavior Modification in Education: Contributions and Limitations." *Developmental Review,* Vol. 1, No. 1, pp. 34–57.

Keller, F. S., and W. N. Schoenfeld. (1950) *Principles of Psychology*. New York: Appleton-Century-Crofts.

Keller, F. S., and J. G. Sherman. (1974) *The Keller Plan Handbook*. Menlo Park, Calif.: Benjamin/Cummings.

Kelley, E. C. (1962) "The Fully Functioning Self," in A. W. Combs, E. C. Kelley, A. H. Maslow, and C. R. Rogers (eds.), *Perceiving, Behaving, Becoming*. Washington, D. C.: Association for Supervision and Curriculum Development.

Kelley, H. H. (1967) "Attribution Theory in Social Psychology," in D. Levine (ed.), *Nebraska Symposium on Motivation, 1967*. Vol. 15. Lincoln: University of Nebraska Press.

Kelley, H. H. (1971) *Attribution in Social Interaction*. Morristown, N. J.: General Learning Press.

Kelley, H. H. (1972) *Causal Schemata and the Attribution Process*. Morristown, N. J.: General Learning Press.

Kelley, H. H. (1973) "The Process of Causal Attribution." *American Psychologist,* Vol. 28, No. 2, pp. 107–128.

Kessen, W., and E. D. Cahan. (1986) "A Century of Psychology: From Subject to Object to Agent." *American Scientist,* Vol. 74, No. 6, pp. 640–649.

Kihlstrom, J. F. (1987) "The Cognitive Unconscious." *Science,* Vol. 237, No. 4821, pp. 1445–1452.

Klahr, D., and J. G. Wallace. (1976) *Cognitive Development: An Information-Processing View.* Hillsdale, N. J.: Erlbaum.

Klaus, M. H., and J. H. Kennell. (1976) *Maternal-Infant Binding.* St. Louis: Mosby.

Klatzky, R. L. (1980) *Human Memory: Structures and Process.* San Francisco: W. H. Freeman.

Klein, D. B. (1977) *The Unconscious: Invention or Discovery.* Santa Monica, Calif.: Goodyear.

Kleinginna, P. R., and A. M. Kleinginna. (1988) "Current Trends Toward Convergence of the Behavioristic, Functional, and Cognitive Perspectives in Experimental Psychology." *Psychological Record,* Vol. 38, No. 3, pp. 368–397.

Knapp, T. J. (1985) "Who's Who in American Introductory Psychology Textbooks: A Citation Study." *Teaching of Psychology,* Vol. 12, No. 1, pp. 15–17.

Kohlberg, L. (1958) "The Development of Modes of Thinking and Choices in Years 10 to 16." Ph.D. diss., University of Chicago.

Kohlberg, L. (1967) "Moral and Religious Education in the Public Schools: A Developmental View," in T. R. Sizer (ed.), *Religion and Public Education.* Boston: Houghton-Mifflin.

Kohlberg, L. (1968a) "The Child as a Moral Philosopher." *Psychology Today,* Vol. 2, No. 4, pp. 25–30.

Kohlberg, L. (1968b) "Moral Development," in *International Encyclopedia of the Social Sciences.* New York: Macmillan

Kohlberg, L. (1971) "From Is to Ought," in T. Mischel (ed.), *Cognitive Development and Epistemology.* New York: Academic Press.

Kohlberg, L. (1976) "Moral States and Moralization: The Cognitive-Developmental Approach," in T. Likona (ed.). *Moral Development and Behavior.* New York: Holt, Rinehart & Winston.

Kohlberg, L. (1984) *The Psychology of Moral Development.* San Francisco: Harper & Row.

Kohlberg, L., and R. Kramer. (1969) "Continuities in Childhood and Adult Moral Development." *Human Development,* Vol. 12, No. 2, pp. 93–120.

Kolominskly, Y. L., and M. H. Meltsas. (1985) "Sex-Role Differentiation in Preschool Children" (in Russian). *Voprosy-Psikhologii,* No. 3, pp. 165–171.

Kris, E. (1947) "The Nature of Psychoanalytic Propositions and Their Validation," in S. Hook and M. R. Konvitz (eds.), *Freedom and Experience.* Ithaca, N. Y.: Cornell University Press, pp. 239–259.

Krohn, M. D., W. F. Skinner, J. L. Massey, and R. L. Akers. (1985) "Social Learning Theory and Adolescent Cigarette Smoking: A Longitudinal Study." *Social Problems,* Vol. 32, No. 5, pp. 455–473.

Kuhn, T. S. (1962) *The Structure of Scientific Revolutions.* Chicago: University of Chicago Press.

Lamal, P. A. (1989) "The Impact of Behaviorism on Our Culture: Some Evidence and Conjectures." *Psychological Record,* Vol. 39, pp. 529–535.

Layzer, D. (1974) "Heritability Analyses of IQ Scores: Science or Numerology?" *Science,* Vol. 183, No. 4131, pp. 1259–1266.

Leahy, A. M. (1935) "Nature-Nurture and Intelligence." *Genetic Psychology Monographs,* Vol. 17, pp. 236–308.

Lee, V. L. (1988) *Beyond Behaviorism.* Hillsdale, N. J.: Erlbaum.

Leff, H. L. (1978) *Experience, Environment, and Human Potentials.* New York: Oxford University Press.

Lerner, D. (1965) "Introduction," in D. Lerner (ed.), *Cause and Effect.* New York: Free Press, pp. 1–10.

Lerner, R. M. (1976) *Concepts and Theories of Human Development.* Reading, Mass.: Addison-Wesley.

Lerner, R. M. (1986) *Concepts and Theories of Human Development,* 2d ed. New York: Random House.

Levin, I. (ed.) (1986) *Stage and Structure: Reopening the Debate.* Norwood, N. J.: Ablex, pp. 40–58.

Lewin, K. (1942) "Field Theory and Learning," in *Forty-First Yearbook, National Society for the Study of Education.* Part II. Bloomington, Ill.: Public School Publishing.

Loftus, E. F. (1975) "Leading Questions and Eyewitness Report." *Cognitive Psychology,* Vol. 7, No. 4, pp. 560–572.

Logan, R. D. (1986) "A Reconceptualization of Erikson's Theory: The Repetition of Existential and Instrumental Themes." *Human Development,* Vol. 29, No. 3, pp. 125–136.

Logue, A. W. (1985) "The Growth of Behaviorism: Controversy and Diversity," in C. E. Buxton (ed.), *Points of View in the Modern History of Psychology.* Orlando, Fla.: Academic Press, pp. 169–196.

Lorenz, K. Z. (1977) *Behind the Mirror: A Search for a National History of Human Knowledge.* New York: Harcourt Brace Jovanovich.

Love, S. Q., T. H. Ollendick, C. Johnson, and S. E. Schlesinger. (1985) "A Preliminary Report of the Prediction of Bulimic Behaviors: A Social Learning Analysis." *Bulletin of the Society of Psychologists in Addictive Behaviors,* Vol. 4, No. 2, pp. 93–101.

Lowrey, G. H. (1978) *Growth and Development in Children,* 7th ed. Chicago: Year Book Medical Publications.

Luria, A. R. (1976) *Cognitive Development: Its Cultural and Social Foundations.* Cambridge, Mass.: Harvard University Press.

Luria, A. R., and R. Yudovich. (1971) *Speech and the Development of Mental Processes in the Child.* Harmondsworth, England: Penguin.

Maccoby, E. (1968) "The Development of Moral Values and Behavior in Childhood," in J. A. Clausen (ed.), *Socialization and Society.* Boston: Little, Brown.

Mackworth, J. F. (1976) "Development of Attention," in V. Hamilton and M. D. Vernon (eds.), *The Development of Cognitive Processes.* New York: Academic Press.

Magary, J. F., M. K. Poulsen, P. J. Levinson, and P. A. Taylor (eds.). (1977) *Piagetian*

Theory and Its Implications for the Helping Professions. Los Angeles: University of Southern California.

Mahoney, M. J. (1989) "Scientific Psychology and Radical Behaviorism." *American Psychologist,* Vol. 44, No. 11, pp. 1372–1377.

Mahrer, A. R. (1978) *Experiencing: A Humanistic Theory of Psychology and Psychiatry.* New York: Brunner/Mazel.

Malina, R. M., and A. F. Roche. (1983) *Manual of Physical Status and Performance in Childhood.* Vols. 1 & 2: *Human Growth: A Comprehensive Treatise.* New York: Plenum.

Marek, J. C. (1988) "A Buddhist Theory of Human Development," in R. M. Thomas (ed.), *Oriental Theories of Human Development.* New York: Peter Lang, pp. 76–115.

Martindale, C. (1987) "Can We Construct Kantian Mental Machines?" *Journal of Mind and Behavior,* Vol. 8, No. 2, pp. 261–268.

Marx, K. (1847) "The Communist Manifesto," in D. McLellan (ed.), *Karl Marx, Selected Writings.* Oxford, England: Oxford University Press, 1977.

Marx, K. (1859) "Preface to A Critique of Political Economy," in D. McLellan (ed.), *Karl Marx, Selected Writings.* Oxford, England: Oxford University Press, 1977.

Marx, M. H., and F. E. Goodson (eds.). (1976) *Theories in Contemporary Psychology.* New York: Macmillan.

Maslow, A. H. (1968) *Toward a Psychology of Being.* Princeton, N. J.: Van Nostrand Reinhold.

Maslow, A. H. (1970) *Motivation and Personality,* 2d ed. New York: Harper & Row.

Maslow, A. H. (1971) *The Farther Reaches of Human Nature.* New York: Viking Press.

Mead, G. H. (1934) *Mind, Self, and Society.* Chicago: University of Chicago Press.

Mead, M. (1968) *Coming of Age in Samoa.* New York: Dell.

Miller, G. A. (1956) "The Magical Number Seven, Plus or Minus Two: Some Limits on Our Capacity for Processing Information." *Psychological Review,* Vol. 63, No. 2, pp. 81–97.

Miller, L. (1988) "Behaviorism and the New Science of Cognition." *Psychological Record,* Vol. 28, No. 1, pp. 3–18.

Miller, P. H. (1983) *Theories of Developmental Psychology.* San Francisco: W. H. Freeman.

Mishkin, M., and T. Appenzeller. (1987) "The Anatomy of Memory." *Scientific American,* Vol. 256, No. 6, pp. 80–89.

Montagu, A. (1959) *Human Heredity.* New York: Harcourt Brace Jovanovich.

Moore, J. (1990) "On Mentalism, Privacy, and Behaviorism." *The Journal of Mind and Behavior,* Vol. 11, No. 1, pp. 19–36.

Mounoud, P. (1986) "Similarities between Developmental Sequences at Different Age Periods," in I. Levin (ed.), *Stage and Structure: Reopening the Debate.* Norwood, N. J.: Ablex, pp. 40–58.

Mueller-Schwarze, D. (ed.). (1978) *Evolution of Play Behavior.* Stroudsburg, Penn.: Dowden, Hutchinson, & Ross.

Muller, P. (1969) *The Tasks of Childhood*. New York: McGraw-Hill.

Munro, D. J. (1977) *The Concept of Man in Contemporary China*. Ann Arbor: University of Michigan Press.

Murray, H. A. (1938) *Explorations in Personality*. New York: Oxford University Press.

Muzika, E. G. (1990) "Evolution, Emptiness, and the Fantasy Self." *Journal of Humanistic Psychology*, Vol. 30, No. 2, pp. 89–108.

Nagel, E. (1959) "Methodological Issues in Psychoanalytic Theory," in S. Hook (ed.), *Psychoanalysis, Scientific Method, and Philosophy*. New York: New York University Press.

Nagel, E. (1965) "Types of Causal Explanation in Science," in D. Lerner (ed.), *Cause and Effect*. New York: Free Press, pp. 11–32.

Neisser, U. (1976) *Cognition and Reality*. San Francisco: W. H. Freeman.

Newell, A., J. C. Shaw, and H. A. Simon. (1958) "Elements of a Theory of Human Problem Solving." *Psychological Review*, Vol. 65, No. 3, pp. 151–166.

Newell, A., and H. A. Simon. (1972) *Human Problem Solving*. Englewood Cliffs, N. J.: Prentice-Hall.

New England Primer: Or an Easy and Pleasant Guide to the Art of Reading. (1836) Boston: Massachusetts Sabbath School Society.

Ochse, R., and C. Plug. (1986) "Cross-Culture Investigation of the Validity of Erikson's Theory of Personality Development." *Journal of Personality and Social Psychology*, Vol. 50, No. 6, pp. 1240–1252.

Ornstein, P. A., and M. J. Naus. (1978) "Rehearsal Processes in Children's Memory," in P. A. Ornstein, *Memory Development in Children*. Hillsdale, N. J.: Erlbaum.

Ouspensky, P. D. (1957) *The Fourth Way*. London: Routledge & Kegan Paul.

Palmonari, A., M. L. Pombeni, and E. Kirchler. (1990) "Adolescents and Their Peer Groups — A Study of the Significance of Peers, Social Categorization Processes, and Coping with Developmental Tasks." *Social Behaviour*, Vol. 5, No. 1, pp. 33–48.

Paniagua, F. A. (1986) "Synthetic Behaviorism: Remarks on Function and Structure." *Psychological Record*, Vol. 36, No. 2, pp. 179–184.

Paris, S. G. (1978) "The Development of Inference and Transformation as Memory Operations," in P. A. Ornstein, *Memory Development in Children*. Hillsdale, N. J.: Erlbaum.

Pascual-Leone, J. (1976) "A View of Cognition from a Formalist's Perspective," in K. F. Riegel and J. Meacham (eds.), *The Developing Individual in a Changing World*. The Hague: Mouton, pp. 89–100.

Peel, E. A. (1976) "The Thinking and Education of the Adolescent," in V. P. Varma and P. Williams (eds.), *Piaget, Psychology, and Education*. Itasca, Ill.: F. E. Peacock.

Pellegrino, J. W., and C. K. Varnhagan. (1985) "Abilities and Aptitudes," in T. Husén and T. N. Postlethwaite, *International Encyclopedia of Education*. Vol. 1. Oxford, England: Pergamon Press, pp. 1–8.

Pepler, D., and K. Rubin. (1982) *Play of Children: Current Theory and Research*. New York: Karger.

Pepper, S. C. (1942) *World Hypotheses: A Study in Evidence.* Berkeley: University of California Press.

Perls, F. S., R. F. Hefferline, and P. Goodman. (1951) *Gestalt Therapy.* New York: Julian Press.

Petermann, F. (1987) "Behavioral Assessment and Reduction of Children's Aggression." *Journal of Human Behavior and Learning,* Vol. 4, No. 1, pp. 48–54.

Peters, R. S. (1971) "Moral Development: A Plea for Pluralism," in T. Mischel, *Cognitive Development and Epistemology.* New York: Academic Press.

Phillips, D. C., and M. E. Kelley. (1975) "Hierarchical Theories of Development in Education and Psychology." *Harvard Educational Review,* Vol. 45, No. 3, pp. 351–375.

Phillips, J. L., Jr. (1975) *The Origins of Intellect: Piaget's Theory,* 2d ed. San Francisco: W. H. Freeman.

Piaget, J. (1930) *The Child's Conception of Physical Causality.* London: Routledge & Kegan Paul.

Piaget, J. (1946) *Le Développement de la Notion de Temps chez l'Enfant.* Paris: Presses Universitaires de France.

Piaget, J. (1948) *The Moral Judgment of the Child.* Glencoe, Ill.: Free Press.

Piaget, J. (1950) *The Psychology of Intelligence.* London: Routledge & Kegan Paul.

Piaget, J. (1951) *Play, Dreams, and Imitation in Childhood.* New York: Norton.

Piaget, J. (1952) *The Child's Conception of Number.* London: Routledge & Kegan Paul.

Piaget, J. (1953) *Logic and Psychology.* Manchester, England: Manchester University Press.

Piaget, J. (1963) *The Origins of Intelligence in Children,* 2d ed. New York: Norton.

Piaget, J. (1969) *The Child's Conception of Movement and Speed.* New York: Basic Books.

Piaget, J. (1970a) *Genetic Epistemology.* New York: Columbia University Press.

Piaget, J. (1970b) *Science of Education and the Psychology of the Child.* New York: Viking Press.

Piaget, J. (1972) *Psychology and Epistemology.* London: Penguin.

Piaget, J. (1973) *The Child and Reality.* New York: Viking Press.

Piaget, J., L. Apostel, and B. Mandelbrot. (1957) *Logique et Equilibre.* Paris: Presses Universitaires de France.

Piaget, J., and B. Inhelder. (1956) *The Child's Conception of Space.* London: Routledge & Kegan Paul.

Piaget, J., and B. Inhelder. (1969) *The Psychology of the Child.* New York: Basic Books.

Piaget, J., A. Jonckheere, and B. Mandelbrot. (1958) *La Lecture de l'Expérience.* Etudes d'Epistémologie Génétique V. Paris: Presses Universitaires de France.

Piaget, J., and A. Szeminska. (1952) *The Child's Conception of Number.* Atlantic Highlands, N. J.: Humanities Press.

Pickar, D. B., and C. D. Turi. (1986) "The Learning Disabled Adolescent: Eriksonian Psychosocial Development, Self-Concept, and Delinquent Behavior." *Journal of Youth and Adolescence,* Vol. 15, No. 5, pp. 429–440.

Posner, M. I. (ed.). (1989) *Foundations of Cognitive Science.* Cambridge, Mass.: MIT Press.

Poulsen, M. K., and G. I. Luben. (1979) *Piagetian Theory and Its Implications for the Helping Professions.* Los Angeles: University of Southern California.

Power, C. (1988) "The Just Community Approach to Moral Education." *Journal of Moral Education,* Vol. 17, No. 3, pp. 195–208.

Pylyshyn, Z. W. (1989) "Computing in Cognitive Science," in M. I. Posner (ed.), *Foundations of Cognitive Science.* Cambridge, Mass.: MIT Press, pp. 52–91.

Reese, H. W., and W. F. Overton. (1970) "Models for Development and Theories of Development," in L. R. Goulet and Paul B. Baltes (eds.), *Life-Span Developmental Psychology.* New York: Academic Press.

Reeves, C. (1977) *The Psychology of Rollo May.* San Francisco: Jossey-Bass.

Riegel, K. F. (1972) "Time and Change in the Development of the Individual and Society," in H. W. Reese (ed.), *Advances in Child Development and Behavior.* Vol. 7. New York: Academic Press, pp. 91–113.

Riegel, K. F. (1973) "Dialectical Operations: The Final Period of Cognitive Development." *Human Development,* Vol. 16, No. 5, pp. 346–370.

Riegel, K. F. (1975) "Toward a Dialectical Theory of Development." *Human Development,* Vol. 18, No. 1–2, pp. 50–64.

Riegel, K. F. (1976) "From Traits and Equilibrium toward Developmental Dialectics," in W. J. Arnold (ed.), *Conceptual Foundations of Psychology.* Nebraska Symposium on Motivation, 1975, Vol. 23. Lincoln: University of Nebraska Press, pp. 349–497.

Riegel, K. F. (1979) *Foundations of Dialectical Psychology.* New York: Academic Press.

Roback, A. A. (1964) *History of American Psychology:* New York: Collier Books.

Rogers, C. F. (1961) *On Becoming a Person.* Boston: Houghton Mifflin.

Rogers, C. F. (1973) "My Philosophy of Interpersonal Relationships and How It Grew." *Journal of Humanistic Psychology,* Vol. 13, No. 2, pp. 13–15.

Romig, C. A., and J. G. Thompson. (1988) "Teen-age Pregnancy: A Family Systems Approach." *American Journal of Family Therapy,* Vol. 16, No. 1, pp. 133–143.

Rose, M. (1986) "The Design of Atmosphere: Ego-Nurture and Psychic Change in Residential Treatment." *Journal of Adolescence,* Vol. 9, No. 1, pp. 49–62.

Rose, S. R. (1987) "Social Skills Training in Middle Childhood: A Structured Group Approach." *Journal for Specialists in Group Work,* Vol. 12, No. 4, pp. 144–149.

Rosenthal, D. A., S. M. Moore, and M. J. Taylor. (1983) "A Study of the Self-Image of Anglo- , Greek- , and Italian-Austrian Working Class Adolescents." *Journal of Youth and Adolescence,* Vol. 12, No. 2, pp. 117–135.

Ross, R. P. (1985) "Ecological Theory of Human Development," in T. Husén and T. N. Postlethwaite (eds.), *International Encyclopedia of Education,* Vol. 3. Oxford, England: Pergamon Press, pp. 1513–1517.

Rotter, J. B. (1954) *Social Learning and Clinical Psychology.* New York: Johnson Reprint Company, 1980.

Rotter, J. B. (1982) *The Development and Application of Social Learning Theory.* New York: Praeger.

Rousseau, J. J. (1773) *Emilius; or, A Treatise of Education.* Edinburgh: W. Coke. In three volumes.

Sandor, D., and D. A. Rosenthal. (1986) "Youths' Outlooks on Love: Is It Just a State or Two?" *Journal of Adolescent Research,* Vol. 1, No. 2, pp. 199–212.

Savin-Williams, R. C. (1976) "An Ethological Study of Dominance Formation and Maintenance in a Group of Human Adolescents." *Child Development,* Vol. 47, No. 4, pp. 972–979.

Schnaitier, R. (1987) "Behavior Is Not Cognitive and Cognitivism Is Not Behavioral." *Behaviorism,* Vol. 15, No. 1, pp. 1–11.

Schneirla, T. C. (1957) "The Concept of Development in Comparative Psychology," in D. B. Harris (ed.), *The Concept of Development.* Minneapolis: University of Minnesota Press.

Schneirla, T. C. (1972), in L. R. Aronson, E. Tobach, J. S. Rosenblatt, and D. S. Lehrman (eds.), *Selected Writings of T. C. Schneirla.* San Francisco: W. H. Freeman.

Schoggen, P. (1989) *Behavior Settings.* Stanford, Calif.: Stanford University Press.

Scholnick, E. K. (ed.) (1983) *New Trends in Conceptual Representation: Challenges to Piaget's Theory?* Hillsdale, N. J.: Erlbaum.

Scriven, M. (1959) "The Experimental Investigation of Psychoanalysis," in S. Hook (ed.), *Psychoanalysis, Scientific Method, and Philosophy.* New York: New York University Press.

Sears, R. R., L. Rau, and R. Alpert. (1965) *Identification and Child Rearing.* New York: Harper & Row.

Shaver, K. G. (1975) *An Introduction to Attribution Processes.* Cambridge, Mass.: Winthrop.

Sheldon, W. H. (1940) *Varieties of Physique.* New York: Harper & Row.

Sheldon, W. H. (1942) *Varieties of Temperament.* New York: Harper & Row.

Sherif, M. (1966) *In Common Predicament: Social Psychology of Intergroup Conflict and Cooperation.* Boston: Houghton Mifflin.

Shuttleworth, F. K. (1935) "The Nature versus Nurture Problem: II. The Contributions of Nature and Nurture to Individual Differences in Intelligence." *Journal of Educational Psychology,* Vol. 26, No. 9, pp. 655–681.

Sidman, M. (1986) "Functional Analysis of Emergent Verbal Classes," in T. Thompson and M. D. Zeiler (eds.), *Analysis and Integration of Behavioral Units.* Hillsdale, N. J.: Erlbaum, pp. 213–245.

Siegel, M. (1982) *Fairness in Children.* London: Academic Press.

Siegler, R. S. (1976) "Three Aspects of Cognitive Development." *Cognitive Psychology,* Vol. 4, pp. 481–520.

Sigel, I. E., and R. C. Cocking. (1977) *Cognitive Development from Childhood to Adolescence: A Constructivist Perspective.* New York: Holt, Rinehart & Winston.

Sigel, I. E., and F. H. Hooper. (1968) *Logical Thinking in Children.* New York: Holt, Rinehart & Winston.

Skeels, H. M. (1940) "Some Iowa Studies of the Mental Growth of Children in Relation to Differentials of the Environment: A Summary," in *Intelligence: Its*

Nature and Nurture. 39th Yearbook of the National Society for the Study of Education. Bloomington, Ill.: Public School Publishing.

Skinner, B. F. (1938) *The Behavior of Organisms: An Experimental Analysis.* New York: Appleton-Century-Crofts.

Skinner, B. F. (1945) "Baby in a Box," in B. F. Skinner (ed.), *Cumulative Record: A Selection of Papers,* 3d ed. New York: Appleton-Century-Crofts, 1972.

Skinner, B. F. (1948) *Walden Two.* New York: Macmillan.

Skinner, B. F. (1950) "Are Theories of Learning Necessary?" *Psychological Review,* Vol. 57, No. 4, pp. 193–216.

Skinner, B. F. (1969) *Contingencies of Reinforcement: A Theoretical Analysis.* Englewood Cliffs, N. J.: Prentice-Hall.

Skinner, B. F. (1971) *Beyond Freedom and Dignity.* New York: Knopf.

Skinner, B. F. (1972) *Cumulative Record: A Selection of Papers,* 3d ed. New York: Appleton-Century-Crofts.

Skinner, B. F. (1974) *About Behaviorism.* New York: Knopf.

Skinner, B. F. (1984) "The Shame of American Education." *American Psychologist,* Vol. 39, No. 9, pp. 947–954.

Skinner, B. F. (1985) "Cognitive Science and Behaviourism." *British Journal of Psychology,* Vol. 76, No. 3, pp. 291–301.

Skinner, B. F. (1987) *Upon Further Reflection.* Englewood Cliffs, N. J.: Prentice-Hall.

Skodak, M. (1939) "Children in Foster Homes: A Study of Mental Development." *University of Iowa Studies in Child Welfare,* Vol. 16, No. 1 (entire issue).

Smith, M. B. (1990) "Henry A. Murray (1893–1988): Humanistic Psychologist." *Journal of Humanistic Psychology,* Vol. 30, No. 1, pp. 6–13.

Smith, P. K., and K. J. Connolly, (1980) *The Ecology of Preschool Behaviour.* Cambridge, England: Cambridge University Press.

Sober, E. (1989) "What Is Psychological Egoism?" *Behaviorism,* Vol. 17, No. 2, pp. 89–131.

Spitz, R. A. (1950) "Anxiety in Infancy; A Study of Its Manifestations in the First Year of Life." *International Journal of Psychoanalysis,* Vol. 31, pp. 138–143.

Spock, B., and M. B. Rothenberg. (1985) *Dr. Spock's Baby and Child Care.* New York: Pocket Books.

Stafford-Clark, D. (1967) *What Freud Really Said.* London: Penguin.

Stemmer, N. (1989) "The Acquisition of the Ostensive Lexicon: The Superiority of Empiricist over Cognitive Theories." *Behaviorism,* Vol. 17, No. 1, pp. 41–59.

Sternberg, S. (1969) "Memory-Scanning: Mental Processes Revealed by Reaction-Time Experiments." *American Scientist,* Vol. 57, No. 4, pp. 421–457.

Stevenson, H., H. Azuma, and K. Hakuta (eds.). (1986) *Child Development and Education in Japan.* New York: W. H. Freeman.

Stevick, D. B. (1968) *B. F. Skinner's Walden Two.* New York: Seabury Press.

Strayer, F. F., and J. Strayer. (1976) "An Ethological Analysis of Social Agonism and Dominance Relations among Pre-School Children." *Child Development,* Vol. 47, pp. 980–999.

Strazicich, M. (ed.) (1988) *Moral and Civic Education and Teaching about Religion.* Sacramento: California State Department of Education.

Suppes, P. C. (1969) *Studies in the Methodology and Foundations of Science.* Dordrecht, Holland: R. Reidel.

Tart, C. T. (1990) "Extending Mindfulness to Everyday Life." *Journal of Humanistic Psychology,* Vol. 30, No. 1, pp. 81–106.

Thagard, P. R. (1978) "The Best Explanation: Criteria for Theory Choice." *Journal of Philosophy,* Vol. 75, No 1, pp. 76–92.

Thomas, R. M. (1960) *Judging Student Progress,* 2d ed. New York: Longmans, Green.

Thomas, R. M. (1985) "Christian Theory of Human Development" in T. Husén and T. N. Postlethwaite (eds.), *International Encyclopedia of Education.* Vol. 1. Oxford, England: Pergamon Press, pp. 715–721.

Thomas, R. M. (1986) "Assessing Moral Development." *International Journal of Educational Research,* Vol. 10, No. 4, pp. 349–476.

Thomas, R. M. (ed.). (1988) *Oriental Theories of Human Development.* New York: Peter Lang.

Thomas, R. M. (1989a) "Moral and Ethnic Identity." *International Journal on the Unity of the Sciences,* Vol. 2, No. 4, pp. 381–403.

Thomas, R. M. (1989b) "A Proposed Taxonomy of Moral Values." *The Journal of Moral Education,* Vol. 18, No. 1, pp. 60–75.

Thomas, R. M. (1989c) *The Puzzle of Learning Difficulties—Applying a Diagnosis and Treatment Model.* Springfield, Ill.: Charles C Thomas.

Thomas, R. M. (1990) *Counseling and Life-Span Development.* Newbury Park, Calif.: Sage.

Thomas, R. M., and D. L. Brubaker: (1971) *Curriculum Patterns in Elementary Social Studies.* Belmont, Calif: Wadsworth.

Thomas, R. M., and S. M. Thomas. (1965) *Individual Differences in the Classroom.* New York: David McKay.

Tinbergen, N. (1951) *The Study of Instinct.* Oxford, England: Oxford University Press.

Tinbergen, N. (1973) *The Animal in Its World: Explorations of an Ethologist 1932–1972.* Cambridge, Mass.: Harvard University Press.

Travers, J. F. (1977) *The Growing Child.* New York: Wiley.

Trivers, R. L., and H. Hare. (1976) "Haplodipoidy and the Evolution of the Social Insects." *Science,* Vol. 191, No. 4224, pp. 249–263.

Tronick, E., and P. M. Greenfield. (1973) *Infant Curriculum: The Bromley-Heath Guide to the Care of Infants in Groups.* New York: Media Projects.

Tryon, C., and J. Lilienthal. (1950) "Development Tasks: I. The Concept and Its Importance," in *Fostering Mental Health in Our Schools.* Washington, D. C.: Association of Supervision and Curriculum Development, National Education Association.

Tulving, E. (1972) "Episodic and Semantic Memory," in E. Tulving and W. Donaldson (eds.), *Organization and Memory.* New York: Academic Press.

Turiel, E. (1980) "The Development of Social-Conventional and Moral Concepts," in M. Windmiller, N. Lambert, and E. Turiel (eds.), *Moral Development and Socialization*. Boston: Allyn & Bacon, pp. 69–106.

Tuttman, S. (1988) "Psychoanalytic Concepts of 'the Self.'" *Journal of the American Academy of Psychoanalysis*, Vol. 16, No. 2, pp. 209–219.

Tyler, L. (1986) "Meaning and Schooling." *Theory into Practice*, Vol. 25, No. 1, pp. 53–57.

Uttal, W. R. (1981) *A Taxonomy of Visual Processes*. Hillsdale, N. J.: Erlbaum.

Valsiner, J. (1987) *Culture and the Development of Children's Action*. Chicester, England: Wiley.

Valsiner, J. (ed.). (1988a) *Child Development within Culturally Structured Environments*. Vols. 1 & 2. Norwood, N. J.: Ablex.

Valsiner, J. (1988b) *Developmental Psychology in the Soviet Union*. Bloomington: Indiana University Press.

van Vliet, W. (1985) "The Role of Housing Type, Household Density, and Neighborhood Density in Peer Interaction and Social Adjustment," in J. F. Wohlwill and W. van Vliet (eds.), *Habitats for Children*. Hillsdale, N. J.: Erlbaum, pp. 165–200.

Vawkey, T., and A. Pellegrini. (1984) *Child's Play: Developmental and Applied*. Hillsdale, N. J.: Erlbaum.

Vonéche, J. J. (1985) "Genetic Epistemology: Piaget's Theory," in T. Husén and T. N. Postelthwaite (eds.), *International Encyclopedia of Education*. Vol. 4. Oxford, England: Pergamon Press, pp. 1997–2007.

Vurpillot, E. (1976) "Development of Identification of Objects," in V. Hamilton and M. D. Vernon (eds.), *The Development of Cognitive Processes*. New York: Academic Press.

Vygotsky, L. S. (1962) *Thought and Language*. Cambridge, Mass.: MIT Press.

Vygotsky, L. S. (1963) "Learning and Mental Development at School Age," in B. Simon and J. Simon (eds.), *Educational Psychology in the USSR*. London: Routledge & Kegan Paul, pp. 21–34.

Vygotsky, L. S. (1971) *Psychology of Art*. Cambridge, Mass.: MIT Press.

Vygotsky, L. S. (1978) in M. Cole, V. John-Steiner, S. Scribner, and E. Souberman (eds.), *Mind in Society*. Cambridge, Mass.: Harvard University Press.

Wadsworth, B. J. (1971) *Piaget's Theory of Cognitive Development*. New York: David McKay.

Waley, A. (1938) *The Analects of Confucius*. New York: Knopf.

Watson, J. B. (1913) "Psychology as a Behaviorist Views It." *Psychological Review*, Vol. 20, No. 2, pp. 158–177.

Weiner, B. (1974) *Achievement Motivation and Attribution Theory*. Morristown, N. J.: General Learning Press.

Weiner, B. (1980) "Dedication to Professor Heider," in D. Gorlitz (ed.), *Perspectives on Attribution Research and Theory*. Cambridge, Mass.: Ballinger.

Werner, H. (1961) *Comparative Psychology of Mental Development*. New York: Science Editions.

White, B. L. (1971) *Human Infants: Experience and Psychological Development.* Englewood Cliffs, N. J.: Prentice-Hall.

Whyte, L. L. (1960) *The Unconscious before Freud.* New York: Basic Books.

Wilson, E. O. (1975) *Sociobiology: The New Synthesis.* Cambridge, Mass.: Harvard University Press.

Wilson, E. O. (1978) *On Human Nature.* Cambridge, Mass.: Harvard University Press.

Winitz, H. (1969) *Articulation Acquisition and Behavior.* New York: Appleton-Century-Crofts.

Wohlwill, J. F. (1976) "The Age Variable in Psychological Research," in N. W. Endler, L. R. Boulter, and H. Osser (eds.), *Contemporary Issues in Developmental Psychology.* New York: Holt, Rinehart & Winston.

Wohlwill, J. F., and W. van Vliet. (1985) *Habitats for Children.* Hillsdale, N. J.: Erlbaum.

Woodworth, R. S. (1929) *Psychology.* New York: Holt, Rinehart & Winston.

Worchel, S., and J. Cooper. (1979) *Understanding Social Psychology.* Homewood, Ill.: Dorsey Press.

Wuthnow, R. (1978) "Peak Experiences: Some Empirical Tests." *Journal of Humanistic Psychology,* Vol. 18, No. 3, pp. 57–75.

Zigler, E. (1963) "Metatheoretical Issues in Development Psychology," in M. H. Marx (ed.), *Theories in Contemporary Psychology.* New York: Macmillan.

Zimmerman, B. J. (1983) "Social Learning: A Contextualist Account of Cognitive Functioning," in C. J. Brainerd (ed.), *Recent Advances in Cognitive-Developmental Theory.* New York: Springer-Verlag, pp. 1–50.

NAME INDEX

This index contains two types of names: (1) those of people whose specific publications are cited in the text and (2) those of people whose ideas are cited but whose specific publications are not.

SUBJECT INDEX